MAXIMUM PC

ULTIMATE PC
PERFORMANCE GUIDE

By MAXIMUM PC

800 East 96th Street,
Indianapolis, Indiana 46240

Maximum PC Ultimate PC Performance Guide

International Standard Book Number: 0-7897-3317-X

Library of Congress Catalog Card Number: 2004110330

Printed in the United States of America

First Printing: September 2004

07   06   05   04   4   3   2   1

Trademarks

Warning and Disclaimer

Bulk Sales

Que Publishing offers excellent discounts on this book when ordered in quantity for bulk purchases or special sales. For more information, please contact

U.S. Corporate and Government Sales
1-800-382-3419
corpsales@pearsontechgroup.com

For sales outside the U.S., please contact

International Sales
international@pearsoned.com

Que Publishing

Publisher
Paul Boger

Associate Publisher
Greg Wiegand

Executive Editor
Rick Kughen

Development Editor
Rick Kughen

Managing Editor
Charlotte Clapp

Indexer
Ginny Bess Munroe

Technical Editor
Mark Reddin

Publishing Coordinator
Sharry Lee Gregory

Interior Designer
Anne Jones

Cover Designer
Anne Jones

Page Layout
Tricia Bronkella
Eric S. Miller

Maximum PC

Publisher
Chris Coelho

Editor-in-Chief
George Jones

Staff Writers
Gordon Mah Ung
Will Smith
Logan Decker
Josh Norem

Cover Designer
Natalie Jeday

Future Network USA

Editorial Director
Jon Phillips

Contents at a Glance

Foreword

Introduction

1 Building

2 Maximizing Performance

3 Tuning Windows

4 Internet & Security

5 Fun & Games

6 Troubleshooting

Index

Table of Contents

Part I: Building

Guide to SpecSpeak 2

Anatomy of a Case 10

How To Pick the Best Case 12

How To Pick the Best Mini-System 14

How To Pick the Best CPU 16

CPU and Chipset Reference 19

Anatomy of a Mobo 24

How To Pick the Best P4 Mobo 26

How To Pick the Best Athlon Mobo 28

Anatomy of a Videocard 32

How to Pick the Best Videocard 34

Anatomy of a Soundcard 38

How to Pick the Best Soundcard 40

Anatomy of a Hard Drive 42

How to Pick the Best Hard Drive 44

How to Pick the Best Monitor 47

How to Pick the Best CD Burner 50

Anatomy of a DVD Burner 52

How to Pick the Best DVD Burner 53

Anatomy of a Power Supply 55

How to Pick the Best Power Supply 57

How to Pick the Best Mouse & Keyboard............ 59

How to Pick the Best Cooler for Your CPU 60

Pick the Best Cooling Device...................... 62

How to Properly Position Your Case Fans............ 64

Build It... 68

How to Build a PC Entertainment Center 80

How to Paint Your Case........................... 84

Part II: Maximizing Performance

How to Supercharge Your PC: One Little
Hack at a Time 90

How to Optimize Your PC's BIOS Settings........... 92

How to Quiet the Vacuum Cleaner You Call a PC..... 100

How to Set Up Your CRT 104

How to Set Up a Dual Display 108

The Overclocker's Handbook 111

Make Use of *Powerstrip*'s 7 Coolest Features 124

Part III: Tuning Windows

Windows XP: Demystified and Dissected 126

Cracking the XP Kernel 128

Windows XP Service Pack 2 129

Customize Your Interface 130

Accelerate, Streamline, and Take Control of XP 136

Windows Services Exposed and Expunged 142

Maintain a Healthy OS. 146

Master the Dark Arts: Be a Power User 152

How to Get Old Programs to Run on XP 158

Power Toys for Power Users 160

Windows Longhorn Sneak Peek 162

How to Make Custom Recovery Disks 164

How to Burn Your Videotapes to DVD 222

How to Make Your Own DVD 228

How to Make a Feature Film on Your PC. 230

How to Make MP3s 234

Turn Your PC into a Rock N' Roll Recording Studio. . . 237

Speakers: Now Hear This! 239

How to Build Your Own Arcade Machine. 242

How to Create a 3-D Model. 252

Part VI: Troubleshooting

CPUs and Cooling: The Need for Speed Lives On 260

Motherboards 270

Videocards 278

Hard Drives 286

Optical Drives 292

Sound Cards 295

CRT & LCDs Monitors. 298

Windows XP Troubleshooting Secrets 304

The XP Doctor Is In!. 310

Index 312

Part IV: Internet and Security

Maximize Your Broadband Connection............172

Share Your Broadband Connection 176

How to Protect Yourself with a Firewall...........180

Turn Your PC into Fort Knox 182

All About Viruses 186

How to Stamp Out Spyware 187

How to Eliminate Spam........................190

Kill Pop-ups!................................194

How to Protect Your Wireless LAN 195

How to Give Dial-Up a Kick in the Pants 198

How to HTMLify Your Desktop 199

How to Make a Linux Router 202

Part V: Fun and Games

How to Set Up Your 5.1 Speaker Rig 206

How to Optimize Your PC for Multiple
Player Mayhem.................................210

How to Kick Ass and Take Names in
First-Person Shooters 214

How to Master Digital Photography 215

Foreword

Behold! The Invigorating Qualities of Pure PC Power

Sometimes it takes an email from Iran to put things in perspective.

You see, the last piece of writing that I finished just prior to starting this *Ultimate Performance Guide* foreword was a response to an email sent from Iran. The Iranian email was cogent, pleasant, and even a bit poignant. And it made me think about what *Maximum PC's* "performance message" stands for in a big-picture kind of way. An excerpt from the Iranian email:

"Ladies and Gentlemen,

Our company is a provider and agent of many kind of magazines and other publications from all over the world. Now your publication is introduced to us and we would like to know more about it to providing for our customers. So, please kindly provide us a sample copy. We are not allowed to importing and distributing foreign publications without a sample copy to offer to 'culture and Islamic Guidance' Ministry in our country for previous authorization to importing the foreign publications.

We understand that it may be against your rules but we request and ask you to have an exception because our country is an Islamic country and has its special laws and we must to accept them.

We shall to appreciate your attention and prompt reply.

Yours Faithfully, [name withheld to protect the letter-writer's anonymity]"

Charming letter, isn't it? I wrote back to the businessman, and let him know that we can't send any packages to Iran—that the U.S. Post Office simply won't send *anything* to Iran. That was the sum total of my response, but after I hit the send button, I couldn't help but think about how Iranian PC users might interpret—and benefit from—*Maximum PC's* twin gospels of "pure PC power" and "minimum BS." There's something very liberating about the *Maximum PC* world view. It's a doctrine that essentially says, "It's OK to want the best. It's OK to want *more*. PC building, hacking, assembling and disassembling isn't just a vocation—it's a hobby for passionate enthusiasts, and the hobby is good."

Listen, I've never been to Iran, but my guess is that the place is teeming with PCs. And where PCs teem, PC technicians naturally follow. Do these geeks-in-waiting have any encouragement, any validation from like-minded enthusiasts? I can't say for sure, but my guess is that in a country where a "culture and Islamic Guidance Ministry" calls some of the shots, magazines like *Maximum PC* don't exactly flourish. So I was entirely smitten by the idea that some day, Iranian PC enthusiasts might find themselves reading our magazine, and marveling at the content, and it's "performance for performance's sake" message.

After all, when we tell our readers how to build the "perfect PC"—that "dream machine"—we're essentially telling them to liberate themselves from a world of restriction and enter a world of possibilities. And when we show readers how to tweak Windows XP according to their own personal desires, we're telling them that OS hacking has a value that exceeds mere utility—that it affirms individuality and personal expression, and these are wonderful things. And when we show people how to mod their computers or otherwise hack their hardware, the message isn't so much "do it for productivity," but rather "do it because it's fun."

That's our pro-performance message, and it resonates pretty damn well on American shores. I submit to you the following: Just three years ago, *Maximum PC* published 12 issues a year. One year later, we upped our schedule to 13 issues a year--12 monthly issues, plus one newsstand special. And a year after that we hit 12 plus two. And this year? By the end of 2004, we will have published *16* issues—12 monthlies plus four newsstand specials.

If this doesn't tell you that our pro-performance messages is playing to people's hearts and imaginations, then, brother, I give up.

As I stated in my preamble on the inside-front cover, this book is a compilation of all the "newsstand-only specials" we've published to date. The entire content herein is focused on increasing PC performance in some tangible way (either directly or indirectly), as well as enjoying all the fringe benefits that these performance boosts might yield.

Now, whether or not you feel that the gospel of pure PC power has a larger significance vis-à-vis politics and the human condition, well, that's your call. You can still enjoy this book as a basic handbook, a how-to guide. The *Ultimate Performance Guide* is chock full and brimming with interesting, helpful, invaluable PC information. Just make no mistake: Beneath all our troubleshooting advice, all our helpful instruction, and all our answer-giving lies a very real subtext: That working on PCs is fun. That working on them is its own reward. That striving for more powerful PCs is righteous and commendable. That this "thing of ours" is all about a celebration of life. A celebration of inventiveness. An exploration of possibilities.

That's the performance story that I personally embrace, and I think you will, too, by the time you finish this book.

—Jon Phillips, editorial director, *Maximum PC*

We Want to Hear from You!

As the reader of this book, *you* are our most important critic and commentator. We value your opinion and want to know what we're doing right, what we could do better, what areas you'd like to see us publish in, and any other words of wisdom you're willing to pass our way.

As an associate publisher for Que, I welcome your comments. You can email or write me directly to let me know what you did or didn't like about this book—as well as what we can do to make our books better.

Please note that I cannot help you with technical problems related to the topic of this book. We do have a User Services group, however, where I will forward specific technical questions related to the book.

When you write, please be sure to include this book's title and author as well as your name, email address, and phone number. I will carefully review your comments and share them with the author and editors who worked on the book.

Email: feedback@quepublishing.com

Mail: Greg Wiegand
            Associate Publisher
            Que Publishing
            800 East 96th Street
            Indianapolis, IN 46240 USA

For more information about this book or another Que title, visit our Web site at www.quepublishing.com. Type the ISBN (without hyphens) or the title of a book in the Search field to find the page you're looking for.

About the Author

Maximum PC is the market-leading special interest PC and personal technology enthusiast magazine. With absolute candor and uncompromising honesty, *Maximum PC* guides its readers through the rapidly expanding world of PC technology: PC building and upgrading, games, digital cameras, PDAs, MP3s, DVD burning and playback, wireless communications and much, much more—all with a direct emphasis on getting the most performance possible. *Maximum PC* serves the specialized information needs of its passionate readers with uncompromising product reviews, in-depth features, step-by-step instruction, and incisive analysis of leading-edge trends.

YOUR GUIDE TO SPECS!

Reading the performance specs on a **hardware box** can feel like reading the menu at a French restaurant. If you don't actually understand the words on the page, you'll have no idea what you're about to sink your teeth into. And so go **hardware specs**. We've included a few spec laden sample products here, but don't think of them as the crème de la crème. Choosing hardware doesn't have to be that tough. Simply learn the language of specs with our handy guide, and you'll never have to worry about buying something disgusting and distasteful. Sweetbreads, anyone? Bon appétit…

MONITORS

Tube: Many CRT companies like to pimp the specific, trademarked name of their monitor technology. Because these hyperbolic names often impart little information about the actual product, skip this hoo-ha and zip on down to the "CRT type" entry.

CRT type: Here you'll learn some legitimately important information about the display—specifically, whether it's a shadow-mask or aperture-grille CRT (that's cathode ray tube, the same technology used in traditional television sets). Shadow-mask CRTs tend to be dimmer than aperture-grille CRTs and have more problems with color consistency (aka "screen mottling"). But shadow-masks do lack the two razor-thin horizontal lines found on all aperture-grille displays (some people find these lines to be distracting). Invar is an iron-nickel alloy that's used in the monitor's mask. The mask is essentially a perforated piece of metal that guides the monitor's electron gun to the precise phosphor dots it needs to illuminate.

Size: You'll most likely find 15, 17, 19, or 21 inches listed here. But the "size" spec only refers to the size class the monitor belongs to, not the actual viewing area.

- **Tube: SupaFlat™ ZFT**
- **CRT type: INVAR shadow mask**
- **Size: 19 in.**
- **Viewable image size: 18.0 in.**
- **Dot pitch: 0.20mm (horizontal)**
- **Maximum refresh rates:**
  - **640x480: 160Hz**
  - **800x600: 160Hz**
  - **1024x768: 155Hz**
  - **1157x870: 140Hz**
  - **1280x1024: 120Hz**
  - **1600x1200: 100Hz**
  - **1600x1280: 95Hz**
  - **1856x1392: 87Hz**
  - **1920x1440: 85Hz**
  - **2048x1536: 75Hz**

Viewable image size: The screen on any CRT features a perimeter that can't display actual colored pixels, so it's only fair that CRT vendors share information on a monitor's actual viewable image area. This area is always expressed as a diagonal measurement.

Dot pitch: A CRT's pitch refers to the distance between two neighboring phosphor dots of the same color. This spec is always described in fractions of a millimeter and is usually measured diagonally. Smaller numbers are always better, because the closer the dots are to each other, the crisper the picture will be. Shadow-mask monitors boast a dot pitch, while aperture grilles boast a stripe pitch. Be aware that some shadow-mask monitor vendors define pitch as a horizontal dot pitch, yielding a number that's a bit smaller than the traditional diagonal pitch measurement. To wit: A monitor with a 0.28mm dot pitch will boast a 0.24mm dot pitch if measured horizontally. Caveat emptor.

Maximum refresh rates: As you increase a monitor's resolution, its refresh rate will drop accordingly. For this very reason, maximum refresh rates and resolutions are usually grouped together in the same spec slot. These numbers should always be as high as possible—you never want to see low refresh and resolution specs. Ideally, your monitor will still be able to support high refresh rates (85Hz and above) at its highest resolution settings. Refresh rates below 75Hz can cause a flickering effect that will eventually strain your eyes. As for resolutions, 1600x1200 is considered the lowest "pro-level" resolution acceptable for serious graphic design work.

SPEAK

VIDEOCARDS

Chipset: It's the driving force behind everything your videocard is capable of. There are two chipsets worth considering right now: the GeForce line from nVidia and the Radeon line from ATI. The GeForce and Radeon lines each boast several subdivisions, so you'll find everything from $80 budget cards to $400 ultimate gaming cards under their umbrellas. Nonetheless, each card in each product line is based on the same chipset.

Memory size: All videocards include a certain amount of onboard, high-speed memory. This RAM is used to store information about the geometry of the 3D models the card is rendering, as well as the actual textures that are being stretched across those models. Many current games use the full 128MB that most cards offer and even take advantage of the extra space that a 256MB card offers. A 128MB card will serve you well for the next few months, but a forward-thinking buyer would get a card with 256MB.

- **Chipset:** ATI R300
- **Memory size:** 128MB
- **Memory type:** 256-bit 330MHz DDR SDRAM
- **RAMDAC:** 350MHz
- **Max resolution:** 2048x1536@85Hz

Memory type: The first portion of our example (256-bit) refers to the amount of data that the card's memory can transfer each clock cycle. Most videocards support 256-bit, 128-bit or 64-bit transfers—the larger the number, the better.

The second number is the speed rating of the memory in megahertz. A larger number is better here as well.

Memory can be single data-rate (SDR) or double data-rate (DDR). SDR memory can complete one data transfer per clock cycle. DDR can complete two, making it effectively two times faster than SDR memory of the same frequency.

When you put all of the memory specs together, they essentially tell you the maximum theoretical memory bandwidth of the card. For example, this card is able to transfer two 256-bit chunks of data 330,000,000 times every second, yielding a maximum theoretical memory bandwidth of 21.12GB/sec.

RAMDAC: The RAMDAC (random access memory digital-to-analog converter) converts the digital signal produced by the videocard into an analog signal that a CRT monitor can display. The faster the RAMDAC, the higher the maximum resolution and refresh rate that the videocard can drive.

Max resolution: This is the maximum resolution and refresh rate that the videocard will drive, and is a direct function of its RAMDAC speed. Most modern videocards should be capable of running 1600x1200 at 85Hz or faster.

NOTE: A videocard's spec box won't typically define which specific 3D visual effects the card supports; this information usually appears on a different part of the product packaging.

Because all spec boxes are different—after all, vendors are going to highlight the specs that make their product look best and avoid those that make it look bad—what you'll see here are "spec lists" we created to deliver details on as many specs as possible. You may not see all of our examples on a given box, but you'll definitely see them as you look over multiple boxes.

256 MB
128 MB

- The Fastest 3D performance on the planet!
- Complete Microsoft® DirectX® 9.0 support
- 128/256 MB Fast DDR memory
- 256-bit supercharged memory interface
- 8-pixel pipeline architecture
- Dual monitor support with DVI-I and TV-Out

CE FC DX9 AGP PnP DVI

RADEON
9800 SERIES

POWERED BY
ATI

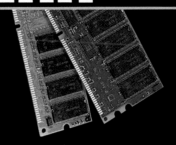

MEMORY

Capacity: This is how much memory is installed on the PCB (printed circuit board—the green board that the memory is stuck onto). RAM slots on most PCs are sparse, so you should try to purchase large-capacity modules whenever possible. In other words, if you want a 256MB upgrade, buy a single 256MB stick instead of two 128MB sticks. This way, you'll still have an open slot for another upgrade in the future.

Formfactor: This refers to the actual physical form of the memory module. Our example has a 184-pin connector and is identified as a DIMM (dual inline memory module). Different mobos are built to house different memory formfactors, so you'll need to refer to your system documentation or peek at the motherboard to determine exactly what kind of RAM you need.

ECC/Parity: Parity memory can detect compromises in data integrity, while ECC (error correction code) memory is not only able to detect errors, but can also correct them. Data-integrity schemes in memory modules are on their way out in most systems, with the exception of critical high-end servers. ECC and parity memory modules are more expensive than traditional memory, and manufacturing processes over the past decade have vastly improved reliability among memory components, so you won't often see error correction offered on memory.

- **Capacity: 256MB**
- **Memory speed: 400MHz**
- **Formfactor: 184-pin DIMM**
- **Type: PC3200 DDR SDRAM**
- **ECC/Parity: None**
- **Voltage: 2.6v**
- **CAS latency: CL2**

Memory speed: There are two methods of classifying the speed of your RAM. Traditional memory speed has been measured in nanoseconds, with ratings that range from 80ns to 50ns. Lower numbers indicate faster access times. But SDRAM (synchronous dynamic RAM) memory chips synchronize themselves with your PC's system clock. (No, it's not the one that tells you the time; it's the one that sends out a regular signal, like a metronome, to which all of the machine's components can synchronize). As a result, the speed of most new memory modules is expressed in megahertz, just like your CPU. In this case, higher numbers are better.

Type: RAM type usually refers to the clock speed of the chips and the technology they use. Our example is DDR (Double Data Rate) SDRAM running at 400MHz. You can sometimes mix RAM configured at different clock speeds, but all modules will synchronize to the speed of the slower module. Regardless, you'll need to refer to your system documentation to match up the proper RAM with your motherboard and processor.

Voltage: This is the amount of power your memory requires. Older systems used memory modules that operated at 5v, but these days, most RAM operates at 2.6v or so. Don't even think about using chips that can't operate at the voltage your motherboard requires.

CAS latency: Column address strobe (CAS) is used in conjunction with row address strobe to locate information in RAM. The CAS latency, or CAS rating, refers to the number of clock cycles it takes to perform this locating function. A CL3 factor means it takes three clock cycles to locate information, whereas memory with a CL2 factor takes just two clock cycles. This doesn't mean you get 33 percent faster performance with CL2. In fact, the difference in most systems will be nominal. Still, memory-intensive applications and overclocked processors may get a boost from lower latency ratings. You can mix CL2 and CL3 modules, but they'll all run at CL3.

NICs NETWORK INTERFACE CARDS

Standards: This lets you know what network protocols your card supports. Our example card supports the classic Ethernet 10BASE-T, which operates at 10 megabits per second, or 1.25MB/sec, as well as the beefier 100BASE-T that ups the throughput to a (theoretical) 100Mbps, or 12.5MB/sec. If that's not enough for you, there's always Gigabit Ethernet which ups the ante to a breathtaking 1000Mbps. Remember, though, that all nodes on your network share this bandwidth, so the actual throughput on any given machine will depend on the amount of network traffic.

LEDs: They're more than just pretty lights. Light-emitting diodes, or LEDs, can help you diagnose problems with your computer. This card conveniently offers separate LEDs that indicate when data is being transmitted over a 100BASE-T network or a 10BASE-T network, as well as a handy extra light that illuminates when you're connected to the network and flashes whenever you're transmitting or receiving data.

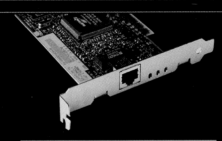

- **Standards: 10Mbps 10BASE-T, 100Mbps 100BASE-T**
- **Interface: PC PCI, Network RJ-45**
- **LEDs: 100Mbps, 10Mbps, Activity**
- **Auto-sensing**
- **Wake on LAN**

Interface: This indicates how your NIC connects to your PC and your network. This card is intended for a PC PCI slot and requires cables with RJ-45 (registered jack) connectors. These connectors look like telephone jacks, but are slightly wider and hold up to eight wires each.

Auto-sensing: An auto-sensing card can identify whether you've plugged into a 100BASE-T network or a 10BASE-T network and configure itself accordingly. Without this capability, you'd have to manually switch the network through software or a hardware jumper.

Wake on LAN: Wake on LAN cards support ACPI (advanced configuration and power interface) remote wake up, which is a long-winded way of saying that they're capable of remotely powering up your Windows 98 or Windows 2000 PC.

OPTICAL DRIVES

Interface: Internal optical drives use either the SCSI or EIDE (also known as ATAPI) interfaces. At the risk of bringing up the age-old SCSI vs. IDE brouhaha, most users will be perfectly happy with the cheaper IDE drives (though SCSI does have the advantage of dedicated controllers that don't place the burden of I/O tasks on your CPU, and the capacity for chaining more than two drives on a single cable).

DAE speed: DAE, or digital audio extraction, indicates how fast an optical drive can extract tracks from an audio CD using the 1x=150KB/sec ratio. Again, higher numbers are better. DAE times tend to be slower than general read times because audio tracks on compact discs aren't recorded in the same way that files are recorded on a hard disk. The laser in your optical drive must not only decode the digital data, but must also use complex algorithms and error-correction bits to play a kind of guessing game about exactly where tracks begin and end.

Max data transfer rate: This is just another expression of the drive's maximum data-read speed. A 52x drive transfers 150KB/sec multiplied by 52, resulting in a maximum data-transfer rate of 7800KB/sec.

Data buffer size: Data buffers are crucial to preventing the buffer underruns that cause you to burn coasters instead of usable CDs. Buffers essentially ensure that a constant stream of information is available to your burner's laser. If the data buffer runs dry during the burning process, the laser stops recording, and the disc is ruined. When writing at 16x speed, a data-starved 2MB buffer can survive for just under a second before it drains completely. Buffer-underrun protection technology (such as Burn Proof) can eliminate the consequences of this problem.

Formats supported: Among the glut of formats out there, these are recognized by most optical drives:

- CD-DA ("Red Book") is a garden-variety audio CD.
  - CD-Text is an audio CD with extended text information containing artist and track names, credits, etc.
- CD-ROM ("Yellow Book") is a standard data CD.
  - Mixed-mode CD-ROM contains audio CD and data CD information.
- CD-ROM XA is a photo-CD format, or a data CD with interactive multimedia content.
- Photo-CD is based on the CDROM-XA format and is used to store photographic images.
  - Video CD ("White Book") is for video compressed in the MPEG-1 standard. Video CDs can be played by most stand-alone DVD players.
  - CD-I ("Green Book") is a precursor to the CD-ROM XA format.
  - CD-Extra ("Blue Book") is another stab at a mixed-mode format, but with a hokier name.

- **Interface: E-IDE (ATAPI)**
- **52x32x52x**
- **DAE speed: 40x**
- **Seek time: 140ms (reading)**
- **Max data transfer rate: 7,800KB/sec**
- **Data buffer size: 2MB**
- **Buffer underrun protection**
- **Recording modes: Disc-at-once, track-at-once (multisession), session-at-once, packet writing**
- **Formats supported: CD-DA, CD-ROM, Photo-CD, Video CD, CD-I, CD-Extra, CD-Text, CD-ROMXA**
- **Flash upgradeable**

Write/rewrite/read speed: Optical drives capable of burning to CD-R and CD-RW always indicate speeds in the AxBxCx format, in which A describes the maximum write speed to CD-R, B describes the maximum write speed to CD-RW, and C describes the drive's maximum data read speed. A speed of 1x is 150KB/sec, so data rates higher than this are multiples of this base figure. Needless to say, higher numbers are better across the board. Note that the maximum speed a drive can actually hit before physics begins to upset the process is around 52-56x. Drives that advertise faster rates, such as Kenwood's True-X drives, have multiple lasers reading simultaneously to achieve higher speeds.

Seek time: This is the amount of time it takes a drive to locate and deliver information. The lower the number, the faster the drive should be. But don't make this the determining factor in selecting a drive. Though most optical drives claim an access time of around 150 milliseconds, there really aren't any specific standards for measuring this type of performance.

Buffer underrun protection: If you're a CD-burning freak, buffer underrun protection is just about the greatest thing since Cocoa Krispies. Branded under such names as Burn Proof, SafeBurn, and JustLink, these technologies can pause recording when the data buffer is empty, then resume recording when it's been refreshed. These pauses, however, can extend burning times and are considered verboten by nitpicky audio-mastering professionals because they leave tiny gaps between data streams.

Recording modes: The options are as follows:
- Disc-at-once: Writes the entire CD in one pass. After writing, your disc is "closed" and you can't add any additional information.
- Track-at-once or multisession: CD can be written to in multiple passes at different times. However, until the disc is "closed," some players—especially consumer devices—may be unable to read the disc.
- Session-at-once: This hybrid mode allows disc-at-once control over gaps left between tracks by track-at-once recording. This method is often used when creating discs in the CD-Extra format, such as audio CDs that include digitized video.
- Packet writing: Formats your disc into small blocks of data holders, like a floppy disk. Data can be added or erased incrementally. Erased blocks can be reused on a CD-RW.

Flash upgradeable: Trust us, you want this. Flash-upgradeable optical drives have a chip similar to your PC's BIOS that can be "flashed" with new instructions from the manufacturer. These updates can fix bugs, improve performance, and add support for new CD formats.

SPEAKERS

Frequency response: The sensitivity of the human ear ranges from 20Hz to 22KHz, and most speaker systems closely approximate that range. Speaker sets without subwoofers, however, may only reach down to 120Hz. Such a set can still pump out bass, but it probably won't rattle windows when you crank up the volume. Speaker sets that do include subs usually come with satellites that boast a frequency response of 150MHz to 250MHz—which is just fine, because the subwoofer takes care of everything below this range.

Crossover points: Take the dust cover off the front of a good stereo speaker and you'll usually see a little speaker (the tweeter) and a big speaker (the woofer). The crossover point is the boundary between the two—the tweeter handles all frequencies above that point, and the woofer handles all frequencies below. In a really good set of PC speakers, the crossover point falls around 200Hz. If individual satellite speakers have two speakers inside, the crossover point usually falls around 5KHz. Dolby Digital speakers have a subwoofer-to-woofer crossover point around 250Hz.

- **Frequency response: 20Hz-22KHz**
- **Maximum output: 100dB at 20 feet**
- **Crossover points: 5KHz high-frequency crossover**
- **Power output per channel or total power output: 400W total output (25W midrange X 4, 85W subwoofer)**
- **Input connectors: 1/8 inch, S/PDIF, optical**

Maximum output: Audio volume is stated in decibels, a figure that's calculated with a complex formula that takes into account the distance between the audio source and where the decibel reading was recorded. That's why manufacturers often include a distance in the maximum output rating, as in "110dB (decibels) at 10 feet." A volume of 60dB is roughly equivalent to the quiet of a golf course. Dance clubs average between 100 and 110dB. For most people, painful sound levels begin at 120dB. At 140dB, run for your life—a jumbo jet is about to land on your head.

Power per channel: Often, a speaker system's power per channel (reported in watts) has more to do with marketing than audio quality. Indeed, an inefficient speaker might use a lot of power to generate average volume levels, while an efficient speaker might use only an average amount of power to generate superior volume levels. Producing bass frequencies always requires more power than producing treble frequencies, which is why subwoofers may draw 65W while satellites may draw only 25W. All of these variables should tell you that the power-per-channel spec is a vague measure of speaker quality at best. As a general rule, though, higher numbers in the power-per-channel spec indicate better-designed speakers.

Input connectors: PC speakers are usually equipped with 1/8-inch "mini" plugs that connect directly into the jacks of your soundcard. Most PC speakers plug into the analog connectors, but some can work with digital connections. These speaker sets have a built-in analog-to-digital converter, and they connect with a mini plug or a S/PDIF digital input that uses an RCA plug. Dolby Digital speakers often come with a box that contains an amplifier, a Dolby Digital decoder, and a digital-to-audio converter, and they often connect to a soundcard with a single optical input. Some PC speakers also have auxiliary inputs, so you can connect more than one PC or other device.

WIRELESS LAN

Standards: If you plan to set up a wireless LAN using hardware from more than one company, be sure it all follows the same standard. The two most popular Wi-Fi standards are 802.11b and 802.11g. 802.11g networks are faster, and the equipment should be backwards-compatible with 802.11b. 802.11a operates in the 5Ghz range, but isn't backwards-compatible with the other standards.

Frequency range: This is the area of the radio spectrum in which your wireless kit works. Wi-Fi and Bluetooth operate in the 2.4GHz spectrum, which is also shared by some cordless phones. Microwaves can also cause interference in that region and can affect the range of Wi-Fi kits.

External interfaces: This details the means by which your router or bridge connects to the Internet. Most routers include a standard RJ-45 port that connects to a 10/100baseT LAN. Some also include an internal modem so you can dial into your ISP.

- **Standards: 802.11b, Wi-Fi**
- **Data transmission rate: 11Mbps/5.5 Mbps/ 2 Mbps/1Mbps**
- **Frequency range: 2400-2483.5MHz**
- **Max distance between terminals: 100 feet indoors, 200 feet outdoors**
- **External interfaces: V.90 56K modem, 10/100baseT**
- **Router or bridge: Router**

Data transmission rate: Usually listed in megabits per second, this is the speed at which your wireless connection moves data. As you move farther from the base station, the speed of the connection will drop. Those diminishing speeds are also listed.

Max distance between terminals: This is simply the maximum distance at which the LAN kit will work, usually reported for both indoors and outdoors. FYI: We've found the indoor settings listed to be very optimistic, especially in crowded urban areas.

Router or bridge: Wireless Ethernet access points are available as either bridges or routers. A bridge is like any other section of network cable—it does nothing but pass data from your wired LAN to your wireless LAN. If you use a bridge, you need an IP address for each wireless machine. A router can share a single IP address with more than one wireless machine by using Network Address Translation (NAT).

SOUNDCARDS

Audio DSP chipset: The digital signal processing (DSP) chip determines the basic features of a soundcard. Creative Labs' Sound Blaster Audigy 2 uses the CA0102 DSP chipset, which caters to digital-music enthusiasts by offering such features as DVD-Audio playback. Among soundcards, there's Creative Labs and then there's everybody else, so the EMU10K1 (in the original Audigy) and the CA0102 are ubiquitous. However there are challengers, with several soundcard makers including Turtle Beach and Hercules offering products based on another DSP from Crystal Semiconductors. Manufacturers like Philips make their own DSPs for exclusive use in their own soundcards.

Hardware voices/hardware audio channels: This is the number of audio streams that a soundcard can play back simultaneously. A single audio stream can be anything from a sound effect to a character vocalization in a game to individual musical notes in a MIDI synthesizer. Most soundcards support 64 hardware voices, which means they can play up to 64 different sounds at one time. Some manufacturers claim simultaneous playback of up to 256 audio streams, but that figure usually combines hardware voices and software voices. Hardware voices run on the soundcard only, while software voices rely on system resources (i.e., your PC's processor and memory). Performance in demanding applications such as 3D games suffers when your soundcard relies on software voices, so be sure your soundcard supports at least 64 hardware voices.

Input/output connectors: PC soundcards output audio at "line level," so you can't connect a soundcard directly to a speaker and get significant volume. Fortunately, most PC speaker sets have a built-in amplifier that brings the audio signal up to "speaker level." If you don't have a set of PC speakers, you can connect the soundcard's outputs to a stereo receiver, which also has a built-in amplifier. In all cases, you'll have to match the soundcard's connectors to your speakers' or stereo receiver's connectors. Most PC soundcards are equipped with 1/8-inch "mini" connectors, to which most PC speaker sets can be directly connected. Some soundcards, such as Creative's Sound Blaster Audigy 2 Platinum eX, come with "breakout boxes" that attach to the soundcard and offer many additional connector options, such as RCA connectors for stereo receivers and optical pass-through connectors for Dolby Digital 5.1 speaker sets.

- **Audio DSP chipset: CA0102**
- **ADC/DAC resolution and sampling rate: 24-bit audio at 192KHz**
- **Hardware voices/hardware audio channels: 64**
- **3D audio formats supported: DirectSound3D, EAX 2.0, EAX Advanced HD**
- **Input/output connectors: 1/8-in., S/PDIF, optical pass-through**

ADC/DAC resolution and sampling frequency: Even if you create music on your PC and play it through digital speakers, all audio must at some point be converted to analog in order for you to hear it. All soundcards support signal conversion, both analog-to-digital (ADC) and digital-to-analog (DAC), but not all have the same resolution and sampling frequency, which are measured in bitrate and hertz, respectively. The higher the resolution and sampling frequency offered by your soundcard, the more precise your PC can be in audio reproduction. Accept nothing less than CD quality in these categories: 16-bit resolution, and a 44.1KHz sampling frequency (most consumer-level soundcards support sampling frequency up to 48KHz.)

3D audio formats: When attached to a set of PC speakers that includes at least four speaker boxes, most soundcards can render 3D or "positional" audio, which generates sounds from any direction around a listener. During gaming or DVD-watching, positional audio sounds like you're standing in the middle of all the action. A good soundcard will support DirectSound3D, EAX (now at version 3.0), and A3D. DirectSound3D, which is part of Windows' DirectX suite, provides a standardized and relatively simple way for programmers to create 3D positional audio. Creative's EAX extends DirectSound3D with additional audio processing features.

HARD DRIVES

Capacity: Even a hard drive's advertised size can be misleading. In the hard-drive industry, 1MB is defined as 1 million bytes, not the more technically accurate 1,048,576 bytes. So what does this mean to you at the end of the day? Well, if you're buying a 75GB drive, be aware that if you believe 1MB to be 1,048,576 bytes, your "75GB" hard drive is closer to 72GB. Better yet, just get a 200GB drive and don't sweat the missing few gigs.

Buffer size: This is the amount of memory, or cache, that's used to store recently read data, or buffer data, that's being written to the disk. Many drives today come with a generous 8MB of cache, but after that, diminishing returns actually make the difference inconsequential. However, super-large buffers do come into play when running servers.

Spindle speed: This describes how quickly a hard drive can spin its disk platters (which are attached to a shaft or spindle), and is measured in revolutions per minute (rpm). Most consumer hard-drive speeds range from 5400rpm to 15,000rpm, with the average performance of an IDE drive ringing in at 7200rpm. A drive's spindle speed and areal density are among the most important specs to consider, because the two combined essentially determine the personality of the drive. A higher spindle speed typically suggests faster drive performance, but not always. To wit, a drive with a high spindle speed and low areal density might actually deliver less throughput than a drive with a low spindle speed and high areal density—in some cases. That stated, given the specifics of the models currently on the market, you should always take a 7200rpm drive over a 5400rpm drive.

Sustained (or sequential) transfer rate: This tells you how quickly a hard drive can serve up a contiguous file and is usually expressed in gigabytes per second. Sustained data rate is among the most telling hard drive specs—but it can be easily misrepresented. Sustained transfer rates describe the speed at which a hard drive can move a single large file that's laid out sequentially on the disk. But if you typically work with smaller files that are scrambled all over the disk, seek time is a more relevant spec.

- **Capacity: 75GB**
- **Seek time: 8.5ms**
- **Buffer size: 2MB**
- **Interface: ATA/100**
- **Spindle speed: 7200rpm**
- **Areal density: 11Gb per square inch**
- **Sustained (or sequential) transfer rate: 37GB/second**

Seek time: Measured in milliseconds (ms) and usually expressed as an average, seek time tells you how long it takes for a drive's read heads to move back and forth across the platters that actually store the drive's data. Seek time can be an important factor in determining how fast a drive performs, but most modern 7200rpm drives have very similar seek times. They all seem to hover in the 9ms range, and the difference between an 8.5ms and 9ms seek time is negligible. You won't see real differences until you're looking at a drive with a seek time in the ultra-high-performance 5ms range (such as that offered in the Seagate X15).

Interface: Don't be fooled by boxes emblazoned with the promise "133MB/s transfer rate!" An ATA/133 drive can indeed handle 133MB/sec transfers, but you'll never experience such speeds during actual use. The problem is that the internal machinery of even the fastest IDE hard drives can't pump data at such a fast rate. In fact, none of the ATA/133 drives currently available will hit even 50MB/sec transfers during peak operation. This doesn't mean you shouldn't buy ATA/133—it is, after all, the fastest hard-drive technology available. But ATA/100 is more than adequate until Serial ATA drives take over. If your immediate consideration is speed, pay more attention to areal density, the number of platters, spindle speed, and seek time.

Areal density: This defines the amount of data that can be packed onto a square inch of magnetic platter surface. The closer together you can corral your data, the higher the areal density. Usually expressed in gigabits per square inch, higher densities generally indicate faster drives. For example, if you double the areal density of a disk platter, the drive head needs to move only half as far in order to read or write the same amount of data on the platter. Increasing areal density also allows for a reduction in the drive's platter size, which gives you other benefits, such as reduced power consumption.

SYSTEM REQUIREMENTS

If game companies told you what your system *really* needed in order to get the most our of their games, you probably wouldn't buy the games at all. The "System Requirements" example below was pulled directly from the box of *Battlefield 1942*.

CPU: A 500MHz Pentium III? For *Battlefield 1942?* Maybe if you don't mind games with frame rates slower than filmstrips. We think that even the recommended 800MHz Pentium III is a farce. To get the most from a game, our rule of thumb is to triple the minimum requirement or double the recommended CPU.

Memory: 128MB of RAM isn't enough for Windows XP alone, much less running a game on top of the OS. We recommend no less than 512MB for optimal performance under Windows XP.

CD-ROM: It's often said that few games take advantage of CD-ROM speeds beyond 4x because they use only low-quality video and because most of a game's levels are installed on your hard drive. For the most part, this adage holds up. The reasoning, however, doesn't take into account the long install times of new games. If a game takes two CDs to load, you'll cut your time by a third—possibly by half—by using a CD-ROM that spins at 32x or better.

Hard drive: The box specs rarely lie in this case. If a game requires 650MB to run, you'd better have that much hard-drive space available. But also consider the fact that many games can now be loaded onto the hard drive in their entirety—where they'll lay claim to a helluva lot of space. We recommend you have between three and 10 times more space available than the game says it needs. Since hard drives tend to slow down when they're almost full, you'll get the most performance from a drive that isn't packed.

MINIMUM

- **CPU: Pentium III 500/AMD Athlon**
- **Memory: 128MB**
- **CD-ROM: 4x**
- **Videocard: 32MB supported Direct3D and Hardware and Transform & Lighting capable video card with DirectX 8.1 compatible sound card**
- **Hard drive: 1.2GB free space**

RECOMMENDED

- **CPU: Pentium III 800 / AMD Athlon**
- **Memory: 256MB**
- **CD-ROM: 16x**
- **Videocard: 64MB supported Direct3D and Hardware and Transform & Lighting capable video card with DirectX 8.1 compatible sound card**
- **Hard drive: 650MB free space**

Videocard: As we may have mentioned, game publishers tend to distort reality when describing the minimum videocard needed to render their masterpieces. We'd be surprised if a 32MB card could run any triple-A game titles. If they did, it would be because you'd turned off so many of the game's details, you might as well load up the text-based *Zork.*

ANATOMY OF A case

Build quality: If you don't intend on stacking components on top of your PC, the strength of your case probably isn't of paramount concern. But keep in mind that a hefty case made of steel or thick aluminum doesn't just prevent crumpling if your supersized friend takes a breather on it—it also helps dampen the noise from your components.

You should also be on the lookout for details such as folded or blunted edges in the interior. It doesn't seem important until you've had some of the truly gross experiences we've had inside cases with sharp, burled edges.

Cooling features: A well-designed case will allow good airflow, with adequate ventilation and plenty of mounts for cooling fans in strategic locations. The ideal case will also include several cooling fans. This particular case includes three fans, one of which is a tilted front intake fan cleverly positioned to pull in cool air from vents in the floor of the case. And please don't block the intake fans by placing them against walls or barricading them with peripherals!

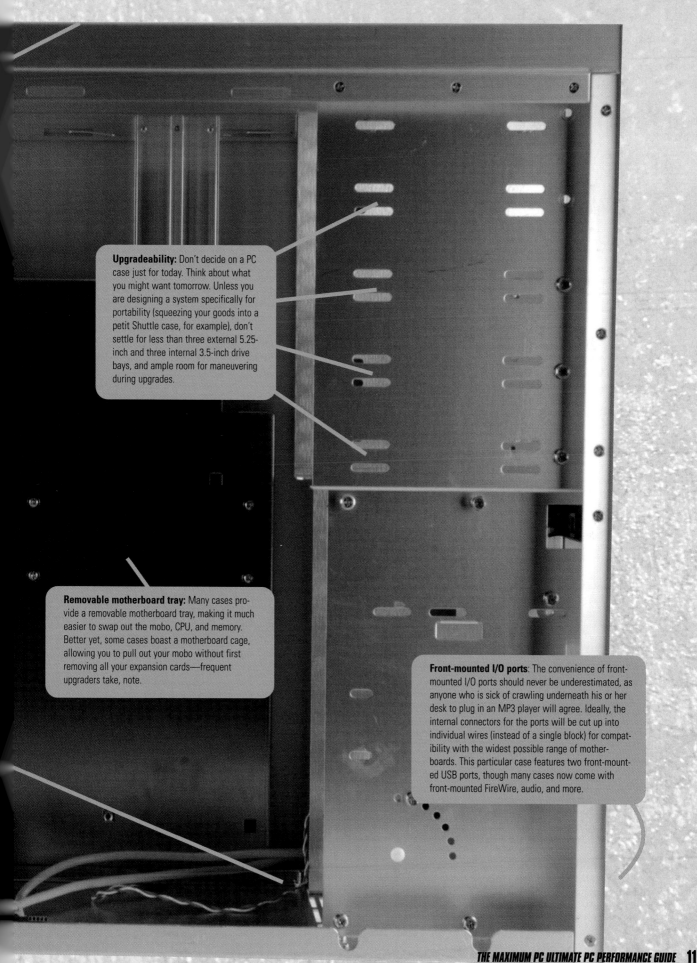

Upgradeability: Don't decide on a PC case just for today. Think about what you might want tomorrow. Unless you are designing a system specifically for portability (squeezing your goods into a petit Shuttle case, for example), don't settle for less than three external 5.25-inch and three internal 3.5-inch drive bays, and ample room for maneuvering during upgrades.

Removable motherboard tray: Many cases provide a removable motherboard tray, making it much easier to swap out the mobo, CPU, and memory. Better yet, some cases boast a motherboard cage, allowing you to pull out your mobo without first removing all your expansion cards—frequent upgraders take, note.

Front-mounted I/O ports: The convenience of front-mounted I/O ports should never be underestimated, as anyone who is sick of crawling underneath his or her desk to plug in an MP3 player will agree. Ideally, the internal connectors for the ports will be cut up into individual wires (instead of a single block) for compatibility with the widest possible range of motherboards. This particular case features two front-mounted USB ports, though many cases now come with front-mounted FireWire, audio, and more.

How To Pick the BEST CASE

Finding the ideal habitat for your components

We've lost track of how many times we've espoused the importance of choosing a quality case, but it's time for a recap. A case is more than just a shoebox for your components. A good case improves the stability of your system by channeling punishing heat away from your parts. It can reduce noise by stabilizing noisemakers such as optical drives and side-panels that resonate. A well-thought-out case makes using your PC more convenient by trundling vital connections like USB and FireWire to the front. And last, but definitely not least, a good case looks *cool*.

While choosing a case is one of the most important decisions you'll make when designing a PC, it can also be one of the most vexing. There are literally hundreds of cases from various manufacturers vying for your attention, all claiming to be the best of the best. Even the hardiest geek would tire of sorting through all the riffraff, but hey, that's why we're here. We've broken down all the important attributes you should look for when choosing a case, and included reviews from our monthly magazine of some of the best cases we've seen recently. So if you're ready to begin your search for the perfect case, let's get started!

BASIC STRUCTURAL DESIGN

The first thing you need to establish before buying a case is whether portability is an important factor. If you often tote your rig to friends' houses or LAN parties, you'll want a smaller, more lightweight case. If portability is paramount, you'll want a mini-case like the one pictured on this page. But for a PC that's going to stay put, we strongly recommend choosing a case that's relatively large—this will improve airflow and give you more room for upgrades.

In any event, the case is bound to be pushed around now and then, so you'll want to consider sturdiness. Steel cases tend to be more rigid, while aluminum cases are generally more flimsy. You should also check out the thickness of a case's material—if it seems no thicker than a Coke can, it's probably no stronger either. Try pushing down firmly on the top of the case when it's fully closed. Any give is a bad sign. You wouldn't think that a case could be *that* fragile, but we've seen a few that are. Lastly, to avoid any undue trips to the emergency room, make sure that any rough metal edges on the interior of the case have been folded over to protect your fingers—you'd be surprised how many cases have carnivorous interiors.

THOUGHTFUL AMENITIES

Planning the interior of your case and installing all your components doesn't have to be a chore. A well-designed case can make the process easy. Seek out a case with enough ventilation holes and strategically positioned fan mounts to keep all your piping-hot components running cool. At the very least, you'll want mounts for front intake and rear exhaust fans; ideally, you should have cool air blowing across your CPU, videocard, and hard drives, as these are the hottest-running components in your system. Some particularly well-thought-out cases even include filters for those vents to help keep out unwelcome dust particles. Premium cases will include wire guides and clips to help you tidy up your PC's internal wiring. Although these features can dramatically reduce internal temperatures, they remain pathetically uncommon.

If you do a lot of upgrading and drive-swapping, look for a case that features thumbscrews for the side panels and expansion slots (thumbscrews don't require a screwdriver every time you want to peek into the works). A case with drive rails—a locking system that lets you pull drives in and out of your system without screwing and unscrewing them every time—will make drive-swapping a snap. One caveat: Given the high speeds that hard drives and optical drives spin at these days, it's absolutely critical to make sure that a drive-rail system is well-designed and sturdily constructed. Make sure you can return the case from where it was purchased without a restocking penalty if you find the drive rails don't fit snugly enough to prevent rattle.

For those who are tired of listening to a PC that sounds like a vacuum cleaner, this may come as music to your ears: Some manufacturers are now offering cases specifically geared toward a quieter computing experience. In these cases, look for features such as rubber grommets on the hard drive mounts (to absorb vibration and noise), bundled-in fans that are quiet and preferably speed-adjustable, and a sturdy construction that helps dampen noise rather than amplify it. This is the kind of thing you may only be able to evaluate after you've bought the case, so make sure you can return it without penalty if it's a dud.

Nothing elicits more swearing from *Maximum PC* staffers than having to crawl around to the back of a PC just to plug in an external device. Front-mounted I/O ports will spare you pitched battles with dust and roaches every time you want to plug in your USB key. Almost every case comes with front-mounted USB ports these days, and some even come with front-mounted FireWire and audio ports. Internally, you'll need to connect these ports to the

Xoxide's UV-reactive case glows under ultraviolet light, illustrating just how crazy you can get with your case if you're game.

appropriate headers on your motherboard. Headers are groups of pins used to hook up devices and I/O ports to your mobo, and the arrangement of these pins varies from motherboard to motherboard. As such, you should look for a case that has its USB and FireWire connectors cut up into individual leads that can be connected in any order, as opposed to a fixed block of leads that may be incompatible with your mobo. Or if you prefer, some cases feature pass-through connectors for their front-mounted I/O ports that simply hook up to the appropriate ports on the back of your system.

LEAVE ROOM FOR IMPROVEMENTS

Any case that can be opened without an engineering degree could be advertised as having "easy access." But the devil's in the details. An upgrade-friendly case should be large enough to hold all your existing components comfortably, as well as any components you think you might purchase in the future. The case should also be easy to work on—features such as drive rails, removable drive cages, and particularly a removable motherboard cage or tray are optimal.

Finally, the ideal case will accommodate a variety of motherboard sizes. If you're interested in running a dual-processor rig, for example, make sure your case can fit a full-size ATX motherboard (few can).

BODY MODS

How do you know when a once-underground craze like case modifying has truly gone mainstream? When your local computer store starts to carry a staggering array of pre-modded cases, all mass-produced and ready for purchase. Many manufacturers now offer enclosures that come complete with side-panel windows, neon-colored LEDs, and even sound-sensitive cold-cathode lights. Some companies also offer their cases in a variety of slick color schemes. That means you can now own a trick-looking rig without the dangers of using a Dremel tool.

Of course, if you're the do-it-yourself type, you may want to bust out that Dremel anyway and do your own custom case-modding job. If that piques your interest, look for a case that facilitates easy modding. A case with thin side panels, or at least panels that aren't particularly thick, is probably best. But at the very least, make sure you get a metal case—cutting holes in a plastic case is almost impossible, and it sure as hell won't be pretty.

BUNDLED-IN EXTRAS

To differentiate their products from the masses of me-too offerings, some manufacturers bundle extra goodies with their cases. Case fans are perhaps the most commonly bundled extras; almost every case comes with at least one. Ideally, the included fans will be temperature-sensing, speed-adjustable, or at least quiet. Some case manufacturers include fans with bright neon LEDs, which look slick when viewed through a window. You may want to spring a few extra bucks for a case that comes with a fanbus to control the speed of your fans, such as Thermaltake's Xaser III.

Power supplies are also commonly bundled with cases, but most of the time, they're cheap throwaway units. Try to find a case that bundles a quality power supply if possible, as this can be a real money saver (see our article on page 71 about how to identify a high-quality power supply). If the case you buy comes with a crappy no-name unit, we highly—*highly*—recommend buying your own add-in power supply.

Another extra you might want to look for in a case is a temperature sensor with an overheating alarm and an LCD readout on the front of the case. And if you move your system a lot, a carrying strap could prove invaluable—yes, believe it or not, some manufacturers are now bundling carrying straps with their cases!

APPEARANCE AND PRICE

Appearance is a highly subjective thing, so we can't really give you

Lian Li's PC-6070A has noise-absorbing foam, a soft rubber seal around the front door, and three nearly silent 80mm case fans.

any advice other than to get a case that is aesthetically pleasing to your own eyes. There are plenty of cases out there that strike a balance between form and function, so you don't need to sacrifice good looks to get a case with all the features you want.

With its sci-fi etchings and blue button halos, the Nexus is one of the most handsome fan buses around. And with four fan dials on its fashionable black (or silver) faceplate, the Nexus is also robust—capable of handling even the biggest, baddest air pushers. (It's rated at 19 watts per channel, which is powerful enough to accommodate even fast 92mm fans.)

Be forewarned that when you find the perfect case with all the features you're looking for, it probably won't come cheap. So be prepared to spend a fair chunk of change on your case, and know that it's a worthwhile investment.

How To Pick the BEST MINI-SYSTEM

Little boxes don't have to mean big compromises

Once upon a time, owning a powerful system meant sacrificing a fat chunk of desk real estate to a massive tower. If you wanted a computer that was slim, stylish, and portable, you pretty much had to buy a Mac (shudder). Thanks in large part to the efforts of a Taiwanese motherboard maker called Shuttle, those days are long gone. The company made a name for itself selling do-it-yourself kits that included a small, attractive case and a tiny motherboard with tons of built-in features.

Shuttle's innovative idea has since been mimicked by countless competitors, and it has become a daunting task to pick out the perfect mini-system kit. Choosing the right mini-system is a critical decision, too. The kits lean toward the expensive side, and since most of the components in a given kit are proprietary (meaning they were designed for that particular case, and not to be used with other manufacturers' products), you can't easily swap out the core parts. So we're going to tell you exactly what to look for in a mini-system, and dish out some of our recent mini-system reviews so you know which ones are hot and which ones are not.

ENGINEERING AND BASIC DESIGN

There are generally three types of people who buy mini-systems: People who lack desk space, people who move their computers around a lot, and people who just can't get over how darned cute the wee things are. Unless you fall exclusively into the third category, you'll want your mini-system to be small, light, and easily portable. Frequent LAN party attendees will also want to look for a model that has a built-in carrying handle. And of course, regardless of your reason for buying a mini-system, chances are you'll want to look for one that's sleek and stylish. Some of the latest mini-systems even come tricked out with case windows and neon LED-adorned fans—if that's your fancy.

If you've ever tried to build a mini-system before, you know what a pain it can be to cram all your hardware into such a tiny space. All mini-system kits are not created equal in this regard, however. Some kits include features such as a removable top and removable drive cage that make component installation less of a chore. Trust us: If you're planning on ever upgrading or replacing the hardware inside your mini-system after the initial installation, you'll want these features. Unless you're a skilled contortionist, of course.

Finally, it is of utmost importance that a mini-system come with a quality power supply. Mini-systems often can't fit more than a 200-watt power supply within their cramped quarters. Thus, it's necessary that this power supply be high-quality and capable of consistently delivering its maximum wattage. Upgrading the power supply in a mini-system is not usually an option, so if you want to run the latest hardware, make sure your mini-system's PSU is up to the task.

Unfortunately, it's difficult to ascertain the quality of a power supply without actually operating the mini-system. So if you decide to deviate from our recommendations at the end of this article, be sure to check out the *Maximum PC* forums and listen in on the chatter about the system you are considering. In particular, look out for posts that complain of instability running the latest hardware under high-stress situations.

KEEPING YOUR COOL

A mini-system's dearth of internal space makes the management of heat an issue. A well-designed cooling

It's probably safe to say that the majority of small formfactor case-modding projects have been based on Shuttle's fine enclosures, such as this XPC SB51G. This case's aluminum chassis helps wick away heat, and also provides a very neutral canvas on which to cut, drill and paint. Note that the air venting is extremely simple in design, allowing for more integration opportunities by the wily hardware hacker.

setup should keep all the parts in your rig from overheating by channeling heat away from components and directing it out of the case. However, it shouldn't sound like a wind tunnel. This is a tricky balancing act to pull off. In our experience, Shuttle comes closest to the sweet spot, thanks to the innovative heat pipe (a hollowed-out tube that transfers heat energy away from your CPU and out the case) that ships with its mini-systems. Many mini-systems will also include wire clips and guides and rounded cables to help improve internal airflow—a nice touch that not only looks good, but is utilitarian as well.

LITTLE CASES, BIG TECHNOLOGY

The wee, proprietary motherboard that comes in a mini-system is generally not upgradeable, so you'll want to make sure it's a good one. Intel fanboys and girls will want a chipset that supports Hyper-Threading technology, as well as an 800MHz (or at least 533MHz) frontside bus. Meanwhile, AMD loyalists should seek out a mini-system that uses nVidia's fast and reliable nForce3 chipset—preferably utilizing the Athlon 64 and 800MHz HyperTransport.

As for memory, it's typical for mini-systems these days to have two DIMM slots. The nForce3 chipset offers dual-channel capability (which doubles memory bandwidth when at least two sticks of RAM are installed)—a boon for performance. If the option is available, pounce on it, since dual-channel technology dramatically boosts P4 performance.

Expansion-wise, most mini-systems come with one AGP slot and one PCI slot—avoid any system that denies you either of these slots. Because a mini-system's expansion capabilities are severely limited, you'll want yours to come with as many integrated features as possible to minimize the need for add-in cards. Most companies' offerings include onboard LAN, audio, and video. Granted, integrated audio and video aren't top quality; if we could get by relying on just one, it would be integrated audio.

Finally, avoid squandering your PCI slot on an add-in USB 2.0 or FireWire card by buying a mini-system that sports built-in USB 2.0 and FireWire (remember that USB 2.0 is about 40 times faster than USB 1.1!). The majority of mini-systems have a plethora of convenient front-panel I/O ports, including USB, FireWire, and even audio. If you want easy access to a headphone jack, or if you often use USB keys or external drives, don't deprive yourself of front I/O.

The Hornet Pro packs a fistful of power, with 10K RAID and nVidia's latest and greatest GeForce 6800 videocard.

HORNET PRO 64

If you're into small formfactor boxes and you're biased towards high-end videocards with the GeForce moniker, you probably already know the two don't mix well these days. Few SFF boxes can accommodate these cards' two-slot design. And no SFF machines we know of have the *cojones* to match the merciless power requirements of nVidia's new GeForce 6800 Ultra.

But somehow, Monarch has managed to not only stuff a GeForce 6800 Ultra into its Hornet Pro 64, it has also integrated a bunch of other high-end components.

The GeForce 6800 Ultra is paired with AMD's brand-new Athlon 64 3700+ in a VIA K8T800-based motherboard. This equates to a smooth 2.4GHz of computing that's damn-near as fast as a FX-53 CPU in most tests. A pair of Corsair Micro DDR400 Pro modules light up to indicate memory access activity, while a pair of RAID 0 Western Digital Raptor 74GB 10K drives handle storage. Also new to the mix: Plextor's PX712A, a recent upgrade to our favorite multi-format burner—the Plextor PX-708A. Rounding out the hardware configuration is a Sound Blaster Audigy 2 ZS card.

The case itself sports a Ferrari red custom paint job that looks fabulous. None of this matters to gamers, though, so much as cold, hard performance results. This is a category where the Hornet Pro 64 doesn't disappoint. In our *Jedi Academy* OpenGL test, the Hornet Pro 64 gave us a Lab record 115fps. In *Halo*, the Hornet Pro coughed up an amazing 78fps, more than double our zero-point reference system. While it's not part of our official suite, we also ran *3DMark 2003* and recorded a shockingly fast 12,034. In *3DMark 2001 SE*, it threw down a 24,747. Needless to say, the nVidia GeForce 6800 videocard is one bad mutha.

In application testing, the Hornet performed well, but the 200MHz speed advantage of its Athlon 64 3700+ was nullified by the dual-channel capabilities of our zero-point Athlon 64 FX-51. With this said, Monarch's little red box posted 12 percent faster scores in our *MusicMatch* test, which measures a PC's ability to encode MP3s. While our software tests consistently demonstrate the power of Intel's architecture with regard to software performance—the Hornet ran behind our P4EE-equipped system—the Pentium 4 is considerably more expensive. In our mind, these savings justify Monarch's decision to go with an Athlon-based CPU.

Front-mounted I/O ports (that let you jack in headphones, USB and FireWire devices, and even line-in audio) are easily overlooked when shopping for a mini-case, but you'll kick yourself later if you don't have them.

How To Pick the BEST CPU

We picked our brains to help
you pick your PC's brains

One of the most important decisions you're going to make when building your new PC is which CPU to use. Choosing an Athlon XP or Pentium 4 (or Athlon 64, P4EE) will dictate what motherboard you buy, what kind of RAM you'll want, and how fast your applications can do what they do.

Before we look at what each of the two major CPU manufacturers has to offer, lets take a quick look at the first thing on everyone's mind when choosing a CPU—the mighty megahertz.

Do your proper research! Only a sucker would invest in the Pentium 4 "Willamette" in Socket 423 trim.

MEGAHERTZ: DOES IT REALLY MATTER?

Watching the meteoric rise of the Pentium 4's clock speeds, we've certainly been conditioned to think that megahertz is the final word on processor speed. But the truth is that given the differences between the architectures of the two leading CPU families, clock speed can be misleading. Although it's still an important metric of brute strength, factors such as application-specific optimizations can be just as crucial.

To give you an idea of how drastically different the design can be from CPU to CPU, consider the original Pentium 4. Launched at 1.5GHz, many people reasonably assumed the Pentium 4 was much faster than the Pentium III, which at the time was limited to 1.1GHz. Due to the core architecture differences, the Pentium 4 was actually *slower* in many applications that were out at the time, despite its 400MHz clock-speed advantage. One reason was that applications weren't yet optimized to take advantage of the P4's architecture. But the other culprit was the P4's

lengthy instruction "pipeline."

If you think of a CPU as a car factory, then there would be 12 people working on the assembly line at the Pentium III factory (in what's called a 12-stage pipeline). Each person performs a few tasks on the job at hand before it's moved to the next person. At the Pentium 4 factory, there are 20 people working on the assembly line (a 20-stage pipeline). Because each person does less at each stage, the assembly line can move much faster than at the Pentium III factory. However, sometimes things go wrong and the entire job has to be scrapped ("oops—we ordered the wrong part"). In a CPU, that's called a "branch misprediction," and it's quicker to get the assembly line back up to speed in a Pentium III because there are fewer stages.

Originally the P-III, as well as AMD's Athlon, gave the Pentium 4 fits by being as fast or even faster than the new flagship Intel chip. Buzzing along at more than twice the speed it was introduced at, the Pentium 4 is the recognized speed leader today. The long pipeline of

the P4, which Intel designed to hit high clock speeds, is now paying off.

That doesn't mean, however, that an Athlon XP running at 2.2GHz is always going to be slower than a Pentium 4 running at 2.5GHz. Because of the Athlon XP architecture, and the amount of older applications that rely heavily on such things as floating-point math, the Athlon XP is still quite a competent performer. Although clock speed still matters, you have to treat the CPUs as though they are on different scales. The megahertz in a P4 and an Athlon may not be equivalent in terms of the amount of work that gets done within each clock cycle.

Enter the next CPU incarnations. The P4 has hit 3.4GHz on the Northwood core along with a 3.4GHz Extreme Edition and also emerged on the Prescott at 3.6GHz (looking to hit stride in the 5GHz range). While AMD has released the Athlon 64 in 3800+ and FX-53 flavors (both topping out at 2.4 GHz).

Nonetheless, the P4's scale probably goes all the way to 5GHz or 10GHz, whereas the Athlon XP stops at 2.25GHz.

INTEL—THE PROCESSOR GIANT

Intel is the largest semiconductor manufacturer on the planet, and as such, they've had a hand in developing a majority of the technologies powering today's PCs, including PCI, AGP, PC100, AC97, USB, and PCI Express. The company's biggest hit has been the Pentium processor and its heirs. The Pentium 4 is the company's flagship CPU today. There are far better ways to shave off costs than going cheapo on this crucial component. We, of course, recommend that you buy the newest, fastest P4 possible.

THE PENTIUM 4

There are several different versions of the original "Northwood" Pentium 4. The P4A with 512KB of cache that ran on a 400MHz bus and used a 0.13-micron core; the P4B, which is the Northwood running on a 533MHz bus; and the P4C, which uses an 800MHz bus.

And that's just the Northwood. Don't forget that Intel surprised us all with another version of the P4EE. For more on it and the aforementioned Prescott P4, see Part VI.

A good portion of a CPU's resources aren't used all the time. If it's calculating something with the floating-point unit, the other portions are sitting idle. To address that, Intel added Hyper-Threading to the core. Hyper-Threading essentially splits a single physical CPU into two virtual CPUs. So while one application is running floating-point operations, another can use the remaining free resources of the CPU. It's a boon to people who run multiple applications simultaneously. Hyper-Threading is generally recognized to be a performance booster, especially for multi-taskers. There are occasions when the CPU can run slower because two floating-point-heavy applications are trying to vie for the same physical resources, but we've mostly found it to be useful. Hyper-Threading is available on the 3.06GHz P4 and newer 800MHz bus Pentium 4 CPUs.

CELERON

Today's Celeron is a Pentium 4 die with just 128KB of cache and is confined to a 400MHz bus. It even fits the same socket and operates in most motherboards built for the 400MHz and 533MHz Pentium 4s. It's more than enough for granny to browse the net, but we can't recommend it for power users.

XEON

If you want a dual processor box, your only option is Xeon. But you'll pay dearly for the privilege. Based on the Pentium 4, the Xeon adds a host of features designed for high-end servers—such as a whopping 2MB of cache—that make these procs enormously expensive.

AMD— THE FEISTY UPSTART

In the five+ years since the introduction of AMD's Athlon line of processors, the Athlon has consistently given the Pentium CPUs a run for the money. The ultimate humiliation came when AMD beat Intel to the 1GHz mark. After years of eating dust, AMD has tasted the sweet nectar of victory and has no intention of giving up.

ATHLON XP

AMD designed the Athlon with a pragmatic approach. Its older CPUs were criticized for having poor floating-point performance, so the Athlon XP was designed to be a screamer at floating-point math. (Intel took the opposite approach— the P4 is fairly weak in floating-point performance, but strong in special instructions, which Intel believes are more appropriate for the future of intense math on computer chips.) The Athlon XP's FPU performance makes it ideally suited for older mathematic and scientific applications that have not been optimized for the Pentium 4.

With the Athlon XP, AMD also implemented a controversial performance rating. Instead of using the standard metric of megahertz, a 2.167GHz CPU with 256KB of L2 cache and running on a 333MHz bus is marketed as an Athlon XP

3000+. What does the 3000+ mean? AMD swears on a stack of *Maximum PCs* that it's not analogous to a 3GHz Intel CPU. Despite this claim, it's just a little too convenient that the performance numbers perfectly line up with Intel's frequencies.

For consumers, the numbering scheme actually makes sense, as the average Joe and Jane don't have the time or technical prowess to understand that a 2.2GHz CPU can run as fast as an Intel 2.8GHz CPU in some applications. For

The "Barton" version of the Athlon XP features 512KB of L2 cache and supports up to a 400MHz frontside bus.

hobbyists though, it's a confusing mess. For example, AMD has two 3000+ CPUs. The original one clocked at 2.167GHz using a 333MHz bus, and a version clocked at 2.1GHz using a 400MHz bus.

AMD CPUs with the larger L2 cache of 512KB are generally preferred, especially when running on a 400MHz bus. You'll have to do a little research when buying the CPU, but most stores and web sites are very clear about labeling the attributes of the Athlon XP so you don't get mixed up.

DURON

This is AMD's version of the Celeron. A budget chip built off a derivative of the Athlon, the Duron has just 64KB of cache and is limited to a 200MHz system bus. In the

The original Athlon XP brought SSE to AMD's plate and introduced the controversial set of performance ratings.

AMD's Athlon 64 series of CPUs brings 64-bit computing to the desktop.

Intel keeps the Celeron in the CPU ghetto by limiting it to a 400MHz bus and cutting the cache down to a mere 128KB.

early days, the Duron could outbox a low-end Celeron, but today it's out-classed by Intel's current generation of Celerons. AMD shelved the Duron in 2003.

OPTERON

The Opteron adds 64-bit extensions to AMD's original processor recipe. The Opteron also breaks from convention by embedding a dual-channel memory controller directly into the die. Combined with the 1MB of L2, the Opteron looks like its well on the way to being a hit even at the low clock speeds of 2.4GHz. Opteron, however, isn't intended for desktop use—it's designed and priced for servers and workstations.

ATHLON 64

Based on the same "Hammer" core as the Opteron, the Athlon 64 has a few key features that differentiate it from its server/workstation big brother. While Opteron supports ECC registered DDR memory at DDR333, Athlon 64 can run non-registered dual-channel DDR400. The socket 939 versions (3500+, 3800+, and FX-53) support a 128-bit memory interface running at a core speed of 2.2GHz or 2.4GHz.

SO WHOSE SIDE ARE YOU ON NOW?

"Intel or AMD?" It can be a tough choice. But it's not all about cache sizes, transistor counts, and which one has the better commercials. The perfect CPU for you will greatly depend on what you intend to do with it. If you're interested in gaming, the Athlon 64 FX-53 seems to hold the advantage even at a 1GHz slower clock.

If you intend to handle a lot of media-intense chores such as MP3 encoding and DV editing with opti-mized apps, or 3D rendering with such programs as Newtek *Lightwave 3D*, go with the P4. We don't recommend building a machine with anything less than a newer P4 or Athlon 64 variant. The higher end Xeon and Opteron CPUs are too expensive and too much to tackle for consumer level, first-time builders. For the most part, you need to look at what you can afford as well as what you spend most of your PC hours doing. Then fire up your browser and check out benchmarks and your favorite app or game manufacturer's recommendations. Also, be sure to check out Part VI for more information.

CPU AND CHIPSET

REFERENCE

Your quick-and-easy cheat sheet on all the silicon chips that matter

BY OMEED CHANDRA

MAXIMUM PC
UTILITY RATING
HANDY

CPUs

Wondering which processor will run on your motherboard's chipset? Then check out this list, which provides all the vital info on every Pentium 4 and socket-based Athlon released thus far. We decided to leave out the Pentium III, Celeron, Duron, and slot-based Athlon processors, because none of these slow-as-molasses CPUs delivers respectable power.

Athlon

Code-name: Thunderbird
Process: 0.18-micron
Die size: 120mm^2
Transistors: 37 million
Frequency: 750MHz–1.4GHz
Interface: Slot A, Socket A

Cache: 256K L2, 128K L1
Voltage: 1.75V
Compatible chipsets: ALi MAGiK 1, AMD 760, ATI Radeon IGP 320, nVidia nForce, nVidia nForce2, SiS 733, SiS 735, SiS 745, VIA KT133/A, VIA ProSavage KM133/A, VIA KLE133, VIA KT266/A, VIA ProSavage KM266, VIA KT333, VIA KT400
Lab notes: When the Classic Athlon started to lag behind the P-III, the Thunderbird restored AMD's lead with full-speed L2 cache. Lower-clocked "T-birds" over-clocked well, but the top-end 1.4GHz versions had very little headroom.

Athlon XP

Code-name: Palomino
Process: 0.18-micron
Die size: 128mm^2
Transistors: 37.5 million
Frequency: 1.33GHz–1.73GHz
Interface: Socket A
Cache: 256K L2, 128K L1
Voltage: 1.75V
Compatible chipsets: ALi MAGiK 1, AMD 760, ATI Radeon IGP 320, nVidia nForce, nVidia nForce2, SiS 735, SiS 745, VIA KT266/A, VIA ProSavage KM266, VIA KT333, VIA KT400
Lab notes: Introduced numerous improvements to the Athlon core including full SSE support, lower power consumption, an on-die thermal diode, and an optimized data prefetch unit. And thanks

to its cooler-running design, the Palomino was more overclockable than the Thunderbird.

Athlon XP Rev A

Code-name: Thoroughbred Rev A
Process: 0.13-micron
Die size: 80mm^2
Transistors: 37.2 million
Frequency: 1.47–1.8GHz
Interface: Socket A
Cache: 256K L2, 128K L1
Voltage: 1.5–1.65V
Compatible chipsets: ALi MAGiK 1, AMD 760, ATI Radeon IGP 320, nVidia nForce, nVidia nForce2, SiS 735, SiS 745, VIA KT266/A, VIA ProSavage KM266, VIA KT333, VIA KT400
Lab notes: Despite being manufactured on a 0.13-micron process, the original Thoroughbred was unable to close the frequency gap with Intel. It has shown particularly poor potential for over-clocking. AMD has since addressed the Thoroughbred's shortcomings in a second revision of the processor.

Athlon XP Rev B

Code-name: Thoroughbred Rev B
Process: 0.13-micron
Die size: 84mm^2
Transistors: 37.6 million
Frequency: 2.0–2.25GHz (top speed at press time)
Interface: Socket A

Cache: 256K L2, 128K L1
Voltage: 1.65V
Compatible chipsets: ALi MAGiK 1, AMD 760, ATI Radeon IGP 320, nVidia nForce, nVidia nForce2, SiS 735, SiS 745, VIA KT266/A, VIA ProSavage KM266, VIA KT333, KT400
Lab notes: By adding one more layer to the Thoroughbred core, AMD was able to attain significantly higher frequencies and narrow the performance gap with Intel. Though initially used solely for 2.0GHz and faster CPUs (i.e, 2400+ and up), the improved core will eventually trickle down to replace the Revision A core for slower-clocked procs. High-end Revision B units (2.17GHz and faster) thrive on a 333MHz FSB. Initial reports

on overclocking potential are promising.

Pentium 4

Code-name: Willamette
Process: 0.18-micron
Die size: 217mm²
Transistors: 42 million
Frequency: 1.4–2.0GHz
Interface: Socket 423, Socket 478
Cache: 256K L2, 20K L1
Voltage: 1.75V
Compatible chipsets: ALi ALADDiN-P4, ATI Radeon IGP 330/340, Intel 845/E, Intel 850/E, SiS 645/DX, SiS 650, SiS 648, SiS R658, VIA P4X266/A, VIA ProSavage P4M266, VIA P4X333
Lab notes: Early P4s trailed the Athlon's performance, but as clock speeds ramped up, the P4 began to flex its muscle. The P4 initially used Socket 423, but Socket 478 quickly replaced this dead-end interface. Despite its long pipeline, the Willamette core showed overclocking potential that was unremarkable at best.

Pentium 4 A

Code-name: Northwood

Process: 0.13-micron
Die size: 146mm²
Transistors: 55 million
Frequency: 1.6-2.4GHz
Interface: Socket 478
Cache: 512K L2, 20K L1
Voltage: 1.5V
Compatible chipsets: ALi ALADDiN-P4, ATI Radeon IGP 330/340, Intel 845/E, Intel 850/E, SiS 645/DX, SiS 650, SiS 648, SiS R658, VIA P4X266/A, VIA ProSavage P4M266, VIA P4X333
Lab notes: The first 0.13-micron P4, the Northwood sports a 512K L2 cache and is known to be very overclockable.

Pentium 4 B

Code-name: Northwood
Process: 0.13-micron
Die size: 131mm²
Transistors: 55 million
Frequency: 2.26–2.8GHz (top speed at press time)
Interface: Socket 478
Cache: 512K L2, 20K L1
Voltage: 1.5V
Compatible chipsets: ATI Radeon IGP 340, Intel 850E, SiS 645DX, SiS 648, SiS R658, VIA P4X333
Lab notes: The "B" version of the Northwood ups FSB speed to a blazing 533MHz and is just as overclockable as the original Northwood. One can only guess how far Intel will push clock speeds on this frequency-friendly process technology.

Chipsets

If you thought your processor choices were deep with variables, check out the chipset scene. There are six vendors for each CPU platform, and most of them offer multiple chipsets, each with a unique set of features and drawbacks. It's enough to make anyone's head spin, which is why we've put together this handy list to use as a field guide for your chipset safari. We collected detailed information on all the popular Athlon and P4 chipsets, but didn't venture into P-III or slotted Athlon territory, because only a Minimum Poser would consider using one of those CPUs in a new system today.

ATHLON CHIPSETS

VIA KT133

Memory support: PC100, PC133, VC133; 1.5GB max
CPU support: Athlon, Duron
Bus speed: 200MHz
I/O interconnect: PCI, 133MB/s

MAX ATA support: 66
Lab notes: The first Socket A chipset on the market, the KT133 was hamstrung by a 200MHz FSB.

VIA KT133A

Memory support: PC100, PC133, VC133; 1.5GB max
CPU support: Athlon, Duron
Bus speed: 200MHz, 266MHz
I/O interconnect: PCI, 133MB/s
MAX ATA support: 100
Lab notes: Adding support for ATA/100 and a 266MHz FSB, this revision of the KT133 was a bit more robust.

VIA KLE133

Memory support: PC100, PC133; 1.5GB max
CPU support: Athlon, Duron
Bus speed: 200MHz, 266MHz
I/O interconnect: PCI, 133MB/s
MAX ATA support: 100
Lab notes: Intended for budget systems, the KLE133 integrated 4x AGP graphics and an Ethernet controller.

VIA ProSavage KM133

Memory support: PC100, PC133; 1.5GB max
CPU support: Athlon, Duron
Bus speed: 200MHz
I/O interconnect: PCI, 133MB/s
MAX ATA support: 66
Lab notes: This version of the KT133 tossed integrated S3 ProSavage4 graphics into the mix.

VIA ProSavage KM133A

Memory support: PC100, PC133; 1.5GB max
CPU support: Athlon, Duron, Athlon XP
Bus speed: 200MHz, 266MHz
I/O interconnect: PCI, 133MB/s
MAX ATA support: 100
Lab notes: Fixed some problems of the KM133 and added ATA/100 and 266MHz FSB capabilities.

VIA KT266

Memory support: PC100, PC133, VC133, DDR200, DDR266; 4GB max
CPU support: Athlon, Duron, Athlon XP
Bus speed: 200MHz, 266MHz
I/O interconnect: V-Link, 266MB/s
MAX ATA support: 100
Lab notes: The first Athlon DDR chipset from VIA, it was quickly succeeded by the KT266A.

VIA KT266A

Memory support: PC100, PC133, VC133, DDR200, DDR266; 4GB max
CPU support: Athlon, Duron, Athlon XP
Bus speed: 200MHz, 266MHz

I/O interconnect: V-Link/266MB/s
MAX ATA support: 100
Lab notes: Featuring an improved memory controller, the "A" revision of the KT266 is one of the best Athlon XP chipsets out there.

VIA ProSavage KM266
Memory support: PC100, PC133, DDR200, DDR266; 4GB max
CPU support: Athlon, Duron, Athlon XP
Bus speed: 200MHz, 266MHz
I/O interconnect: V-Link, 266MB/s
MAX ATA support: 100
Lab notes: Sporting integrated S3 ProSavage8 graphics, this variant of the KT266A is targeted at budget systems.

VIA KT333
Memory support: DDR200, DDR266, DDR333; 4GB max
CPU support: Athlon, Duron, Athlon XP
Bus speed: 200MHz, 266MHz
I/O interconnect: V-Link, 266MB/s
MAX ATA support: 133
Lab notes: Builds upon the KT266A by adding support for DDR333 and ATA/133.

VIA KT400
Memory support: DDR200, DDR266, DDR333 (unofficially supports DDR400); 4GB max
CPU support: Athlon, Duron, Athlon XP
Bus speed: 200MHz, 266MHz, 333MHz
I/O interconnect: V-Link, 533MB/s
MAX ATA support: 133
Lab notes: Throws AGP 8x, USB 2.0, a faster interconnect, and 333MHz FSB support into the mix.

AMD 760
Memory support: DDR200, DDR266; 2GB unbuffered/4GB buffered max
CPU support: Athlon, Duron, Athlon XP
Bus speed: 200MHz, 266MHz
I/O interconnect: PCI/133MB/s
MAX ATA support: 100
Lab notes: The first Athlon DDR chipset, the 760 was a heavyweight in its time. Unfortunately, Athlon XP support is iffy on many 760-based mobos.

ALi MAGiK 1
Memory support: PC100, PC133, VC133, DDR200, DDR266; 3GB max
CPU support: Athlon, Duron, Athlon XP
Bus speed: 200MHz, 266MHz
I/O interconnect: PCI, 133MB/s
MAX ATA support: 100
Lab notes: Though comparable to the AMD 760, the MAGiK 1 can't hold a candle to newer VIA offerings.

SiS 733
Memory support: PC100, PC133; 1.5GB max

SiS 735
CPU support: Athlon, Duron
Bus speed: 200MHz, 266MHz
I/O interconnect: MuTIOL, 1.2GB/s
MAX ATA support: 100
Lab notes: Integrates north and south bridge functions on a single chip for cheap SDRAM systems.

SiS 735
Memory support: PC100, PC133, DDR200, DDR266; 1.5GB max
CPU support: Athlon, Duron, Athlon XP
Bus speed: 200MHz, 266MHz
I/O interconnect: MuTIOL, 1.2GB/s
MAX ATA support: 100
Lab notes: With built-in LAN and performance rivaling the KT266A, this is a solid single-chip DDR solution.

SiS 745
Memory support: DDR200, DDR266, DDR333; 3GB max
CPU support: Athlon, Duron, Athlon XP
Bus speed: 200MHz, 266MHz
I/O interconnect: MuTIOL, 1.2GB/s
MAX ATA support: 100
Lab notes: Drops the 735's integrated Ethernet, but adds FireWire and DDR333 support.

nVidia nForce 420-D
Memory support: DDR200, DDR266, 1.5GB max
CPU support: Athlon, Duron, Athlon XP
Bus speed: 200MHz, 266MHz
I/O interconnect: HyperTransport, 800MB/s
MAX ATA support: 100
Lab notes: Sports realtime Dolby Digital 5.1 encoding, built-in GeForce2-level graphics, and 128-bit memory support.

nVidia nForce 415-D
Memory support: DDR200, DDR266; 1.5GB max
CPU support: Athlon, Duron, Athlon XP
Bus speed: 200MHz, 266MHz
I/O interconnect: HyperTransport, 800MB/s
MAX ATA support: 100
Lab notes: A cheaper version of the 420-D that lacks integrated graphics.

nVidia nForce2
Memory support: DDR200, DDR266, DDR333, DDR400; 3GB max
CPU support: Athlon, Duron, Athlon XP
Bus speed: 200MHz, 266MHz, 333MHz
I/O interconnect: HyperTransport, 800MB/s
MAX ATA support: 133
Lab notes: Boasts built-in GeForce4 MX-level graphics and DDR400 compatibility. The first Athlon chipset to officially support a 333MHz FSB.

ATI Radeon IGP 320
Memory support: DDR200, DDR266; 1GB max

CPU support: Athlon, Duron, Athlon XP
Bus speed: 200MHz, 266MHz
I/O interconnect: A-Link, 266MB/s
MAX ATA support: 100
Lab notes: ATI's Athlon chipset includes Radeon-level graphics and USB 2.0.

PENTIUM 4 CHIPSETS:

Intel 845
Memory support: DDR200, DDR266; 3GB max
CPU support: P4, P4A
Bus speed: 400MHz
I/O interconnect: Hub Architecture, 266MB/s
MAX ATA support: 100
Lab notes: The original 845 was originally limited to SDRAM support, but Intel eventually added DDR200 and DDR266 support as well.

Intel 845E
Memory support: DDR200, DDR266; 2GB max
CPU support: P4, P4A, P4B
Bus speed: 400MHz, 533MHz
I/O interconnect: Hub Architecture, 266MB/s
MAX ATA support: 100
Lab notes: Responding to criticism that RDRAM is too costly, this chipset brings DDR support to the P4.

Intel 845PE
Memory support: DDR266, DDR333; 2GB max
CPU support: P4, P4A, P4B
Bus speed: 400MHz, 533MHz
I/O interconnect: Hub Architecture, 266MB/s
MAX ATA support: 100
Lab notes: Includes DDR333 support, but not AGP 8x support.

Intel 845GE
Memory support: DDR266, DDR233; 2GB max
CPU support: P4, P4A, P4B
Bus speed: 400MHz, 533MHz
I/O interconnect: Hub Architecture, 266MB/s
MAX ATA support: 100
Lab notes: The increased bandwidth of DDR333 gives the integrated "Extreme Graphics" in this chipset a little more boost.

Intel 845GV
Memory support: DDR266, DDR333; 2GB max
CPU support: P4, P4A, P4B
Bus speed: 400MHz, 533MHz
I/O interconnect: Hub Architecture, 266MB/s
MAX ATA support: 100

THE MEGAHERTZ RACE

AMD trounced Intel in June 2000 when it pushed the classic Athlon to the historic 1GHz mark. Since then, however, the two companies have been locked in a bitter battle, with Intel gaining the upperhand (in clock speeds, at least) once it released the Pentium 4. To give you some perspective on the race to the 3GHz finish line, we dug into our archives to track just who launched what and when.

Please note that all AMD Athlon XPs are referred to by their performance ratings. For example, the 2800+ runs at 2.25GHz.

INTEL	DATE INTRODUCED
Pentium 4B 2.8GHz, 2.66GHz, 2.60GHz, 2.50GHz	August 26, 2002
Pentium 4B 2.53GHz	May 6, 2002
Pentium 4A 2.40GHz	April 2, 2002
Pentium 4A 2.2GHz	January 7, 2002
Pentium 4 2GHz, 1.9GHz	August 27, 2001
Pentium 4 1.8GHz, 1.6GHz	July 2, 2001
Pentium 4 1.7GHz	April 23, 2001
Pentium 4 1.5GHz, 1.4GHz	November 20, 2000

AMD	DATE INTRODUCED
Athlon XP model 2800 (2.25GHz), Athlon XP model 2700 (2.17GHz)	October 2002
Athlon XP model 2600 (2.13GHz), Athlon XP model 2400 (2GHz)	August 21, 2002
Athlon XP model 2200+ (1.8GHz)	June 10, 2002
Athlon XP model 2100+ (1.73GHz)	March 13, 2002
Athlon XP model 2000+ (1.67GHz)	January 7, 2002
Athlon XP model 1900+ (1.6GHz)	November 5, 2001
Athlon XP model 1800+ (1.53GHz), Athlon XP model 1700+ (1.47GHz), Athlon XP model 1600+ (1.4GHz), Athlon XP Model 1500+ (1.33GHz)	October 9, 2001
Athlon 1.4GHz	June 6, 2001
Athlon 1.33GHz	March 21, 2001
Athlon 1.2GHz	October 17, 2000
Athlon 1.1GHz	August 14, 2000
Athlon 1GHz	June 5, 2000

Lab notes: Think of this as the 810 of the P4 chipset family. It includes integrated graphics, but is intended for boards lacking AGP slots. Also lacks DDR333 support.

Intel 850
Memory support: PC600, PC800; 2GB max
CPU support: P4, P4A

Bus speed: 400MHz
I/O interconnect: Hub Architecture, 266MB/s
MAX ATA support: 100
Lab notes: The original RDRAM chipset for the P4 has remained a contender.

Intel 850E
Memory support: PC600, PC800; 2GB max
CPU support: P4, P4A, P4B

Bus speed: 400MHz, 533MHz
I/O interconnect: Hub Architecture, 266MB/s
MAX ATA support: 100
Lab notes: Blazes on a 533MHz FSB, but only officially supports PC800 RDRAM. Many mobo vendors offer PC1066 support nonetheless.

VIA P4X266
Memory support: PC100, PC133, DDR200, DDR266; 4GB max
CPU support: P4, P4A
Bus speed: 400MHz
I/O interconnect: V-Link, 266MB/s
MAX ATA support: 100
Lab notes: This chipset was made without a license, landing the company in a lawsuit from Intel. Slower than the 845E, too.

VIA P4X266A
Memory support: PC100, PC133, DDR200, DDR266; 4GB max
CPU support: P4, P4A
Bus speed: 400MHz
I/O interconnect: V-Link, 266MB/s
MAX ATA support: 133
Lab notes: Refines the P4X266's memory controller and adds ATA/133, but still lacks a license.

VIA ProSavage P4M266
Memory support: PC100, PC133, DDR200, DDR266; 4GB max
CPU support: P4, P4A
Bus speed: 400MHz
I/O interconnect: V-Link, 266MB/s
MAX ATA support: 133
Lab notes: Adds integrated S3 ProSavage8 graphics to the P4X266A chipset.

VIA P4X400
Memory support: DDR266, DDR333; 32GB max
CPU support: P4, P4A, P4B
Bus speed: 400MHz, 533MHz
I/O interconnect: V-Link, 533MB/s
MAX ATA support: 133
Lab notes: This is really the P4X333A with unofficial support for DDR400, 8x AGP, and USB 2.0. Unfortunately, there's still no license from Intel.

SiS 645
Memory support: PC133, DDR200, DDR266, DDR333; 3GB max
CPU support: P4, P4A
Bus speed: 400MHz
I/O interconnect: MuTIOL, 533MB/s
MAX ATA support: 100
Lab notes: The first DDR333 chipset for the Pentium 4.

SiS 645DX

Memory support: DDR200, DDR266, DDR333; 3GB max
CPU support: P4, P4A, P4B
Bus speed: 400MHz, 533MHz
I/O interconnect: MuTIOL, 533MB/s
MAX ATA support: 133
Lab notes: This variant of the 645 tacks on 533MHz FSB capability and ups the IDE controller to ATA/133.

SiS 650

Memory support: PC133, DDR200, DDR266; 3GB max
CPU support: P4, P4A
Bus speed: 400MHz
I/O interconnect: MuTIOL, 533MB/s
MAX ATA support: 100
Lab notes: Intended for mini-PCs and cost-conscious OEMs, this chipset bears similarities to the SiS 645 but adds integrated graphics.

SiS 648

Memory support: DDR200, DDR266, DDR333; 3GB max
CPU support: P4, P4A, P4B
Bus speed: 400MHz, 533MHz
I/O interconnect: MuTIOL 1G, 1GB/s
MAX ATA support: 133
Lab notes: Set to challenge the 850E with AGP 8x compliance and integrated Ethernet and FireWire.

SiS R658

Memory support: PC600, PC800, PC1066; 4GB max
CPU support: P4, P4A, P4B
Bus speed: 400MHz, 533MHz
I/O interconnect: MuTIOL 1G, 1GB/s
MAX ATA support: 133
Lab notes: The first non-Intel RDRAM chipset is also the first to officially support PC1066 memory. Other perks include AGP 8x and built-in Ethernet and FireWire.

ATI Radeon IGP 330

Memory support: DDR200, DDR266; 1GB max
CPU support: P4, P4A
Bus speed: 400MHz

I/O interconnect: A-Link, 266MB/s
MAX ATA support: 100
Lab notes: Targeting budget OEMs, the Pentium 4 version of the IGP 320 is held back by a lack of support for the 533MHz FSB.

ATI Radeon IGP 340

Memory support: DDR200, DDR266; 1GB max
CPU support: P4, P4A, P4B
Bus speed: 400MHz, 533MHz
I/O interconnect: A-Link, 266MB/s
MAX ATA support: 100
Lab notes: Adds support for a 533MHz bus speed.

ALi ALADDiN-P4

Memory support: PC100, PC133, DDR200, DDR266, DDR333; 3GB max
CPU support: P4, P4A
Bus speed: 400MHz
I/O interconnect: PCI, 133MB/s
MAX ATA support: 133
Lab notes: This P4 chipset from ALi hasn't managed to achieve popularity. ∎

ATHLON XPs DECODED!

Can't figure out what the heck a 2400+ is? Then use our handy-dandy decoding chart to help you wade through AMD's mystifying model classifications.

MODEL NAME	CLOCK SPEED	BUS SPEED	PROCESS	CODE-NAME
Athlon XP model 2800+	2.25GHz	333MHz	0.13	Thoroughbred B
Athlon XP model 2700+	2.17GHz	333MHz	0.13	Thoroughbred B
Athlon XP model 2600+	2.13GHz	266MHz	0.13	Thoroughbred B
Athlon XP model 2400+	2GHz	266MHz	0.13	Thoroughbred B
Athlon XP model 2200+	1.8GHz	266MHz	0.13	Thoroughbred A
Athlon XP model 2100+	1.73GHz	266MHz	0.18	Palomino*
Athlon XP model 2000+	1.67GHz	266MHz	0.18	Palomino*
Athlon XP model 1900+	1.6GHz	266MHz	0.18	Palomino*
Athlon XP model 1800+	1.53GHz	266MHz	0.18	Palomino*
Athlon XP model 1700+	1.47GHz	266MHz	0.18	Palomino*
Athlon XP model 1600+	1.4GHz	266MHz	0.18	Palomino*
Athlon XP model 1500+	1.33GHz	266MHz	0.18	Palomino*

*Eventually all Athlon XPs will use the improved Thoroughbred B process.

ANATOMY OF A MOBO

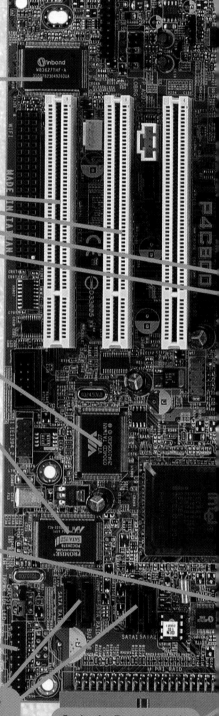

Audio CODEC: Most new motherboar[d]s feature integrated audio that's quite advanced from stereo output. The Anal[og] Devices chip here supports multichann[el] output and advanced 3D audio.

I/O controller: The keyboard controller, PS/2 ports, serial port, parallel port, and floppy drive are controlled by this chip.

PCI slots: The peripheral component interconnect, or PCI, slot pushed aside the creaky old VESA local bus and ISA slots for peripheral cards. But with a 32-bit bus, a 33MHz pipeline, and a 5V power requirement per slot, it's now looking pretty old itself. Although PCI Express will replace it soon, we'll see motherboards with both PCI and PCI Express for the next few years. Don't settle for less than five slots on an ATX motherboard.

RAID and FireWire: Motherboard manufacturers build features into a motherboard by simply adding additional chips to the PCB, such as the Serial ATA RAID and FireWire A support on this board.

BIOS: The basic input/output system of your motherboard is contained in a small nonvolatile piece of memory. When you update the BIOS, this is the chip that gets reprogrammed. Generally, socketed designs are preferred. If you kill the BIOS during an update, or corrupt it with static electricity, you simply pry out the old one and replace it.

Front panel connectors: Plug your case's power-on switch, reset switch, hard drive light, and power lights into these pins.

Serial ATA: Serial ATA is on a rapid pace to replace parallel ATA. These slim ports support only one device per port. The two shown here are controlled by the south bridge, and another two are controlled by the Promise RAID controller chip.

Fan header: These three pins let you hook up auxiliary fans to your motherboard that can be intelligently controlled by the board (if it supports software control).

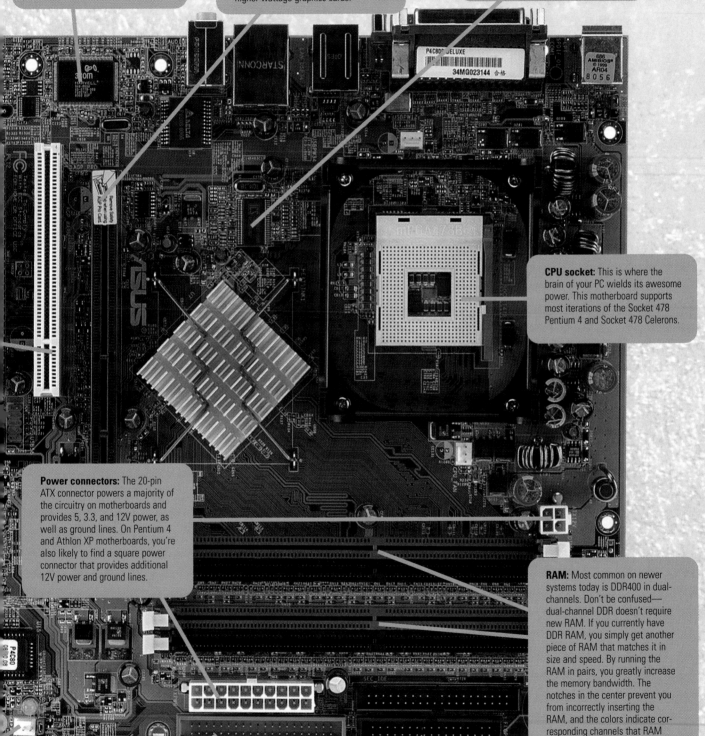

AGP slot: Intel introduced the accelerated graphics port as a kind of express lane to the north bridge, so that graphics data wouldn't get tied up in traffic with data from other PCI cards. The most modern form of AGP is 8x, which can theoretically transfer 2.1GB/s of data. This motherboard sports an AGP Pro slot which adds additional ground and power lines for higher-wattage graphics cards.

NIC: Most modern motherboards have built-in networking. The chip here is a 3Com Gigabit Ethernet chip.

Clock generator: The clock generator on a motherboard does what it sounds like; it controls the clock on the PC that determines the clock speed. Don't confuse this with the real-time clock which controls the time and date stashed in a battery-backed chip called the CMOS.

CPU socket: This is where the brain of your PC wields its awesome power. This motherboard supports most iterations of the Socket 478 Pentium 4 and Socket 478 Celerons.

Power connectors: The 20-pin ATX connector powers a majority of the circuitry on motherboards and provides 5, 3.3, and 12V power, as well as ground lines. On Pentium 4 and Athlon XP motherboards, you're also likely to find a square power connector that provides additional 12V power and ground lines.

RAM: Most common on newer systems today is DDR400 in dual-channels. Don't be confused— dual-channel DDR doesn't require new RAM. If you currently have DDR RAM, you simply get another piece of RAM that matches it in size and speed. By running the RAM in pairs, you greatly increase the memory bandwidth. The notches in the center prevent you from incorrectly inserting the RAM, and the colors indicate corresponding channels that RAM should be paired up in.

ATA/IDE ports: Most motherboards support two IDE/ATA ports for up to four devices. ATA100 is the industry standard. Sadly, we've observed no real performance improvement from drives supporting the latest ATA133 spec.

Floppy port: Hook your ancient floppy drive to this port if you must. Enough said.

How To Pick the BEST P4 MOBO

A quality processor deserves a quality home

Intel's Pentium 4 line of processors has scaled to enormously high frequencies, going from a mere 1.3GHz to an unprecedented 3.6GHz in three years. Today, Intel dominates the high-performance computing sector almost indisputably. We think that AMD's Athlon XP or 64 is a better value, but if you care only about getting the absolute fastest performance possible, then you need a P4.

But you can't just drop a P4 CPU into any old motherboard and expect to get bruising performance—mobos are definitely not created equal. Your motherboard choice will have a major impact on your system's stability, upgrading potential, and overclockability. A good

Modder alert: If you're going to install a case window, make sure you get a foxy looking motherboard, like DFI's fluorescent LAN Party Pro875.

motherboard can also save you money by integrating features such as a RAID controller or sound chip, so you won't have to buy them separately.

There's a dizzying array of motherboard choices out there for the Pentium 4 right now, each offering support for different kinds of memory, bus speeds, and CPUs. Here's a guide to everything you need to know when selecting a P4 motherboard, with reviews of our top picks at the end

for those who know a good shortcut when they see one.

CHOOSING A CHIPSET

Before you can begin your search for the perfect motherboard, you need to know what chipset you want—and there are a lot to choose from. Intel's top of the line consumer chipsets include the 915P (P4) and 925X (P4EE), which include PCI Express, DDR2 support, SATA 150, and an 800MHz system us. The venerable 875P is also woth a mention, sporting a dual-channel DDR400 memory controller, 800MHz frontside bus support, AGP 8x, and Hyper-Threading. Meanwhile, the 865PE is targeted more toward the budget market; it supports the same technologies as its older sibling, but can't sustain the same level of performance.

However, many motherboard manufacturers have successfully hacked the 865PE to bring its performance to near-875P levels.

ATI's Radeon 9100 Pro IGP is another excellent chipset. It supports all the latest technologies—dual-channel DDR400, 800MHz FSB, AGP 8x, Hyper-Threading—and also boasts an integrated graphics core. Hardcore gamers and true performance enthusiasts will want to buy an add-in graphics card, but if your budget is tight, the 9100 Pro IGP offers one of the best integrated graphics core of any chipset on the market. It's also the *only* chipset with integrated graphics to offer programmable shader support (which you'll need if you want to see

next generation games like *Doom3* and *Half-Life 2* in all their glory).

Now that you've seen the contenders, let's look at the pretenders—the P4 chipsets you want to avoid at all costs. Intel's 865G and 865P chipsets are the bastard children of the 865 family. The former offers a GeForce2 MX-level integrated graphics core, but lacks the raw performance of the 865PE, while the latter is restricted to FSB speeds of just 533MHz. Meanwhile, from outside the Intel camp come the VIA PT600 and SiS 655FX. Both are dual-channel DDR400 offerings with 800MHz FSB support, but neither can match the speed or robustness of Intel's finest.

VIA has two chipsets. The PT880 has a dual-channel DDR400 memory controller as well as support for quad-band memory (QBM)—a special type of memory that offers twice the bandwidth of normal DDR.

BASIC FEATURES TO LOOK FOR

Chipset aside, there are certain basic features you should look for in any P4 motherboard. For one, you'll want support for dual-channel DDR400 memory. When sticks of memory are installed in pairs in a dual-channel-capable motherboard, the effective memory bandwidth of the system is doubled. This nifty trick works with standard DDR memory—no expensive special memory is required. The Pentium 4 processor thirsts for the bandwidth afforded by dual-channel DDR; when sandbagged by single-channel memory, the P4 loses much of its performance edge.

You'll also want to make sure the motherboard you choose can support the CPUs of today and tomorrow. Don't even consider a mobo that can't get on the 800MHz bus or run a 3.2GHz Pentium 4, which is the final Northwood core CPU released. You may even want to consider emerging technologies such as DDR2 memory support, PCI Express slots, and possibly SATA connections. Oh, and at least get AGP 8x or hold out just a bit for PCI Express graphics.

Finally, insist on a board that offers USB 2.0 and FireWire I/O, so you'll have high-bandwidth connections to your MP3 player, digital camera, external hard drive, and any other peripherals you may have that support these high-bandwidth connections.

Some motherboard manufacturers offer an insane number of extras, including front bay-mounted media readers and even remote controls!

OVERCLOCKING FEATURES

Pentium 4 owners don't have as many overclocking options as Athlon owners, simply because the multipliers on a P4 can't be unlocked. Still, a good motherboard will allow you to make the best of the options you do have. If you're planning to do any overclocking at all, you'll want a mobo that allows FSB speed adjustments through the BIOS, at the very least. Otherwise you'll be stuck with the chore of fiddling with hardware jumpers on the board itself. An ideal overclocker's board will allow the speeds of the FSB and memory to be set independently of the AGP and PCI bus clocks. In the past, overclocking the frontside and/or memory buses caused the AGP and PCI buses to run out of spec as well, which often limited the extent to which a system could be overclocked. Lately, however, some enthusiast boards have begun offering the ability to set these bus speeds independently.

Abit motherboards are synonymous with overclocking, and the IC7-G Intel board lives up to expectations with a galore of features for practitioners of the dirty deeds. Although it may be getting a little long in the tooth, it's still a great 875 board.

EXTRA FEATURES

These days, integration is the name of the motherboard game. In a mad dash to one-up each other, motherboard and chipset manufacturers have started offering all sorts of extra features that can save you both money and expansion slots. Any motherboard you buy should offer integrated 10/100Mbps Ethernet at the very least. Depending on your needs, you may want to get a mobo with dual-Ethernet capability or Gigabit Ethernet. Should you decide to get a board with Gigabit Ethernet, look for one with a network controller that takes advantage of Intel's communications streaming architecture (CSA), such as the Intel Pro/1000. CSA allows the network controller to plug directly into the northbridge, so it doesn't suck bandwidth from the PCI bus—especially

critical for the 1000Mbps transfer rates of Gigabit Ethernet.

Many boards these days also include a built-in RAID controller, allowing you to stripe your hard drives (for better performance) or mirror them (for data backup). The latest RAID controllers, however, offer what's known as RAID 1.5, a new spec that allows you to simultaneously perform striping *and* mirroring using just two hard drives. RAID definitely isn't for everyone, but if you're interested in taking advantage of it, look for a board that supports RAID 1.5, so you can get the best of both worlds. Meanwhile, if you want to plug in a next-generation 10,000rpm hard drive, make sure the motherboard you choose has a built-in Serial ATA controller.

Almost every motherboard now includes integrated audio, but it's

hard to find one with *quality* integrated audio. In fact, for the Pentium 4, it's almost impossible—if you care at all about sound quality, we recommend you get an add-in soundcard, like Creative Labs' Audigy 2. You should also keep an eye out for any cool peripherals that may come bundled with a motherboard. Many boards now come with bonus-round toys like a remote control or even a carrying case for your PC. Others come dressed in sexy color schemes complete with fluorescent expansion slots, catering specifically to the case-modding crowd. And lastly, don't brush off the software bundle—while most mobos ship with a bunch of trashy programs, some come with useful apps such as a temperature monitor or virus scanner.

How To Pick the BEST ATHLON MOBO

Bad mobo's mean bad mojo. Here's how to pair your Athlon with the right motherboard

Years after the debut of the Athlon, AMD is still giving Intel—once the unchallenged king of the desktop—a run for its money. But the Athlon XP can't take on the P4 without the proper support infrastructure, so choose your motherboard wisely. As the backbone of your rig, the motherboard has the most profound effect of any component on the overall stability of your system. What's more, today's motherboards come with tons of extra features, such as built-in networking and onboard RAID controllers, that can save you expansion slots and money.

Perhaps most importantly, the motherboard you choose today will determine what upgrades you'll be able to plug into your system tomorrow, and next year. As such, you'll want to be as informed as possible before making this critical choice—and we've got you covered. We've come up with this short list of everything you need to know about picking the right mobo for your needs.

DEBUNKING THE MYTHS

Before we get started, there are a few misconceptions out there that may need to be cleared up. First of all, contrary to what Intel fanboys would have you believe, the Athlon XP is still a perfectly viable alternative to the Pentium 4. Is the P4 faster right now? Yes, but not by a particularly large margin, and AMD still offers more bang for the buck. So if you're looking for the most performance for the least price, the Athlon XP is your processor. That said, the 32-bit Athlon series has reached the end of the line—the future lies with the Athlon 64 and its 64-bit instruction set.

There are also some popular misconceptions out there that apply to motherboards in general. Many people believe that having more PCB layers—in other words, a thicker motherboard—makes for better quality and reliability. Though this may be true in some cases, it is not a valid rule of thumb. A skilled engineer may be able to accomplish in four layers what an incompetent engineer needs six layers to do. Thus, it's not a good idea to use "more is better" as a general rule when it comes to motherboard layers.

The same thing applies to capacitors, which can be thought of as tiny "storage tanks" that hold an electrical charge. The stored charge helps compensate for an uneven flow of electricity to the motherboard. While some folks think that having bigger capacitors makes a motherboard more reliable, it's not necessarily the case. As with PCB layers, more is not necessarily better, and good design in this instance isn't apparent to the naked eye.

CHOOSING A CHIPSET

The first decision you need to make when shopping for a motherboard is what chipset you want. There are really only two companies making performance chipsets for the Athlon platform today: nVidia and VIA. SiS also makes Athlon chipsets, but they tend to be targeted at the budget market, and generally aren't as refined or feature-filled as those from nVidia and VIA.

Of all the Athlon chipsets out there, nVidia's nForce2 Ultra earns our highest recommendation. The nForce2 line sports such features as built-in Dolby 5.1

The A7N8X Deluxe motherboard from Asus goes nuts with sweet features like built-in Ethernet, USB 2.0, and FireWire, all piped in through the high-bandwidth HyperTransport interconnect.

audio, 10/100Mbps LAN, AGP 8x support, a dual-channel DDR400 memory controller for maximum memory bandwidth, and optional GeForce4 MX-level integrated graphics. The Ultra version adds excellent support for the 400MHz frontside bus—earlier versions of the nForce2 promised this support, but didn't deliver it consistently. If you don't care about 400MHz FSB support, though, any version of the nForce2 should give you great performance and rock-solid stability.

VIA's KT400A is the other main contender for the Athlon XP chipset throne. It offers DDR400 memory support, but only in single-channel configurations, and lacks 400MHz FSB support. The KT400A does include built-in networking and AGP 8x capability, but feature-for-feature it's still outclassed by the nForce2 line. The KT600 chipset will soon succeed the KT400A, boasting such amenities as 400MHz FSB support, six-channel audio, and built-in RAID support. Performance-wise, the KT600 could put nVidia and VIA neck and neck. Be forewarned, however, that VIA has a reputation for problems with stability and robustness, both of which are hallmarks of the nForce2.

upgrades. It's not a bad idea to check www.amd.com/us-en for Athlon 64 and 64 FX recommended motherboards that use these chipsets.

BASIC FEATURES TO LOOK FOR

Having chosen your chipset, it's important to know what basic features to look for in a motherboard. Most important is processor support—any motherboard you buy should be able to work with the Athlon XP 3200+, the final Athlon XP to be released. The 3200+ chip runs on a 400MHz FSB (frontside bus), so this means that whatever motherboard you choose should support this bus speed as well (if your motherboard has a slower FSB, the Athlon XP 3200+ will still function, but at nowhere near its full potential).

Surprisingly, even if the chipset on your motherboard claims to support a certain FSB speed, that's no guarantee that the motherboard itself will support it. Some Athlon boards only offer 400MHz FSB support on certain revisions, so make sure to check the manufacturer's web site or motherboard documentation for this important feature.

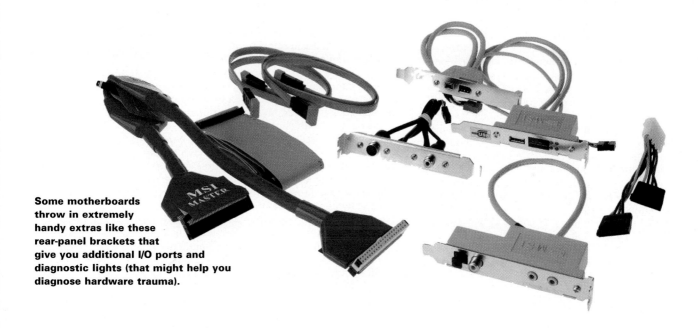

Some motherboards throw in extremely handy extras like these rear-panel brackets that give you additional I/O ports and diagnostic lights (that might help you diagnose hardware trauma).

For the Athlon 64–minded, again manufacturers turned to VIA for the K8T800 and nVidia for the nForce3. At press time, even the 939 socket versions were being paired with the nForce3 and K8T800 with the advantage going to VIA. Both chipsets offer up to 1GHz HyperTransport capability, dual-channel DDR, AGP 8x, and SATA support. The notable exception is the original nForce3 150, which had limited bandwidth and SATA support only with an additional chip. For PCI Express options, VIA's K8T890 will allow for future

Next up is memory. To maximize your performance, you'll want a board that uses a dual-channel memory controller, such as that of the nForce2. When at least two sticks of memory are installed in a dual-channel-capable motherboard, the system's effective memory bandwidth is doubled—no special type of memory is required. In general, you'll want to synchronize the speed of your memory with the speed of your frontside bus, e.g. DDR333 memory with a 333MHz FSB. So, make sure the mobo you buy supports a high enough grade of DDR for your

CPU's FSB. Also, try to get a board with three memory slots; some cheapo boards offers just two.

Another basic feature you'll want to look for is an AGP 8x slot with a retention clip at the end. A retention clip is a good safety measure to have, helping to keep your videocard from coming loose in its slot over time. Support for USB 2.0 and FireWire is important as well, so you can hook up all the latest peripherals to your rig.

Motherboards with a jumperless design are always preferable. If you catch overclocking fever someday, you'll be able to manipulate clock settings without messing around with physical jumpers.

Comprehensive thermal monitoring is another invaluable feature—you'll want a mobo that can automatically shut down your PC if the CPU overheats or its fan dies. Lastly, make sure the motherboard you want doesn't have capacitors positioned too close to the processor socket, as this can make it difficult to install a CPU cooler.

OVERCLOCKING FEATURES

Hoping to overclock your system to get the most from your investment? If so, there are a few additional motherboard features you'll want to look out for. For instance, the ability to adjust frontside bus speeds and clock multipliers through the BIOS is very desirable. Some mobos still use jumpers or DIP switches for this task. Even worse, others simply don't allow you to overclock at all—so make sure you're getting the real deal.

Lately, some motherboards have begun offering the ability to adjust memory and FSB speeds independently of AGP and PCI bus speeds. If you're planning significant overclocking, this is a feature you'll definitely want to have. Traditionally, overclocking the frontside and/or memory buses resulted in the AGP and PCI buses being overclocked as well, thus increasing the number of possible failure points. A motherboard that allows your AGP and PCI devices to run at spec even when other parts of your system are overclocked will significantly increase your chances of overclocking success.

EXTRA FEATURES

Today's motherboards are so feature-filled that it's quite possible to build a complete system without buying a single expansion card. Many once-exotic features, such as onboard networking and RAID, are practically standard fare on today's motherboards. Any motherboard you buy should at least have built-in 10/100Mbps Ethernet—though, depending on your needs, you may want to look for one with dual Ethernet ports or even Gigabit Ethernet.

Integrated RAID is another common feature, but one that's definitely not for everyone. Should you decide to spring for a mobo with a RAID controller, look for one that supports the new RAID 1.5 spec, which allows you to perform both striping and mirroring simultaneously with just two hard drives—a very cool feature. Meanwhile, if you want to run the new generation of 10,000rpm hard drives, make sure you get a board that boasts a Serial ATA controller.

A hard-to-find feature that might be worth seeking out is quality integrated audio. Most chipsets offer little more than crappy-sounding generic sound circuitry. However, nVidia's nForce2 can pump out some high-quality vibes, roughly matching the audio prowess of a Sound Blaster Live! card. Additionally, it features real-time Dolby 5.1 encoding and decoding. If you're planning to buy (or already own) a soundcard you're happy with, you don't need to worry about the quality of your motherboard's integrated audio.

There are also a few other features you may want to keep an eye out for. Many motherboards now come bundled with cool bonus peripherals, such as flash memory reader/writers or a remote control. In addition, some mobo manufacturers have started catering to case modders with features such as colorful PCBs or fluorescent expansion slots that look positively slick through a window. And finally, don't underestimate the value of a decent software bundle. Most mobos come with a bunch of crusty old apps that you'll never use, but some toss in a temperature monitoring program or free antivirus software, both of which are good to have on hand.

All of that should give you a pretty good idea of what to look for in an Athlon XP motherboard.

The K8N Neo supports single-channel DDR Athlon 64s in Socket 754 trim.

MSI K8N NEO PLATINUM EDITION

Sometimes you have to make sacrifices to be first. Such was the tale of the first Athlon 64 chipset, the nForce3 Pro 150. It lacked native Serial ATA, Gigabit Ethernet, and a high-speed HyperTransport link. Yawn.

MSI's K8N Neo Platinum Edition mobo, which uses nVidia's new nForce3 Pro 250Gb chip, aims to correct these previous blunders. Like the nForce3 Pro 150, the nForce3 250Gb is a single-chip solution (a benefit of having the memory controller for the Athlon 64 series on the CPU itself), which offers improved latency over the standard two-chip design that Intel and VIA use. But unlike the nForce3 Pro 150, the 250Gb's single chip boasts a Gigabit Ethernet core, which is even faster than Intel's blazingly fast CSA port and far superior to any PCI-based card.

Another improvement afforded by the new nForce3/K8N Neo product is a faster HyperTransport link between the CPU and the chipset. Although we've never been able to prove that the nForce3 150's 600MHz link hurt performance, the 250Gb supports a more confidence-inspiring 800MHz link, and can be bumped up to 1GHz.

In Lab testing, the K8N Neo ran faster than the Soyo CK8 board we used in June 2004's speed trials, but the difference was far from spectacular. In our real-world gaming benchmarks, the K8N Neo also outpaced VIA's K8T800-based Albatron K8X800 Pro II mobo, but again just barely. That's the nature of the Athlon 64 platform[md]the memory controller's placement on the CPU has greatly diminished the potential for performance differences among competing chipsets.

Fans of the nForce2's APU audio system will be disappointed that nVidia didn't include the real-time Dolby Digital encoding capabilities in its new chipset; the nForce3 offers a snazzy built-in hardware firewall as a consolation.

The K8N Neo also packs two parallel ATA133 ports, four Serial ports, and a rather unique RAID arrangement. You're offered RAID 0, 1, and 0+1 but, unlike conventional implementations, the K8N Neo lets you create a RAID partition across SATA *and* PATA drives. Using this capability on our evaluation board felt clunky[md]for example, it took us five minutes just to figure out which drive was on which chain before we could activate the RAID[md]but nVidia says its *NVRAID 2.0* software will move the work out of the BIOS and into the operating system. Unfortunately, running RAID still requires the use of F6 drivers.

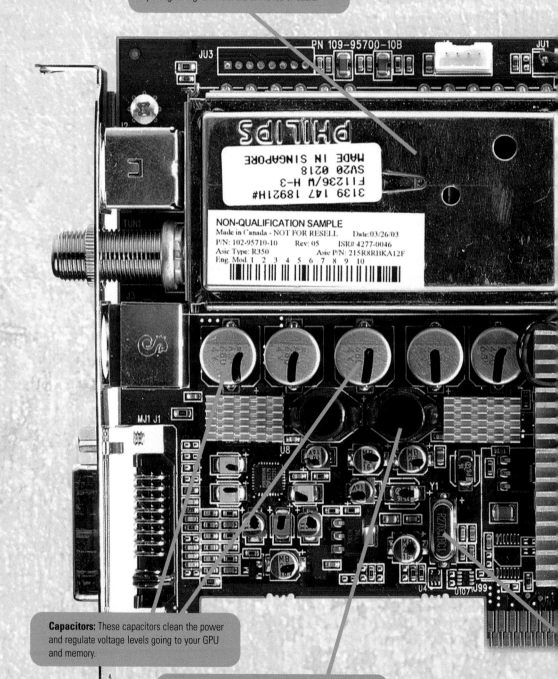

TV tuner: This metal box, sometimes called a "tuner can," houses an analog tuner capable of pulling TV signals from the airwaves or cable.

PN 109-95700-10B

PHILIPS

MADE IN SINGAPORE
SV20 0218
F11236/W H-3
3139 147 18921H#

NON-QUALIFICATION SAMPLE
Made in Canada - NOT FOR RESELL   Date:03/26/03
P/N: 102-95710-10   Rev: 05   ISR# 4277-0046
Asic Type: R350   Asic P/N: 215R8RBKA12F
Eng. Mod. 1   2   3   4   5   6   7   8   9   10

Capacitors: These capacitors clean the power and regulate voltage levels going to your GPU and memory.

Switching regulator: The switching regulator works in tandem with the capacitors to ensure that the proper voltage levels go to the GPU and memory.

Diodes: Handy diodes do a neat trick: They conduct electricity in only one direction. By placing them on a circuit, these diodes prevent ESD (electrostatic discharge) from damaging the videocard's sensitive components, such as the GPU. Still, they can't block every shock, so we consider the antistatic wrist strap a must every time you handle a component with an exposed circuit board. Especially the videocard—it probably cost you a bundle.

Auxiliary power connector: Scotty, we need more power! Even the AGP slot can't provide enough juice for today's enormous graphics processors that have millions and millions of transistors. This auxiliary power connector draws additional power from the system's power supply to supplement the juice provided by the AGP slot.

More capacitors: These capacitors sit on the signal lines going to memory and scrub the juice of any spikes or irregularities before it's introduced into the delicate RAM modules. This clean, consistent power allows card manufacturers to crank up memory clock speeds without having to worry about shoddy power preventing the card from completing important calculations.

Onboard RAM: The graphics card's DDR memory will give the R350 processing unit anywhere from 128MB to 256MB of fast storage (the model pictured here has 128).

Graphics processing unit: Also known as the GPU, the whole enchilada lies underneath this heatsink and fan. The ATI R350 core is designed to perform millions of specialized graphical calculations every second. Its design is, believe it or not, far more complex than the Pentium 4 or Athlon XP.

Crystal: The crystal inside this housing vibrates at a specific frequency, providing a reference clock that controls your card's memory and core clocks (just like a quartz crystal keeps time in a watch).

How To Pick the BEST
VIDEOCARD

It's a life-and-death decision for gamers

The GeForce FX 5800 used uber-high memory and core clocks to maximize performance, and needs a massive heatsink/fan combo to cool its chips.

The single-most important PC component for gamers—trumping even the almighty CPU—is the videocard. The videocard is responsible for drawing every polygon, texture, and particle effect in every game you play. A fast videocard will carry you into videogame nirvana, where everything runs at 60 frames per second and graphic detail is set to "Maximum." A slow videocard will doom you to frame rate hell, where your games will resemble a slideshow.

For the uninitiated, reading the specs of a typical videocard can be a terrifying experience. But you don't have to be cowed into picking up the most expensive card on the shelf and hoping for the best. We're going to explain everything you need to know about buying the right graphics accelerator for your PC, whether you're a gamer, a graphic artist, or an evil genius. And by the time we're done, you'll know everything we know.

(At least until the next generation of videocards arrives.)

THE BASICS

At the heart of every videocard is a chip called a graphics processing unit, or GPU. Two major players design most of the GPUs suitable for gaming 3D accelerators: ATI and nVidia. Both companies sell their chips—which are significantly more complex than CPUs—to other companies, which then build the actual videocards you buy at Ye Olde Videocard Shoppe. These boards are generally labeled with either the ATI or nVidia logo. (ATI also sells its own ATI-branded boards.)

If somebody tells you that one company's GPU is superior, take that advice with a big fat grain of salt, because the technologies each company deploys are leapfrogging over each other constantly. In fierce competition with each other, ATI and nVidia release new versions of existing chips at least every six months, with entirely new chip generations appearing every year to 18 months. As

a result of these grueling product cycles, the fastest card can change three, four, or even more times a year.

There are two different types of videocard interfaces inside your PC. The accelerated graphics port (AGP) is designed specifically for 3D accelerators, which require massive data transfers between the videocard and the rest of the system. The other interface is the classic PCI slot that your other cards use (soundcard, network adapter, etc.). Because PCI slots aren't capable of transferring graphics data as fast as AGP slots, you'll want to avoid buying a PCI videocard unless it's absolutely necessary. Your motherboard, for instance, may have a videocard built into it and not have any AGP slot at all. If this is the case, we recommend upgrading to a better motherboard if you're up to the task.

REGULAR OR EXTRA STRENGTH?

There is a wide price range for videocards. For the most part, all the cards from the same vendor (ATI or nVidia, for example) use the same basic chip, but performance-enhancing functions are disabled as the cards get cheaper. The highest-end cards are priced between $400 and $500, and have more memory and higher clock speeds than anything else on the market (we'll talk about what those specs mean in the next section). These are the brawniest of the videocards, capable of drawing more polygons at higher resolutions and higher frame rates than anything else at the consumer level.

In the $300 range, the boards are generally based on the same basic chip as the hyper-expensive cards, but have less onboard memory or have features intentionally disabled to slow them down. Videocards priced in the $200 range generally have less memory and are even more crippled than the $300

cards, but still include the same basic functionality as the $500 cards. Generally, cards under $200 are at least one generation old, include even less memory, and are significantly slower than the other cards.

What you sacrifice by purchasing a $200 card versus a $500 card varies from manufacturer to manufacturer, but speed is virtually always the first victim. Read on to understand why.

CLOCK SPEEDS

Just about every component in your PC has a "clock" speed, including your videocard. In fact, there are two different clocks on the videocard. One controls the speed of the GPU, while the other sets the speed of the memory. The GPU clock is called the "core" clock, and the other is called the "memory" clock. Increasing the core clock ups the number of calculations the GPU can do every second, while adjusting the memory clock changes the bandwidth, or amount of data the memory can transfer to the GPU every second. If everything else is equal, a card with faster core and memory clocks will be faster than a card with slower clocks.

Even though high-end videocards use the same basic core as cheap videocards, GPU cores that will run at the requisite super-high speeds are rare. Only a small percentage of GPUs can run at the 400MHz+ speeds required by a high-end videocard. Memory is much the same. System memory that's in most PCs runs somewhere between 100MHz and 200MHz—one MHz, or megahertz, is one million memory transfers per second. The memory on high-end videocards runs at 500MHz. Memory this fast doesn't come cheap.

The easiest way for a GPU manufacturer to slow down a videocard is to lower the core and memory clocks. The default clocks for each card are programmed on a BIOS chip that's soldered to the motherboard, but those clock speeds are easy to adjust by an adventuresome end-user. Using an application like *Powerstrip* (www.entech.co.tw), it's easy to overclock most videocards' GPU and memory. But overclocking isn't for everyone. It can create heat-related visual glitches in your games, jeopardize your machine's stability, and even permanently damage your videocard if it isn't properly cooled. You've been warned.

MEMORY BANDWIDTH

The amount of data your card can move between the GPU and the videocard's onboard memory (called memory bandwidth) is the biggest bottleneck on the videocard. The memory bandwidth is controlled by three things, the memory clock, the size of each 'chunk' of data transferred every clock cycle, and the number of chunks of data transferred

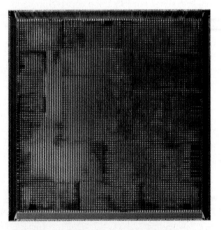

Half-Life 2 will use programmable shaders to make every surface in the game look more real. It will bring old 3D cards to their knees.

each cycle.

The GPU reads and writes small chunks of data to the memory almost a billion times per second. Right now, most videocards use double data rate (DDR) memory. DDR memory can transfer two chunks of data every clock cycle instead of just one. (The type of memory supported by a board is configured at the chip level, and it's not user configurable.) In addition to original DDR memory, which is in wide use now, there are also newer DDR-II and G-DDR memory specs. DDR-II is designed to run at much higher clock speeds than vanilla DDR and will be used for main system memory and some videocards. G-DDR (or graphics DDR) memory is designed specifically for videocards, but it's not available yet. When it is, we expect it to become the standard on high-end videocards. It doesn't require as many extra components soldered on the graphics board, and it runs at higher clock speeds than even DDR-II. We don't expect to see any videocards equipped with anything other than one of these flavors of DDR memory going forward.

GPU manufacturers design their chips to accommodate specific-size chunks of data; this isn't user configurable either. The size of the data chunks is also referred to as the width of the memory pipeline. A wider pipeline means more memory bandwidth for the GPU. Most high-end cards today transfer 256-bit chunks of data at a time, while budget boards transfer just 128-bit or 64-bit chunks. It's always best to get a card with the widest pipeline possible. You can always overclock your memory to make it faster, but you can't adjust the width of the memory pipeline on most cards. There are some hardware hacks that enable wider pipelines on some videocards, but this is the exception, not the norm.

MEMORY SIZE

The fastest memory in the world won't do you any good if there's not enough of it to hold all the data your games and applications will toss at it. Even crappy-looking old games can fill a 64MB card's onboard RAM, and when

that happens, the game will have to store its data in your significantly slower system memory. As a result, your frame rates will tank.

Games use onboard memory to store both the textures and models that make up a 3D scene, and the work in progress as an image is rendered. Modern GPUs read and write to video memory just like a CPU does with system memory, but video memory is an order of magnitude faster than the memory the CPU has to work with. Where even the fastest system memory can only transfer 2GB/sec, video memory on a high-end card can transfer more than 20GB/sec of data.

We recommend a minimum of 128MB of RAM for optimum results in most games. People who primarily favor single-player games can probably get by with 64MB, but online multiplayer gamers need as much video memory as possible. Even 256MB isn't out of the question. Consider going with less than 64MB of RAM only if you don't intend to play any games at all.

The GPU is the heart of your 3D accelerator. It's responsible for drawing, texturing, and lighting everything 3D on your PC.

GPU ARCHITECTURE

Memory bandwidth is an important part of the videocard speed equation, but the inner workings of the GPU have a lot to do with it too. To understand how GPU architecture affects performance, you need to understand a bit about how 3D accelerators work.

The image displayed on your monitor is made up of many tiny dots of color called pixels. The 3D accelerator has to draw each pixel and form them into a single frame, which is then displayed on the monitor. This has to happen at least 30 times a second to create the illusion of motion.

Drawing individual pixels isn't a simple process. To draw a 3D scene, the videocard first determines the shape of the world from the program that's running, then it draws wireframes out of polygons. At this point, the hardware T&L (transform and lighting) engine converts the polygon-based wireframes into individual pixels that make up the scene. After that, textures are applied to each pixel. For example, a wall might get a stone texture applied to it, while a human model will get a skin texture. More advanced techniques, like bump maps, are then applied to the textures to make them look less flat and more real (a bump map would help the stone wall look rougher, more dimensional, and realistic). If the pixel being drawn is behind glass or fog, those effects are blended in too. Finally, any lighting calculations are performed and applied to the texture. In today's games, each pixel can sometimes have 12 or more effects applied to it!

To speed up this process, modern 3D accelerators can process more than one pixel at a time. High-end 3D cards sport four or even eight pipelines capable of applying one texture or effect to a pixel per clock cycle. Because 3D accelerators perform the same functions over and over for millions of pixels each frame, adding extra pipelines makes them significantly faster. Budget cards usually have just two or four pipelines.

PROGRAMMABLE SHADERS
An important advance of the last two generations of videocards are programmable

This pachyderm's textures weren't made in *Photoshop*. His skin (and the marble pedestal on which he stands) are dynamically textured with shader programs.

shader units, which let developers create much better looking games. Before programmable shader cards were introduced, the fixed-function 3D pipeline was highly specialized. Although it worked much faster than a more general-purpose processor, such as a CPU, it was also extremely inflexible.

Programmable shader units make GPUs more CPU-like. In addition to the basic 3D tasks that fixed-function cards perform, shader units can execute shader programs that run complex algorithms on pixels, which are similar to regular computer programs. These shader programs can be thousands of instructions long and calculate everything from the lighting for an entire scene to the reflections in a simple mirror.

Like everything else we've talked about, high-end videocards will have the most powerful, most flexible shader units. These days, even sub-$200 videocards support rudimentary shader programs, but to run upcoming shader games (like *Half-Life 2* and *Doom3*) at reasonable resolutions and frame rates, a high-end card is necessary.

DRIVERS
In the early days of 3D accelerators, different hardware manufacturers wrote customized drivers with special features—including exhaustive monitor databases and support for funky 3D glasses. Now driver development is too onerous a task for a mere board vendor. Drivers that used to take small teams a few weeks to write, now take massive teams of a hundred or more people several months to complete. Board vendors just don't have the resources to do much more than add their logo to a driver. The practical upshot is: If you want the most up-to-date, reliable driver, you should go to your chipset's vendor, *not* the board vendor. Driver updates are easily accessible from **www.ati.com** and **www.nvidia.com**.

THE WORKSTATION QUESTION
We're frequently asked if professional-level workstation videocards are faster than consumer-level gaming cards. For a long time, it was true that workstation boards, which cost thousands of dollars,

would provide faster frame rates in early 3D games, such as *GLQuake*.

That's not the case anymore. Modern workstation boards are based on the same chipsets as the consumer boards, but those consumer boards are usually significantly faster than their workstation kin. Consumers need speed for games, but workstations need precision and accuracy above all else. Besides, most pro-level applications are much less intensive than even an old game. One thing hasn't changed: Workstation boards are significantly more expensive than consumer parts, starting at about $500. People who shell out the additional scratch for a pro-level part usually get 24/7 customer support—including help for specific apps—and drivers guaranteed to work perfectly with CAD and content creation applications.

GENERAL GUIDELINES
We can't give hard and fast rules for videocard purchases because the market changes so quickly, but we can give soft and slow suggestions to help you make a more informed decision.

For gamers who infrequently upgrade their videocard, it makes sense to spend the money for a high-end videocard. A $400 investment now gets you a card that's damn fast and will continue to perform acceptably for two or more years. As a general rule, high-end boards don't overclock terribly well, though. Overclockers can find great deals in the $150 price range, if they don't mind slightly more frequent upgrades. Non-gamers needn't shell out the big bucks for great 2D performance. There's no reason to pay big for all that 3D research and development if you don't play PC games, and even the cheapest 3D cards are extremely fast 2D accelerators.

We're starting to see some specialty cards designed for people who spend a lot of time manipulating large digital images. Creative Labs announced a new Graphics Blaster Picture Perfect board based on a 3Dlabs workstation chip that claims to be significantly faster than a standard videocard when manipulating large image files. The board is available for about $150. We think the image manipulation sounds cool, but we're concerned that these cards won't be able to handle even minor 3D applications.

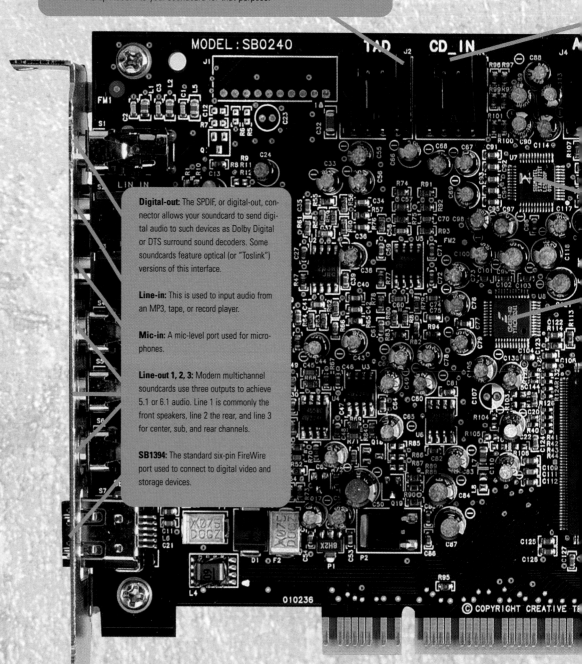

TAD: For about 10 minutes in the early 1990s, some people thought it would be clever to use their $4,000 PCs as telephone answering machines. This connector hooked your internal dialup modem to your soundcard for that purpose.

MODEL: SB0240

Digital-out: The SPDIF, or digital-out, connector allows your soundcard to send digital audio to such devices as Dolby Digital or DTS surround sound decoders. Some soundcards feature optical (or "Toslink") versions of this interface.

Line-in: This is used to input audio from an MP3, tape, or record player.

Mic-in: A mic-level port used for microphones.

Line-out 1, 2, 3: Modern multichannel soundcards use three outputs to achieve 5.1 or 6.1 audio. Line 1 is commonly the front speakers, line 2 the rear, and line 3 for center, sub, and rear channels.

SB1394: The standard six-pin FireWire port used to connect to digital video and storage devices.

CD-in/aux-in/CD SPDIF: CD-in and aux-in were used for analog audio playback from your optical drive and other multimedia devices (such as TV tuners). CD SPDIF introduced a cleaner digital connection to your optical drive. When manufacturers figured out how to pull digital audio through the IDE cable, all three connectors became instantly obsolete. *"Buh bye."*

SB1394: Creative gave soundcards a cool twist when it began embedding IEEE 1394 or "FireWire" into its soundcards. These six-pin ports can be used to connect with DV cams, iPods, and other storage devices. This internal header brings a FireWire port to the front of your case.

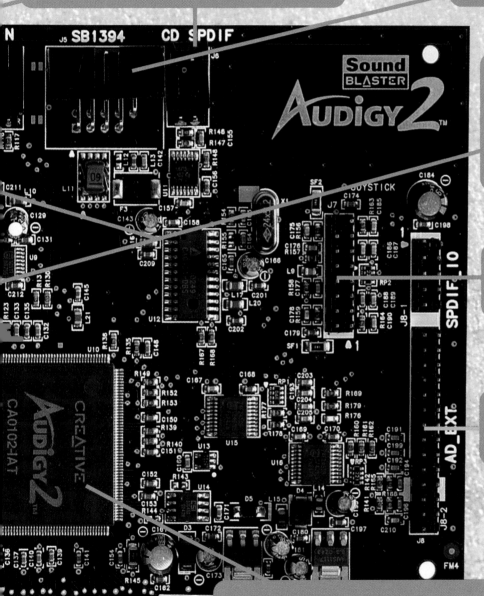

DAC: The second-most important chip on any soundcard is the digital analog converter. Its job is to convert the digital sound the computer understands to analog that you can hear. The Audigy 2 features a Cirrus Logic CS4382 chipset which supports 24-bit audio in multiple channels. The second Sigmatel chip functions as an analog mixer for the CD, line-in, mic, and aux-in ports on the board.

Joystick header: In the unlikely event your joystick uses the old-fashioned game port instead of USB, this header allows you to add a joystick/MIDI port to the back of your PC.

AD EXT / SPDIF_IO: This port is used to plug the Audigy 2 drive into the soundcard, which adds front-mounted optical, FireWire, analog I/O, and MIDI ports to the card.

DSP: The digital signal processor is the heart of the soundcard, the equivalent to the GPU on a videocard. DSPs are special chips designed to, well, process signals. DSPs can be much more efficient than general purpose CPUs when crunching audio signals—you might say that these chips are "trained" to do audio processing tasks very quickly. The DSP not only handles the processing of environmental sounds for gamers, but it's also integral to home audio production and effects processing that used to cost thousands of dollars in outboard equipment.

How To Pick the BEST SOUNDCARD

Advice that's music to your ears

There's a popular adage in the soundcard industry: If you show an audience a movie using a busted speaker running in mono, and then you show the same audience the exact same movie but with state-of-the-art speakers and in surround sound, they're bound to say the second movie *looked* better. The parable highlights the genral perception of PC audio—it's often an afterthought to concerns about megahertz, pixels, and gigabytes.

But PC audio has come a long way since its days of scratchy hiss. Today's PCs sing in full surround sound and can play full 24-bit audio, producing realistic audio that seems to be emanating from all sides.

The first soundcards, most notably the original Creative Labs Sound Blaster, fit into the ISA slot. Today's soundcards are all PCI-based. When choosing a soundcard, you'll first have to decide how many channels you want. Several different multichannel outputs are supported today:

➤ **Two-channel:** Common stereo output from two speakers arranged in front of you, with one on each side of your monitor.
➤ **Four-channel:** PCs first adapted to "surround sound" by adding two speakers positioned to the left and right behind a user.
➤ **Five-channel:** To help fill the gaps, a center channel gets positioned directly between the left and right front speakers. In most DVD movies, dialog is played through the center channel.
➤ **Six-channel:** A sixth speaker positioned directly behind the listener's head helps fill out the rear audio.
➤ **Seven-channel:** Although there's little speaker support for it, the 7.1 configuration adds two speakers behind you for even higher precision in distinguishing rear audio cues.

Of the choices here, two-, four-, and five-channel are the most common. You'll easily be able to find speakers of these configurations. You'll see a ".1" behind the channels, as in 2.1 or 5.1. The .1 refers to a separate subwoofer in the speaker set. If you have a 2.1 set of speakers and you're worried about buying a soundcard with 7.1 support, don't sweat it. All consumer soundcards are capable of running with fewer than the maximum number of speakers. A 5.1 soundcard,

for example, will support 4.1 and 2.1. Soundcards cannot, however, run more than their maximum, so an older Sound Blaster Live! 4.1 soundcard will not support 5.1 audio.

Although multichannel soundcards are common, the majority of PC users run 2 or 2.1 speakers, or use headphones. Because of that, most soundcard vendors spend an inordinate amount of time trying to develop filtering algorithms that will fool you into believing that the audio from just two speakers is coming from behind you. It's an inexact science and the faux surround sound will not be equally satisfying to everyone. So we don't recommend basing a soundcard purchase on "virtual" surround sound.

The most effective technique for most people is nothing less than full 4.1, 5.1, or better, with speakers positioned behind their heads.

DIRECTSOUND, DIRECTSOUND3D, AND THE API WARS

It's difficult to discuss soundcards without dredging up the past. In the beginning, DOS-based video games, such as the original *Doom,* required that game developers write drivers for each videocard. On the other hand, Microsoft's API DirectSound and DirectSound3D let developers write to a common API (application programming interface) and not worry about the different soundcards.

But soundcard vendors, eager to differentiate themselves from each other, continued to develop their own APIs and features. Aureal's A3D was one of the strongest rebel APIs and garnered a fair amount of support from gaming developers, while Creative Labs pushed its own EAX API, which worked in conjunction with DirectX.

In the end, Creative's simpler API won out. Today, DirectSound3D and Creative's EAX are the prevailing API's for games. EAX has also vastly improved with more subtle controls that affect how something sounds going through an object or reflecting off an object. As long as the soundcard you buy supports

Creative Labs' Audigy 2 is the prince of consumer soundcard families, offering 24-bit audio, a popular API, and niceties such as built-in FireWire.

DirectSound3D and some level of EAX, you're in good shape.

WHAT ABOUT ONBOARD AUDIO?

Just as soundcards have evolved, so has the audio on motherboards. Years ago, motherboard makers simply bought audio chips, such as a Sound Blaster, to embed on their boards. Onboard audio offered few frills then, but today onboard audio provides an amazing amount of functionality such as multichannel, coax, and optical digital links for truly finicky audiophiles, and even the ability to sense whether a microphone is plugged into a speaker jack. The overwhelming majority of today's onboard audio, however, relies on the CPU and drivers to do most of the heavy lifting. We remain suspicious of onboard audio, not so much because of the hardware, but because on many motherboards that we've reviewed, the audio software has been poorly implemented.

Among the most popular onboard vendors are Analog Devices, C-Media, VIA, RealTek, and nVidia. nVidia's nForce2 MCP-T audio solution is fairly unique in the audio space. Unlike the other onboard competitors, the nForce2 MCP-T is an audio "accelerator," and just like a graphics accelerator, it offloads processing of audio from the CPU. The nForce2 is also unique because it can encode audio in real-time to Dolby Digital. Hook any of the other audio solutions to a home entertainment system's Dolby Digital decoder, and all you'll get is DVD audio or stereo for games. Because the nForce2 MCP-T uses technology developed for the Xbox, it can output games in multichannel to a decoder.

Although onboard audio is clearly becoming increasingly sophisticated, we still prefer the feature orgy associated with add-in cards. The Audigy 2, for example, does 24-bit audio, offers a multitude of I/O options (including a FireWire port) and is unique in its ability to play DVD Audio discs (in the event you happen to have one of those lying around).

THE 24-BIT QUESTION

Creative Lab's original Audigy helped take PC audio to the next level. Offering limited 24-bit audio support, the Audigy sounded head and shoulders better than the Sound Blaster Live! and the majority of other consumer PC soundcards. As its name implies, 24-bit audio simply packs in more audio information than 16-bit audio. If you imagine a sound file as a gentle curve, 16-bit is a jagged stair-step approximation of that curve. By increasing it to 24-bit, the jaggedness is reduced significantly and the sound is smoother and richer. Creative has been the sole retailer of consumer-level 24-bit audio cards for the last few years (as opposed to brawny, but expensive professional audio soundcards) but the competition is heating up. AudioTrak and M-Audio are among several vendors now offering affordable, multichannel 24-bit products. One limiting factor of the higher resolution is the lack of source material. Since the majority of PC audio is 16-bit (audio CDs are 16-bit as well), the benefit of 24-bit isn't as noticeable. The higher resolution, however, can benefit even the average game or MP3 file. Because 24-bit soundcards generally use higher-quality digital audio converters and codecs, 16-bit audio source material can sound improved over the garden variety 16-bit soundcard. Our endorsement of the Audigy 2 for consumer use stands.

LOOKING AHEAD: INTEGRATED SOUND LEAPS AHEAD

Where do soundcards go from here? Intel's Azalia could revolutionize the integrated soundcard market—and put some pressure on Creative.

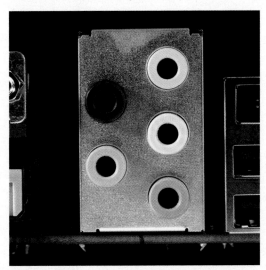

By integrating advanced audio capabilities into motherboards, Intel hopes to bring 32-bit, multichannel audio to the masses in late 2004 with its High Definition Audio spec. So what does this mean for Creative's add-in soundcard market? Read on to find out.

Undoubtedly, the big news around soundcards over the next year will be the impact Intel's new integrated sound spec has on the PC market.

In early 2003, Intel announced plans to push an eight-channel audio spec with support for up to 96KHz (192KHz in stereo mode) as well as 32-bit multichannel support. Dolby has been a key partner in developing this high-def spec, code-named Azalia and later dubbed Intel High Definition Audio. Several of its technologies will be options in HD motherboards, including a software decoder that runs off the CPU.

The technology replaces the current AC'97 specification used since 1997 and will complement Microsoft's Universal Audio Architecture, in the process paving the way for broader adoption of "next-gen" audio. More than 80 different companies, including PC and CE manufacturers, codec vendors, software providers, and other industry leaders have teamed with Intel to develop version 1.0 of the spec, which also extends to handheld devices.

Scheduled to be integrated into motherboards by the end of 2004, this new advanced spec will allow consumers not interested in purchasing add-in boards an affordable method of experiencing high quality, multichannel sound in their PC gaming and movie-watching.

Interestingly, Creative's level of concern about motherboard manufacturers beginning to incorporate High Definition Audio into their mobos was very low. And it should be. Like us, the company expects soundcard sales to remain brisk—PC enthusiasts seeking high-quality audio without affecting CPU usage will continue to snap up soundcards like the Audigy 2 ZS Platinum.

And, given the company's new stake in British technology firm Sensaura, Creative will also likely realize a small financial gain with each new integrated mobo sold.

And What About the Audigy?

We asked Creative what their plans were outside of the realm of integrated sound, and the company, which also has a successful business selling speakers, portable music devices, and other sound-related products, declined to publicly comment upon its future soundcard plans.

Sometime in the beginning of 2005, we expect to see a new, revised Audigy soundcard. Whether that add-in board is named the Audigy 3 or is another variant of the Audigy 2, we expect this product to feature increased audio clarity via a more refined signal processor.

At some point in the near future, we also expect to see an Audigy card that supports 32-bit audio—not that our mortal ears will be able to notice a significant quality difference.

It seems as if the speaker market is reaching its peak with eight channel, 7.1 sound. If this is indeed the case, we will likely see no further increase in the number of channels output by soundcards.

HaRD DR

Logic board: Once upon a time, drives were pretty dumb and needed to be plugged into controller cards (via a PC slot) in order to work. These days, the controller is built right into the PCB beneath the drive, along with the drive cache, and lots of shiny things.

Voice coil/voice coil magnet: Hidden beneath this curved piece of metal is an extremely strong rare earth magnet. If you were to look closely underneath the metal shield, you'd just barely see the copper wire coiled beneath. When current is passed through the wire, the resulting electromagnetic field pushes or pulls the drive head assembly across the platters. The drive head assembly can sweep across the platter hundreds of times a second; each sweep causes a faint click that is the sound of a hard drive earning its keep.

IDE cable connector

ve

Read/write head assembly: Like the old cassette recorders of yore, there are two separate heads in a hard drive head assembly for reading and writing data. We're pointing out the "assembly" here because the actual read/write heads could be hidden behind the leg of a gnat.

Most modern hard drives employ GMR heads, which, oddly enough, is an acronym for "giant magnetoresistive" heads. Nobody was trying to be funny or ironic; the name comes from the "giant magnetoresistive effect," a sly technique discovered in the 1980s that allows weaker magnetic fields from the disk media to be picked up by the read/write heads. The result is more data packed into less space.

Disk media: Modern drives have several platters stacked one on top of the other like a stack of pancakes. Each platter is two-sided, and both sides are used for data storage. On the surface of each platter is an extremely thin layer of magnetic particles. Using a very delicate electromagnetic write head, these particles are organized and reorganized into neat groups that represent either 1s or 0s. The read head then reads these "bits" and translates them back into digital data.

Spindle motor: This is the motor that spins the platters of a hard drive. Each platter is supported by ball bearings around the circumference of the spindle motor to prevent excess wobbling. Newer hard drives use fluid dynamic bearings, however, which use a thick oil to stabilize the platters without the whirring racket of ball bearings.

Flex circuit: This thin ribbon provides power to the head assembly. It also has a tiny pre-amp built into it that amplifies the wee signals picked up from the platters.

Master/slave jumpers

Power connector

How To Pick the BEST HARD DRIVE

Bigger, faster, and smarter—meet the new crop of hard drives

Your CPU and videocard are glamorous components, with impressive-sounding descriptors like "gigahertz," and faster iterations popping up every few months. But the hard drive is the heart of your PC. It's the basket where your PC puts all the goods—your OS, your applications, and, of course, all your valuable data.

Not much more than a decade ago hard disk storage was expensive and fairly limited in capacity. But today, it's almost an afterthought. A high-performance drive from a major manufacturer like Western Digital will cost you less than a buck per gigabyte. So it's tempting to just grab the biggest one you can find and assume you're set for a year or so.

Not so fast, big guy.

Your hard drive is a mechanical device, and it won't ever challenge solid-state components like your CPU and RAM in the speed category. But it does do its job—keeping your CPU and RAM fed with the data they hunger for—reliably and cheaply. So given that we're stuck with the technology for the time being, we may as well minimize the drag on our system's performance by intelligently selecting the right hard drive.

A FEW NANOSECONDS IN THE LIFE OF A HARD DRIVE

If you want to understand what makes one hard drive faster than another, well, wouldn't you know, you need to understand a bit about how they work. It's a lot more interesting than you might imagine.

Suppose a program is looking for a file. Your operating system and hard drive work together (mediated by a disk controller built into the drive) to find out where the file is physically situated on the disk. Disk addressing is done in terms of tracks and sectors (which can be thought of as rings and points on the rings). If the data has already been read and stored into a small amount of built-in memory called the "cache," then the data is served up directly from the chip. This would be the case, for example, if you reopened a document that you just closed. If the data isn't there, then the drive needs to retrieve the data by moving the read and write heads to the right disk location.

The read and write heads (they are separate) are mounted at the very tip of the arm assembly. The assembly is similar to the arm and stylus of a classic record player, except that instead of being driven by a motor and belt, the arm is moved by a very strong and precise magnet capable of rapidly twitching the arm to and fro. The read and write heads float above the surface of the drive platters, which store digital information in a thin layer of magnetic particles (like cassette tapes).

Once the read head arrives at the correct track, the drive needs to wait for the platter to spin to the correct sector before reading. Once the data is picked up, it is passed to the cache, and then on to the rest of your PC for processing.

SPEED METRICS FOR POWER USERS

Now that you know some of the essentials of how a hard drive works, let's look at the attributes that determine what kind of performance you'll get from your drive. Again, it comes down to the efficiency of physically moving parts.

Rotational speed is the speed at which the spindle motor spins your drive platters. The faster the rotational speed, the less you'll have to deal with the effects of rotational latency, which is the time it takes for a disc to spin the right sectors past your drive's read or write head. Think about it like this: If a bus runs through a city loop at 10 miles per hour versus one that runs at 20 mph, and you just missed both of them, the 20mph bus will come back your way sooner. Faster rotational speeds also help with transfer rates, by way of passing more bits under the head with every rotation. Don't settle for a desktop drive that runs at less than 7200rpm.

Another number getting a lot of attention in the past few years is the cache size. Western Digital turned over the desktop drive industry with 8MB caches (compared with the then typical 2MB) and other vendors soon followed

"Are you sure we can't fit in one more?" Jeff, Betty, and Bernard check out the first IBM hard drive, boasting 50 platters, each 24 inches across.

suit. A larger cache has more room for stored data, thus increasing cache "hits," which are successful retrievals from the fast cache instead of the relatively pokey drive platters. A 2MB cache

YOUR GUIDE TO SERIAL ATA

Why the PC industry is rushing away from parallel ATA

Take a look at a machine equipped with Serial ATA, and its most striking feature will be the skinny data cables. While skinny cables have a positive impact on a case's internal airflow, this isn't the main reason why the PC industry is dropping parallel ATA (and its flat, wide cables) for SATA. The main reason is that the current parallel interface is facing a performance wall.

Parallel ATA cables send data along multiple wires. Each piece of data must travel along the length of the familiar ribbon cable, and arrive at the same time in order to maintain data integrity. In order to get more speed from this scheme, the only option is to push the data to higher frequencies or make the data path wider. That's where the problems lie. Making the data path wider is impractical, as there are already 80 conductors in the ribbon. And increasing speed adds to the likelihood of data corruption.

Because serial interfaces don't have to deal with coordinating multiple lanes of data, we're able to push them to much higher speeds. SATA is currently rated for 150MB/s, slightly higher than the 133MB/s offered by the fastest parallel ATA spec (which still hasn't been widely adopted). SATA will soon reach 300MB/s and eventually double to 600MB/s by 2007.

The first SATA implementations on motherboards were kludgey: Serial ATA chips were piped through the PCI bus. This limited the 150MB/s potential of SATA to PCI's 133MB/s throughput, and required the loading of drivers just to recognize the chip. But current-generation SATA-equipped motherboards should be plug-and-play. In Intel's new ICH5 southbridge chip, for example, SATA is native. Plug a SATA hard drive into an 875P motherboard, and you can load WinXP without needing to install any drivers.

Because of the glut of parallel devices, it'll probably take two to three years for the PC industry to drop parallel ATA entirely.

Although current hard drive data rates fall far short of the maximum throughput of even parallel ATA specs, companies are laying the foundation for the future. You don't, after all, wait for the traffic jam before you try to build the roads (unless you run the state of California).

is acceptable, but we've observed dramatic improvements in performance with hard drives that utilize the brawnier 8MB cache.

The most misunderstood performance stat is the interface speed. Interface speeds like ATA66, ATA100, and ATA133 are, for the most part, much faster than what your desktop drive is able to continuously transfer, and rarely, if ever, constrict your data flow. These standards (representing megabytes per second) are more than capable of handling the 60MB per second or so of traffic that a drive can continuously deliver. For proof, we tested an identical ATA133 capable drive with an ATA100 and ATA133 controller, and came out with identical scores. Even the new SATA150 interface had virtually no performance advantage over an identical drive with an ATA100 interface. You don't need an ATA133 drive if you've already got an ATA100 drive. In fact, we question whether buying an ATA133 is wise at all—you'd be better off trading up to a Serial ATA drive (but make sure you get a motherboard or controller card that supports it).

Note that more than one drive on a single channel *will* overload an ATA66, and will likely strain even an ATA100 interface at times. The lesson: Always keep your hard drives on separate channels!

Seek time describes how quickly a drive can move from one place on the drive platter to another. It can be expressed as average seek time (meaning how long it takes to go from

one random position to another), and full stroke (which measures the travel time between the outermost and innermost tracks). Most current drives post average seek times between 8 and 10ms (milliseconds). These numbers are useful, but don't go overboard. For example, some SCSI drives have average seek times as low as 5ms; you'll notice a difference between this and your bread-and-butter 9.5ms desktop drive. Less urgent is the difference between a drive with 8.5ms and a 10ms average seek time—and the lower rated one may be much more expensive. Stick with a high-rpm drive, and use common sense. Lower average seek times are better, but you won't want to pay through the nose for a slightly lower figure. If performance is that crucial, consider a RAID setup.

DESKTOP VS. SERVER DRIVES

Hard drives are designed for specific tasks that generally fall into two categories: server and desktop duties. The high-rpm SCSI drives can handle many simultaneous tasks—essential for servers that get requests from many different users at the same time. Desktop IDE drives are designed to work most efficiently when data is requested in relatively bulky chunks, although many contemporary drives are handling server-type requests with greater efficiency. Server drives are much more expensive, however. Overall, you'd be better served by a Serial ATA or IDE RAID setup.

How To Pick the BEST MONITOR

CRT or LCD—what's the diff, and which one is best?

The Cornerstone P1750 is a good, honest, inexpensive 21-incher. It doesn't offer the exacting visual quality of the Sony F520, but it's a very respectable $600 monitor.

Very few power users consider the CRT monitor to be a glamour component. After all, cathode ray tube displays are based on essentially the same technology found in common TV sets—that old-school technology was invented way, way back in the 1920s (the date of television's official birth is open to debate, but that's another story altogether).

Yes, CRTs are completely "yestertech" compared with videocards and optical drives, which seem to be reinvented every six months, but they cannot, must not, be underestimated. Think about it. A good CRT can potentially be a system's most expensive component. Even more importantly, CRT life cycles are relatively long, so the monitor you buy this year will likely be the same one you're using in 2006. Think you'll be running the same CPU, hard drives, and videocard in 2006? For the sake of your games and applications, we certainly hope not. But you'll probably be running the same CRT, so you best take your CRT purchasing decision seriously.

CRTs offer a few key benefits over flat-panel LCDs: (1) In most cases, they offer more square inches of screen real estate for every dollar spent. (2) They can display quick-moving video and 3D gaming content without any hint of streaking and trailing whatsoever. (3) They can display every single color a videocard can produce—no excuses, no ifs, ands, or buts. (4) They can display multiple resolutions, from 640x480 to 1600x1200 and beyond. (LCDs have only one "native" resolution, and this can lead to problems.)

But CRTs are not without their foibles: (1) Compared with LCDs, they're heavy as all get-out, emit more heat, and consume much more desk space. (2) Their screen image is more prone to geometric distortion. (3) Bad CRTs can exhibit a fuzzy picture.

Maximum PC prefers CRTs over LCDs for gaming and image-editing work. A flat-panel LCD is easier to transport to LAN parties, but we are loath to give up native support for multiple game resolutions. As for image editing, very few LCDs can accurately display the full range of color and grayscale gradation in continuous-tone images. That said, if you're only going to be typing and web surfing on your new computer, we think that high-quality, high-resolution LCDs are hard to beat.

OK, so you've weighed the strengths and weaknesses, and you've decided a good CRT is the best monitor for you. The next step is to choose between shadow mask and aperture grille technology.

POKING HOLES

Shadow mask and aperture grille are two different technologies that perform the same function: By using either a perforated sheet of metal (a "mask," if you will), or a series of narrow, vertical metal strips (a grille, by any other name), shadow masks and aperture grilles help confine a CRT's electron beam, ensuring that the beam triggers only the red, green, or blue phosphor dots that need to be illuminated (these dots congregate in triangular arrangements called triads). Once a phosphor dot is triggered, it glows with color, and, voila, you have a screen image. This is a gross simplification, of course, and we wish we had enough space to explain how CRTs *actually* work. But for the purpose of this article, we'll simply explain the pluses and minuses of each "masking" approach.

➤ **Shadow Mask:** Shadow mask CRTs tend to be less expensive than aperture grilles. They also lack the faint, horizontal lines that span the screens of aperture grille CRTs. On the downside, shadow mask CRTs usually offer dimmer, less vibrant screens than aperture grilles, and they typically don't match their cousins' fine detail reproduction.

➤**Aperture Grille:** Every CRT monitor company's highest-quality, pro-level offering is an aperture grille display—does that give you an idea of which technology is superior? The key thing to remember is that grilles allow more electrons (and thus light) to pass through to the phosphor layer, and this fosters a brighter, more brilliant screen image. The best aperture grille CRTs also boast the finest pitches.

SPEC TECH

Buying a monitor based on its advertised specs is always a dubious proposition. Still, the specs you see on CRT cartons do mean something, so let's get to the bottom of them:

➤ **Size/viewing area:** You've probably already figured out that a "19-inch" monitor doesn't offer 19 diagonal inches of screen real estate—it actually comes in at around 18 inches. Then you have the problem of 21- and 22-inch monitors essentially falling into the same size category. Sony specs its best 21-inch CRT at 19.8 viewable inches, while NEC specs its primo-grande 22-inch CRT as having 20.0 viewable inches. NEC's viewable diagonal is just 0.2 inches longer than Sony's, but

box advertising would suggest a full inch of difference. Buyer beware.

Our overall advice is to pay closest attention to actual visible viewing area specs, and always purchase the largest, most brilliant CRT that your desk (and budget) can support. Actual visual quality is very important, yes, but we'd still rather have a 21-inch CRT with "good" visual quality over a 17-inch CRT with "category-leading" visual quality. There's just no replacement for screen real estate.

➤ **Dot and grille pitch:** A CRT's sharpness is directly related to its dot or grille pitch (dot pitch applies to shadow mask displays; grille pitch to aperture grille displays). In simple terms, a monitor's pitch describes the distance between one of its phosphor dots and the next closest dot of exactly the same color. The CRT industry doesn't use a standard way to measure this distance, but, in general, regardless of which type of

CRT you buy, you'll want to go with the lowest pitch spec possible. For example, Sony's 0.22mm grille pitch CRT is preferred to its 0.24mm pitch CRT. The smaller the pitch, the finer your screen pixels will be, and thus the sharper your overall image.

With some aperture grille monitors, you'll see a grille pitch spec that describes a range; for example, "0.25mm-0.27mm." This means that the pixels in the center of the display are sharper than the pixels on the display's perimeter—they ramp from a 0.25mm pitch to a 0.27mm pitch. Is the gradation noticeable? We don't think so.

However, you should be concerned with shadow mask specs that describe a "horizontal dot pitch" of a super-low figure like 0.22mm. Shadow mask vendors have

traditionally quoted diagonal pitch specs, despite the fact that diagonal pitch numbers never look as attractive on a spec sheet. To wit, a CRT's horizontal dot pitch equals 0.866 times its diagonal dot pitch. The upshot is that a 0.22mm horizontal dot pitch offers the same level of screen sharpness as a 0.25mm diagonal dot pitch.

➤ **Resolutions/refresh rates:** Every CRT displays a matrix of dots to describe whatever image is being presented on screen. This matrix is called its resolution. The lowest standard resolution you'll ever see supported is 640x480 (480 lines of 640 individual dots), but the best consumer CRTs can display 2048x1536. The higher your resolution, the more visual information can be displayed on your screen. Do you really need a 2048x1536 display? Probably not, unless you're doing high-end graphic design. Still, high-resolution support is the hallmark of a good CRT.

A monitor's refresh rate is directly related to its resolution. In simple terms, the refresh rate describes how many times per second a CRT redraws its screen. But here's the catch: The higher the resolution setting, the more difficult it is to redraw the screen. Thus, as resolutions go up, refresh rates go down. This is true for all CRTs. The key is finding a CRT that can maintain high refresh rates (75Hz and above) at high resolutions.

We suggest that you avoid any CRT that can't maintain a refresh rate of at least 85Hz at 1600x1200. A refresh rate below 75Hz will give you eyestrain, and any rate above 85Hz could possibly lead to blurry pixels.

AIN'T LCDs GOOD FOR NOTHING?

Flat-panel LCDs are seemingly taking over the PC market. But are they really the best choice? First, let's consider their pluses: (1) They're light and easy to carry, they don't take up much physical desk space, and they don't consume much electricity or emit much heat. (2) Because LCD pixels are arranged on a fixed, physical grid, geometric distortion is an

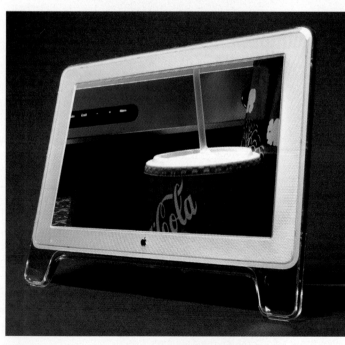

Apple's LCDs do in fact work with PCs. And their visual quality is absolutely kick-ass. Just be aware that all of Apple's display controls are accessed via a MacOS menu, so if you run the 23-inch, 1920x1200 Apple Cinema Display on your PC, you will not be able to tweak its pixel properties!

impossibility. (3) They offer a sharp, crystal-clear image when running in their native resolution.

Sounds like one big pixel-loving party, right? Well, LCDs also have their problems: (1) They still cost more than CRTs, all screen sizes being equal. (2) Some can't display fast-moving video and games without streaking (for example, a quick-moving hockey puck might look like a comet with a tail). (3) They don't have the color accuracy of CRTs, thus they're not ideal for image-editing work. (4) When running in their non-native resolution, they must "interpolate" pixels, and this leads to horribly degraded visual quality.

OK, so let's say you're copasetic with the inherent weaknesses of LCDs. It's now time to deconstruct their specs.

➤ **Viewing area:** When an LCD is marketed as a 17-inch display, you really do get 17 diagonal inches of screen real estate. More is better—buy as much screen as you can possibly afford.

➤ **Pixel pitch:** A smaller pitch is better, and will provide a sharper screen image. And unlike CRTs, all LCD pixel pitches are measured in a consistent manner. So when comparing flat-panels, you might as well opt for those with the smallest pitch specs.

➤ **Resolution:** Because your LCD will essentially be fixed at a single resolution, you better make sure it's the right resolution for your screen size. For 17- and 18-inch LCDs, we prefer 1280x1024. For larger monitors, 1600x1200 is preferred. (Note: LCDs don't have refresh rates, per se, so don't be worried if you see that an LCD is preset to run at a low 60Hz or 75Hz.)

➤ **Pixel response:** This spec, expressed in milliseconds (ms), refers to the speed at which the LCD's pixels can change color. Speed is important because if the pixels can't switch quickly enough, fast-moving screen content will exhibit streaking. Generally speaking, any LCD with a pixel response spec of 25ms or faster should be problem-free. That said, just because an LCD is advertised to hit 25ms doesn't mean it can switch at 25ms, so buyer beware. It always pays to run some content on the LCD before purchasing. But for what it's worth, even today's lamest LCDs can switch pretty damn quickly, and we haven't seen horrible streaking problems in a while, even in budget models.

➤ **Brightness:** This spec is expressed in candelas per square foot or meter (a candela is the total amount of light emitted by a single, standard candle). For example, a particular Sharp LCD can display 200cd/m2 —200 candles per square meter. Higher brightness specs are preferred.

How To Pick the BEST CD BURNER

Spinning the newest generation of CD burners

Even Luddites who once scoffed at the idea of owning a personal computer fell under the seductive spell of CD burning. At the same time CD burners were plunging in price, certain applications that could be used with them (read: *Napster*) were growing in popularity, reinforcing the PC's inextricability in *all* our lives.

Today, ultra-fast CD burners are so ubiquitous, they may as well be sold in blister-packs at the local drugstore. But make no mistake: "High speed" does not mean "high quality." It's worth it to pay a premium for a quality drive and brand-name media. Those extra dollars today will pay big dividends tomorrow.

Before we talk about the features you need in a CD burner, let's look at the basics of how a burner works.

THE EZ BAKE OVEN OF YOUR PC

Compact discs store data in a single, continuous track that begins at the inner ring of the disc. The data is stored digitally—that is, every bit of text, imagery, or sound is stored as a sequence of 1s and 0s. On a commercially pressed disc, these 1s and 0s are represented by pits (areas that have been microscopically indented) and lands (areas that have been left flat). The laser on your CD-ROM drive or CD player is reflected to an optical sensor when it hits a land, which results in a "1." When the laser hits a pit,

Yamaha's cool image-burning CRW-F1 is no longer manufactured—Yamaha ditched its optical drive division—but that's what eBay is for.

the light is reflected away from the sensor, resulting in a "0."

Home CD burners don't really create pits and lands like commercial CD presses do, but they function in the same manner. Instead of pressing an indentation into a disc's surface, a consumer drive "burns" a mark into a photosensitive dye on the disc that's protected by a transparent plastic layer. Wherever the disc is left untouched, the laser light is reflected and a "1" is registered. Wherever the disc has been burned, the laser light is absorbed and a "0" is registered. When you finish burning a disc, you can actually see the difference between the used and unused portions of a disc—the burned areas are slightly darker. (In its day, Yamaha's clever CRW-F1 allowed you to burn images and text in the unused portions of a disc by taking advantage of the difference in reflectivity of burned and unburned areas.) Rewriteable media works similarly, except that the photosensitive layer is replaced by a polymorphous layer. Like the T-1000 Terminator, this layer can change from one form to another and back again; from burned to unburned, in other words.

WHY MEDIA MATTERS

How a particular CD burner interacts with a particular type of media is called a "write strategy." Believe it or not, optical drive manufacturers tailor the strength of their laser to different brands and dye formulations on different kinds of media. This information is stored in the drive's firmware, a piece of rewriteable, non-volatile memory in your CD burner. When you pop in a disc, the CD burner reads information about the disc imprinted in a small area called the ATIP, and adjusts itself accordingly. Quality drive manufacturers like Plextor and Lite-On constantly update their firmware to accommodate different kinds of media

and implement new write strategies for them. No-name manufacturers are more apt to let this kind of thing slide.

This is your hint to buy quality, brand-name media. You'll find that manufacturers such as Verbatim and Memorex consistently deliver a more reliable product as a result of using higher-quality dyes that not only provide higher reflectivity, but longer-lasting discs as well.

BUFFER-UNDERRUN PROTECTION

Insist on a drive that offers some kind of buffer-underrun protection. (Actually, the point is somewhat moot as virtually every CD burner has it these days.) There are times when a PC can't feed data to the CD burner fast enough; this is known as buffer-underruns. If a drive is unequipped to protect against buffer-underruns it will stop running at the moment the buffer is depleted, resulting in an unreadable disc. Buffer-underrun protection enables a drive to pause while the buffer is replenished and then resume burning chores where it left off.

DIGITAL AUDIO EXTRACTION: GETTING EVERY LAST DROP

The "Red Book" CD Audio specification was designed for fault-tolerant playback, not flawless digital audio extraction (aka "ripping" music tracks from audio CDs). In order to understand why a good optical drive matters, it's important to understand how error-correction schemes work, and why digital audio extraction can be such a tough job.

The pits and lands that represent digital information on an audio CD are microscopic, so a scratch on the surface, even a tiny one, is bound to obliterate a few bits of data. The CD spec was designed to compensate for this inevitable wear and tear with a number of error-correcting schemes. The first, and relatively simplest, is called C1 correction. Data written to a CD is surrounded by a matrix of confirmation bits that are referenced when data is obscured. It works a lot like algebra: When you see the equation $9 + x = 10$, you know x has to represent the number 1, even though the middle digit is missing. By the same token, if 9 is the available audio data, and 10 is the confirmation bit, the error-correction scheme knows the missing audio data is 1.

C2 error correction is far more complex. With C2, one block of audio CD information is interleaved with information from many other blocks. This way, a surface scratch will affect only small parts of many blocks, instead of a large part of one block (for this very reason, you should never clean a CD by wiping in a circular motion—you're far more likely to scratch several contiguous blocks that way). Just look at C2 error correction this way: It's fairly easy to guess the evenly distributed missing letters in "M_XIMU_ PC MAG_ZIN_" but much more difficult with a contiguous missing block such as "M___UM PC MAGAZINE" (which could be "MAGNUM PC MAGAZINE"). C2 error correction performs an analysis similar to C1 error correction, but across many interleaved frames instead of within just one.

If error correction somehow fails, then the player attempts to hide the glitch by essentially guessing what a value should have been. It does this by referencing the information in nearby blocks, a process called *interpolation* that results in signal degradation and distortion. Even worse, during the ripping process, your optical drive may just skip errant blocks altogether, resulting in clicks, pops, and dropouts.

Your best defense against audio flaws is to get an optical drive with good hardware error correction that is capable of reporting C2 error information to your PC. Our favorite drives for digital audio extraction—by a long shot—come from Plextor. This manufacturer's drives are legendary for their reliability, and offer optimized circuits for cleaner power and black CD trays that absorb laser light to reduce disc errors caused by stray bits of light.

Lite-On may not be a household name, but in our tests, its drives consistently hit the top speeds for the bottom dollar.

HOW FAST IS FAST ENOUGH?

A 52x burner sounds sexier than a 40x, no doubt about it. But the difference in speed is minute—about 45 seconds at the most, and you'll only realize that advantage when writing to the full capacity of a 700MB disc. That's because the top burning speed of the drive is reached at only the outer extremities of a disc (where the track circumferences are longer and the data rate increases). If you've already got a 32x drive or above and are happy with its features, there's no compelling argument to upgrade to a faster drive. But then again, optical drive prices are so low these days, you might not have to pay much simply to have 52x burner bragging rights.

ANATOMY OF A DVD BURNER

Interface PCB (underside of drive): This is the main PCB (printed circuit board) that contains the chips and connectors for interfacing the drive to the PC. It also contains special chips for adding all the control information necessary for creating the DVD structure on the disc.

Optics control PCB: This PCB accepts the signals from the interface PCB and translates them into the laser pulses needed to actually burn the disc, and to control the focusing and tracking of the laser.

Spindle motor: This motor controls the rotation of the DVD or CD when it's loaded into the drive. Unlike a typical hard drive which has only one fixed rotation speed, the motor in this DVD burner has to spin at different speeds depending on the burning task and the media being used. And it has to maintain these speeds with absolute precision.

Laser optics: This is an amazing assembly consisting of the laser, prisms, and servo motors for focusing and tracking the laser on the DVD or CD for reading and writing. The Sony DRU-510A pictured here can read/write to a staggering number of optical formats, including CD-R, CD-RW, DVD-R, DVD+R, and DVD-RW, among others. Each format has its own finicky positioning and burning requirements, which makes this assembly one of the most versatile of the mechanical components in your PC.

Loading tray motor: This motor controls the opening and closing of the drive's loading tray. A good motor should be quiet, and smoothly open and close the tray without funky rattling noises.

How To Pick the BEST DVD BURNER

Formats, shwormats...here's all you really need to know about DVD burning

I f the launch of recordable DVD drives for consumers went the way it should've, this section wouldn't be necessary. But it didn't, and it is.

The good news is that choosing the right DVD burner isn't as difficult as it might first seem. In fact, we're going to *tell* you which burners are the best. But first, let's recap the individual DVD formats so you'll understand what all the fuss has been about.

DVD-RAM

DVD-RAM was the first recordable, rewriteable DVD standard introduced at the consumer level. DVD-RAM discs hold up to 4.7GB per side, so double-sided discs can hold up to 9.4GB per disc. In our opinion, the format wasn't particularly well thought out. Although the discs themselves resemble typical DVDs, they are encased in cartridges. *Ick.* DVD-RAM wasn't designed to be compatible with set-top DVD players, so you couldn't author your own videos to play for a bunch of bored

DVD-RAM starts to look good for home use only when it's combined with DVD-R, as in Panasonic's MultiDrive II.

house guests. And although you can remove the discs from the cartridges, there isn't much point, because not even DVD-ROM drives can read the discs without support for the MultiRead2 spec, which is common today, but wasn't back when DVD-RAM was introduced. The format lives on today as a storage and backup device for businesses. In this regard, the cartridges are an effective deterrent against wear and tear. But for home use, there isn't much argument for DVD-RAM.

DVD-R/W

The write-once DVD-R format was developed by Pioneer Electronics and had the distinction of being the first format that offered some compatibility with set-top players and DVD-ROMs.

We say "some" because not all DVD readers could handle the subtle differences between commercially "stamped" DVDs and the less reflective DVD-Rs. DVD-R discs hold 4.7GB per side, although double-sided discs are rare.

Pioneer introduced rewriteable DVD-RW discs two years later, but the thrill of being able to reuse media was mitigated by DVD-RW's far lower compatibility with set-top players and DVD-ROM drives compared with the write-once DVD-R.

DVD+R/W

Although Pioneer's DVD-R/W technology worked fairly well as a consumer format, other manufacturers balked at having to pay Pioneer for every drive they produced and sold. So a

Sony's DRU-500A was the first burner to offer both leading DVD formats in a single drive.

cadre of companies including Sony, Philips, and Hewlett-Packard got together and created their own format. The first DVD+RW drives appeared in March 2001, accompanied by a huge marketing push that touted the technical advantages of the format, such as "lossless linking" and "defect management." But the rewriteable 4.7GB discs had an even lower rate of compatibility with set-top players and DVD-ROMs than did DVD-RW.

The write-once DVD+R format was released later in the year. Although DVD+R offered greater compatibility with other players, many early adopters of recordable DVD drives were surprised to find that their drives weren't upgradeable to the new format, even though some manufacturers suggested they would be able to do just that.

Let's see: a confusing VHS vs. Betamax–style standards slugout, broken promises, and compatibility issues. Talk about a traumatic birth. What kept the momentum going for DVD burners despite all of this was plummeting prices. Once sub-$300 burners were released (not to mention software packages that decrypted and copied commercial DVDs), the prospect became irresistible. Which led to yet another embarrassing problem: product returns. Happy consumer walks into a store, buys a DVD-RW drive, and then picks up some DVD+RW media on his way out, not realizing that the two different standards are incompatible. The disc won't work in the burner, so the whole

kit and caboodle is brought back to the store for a refund. How do you impress upon people the differences between formats? You don't. Hence, the introduction of the dual-format DVD burner.

Sony was the first to bite the bullet with the DRU-500A, a sparkling, silvery beaut that wrote to both DVD+R/W and DVD-R/W discs. It was the first DVD burner to allow consumers to experiment with different types of media to figure out which format or formats were most compatible with their players. In our experience, DVD-R remains the compatibility leader for DVD Video, while DVD+RW is the most efficient for data storage and retrieval.

Today's dual-format DVD burners are quite affordable for most 8x drives. At press time, Sony announced the DRU-540A, a 12x (using certified 8x media) model for those that have the need for speed.

Now that the format issue is moot, you need only pick your manufacturer.

Sony's DRU-500A was the first drive to offer both leading DVD formats in a single drive.

DOUBLE-SIDED VS. DUAL-LAYER

Double-sided DVD-RAM discs can hold up to 9.4GB of data and video, but you have to literally flip the disc to access the latter half of the information. Commercial DVDs can also hold up to 9.4GB of data and video, but disc-flipping is unnecessary. That's because they have two layers: When the end of one layer is reached, the reading laser adjusts its focus to zoom onto the second layer of the disc. That's why, on some very long movies, you'll notice a brief pause or stuttering as the laser adjusts itself to read the second layer. In *Titanic*, this happens just after Leonardo de Caprio gets hauled away for stealing the necklace.

You say you want to create dual-layer discs? Until recently you would have been out of luck, but leave it to Sony to be first again with a consumer dual-layer DVD burner—the DRU-700A.

ANATOMY OF A POWER SUPPLY

Power factor correction circuit: Computers, like many electrical appliances, draw a lot more power at the instant they are turned on—as much as four times the amount drawn under regular use. While this spike in power demand lasts just a fraction of a second, it may be enough to trip a circuit breaker in a home or office that has numerous electrical appliances. The duty of the power factor correction circuit is to smooth out this initial spike as much as possible, reducing its amplitude and preventing circuit overloads.

Output capacitors (underneath): Essential for system stability, these help the PSU provide the excess muscle required when the electrical demands from your PC's components suddenly changes, such as when two optical drives spin up simultaneously.

Heatsinks: Transistor switches and power diodes in the PSU produce loads of heat. The heatsink helps whisk away the heat from these components, a vital task considering that a power supply becomes less efficient as its temperature rises.

Line-conditioning circuitry: This is another of the phalanx of components within your power supply that help maintain consistent power levels from notoriously unreliable home sockets. Generally, you'll find line-conditioning circuitry only in top-tier power supplies.

Input capacitor: Usually the largest capacitor in a PSU, this provides reserve power when input power suddenly plummets (like, for example, when someone fires up the blow-dryer). In fact, it's one of a battery of devices built into a power supply (including the EMI filter and line-conditioning circuitry) that are intended to compensate for the unstable and interference-prone electricity from common household power outlets. In general, the bigger the capacitor, the better.

Fan: Heatsinks alone are not enough. The fan is necessary to prevent your power supply from becoming an EZ Bake Oven.

Electro magnetic interference (EMI) filter: Found in better power supply units, EMI circuitry smoothes out the small fluctuations in the incoming AC current.

How To Pick the BEST POWER SUPPLY

Don't starve your prized components of power!

You don't hear a lot of folks bragging about the power supply in their custom rig. With the frantic arms race between AMD and Intel, and the leapfrog of one video-card technology over another, it's easy to forget the basic necessity of a steady and ample supply of power.

Granted, even the brawniest power supply unit (PSU) won't yield an extra ounce of computing power, but an inadequate power supply could result in unreliable operation, component damage, or even the inability to boot your PC in the first place.

If you don't want to get into the nitty-gritty of power supplies, we understand. Here's some simple advice: You'll want at least a 350-watt PSU from a *name-brand* company like PC Power and Cooling (www.pcpowerandcooling.com), Antec (www.antec-inc.com), or Enermax (www.enermax.com.tw).

But if you want to get down and dirty with us, here's some clear guidelines that will help you select a PSU that meets all your needs.

GET THE POWER YOU NEED

Before shopping for a PSU, it behooves you to first tally up how much power you need. You do this by adding up the power requirements of each component in your PC. Most components in your PC will display the power requirements (either on the part itself or in the documentation) in the form of voltage and current ratings. For example, a 7200rpm Seagate Barracuda 160GB hard drive has the following power information imprinted on it: +5V (volts) 0.72A (amps) and +12V (volts) 0.35A (amps). This means it uses both 5V and 12V power (one for the drive and another for the circuitry). First, we need to multiply the volts and amps of each line to find the total wattage the drive needs: 5 volts multiplied by .72 amps gives us 3.6 watts, and 12 volts multiplied by .35 amps gives us

a total requirement of 7.8 watts. The drive should be given plenty of head-room, so we'll round this up to 10 watts total. Tally up the requirements for the rest of your components to find out the minimum wattage you need from your power supply.

If you're upgrading, or just afraid of math, refer to the chart below to estimate the amount of power some components typically require.

When you are figuring out how much power you'll need, don't forget to leave plenty of room for the components you may want to add later, such as a second optical drive or a video-card that requires additional power beyond what the AGP bus can provide (some recent videocards demand as much as 50 watts!). In addition to the total power requirement of your system, it is often useful to calculate a separate power requirement for all the devices that use 3.3V and all those that use 5V power. This is helpful because most PSUs list a separate (lower) rating indicating the maximum power draw possible in each of these categories.

We can't emphasize enough how important it is to allow for plenty of

3.3 volt connector

5 volt connector

12 volt connector

COMPONENT	POWER REQUIREMENT	LINE(S) USED
P4 or Athlon XP CPU	70~90 watts	+3.3v or +12v
RAM	16 watts per 256MB	+3.3v
CD/DVD drive	10~20 watts	+5v and +12v
Hard drive	10~20 watts	+5v and +12v
Floppy	5 watts	+5v
AGP videocard	20~50 watts	+3.3v
Typical (non-video) PCI card	5~10 watts	+5v
Motherboard	20~40 watts	+3.3v, +5v, and +12v
CPU/case fans	2~4 watts	+12v

headroom—in fact, we recommend *at least* 30 percent more wattage than you've calculated. This provides more than just headroom for upgrades.

PSUs actually lose efficiency as heat rises. Remarkably, under a typical operating temperature of around 100° F, many PSUs can lose 25 percent or more of their posted power ratings! (The problem is that there is no legal or conventional requirement for a power rating to be accompanied by a temperature rating. That is, manufacturers aren't required to say "This power supply outputs 400 watts—but only at 40° Fahrenheit." That's nearly freezing, and it's *never* that cold inside your computer. The truth is that the unit may only be worth 250W at a more likely 100° F!)

The bottom line is that you should purchase a PSU with as high a power rating as you can afford, given that it has the features you want.

Contrary to a widely held misconception, a PSU with a higher rating *will not use more power than one with a lower rating*; both will draw only as much power as your components demand.

GET THE FEATURES YOU NEED

With the exception of very small or "slimline" designs, most PC enclosures accept a standard-size power supply. However, newer motherboards typically require a PSU that complies with the ATX12V standard. These PSUs have the same dimensions as traditional power supplies, but they also include an additional four-pin 12-volt power connector and an increased wattage rating for +12V output. Therefore, if you're planning to build a Pentium 4 machine or any computer using a recent Athlon mobo—and you are, aren't you?—be sure to get a PSU with an ATX12V connector. In addition, if you plan on running a Serial-ATA drive, you'll need a PSU with the new Serial-ATA power connectors. It's possible to buy adapters that will allow you to use the standard

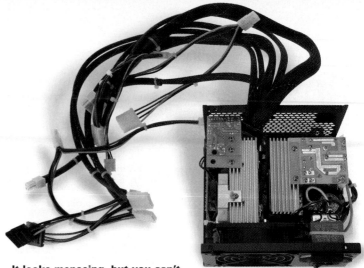

It looks menacing, but you can't accidentally plug a power connector into the wrong socket and blow up everything, because they're all different sizes.

If you plan to purchase Serial ATA drives, make sure you buy a power supply with Serial-ATA connectors, pictured above.

hard drive power connectors, but there's a catch: These adapters will not supply 3.3 volt power. Although no Serial ATA drives require this voltage at this time, future drives may—and then you'll be out of luck.

For utmost reliability and stability—and especially if you're planning to overclock—you should also look for a PSU with line-conditioning circuitry. The power we get from the AC outlets in most U.S. homes and offices is full of ripples and spikes. This is just fine for your hair dryer, but can lead to harmful voltage instabilities in your computer. Line conditioners keep your system fed with clean, consistent power, thus reducing the chances of a brownout causing hard drive write errors or system lockups.

Because a power supply generates considerable heat, a good PSU should feature the more durable ball-bearing fan(s). These fans are less likely to get rattly or even fail over time. Ball-bearing fans are significantly more costly than conventional fans, so if a manufacturer puts one in a product, you can be sure that the packaging and/or documentation will state as much. Just be sure to look for it!

If you plan on using your system beyond the boundaries of North America, pick up a PSU that will accept both 110~120v (the U.S. standard) and 220~240v AC inputs. Many PSUs sport universal voltage capability as a fea-

ture. These can be identified by either a label stating their voltage compatibility range (e.g.,110~240v) or a switch in the back marked with two input voltages you can select from.

THE UNSCIENTIFIC METHOD

If you're trying to gauge whether or not to go with a lesser-known manufacturer, or if you can get away with the power supply included with your case, you may be surprised to know that weight is often a reliable indicator of quality. When it comes to the innards of a PSU, bigger is better. A good power supply typically has huge capacitors and beefy heatsinks. Hence, a good PSU usually has substantial heft, while featherweight units are likely to be system-damaging junk.

ELECTRON TALK

Voltage is a measurement of electrical potential difference, while current is the rate of the flow of electrons. Voltage is expressed in volts (V) and current in amperes (A). If you imagine electricity as water in a garden hose, voltage is the pressure of the water and current is the rate at which water is flowing.

How To Pick the BEST MOUSE & KEYBOARD

Our input on your input

Yes, we've proselytized about the importance of every single component in your PC, and the mouse and keyboard, however unglamorous, are no exception. Think about it: The right keyboard can keep you merrily typing away after 10 hours at the office (we know this all too well). The wrong keyboard can put you in the hospital. The right mouse can make you the badass *Counter-Strike* god; the wrong mouse will have you serving snacks to your compadres after they've owned you in deathmatch.

Please, *please*, dump the craptacular $3 mouse and $10 keyboard that came with your PC. By now, you're probably tired of hearing about the freaky mechanics of every component. Well, you're in luck. Choosing a good mouse and keyboard for optimum gaming and ergonomics is pretty easy.

The keyboard part doesn't require any brainwork. Go to the store and fiddle with them all—standard keyboards, split keyboards, quiet ones, "clicky" models. Keep going until you find one that's comfortable. Even the *slightest* discomfort you feel is going to be magnified several times over within an hour or two of typing. Many keyboards also offer bells and whistles like multimedia control, wireless transmitters, and the like. If you want those features, great. But *only* on those keyboards that pass the comfort test.

Now on to our little rodent friends. There are a few things every mouse should have. Three buttons are absolutely mandatory, as is a scroll-wheel, preferably positioned in the center of your mouse. More buttons are optional, but not required. Truth be told, we don't use them that often, even though they can be extremely handy for web designers and *Excel* wonks who can program the buttons to do all sorts of parlor tricks.

In addition to the aforementioned prerequisites, there are really just two other things to consider before purchasing a mouse: comfort and accuracy.

Comfort's self-explanatory. You want a mouse that's sized for your hand, has buttons within easy reach, and can be used for extended periods without discomfort. If your fingers seize up after a marathon *Rise of Nations* session, you're going to have serious carpal tunnel problems down the road. If a demo unit is unavailable, don't hesitate to take your prospective mouse out of the package right there in the store. Fondle it. Skim it across the display shelf. Knock yourself out (not literally, of course).

Gamers need an optical mouse that senses movement via a small beam of red light at the base. These can be far more accurate than the old-fashioned roller-ball mice, which have to be cleaned periodically (another chore you don't need). But not all optical sensors are created equal. A slow optical sensor will turn your smooth-as-buttah mouse movements into stuttery cursor spasms. Not everyone measures mouse responsiveness the same way, but testing a mouse for gaming is easy. To test the rodent, firmly grab it, then move it from one side of your mousepad to the other as fast as you can. Watch the cursor as you do this. If it matches your movements across the screen, the mouse is golden. If it jumps madly across the desktop, ditch that mouse for another one.

Some of us are driven crazy by the constant tug-of-war with mice cords, so cordless mice can be a relief. But cordless-mice manufacturers have been slow to provide transmission rates sufficient for gaming. In fact, we think there's only one cordless mouse that comes close to performing well enough for gamers, and that's the Logitech MX700. Most other mice sacrifice update frequency for longer battery life, and the result is piss-poor game performance.

How To Pick the BEST COOLER FOR YOUR CPU

Fever reducers for your binary reactor!

Modern CPUs pack millions of transistors into a tiny amount of space. As a result, they're not just highly advanced silicon brains, they're also intense furnaces that generate massive amounts of heat. And heat reduces performance, introduces instability, and can seriously abbreviate the life of your components.

If you don't plan to overclock your CPU (running it at a higher clock frequency than its official, posted rating) you'll most likely be satisfied with the heatsink and fan combo that came with your CPU. But if you intend on raising some overclocked hell with your processor, or if you bought a "bare" CPU in some shady back-alley deal, you'll need to devise your own cooling strategy. Here's how to go about it .

The more surface area your heatsink has, the more it will be able to transfer your CPU's heat to the air inside your case. Hence the "blooming flower" design of Zalman's CNPS6500B-CU.

FUN WITH CLASSIC AIR COOLING

The job of any CPU cooling setup is to move heat from your CPU and dissipate that heat into the air. Heatsinks squat directly on your CPU and transfer heat from the die (or, in Intel's case, a heat spreader plate) to its fins or spires, which pass the heat into the air, which should then be swept out of the case by your case fans (as long as airflow isn't obstructed by tangled cables and whatnot).

There are four major factors affecting cooler performance: the kind of metal the heatsink is cast from, the design of the radiating fins, the fan (if present as part of a heatsink/fan combo), and the contact surface between the heatsink and the CPU.

As far as the material goes, copper is the finest material a heatsink can realistically be made from. It's the third-best conductor of heat after silver and diamond, which are somewhat more expensive. So look for a cooler with a copper heatsink, or at the very least, a heatsink with a copper contact plate.

Heat is dissipated from the heatsink through contact with air, so the more surface area on your heatsink, the better. That's why you want to look for heatsinks with numerous thin fins or spires rather than a few thicker ones.

A heatsink alone won't cut it for overclocked CPUs. A heatsink/fan combination will wick the heat off the heatsink radials much faster. Keep in mind, however, that the bigger the fan, the more noise it's likely to make.

Finally, it's important that the surface where the cooler contacts the CPU be as smooth as possible. Although the base of a heatsink may look smooth to your eye, it's actually replete with microscopic gaps and crevices that inhibit maximum heat transfer. That's where thermal paste enters the picture. Thermal paste, like our preferred Arctic Silver 5 (www.arcticsilver.com), fills in these tiny gaps to improve the conductivity of your heatsink. But don't go crazy with this stuff; more is *not* better here. When applying thermal paste, apply just enough to create a *very* thin film over the CPU. Remember, we're just trying to fill in microscopic gaps, not to smother your CPU or clean up goop that spills out over your mobo's circuitry!

HARDCORE COOLING FOR HARDCORE GEEKS

Good heatsink/fan combos can be very efficient, but they may not be good enough for hardware fanatics who plan on pushing their CPUs to insane speeds. If you fall into this category, you should consider more robust cooling options. One is water cooling.

Water-cooling systems send liquid to "heat blocks" attached to your key components (candidates include your CPU, GPU, and hard drive). The cool liquid draws heat away from your searing component, then transports it to some type of cooling device (usually a fan-cooled radiator), which dissipates the heat outside of your case. The liquid is circulated through each heat block with the help of

AMD FANS BEWARE!

Massive heatsinks may look impressive, but we've seen many tragedies involving colossal contraptions that have been slapped onto delicate AMD CPUs. Unlike Pentium 4 processors which are protected by thick metal heat spreaders, AMDs have exposed cores that are easily damaged by applying too much pressure to the CPU when locking down the heatsink. A single scratch could take out a whole neighborhood of transistors, while a fracture could mean a very short life for your CPU. AMD's specification for Socket A processors requires the heatsink and fan combo to be no more than 300 grams. But even with a cooling setup lighter than this, be careful to latch it down slowly while applying steady pressure.

a pump—the literal heart of the water-cooling system. This ticker, usually a high-end fish tank pump, can cycle the equivalent of a thousand of gallons a day throughout your rig.

The water within a heat block can absorb four times the heat of a traditional heatsink/fan combo. Even better, it can transfer heat 30 times more effectively than regular cooling methods, and doesn't produce excessive noise. In short, water-cooling is an extremely effective tool for overclockers—it not only cools key components, it also helps keep heat away from your case's general interior. That said, be aware that there is, after all, liquid running through your system. If it's installed incorrectly, or if there is a manufacturing defect and a circulation tube pops loose, well, there goes the neighborhood.

There's another way to achieve overclocking-class cooling that doesn't involve a fish-tank pump. It's called phase-change cooling, and to understand how it works, you'll need to brush up on some basic physics.

A "phase change" occurs when matter shifts between any of its liquid, gaseous, or solid states. For example, water phase-changes when it turns to ice in your freezer, when it boils away in a cooking pot, and when steam condenses back into water.

In order to change from liquid to gas, water (like all matter) needs a significant amount of energy. At room temperature, for example, one gram of water needs just one calorie of energy to increase in temperature by 1 degree Celsius. But at 100 degrees Celsius (the boiling point of water), water needs to absorb 540 times that

No, this isn't a menacing lab experiment—it's the apparatus for a water-cooling kit, including water blocks for videocards and hard drives.

amount of energy to phase-change into steam. Conversely, all that energy is released again when the steam vapor condenses back into a liquid.

Here's the plot twist that makes phase-change cooling possible: Boiling and condensation can be forced to occur by manipulating pressure, and if you put water in a container holding a vacuum, the water will boil at a lower temperature than it would at regular room pressure. Water in this vacuum still requires 540 calories of energy to convert to steam, and it will absorb this energy from the most convenient heat source—such as a scorching-hot CPU. Fantastic, yes, but true: By boiling refrigerant over your CPU and "stealing" its heat energy to do so, the processor is cooled.

Now *that's* exotic cooling, and the prices reflect it.

Hard Drive Coolers

Aside from a defrag every now and then, do you really need to concern yourself with hard drive health? You do if you want to protect that 5,000-song MP3 collection. And now that hard drives are capable of moving up to 160GB of data and spinning at a staggering 15,000rpm, it's about time you start seriously thinking about cooling. Hard drives are built from mechanical, moving parts, and just like car engines they break down if allowed to run too hot. And if you're fortunate enough (let alone rich enough) to run SCSI drives, you already know that those suckers can get hot enough to sear a steak.

In this roundup, we pit hard drive coolers from GlobalWin, Antec, and PC Power & Cooling against the heat of a 10,000rpm Seagate Cheetah drive. To test each cooler, we ran the file system benchmark in SiSoft *Sandra* for a half-hour, then used a Raytek thermometer gun to take temperature readings from two loca-

■ PC Power & Cooling Bay Cool

The Bay Cool is your basic, working man's hard drive cooler. The solid construction and simplistic design make it ideal for entry-level computer hobbyists who want to "set it and forget it." Once you've installed your hard drive in the Bay Cool's mounting bracket, you just slide the assembly into an open 5.25-inch drive bay. Then you simply plug it into your power headers, and

you're swinging to the low purr of two 40mm fans. The whirling duo whisks 6.5 CFM of air over the hard drive. A small air filter on the front of the assembly keeps harmful dust from clogging up the fans but still allows cool air to make its way into the interior of the case.

The two minis worked pretty well considering their size. While the SCSI drive was churning away on its meal of data bits, the Bay Cool dropped the top of the drive from 120 to 95 degrees. And while it appeared that the fans blew most of their air over the top of the drive, the chip underneath was cooled from 139 to 113. We were

■ GlobalWin I-Storm II

The I-Storm II is a unique hard drive cooler in more ways than one. The first thing we noticed was that it looked a little too porky to fit all the way inside a 5.5-inch bay. Turns out we were right. The ugly cooler actually extended about two inches beyond the front of what had previously been a stylish case. Are we scaring you? Well, if you

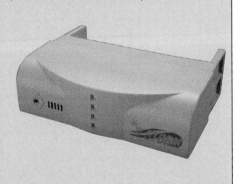

don't mind being ridiculed for having one of the most ridiculous-looking hard drive coolers ever made, read on.

Affectionately nicknamed "Elephant Nose" by our editors, the I-Storm II actually yielded decent performance. Even more amazing, it cooled our SCSI drive without all the noise of its competitors. The cooler's distinctive fan uses a single ball-bearing, rotary-style assembly to push a rated 35 CFM of air, all at low rotation. This engineering adds up to less noise. In fact, the only noise you'll hear is from the built-in alarm, which sounds if the I-Storm senses a problem.

So it looks stupid and runs silent. But what about job one—cooling the damn hard drive? The I-Storm got the temperature of the top of the drive down to 96 degrees. The bottom, meanwhile, hit 121 degrees. Aside from its goofy design, the I-Storm is a nice buy. It offers good cooling without all the eardrum punishment. Just be prepared to ruin the beauty of your case.

■ Antec Hard Drive Cooling System

When *Maximum PC* first heard of Antec, the company was making its mark with well-designed PC cases. Flash forward a few years, and now we're reviewing an Antec hard drive cooler. At first glance, we could tell this thing meant business. It's the only drive cooler in the roundup to feature a heatsink, and it comes with a digital readout. The digital display is connected to a pair of thermal sensors. The first sensor monitors ambient case temperature, while the second monitors the hard drive and controls the drive cooler's fans. If your drive reaches a critical temperature, the fans kick in to

high gear. Once the drive cools, the fans slow down again. Ingenious!

The Cooling System's stylish front panel pops off to reveal fans similar to the ones used in the PC Power & Cooling Bay Cool. The Bay Cool's fans are positioned farther apart than the Antec's fans, and one would think this would promote better cooling across the entire hard drive—but this wasn't necessarily the case. With the Antec, the bottom of the drive was cooled to 119 degrees after a half-hour of duress. That's a 20 degree drop. We couldn't get a direct reading off of the top surface of the drive because of the heatsink. But it's worth noting that the temperature of the heatsink was a "chilly" 95 degrees, which is probably a few degrees cooler than the drive itself. The Antec has style, features, and cooling. With its slick design and thermal sensor display, it's a total package.

Slot Coolers

Many PC enthusiasts doubt the effectiveness of slot-based coolers for add-in cards. Some claim that these devices don't move enough air because their fans are too small. Others say the coolers' basic design is flawed; that they just move hot air over even hotter components. Well, enough bellyaching. It's time to enter the Lab and debunk these weak-hinged arguments. In this segment, you'll met three types of coolers, each working in different ways to achieve the same objective—to get your components to "simah down now!"

The Vantec is an exhaust fan. Its goal is to flush hot air out of your case, and away from hot components. The Buss-Cool from PC Power & Cooling sits in the PCI slot closest to your videocard and blows cool air directly onto one side of it (the rest of your case fans then take care of the heat exhaust). Finally, the Card Cooler from TheCardCooler.com mounts at a 90 degree angle over your videocard, and blows air over both the top and bottom.

Unless you're downloading MP3s 24/7 and your modem is overheating, most people will use these products to cool videocards. Because of its massive heat production, we decided to use an ATI Radeon 8500 for testing. In order to generate near-meltdown temperatures, we ran *3DMark2001*—specifically, the Nature demo at 1280x1024, 4x AA, and 32-bit textures, looping without pause for a half-hour. This is sort of like the videocard version of the Navy Seals' "hell weak." To record baseline temperatures, we aimed a Raytek thermometer gun on the card's core (the bottom of the card), heatsink (the top of the card), and RAM. Under extreme duress, these three components hit 141, 119, and 142 degrees, respectively.

■ Vantec Exhaust PCSC-100

The Vantec Exhaust's simple design and solid construction make it a good value for anyone looking to simply move air away from components. But while it lagged behind the other two coolers as far as performance, it was nearly silent in comparison, in large part due to its single brushless fan. During our stress test, it dropped the core down to just 137 degrees and the heatsink to 115 degrees. In both cases, that's only a 4 degree difference from no cooling at all. The Vantec did have more success cooling the RAM—it dropped 12 degrees.

We weren't expecting much from the Vantec, and that's exactly what we got; the fan just doesn't have enough cooling prowess to keep videocard overclockers feeling safe and secure. You see, in order to offer the most effective cooling, a fan must blow air directly onto a videocard, instead of just pulling air away from it. That said, while exhaust-type coolers aren't very popular with overclockers, OEM system builders are beginning to see their advantages. Take, for example, the PCFX Xbrat system, which *Maximum PC* reviewed in August 2002. It was one of the smallest systems we've ever reviewed, and all of its components were packed in tight together. Due to the small size of the case, there wasn't much room for a large exhaust fan, so PCFX installed one of these exhaust coolers, placing it in the heart of where the PCI cards reside. This is an ideal application for a cooler like the Vantec Exhaust—inside a small case, where *any* extra cooling is helpful.

■ PC Power & Cooling Buss-Cool

Since 1985, the folks over at PC Power & Cooling have been coming up with unusual and innovative components. The Buss-Cool is no different. Its two superthin fans are spec'd to rush 26 CFM of air onto the card sitting adjacent to it. Out of all the components we tested, this one was the easiest to install. Forget about messy fan wires; the two fans simply draw power directly from the PCI bus. Worried about the electrical stress on your motherboard?

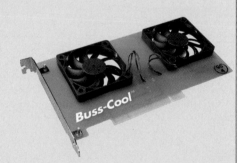

Don't be. The device demands a mere 3.2 watts of power; less than most high-end videocards.

When we fired up *3DMark2001*, we noticed that the fans were quieter than we expected, but still noticeably noisier than the Vantec Exhaust cooler. The Buss-Cool's performance, however, makes up for the added noise. Although the heatsink didn't get much cooler (it dropped 5 degrees to 114), the core dropped 8 degrees, hitting a low of 131. Considering the size of the fans, we were also surprised so see that the Buss-Cool chilled the RAM to 117 degrees—that's a 25 degree difference!

The Buss-Cool offers solid performance without creating too much noise, and its installation couldn't be simpler. And considering that it draws power directly from a PCI slot, it doesn't add any wiring jumble to your case interior. The Buss-Cool may not be the highest-performing slot cooler available, but with all of its nice features, it's definitely worth considering.

■ Card Cooler featuring Sunon Fans

With two huge fans whooshing about 70 CFM of air above and below the videocard, we expected big things from the Card Cooler. And it did not disappoint us.

The device's massive airflow comes from two 80mm Sunon fans, each spinning at 2800rpm. The Card Cooler also benefits from its unique mounting approach. Both the Vantec and the Buss-Cool move air on only one side of the card, but when properly mounted perpendicular to a videocard, the Sunons will cool both sides of the card. The benchmarks pretty much speak for themselves. The core temperature plummeted from 141 to 111 degrees. Yikes! Both the

heatsink and RAM dropped to 97 degrees—that's a 44 degree drop in RAM temperature!

With performance like this, who wouldn't want the Card Cooler? How about gamers who are trying to enjoy a late-night fragging session without waking their girlfriends, or their parents, or their girlfriends' parents. Adding the Card Cooler is essentially like putting in two additional case fans. Since these fans are installed on two metal brackets that use PCI mounting screws, the Card Cooler is also a bitch to install. And any time you want to swap out or move an expansion card, you'll have to fiddle around with the Card Cooler, which usually means placing the case on its side.

Still, if you can handle the significant noise this thing puts out, it's definitely worth the purchase price.

How To...

PROPERLY POSITION YOUR
CASE FANS

We blow smoke in search of a climate-controlled case

BY WILL SMITH AND GORDON MAH UNG

MAXIMUMPC
DIFFICULTY RATING
EASY
HARD
XXX

With CPU speeds exceeding 3GHz, hard drives hitting 15,000rpm, and videocards generating enough heat to deep-fry an Arkansas pickle, the flow of fresh, cool air through case interiors is becoming increasingly important. Heat causes instability, and instability causes Blue Screens of Unhappiness.

But how do you promote the best airflow possible? How do you know whether your fans should be sucking air in, or blowing air out? How do you determine if you should have a fan mounted on top? And what about drive-bay coolers? We decided to find out.

To help us determine the best fan placement spots, we pumped "movie fog" into two computer cases, and observed exactly how each rig's interior fans affected the flow of the smoke within. If the smoke wasn't properly whooshing past critical components, we knew we'd need to reevaluate fan placement. Our first case study focused on a home-built dual-Celeron rig. It was loaded with a bazillion fans and wrapped in a SuperMicro full-tower case. Our second case study involved a factory-built Dell rig featuring a 733MHz Pentium III. It came with a default two-fan config.

Here's what we gleaned from our airflow tests. Apply what we learned to your own case at home.

Getting Started

For our experiments, we bought a sheet of Plexiglas, a Plexiglas cutter, duct tape, five feet of flexible heater vent tubing, and a smoke/fog machine. The device works by vaporizing a "fog fluid" mixture into superfine particles.

First we cut sheets of Plexiglas to replace the case sides, and used the duct tape to seal leaks all around the edges of the Plexi. After some experimentation with different methods of introducing smoke into the systems, we found that we got the best results by feeding smoke into the cases via a heater hose. The hose was connected to the smoke machine on one end, and to a cardboard box on the other end. We then fitted the cardboard box over the PCs' front air intakes.

We filled each system with smoke to make airflow patterns visible. While we were able to clearly see distinct patterns emerge when we turned on the smoke-filled PCs, the photographs in this article don't illustrate the patterns very well, so we've added arrows to highlight our observations.

Anyone can conduct airflow tests at home. Just be aware that there's always risk associated with pumping any kind of vapor into an electrical device. Electric shock is certainly a consideration, and you can also destroy your delicate electronics. For this reason, you might want to eschew home-testing, and just use this article for general advice.

Case Study 1: SuperMicro SC-750A

To see how airflow works in a full-tower rig, we performed our first test on SuperMicro's SC-750A case. Twin 8cm fans were mounted in the front bezel, a 10cm fan sat above the power supply (complementing the existing power-supply fan), and three different fans served the motherboard's chipset and two CPUs. An 8cm case fan for blowing air onto the CPU, and a 4cm fan mounted on the back of the case (directly behind the CPU) were notably absent. We chose this elderly system because it was positively stuffed with peripherals, including three hard drives, two optical drives, four PCI cards, and a smoking-hot GeForce DDR videocard warming the AGP slot.

The first thing we noticed about the SC-750A was that the triple CPU/chipset fan combo created massive air disturbance. The fans threw up small funnels of smoke as they sucked air down onto their respective chips. This, of course, doesn't necessarily aid in cooling; such a system might simply blow hot air to other parts of the case. Also, in order for the smoke to exit, it had to flow from the front of the case, through the turbulent air above the CPUs, and into the power supply, where it was evacuated—a convoluted, inefficient course. Moral of the story: If you want to really cool your CPU and chipset area, you should install an exhaust fan behind the CPU, below the power supply. This will push hot air out of your case and into the room at large.

Our test also confirmed the need for the svelte cables that will be afforded by Serial ATA. Our 750A hid a veritable rat's nest of SCSI, IDE, and floppy ribbon cables that acted like a wind drogue, blocking the flow of air from the two front fans. Serial ATA's I/O cables, which are about 1/4-inch in diameter and more than twice as long as current IDE ribbon cables, will be a welcome change for PCs.

Another problem we encountered concerned dead air surrounding peripheral cards. Because the I/O cables prevented bezel fan air from blowing directly onto the PCI cards, air movement in the PCI card area was stilted at best. Although the SC-750A alleviates some of this by including passive vents near the PCI cards, we didn't find them adequate for cooling today's hot peripherals. So we added a PCI exhaust fan to better evacuate the air near the PCI slots.

The SC-750A was properly configured in respect to its placement of storage devices. The two optical drives were wisely mounted with plenty of room between them, encouraging airflow. If you have problems cooling drives, the 750A actually lets you mount fans on both sides of your drive bays. If your case has that option, we recommend installing the fans, particularly if you're running a lot of hot, high-speed drives.

We didn't expect the auxiliary fan mounted above the power supply to do much good, because we thought the power supply fan would

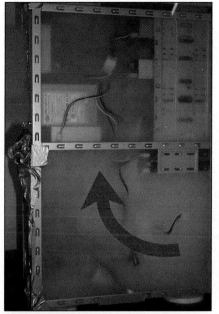
Air entered the 750A's case along the arrow's path but was not sufficiently vented through the area around the power supply.

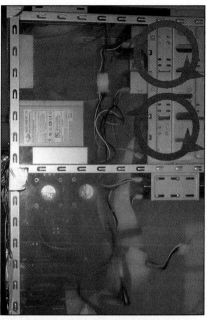
Though the 750A's optical drives are staggered for better airflow, they still could have benefited from the optional drive bay fans. In their current config, the drives suffer from dead air zones.

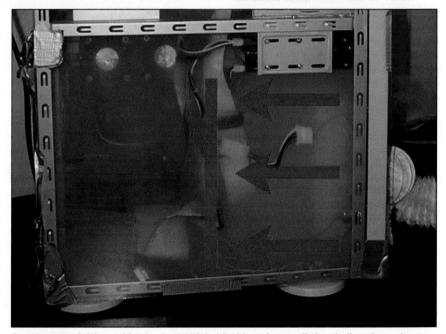
A rat's nest of drive cables in the 750A is blocking almost all the air flow from the two front bezel fans.

"steal" most of the air before it reached the top of the case. To test our theory, we ran the system both with and without the top fan enabled. Surprisingly, airflow was reduced considerably when the top fan was disabled, causing the air to bog down in the lower half of the case. When the top fan was on, air moved well from the lower intakes and over the drive bays before it was blasted out of the system. To see if we could mimic this action for those of you with mid-

tower cases, we shut down the top fan and added PC Power and Cooling's Turbo Cool 2X, an additional fan that screws to the back of the power supply and is purported to increase the airflow through your system. The Turbo Cool's high-velocity fan made quite a difference in clearing the smoke, working almost as effectively as the auxiliary fan that lives above the power supply. Unfortunately, this fan also sounds like a DC-3.

Case Study 2: Dell XPS B733r

The second system we ran through the grinder was one of our old Dell test rigs. It used the standard "Palo Alto" case employed by Dell and a number of other OEMs, a 733MHz Pentium III, 128MB of RDRAM, and just two fans. The Palo Alto is designed for power users who don't need a ton of expansion capabilities. Like most OEMs using the Palo Alto case, Dell relied on a custom-fitted "wind tunnel" that reaches from the CPU to an 8cm fan mounted inside the back of the case. The wind-tunnel design has the advantage of directly venting air from the CPU rather than just moving it around inside the case. It also allows the use of larger fans that spin at lower RPMs—and thus produce lower decibel levels.

With only the wind-tunnel fan and the power supply fan aiding exhaust, how well does this system work when compared with a system with a zillion fans? It turns out that the wind tunnel performs much better than we expected. In the Dell, smoke moved at a good clip from the lower front bezel, past the hard drive, and out through the gaps in the wind tunnel. The pattern was much clearer than the wind chop that affected the configuration on the SC-750A case.

As is to be expected in a case with few fans, there were several dead-air spots, specifically around the lower PCI slots and drive bays. We'd recommend installing a PCI exhaust fan, a supplemental external power supply exhaust fan, and also a hard drive cooler to wipe out excess heat in the trouble areas.

What to Do at Home

Every PC case is different, so we don't recommend that you immediately tweak your PC based on what we learned from our two case studies. Instead, grab a thermometer gun (like the Raytek MiniTemp), and set up your own tests. Measure the temperature around typical hotspots (memory, CPU, 3D accelerator, and hard drives), then tailor your cooling solution to fit your case's needs.

As a general rule, we found that having more intake fans than exhaust fans can actually impede airflow. If anything, you'd do well to have extra exhaust fans to complement your puny power supply fan (which also exhausts air, but at a meager pace). The extra exhaust fans will actually draw a small amount air into the case as a natural part of their functionality, then scoot

In the Dell's case, cool air is sucked in past the hard drives, making a beeline for the wind tunnel where it is vented. However, a massive dead spot covers the PCI cards.

out all the hot air generated by your components. Bottom line: It's better to blow air out than to suck air in.

If you have a hot AGP card, or PCI cards that generate excess heat, some form of active cooling around the expansion slots could benefit your case's climate. Consider a fan that fits into a spare expansion slot. Any type of device that can get air moving in this area is good.

We can't wait for Serial ATA to become common. Until then, consider using zip ties or velcro straps to lash down the cables in your case. If you have lots of ribbon cables floating around your system, consider buying some pre-split IDE cables that are a little more aerodynamic. Also check www.plycon.com for more info on rounded

IDE ribbons.

Unless you have a proper exhaust system, CPU fans do little more than blow hot air around your case. So if you have an unused fan mount behind your CPUs, take advantage of it by adding another fan that blows air out. If you don't want to fool with adding additional fans, consider picking up a power supply equipped with a better fan. We recommend something from PC Power and Cooling.

If nothing else, our little experiment proved that brute force isn't necessary when cooling your PC. A well-designed cooling scheme using two fans is just as effective at ventilating your case as adding 15 fans but not having any overall plan. ■

By the Maximum PC Staff

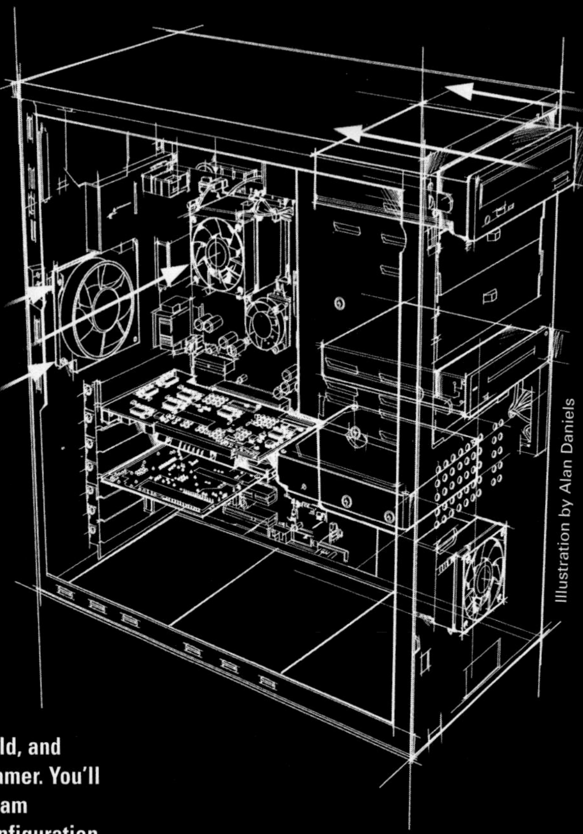

Been thinking about building your own Dream Machine? We bet you have. If you're like most PC enthusiasts, you want to experience true pride of ownership—that indescribable feeling one gets from having built a computer completely from scratch. Sure, you can have fun with a prefab machine, but you'll never really be able to call it your own flesh and blood.

So it's time you built your very own. On the following pages, you'll find the necessary blueprints to conceive, build, and troubleshoot your own PC screamer. You'll get to decide your personal Dream Machine's exact component configuration, one tailored to your personal passions and proclivities. Gamers can splurge on the very, very best videocard and dispense with the funky RAID setup. Videographers can ditch the DVD-ROM and CD-RW drives in favor of a do-it-all DVD/CD combo burner. You make the choices, and you decide on the compromises—that is, if you intend to make any compromises at all.

This guide is just a starting point to help you get moving on the fundamentals of PC building. What you make of this project is limited by only your budget and imagination. You can buy every part we used in the step-by-step tutorial, and configure your PC as a mirror image of our own. Or you can go hog wild with 1GB of memory, SCSI

RAID, and twin plasma screens hooked up to a dual-monitor videocard. Get the idea?

Before you take the plunge, we've got two pieces of advice. Make sure you read this entire article before you begin buying components. It's an important precaution that will help you avoid, for example, pairing a Serial ATA drive with a motherboard that doesn't have a Serial ATA connector (doh!). Then, thoroughly read this "Build It" article, from beginning to end, before snapping Part A into Part B so you get the "big picture" of the process. Building a PC isn't difficult, but paying close attention to details is absolutely essential if you want a quick, trouble-free assembly.

Illustration by Alan Daniels

How to construct the ultimate PC in less than three hours. All your questions answered, every step explained.

BUILD IT

BUILD IT

Putting It All Together

Here's a step-by-step guide to putting all of your PC's pieces together. Although your components may differ from the ones we chose, the basic assembly is the same. Just remember to read this whole how-to before diving into your own project.

1 Remove Mobo Tray

Using a case with a removable motherboard tray can make your assembly job much easier. Luckily, our mid-tower case from PC Power and Cooling has a removable tray. The case comes without a power supply, so we ordered the company's 300W Turbo-Cool supply. A good place to build your project

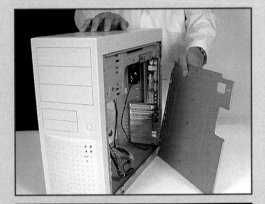

Fewer and fewer companies use removable motherboard trays these days. Fortunately, PC Power and Cooling's mid-tower case includes this amenity.

is in the kitchen, where there's plenty of light and no carpet to create static electricity. If you're in a particularly dry environment where the risk of static discharge is higher, consider getting an antistatic wrist strap from a local electronics store before you touch any items of value.

2 Mount the Motherboard

Begin by matching the mounting holes in the motherboard with the holes in the tray. Ideally, brass or aluminum standoffs should be used to support the motherboard in all four corners, as well as in the center. If your tray doesn't have a screw hole in a section of the motherboard that you'll be applying pressure to (such as near the IDE cables or PCI slots), then you can use plastic standoffs for additional structural integrity.

Make sure you can account for all the metal standoffs you've used. An errant metal standoff that's poking into a random point of the motherboard could potentially short out the PC. Also, be sure to firmly screw down any brass standoffs so they don't back off by accident. Once you've mounted the motherboard, you should push on different sections of it to make sure it feels solid.

Our Soyo motherboard uses a BIOS setup menu to configure most of the board's essential settings, but other motherboards may require that you switch physical jumpers to change settings. Now would be a good time to familiarize yourself with where these jumpers reside and what they do. For our motherboard, we did have to throw a jumper to instruct the onboard RAID controller to act as a normal ATA/100 controller for our single IDE drive.

(a) Make sure the I/O shield that came with your case or motherboard matches the I/O holes on the motherboard.
(b) Make sure the standoffs are tightened so they don't back off.
(c) When screwing the motherboard into the backplate, leave it a little loose while you ensure that PCI cards will fit properly, then tighten the screw.

3 Install the CPU

Modern CPUs are as delicate as butterflies. Don't manhandle them. To install a socketed CPU, lift the arm on the socket straight up in the open position. You'll notice that pins are missing from two corners of the Athlon XP (only one corner is missing pins on a Socket 478 Pentium 4). These notched corners should match the two notched corners of the socket. Drop the CPU straight into the socket, and take care not to bend any pins

(see a). Once the CPU is sitting flat in the socket, lock the arm back down.

If you're sure your heatsink already has a thermal pad or thermal tape on it, you don't need to apply thermal compound. Our heatsink came "raw," so we used Arctic Silver II thermal compound for its low electrical conductivity and good heat transfer characteristics. A tiny 1mm or 2mm dab of goop is generally sufficient; apply it to the core (see b). Use enough to cover the core, but not so much that it oozes all over the CPU and motherboard. Obviously, you'll want to use more thermal compound for Pentium 4s with their larger cores. You can find more instructions at **www.articsilver.com**.

Mount the heatsink fan by placing the fan flat against the CPU. Clip one side of the heatsink to the socket. To clip the other side, use a screwdriver or needlenose pliers to nudge the other clip into place (see c). Press on only the clip and keep the heatsink flat on the CPU, not at an angle. BE VERY CAREFUL—it's ridiculously easy to crush AMD CPUs during heatsink application. While you're here, plug the fan into a nearby power header that's marked CPU1.

Accessorize the Mobo with Memory, Cables, and Wires

4

It's time to install RAM, cables, and the front-panel connectors. Open your motherboard manual and determine which memory slot should be populated first. Some motherboard makers actually label the slots 1, 2, and 3. While your RAM may ostensibly work fine in any memory slot, using the correct slot can help ensure trouble-free performance. PC100 and PC133 memory modules boast two notches that make it easy to determine which way the memory fits into the slots. But the DDR memory module that we used has just one notch, and it's nearly in the middle of the module, making it easy to inadvertently insert the memory in the wrong direction. Line up the notches and press the memory into the slot until it locks into place (see a).

Now insert the IDE cables. The cables should be notched to fit in only one direction (see b). Use the fine-wired 80-pin conductor cables for your hard drives, and the coarse-wired 40-pin cables for your optical and removable storage drives. Try to keep the boot hard drive on the primary IDE channel, and try to keep optical drives on separate channels— high-speed CD burners won't perform at full spec if they're pulling data from a CD-ROM drive that's sitting on the same channel. In our case, we actually isolated all of our IDE drives on their own channels by using the mobo's two regular IDE channels, as well as the two extra IDE channels enabled by the motherboard's onboard IDE RAID controller. (Unless your system is equipped with an IDE RAID controller, you'll have only two IDE channels total.)

Finally, carefully examine the motherboard and its manual to determine which way to connect the power-on, reset, and hard-disk activity lights located on your PC's front panel (see c). If you put the connectors in backward, you won't kill anything, but the lights won't work.

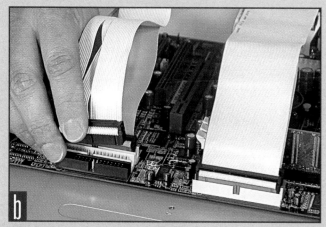

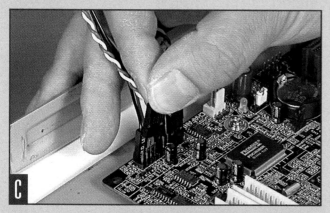

(a) Before you rush out and buy the largest chunk of memory you can find, make sure the memory type is supported by your motherboard. You should also verify which slot to use if you're populating your board with only one stick of memory.
(b) Most motherboards come with their own IDE cables. Usually, the blue connector goes on the motherboard.
(c) No one ever connects the front panel connectors correctly the first time. If your new PC won't boot at first, make sure your power switch connector has been inserted properly.

Set IDE Master/Slave Jumpers

5

This step is for everyone who doesn't have access to four IDE channels and might need to put two IDE devices on a single channel.

Let's say you have three IDE drives: one hard drive, one DVD-ROM drive, and one CD-RW drive. Because each IDE channel supports two devices, you can accommodate all your drives—but you'll need to set each drive in the proper position. You'll want to plug the hard drive into the master interface of the primary IDE channel; the DVD-ROM drive into the slave interface of the primary channel; and the CD-RW drive into the master interface of the secondary channel. Now for the kicker: Each IDE device must be appropriately set as either a master or slave device. You can do this by setting a jumper on the back of each drive; a little map next to the jumpers will indicate proper settings. To ensure reliable operation, we recommend that you eschew the "cable select" option and instead opt for either a master or slave setting.

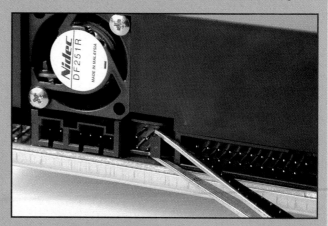

The jumpers on the back of an IDE drive usually let you choose master, slave, or cable select. Move the jumper around to change the relationship.

BUILD IT

6 Slap in the Drives

We staggered our CD-RW drive and DVD-ROM drive in order to keep an empty drive bay between the devices. Stacking optical drives on top of each other usually won't hurt anything, but it makes sense to encourage as much airflow as possible inside your case. Because our mid-tower case is intended to sit on the floor, and because our DVD-ROM drive will be used to play DVD movies and audio CDs, we placed the DVD-ROM drive in the top bay for convenience. We have a small case, so we weren't worried about the length of our IDE cables. But if you're using a relatively tall case, remember to get extended IDE and floppy cables.

When actually screwing your drives into the case, we recommend that you do so on both sides of the drive—this will require removing the starboard-side case cover. Today's optical drives spin at increasingly high speeds, and excessive vibration or rattling can actually hurt performance, so you'll want your drives properly secured to your chassis. We recommend that you use a non-magnetized screwdriver for this type of work.

Go ahead and mount your optical drives and floppy drive (if you have one), and pop in the front case bezel if it's been removed. Since both sides of your case are open at this point, take the time to align the floppy and optical drives so they sit flush with the front case bezel. If you have a hard drive gondola like the one that came with our case, screw your hard drive into it. Just don't insert the gondola back into the case; we'll get to that later.

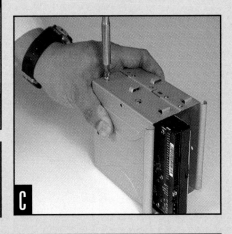

(a) We put the PlexWriter CD-RW drive on the bottom and the Pioneer DVD-ROM drive on top because we'll want quicker access to the DVD-ROM drive—but that's just us. (b) The floppy drive is the PC's appendix—but we kept it in our project for sentimental reasons. (c) It's important to tightly fasten screws on both sides of your IDE drives, such as this 7200rpm hard drive. Excessive rattling may hurt the performance.

7 Put the Motherboard in the Case

It's now time to fit the whole motherboard enchilada into the case—but before you do, make sure the holes in your case's metal I/O shield match the I/O ports on your motherboard. Also, make sure all the shield's metal holes are punched out. If the holes don't match the ports, don't proceed! Get a proper I/O shield to save yourself heartbreak down the line. When you install the motherboard tray into the PC, make sure you don't crimp any cables. We usually leave the motherboard screws a tiny bit loose and tighten them only after we're sure there's enough space between the back of our PCI add-in cards and the edge of the motherboard.

Fold in the motherboard tray carefully, and check to see if the case's I/O shield matches your motherboard I/O ports.

8 Connect the Power

Match the clip of the 20-pin power connector with the notch in the plug, and firmly clip it in place. Like most desktop Athlon mobos, our Soyo needs just the 20-pin for power. Motherboards for the Pentium 4 add a small four-pin connector (labeled 12V) for additional 12-volt power needed by the CPU. So, if you're building a Pentium 4, attach that connector as well. For all power connections, check your motherboard manual for anomalies. Some boards, such as the original Athlon MP mobos, use proprietary plugs. Many dual Athlon boards also make use of the 12V connector, and may require that you plug a hard drive power plug directly from the power supply into the motherboard.

Make sure you plug the ATX power connector to the motherboard in the correct direction. The power plug will usually include a notch that prohibits improper insertion. An incorrectly inserted power plug will kill your PC.

9 Connect Your Drives

It's now time to connect your IDE cables to your optical drives. The cables are notched and should fit only one way into the drives and motherboard.

If your case is so cramped that you can't see where the notch is, remember that the red stripe on the IDE cable corresponds with pin 1 on an IDE drive, and pin 1 is the pin closest to the drive's power connector.

After you've hooked up the IDE cables, insert the four-pin power cables to the optical drives. The power cables are keyed so they'll fit in only one way, but we've seen worn-out and cheap power cables that magically fit in the wrong direction. The short lesson is to make sure you have your power plugs facing the right direction.

(a) First goes the IDE cable…. (b) Then goes the power connector. For both insertions, be gentle and make sure everything is facing the correct direction.

10 Hook up the Hard Drive

In our PC Power and Cooling mid-tower, we used the included hard drive gondola to mount our hard drive. While the gondola design restricts the use of tall fans and heatsinks, it does aid in cooling the 7200rpm hard drive—because the gondola is more or less suspended in the middle of nowhere, air gets to flow all around it.

If you're not using a gondola, just screw the hard drive into an available 3.5-inch drive bay and remember to leave open space for cooling. Once we screwed our gondola back into its original position, we hooked up our IDE and power cables, just as we did with our optical drives. Your CD-ROM drive probably doesn't need the dense 80-conductor cables, but all ATA/66 and ATA/100 hard drives do. You can tell the difference between 80- and 40-conductor cables by looking at their wires. 80-conductor cables use very fine wires; 40-conductor cables use relatively thick wires. Because we have four independent IDE channels available, we set the hard drive to master and plugged it into the master interface of the primary IDE controller.

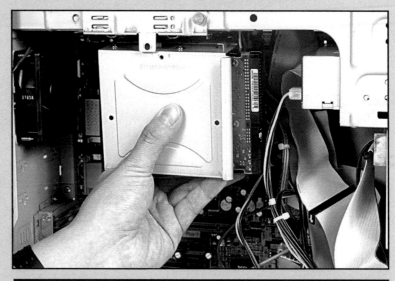

The gondola in our PC Power and Cooling case provides our 7200rpm hard drive with a slightly cooler environment than a drive bay would.

11 Adding the Videocard and the Soundcard

The first add-in card we installed was the Leadtek GeForce3 AGP card. The Soyo Dragon, like many Athlon motherboards, features the slightly longer AGP Pro slot to accommodate cards that need to draw extra power. Our GeForce3 card, however, is a normal AGP card (a). Both the card and slot are keyed so it's near impossible to screw up the insertion of the card—but we have heard of people jamming the card into the wrong slot and frying their systems. If your motherboard has a sticker or small piece of plastic that plugs up part of the slot, leave it in place; this will prevent the card from shifting backward and shorting out.

Back in the day, we would have recommended that you boot your system and verify its health before installing your PCI cards. But because we have so much confidence in today's hardware, we went ahead and also installed a Creative Labs Sound Blaster Audigy soundcard. Because videocards generate so much heat, we placed the Sound Blaster in an open slot away from the AGP card (b).

We're not going to tidy up our wiring until we've "burned in" the PC for a 72-hour period. In fact, you should never, ever, ever put the side back on your case before you boot. If you do, your PC will refuse to boot just to spite you.

12 Set up the BIOS

We've come this far without detecting the acrid smell of charred silicon—so far, so good. Now it's time to set up your PC's BIOS. The term BIOS stands for "basic input/output system." This is the software that contains all the rudimentary instructions on how your operating system should communicate with your hardware.

First, turn on your newly constructed PC and punch the key that lets you enter the BIOS. It's normally the F1, F2, or DEL key. If you get a full-screen logo but no key prompt to "enter setup," hit the ESC key. This will spawn your hidden boot sequence. Now you can hit F1, F2, or DEL to enter the BIOS setup screen. Once you're inside the setup menus, you can adjust a number of parameters that will affect OS-hardware communication. But for the purpose of this tutorial, we'll focus on just a few necessities:

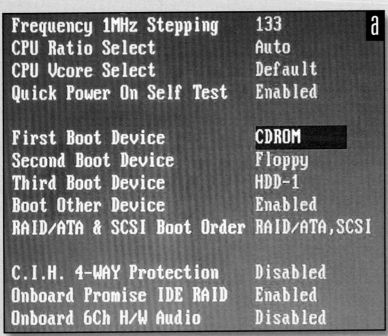

■ Because you'll soon be loading Windows XP Home from scratch, directly off its CD, the first thing you'll want to do in the BIOS is set the First Boot Device to the CD-ROM drive (see a). This tells the computer to boot from the CD drive before trying to boot from the hard drive, which is still blank. While you're in the BIOS, you'll also want to disable the onboard audio to make way for the Sound Blaster Audigy card.

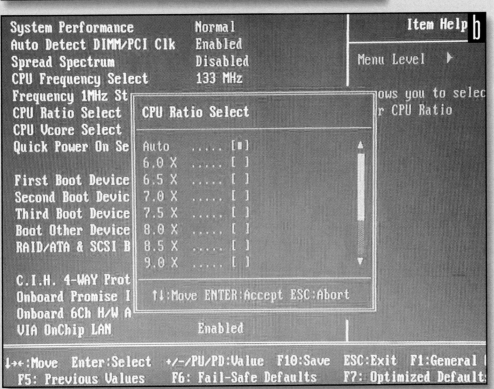

■ Make sure your system bus is clocked correctly. For AMD systems, like ours, this means a setting of either 100MHz or 133MHz, depending on the CPU you have—100MHz for Duron and 133MHz for Athlon XP. Remember that you can't manually set the CPU multiplier (or ratio) for Athlon XP or any Intel processors, so leave the BIOS setting at Auto (see b). If at any place in the BIOS you encounter options for "Maximum" or "Normal," go with the normal setting—you want to make sure everything is working fine before you try to optimize for maximum performance.

■ Check the System Health or Status tab for details on your CPU temperature and CPU fan speed. Our 1.53GHz Athlon XP was running at a mere 111 degrees Fahrenheit, and the fan was turning at about 5500rpm—all within spec.

■ See Part II, "Maximizing Performance," to learn more about the BIOS.

Install Windows XP

We're in the final stretch, and lucky you, the Windows XP setup routine is much easier than that of earlier versions of Windows.

After following our BIOS instructions, your system should be set to boot from the CD, so insert your WinXP disk and reboot your computer. You should eventually see a screen prompting you to "Press any key to boot from CD," at which point you'll need to press the "any" key.

Before the GUI

After your system has booted off the CD, the installer will start the non-GUI portion of setup (GUI stands for "graphical user interface"). If you want to install Windows on a SCSI drive or RAID array that XP doesn't include built-in drivers for, you'll need to press F6 as soon as you see the blue screen. Otherwise, you can wait for the Welcome screen (a).

Follow the prompts until you get to the partitioning screen (b). Assuming you're using a new hard drive, you'll need to tell Windows how you want to configure your disk. If you're using your old drive, be extra careful at this step—this part of the installer is the WinXP equivalent of *FDISK* and can easily wipe your drive. For maximum performance with XP, we recommend creating one big partition that spans the entire drive. If you decide you need two partitions later, it's easy to repartition the drive using a utility like *Partition Magic* (www.symantec.com). Unless you plan on dual-booting Win98 or WinME, we recommend that you use the NTFS format for your new drive. And *always* do a thorough format on a brand-new hard drive!

Once you've started the format, it's usually safe to leave the machine for 20 or 30 minutes. The formatting process is even more mind-bogglingly dull than watching paint dry.

Halfway there!

When you return, your PC should be into the GUI stage of the install. The first screen you'll see is the language options screen (c). Unless you have a nonstandard keyboard layout, or don't live in the U.S., you can safely continue to the next step.

Next, you'll need to enter your name (d). Since we're giving this machine to our friend Dick Matthews, we used his name.

The last major step you have to wade through is the setup of your network. Typical settings work for most cable modems and DSL connections, although you'll need to use manual settings if you have a statically assigned IP address or use some sort of wonky PPPoE connection. After the network is configured, Windows should reboot one last time.

Finishing up

Following the final reboot, you'll be prompted to activate Windows. We recommend that you hold off until you have all the drivers set up for your hardware and everything is working properly. You should have at least 30 days before your unactivated copy of Windows stops working, so take your time.

Now that WinXP is installed, hit the web and grab the latest drivers for your motherboard, 3D accelerator, soundcard, and anything else that might need an update, including Windows XP itself (always install new motherboard drivers first). Finally, have fun with your new system!

Learn More

See Part III, "Tuning Windows," to learn how to get the most out of XP.

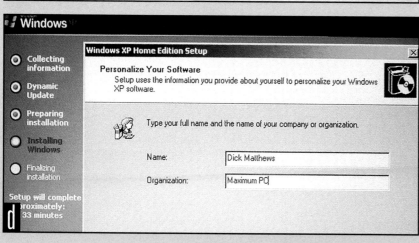

Top 10 Troubleshooting Tips

A rogue's gallery of the most common problems that plague new PCs

1 Can't See the Optical

If your PC ignores the CD-ROM during the boot process, preventing you from booting off the Windows XP disc in the drive, double-check the boot sequence in the BIOS. The BIOS is a set of all the hard-coded instructions and drivers needed to start your PC before other software—namely, your OS—can take over. It's easy to get into the BIOS. With most motherboards, you can enter the BIOS by hitting the F1, F2, or Delete key during the initial boot sequence. If the onscreen instructions indicating which key to press go by too quickly, just press the Pause key.

Once you're in the BIOS, you'll need to find a menu or menu option called "Boot Device Priority." This is where you establish the order in which your PC turns to different components looking for an OS. Make sure CD-ROM is designated as the first boot device. After you're finished installing the OS, you can speed up future boot times by making the hard drive your first boot device.

2 Mayday, Mayday!

Sometimes your PC simply won't boot at all, and only emits a series of beeps from your PC speaker. This is called a POST, or "power on self test," error, and it means that a component crucial to booting (like a videocard or hard drive) is broken, improperly seated, or improperly configured.

The sequence of beeps you hear isn't random. The number and/or length of the beeps describe the nature of the problem. For instance, two beeps on a motherboard that uses an AMI-manufactured BIOS means there's something amiss with your RAM modules.

Your motherboard's manual will help you decode the sequence of beeps for troubleshooting.

3 Sound Off

If your system powers up, but won't boot and doesn't elicit any beeps, make sure you have your case speaker connected to the motherboard; you'll want to hear any error messages that the system might issue. Some motherboards come with their own onboard speakers, precluding the need to connect a case speaker.

4 Code Red

If your system doesn't respond at all when you press the power button—no whirring of fans, no beeps, no nothing—don't panic. The first thing to do is make sure it's plugged in. No need to be embarrassed—it still happens to us on occasion. Make sure the plug is firmly inserted into the power supply as well as the outlet. If you're using a UPS (uninterruptible power supply), make sure that's plugged in too. If that doesn't do the trick, reseat the graphics card, RAM, and any PCI cards you've connected, and then make sure the motherboard power connector is firmly plugged in. Take it out, and reattach it.

5 Exile the Riffraff

It's always possible you were sold a bum part that's preventing your PC from booting, or that you're using a fully functioning part that's saddled with broken drivers. To determine if this is the problem, follow this most basic of troubleshooting methods: the process of elimination. Working backwards from the order in which you installed the cards and/or drivers, remove a card or driver, and try rebooting. If that doesn't work, replace the component and/or driver, and try removing the next part down the line.

If you've got a replacement part that you know is healthy, like an older network card that you're replacing with a new wireless card, try swapping that and rebooting.

It takes patience, but eventually you'll find the driver or subsystem that's giving you trouble.

6 Drive on the Left Side

PC power supplies support both the 115-volt power used in the U.S. and the 230-volt power used in other parts of the globe. Most power supplies are already set to 115, but we have occasionally seen them set to 230. Make sure your supply is set properly before you fire it up. This problem is rare, but when it happens, it stumps even the pros.

7 Hot Flashes

If your system starts up fine but reboots after a few seconds, it's likely you have an overheating problem. You're heatsink may be inadequate for your CPU, or you may have forgotten to install the thermal pad or thermal compound between the CPU and heatsink. If you have indeed applied the pad or compound properly, make sure your CPU/heatsink fan is connected to the motherboard headers for power. If it does work, you may have to upgrade to more advanced cooling paraphernalia (see page 74 for more information on this subject). Also, make sure your CPU is clocked within its specified range.

8 Lights On

If the floppy drive refuses to work and the access light stays lit, then the cable was attached incorrectly (this is very common, because there isn't any notch or block to prevent the cable from being installed the wrong way). Power down the system, and simply flip the cable over on the floppy end of the chain.

9 Disappearing Drives

If your PC can't detect your hard drive, the first thing to do is completely power off the PC, reseat the IDE cables on both ends, and power back on. If you've got more than one hard drive, and your PC can't see either of them, double-check their master/slave settings. Each IDE channel can support two drives: one master, and one slave. The drive that will house the OS should be set to master, and the other drive set as slave. These settings are determined by moving a jumper next to the IDE

connector on the drive itself. On most drive labels, you will find a diagram that indicates jumper placements for master and slave designations, but sometimes you'll have to refer to the documentation for instructions.

If your PC can't see your hard drive and your motherboard comes with built-in IDE RAID, make sure your jumper settings or BIOS are properly configured. Check your documentation to determine how to switch between RAID and Ultra DMA settings, depending on which you are using.

10 Underclocked CPU

The initial boot screen should post your CPU's speed (although with Athlon XP CPUs, you won't get the clock speed, but rather AMD's "performance rating"). If it's lower than you expected, the frontside bus speed is probably underclocked. On a Pentium 4 motherboard, the frontside bus will run at either 400MHz, 533MHz, or 800MHz. On an Athlon XP motherboard, it will be either 133MHz, 166MHz, 200MHz, or 266MHz. Make sure you know what frontside bus your CPU supports before you clock it up.

Most modern motherboards allow you to set the frontside bus in the BIOS, while others require that you configure jumpers on the board's surface for the correct speed. Your motherboard manual will tell all.

Safety Tips

An ounce of prevention is worth a pound of fried hardware—five crucial safety tips for PC builders

Unplug the Power Supply!
Don't work on your PC with the power supply still plugged into the wall. Even when the PC is off, the power supply transmits a small amount of electricity to the motherboard, and removing components with the PC still plugged in could fry them.

Static Be Gone!
Static electricity can, and does, kill computer components. So pick up a cheap antistatic strap at the local electronics store, and make sure it's connected to something grounded. Don't start your building project on the shag carpet of your living room, and for God's sake, don't build the PC while dressed in a polyester leisure suit. At the very least, touch your PC's power supply, or some type of metal object that's grounded, before working on your PC.

Clean the Sink!
Today's high-performance heatsinks and CPUs need to be in firm contact with each other to dissipate heat properly. If they're not, your CPU can crack. If you're reusing an old heatsink, make sure you use rubbing alcohol to thoroughly clean off the old thermal goop, and apply just enough thermal compound to cover the core. Don't apply so much that it oozes out and shorts contacts.

Be an AGP Pro!
When inserting a regular AGP card into an AGP Pro socket, make sure you don't hammer the card into the wrong part of the socket, as it may short out your mobo or videocard. Most AGP Pro sockets have safety tabs to keep the card from being inserted incorrectly, so don't remove these tabs unless you absolutely need to.

Insert Your Cable Slowly!
As with any cable connector, be especially careful when inserting the flat IDE cable into your hard drive or optical drive. If the cable doesn't have a safety tab that prevents it from being put in upside down, you can easily destroy a pin—or two or three or four—on your brand new 200GB hard drive.

BUILD IT

The 10 Tenets of Effective Case Cooling

Don't let your 2GHz PC turn into a four-alarm fire!

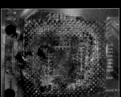

Edmar Dominicci sent us this grim example of what happens when you fail to plug in your heatsink's fan.

When their circuit counts are combined, the Athlon XP CPU and GeForce3 graphics processor account for more than 90 million transistors—and every single one of those transistors gets hot, hot, hot when under duress. Worried about heat stroke? You should be. So before you put your PC together, develop a cooling strategy to prevent a serious meltdown. Here are the 10 most important things to consider when contemplating meltdown-prevention. If you follow these tips—and don't overclock your parts—you should never run into problems.

1 Front to back, top to bottom
Your rig's airflow should be the same regardless of the number, shape, and size of your fans. Air should come in at the bottom of the case and be blown toward the back. It should then be sucked up and out the top of the system. To this end, fans at the front and bottom of your case should draw air into the case, while fans at the back and

top of the case should blow air out. This includes blowhole fans, drive bay fans, and PCI slot fans.

2 Keep a clear path
When you design the cooling scheme for your case, make absolutely certain you maintain a nice "jet stream" through your case's interior. This essentially means removing unnecessary obstructions. Using cable ties to reduce the clutter of IDE and floppy cables can dramatically improve your cooling.

3 Basic cooling precedes exotica
Before you add a heat pipe or peltier cooler in order to overclock your CPU, devise a good cooling layout based on a normal system bus speed and rudimentary case fans. If your rig doesn't behave properly with basic cooling, it probably won't appreciate being overclocked with exotic cooling.

4 Know what's hot and what's not
Take advantage of the temperature monitors that are built into your motherboard, but don't rely on them exclusively. To this end, you should pick up a good electronic wired thermometer at your local Radio Shack. Attach its probe to a suspect area of your case interior, close the case's side panel, run the PC for a few hours, then check the probe's digital readout. Record the temperature, then move the probe to a new location. Repeat this procedure for different parts of your case—if you find any hot spots, consider additional cooling for those areas.

5 Optimize airflow!
A good way to perfect your system's flow (assuming you have a sufficient number of fans) is to use clear packing tape to seal any extra case holes, or cool air will leak from the back of your PCI slots before it can run over your CPU and memory. Also ensure

that you have an equal number of fans blowing air into and out of your system. You don't want to have more air coming in than going out, and you don't want to create a vacuum inside either.

6 Use a filter over your intake fans
Dust kills PCs, so grab some "filter media" to protect your computer. It's the same stuff that filters air going into your house's central air system, and most hardware stores stock it (but you'll need to cut it to the proper size). Electrostatic filters grab more dust, so they're preferable. Just remember to clean out your filter every month or two!

7 Hot, hotter, hottest
In most systems, the CPU is the hottest component, followed by the videocard, the motherboard's core-logic chipset, the memory, and finally the hard drives. Don't neglect any of these components, but remember to make cooling the CPU and videocard a priority.

8 Keep your hard drives cool
High-speed hard drives—such as the 7200rpm beasts that are common today—generate a lot of heat. Make sure you have sufficient air flowing over them to increase their lifespan.

9 Don't overstress your mobo
Don't plug massive dual fans into your motherboard fan headers. Those headers are designed to power a single 8cm fan, not three 10cm fans.

10 Get the right fan/heatsink combo
If a reseller sold you an AMD processor that didn't come with a companion heatsink and/or fan already attached, go to **www.amd.com** and search for "thermal solutions" for a list recommended by AMD for its entire line-up of CPUs.

Intel doesn't have an equivalent table on its web site, but it does have voluminous notes on thermal management for its CPUs; go to **support.intel.com/support/processors**. When you buy a fan/heatsink combo for your Intel processor, make sure it is specifically designed for your type of proc. ∎

Thermaltake's Volcano fan is a heavy-duty fever-reducer for today's monster CPUs.

How To...
■ **A step-by-step guide to tweaking your PC Experience**

BUILD A PC Entertainment CENTER

MAXIMUM PC
TIME TO COMPLETION
04:30
HOURS   MINUTES

BY WILL SMITH

Throw away your game console, DVD player, and TiVo. Here's how to make the perfect PC for living room deployment

HP and Alienware are doing it, so why aren't you? Media Center PCs—which play DVDs, record live TV, and manage entire digital music collections—are the latest craze.

Unfortunately, the Windows XP Media Center Edition isn't available for retail purchase. You can get it only if you buy a prefab Media Center system from a system manufacturer. The Media Center extension to the basic WinXP operating system is expressly designed to work with a hardware remote control unit and lets you use your PC as a turnkey digital media command center. We

can understand why the Media Center software isn't going retail: Our OEM friends tell us it works with just a very short list of approved hardware configurations.

The good news is that you don't need Media Center software to enjoy Media Center features. The software just streamlines the entertainment experience for couch-potato convenience. In this article, we'll show you how to build a PC entertainment center, using readily available (mostly economical), off-the-shelf parts.

Shopping List

We used the following parts, but substitutions are discussed later in the article.

► **Shuttle SN45G nForce2 XPC (a bare-bones mini-case with a preinstalled nForce2 motherboard)**

► **Athlon XP 2000+ processor**

► **512MB PC2400 DDR SDRAM**

► **200GB Maxtor DiamondMax Plus 9 hard drive**

► **Sony DRU510A DVD recorder**

► **ATI All-in-Wonder 9800 Pro videocard**

► **Mini headphone-jack extension cable**

► **A TV, HDTV, or PC monitor**

► **5.1 speaker set with a digital decoder**

► *MusicMatch Jukebox Plus*

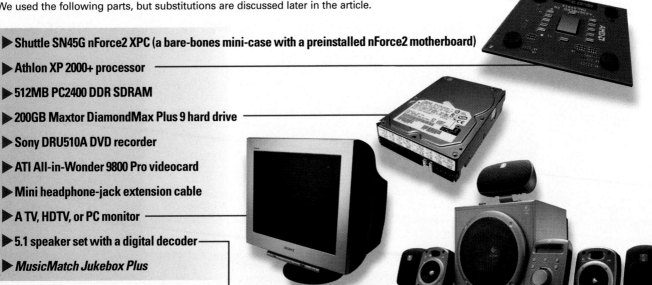

Components in Detail

Before you configure your entertainment center, you need to decide exactly what you want to do with it. We wanted to play DVDs; play, pause, and record live TV; play digital music; enjoy an occasional game; and archive everything to a recordable DVD. We tailored our project PC to these specifications, but in the following paragraphs, we tell you where you can scrimp if you want to ditch some of these features.

CPU, CHIPSET, AND MEMORY

The nForce2 core-logic chipset can do Dolby Digital 5.1 encoding in real-time, so we were intent on buying a bare-bones Shuttle case that features this chipset. This chipset is compatible only with Athlon CPUs, so if you don't want to be locked into the AMD platform, you might consider the Shuttle SB51G, which runs Pentium 4s.

As long as you have sufficient CPU speed and memory capacity (1.5GHz and 256MB, respectively), you should be fine, even if you're using ATI's software encoder for TV recording duties. If you're *not* planning to use your PC as a TiVo replacement, you can skimp on CPU power. DVD and MP3 playback are much less CPU-intensive than on-the-fly video encoding.

3D ACCELERATION AND TV FUNCTIONALITY

For TV viewing and recording and 3D acceleration in a single AGP slot, there's really no better alternative than the ATI All-in-Wonder 9800 Pro. It combines the awesome 3D speed of a Radeon 9800 Pro with the multimedia prowess of previous All-in-Wonder products, and even includes a handy wireless remote control.

If you're looking for the TV viewing goodness, but don't need top-shelf 3D power, consider the ATI All-in-Wonder VE. It has all the same TV functionality as the 9800 Pro without the expensive 3D accelerator.

MASS STORAGE

When it comes to your storage subsystems—i.e., your hard drive and optical drive—bigger is always better. However, if you're not planning on using your entertainment PC for TV recording and "timeshifting"

duties, your hard drive can be significantly smaller. While 40 hours of recorded TV can consume 128GB of hard drive space in a flash, even a massive MP3 collection with more than 3,000 tunes will absorb just 15GB of space.

If burning DVDs isn't your bag but you still want to watch DVDs and burn music CDs, you should get a CD-RW/DVD-ROM combo drive. We recommend the Samsung SM-332. It will burn CDs at 32x, and rips audio quickly, too. It's also significantly cheaper than the Sony DVD-RW/+RW drive.

INPUT OPTIONS

Even though the All-in-Wonder ships with a good remote, you'll still want a reliable wireless keyboard and mouse, for games if nothing else. Logitech's Cordless Keyboard is quite nice and reasonably priced. We're also fans of the Gyration Ultra mouse, which works as either a normal optical mouse or by waving it around in mid-air. It's perfect for couch gaming! Gyration also sells a compact wireless keyboard, but we haven't yet tested it.

Putting It All Together

You'll need to install the CPU, memory, drives, and AGP card before you can start using your new PC. If you have built a PC before, but are nervous about digging around the Shuttle box's guts, here's a short cheat sheet.

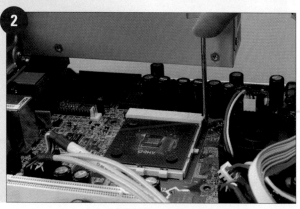

STEP ONE CPU AND MEMORY

First, you'll need to open your Shuttle case and remove the drive cage (the big U-shaped metal thing near the optical bays at the front of the case). Next, you'll need to remove the CPU cooling assembly. First, unscrew the thumbscrews holding the fan mount on the outside of the back of the case. Second, lift the fan assembly off the radiator, and remove the screws that hold the heat pipe to the CPU socket (figure 1).

Now you can lift the CPU locking lever and gently drop the CPU into its socket, making sure not to force it in. Push the lever back down until it clicks into place (figure 2). After the CPU is seated, apply a small amount of thermal grease to the core, then replace the CPU cooling mechanism. Make sure not to over-tighten the heatsink when you lock it down. You should tighten the screws by hand, and then give them a quarter twist with your screwdriver. Over-tightening can kill your Athlon.

Next, install the memory. All you need to do is slide it into the slot, then push down until it clicks into place. It's an absolute pain in the ass to install the RAM after you've reinstalled the drive cage, so make sure you do things in order!

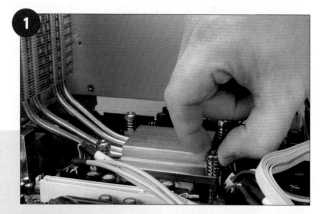

STEP TWO INSTALLING YOUR DRIVES

Now that your CPU and memory are installed, it's time to plug in your drives. Take a look at your Shuttle's drive cage. We recommend putting the hard drive in the bottom slot and the optical drive in the top slot, and forgoing a floppy drive—1.44MB just isn't enough space to fool with these days. There are specific holes lined up in the bottom slot of the drive rack for the hard drive, but you'll need to make sure the optical drive's front panel lines up properly with the front of your Shuttle case. You can do this by lining up the bezel of the drive with the 3.5-inch slot cover that's mounted in the drive caddy (figure 1).

Once the drives are mounted in the drive cage, you'll need to

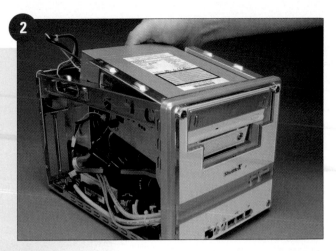

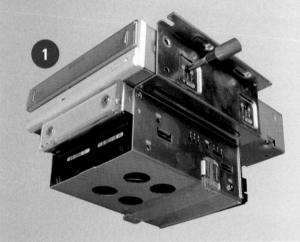

slide the cage into the case. Before you do, make sure the jumpers for the drives are set properly. The hard drive should be set to be master and the optical drive should be set to slave. We recommend plugging the IDE and power cables into your hard drive before you set the cage in your case. They're difficult to access once the drive cage is screwed down.

Slide the drive cage into the case bezel first, and then lower the back end until it's flush with the top of the case (figure 2). Be very careful not to force it. You may need to adjust the IDE and power cables to get everything in. If you're using an All-in-Wonder 9800 Pro, you'll also need to keep a floppy power connector available on the left side of the case to give the board the additional juice it needs. Once the cage is in the case, you can slide it all the way forward and lock it in place using the screws on the top.

STEP THREE INSTALLING YOUR VIDEOCARD

All that's left on the hardware front is the All-in-Wonder 9800 Pro. Turn the case around until you have easy access to the left side, and remove the slot cover from the AGP slot's faceplate. Next, slide the 9800 into the slot and screw it into the mounting bracket. Last, you'll want to plug a floppy power connector into the All-in-Wonder's power jack (see image).

Make sure you pick the proper output dongle for the videocard. If you're going to use a monitor or normal TV as your display, use the black dongle. HDTV users will need the red dongle. Connect the audio output on the dongle to the microphone input on the front of the PC using your headphone extension cable.

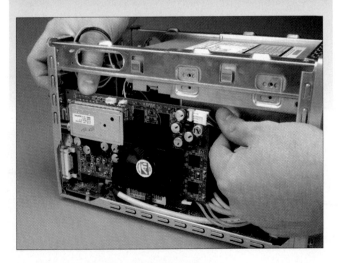

STEP FOUR CLOSING THE CASE

Everything's installed, so you can plug the keyboard, monitor, and power into the PC and power it up to make sure it passes the power on self test (POST). If the PC POSTs properly and all your drives are detected by the BIOS, you can pull the power and put the cover back on the Shuttle box. Make sure you don't catch any wires when you're closing the cover, and that the sides get into their guide grooves.

Getting the Software Working

Next up, we'll install the software you'll need to run your entertainment PC. You'll need a copy of Windows XP Home or Professional and some of the bundled software that comes with the videocard (the ATI drivers, *Pinnacle Studio,* and *Mediator*).

INSTALLING WINDOWS
Installing Windows XP is generally pretty easy. If you have a hard drive that's larger than 133GB, you'll need to pay close attention during the hard drive partitioning sections of the install.

If a hard drive is larger than 133GB, anything beyond the 133GB mark won't show up in the Windows XP partitioning tool. To fix this, we recommend that you create a small 40GB partition using the XP installer, install the OS on that partition, install the chipset drivers for your motherboard, and then create a large partition using the rest of the drive.

Why create just a 40GB install partition? Because we plan on using that drive only for the OS, the important applications, and digital music. Even a massive music collec-

tion probably won't be more than 20 or 30GB, leaving plenty of room for Windows XP and your applications on the C: partition. Don't partition or format the rest of the drive until Windows and the chipset drivers are installed.

Once your Windows install is up and running, go into the Computer Management tool by going to Start, then Run, and typing `compmgmt.msc`. From there, go to the Storage section and look under Disk Management. Right-click the unformatted section of the drive, select Create partition, and make a primary partition. Then you'll need to format your new partition by right-clicking it and choosing Format.

After you've installed XP, you'll want to install Service Packs 1 and/or 2 (available at www.windowsupdate.com) and reboot. You'll also need to install your chipset drivers and ATI's All-in-Wonder 9800 Pro drivers, rebooting as prompted.

RECOMMENDED SOFTWARE
Once your drivers are installed, we recommend installing the software bundled with

the All-in-Wonder. The ATI *Multimedia Center* and remote control software will let you use the PC without a keyboard and mouse, and seamlessly switch between watching TV, listening to music, and viewing DVDs.

The first time you launch the ATI's TV app, you'll be prompted to start a setup wizard. When you're in the wizard, make sure you set ATI's TV timeshifting app to use the large hard drive partition you just created instead of your smaller C: partition. By isolating the video on the large partition, you'll maximize the amount of video you can record as well as minimize the drive fragmentation that inevitably occurs during TV timeshifting.

Pinnacle Studio and *Mediator*—which are bundled with the All-in-Wonder—will let you encode captured TV shows in the proper MPEG-2 format so they will work on set-top DVD players. You'll then be able to burn your videos and captured TV shows to disk using *MyDVD 4.5*, which is bundled with the Sony drive we recommend.

Finally, we like *MusicMatch Jukebox* to play all our digital music, organize playlists, manage ID3 tags, and burn songs to CD.

Output Options

Now that your media center is set up, you need to configure it for your particular output options. Everyone knows how to plug a normal PC monitor into a PC, but using a normal TV or an HDTV as your display can be tricky. Besides discussing display connectors in this section, we'll also show you how to hook up your home stereo speakers to your PC (in the event your "multimedia speakers" are $10 throwaway jobbies).

Before you disconnect the monitor you used during setup, make sure you set the resolution in the Display control panel to the minimum. That will help ensure that you'll be able to see and configure your new display when you connect it.

USING AN HDTV AS YOUR MONITOR
The All-in-Wonder 9800 Pro includes an HDTV output that will work with any HDTV at any of the HDTV resolutions. The dongle is red, and has five outputs. You'll use the red, green, and blue RCA outputs to connect to your HDTV. The orange is a coaxial digital output, which you won't use. The blue mini-headphone plug needs to be connected to the microphone input on the front

of the PC (if you don't connect it, you won't get any audio when you're watching TV).

USING A NORMAL TV
The resolution of a normal TV is pretty shameful in this age of 1600x1200 flat panels. However, the low resolution doesn't preclude you from using your entertainment PC to watch TV, view DVDs, and listen to tunes. Just connect either the RCA composite or S-video outputs of the videocard to your TV (your videocard should have the necessary cables).

The max resolution most TVs will display is 800x600 at 60Hz, so you'll need to make sure that your PC's display settings are adjusted to these specs before you connect your TV to your PC. Also, the OS is much easier to use if you set it to use large fonts and icons. Go to the Appearance tab in Windows' Display Properties control panel, and change the font size to Extra Large. Then click the Advanced button, select the Icon item, and change the size from 32 to 45. Press OK and then press Apply.

USING A DIGITAL 5.1 SPEAKER RIG
If your home theater receiver has a free

Toslink optical SPDIF input, use it—it's the best interface for PC connections, and it's simple as pie to use. All you need to do is plug one end of the optical cable into your receiver and the other end into your PC. Then go into the nForce control panel (by double-clicking the system tray icon), and make sure that the Digital output box is checked. Select the proper digital input on your receiver, and you should be good to go.

USING AN ANALOG SPEAKER RIG
To connect your PC to a stereo, you'll need a mini headphone-to-stereo-RCA cable. You can get these at Radio Shack for less than $10. Plug the headphone end into your PC's main sound output (the green jack), and the other end into a spare set of inputs on your receiver.

If your receiver has 5.1 analog inputs, you might be able to use the analog 5.1 outputs on the back of the Shuttle box and three mini headphone-to-RCA cables. Unfortunately, we weren't able to test this config with the hardware we had in the lab.

Believe it or not, you now have a fully functioning PC that's perfectly outfitted for living room entertainment. Have fun! ■

How To...

PAINT YOUR CASE

Learn how the pros at Falcon Northwest turn an ordinary computer case into something extraordinary, and how you can paint your own case at home

EDITED BY KATHERINE STEVENSON

MAXIMUMPC
DIFFICULTY RATING
EASY
HARD
XXX

Our virgin case sans the paint and decals.

Regular readers of *Maximum PC* are probably familiar with the spectacular paint jobs that adorn Falcon Northwest's gaming PCs. Indeed, the Medford, Oregon-based company actually commissions a professional auto-painting operation to provide the craftsmanship and customization that characterize Falcon PCs.

So it should come as no surprise that we chose Falcon Northwest to paint and decal Dream Machine—a no-holds-barred celebration of the best a desktop computer can be. We asked Kelt Reeves, Falcon Northwest's president, to take us on a guided tour of the PC's aesthetic transformation, from its humble beginnings to beauteous end. Follow along as the unassuming CoolerMaster ATC-110 you see pictured here becomes the looker that is *Maximum PC's* Dream Machine.

Wherever possible we've provided our own tips for painting a case at home—thanks goes out to all the *Maximum PC* readers who contributed suggestions.

Step 1: Get Yourself an Art Department

Creating your basic design can be the most challenging part, because practically anything you can imagine can be applied to a case. The inspiration for *Maximum PC's* Dream Machine was a BMW 2002 Turbo sports car, and our goal was to translate the classic car's aesthetic to a square-shaped box. *Maximum PC* made this step easy on us: Art Director Natalie Jeday created her own design in Adobe *Illustrator*, a vector-based drawing program, which is exactly what vinyl graphics shops like to work from.

Falcon Northwest has executed case designs that range from a simple single-color paint job to any combination of vinyl lettering, graphics, airbrushing, and even embedded full-color photographs and artwork. The *Maximum PC* Dream Machine called for just paint and vinyl—lots of vinyl. Vinyl can be used for actual decals that are embedded in the paint, or to mask areas of the case during painting. Since we were able to obtain vinyl in all the colors *Maximum PC* had specified, we decided to apply the vinyl to the case instead of having masks made.

Step 2: Off to the Vinyl Shop

Vinyl graphics are used on everything from street signs, to race cars, to those annoying decals of a peeing Calvin that you see on the back window of pickup trucks. Luckily for us, Nick and Gary from Razor's Edge vinyl shop in Medford can create all types of vinyl graphics. You, too, almost certainly have a vinyl shop in your hometown.

Vinyl graphics cutting is done on a specialized machine called a "plotter." The plotter essentially draws a line between two points. But instead of using pen on paper, vinyl plotters use a wickedly sharp blade on paper-backed vinyl. Before the vinyl can be cut, the vinyl artist will go over every vector in the design to ensure that every line of every letter is complete and will cut properly. Once the design is ready, it's then translated into special vinyl-cutting software. In this case, it's *Flexisign Pro*, a $5,000 program designed for signmakers. One of the unique features of this program is that it allows printing by color. Since the vinyl sheets have to be loaded and cut one color at a time, this software makes it easy to cut only the parts of the design that use the color you're currently working on.

Step 3: Cutting the Vinyl Graphics

The vinyl itself is interesting stuff. It's waterproof, fade resistant, comes in hundreds of colors, metallics, and even reflective surfaces (as you've probably seen on emergency vehicles). The vinyl is actually a soft PVC film with an adhesive backing, mounted on silicon paper.

The plotter that Razor's Edge uses is an amazing piece of precision equipment. Just the blades for this beast run $30 a piece, and typically last just two weeks. With tolerances literally down to millionths of an inch, the plotter can score the 2-millimeter thick vinyl just deep enough to cut it, without cutting all the way through its paper backing. One-millionth of an inch too shallow, and the vinyl won't cut. One-millionth of an inch too deep, and the paper will cut through—outputting your job as a horrendous pile of confetti. Here we see the SummaGraphics plotter in action.

Maximum PC suggests: If you want to apply vinyl to your case, we strongly recommend that you have it cut at a vinyl shop. Creating your own decal would require you to trace a printout using a razor blade knife. The vinyl itself is not printable with either an inkjet (remember, it's waterproof) or laser printer (it will melt, and could catch fire).

Step 4: Weeding Sucks

I asked Nick why he was cutting out several copies of each vinyl graphic when the case design called for just one set. The answer became clear when Nick pulled excess vinyl from around the freshly cut graphics, a process called "weeding." While the large stripes stayed put, fully one-third of the small letters pulled off with the excess material. "Acceptable losses," Nick said. Evidently, in the vinyl game, you throw away much more material than you actually keep. Vinyl is very elastic, and thin pieces are easily pulled off (or stretched by accident) during weeding. For this reason, pinstripes of 1/8-inch or less are nearly impossible to create with vinyl. And, as if that weren't enough, every center of every closed letter has to be painstakingly removed from the paper backing with a razor blade—by hand. Surprisingly, Nick still has his eyesight and most of his sanity.

   Maximum PC suggests: As you might surmise, it pays to have your vinyl shop run off multiple copies of whatever you want to apply to your case. If you somehow stretch your decal or get it all stickied-up, you'll want a backup copy. We should also note that some shops won't even do single-logo jobs; minimum quantities will vary.

Step 5: Get Yourself the Best Auto Painter on the West Coast

I thought it was a crime to paint the beautiful aluminum CoolerMaster cases—until I saw Jim's work. Jim (we'll just call him Jim because he's in the Witness Relocation Program) is a Master car painter. I say "Master" with a capital "M" because that's actually a level in his trade. Jim has been painting cars for more than 20 years and has won many awards and car show competitions.

   Jim works at the largest auto-body shop on the west coast. We'd give you the name of the shop, but it too is in the Witness Relocation Program. This 40,000 square foot shop paints more than 400 cars every month and has five car-size ovens for baking on the auto paint. Each of these "thermal downdraft" car ovens costs upwards of $250,000, has its own built-in life support system, and can bake a car (or PC) at up to 300 degrees. After seeing the work Jim does on cars and motorcycles like this one, we knew he was up to the challenge of our PC cases.

   Maximum PC suggests: You may be able to find an auto body shop in your area that will take on your job. Call around. Or finish reading

Step 6: Smells Like... Brain Damage

For the Dream Machine to remain true to its 1973 BMW 2002 Turbo inspiration, we needed an exact match of the classic car's original factory paint—"Polaris Silver." But how do you match a car that hasn't been manufactured in almost 30 years? A specialized Sartorius ColorMix computer is used for the task. The machine contains a database of every color on every car ever manufactured and the color elements that comprise them. The computer tells the "mixmaster" which pigments to mix, by weight, and he pours them into a can on a scale connected to the computer.

   Because the Polaris Silver we mixed is an exact replica of the 1973 BMW factory paint, it's not as bright or "metallic" as paints made today. Evidently, in 1973, paint makers couldn't achieve the suspension of the courser metallic flakes used in today's metallics and pearlcoats. *Maximum PC* intentionally sacrificed some flashiness to be faithful to the original automobile.

   Professional auto paints consist of chemicals that are much tougher and more beautiful than anything you can find at your local paint store. But they're also much more dangerous. For this reason, most professional paint stores will not sell to the general public.

   Maximum PC suggests: Your paint options may be limited, but be sure to choose an automotive-grade paint, or one that's recommended for the surface you're working on. A spray can is the recommended method of application in the absence of a professional spray gun.

Step 7: Reduce Your Case to Pieces

Auto paints require intense heat to dry, and auto ovens can melt a plastic grill right out of a car should a painter neglect to remove it. So a baked-on finish is not something to attempt with any plastic or plastic-fronted PC. Even the Dream Machine's all-aluminum ATC-110 has plastic fans, wiring, and LEDs that must all be removed by hand, lest they turn into a puddle of goo during the baking process. Here Randy is using heavy-duty tape to secure each piece of the case to the spray tables.

Maximum PC suggests: Obviously, if you decide to have a plastic case painted, baking is out of the question.

Step 8: Totally Ruin a Fine Finish

If you want to make a new paint job stick, you've got to first strip off all traces of its original finish. You'll notice the painter's working with rubber gloves. Any salts or acids from your fingers will soak into aluminum (a very porous metal) and ruin the paint later on. It's possible to have a fingerprint show through 15 layers of paintwork, so wearing gloves is critical.

Maximum PC suggests: An orbital sander and 220 sandpaper is another way to take the finish off a metal case. On a plastic case, your concern is cleaning the surface of release agents (chemicals used to release the case from its mold). For this, stick to a Scotch Brite pad and soapy water.

Step 9: Fun with Acid

Please add phosphoric acid to the list of products "our lawyer says we can't recommend you use at home." This lovely substance is a light acid wash that Jim uses to rub down all the painted surfaces. The phosphoric acid eats away a tiny bit of the aluminum, removing microscopic corrosion already present in any exposed metal. It provides good clean metal for the paint to bond with, and without this vital step, the paint won't adhere correctly and may flake off.

Maximum PC suggests: A product such as Jasco Metal Etch contains phosphoric acid and is suitable for prepping metals before painting. It costs about $4 a bottle and can be purchased at most hardware stores. Follow the safety instructions, and be sure to rinse the case's surface with water when you're done.

Step 10: First Layer... And It's Still Not Paint

Our panels are finally ready for the first of the 15 layers that will be applied to them. The first layer is Zinc Chromate, known more commonly as aluminum etch. This yellowish goo provides a layer of corrosion protection for the freshly exposed aluminum. Yes, aluminum rusts, but it's not the normally reddish-brown rust. Aluminum oxidization actually looks like fine white powder, and it will ruin a paint job.

Maximum PC suggests: Because it's a highly toxic substance, Zinc Chromate cannot be found just anywhere. In California, for instance, its use is strictly regulated. So you may just want to play it safe and substitute Zinc Chromate with a couple layers of sprayed-on primer (be your case metal or plastic).

Step 11: Let's Mix Toxins!

I mentioned before that the Polaris Silver brew was just the pigment. Now Jim is going to mix in the chemicals that will turn it into paint: reducer and activator. Jim, an avid *Maximum PC* reader, explained that the "reducer is like the PCI bus, it carries the paint through the system to its destination." The activator is a hardener that quickly dries the paint layers and makes them tougher. It does this via a process called "gassing out"—essentially the solvents vaporize leaving behind a tough layer of pigment. The whole concoction is loaded into Jim's Satajet 90 pneumatic spray gun that he uses specifically for base-coat jobs.

Maximum PC suggests: It's unlikely you'll have access to professional acrylic-urethane paint, so you'll probably be using enamel paint in a spray can. While enamel isn't as strong or chemical resistant, it also doesn't need to be baked.

Step 12: Applying the Base Coat

While many colors require just two base coats to achieve the desired shade, silver is very "transparent." So three layers are necessary for a proper coating. Between each layer of silver base coat, Jim lets the paint gas out for five to seven minutes. If the solvents aren't allowed this time to evaporate, the paint will eventually blister and pop where the gas has been trapped.

Maximum PC suggests: With enamel, you'll want your paint to gas out for at least 30 minutes between coats. When applying coats, use smooth, even strokes that go in the same direction. Multiple thin coats are better than a single thick coat. Always gas out in between.

Step 13: Clear Coat Can Kill

You may remember the Jonestown massacre in 1978, wherein a cult leader killed more than 900 followers by giving them Kool-Aid laced with isocyanate—a deadly poison if ingested. Since paint manufacturers seem to love deadly chemicals, they use isocyanate in making high-solids acrylic urethane, or clear coat. And the fact is, clear coat makes all paint jobs look better; it gives both cars and Falcon PCs that gorgeous sheen. It's perfectly safe after baking, but in its liquid state it must not be touched, inhaled, or mixed with Kool-Aid because it can kill you.

In fact, isocyanate vapors can permeate your skin, causing cirrhosis of the liver, internal bleeding, and the whites of your eyes to turn yellow. Jim said that many old-school car painters refused to use the carbon filter gasmasks that allow safe use of isocyanates. Since your body cannot purge isocyanates, once you've inhaled enough of this stuff over the years, a mere whiff of it will make you vomit. According to Jim, a lot of the older guys doing car pinstriping today were once painters who inhaled too much isocyanate and can no longer tolerate being near the stuff.

But clear coat looks really sexy, so we decided to use lots of it. We started by applying clear coat over the base coat to give our vinyl graphics a perfect, smooth surface to adhere to. There will be much more clear coating later on. For the clear coats, Jim uses a different spray gun, a SataJetRP. It provides very quick atomization of the acrylic urethane as it's ejected form the spray gun, and this prevents clumping.

Maximum PC suggests: You can buy cans of enamel clear coat at the same shop where you buy your enamel paint. The two substances work fine together, but for best results you should stick with the same manufacturer for both your paint and clear coat. And to be extra safe, do a test run on a small area (such as drive rail) to ensure your paint and clear coat work well together.

Step 14: Preheat Oven and Bake

After the first clear layer has been applied, the finish needs to be baked on. For standard paintwork without vinyl graphics, we would have applied three layers of the clear coat, and then done the baking. However, the vinyl graphics need to be applied to an already baked, "finished" paint job. So after applying aluminum etch, three layers of base coat, and a first layer of clear coat, we put our parts into the oven.

Maximum PC suggests: While we do know of a few readers who've baked painted PCs inside their kitchen ovens, we can't recommend that you go down this dubious path. Also, most do-it-yourselfers use enamel paint, and baking is therefore a non-issue.

Step 16: Sweet, Sweet Clear Coat...

When you apply two layers of vinyl to a case panel, the vinyl naturally sticks above your paintwork in places. This vinyl has to be protected by submerging it in clear coat until the surface of the case is once again smooth and perfect. We did this with five more layers of clear coat. Once two or three new layers of clear coat have been applied, they again need to be baked. You can't do too many layers of clear without baking them on, as they'll start to pool and get uneven if applied too thickly when wet. So after we baked our second layer of clear coat, another two layers of clear coat were added and the PC was baked for a third time.

Step: 15: Laying Down the Vinyl

Once our clear coat was ready, we needed to lay our vinyl stickers in the approximate positions dictated by *Maximum PC's* art director. In order to position the decals accurately we applied tape as guides to keep our lines exactly straight, and used "application fluid"—a slippery substance that allows the decals to be moved around a bit after their sticky backing has been exposed. You can also use soap and water for this stage. Many of our graphics, such as "speed tested" were actually multilayered. The black layer went down first, we let it dry a bit, and then the white layer was wet down and placed on top. Lastly, we soaked the transfer paper so it could be carefully peeled away.

Step 17: Mmmm... Fresh Baked Viper!

Since Jim's oven burns $100 worth of electricity every time its run, the Master painter usually bakes our parts along with a car he's working on. In this shot, you can see *Maximum PC's* case baking alongside an $80,000 Dodge Viper! (Let's hope the owner of the car understands the honor he was bestowed.)

Step 18: Finishing Up

After all the larger pieces of the case were decaled, there was still some detail work to attend to. It turns out the vinyl stripes we had made for the front air grill were exactly the width of the grill, but we needed that color to wrap around the edges a bit so no gaps would show when it's installed. So Jim had to match tiny bits of blue, purple, and red paint to the color of the vinyl, and he used a small artist's airbrush for this detail work. Here we seem Jim carefully masking and painting half of the tiny reset button where a stripe crosses it.

Step 19: How to Scratch That Beautiful Clear Coat

Despite Jim's precision gunning, clear coat is never 100 percent perfect at first. It will have a few broken bubbles and imperfections that need to be sanded out. For this, Jim uses the application fluid again, and a fine grit sandpaper.

Once sanded, the clear coat's imperfections will be gone, but the sandpaper will make it look hazy due to the thousands of fine scratches just made. To bring out its brilliant shine, Jim uses 3M's "Perfect-It" rubbing compound. Rubbing compound is basically very fine grit liquid sandpaper. He applies it with a pneumatic polisher and two different grades of foam discs (one soft, one really soft), and polishes it to a gorgeous shine.

Step 20: "He never drives it, Ferris, he just polishes it with a diaper"

Just like any other fine automobile finish, the Dream Machine looks best when you can see your reflection in the shine. To achieve this effect, Jim applies a thin layer of car wax. Not just any car wax, mind you. New paint jobs are "soft" for about their first six months of life. Tiny bits of solvents will gas out of the finish during this time, hardening the paint to a tough protective shell. It's important during the first six months that these solvents not be trapped in the paint, lest they cause blistering and cracking. So be sure to use a wax that's labeled "breathable," or that's specifically intended for new paint jobs. ■

Step 21: Enjoy!

For more case painting tips, see the "Sub-Zero" how-to in the Extras folder on the disc that came with this magazine.

Master painter Jim Saling will take questions regarding home projects at his web site: **www.smoothcreations.com** (*oops*, did we just blow his cover?).

How To...

Supercharge your PC

ONE LITTLE HACK AT A TIME
Forty-one of Maximum PC's best tips and tricks, from our brains to your PC

---

10 EASY WAYS TO TOUCH UP WINDOWS XP

1 CLEAN OUT YOUR SYSTEM TRAY: Every unnecessary app running on your PC saps precious CPU cycles and memory.

2 UPDATE YOUR DRIVERS: New video-card and chipset drivers can help you reap performance dividends.

3 ENABLE DMA FOR YOUR DRIVES: Go to the Device Manager and take a look at the properties of your Primary IDE Channel. On the Advanced Settings tab, make sure that DMA, if available, is checked for both devices. Rinse and repeat for the Secondary IDE Channel

4 VISIT WINDOWSUPDATE.COM REGULARLY: Patches don't just protect your PC, they also improve performance.

5 CONVERT YOUR DRIVES TO NTFS: Get the most from your drives by converting them to NTFS. Open a command line, and type `convert x: /fs:ntfs`, but replace x with your drive letter. Back up your important files first!

6 USE QUICK LAUNCH: Instead of cluttering your Desktop with loads of shortcuts, right-click the Taskbar, go to Toolbars, and make sure Quick Launch is

checked. Then drag your favorite shortcuts to the Quick Launch bar for easy access, anytime.

7 SPEED UP YOUR UI: Bells and whistles are great, but faster is better. Go to the Display control panel, click the Appearance tab, and hit the Effects button. Uncheck the first two options, as well as "Show shadows under menus."

8 ONE CLICK TO DEVICE MANAGER: To open Device Manager in Windows XP without the hassle of going to System Properties, just create a shortcut to devmgmt.msc.

9 FIRE UP THE ONSCREEN KEYBOARD: If you need to type something and your keyboard's not available, Open My Computer and browse to C:\Windows\System32 and double-click osk.exe. You can use the onscreen keyboard by pointing and clicking at individual characters.

10 DEFRAG: Regular defragmentation can improve your machine's hard drive performance by massive amounts. To start Defrag, right-click your hard drive in My Computer, select Properties, go to the Tools tab, and then Click Defrag.

5 Software Tools Every PC Should Have

COMPRESSION UTILITIES:
1 *Winzip* is the best utility around for managing pesky zip files. You don't have to settle for the puny Compressed Files tool built into XP anymore! Get it at **winzip.com**.

ANTIVIRUS:
2 In today's dog-eat-dog Internet world, you must have antivirus software. We recommend *Norton AntiVirus 2004* (www.norton.com). It's easy to use and provides excellent protection.

FIREWALL:
3 Running a PC without a firewall is like using a blood-based sunscreen in shark infested waters. Learn to install and use a software firewall. See the section, "How to Protect Yourself with a Firewall" (Part IV).

BROWSER:
4 Only schmucks are still using *Internet Explorer*. Download Mozilla *Firebird 0.7* (www.mozilla.org) and browse with the power users.

DEFRAG:
5 The hard drive defragging utility built into Windows XP is acceptable for your grandmother, but if you want to keep your disks in tip-top shape, you need a more powerful tool. Get *Diskeeper* from **www.executivesoftware.com**.

5 Top-Secret Registry Hacks

Adding new functionality to Windows is as easy as opening regedit.exe and making some minor changes. *Changes here can break Windows, so make sure to back up your system before you touch anything!*

1. MINIMIZE OUTLOOK TO THE SYSTEM TRAY: Browse to HKEY_CURRENT_USER\Software\Microsoft\Office\10.0\Outlook\Preferences. Add a new DWORD value named MinToTray, and set it to 1. Next time you restart *Outlook*, it will minimize to the System Tray!

2. MAKE PASSWORD PROTECTED SCREENSAVERS LESS ANNOYING: You enable a password protected screensaver to help keep meddlers out of your machine, but you're annoyed when the screensaver starts and you're locked out. The solution: add a grace period. If the screensaver activates, but you move the mouse during the grace period, you can get right back to work, without typing your password again. Browse to HKEY_LOCAL_MACHINE\SOFTWARE\Microsoft\Windows NT\CurrentVersion\Winlogon and modify ScreenSaverGracePeriod. The value is stored in seconds. We like to set the value somewhere between 5 and 30 seconds.

3. SECURE YOUR PAGEFILE: The swapfile can contain anything that might be in RAM, including sensitive data like passwords. To set XP to automatically erase any info contained in it, go to HKEY_LOCAL_MACHINE\SYSTEM\CurrentControlSet\Control\Session Manager\Memory Management and add a DWORD value named ClearPageFileAtShutdown. Set it to 1, reboot your PC, and your machine will automatically erase the contents of your pagefile when you shut down. Be aware that this will make your PC take longer to shut down.

4. REMOVE THE ANNOYING COMPRESSION OPTIONS FROM THE DISK CLEANUP WIZARD: The Disk Cleanup wizard is a handy way to find out what unused files you can get rid of, but it also calculates the space you'll save by compressing your drive. We don't like to use compression, so we're going to disable it by browsing to HKEY_LOCAL_MACHINE\SOFTWARE\Microsoft\Windows\CurrentVersion\Explorer\VolumeCaches\Compress old files. Clear the value from the Default key. The next time you start Disk Cleanup, it will skip the compression analysis.

5. CUSTOMIZE THE FOLDERS LISTED IN YOUR OPEN DIALOG BOXES: Whenever you open a file in *Notepad* or *Paint*, there's a default list of folders on the left side of the Window. Unfortunately, those folders are just not that useful for most people. To customize them, point Regedit to HKEY_CURRENT_USER\Software\Microsoft\Windows\CurrentVersion\Policies\comdlg32 and create a new key called Placesbar. Inside that new key, create a String called Place0 and point it to the folder you want to appear on the open dialog, say, C:\CurrentWork. Create another String called Place1 and point it to another location on your drive. You can use variables (%USERPROFILE% will point the folder to the profile of a currently logged-in user) or URI's, so you can even use network shares. This hack won't change the same dialogs in *Office*, but if you have *Office XP*, you can add new folders to the Placesbar by going to File, Open, and browsing to the folder you want to add. Once you have it selected, go to Tools and click "Add to My Places."

10 THINGS TO DO TO YOUR BRAND-NEW PC

1 Get your Internet connection up and running. Without net access, your PC is damn near worthless!

2 Install the latest drivers for your motherboard's chipset. They'll be at your mobo manufacturer's web site. Many system crashes can be traced directly to either old chipset drivers or evil, evil gnomes.

3 Download and install the latest drivers for your videocard and soundcard. They'll work with the chipset drivers to have your PC performing at its peak potential.

4 Install Windows XP Service Pack 1 (or SP2, which will contain all SP1 updates) and all the updates from **Windowsupdate.com.** Don't ask questions, just do it.

5 Give your BIOS a little tweak. Make your PC faster and more reliable. Turn to the section, "How to Optimize Your PC's BIOS Settings," for the full scoop.

6 Install and tweak all those apps you use every day. Install *Winzip*, an MP3 player, a word processor, your e-mail app, and Mozilla *Firebird*.

7 Activate Windows, register all your apps—or click the "Never bother me again" button—and make a backup image of your minty-fresh system. For more on backups, turn to the "Maintain a Healthy OS" section (Part III).

8 Now that you have a set of custom recovery disks, it's time to see how she performs. Install your favorite benchmark app and take her for a test spin.

9 Burning in your PC will help you ferret out faulty components and give you a pretty good idea of your system's stability. We like *SiSoft Sandra's* burn-in utility. Download the free version at **Sisoftware.net.**

10 Open a tasty beverage, fire up your favorite game, and let the frags roll in. Your PC is ready to rumble!

11 Web Sites That Every Geek Should Bookmark

1 GOOGLE.COM: It's the only web site we know of that's used as both a noun and a verb. Learn to make Google work for you, and you'll never regret it.

2 WINDOWSUPDATE.COM: Update Windows regularly! It's good for you, it's good for your friends, and it's good for those tiny baby seals that live down by the sea. Really.

3 ARSTECHNICA.COM: Hardware- and software-agnostic computing news is only a bookmark away. Ars Technica has something for computer geeks of every persuasion.

4 SLASHDOT.ORG: "News for Nerds. Stuff that Matters." Slashdot's tag line says it all.

5 SHACKNEWS.COM: If it's gaming, Shacknews covers it. Get all the latest news about games here.

6 THEINQUIRER.NET: More than 90 percent of computer-related news on the net originates here. OK, we made that up, but The Inquirer is always five minutes ahead of the rest of the web.

7 PENNY-ARCADE.COM: Every once in a while we all need a laugh. The wacky-asses at Penny Arcade will provide just that, if you read the column too!

8 GIZMODO.COM: If you ever wondered where that gadget-savvy pal finds out about all his wonderful toys, it's probably Gizmodo. Get the latest on PDAs, wireless tech, and just plain cool stuff.

9 HYPERDICTIONARY.COM: Every word a link. Every link a definition. This is the way dictionaries should be.

10 WIKIPEDIA.COM: The Internet's own free encyclopedia. With more than 170,000 articles, the Wikipedia holds answers to many of your burning questions.

11 MAXIMUM PC COMMPORT: With 2 million-plus posts, the Commport holds the collective wisdom of hordes of helpful *Maximum PC* readers: **http://forums.delphiforums.com/maxcommport.**

How To...

OPTIMIZE YOUR PC'S
BIOS Settings

BY MARK SOPER

Better performance, reliability, and boot speed. Our guide will show you how to get the most from your PC's BIOS

The BIOS controls your PC's hardware at the very lowest levels. It determines the speed of your CPU, memory, and even some components. Because of this, tweaking your PC's BIOS can net you huge gains in performance and reliability. Changing one minor setting can net you a 10 percent performance boost, while another option could cost you as much as 40 percent. How do you know which settings will give your system a lift or bring it to its knees? Motherboard manuals usually leave something to be desired when it comes to explaining the workings of the BIOS. Not to fear, you're reading the most comprehensive BIOS optimization guide we've ever run in the pages of *Maximum PC*. We'll show you how to tweak your BIOS three different ways: to maximize performance, to minimize boot times, and to make your PC more reliable.

We'd be remiss if we didn't warn you that setting your BIOS incorrectly can keep your PC from booting. Before you make any changes to your BIOS, make a note of all the original settings. And make sure you follow our instructions explicitly, as any deviation may do

damage. If you're not comfortable with the possibility of breaking your system, you shouldn't be tweaking your BIOS.

You also need to know that every motherboard manufacturer's BIOS is a little different. Different manufacturers make different settings available to end users. Large PC manufacturers, such as Dell and MPC (formerly Micron PC), lock end users out of the really dangerous stuff, so don't expect to do a lot of tweaking to one of their PCs.

Before you begin, reread this page. Done? Let's get started then!

TWEAK YOUR BIOS FOR MAXIMUM PERFORMANCE

TWEAK 1 Correct Your Memory and CPU Speeds

Overclocking can give your system a big performance boost, but before you can try upping your system's clock speeds, you should make sure the processor's frequency and clock-multiplier are set correctly. Your CPU's speed is determined by

taking your system's frontside bus speed and multiplying it by the clock multiplier. Both of these values are set in your system's BIOS. Overclockers are generally limited to adjusting the frequency, since most modern processors will operate at

just one clock multiplier.

Many BIOSes correctly detect the processor frequency and clock multiplier for you. However, a lot of systems switch to a default fail-safe setting of 100MHz if the system locks up or powers-down during initial startup. Fail-safe mode will cause your PC to suffer a huge performance loss. The processor or FSB frequency is multiplied by a factor of two (most AMD CPUs) or a factor of four (most Intel CPUs) to obtain the processor's rated frontside-bus (FSB) speed. Thus, a 100MHz memory setting in the BIOS is equivalent to a 200MHz FSB on an AMD system or a 400MHz setting on an Intel system.

If your proc requires a faster FSB speed (as most newer CPUs do), this fail-safe setting results in a significant performance drop. You should find this setting in the Frequency/Voltage Control menu or the Advanced menu. To determine the correct frequency to use, check the data sheet for your processor model at the vendor's web site.

```
AMIBIOS NEW SETUP UTILITY - VERSION 3.31a

Freqency/Voltage Control                          [ Setup Help ]

Spread Spectrum            ±0.25 %          Please keyin/select ur
CPU FSB Clock              [ 133 MHz ]      desire FSB. FSB range
CPU Ratio                  Auto             100 ↔ 280 MHz.
CPU Vcore (V)              Auto             Select: [Up]/[Dn].
DDR Voltage (V)            Auto             KeyIn: Number+[Enter]
  Termination Vol (V)      Auto
AGP Voltage (V)            Auto
```

TWEAK 2 User-Defined Memory Timing

STEP 1:
ADJUSTING CAS LATENCY

Manually tweaking your memory settings can yield big performance gains. The memory timing menu is usually located in the Advanced Chipset screen or a sub-menu of this screen. Before you can adjust memory timing, you must change the Configure SDRAM Timing setting from the default of SPD to User (compare this screenshot with the screenshot below). The default SPD setting uses the settings built into a chip on the memory modules to determine the proper memory timings. If you need to determine what the standard timing values are for the memory modules you use and the BIOS doesn't show the actual values, check the memory vendor's web site for the modules' data sheet.

There are two major ways to rate the speed of memory: frequency (measured in MHz) and latency (how quickly the module can send data after receiving a request). SDR memory usually features CAS Latency values of 2 and 3 (lower is faster); DDR SDRAM is available with CAS Latency values of 2.5 and 2. CAS stands for column-address-strobe. Some systems display the CAS Latency value during startup.

To improve performance, try using a lower latency value. For example, if your memory has a CAS Latency value of 2.5, use 2 instead. If the system won't run properly, go back to the default CAS latency and try other adjustments.

```
AMIBIOS NEW SETUP UTILITY - VERSION 3.31a

DRAM Timing Control                               [ Setup Help ]

Current Host Clock         133 MHz
Configure SDRAM Timing by  SPD
  SDRAM Frequency          Auto
  SDRAM CAS# Latency       Auto
  Row Precharge Time       Auto
  RAS Pulse Width          Auto
  RAS to CAS Delay         Auto
  Bank Interleave          Auto
DDR DQS Input Delay        Auto
SDRAM Burst Length         4 QW
SDRAM 1T Command           Disabled
Fast Command               Normal
Fast R-2-R Turnaround      Disabled
```

STEP 2:
ADJUSTING MEMORY TIMING AND ACCESS FACTORS

Depending on the BIOS your system uses, you can also adjust other memory timing factors, such as Row Precharge Time, RAS Pulse Width, and RAS to CAS Delay. Row precharge time (also referred to as tRP) refers to the amount of time needed (in clock cycles) to activate the memory bank. RAS pulse width (tRAS) refers to the amount of time (in clock cycles) to leave the row of memory open for data transfers. RAS to CAS delay (tRCD) refers to the amount of time needed to switch to a different row of memory to access data not found in the current row. For maximum speed, these should be set as fast as possible (smaller values are faster).

The following options have variable impacts on performance:

Enable SDRAM 1T to synchronize RAM with the CPU's FSB if both run at the same speed. SDRAM Burst Length can sometimes improve performance when set to 8QW (que words). Fast Command controls how quickly the CPU interacts with memory (Normal, Fast, Ultra). Many systems default to Fast, but Ultra can be used in some cases to improve

performance. Fast R-2-R Turnaround, when enabled, improves the speed of recovery from a burst operation.

```
AMIBIOS NEW SETUP UTILITY - VERSION 3.31a

DRAM Timing Control                               [ Setup Help ]

Current Host Clock         133 MHz
Configure SDRAM Timing by  User
  SDRAM Frequency          Auto
  SDRAM CAS# Latency       2
  Row Precharge Time       2T
  RAS Pulse Width          5T
  RAS to CAS Delay         2T
  Bank Interleave          4-Way
DDR DQS Input Delay        Auto
SDRAM Burst Length         8 QW
SDRAM 1T Command           Disabled
Fast Command               Ultra
Fast R-2-R Turnaround      Enabled
```

TWEAK 3 Adjust AGP Settings

The AGP menu might be located on its own or be incorporated into the Advanced Chipset menu. The first setting to check is the AGP mode. It should be set for the maximum speed supported by your motherboard and AGP card (usually 4x or 8x with today's hardware).

As you might expect, other AGP settings fall into the trial-and-error category. AGP FastWrite bypasses main memory when performing writes to AGP memory, which can boost write performance by as much as 10 percent when enabled. However, some games have problems with this

setting. AGP Master 1 W/S Read and Write settings can be enabled to use one wait state (a memory cycle that performs no operation) instead of the default of two wait states for memory transfers to and from the AGP card. However, if your system uses a default of zero wait states, enabling these options can slow down your system instead of speeding it up. AGP Read Synchronization can cause stability problems if enabled, so it should be disabled. AGP Aperture Size controls the size of the GART (graphics address relocation table) and the amount of memory address space

used for AGP memory addresses. A value of 64MB to 128MB is recommended.

TWEAK 4 Improve PCI Bus Performance

Enable the PCI Delay Transaction option (also referred to as PCI 2.1 Compliance or Delay Transaction) to improve performance if you have ISA cards. Enable the PCI to DRAM Prefetch option to improve the performance of IEEE-1394 and PCI-based soundcards. Enabling PCI Master Read Caching uses the processor's L2 cache to cache reads from the PCI bus. Disabling this option can sometimes help performance by keeping the processor's L2 cache available for other processes. However, enabling this option in some Athlon-based systems helps lower the temperature of the processor. These options are usually located in the

Advanced Chipset Features menu.

The PCI Latency Timer option might be located in the PnP/PCI Configuration menu. It configures how long each PCI device gets to control the PCI bus before allowing another device to take over. The maximum range of settings is 0 to 255, but some BIOSes provide only certain values in this range. Reducing the value from the default of 32 can improve the response time of each PCI device (0 provides the fastest response time; 255

the slowest) to fix problems with some cards. However, PCI bandwidth suffers as a result. Increase this value to increase bandwidth across the PCI bus if your PCI devices work acceptably.

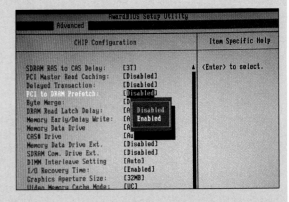

TWEAK 5 Power Up Peripherals

If you still use parallel ports for printers and other devices, you should configure the parallel port to run in EPP or ECP mode (EPP is recommended for single printers; ECP is recommended for daisy-chaining printers and other devices). These settings provide the fastest input-output support available and are typically located in the Integrated Peripherals menu. Make sure you use an IEEE-1284-compliant parallel cable to get the full benefit of this setting.

If you have switched to USB, keep in mind that using a hub to connect several USB 1.1 peripherals on a single USB 1.1 port (still the dominant type of USB port

on most systems) can cause device slow-downs. Slowdowns are particularly likely if you connect low-speed USB 1.1 devices, such as keyboards and mice, to the same port as faster devices, such as printers or disk drives. If you have more than two USB ports, make sure you enable all of them. Then, use separate ports for full-speed and low-speed

devices. The USB setting is also typically found in the Integrated Peripherals menu.

TWEAK YOUR BIOS FOR MAXIMUM RELIABILITY

TWEAK 1 Protect Your PC from Viruses

Although boot sector viruses are no longer the most common type of virus threat, anytime you use a floppy disk, you put your system at risk of an infection. Boot virus protection is a step beyond write-protecting the boot sector, because it can distinguish between legitimate changes to the boot sector caused

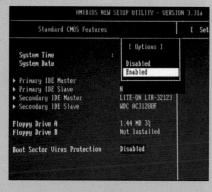

by operating system upgrades and boot managers and virus infections. You can find this option in the Standard CMOS Features, Advanced CMOS Features, or Boot menu of most BIOSes.

TWEAK 2 Watch for Hard Drive Failure

Enabling your disk system's Self-Monitoring and Reporting Technology feature will help you avoid problems with ATA/IDE hard disks. S.M.A.R.T.-enabled drives can report impending problems before they occur, giving you time to back up the drive and test it with ven-

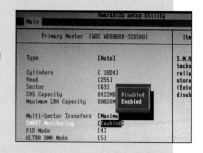

dor-supplied utilities. If you don't run S.M.A.R.T.-compatible software such as *Norton System Works,* you will only see a warning of a problem with a compatible drive at system start-up. You can usually find the option to enable S.M.A.R.T. on the Advanced CMOS/BIOS Features menu, or as an individual configuration option for each ATA/IDE drive.

TWEAK 3 Monitor Vital System Temps

CPU Critical Temperature is found in the Power Management menu of newer systems. When you enable it, you will be warned when your CPU exceeds the temperature you specify. Typical temperature options include 70 degrees Celsius (158

degrees Fahrenheit) up to 95 degrees Celsius (203 degrees Fahrenheit) in five-degree increments. Don't rely on this as a substitute for adequate processor cooling, but use it along with other stability options to warn you of problems.

TWEAK 4 Watch for Faulty Fans

If a CPU- or chassis-fan fails, your system will crash in short order due to overheating, and you might also fry your processor as an unwelcome bonus. Some systems monitor the CPU- and chassis-fans automatically if they are connected to the moth-

erboard. However, in other cases you must enable this feature on the PC Health screen. If your motherboard or system includes software that can receive fan-status messages from the BIOS, this setting provides cheap insurance against fan and system failure

TWEAK 5 Don't Fear Losing Power

If you're running a system that stays on around the clock, such as an Internet Connection Sharing gateway, setting After AC Power Loss to Power On in the Power Management Features menu will automatically restart your system in the event of a power loss. Last State will restore the system to whatever state it was in when the lights went out.

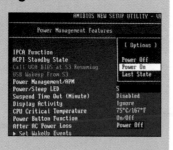

TWEAK 6 Free Unused Resources

Serial and parallel ports are ISA devices that can't share IRQs with newer PCI devices such as USB ports. Although systems with ACPI power management can assign multiple PCI devices to the same IRQ, doing so can reduce system reliability and cause conflicts between devices. If you don't use Serial and parallel ports anymore, disable them in the Integrated Peripherals or I/O Device Configuration menu to help free up the settings for use by newer devices. Serial ports use IRQ 4 (COM 1) and IRQ 3 (COM 2) by default, and the parallel port uses IRQ 7 by default.

TWEAK 7 Reserve Resources for Legacy Hardware

Some systems assume that IRQs 3 to 15 are fair game for PCI/PnP devices. However, if you still have non-PnP ISA devices, you'd better reserve the IRQs they use. Disabling legacy ports helps free up IRQs, but some systems won't use IRQs below 9 for PCI/PnP devices unless you specifically adjust the PnP/PCI menu to enable these IRQs.

TWEAK 8 Minimize Component Interference

The Spread Spectrum feature in some modern systems' Frequency/ Voltage Control menu is designed to help systems pass European electromagnetic interference tests. However, leaving this feature enabled, especially with large values for the voltage fluctuation, can cause disruption to Internet connections and stability problems in overclocking. You can sometimes adjust the voltage value as an alternative to disabling the feature completely.

TWEAK 9 Only Use USB Legacy Settings if You Have To

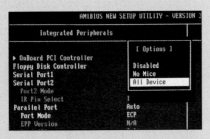

Originally, USB Legacy mode was intended to support USB keyboards when used at a system-command prompt or the BIOS setup program. Modern systems can also support mice and USB floppy drives. In some cases, enabling USB Legacy support for devices you don't use can cause other devices to stop functioning when you try to come out of a hibernate or standby mode. The USB Legacy mode is usually located in the Integrated Peripherals, Advanced, or other menus.

TWEAK 10 Use a Standby State that Makes Sense for You

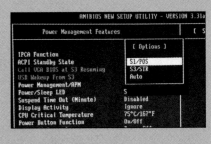

The Advanced Configuration and Power Interface (ACPI) standard supports several different standby modes. The most common are S1/POS and S3/STR. The S3 (Suspend to RAM) option saves more power, but doesn't work with devices that aren't 100 percent ACPI compliant. If you're using older peripherals or aren't sure if the devices you have connected to the computer work in S3 mode, enable S1 mode. You can find this option in the Power Management Features menu.

TWEAK 11 Don't Cache the BIOS

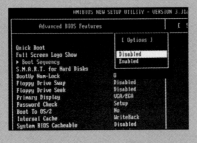

The contents of the system BIOS are copied to L2 cache when System BIOS Cacheable is enabled (it's usually found in the Advanced BIOS Features menu). This feature can cause problems, including system crashes if programs try to write to the BIOS area. Disable this option to avoid headaches, and you'll suffer little if any real-world impact on system performance.

TWEAK 12 Check Your Cache

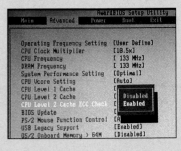

Most systems don't support ECC memory, but if your BIOS (and your processor's L2 cache) supports CPU Level 2 Cache ECC Checking, you can get much of the benefit of ECC memory with off-the-shelf non-parity memory. It also helps improve reliability when you overclock your system. This option is typically located in the Advanced or Chipset BIOS menu. To determine if your processor's L2 cache supports ECC, get the CPU data sheet from your proc vendor's web site.

TWEAK YOUR BIOS FOR MAXIMUM BOOT SPEED

TWEAK 1 Switch Hard Disks from Auto to User-Defined

STEP 1:
FIND YOUR DRIVES IN THE BIOS

By default, most modern systems are configured to detect the specifics of your hard drive every time you boot your PC. Switching the setting for installed drives to User-Defined, bypasses the drive-detection process and speeds boot times. The first BIOS setup screen on many systems is the Standard CMOS Feature screen. It'll display a list of drives currently installed in your PC. If you don't see a list of your drives, look for a setting called IDE Drive Auto-Detect on the main BIOS screen. It works the same way.

Before proceeding keep in mind that there's one good reason for keeping the Auto-Detect option enabled: If you use a hardware boot selection device, the auto-detect feature lets you select which drive(s) to use at startup.

```
                    AMIBIOS NEW SETUP UTILITY - VERSION 3.31a

        Standard CMOS Features                          [ Setu

    System Time                 :  16:42:31
    System Date                    Oct 03 2003 Fri        Primary
                                                          Confi
  ▸ Primary IDE Master            Maxtor 6E040L0
  ▸ Primary IDE Slave             Not Installed
  ▸ Secondary IDE Master          LITE-ON LTR-32123
  ▸ Secondary IDE Slave           WDC AC31200F

    Floppy Drive A                 1.44 MB 3½
    Floppy Drive B                 Not Installed

    Boot Sector Virus Protection   Disabled
```

STEP 2:
RECORD DRIVE SETTINGS

On most modern systems, the Automatic setting displays the drive's configuration. This configuration is read by the system BIOS from the hard disk's firmware using a feature called the Identify Drive command. This feature enables your BIOS to accurately install a hard disk, even if you don't know the correct settings for the drive.

Write down the info corresponding to the Cylinders, Heads, Write Precompensation, and Sectors (per track). Also write down settings for LBA Mode, Block Mode, Fast-Programmed I/O (PIO), and Ultra DMA Mode settings. Alternately, you can check the drive vendor's web site for this information.

Record this information accurately because you'll manually duplicate these settings in the next step. If you make an error recording the information, you will set the system incorrectly, and your computer won't boot.

```
                    AMIBIOS NEW SETUP UTILITY - VEI

        Primary IDE Master:Maxtor 6E040L0


    Type                          Auto
    Cylinders                     19680
    Heads                         16
    Write Precompensation
    Sectors                       255
       Maximum Capacity           41111 Mb
    LBA Mode                      On
    Block Mode                    On
    Fast Programmed I/O Modes     4
    32 Bit Transfer Mode          On
```

STEP 3:
CONFIGURE THE DRIVE AS USER-DEFINED

After you record the drive's settings, move the cursor to the Type field (currently set as Auto) and change it to User or User-Defined. The values for Cylinders, Heads, Sectors for track, and so on are now blank.

Enter the values you recorded in Step 2. Use the arrow keys to move from field to field. It's essential that the drive is configured manually the same way it was detected by the system. If you screw up one or more of the settings, the computer won't boot from the drive or be able to recognize its contents.

Repeat Steps 2 and 3 for each ATA/IDE drive installed (select CD or CD/DVD for CD-ROM or other optical drives). If you don't need to make any additional changes, press the key to save changes to the system BIOS setup. Your computer will restart.

```
                    AMIBIOS NEW SETUP UTILITY - VERSION 3.31a

        Primary IDE Master                              [ Set

    Type                          User               Select <A
    Cylinders                     19680              hard disk
    Heads                         16                 under DOS
    Write Precompensation         0                  Select <D
    Sectors                       255                Nerware a
       Maximum Capacity           41111 Mb
    LBA Mode                      On
    Block Mode                    On
    Fast Programmed I/O Modes     4
    32 Bit Transfer Mode          On
```

TWEAK 2 Streamline the Boot Sequence

STEP 1: DETERMINE THE CORRECT BOOT SEQUENCE

```
                    AMIBIOS NEW SETUP UTILITY

            Boot Sequence

1st Boot Device      Floppy:1.44 MB 3½
2nd Boot Device      CD/DVD:LITE-ON LTR-32123S
3rd Boot Device      IDE-0:Maxtor 6E040L0
Try Other Boot Devices              No
```

Even when you configure your drives as User-Defined, the typical system that boots off a hard drive still spends a lot of time looking for boot devices that you're probably not using, such as CD-ROM and floppy drives, Serial ATA, and others.

In most systems, the boot menu is part of the Advanced BIOS Features or Advanced BIOS Setup menu, or a submenu of that menu. Note that the floppy drive is listed first, followed by the CD-ROM drive and then the hard disk. On systems configured this way, the floppy and CD-ROM are checked for boot files before the hard disk, wasting valuable time at each reboot.

STEP 2: MAKE THE PRIMARY ATA/IDE DRIVE THE FIRST (OR ONLY) BOOT DEVICE

```
                    AMIBIOS NEW SETUP UTILIT

            Boot Sequence

1st Boot Device      IDE-0:Maxtor 6E040L0
2nd Boot Device      Disabled
3rd Boot Device      Disabled
Try Other Boot Devices              No
```

Select the first boot device and change it to the first ATA/IDE drive (might be referred to as IDE-0). Because this drive will always be used to boot the system, you can disable the other boot devices. If you need to boot from a CD or a floppy disk in the future (such as for an operating system upgrade or repair), you can restart the BIOS setup program and reconfigure the boot sequence menu accordingly.

TWEAK 3 Disable Memory Check and Floppy Drive Seek

```
                    AMIBIOS NEW SETUP UTILITY

            Advanced BIOS Features

Quick Boot                          Enabled
Full Screen Logo Show               Disabled
▶ Boot Sequence
S.M.A.R.T. for Hard Disks           Disabled
BootUp Num-Lock                     On
Floppy Drive Swap                   Disabled
Floppy Drive Seek                   Disabled
```

Many systems waste time at startup by performing a memory check and a floppy drive seek. The memory check seldom finds memory problems (even if they exist). If you don't boot from the floppy drive, there's no reason to check the drive at boot time for a boot disk. To disable the memory check, open the Advanced BIOS Features or Boot menu and enable the Quick Boot or Quick Power On Self Test options. Disable the Floppy Drive Seek option in the Advanced BIOS Features or Boot menu.

TWEAK 4 Disable Serial ATA (SATA) Host Adapter

If the SATA host adapter built into many modern systems is enabled but no drives are present, the BIOS wastes time trying to detect drives before giving up and continuing the boot process. The SATA Host Adapter setting is usually located in the Integrated Peripherals menu or a submenu of this menu.

In this BIOS, it is located in the OnBoard PCI Controller menu within the Integrated Peripherals menu. Disable it to more speedily boot!

```
                    AMIBIOS NEW SETUP UTILITY

        OnBoard PCI Controller

rial ATA Controller                 Disabled
dio Controller                      Disabled
```

TWEAK 5 Disable Onboard ATA BIOS

If your system has three or four ATA host adapter connectors instead of the normal pair, it's designed to support additional ATA drives in either normal mode or as an ATA RAID array. We love ATA RAID arrays here at *MaximumPC*, but if you don't have any drives connected to the hard drive controllers, leaving them enabled just wastes precious time at boot. The ATA BIOS option should be located in the Boot menu or in the Onboard Peripherals menu.

```
Main    Advanced    Power    Boot    Exit

1. IDE Hard Drive          [WDC WD800BB-32BSA0]
2. ATAPI CD-ROM            [PLEXTOR CD-R   PX-W]
3. Removable Device        [Disabled]
4. Other Boot Device       [INT18 Device (Netwo]

Plug & Play O/S            [Yes]
Reset Configuration Data   [No]
Boot Virus Detection       [Enabled]
Quick Power On Self Test   [Enabled]
```

TWEAK 6 Enable PCI IDE BusMaster

Bus mastering ATA/IDE host adapters provide a huge speed boost when enabled, but if they're disabled, your drives will be stuck using slower PIO access methods. Look for this option on the PnP/PCI menu or Integrated Peripherals menu. Don't forget to install the appropriate bus mastering drivers for your motherboard chipset in Windows to finish the job. ∎

```
                    AMIBIOS NEW SETUP UTI

        PNP/PCI Configurations

Plug and Play Aware O/S             Yes
Clear NVRAM                         No
PCI Latency Timer                   32
PCI IDE BusMaster                   Enabled
Primary Graphics Adapter            AGP
PCI Slot1 IRQ                       Auto
```

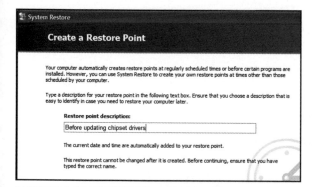

Before installing chipset drivers--or any drivers for that matter--be sure to create a system restore point just in case the new drivers cause instability.

Don't forget your chipset drivers!

Believe it or not, most of the computer problems we hear about at *Maximum PC* can be solved simply by updating the chipset (or "4-in-1") drivers. To get the latest drivers, go to the web site of the company that made your chipset. Drivers will probably also be available from your motherboard's manufacturer, but they may not be the latest and greatest. Chances are your chipset was made by one of the following companies: Intel (www.intel.com), AMD (www.amd.com), nVidia (www.nvidia.com), SiS (www.sis.com), VIA (www.viaarena.com), ALi (www.ali.com.tw), or ATI (www.ati.com). Once you've downloaded the drivers, close all open applications and disable any antivirus software that may be running in the background. At this point, we recommend setting a Windows XP System Restore Point in case the new drivers cause any problems. From the Start menu, open Programs, Accessories, then System Tools, and click on System Restore. Follow the step-by-step instructions to create a restore point. Finally, go ahead and install the chipset drivers, rebooting your computer when prompted to.

How To...

QUIET THE VACUUM CLEANER
You Call a PC

MAXIMUM PC
TIME TO COMPLETION
00:45
HOURS   MINUTES

Silencing tricks for a more peaceful PC experience, in less than an hour's time

BY JOHN TUMMINARO

Once upon a time, your average PC builder worried about excessive heat about as much as people in Antarctica do. PCs of yore didn't run all that hot, so only minimal cooling was required. But in today's world of 2GHz CPUs, 15,000rpm hard drives, and GeForce FX videocards, proper cooling has become essential for any system. The trouble is, most people worry so much about keeping temperature levels down that they sacrifice their tranquility with tons of loud fans.

If you want to quiet a noisy PC, there are some things you can do to knock off a few decibels and make your PC sound a little less like a nuclear reactor. The following three tips are stand-alone, so you can do as many or as few as you feel comfortable with.

Keep in mind that quieting your PC *will* increase your case temperature. If you're planning on over-clocking your PC, you might look to more exotic techniques such as water cooling.

What You'll Need

▶ **Papst 80mm 8412-NGL fan**
  (www.plycon.com)

▶ **Noise Control Magic Fleece**
  (www.plycon.com)

▶ **PC Power & Cooling Silencer 400 ATX**
  (www.pcpowerandcooling.com)

▶ **Foam padding or standard**
  air-conditioner filter

▶ **Felt pen**

▶ **Sharp scissors**

▶ **Ruler or measuring tape**

▶ **Phillips-head screwdriver**

▶ **Duct tape**

Fan, Fan, Thank You Fan

The biggest contributors to noise in any modern system are the fans. Adding a superquiet hard drive or power supply won't quiet your PC at all if you don't also do something about those bloody fans. The problem is that, as a general rule, quiet fans don't move as much air as loud fans, so they're less effective at cooling your hot components. The trick is to find the balance between noise and heat. For our PC we tested the 80mm Pabst fans that are sleeve-bearing and run at a superquiet 12dB, but move just a paltry 19.5 cubic-foot/minute (CFM) of air. At the other end of the spectrum would be the 80mm overclocker Delta fan that puts out an amazing 80CFM of air, but at a deafening 52.5dB. Remember that the decibel scale is logarithmic not linear. A 6dB sound is twice as loud as a 3dB sound, but a 9dB sound is twice as loud as a 6dB sound. Funky, ain't it?

BUY A BETTER FAN

First take stock of your case's cooling system. Determine which fans you want to replace with quieter ones. Measure them diagonally to determine the fan size before ordering replacements (most case fans are 80mm, while most CPU heatsink fans are 60mm).

Next, locate the retention mechanism (either screws or plastic clips) and remove them. Then disconnect the fan power cable from the source, either the motherboard or a four-pin Molex, and remove it from the case. Install the new fan by securing it with the retention mechanism, then plug it into either the motherboard or four-pin Molex. Make sure the fan is blowing in the correct direction—most fans have small arrows on one side that show both the direction of airflow and the rotation of the blades.

Take care not to start up your PC while the CPU fan is unattached. You'll be able to roast a tamale on the heatsink if you do.

This is a typical clip mount system for an 80mm fan. They're not standardized, so make sure you know what you're doing before you try to swap fans.

FILTERS LOOK HOOPTIE, BUT THEY WORK

Filters are a cheap way to reduce fan noise while keeping the inside of your case dust-free. First, find the appropriate material; we used the foam padding that came with our motherboard box, but you can buy cheap air filters at almost any hardware store that'll do the same thing.

Next, cut a square section of your filter material to go over your fan's air hole. Then simply apply tape (duct tape works best). You can either mount the filter on the inside or outside of the case, but if it's outside, make sure it's underneath the case panels to prevent your case from looking hooptie. You may need to use more than one layer if the material is thin, but verify that there's adequate airflow by placing your hand in front of the filter while the fan is blowing.

It may look undignified, but making a filter is highly effective and won't break the bank.

DISABLE THOSE EXTRANEOUS FANS

If you feel like your case is stacked with a few too many fans, you can always remove or disable a couple. To do this, simply unplug the fan's power connector from the motherboard, or the power supply if you're using a four-pin plug. To remove the fan, either unscrew it or unclip it from its mount and simply pull it out. It should be said that unless your case is absolutely jammed with fans, it's probably best to replace the fans with quieter ones rather than removing them altogether. But if you're on a budget and your CPU temps are south of 100° F, it won't hurt to excise a few of these little noisemakers.

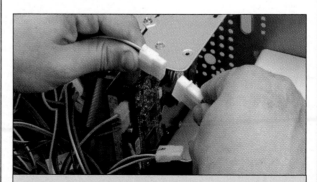

Don't go crazy and disconnect every single fan unless you want to start booking beach vacations inside your case.

Sound Dampening—Add a Little "Magic" to Your PC

Noise-dampening materials work by absorbing sound, keeping noise inside your case, where it belongs. European manufacturer Noise Control meets this need with Magic Fleece—a polyester microfibre specifically intended for quieting a noisy PC. Magic Fleece can greatly reduce your PC's noise levels, but at the price of higher case temperatures.

Before you begin, you'll want to make sure the airflow in your case is adequate. The catch is that installation of the Fleece is pretty much permanent. We recommend taping the material to your case

before you install it permanently, so you can make airflow adjustments if your PC overheats.

First decide which sides of your case you want to apply the Magic Fleece to. We recommend hitting both sides and the top. Then measure the dimensions of the piece you're going to apply. Make sure that when covering side panels you take pains not to cover pieces that affix the panel to your case. You should also make sure you have enough room between the side panel and the motherboard tray. Magic Fleece is 12mm thick and doesn't fit in many cases without

some adjustments.

Once you have the measurements of the sheets you need, use a felt pen to mark your cut out on the plastic covering the adhesive side of the Fleece. Then use scissors—sharp ones, this stuff is hard to cut—to cut your desired segments.

Next you'll want to lay the surface of the case panels flat and mark with a felt pen where the corners of the sheet will be placed. Then remove the plastic adhesive cover and apply the sheet, corners first, to the panel. Be very careful—this stuff is an absolute nightmare to reapply, so take care to do it right the first time.

First measure...

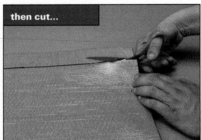
then cut...

then apply.

Power Supply Replacement

A power supply replacement is a nifty way to take your PC's noise level down a notch, but it's not for the faint of heart. Replacing a power supply is a major system upgrade, on par with a motherboard replacement. The PC Power & Cooling's Silencer line of power supplies are reliable, really quiet, and can be had with up to 400W total output.

First open your PC's side panel, and put the case open-side up on a table. Locate all the power connections to your current supply and remove them; this includes optical drives, hard drives, floppy, fans, and the big 20-pin connector on the motherboard (plus possible four-pin 12v connectors for P4 systems). You might want to write down the number of connections you're discon-

necting so you won't miss any when you plug them back in. Next, locate the four screws on the back of the PC that are holding the power supply in place, and remove them. Then simply pull the supply out of the case making sure not to snag anything.

To install the new supply, put it in the case where the old one was. Then make sure that the four screw holes line up; if they do, screw them in. Next reconnect all the power leads you just unplugged. Take your time and make sure you reconnect everything, or else your stuff won't function. After you do that, power on your PC and make sure all the drives are recognized and all the fans are spinning.

If you're using the power supply that came with your case, you might be able to upgrade to something quieter.

Conclusion

To test the effect your changes have had on your noise levels, take your PC into a quiet room and close the door. Then power it up and see how much quieter it has become. The test PC we quieted sounded like a Dustbuster mini-vac before we worked on it. Afterwards, it was near whisper quiet, and the CPU core ran a substantial but not extreme 21° F hotter than it had before (going from 101° F to 122° F). ∎

How To...

SET UP YOUR

MAXIMUM PC
TIME TO COMPLETION
01:00
HOURS MINUTES

CRT

Monitor tweaking instructions from the man who develops *DisplayMate*, the industry-standard software for tuning displays

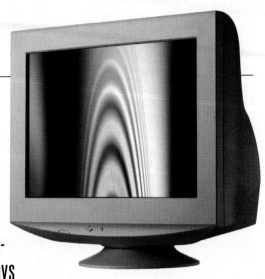

BY RAYMOND M. SONEIRA

PRELIMINARIES

First, it's important to select the right location for your CRT. Make sure the screen isn't facing any windows or areas of high glare. Position the monitor so that the screen is about 18 to 24 inches away from your face, with the top of the screen just below eye level.

Use a single video cable—extension cables will degrade the image quality substantially. Use the shortest cable length that will work. Compared with the standard VGA DB-15 cable, BNC-5 cable connections provide noticeably better image quality only

with cable lengths greater than 15 feet. So for short runs, the standard 6-foot cable that comes with most monitors will likely do fine.

As for the optimum room lighting, use indirect, medium-intensity lighting that's neutral in color. If possible, have the wall area behind your monitor gently backlit. Excessively dark environments or fluorescent lighting will heighten your eye's flicker response.

SET THE REFRESH RATE

Set the refresh rate to the lowest rate that doesn't produce any annoying or uncomfortable flicker sensation. For just about everyone, this is 75Hz. Setting it lower than this value isn't recommended. Setting the refresh rate higher than necessary will needlessly degrade image sharpness due to video bandwidth effects (the pixel clock rate increases with the refresh rate, and this can lead to blurriness). Of course, if you're a 3D gamer and a low refresh rate is bottle-necking your frame rates, follow your best judgment when raising rates.

To check for subliminal flicker that's slightly below your threshold of sensation, you need to maximize the conditions needed for detection. First, turn off all of the lights, then look at a screen that is predominantly peak white, such as a blank page in a word processing program. Now, turn up the Contrast control to maximum, and put your face close to the screen. If you experience a fluttering brightness sensation, you may need to increase the refresh rate.

Video System Information

```
Current Windows Video Mode Information
          Screen Pixels : 1280H x 1024V
          Screen Colors : 16,777,216
          System Colors : 16,777,216
         Intensity Levels : 256

      Screen Orientation : Landscape 4 : 3
     Reported Screen Size : 320 x 240 millimeters
      Screen Aspect Ratio : 1.33 H / V
       Pixel Aspect Ratio : 0.94 H / V
            Square Pixels : Almost

         Color Capability : True Color
             Color Depth : 24 Bits per Pixel
            Color Palette : Not Available
            Color Planes : 1
```

[OK]
[Print]
[Help]

SET THE RESOLUTION AND ASPECT RATIO

One of the great advantages of CRTs is that they perform nicely over a wide range of resolutions and aspect ratios. Here are the recommended operating resolutions for typical CRT monitors:

▶ 17-inch: 1024x768 to 1152x864
▶ 19-inch: 1152x864 to 1280x1024
▶ 21-inch: 1280x1024 to 1600x1200

Your videocard also plays an important role in image quality. For the higher resolutions be sure to use a high-end graphics board.

Note that the popular resolution of 1280x1024 has a native aspect ratio of 5:4=1.25, which is noticeably smaller than the 4:3=1.33 native aspect ratio of almost all CRTs. Most CRT users will fill the screen at this resolution, stretching the image horizontally, resulting in non-square pixels. That's OK most of the time, but may result in aspect ratio errors for some applications; circles will appear slightly elliptical, for example. In photographic images, people will appear 7 percent fatter.

It's also important to find out what Screen Aspect Ratio the Windows driver is reporting. For most resolutions it should be 4:3=1.33, but it's important to check because it's sometimes wrong. For example, on my brand-new Dell Inspiron notebook, the driver reports a 1.40 Aspect Ratio when it's actually 1.33. At 1280x1024, it's a toss-up whether you'll see 1.25 or 1.33. If you have an LCD, it should be 1.25, and if you have a CRT it should be 1.33. You can use any *DisplayMate* product (including the demo) to check this. Select "Video System Information" and look under "Screen Aspect Ratio" (see figure 1). If it's wrong, call the manufacturer to get an updated driver with the right value.

DEGAUSS THE SCREEN

All CRT color monitors are affected by the Earth's magnetic field and need to be regularly degaussed. Monitors automatically do this when they are turned on (that's the source of the buzzing sound). Many CRT monitors also have a front-panel degauss button or a menu option to do this manually. If you keep your monitor on all the time, you should hit the button periodically. The schedule will depend on both your monitor and the magnetic environment it's in. If you notice a change after degaussing, do it more frequently. If not, do it less frequently. Moving the monitor or allowing any steel objects to come near it also

This line is written in Dark Gray and should be dim but visible.
To adjust the intensity of this line use the Brightness Control.

This line is written in Gray and should appear intermediate in intensity between Dark Gray and White.

This line is written in White but should not appear too bright or blurred. Use the Contrast Control to adjust the intensity of this line.

Brightness and Contrast

calls for immediate degaussing. Please note that you can get only one full-power degauss about every 20 minutes.

Keep magnetic appliances away from your monitor. Also keep all of those black box transformers and power supplies away from the monitor. Finally, nearby CRTs can affect each other, so try to keep them at least a foot apart.

WE'RE ALMOST READY TO TWEAK

Most monitors need a full 30 minutes to warm up and stabilize. Make sure the monitor has warmed up before you begin setting the controls. You should also record all your existing monitor control values. If your control settings show digital values, record them so you can restore the values should you need to later on.

Most monitors have a menu selection to restore all settings back to their factory values. Consider resetting the monitor if you're having trouble with it, or if it was attached to another computer previously. Otherwise, it's probably best to keep the current values so you're not starting from scratch.

The settings for most of the controls interact to varying degrees, so you may need to go through this setup procedure more than once. Familiarize yourself with all the available user controls by either reading the manual or systematically going through each of the onscreen menus and buttons. Some buttons may have special dedicated functions when you're not in menu mode, so check each one in turn. For a quick first pass, roughly set the Brightness, Contrast, Size, and Position controls so they look about right. We'll set each one more carefully in due time.

DISPLAYMATE

DisplayMate software is designed to help you set up and tune monitors for optimum image and picture quality using all the controls available on your monitor and videocard control panel. It does this with a series of specialized test patterns that you look at while making adjustments. Each test pattern within *DisplayMate* includes a Test Information screen that tells you what to look for and what adjustments to make. In many cases, the software can help you work around image-quality problems.

DisplayMate for Windows is designed for non-experts. *Maximum PC* uses the advanced *DisplayMate Multimedia Edition* for testing and reviewing monitors in the magazine. To try out the demo version, head over to www.displaymate.com/patterns.html.

BRIGHTNESS CONTROL

Your CRT's brightness control is poorly named because it has very little effect on the screen brightness. In fact, it's used to adjust the black-level of the monitor so that the dark end of the gray-scale is properly reproduced. If it's set too low, the darkest grays are reproduced as black instead of gray. If it's set too high, black is reproduced as dark gray. This is bad, because losing the ability to produce black significantly reduces the contrast capability of the monitor.

Accurately setting the brightness control is the single-most important adjustment on any display. *DisplayMate* includes a number of test patterns that help you accurately set the black-level of the monitor. The first screen in the

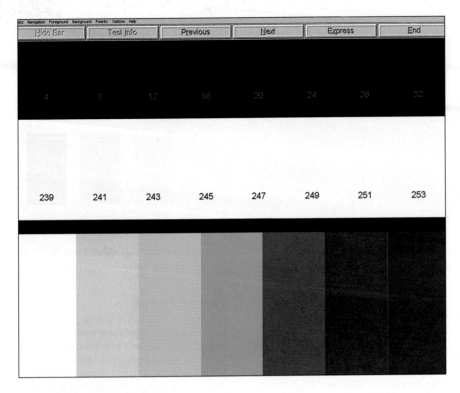

Figure 3: Extreme Gray-Scale

SIZE AND POSITION

Your next step is to carefully frame the image on the screen. Adjust the Horizontal and Vertical Size and Position controls to fill the screen almost to the outer edge. Leave one or two millimeters of border space to allow for some variation and drift in the image. If the monitor isn't performing well, it may be best to restrict the image size and stay away from the edges of the screen. Use the "Screen Framing and Aspect Ratio" test pattern (available in all *DisplayMate* products) for the adjustments (see figure 4).

GEOMETRY

Most monitors will provide additional controls to reduce or eliminate different types of geometric distortion. The controls you're most likely to find are pincushion (which gives the monitor a waist at the middle); bow (similar to pincushion, but both sides curve in the same direction); keystone (like a trapezoid); skew (like a parallelogram); and rotation. Play with each control so that you understand exactly what each one does.

DisplayMate has quite a few specialized test patterns for adjusting screen geometry. If you're using the *DisplayMate* demo, bring up the "Screen Framing" test pattern.

(a) The first control to adjust, if you have it, is screen rotation. Adjust the control so that the line at the bottom of the frame is as parallel as possible with the edge of the screen. If there is any curvature along the bottom or top of the frame, you'll need a vertical pincushion adjustment (which is seldom found on low-end monitors).

(b) Because all monitors have either flattened or perfectly flat screens, they all experience pincushion distortion

DisplayMate demo, "Brightness and Contrast Adjustment," includes dark gray, light gray, and peak white text that tells you how to make the initial adjustments of both the brightness and contrast controls (see figure 2). Basically, you increase the brightness control until the screen background becomes just visible. Then you decrease it until the background becomes black again. The second test pattern in the demo, "Extreme Gray-Scale," will guide you through making a more accurate setting of the brightness control (see figure 3). Look at the top row of dark blocks, labeled 4 to 32. Adjust the Brightness control so you can see just the 8 Block, and the 4 Block is indistinguishable from the black background.

CONTRAST CONTROL

The contrast control sets the monitor's peak brightness. It controls the white-level but has little effect on the black-level. If the monitor appears too bright to you, use the contrast control to lower the brightness to a more comfortable level. On the flip side, you have to be careful about turning up the contrast control too high because the image can be substantially degraded. Here's the proper setup method: On the demo test

pattern "Extreme Gray-Scale," increase the contrast control until the 251 or 253 Blocks are indistinguishable from the white background. Now back it off until they just reappear. On some monitors you may reach the maximum limit for the control before this happens. Don't worry, that's perfectly fine. If the image is now too bright for comfort, decrease the contrast control until the screen looks good to you.

Next, in the demo, look at the first "Brightness and Contrast" screen. The text that's written in bright white should appear almost as sharp as the text written in gray. If it appears blurred, you'll need to reduce the Contrast Control until the text appears relatively sharp again. Now move to the second test pattern, "Extreme Gray-Scale." Look at the frame that encloses the dark and bright blocks at the top of the screen. If there's a kink in the frame, with the bright row appearing wider than the dark row, then there is a screen regulation problem. Decrease the contrast control until this effect mostly goes away.

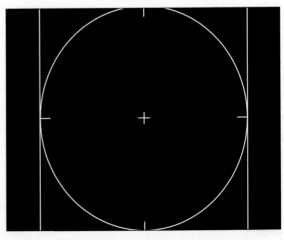

Figure 4: Screen Framing and Aspect Ratio

that needs to be electronically removed. Most monitors give you a horizontal pincushion control. If it's turned too low, the frame will be pinched in on both sides; if it's turned too high, the frame will be turned out on both sides and look like a barrel. Adjust it so that both sides are as straight as possible. It's likely that both sides won't be perfectly symmetric, so pick the best compromise.

(c) Many monitors will have a Bow or Pincushion Balance Control that will let you adjust the left and right sides of the frame so that the pincushion is symmetric. After you do this, go back to step (b) above and repeat it. Then repeat this step also.

(d) If the top and bottom sides of the frame aren't the same length, use the Keystone control to make them equal.

(e) If the left and right sides of the frame aren't square, use the Skew control to transform the parallelogram frame into a square frame.

(f) Because the Keystone and Skew controls interact significantly, you'll need to repeat steps (d) and (e) until you find the best compromise.

(g) All of the geometry controls interact to some degree, and by jockeying each of them a bit, you can generally improve your screen image. For example, if there's some residual pincushion curvature that you just can't seem to get rid of, use the Keystone and Skew controls together with the Pincushion and Bow controls to reduce it. You're transferring geometric errors from one place to another so that they all balance out as best as possible. It's all about managing visual error budgets.

CONVERGENCE

A color CRT is actually made up of separate red, green, and blue displays inside a single tube. The images all have to line up really well in order to show fine detail. For example, on a 17-inch display at 1024x768, the individual pixels are just a bit more than 1/100th of an inch apart. The alignment of the red, green, and blue primaries is called convergence. Their misalignment is called misconvergence, which leads to color fringing and loss of sharpness.

For example, if red and green aren't perfectly converged, when you draw a

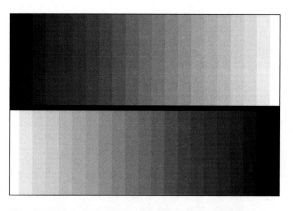

DisplayMate's **various grayscale ramps (found in the full versions of the app) graduate from five to 256 steps, and can teach you volumes about your monitor's ability to properly render gray tones (which are important in photographic images).**

yellow line it will have a red fringe on one side of the yellow core and a green fringe on the other. Similarly, when you draw a black character on a white screen, and R, G, and B aren't properly converged, the black strokes will be filled in to some degree, and the image will look a bit colored and fuzzy. Convergence is very important, but bear in mind that no monitor is ever perfectly converged. Generally, convergence is best at the center, and worst in the corners.

If your monitor includes Static Horizontal and Vertical Convergence controls, you can control the overall alignment of the red, green, and blue images. They won't fix problems in any one particular part of the screen, but will allow you to adjust the relative alignment over the entire screen. Most of the time you want the best agreement at the center, but if one part of the screen is really bad, you have the option of improving it at the expense of the other parts of the screen. It's a compromise, and you have to decide on your error budget.

Green is the brightest of the primaries, so red and blue are varied for the best agreement with green. *Display Mate* has a number of very sensitive test patterns for detecting misconvergence. In the demo, you can use the "Screen Framing" test pattern to adjust the Static Convergence. Convergence is generally worst on the outer borders, particularly the corners, so use the outer frame to look for

color fringing around white. The central cross lets you check for color fringing at the center. Vary the Convergence Controls to see how they affect the fringing. Find the setting that provides the best overall convergence. For higher sensitivity, switch from white (which has all three primaries) to one of the secondary colors, like magenta (which is made up of only red and blue, and will let you track more easily the two colors that are generally off the most).

MOIRÉ REDUCTION

Annoying moiré interference patterns arise from interactions between the pixels in an image and the phosphor elements (the red, green, and blue dots or lines) that coat the screen. All CRTs have some degree of moiré, and in fact, the sharper the CRT, the stronger the moiré will be. Fortunately most monitors have some form of moiré reduction control. Because moiré reduction actually blurs the image a bit, you want to use the least amount that works.

To adjust for moiré, you first need a pattern that accentuates the moiré; *DisplayMate* has a dozen moiré test patterns that you can use. The *DisplayMate* demo has a pattern for adjusting pixel tracking on LCDs that will also let you adjust for moiré on a CRT. First turn off the moiré reduction, or set it to zero. Slowly increase the moiré reduction until the wispy pattern weakens significantly. Don't try to make it go away entirely. If you overdo it, you will wind up blurring the image excessively. ■

Dr. Raymond M. Soneira is President of DisplayMate Technologies Corp. For more information, go to www.displaymate.com.

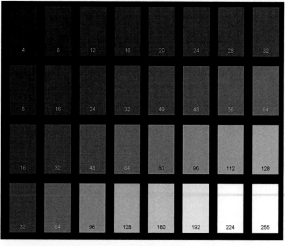

The color tracking screen, found in the full versions of *DisplayMate,* **helps you identify color-tint variations in otherwise neutral grays.**

How To...

SET UP A
DUAL DISPLAY

Why settle for a single monitor when you can easily have twice the screen real estate?

BY DAN DINICOLO

MAXIMUM PC
TIME TO COMPLETION
01:12
HOURS   MINUTES

Imagine having twice the desktop space to work on your *Photoshop* files. Or to accommodate a multitude of open browser windows. Think of all the multitasking you could accomplish if you weren't confined to a solitary computer screen. It's not such a lofty fantasy, folks. As long as you have the physical space for two screens, a dual-display setup is within your reach.

Whether your loyalties lie with nVidia or ATI, both companies offer multi-monitor support in any of their modern videocards. And their respective setup applications are feature rich and user friendly.

For more on doubling your display pleasure, read on.

DISPLAY HARDWARE
The benefits of using multiple monitors to increase the size of the Windows desktop are obvious. You have more screen to work on, plain and simple. In the old-school multi-display scenario, a PC had to be outfitted with a separate videocard for each screen, a configuration that has been supported since Windows 98. However, both nVidia and ATI now make multiple-display capabilities standard fare on their modern videocard models, enabling two monitors to be connected to a single card.

While different video output configurations are available, both vendors prefer to use a common configuration that employs one traditional VGA connector and one DVI connector. CRT monitors generally use a standard VGA connection to pass an analog signal between the videocard and monitor. The DVI connector is the preferred digital input for flat-panel displays. ATI and nVidia also provide an adapter that converts the DVI connector to standard VGA, so dual CRTs can be accommodated.

NVIEW VS. HYDRAVISION
Whether you use the *nView* or *HydraVision* app to run your dual-display setup depends entirely on your videocard. Is it from nVidia or ATI? However, if you're in the market for a new videocard, it's well worth knowing the differences and similarities between the two.

First, both nVidia's *nView* and ATI's *HydraVision* support features such as user profiles, hotkey assignments, application position memory, and virtual desktops. But the respective products do incorporate some different feature sets that may be important to you.

For example, let's say you intend to play a variety of 3D games on your multiple-monitor system. While *nView* provides 3D acceleration for DirectX and OpenGL across both screens, *HydraVision* provides such support for only DirectX. Another neat feature included with *nView* is the ability to manipulate various multiple-monitor properties on an application-by-application basis. For example, you could have *Outlook*

Express open in a different resolution than *Internet Explorer* if that was your preference. *HydraVision* does not include this capability.

Finally, for users running Windows 2000, only *nView* enables you to configure the properties of individual monitors independently—for example, having two monitors work at different refresh rates and resolutions. Windows XP users need not worry as both packages support this capability with the OS.

MONITOR POSITIONING
The first thing to consider in any multiple-monitor configuration is the positioning of the monitors themselves. For example, after plugging in both monitors you might notice that the manner in which they display output is effectively reversed from what you want—the monitor on the right displays your Start menu, and the monitor on the left extends your desktop. Instead of physically repositioning the hardware, you can use the Display applet in Control

Assign Hotkeys in HydraVision

Quickly accomplish multiple display tasks by setting up custom hotkeys

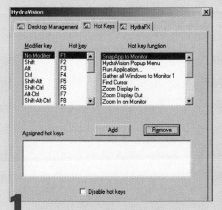

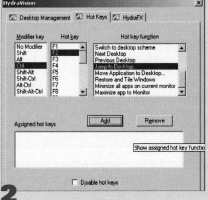

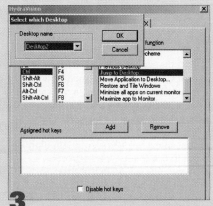

1 Click Start, point to Programs and then choose HydraVision. The HydraVision program opens to the Desktop Management tab by default. Click the Hot Keys tab.

2 Click a Modifier key, such as Ctrl, and Hot key such as F4 in their associated text boxes. Pick an action in the Hot-key function text box, such as Jump to Desktop. Click Add.

3 When prompted, select a desktop in the Desktop name drop-down box and click OK. Additional hotkey combinations can be added or removed as necessary according to your needs. Click OK to exit.

Panel to switch positions. Access the Settings tab and then drag the monitor icons to match the physical positioning of the monitors themselves. To change the display properties of either monitor, click that monitor and then edit the resolution or color quality as you normally would.

DESKTOP MODES

Once you have multiple monitors configured and connected, there are a number of different ways they can be utilized. For example, *nView* enables you to configure your monitors in four modes known as Standard, Clone, Horizontal span, and Vertical span.

Standard mode effectively disables *nView*, limiting you to a single monitor. In Clone mode, the contents of both monitors is identical. While this may not seem practical, it's a great feature if you're giving a presentation and wish to view your desktop both on your own screen and, say, a large television simultaneously. Horizontal span literally spans your entire desktop, including the taskbar, across two screens. So, you'll find your Start menu at the far left of one screen and your System tray on the far right of the other. The Vertical span mode provides a similar effect – just don't try to balance one monitor on top of the other! To get at these settings, access the Advanced section of your display settings, click the nVidia

GPU tab, select Advanced Properties and then press the Desktop Manager Configuration button on the Desktop Utilities tab.

If you're looking for more desktop space, use the Extend my Windows desktop on to this monitor checkbox on the Settings tab of the Display applet. An extended monitor doesn't extend your taskbar, instead the second display adds more to your desktop area. This can also be controlled from the Desktop Utilities tab.

VIRTUAL DESKTOPS

As if two desktops weren't enough, both *nView* and *HydraVision* provide support for multiple virtual desktops. This means you're able to create multiple desktop environments that you can switch between to reduce clutter.

For example, you might run *Internet Explorer* on one virtual desktop and Adobe *Photoshop* on another. This is a great feature if you commonly run multiple applications simultaneously, and have trouble identifying them on a cluttered taskbar. While it takes a little while to get used to the feature, it quickly becomes useful.

In *HydraVision* this capability is called MultiDesk and provides for up to nine individual virtual desktops. The *nView* equivalent provides access to 32 virtual desktops. *HydraVision* uniquely includes the ability to switch between desktops using the scroll wheel on your mouse.

APPLICATION POSITION RECALL

An excellent feature of both *nView* and *HydraVision* is the ability to have your system remember where and how you want your applications to be opened. Known as application position memory, this feature must be user-enable and subsequently provides great dividends.

For example, let's say you want *Outlook Express* to always be opened to your second monitor. If you position it there (by dragging it from the first monitor) and then maximize it, the next time you open the app it will open at that same location. This saves you the trouble of having to reposition individual windows.

In *HydraVision*, this feature is implemented by a single checkbox. Open *HydraVision* from your Start menu, and then check the Automatic position memory checkbox on the Desktop Management tab. Opening the *nView* Desktop Manager applet in Control Panel, and then checking "Enable application position memory on the Windows tab" accesses this setting for *nView* systems.

APPLICATION INTEGRATION

For those who do a lot of Web surfing, both nView and HydraVision offer some great browser integration features. One of our favourites is the ability to open links on a new screen. Instead of just clicking on a link and having it open in the same window or a different window on the same monitor, you can choose to 'send' the link to a different window, or even a different virtual desktop. This is a handy feature when using search engines such as Google, enabling you to leave your search open in one monitor while viewing the new pages on the second monitor.

Along the same lines, *nView* also makes it possible to send applications to other windows or desktops in the same manner. To enable this feature, open Desktop Manager and check the "Extend application system menus with nView options" checkbox. It's also worth digging around in the Menu Options section of the nView Extensions in the shortcut menu, since this allows you to control individual application settings.

HOTKEYS AND ZOOMING

Time is money, right? Well, both *nView* and *HydraVision* have the facility to assign shortcut hotkeys to a variety of different system functions. For example, you could assign Ctrl + F4 to jump to a certain virtual desktop, or you could assign a different key to start a particular program. See the walkthrough section on the previous page for more on assigning hotkeys in *HydraVision*.

Both programs include the ability to zoom a selected area on one monitor over to the second monitor. In *nView*, open the Desktop Manager and then access the Effects menu. This will enable you to configure zoom settings, such as

whether the tool should work using a magnifying-glass effect, be centered on the cursor, or work using your mouse's scroll wheel. Overall, this is a valuable feature for anyone doing precision graphics editing.

PROFILES

If you've got multiple users using a single PC, or have different multiple-monitor requirements based on different situations, you can easily address the issue with profiles. Think of a profile as being much like your desktop settings in Windows—every time you log on, the same settings appear.

Profiles in a program like *nView* are similar, except that you can have multiple profiles and easily switch between them. For example, you could create one profile for graphics editing, another for doing presentations and so forth. Furthermore, you can easily assign hotkeys that would enable you to switch between them.

To create a new profile, access the *nView* Desktop Manager Profiles tab, create a new profile, load it, make your changes, and then save it. When done, be sure to assign hot keys to the profiles to make switching a breeze.

SPECIAL EFFECTS

Finally, both programs also provide some advanced effects that will help make managing your desktop environment easier. The best of these is

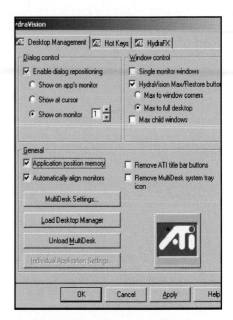

Enable application position memory to remember the location where a window was last used.

the transparency feature, which means you're able to set transparency levels to windows so you can see what's beneath them. This is a far preferable alternative to minimizing and maximizing windows endlessly to try to find a rogue dialog. Configure transparency settings from the Effects window in *nView* Desktop Manager, or from the HydraFX menu in *HydraVision*. ∎

Dual-Display the Old-Fashioned Way

Enable your PC for multiple displays using a second videocard

So you don't have an nVidia or ATI dual-display videocard? Well, the good news is that Windows versions since 98 (although not NT) all support the use of two graphics cards for multiple-monitor configurations. Although you'll be missing some of the features included with the *nView* and *HydraVision* software packages, you'll still have the benefits of more desktop space to work with. Furthermore, a variety of utilities (including some found in Microsoft's Power Toys) provide some of the features mentioned in this article, such as virtual desktops.

To configure your system to use two graphics cards, the cards used must be either AGP- or PCI-based. Windows can support up to nine displays in this type of

configuration, although finding this many free PCI slots may present you with a small problem. Unfortunately, older ISA cards are not supported. One display will be configured as the primary display and another as the secondary, but it's not possible to configure which is which. The primary display will be the one visible during the boot process and you may be able to change the settings there if your BIOS permits it.

If your second desktop does not function correctly after rebooting, access the Display program and ensure that the option to extend your desktop to the second desktop is checked. In addition, be sure that you have the correct driver installed for each device, since each is still an independent card with its own requirements.

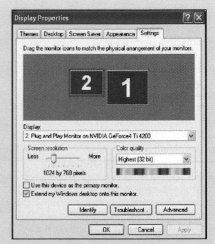

Use the Settings tab to configure individual monitors in a multiple monitor configuration

CPU Overclocking
The Overclocker's Handbook

Increase your CPU speed—*for free.* Here's how in vivid detail....

In this section, we show you how to overclock your CPU, adding a few extra horses to your already ragin' mod. The tricks you learn here will help you match your mod's actual performance to its already tight look.

All Men Are Created Equal . . . Processors Are Not

All PC processors are *not* created equal. Sure, your Pentium 4 and your buddy's Pentium 4 might both be clocked at 2GHz, but this is only because Intel rated the processors for 2GHz before the two CPUs left the factory. But when it comes right down to it, every processor is a unique entity. One marked to run at 2GHz might actually run just fine at 2.2GHz, while another marked for 2.2GHz might not have any headroom at all.

These speed tolerance variances are inevitable—each CPU is unique, and on the microscopic circuit level, some are more accepting of higher frequencies than others. That's why each CPU is individually tested for its speed potential after it pops out of the toaster, so to speak. If a proc can run days on end at, say, 2.2GHz without giving up the ghost, then it's labeled accordingly and tossed into the 2.2GHz bin. If not, it's given a more modest rating. This way, CPU manufacturers can reasonably guarantee 100% reliable performance—and thus reduce warranty claims.

CPUs manufactured during the launch of a new processing technology tend to have less frequency headroom than CPUs manufactured at the end of a processing technology's lifetime. That's because after the initial CPU launch, chip designs are tweaked and refined and manufacturers such as AMD and Intel find craftier and craftier ways to produce CPUs capable of running at faster speeds. So, for example, a 1.6GHz P4A manufactured at the launch of Intel's Northwood process technology might have much less frequency headroom than a 1.6GHz P4A manufactured at the end of the Northwood's run. And get this: It's typical for CPU companies to manufacture a whole slew of extremely capable processors and then label them with lower speed grades to fulfill orders for lower-priced CPUs! That's right—the processor that's been sitting inside your system for two years might actually have been created to run at faster speeds.

And you can make it run at faster speeds if you practice the dark art of overclocking. In the following pages we teach you the basics, walk you through four case studies, and show you how to exploit the quirks of chip production to realize the full potential of your CPU.

The Basics

So, what is overclocking? Simply put, it's the practice of running a computer chip at a higher frequency than it's been originally set to run. CPU overclocking can be accomplished in two ways: by increasing the speed of a system's frontside bus (abbreviated to FSB, the bus that connects the CPU with the chipset) and by changing the CPU's multiplier setting. Because a CPU's frequency is determined by multiplying FSB speed by the multiplier setting (for example, a 133MHz FSB paired with a 10x multiplier equals 1333MHz), you can increase the frequency of your CPU by upping either value.

The overclocking process varies from motherboard to motherboard, but in most cases, settings for the frontside bus speed can be changed by making an adjustment in your system BIOS. The multiplier ratio setting is often located here as well, but with some mobos, you can only change the multiplier ratio via a physical switch on the motherboard itself. Sometimes you also need to increase your CPU's core voltage because a faster chip has a larger appetite for power. The voltage setting usually hides in your BIOS as well. Consult your motherboard user's manual for specifics on where your FSB, voltage, and multiplier settings might be hiding.

Overclocking involves many risks, the least of which is invalidating the warranties on your processor and related system components. System instability is also a possibility, and in extreme cases, you could irreparably damage your computer—though this is usually caused by an inadequate cooling setup. So, as you consider overclocking as a feasible means of increasing CPU performance, you must also consider adding extra cooling to your rig. At the very least, this might mean adding a high-performance fan/heatsink to your CPU. This will get you through a "modest" overclock. If, however, you're considering a drastic overclock or are dealing with a CPU that just doesn't take well to *any* overclocking, you might need to consider exotic cooling—namely watercooling—to prevent system instability and damage.

For purposes of this section, we will simply encourage you to use the following products for your ventures into the world of overclocking:

- **Conventional heatsink/fan combos for P4s**—Intel's newer bundled P4 coolers are very efficient, featuring a powerful fan, radial fins, and a copper central post. Chances are you'll find this combo to be adequate for modest overclocking adventures. For a more serious solution, try Swiftech's MCX478V, combined with a quality 92mm fan. As to fan choice, the Tornado TD9238H is the best performing but loudest (56.4dBA) 92mm available: 119CFM at 4800rpm. If noise is a concern, the Thermoflow TF-9225 is good choice. It features a thermal probe for active rpm throttling between 1850rpm and 3100rpm, with peak ratings of 58.5CFM at 40dBA.

- **Exotic cooling for P4s**—If you plan to throttle up your CPU into the red, we recommend investing in either liquid cooling of Koolance's Exos system (www.koolance.com) or a phase-change system care of the Chip-Con Prometeia www.prometeia.com). Both the Exos and Prometeia are mainstream designs with superb efficiency. An additional possibility is thermoelectric peltier cooling, such as the Swiftech MCW5002-PT hybrid peltier/liquid cooler. See http://www.swiftnets.com/products/mcw5002-PT.asp.

A cooling enhancer for liquid systems is available in the form of the Swiftech MCW-CHILL 452, an inline peltier cooler. See http://www.swiftnets.com/products/MCWCHILL-452.asp.

- **Conventional heatsink/fan combos for Athlon XPs**—If you have a late-model AMD that came with a copper-based cooler, you'll find that it works well for sober overclocking. Otherwise, try the Cooler Master Aero7 (www.coolermaster.com.hk), which features a quiet and powerful centrifugal blower. The Swiftech MCX6400-V is the AMD64 premier air-cooled heatsink currently on the market when combined with a quality 92mm fan.

- **Exotic cooling for Athlon XPs**—If you're going to really turn up the heat on your Athlon XP, we recommend the same water and phase-change systems previously noted for the P4.

Do You Feel Lucky, Punk? Well, Do Ya?

CPU overclocking can sometimes result in destroyed processors, motherboards, and other system components. Don't even consider overclocking unless you feel comfortable with the risks. Overclockers who approach the dark arts with patience, caution, and reason will rarely (if ever) hurt their hardware. But you never know when science will go awry...

Please note that frontside bus overclocking is riskier than simply changing the CPU multiplier ratio because on most mobos, every increase in FSB frequency also causes an increase in PCI bus frequency. And if the PCI bus speed deviates too far from its 33MHz spec, some PCI devices can experience problems. If at all possible, use a motherboard that allows you to keep the PCI bus at or near 33MHz, even when system bus speeds are increased. Check motherboard manuals and spec sheets for details.

Is Your CPU a Prime Candidate?

The quickest way to find out how much extra sauce you can squeeze from your CPU is by researching how far others have pushed similar CPUs. That's what makes online forums so helpful (at the end of this chapter, we point you to our favorites). If you have an Athlon XP 3000+, just ask other owners how much success they've had with the same type of chip.

As a general rule, "mature" CPU technologies tend to be more overclockable. For example, while the original Thoroughbred Athlon processors were fabbed on a 0.13-micron process, they were often less overclockable than the 0.18-micron Palomino Athlons—a seemingly strange anomaly because "thinner" process technologies definitely run cooler than "thicker" process technologies, and coolness aids overclocking. But sometimes even a particularly efficient, cool-running process technology can't mitigate the overclocking constraints of a core design that resists speed increases, and the design will have to be finagled. In the case of the Thoroughbred, AMD said the chip had low frequency headroom because of "congestion" in the circuits. By adding an extra layer to the chip for routing signals, AMD says it was able to accelerate the clock speeds of the Athlon XP.

Most people would agree that Intel's Northwood P4s have been overclocker darlings. The Northwood chip's heat spreader—a slug of metal that helps pull heat from the tiny core—is just one of the features that make that P4 overclocking friendly.

Nonetheless, the Athlon XP has always been quite popular among overclockers because it can be "unlocked." All P4s and many Athlon XPs sold to the general public are multiplier-locked, leaving the frontside bus as your only overclocking path. Intel CPUs can't be unlocked, but most Athlons can be unlocked with a bit of finesse, making them quite popular with speed freaks.

The Athlon 64 and Opteron processors are FID locked. Only the Athlon FX is unlocked at this time.

Thunderbirds can be unlocked with just a pencil. Palominos require an unlocking kit, such as Highspeed PC's XP Unlocking Kit (www.highspeedpc.com). Thoroughbred B and Barton CPUs, however, require a bit more tinkering to unlock the lower multiplier settings you need for overclocking. Some tricks require shorting pins. Yikes!

Of course, some lucky (or well-connected) individuals have managed to obtain unlocked P4 engineering samples. To see if you're the owner of a rare unlocked P4, head to your BIOS and try changing the multiplier ratio. If it works, thank the processor god for making you one of the lucky ones.

The right motherboard is just as important as the right CPU for overclocking. Boards that allow adjustments to FSB speed, multiplier ratio, and CPU core voltage are your friends. This means most Intel-branded motherboards are not your friends. Even the Intel Bonanza boards, which let you do some mild overclocking tweaks, aren't ideal for overclocking. We suggest you turn to motherboards from Abit (www.abit.com.tw) and Asus (www.asus.com) for features such as voltage controls and PCI/AGP dividers. (These dividers let you lock down PCI and AGP bus speeds while simultaneously increasing system bus speeds—a boon for maintaining overall system stability. After all, the idea is to overclock your CPU, and not the other devices that plug into your mobo.)

Good overclocking mobos also offer temperature monitoring and an emergency shutdown feature to help prevent CPU meltdown. Athlon XP users should seek out a motherboard that supports the thermal diode integrated onto the core of an AMD processor. It's also a good idea to use software that allows you to monitor your hardware sensors while in Windows. Check out Hardware Sensors Monitor (www.hmonitor.com), which allows you to throttle down Intel CPUs.

The very best motherboards include plenty of documentation on overclocking features and allow memory and FSB speeds to be set independently of one another. Because many mobos don't fall into this category, speed freaks opt for memory that is spec'd higher than the speed of their FSBs (for example, they put DDR333 memory on a 266MHz bus). That way, even if the FSB is overclocked, the memory will still run within spec.

Preparations and Precautions

A few simple precautions can minimize the risks of overclocking. For one, you should ensure that your cooling setup—especially the CPU fan—is ready for increased heat. Although Northwood P4s can often be overclocked considerably with just stock Intel cooling, the same cannot be said for Athlons and older, 0.18-micron Pentium 4s. We've said it before, and we'll probably say it again before this article is over—for significant overclocking, we strongly recommend investing in a more powerful heatsink/fan unit and even liquid cooling or phase-change cooling systems for radical speed freaks.

It's also important to use a high-quality thermal compound, which helps to wick heat from the CPU to the heatsink. Our favorite is Arctic Silver 5 (www.arctic-silver.com). Also, if you're planning on overclocking your FSB (and thus your memory) by a large margin, it might be worthwhile to buy memory heatsinks.

Make sure you have time to do the overclocking process thoroughly and with patience. And if there were ever a golden rule of overclocking, it's this: Always overclock in small increments. Don't try to jump straight from, say, 1.5GHz to 1.8GHz. Play it safe, and you're more likely to achieve success.

Let's Get Ready to Ratchet

Now that you know the concepts behind overclocking, it's time to get some real-world experience. First, we provide a numbered step-by-step list of the basic overclocking operating procedure, and then we show you four overclocking case studies to give you a better idea of obstacles and how they can be surmounted.

1 Verify the make and model of your CPU by right-clicking My Computer and selecting Properties. Next, check the online resources at the end of this chapter to get a good idea of how far others have pushed that particular CPU. Before you begin, also make sure your mobo manual is handy.

2 Consider whether your present cooling solution is up to the task, or if you want to invest in a hardier method. After all, the point of overclocking is to get the most out of your processor, so you'll want the most aggressive cooling setup you can afford.

3 After you've installed your CPU and cooling solution, you need to get into your PC's BIOS. Most systems indicate how to access the BIOS during bootup. Watch the screen for clues like "Press Del to enter BIOS," the most common method.

BIOS screens follow basic computer interface navigation rules. Just make sure you don't save changes unless you truly want to change these very critical, system-level controls. That's your only warning.

4 If you're running an unlocked Athlon XP, you can try increasing the multiplier to affect your overclocking (remember, just ratchet up speeds one tick at a time). Dig around in your BIOS until you find the setting that lets you alter the multiplier. If your Athlon XP is an 1800+ that was made when AMD was popping out 2200+ CPUs, there's a chance you might be able to increase the multiplier without having to resort to a bus overclock.

If you're denied multiplier tweaking, or if you have an Intel CPU (which are always multiplier-locked at the factory), dig around for your FSB controls. You'll usually find that the FSB has been set to 100MHz, 133MHz, or 166MHz (these bus speeds do not reflect the double-pumped and quad-pumped strategies that AMD and Intel use, respectively). Take baby steps when adjusting the FSB. For example, if your default is 133MHz, try 135MHz, check for system stability via all the suggestions that follow these steps, and then try a little bit more speed if 135MHz performs okay.

If you push your FSB too far, the mobo may even deny you access to the BIOS screen upon reboot. If this occurs, you need to refer to your motherboard's instructions to clear the CMOS memory and return the BIOS to its ultra-safe default settings. With many new motherboards, rebooting automatically resets the board to low CPU speeds. Older models might reset when you hold down Delete during the boot. Again, refer to your manual.

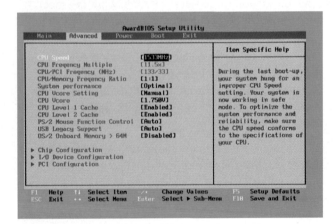

If your Athlon XP is unlocked, you can simply go into the BIOS and crank up the multiplier a notch at a time for a speed increase.

5 You need to check for stability after every incremental increase in speed. To do this, allow your PC to boot into Windows. If it freezes during booting or within a few minutes thereafter, you've got two options: (1) Return to the BIOS and drop the multiplier or FSB speed, or (2) increase the voltage.

Increase the voltage one increment at a time, and don't exceed an overall increase of 10% unless you have a

spare processor or two lying around (voltage tweaking is arguably the most dangerous part of overclocking). And if you do increase voltage, it's absolutely necessary to increase your cooling.

6 When you're satisfied with the initial stability of your overclocked system, you need to put it under some stress. Our initial stability tests begin with simultaneously running Folding@Home and SETI@Home for an hour or two. If the system runs normally without lockups or apparent glitches, we then run a looping Quake III demo—all night long. Another option is CPU Burn-in, a free utility available at users.bigpond.net.au/cpuburn. This useful app performs a series of intense floating-point calculations and error-checks to detect subtle chinks in the armor of an overclocking job.

The next thing to do is run some benchmarks to gauge the performance gain you've netted. Which benchmarks you use is a matter of personal preference, but *Maximum PC* usually runs SYSmark, 3DMark, and a game based on a punishing 3D engine.

That's it—the overclocking process in a nutshell. But, alas, overclocking is a tricky craft that sometimes requires a little improvisation. Things don't always go the way you hope, and the unexpected arises at, well, unexpected moments. So, before you drop this book and begin spelunking in your BIOS, check out our case studies on the following pages. These are real-life overclocking experiences from the *Maximum PC* Lab. A study of these examples will give you a good idea of what to expect on your own. If you can read our examples without breaking into a nervous sweat, award yourself an Overclocker's Certificate and get ready to burn.

How to Break into Your BIOS

Don't let clock-blockers ruin your fun!

Dell, HP, and other large OEMs write custom BIOSs that don't include any FSB controls, so overclocking is effectively denied. There are, however, a few options for the truly determined. Just remember that over-clocking an OEM system will void the warranty—and not just for your CPU, but for the whole config.

Your first option is a software utility called CPUcool. This program lets you adjust your FSB speed directly from within Windows. We used it our-selves to ratchet up an HP system armed with a Pentium 4B mobo. Unfortunately, we weren't able to overclock beyond 50MHz without system crashes. We also had no luck getting the utility to work on any of the Dell machines floating around our office. You can also try CPUFSB and SoftFSB. These utilities also tweak FSB speeds but don't seem to cooperate very well with modern CPUs.

If you're uncomfortable using a software program that might bork your entire system, you can take the drastic step of replacing your mobo with something more overclockable. Open your case and make sure it contains a standard ATX power supply, as well as mounting points lined up in the standard ATX form factor. Also make sure your rig has a front-panel con-nector (for your power switch, reset switch, and front panel LEDs) that will connect to another motherboard. We've had okay success in upgrading older HP and Compaq machines, but Dell machines usually require a new power supply and serious modifications to their front-panel connectors.

Vamping Your Videocard Velocity

One Small Step for the Clock, One Giant Step for Performance

Videocard overclocking is simple but shouldn't be taken lightly. It's much easier to fry a videocard than a CPU because most videocards don't automatically clock down when they overheat. If you push your card too far or too fast, you can destroy it or drastically shorten its lifespan. Consider yourself warned.

The only tool you need is EnTech's PowerStrip (www.entechtaiwan.com). When it's installed and running, right click the taskbar icon; then go to Performance Profiles and then Configure. In that screen, you can decrease and increase your videocard's memory and core speeds. After making a modest speed adjustment, test the settings before pushing your card further. We recommend that you start by bumping up your core GPU speed in 5MHz increments and then running a punishing game or benchmark before bumping it further.

When you see artifacts and other visual glitches during testing, you should crank your GPU clock back a notch and then start tweaking the memory clock speeds in the same way described previously. Texture corruption is usually indicative of memory that's been clocked too high. Screen-wide artifacts, meanwhile, suggest that the core is clocked too high. After you've tweaked your card to taste, you still need to spend a few hours doing some additional hard-core testing—preferably by playing your favorite game.

The Official Word from Intel and AMD:
Tom & Jerry Have Choice Corporate-speak for Silicon Hot-rodders

AMD: "AMD places a very high value on its reputa-tion as a supplier of PC processors. Our reputation for quality and reliability rests in part on operation of our products within the specified range of perform-ance parameters for each product. AMD is especially concerned that consumers receive products that have not been altered or modified without AMD's authori-zation…. We appreciate your understanding, cooper-ation, and your recognition that AMD does not sup-port the unauthorized alteration of AMD products."

Intel: "Intel does not advocate overclocking. Running beyond the speed, temperature, and volt-age specifications of your CPU may void your war-ranty and could damage your hardware. Intel is especially concerned about overclocking where the CPU or system may be remarked and sold to an unknowing consumer at a higher speed than it is rated…. Users who suspect that they have pur-chased an overclocked CPU can download our Frequency ID utility at http://support.intel.com/."

Overclocking Case Studies

Case Study 1—P4 Northwood A: 2.0GHz to 2.52GHz on Abit IT7-MAX2

Entry-level P4s are excellent OC candidates. Featuring the Northwood A core fabbed on a 0.13-micron process, most of these processors have a good amount of frequency headroom. At stock speeds, they run a 100MHz bus, quad-pumped to 400MHz.

We mounted our 2.0GHz CPU on an Abit IT7-MAX2 motherboard using Intel's bundled heatsink and cooler. The mobo's illustrious roll call of BIOS features includes everything an overclocker could want. With the PCI bus set to a fixed rate of 33MHz, we stepped up the FSB speed from 100MHz—5MHz at a time—until the system failed to boot at 130MHz. We then reduced the FSB 1MHz at a time until we were able to attain rock-solid operation with a 126MHz bus. This yielded a processor speed of 2.52GHz—a mighty 26% increase over the CPU's rated speed. We also increased the BIOS's CPU core voltage settings from 1.5V to 1.55V for an added stability margin.

By adopting a 3:4 FSB-to-memory clock ratio, we were able to operate the DDR memory at 336MHz, which was pretty close to the 333MHz rating the Abit motherboard was designed for. We used two sticks of 512MB Corsair DDR400 CL2 memory, but running at 336MHz shouldn't be a problem with the majority of high-quality DDR333 CL2 memory modules. Other testing organizations running Northwood A P4s have taken their buses from 100MHz to 133MHz, so we believe that our actual CPU specimen, one of the first Northwoods ever fabbed, limited our overclocking attempts. An ambitious overclocker with a late-run chip and a more elaborate cooling solution might achieve even better results.

The BIOS in the Abit IT7-MAX gives you an assortment of OC options, but we're partial to the bus speed setting. We took our FSB from 2.0GHz to 2.52GHz.

The BIOS in the Abit IT7-MAX gives you an assortment of OC options, but we're partial to the bus speed setting. We took our FSB from 2.0GHz to 2.52GHz.

Case Study 2—P4 Northwood B: 2.8GHz to 3.21GHz on Gigabyte Titan CA-SINXP1394

Featuring a 133MHz FSB quad-pumped to 533MHz, the Northwood B is a clean-up version of the original Northwood A. The chip is available today with factory speed ratings from 2.26GHz to 3.06GHz, which puts our 2.8GHz specimen near the top of the CPU type's frequency spectrum. Conventional wisdom says the 2.8 shouldn't have much headroom, but we were able to push our example relatively far with stock cooling.

Seating the P4 in a Gigabyte Titan CA-SINXP1394 motherboard along with Intel's efficient bundled cooler, we increased the FSB in 5MHz increments until our system crashed upon booting at 158MHz. We then dialed back the FSB until rock-solid stability was achieved at 154MHz. In the final configuration, our 400MHz CL Corsair memory module was operating in dual-channel mode at 384MHz CL2 (192MHz memory clock)—the highest available setting that doesn't exceed the module's 400MHz rating.

During our OC attempts, we didn't attempt to manually increase the core voltage beyond the "normal" BIOS setting, but we noticed that the BIOS's own PC health status screen showed a core voltage of 1.602V— 0.1V higher than the factory specification of 1.5V. It seems that the folks at Gigabyte, perhaps to foster stability in overclocked systems, had programmed their mobo to default to a higher-than-normal core voltage. While we don't feel that the 0.1 over-volt was harmful or objectionable, we would prefer that the user make such decisions.

All in all, our efforts netted a 14.6% increase in clock speed. We think that's impressive, considering we were upclocking one of the fastest-rated Northwood Bs. All things being equal, a 2.8 Northwood B should have much less headroom than, say, a CPU with an assigned speed of 2.6GHz.

The Gigabyte SINXP1394 features a six-phase power module (next to the CPU fan) to make overclocking more stable.

Case Study 3—Athlon XP Palomino 2000+: 1.667GHz to 1.813GHz on Asus A7V333

We expected a lot from this combination—late-production Palomino silicon on a hearty Asus A7V333 motherboard, with the same cooler AMD uses on its 3000+ Barton and 400MHz CL2 Corsair memory. Unfortunately, as with many overclocking ventures, things didn't turn out the way we hoped. As usual, we started edging up the FSB speed in 5MHz increments but slammed our heads into an unexpectedly low ceiling. The system crashed at 148MHz, prompting us to decrease the FSB until reaching stability at 145MHz. It came as a huge surprise that our Athlon XP 2000+ absolutely refused to accept a faster FSB speed. After all, for our Lean Machine 2002 project, we pushed a 2000+ to run its FSB at 166MHz on the exact same motherboard.

We've hit far higher speeds using this Asus A7V333 before, but with the 2000+ we dug up, we couldn't get past 1.8GHz.

At first, we suspected that we'd hit the core clock limit. However, after unlocking the chip using High Speed PC's Athlon XP unlocking kit and setting the CPU clock multiplier down to 8x (from 12.5x), we still couldn't reliably run the processor above a modest 145MHz FSB setting. Not even a core voltage boost to 1.85V remedied the situation. Because Athlon XPs rated at 2000+ and slower support a core multiplier between 5x and 12.5x (even when all the L1 bridges are connected), we were stuck at 1.813MHz (12.5 × 145MHz). Oh well. So goes the bad luck of the CPU draw.

Case Study 4—Athlon XP Barton 3000+: 2.167GHz to 2.327GHz on MSI K7N2G

Back in their heyday, AMD's fastest-rated Athlons were quite OC-friendly. But today, as AMD struggles to squeeze more clock frequency from a relatively short-pipeline architecture, some recent top-rated Athlon XPs have proven to be poor overclockers. So, when we got our hands on an Athlon XP 3000+ featuring the Barton core and a 166MHz FSB (double-pumped to 333MHz), we were anxious to see if it would buck the trend and make the Socket A platform the overclocker's preferred diet once again. The Barton core uses the now-dated 0.13-micron process (moving to 90nm would certainly provide more frequency headroom) and is almost identical to the older Thoroughbred B save for a double-size L2 cache. We didn't expect tremendous overclocking potential, but we had to give it a try.

We installed the Athlon XP 3000+ on an MSI K7N2G mobo (featuring the new nForce2 chipset) and threw in two sticks of 512MB Corsair DDR400 CL2 memory. Edging the FSB gingerly forward, we were able to go from 2.167GHz to 2.4GHz (that's a bus speed of 185MHz). However, trouble soon reared its head. The system worked fine as long as we didn't run any serious graphics benchmarks, which ended in abrupt crashes.

Eventually, we were able to achieve unwavering stability with an FSB of 179MHz and a corresponding CPU speed of 2.327GHz. Running a 1:1 FSB-to-memory ratio, we were operating the DDR memory at 358MHz in dual-channel mode—well below the 400MHz speed the modules were rated for. At this setting, everything ran beautifully and CPU temperatures stayed at a comfortable 52° Celsius using AMD's bundled cooler and heatsink.

By using the straight bus overclock, we goosed our Athlon XP 3000+ to 2.32GHz.

If you're willing to undertake the tricky process of unlocking an Athlon's CPU multiplier, you might get better results. Just don't expect any stratospheric headroom built in to the Barton core.

The Proof Is in the Benchmarks

CPUs	Clock Speed[1]	SiSoft ALU[2]	SiSoft FPU[3]	Quake III Arena[4]
Northwood A	2.000	5385	2632	187
Northwood A	2.520	6624	3318	217
Barton 3000+	2.167	8046	3267	285
Barton 3000+	2.327	8676	3512	305
Northwood B	2.800	7226	3714	348
Northwood B	3.210	8305	4240	375
Palomino 2000+	1.667	6211	2504	214
Palomino 2000+	1.813	6756	2708	237

1. Gigahertz 3. MFLOPS
2. MIPS 4. Frame rate

The Five Most Overclockable CPUs

Pentium 4 Northwood 2.4GHz

The 2.4GHz P4 (running a stock FSB of 533MHz) is a favorite and can often be OC'd beyond 3200MHz, even with traditional forced-air heatsink coolers. The average overclock often reaches upwards of 3000MHz with minimal tweaking, often needing only a quick FSB BIOS bump. An Intel i875 Canterwood chipset motherboard is a definite recommendation, as this CPU has great performance potential when paired with dual-channel DDR memory.

Athlon XP Barton 2500+ Mobile

The Barton core Athlons, especially the elusive power-efficient mobile models, have become particular favorites from a price perspective because they yield above-average overclocking results due to their advanced 0.13-micron core technology. Average returns are usually in the 2200MHz–2300MHz range (up from 1.83GHz). Top-end cooling combined with an NVIDIA nForce2 or VIA KT600–based motherboard should yield results up to 2500MHz, but don't expect to go much further with even the most radical of cooling configurations.

Athlon XP Thoroughbred 2100+

The 2100+ (1.73GHz) was once the most popular Athlon model for overclocking. While not as speedy as the latest Barton core models, this chip is generally good for clocking past 2000MHz with a minimal core voltage increase. Extreme cooling and high voltages can offer the best overclocking reward, often in excess of 2200MHz with a quality nForce2 chipset motherboard.

The Book of Overclocking

The remainder of this chapter was written by Scott Wainner, president/CEO of online retailer reviews and price comparison site ResellerRatings.com and coauthor (with Robert Richmond) of *The Book of Overclocking* from No Starch Press (ISBN 1-886411-76-X) a book that we've dog-eared here in the *Maximum PC* Lab. This material appeared in the July 2003 issue of *Maximum PC*.

Please note that while there are newer processors that could be added to this list, we still believe the processors we identified in the July 2003 issue remain the most overclockable processors available.

Athlon XP Thoroughbred 1700+

Although it's becoming difficult to find, the low-cost Athlon XP 1700+ (1.47GHz) provides a great offset when purchasing a more expensive NVIDIA nForce2 chipset mobo. Average overclocks often reach well beyond 2000MHz, often at default core voltages with the low-power DLT3C core models. Extensive cooling and a slight core voltage increase can offer the bump needed to push this inexpensive chip beyond 2200MHz.

Pentium 4 Northwood 1.8GHz

The 1.8GHz Northwood P4 (running a stock FSB of 400MHz) is a great overclocking option for true hardcore enthusiasts. Its low fixed multiplier, combined with a quality Intel i845 chipset motherboard, can allow for tremendous overclocking potential. Overclocks in excess of 2600MHz are not uncommon, and getting beyond 2800MHz is even possible with radical peltier or water cooling.

And 4 Others That Might Just Break Your Heart

(In order from least generous to most generous in terms of overclocking potential)

VIA C3 (Any Model)

VIA processors are currently attracting a lot of attention for their low power demands and minimal cooling requirements. Oddly, however, even with a thermally efficient core, the C3 offers only minimal overclocking potential at best. Expect maximum overclocking returns in the 50MHz–100MHz range. Whee.

AMD Athlon Thunderbird 1400MHz

The Athlon Thunderbird was put out to pasture after hitting 1400MHz. With an early-generation 0.18-micron core, this processor has massive power demands and dissipates tons of heat. Overclocking upwards of 1600MHz–1700MHz might be possible, but only with quality cooling and potentially dangerous voltages.

Pentium III EB 1000MHz

The Pentium III Coppermine core was hitting its maximum frequencies when the 1GHz chip was released. In fact, its limitations were clearly evident when Intel released—and eventually withdrew—the P-III 1.13GHz from the marketplace. Lucky overclocks are generally in the 1150MHz–1250MHz range with traditional heatsink cooling.

Athlon XP Barton 3200+

The Athlon 3200+ (2.20GHz) is one of the best-performing processors, but its overclocking potential leaves much to be desired because of the limited frequency scaling of the Barton core. The expensive 3200+ often slams the proverbial wall around 2400MHz, even with the best cooling and maximum voltages.

Top 10 Tips for the Hardcore Overclocker

Tricky, dangerous, over-the-top, foolhardy, brazen, gonzo, imprudent...

1 **The Crayola Trick**—When trying to connect a CPU's L1 bridges with conductive fluid to unlock the multiplier, do those pesky holes in the surface of the Athlon XP annoy you beyond belief? Sure, you could break out the epoxy or superglue, and spend countless hours trying to fill the holes, but there's an easier way, and it's often the simplest ideas that are overlooked. A cheap coloring crayon can fill the surface pits with just a few passes and a little pressure.

2 **Smoking the Core**—Processor burn-in is perhaps the most controversial topic you'll hear discussed in overclocking circles. Start by running the processor at its default frequency with an increased core voltage for several days. Assuming the chip runs fine in this condition, drop the voltage back to default and then push the chip to its maximum stable frequency. Now adjust the voltage as necessary to reach the desired

overclocking range. Do you actually "break in" the electronic circuits? Probably not. The benefits of the procedure probably have much more to do with getting the CPU's thermal paste to settle and even out. Regardless, burn-in seems to help in pushing a chip to its maximum limits.

3 **String 'em Up**—Have a motherboard that offers no way to change the CPU voltage? Coated magnet wire might be the key to overclocking bliss. Strip the ends and wrap the small wire around specific pins on the bottom of the processor to unlock many features, such as voltages and multipliers. A quick glance at the Intel or AMD technical documents of your CPU model will serve as a guide to the maze of socket pins. Be sure to pay close attention to your heatsink when installing the processor in your motherboard because the magnet wire can cause the CPU to seat differently, requiring either heatsink clip retensioning or wiggling the heatsink a bit to realign its base with the chip.

4 **Computer and a Beer?**—You've probably already seen slick hobbyist systems mounted inside coolers

and micro-fridges. But while nice to look at, they can cause water condensation on electronics parts, which is never good. Refrigeration can work, but all water vapor must be removed before the system can be operated long-term. Damp Rid is a commercial product used to remove humidity from basements. Just fill up the fridge with this powdery substance, crank up the cooling, and wait a couple of days before firing up the system. Those without patience need not apply.

Billed as an "air freshener," DampRid (www.damprid.com) is really a box of calcium chloride salts that harden as they absorb moisture.

5 **Conform to the Rules**—Conform to the rules of condensation, that is. Conformance sealant is a must for any system being cooled below the air's dew point. The sealer is available in an aerosol and can be applied in the same manner as spray paint. Cover the entire

motherboard as well as any other electronics surfaces that are near the contact point of the active cooling solutions, such as a chilled liquid waterblock or thermoelectric peltier circuit, to keep water from ruining your day. The stuff is almost impossible to find, but you can go to HMC

Konform is an acrylic resin that can protect your PC's delicate innards from the effects of moisture. Basically, it laminates your electronics.

Electronics (www.mcelectronics.com) and look up "Chemtronics CTAR12 Acrylic Konform AR."

6 **Get the Lead Out**—Magnet wire can also be used along with 60/40 lead solder to manipulate CPU pins. Instead of wrapping the wire around the processor pins, solder it to the matching pins on the back side of the motherboard CPU socket. A micro-DIP switch can be installed inline to allow for easy customization of many different processor models.

7 **The Bling Bling Effect**—Why not pimp out your system with a little silver? Silver-based thermal pastes represent today's top choice for heatsink interface material. Popular brands like Artic Silver 5 can lower core processor temperatures by 5%–10% compared with traditional silicon thermal pastes. Follow the directions to the letter, being careful not to over apply. Keep in mind that it will take about 72 hours to realize the full benefits of thermal paste. But the increased thermal efficiency can often raise a processor's maximum attainable frequency, sometimes upwards of 50MHz.

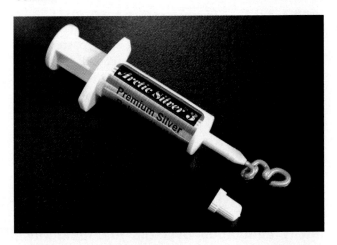

The makers of Arctic Silver ($8, www.arcticsilver.com) advise that thermal compounds can take from 72 to 200 hours after the initial application to achieve their maximum thermal conduction.

8 **The Final Lap**—Most heatsinks lack a smooth finish on the base side of the cooler, but this can be addressed by *lapping*, a process that entails using ultra-fine sandpaper to remove imperfections in the contact surface. Attach the sandpaper to a glass surface and move the heatsink in alternating figure-eight rotations to evenly sand the bottom finish. Start with 800-grit sandpaper and work toward 1600-grit polishing paper. A high-speed rotary tool with polishing cream can finish off the process to provide a mirror like finish for the heatsink base, ensuring maximum thermal transfer for improved cooling efficiency.

9 **Mr. Snow Miser**—Liquid nitrogen has become a favorite of the hardcore overclocking elite—but it's not kid's stuff. LN2 is available through a variety of scientific suppliers for a relatively cheap price. This super-cooling liquid can be placed in a reservoir mounted atop the processor to max out a chip's top speed for short periods. Sadly, liquid nitrogen is not a long-term solution, but rather a hardcore trick for demonstrating one's overclocking prowess. Beware: This cooling method can easily snap off a few fingers of anyone not understanding how to handle this dangerous material!

11 **Deadly Intentions**—Ever thought about drowning your PC? Immersion cooling is used by supercomputers from Silicon Graphics, and now this technology can be deployed in desktops and servers. Fluorinert is the fluid of choice, but it can be expensive at $500 a gallon. 100% pure mineral oil works nicely, but any contaminants like fragrances or colorings will short out your system. A multimeter is recommended to test the fluid for capacitance, and never attempt to submerge any power supplies or drives into any electronics cooling fluid.

Choosing Your Motherboard
A fast car needs a good track

Before you even think about buying a specific motherboard—particularly for overclocking—download the board's manual off the Internet and read it word by word. Make sure the board offers access to frontside bus speed controls. This is the most basic, entry-level feature offered in an "overclocking board." You'll also want the ability to increase core voltage to the CPU. Some boards (such as the Abit IT7-MAX2 used in case study 1) also allow you to independently increase voltage to your AGP card and RAM—a fantastic level of control for hardcore practitioners.

Because overclocking your FSB increases the speed of your PCI and AGP devices, you might suffer instability problems caused by add-in cards that can't handle the faster frequencies. This is why it's always smart to pick a board that lets you adjust AGP and PCI dividers. A healthy list of dividers will let you keep your PCI and

AGP slots within spec (or at least closer to spec) even when increasing the FSB in zany increments.

OC success (or the lack thereof) can also be traced back to a mobo's design layout and power dynamics. Some boards are simply much more prepared to handle the electrical stress. Unfortunately, a board's "over-clockability quotient" is difficult to quantify, and you won't find anything about "stability under intense duress" mentioned in the mobo manuals. So, talk to your friends and check online message boards for info on a specific model's OC potential.

In our experience, Abit continues to be the premier brand for overclockers. The company generally exploits every overclocking trick when designing its boards. Asus, MSI, Gigabyte, DFI, Chaintech, and I will also have nice features for OC tomfoolery.

Online Resources
The most overclocking-friendly websites around

The most comprehensive site for overclockers and overclockers-to-be is, not surprisingly, www.overclockers.com. The information here runs the gamut, but the real jewel is the CPU database, a massive, user-maintained compendium of CPUs and their overclocking potential (the database is also available at www.cpu-database.com). Start here for an idea on how far to push your proc.

At www.octools.com you'll find plenty of traditional fare, such as reviews of motherboards and water-cooling systems, as well as hardware news. But dig a little deeper in the site to find treatises on budget overclocking, condensation prevention, and lapping techniques. And don't pass up Mission: Submersible, a photo essay on total-submersion cooling.

Online forums can also yield a wealth of information, especially if you need quick answers when faced with an overclocking roadblock. Check out the Overclock Intelligence Agency forums at www.ocia.net/forums/ and the forums at Overclockers Online at http://forum.overclockersonline.com/.

MAKE USE OF *POWERSTRIP'S*
7 Coolest Features

PowerStrip is a powerful utility you can use to unlock much of your videocard's hidden potential. You can find the trial version at www.entechtaiwan.net, from there just click utilities. In this how-to, we'll walk you through its 7 coolest features.

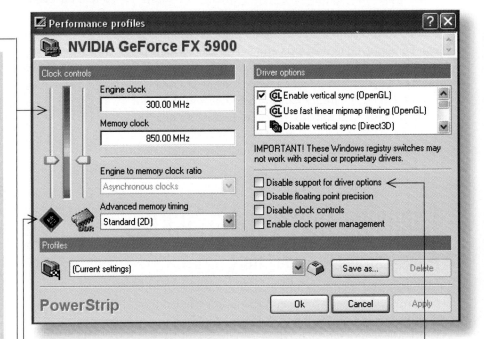

#1: Overclocking

If you have one of the new generations of videocards that include overclocking utilities, you may want to use the clock controls supplied with the display driver. For practically everything else produced since 1995, you'll find clock controls here: **PowerStrip menu > Performance profiles > Configure.** You can control multiple graphics cards from this screen, and—if the hardware design permits—set engine and memory clocks independently; then save different speeds to various profiles and invoke them at the touch of a hotkey. Go easy on these controls and use common sense. If your card could run stably at a much higher speed and under all conditions, the manufacturer would have shipped it that way to begin with. Start by increasing the engine clock just 5MHz at a time, and then test each increase extensively for stability using your favorite games. When you reach the limit, back off 5MHz or 10MHz to provide a safety margin. Once you've discovered the limit for the graphics engine, leave it there and repeat the same procedure with the memory clock, watching closely for early, visible signs of pixel corruption and garbage. Note that the video BIOS will restore the manufacturer's defaults each time it initializes. You don't have to have *PowerStrip* running all the time, but you do need to run it after Windows loads in order to override the manufacturer's defaults and restore your own clock preferences.

#2: Raising the limits

The first time *PowerStrip* meets up with your graphics card, it records the current detected clock speeds as your defaults, then calculates a reasonable range based on those values. Typically, the max is set to 133 percent of the default and the minimum is set to 80 percent. So if your card runs by default at 300MHz, *PowerStrip* probably will offer up a range of between 250MHz and 400MHz. If you need to go higher—or, heaven forbid, lower!—than those numbers, double-click on the icon immediately below the clock slider(s), then enter the multiplier of your choice. Just remember that increasing the multiplier will not in itself make your card faster. It just allows you to experiment with higher speeds.

#3: Eye candy

While you are still on the **Performance** page in *PowerStrip*, uncheck the option to "Disable support for driver options" and have a look at the list of switches in the box above. If you want to disable vertical sync or set antialiasing and/or anisotropic filtering to their highest levels while you play, then a *PowerStrip* Performance profile may be just the ticket. But keep in mind that, unlike the clocks (which can be changed anytime), these switches have to be set *before* you load a game.

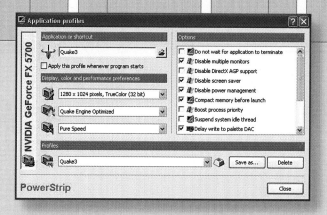

#4: Using profiles

Most people leave their videocards overclocked at all times, mainly because it's a pain in the butt to keep switching the clock and memory speeds back and forth. Luckily, *PowerStrip*'s Application profiles make it easy to customize your card settings for different circumstances. Create a couple of overclocked Performance profiles—one named, say, "Max visual quality" with all the eye candy enabled, and another named "Pure speed" with v-sync off and the eye candy disabled. Then go here: **PowerStrip menu > Application profiles > Configure**. Create a profile for your game or benchmark and assign the appropriate Performance profile to it. Then start the game or benchmark from the *PowerStrip* menu instead of the Windows Start menu. *PowerStrip* will change the clocks, turn on/off the eye candy, and then launch the game or benchmark. When you're finished, *PowerStrip* will automatically restore everything to the way it was *before* you clicked on the Application profile.

#5: Custom resolutions

Graphics cards are capable of generating practically any resolution, but Windows display drivers usually include only the most commonly used. Fortunately, the latest display drivers from ATI, Matrox, and Nvidia can accept a wide range of custom resolutions, which you can define in *PowerStrip* here: **PowerStrip menu >**

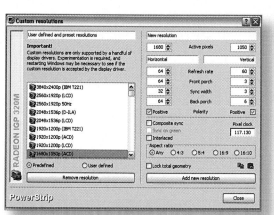

Display profiles > Configure > Advanced timing options > Custom resolutions. You also can specify your own custom resolution!

#6: Locking refresh rates

When gamers made the transition from the old Win9x/Me platform to NT/2000/XP, they discovered that games that changed resolution without specifying a refresh rate usually ended up running at just 60Hz. There are ways to "force" the refresh rate through the registry and driver, but nothing comes close to the power and precision of *PowerStrip*'s geometry controls, which can be found here: **PowerStrip menu > Display profiles > Configure > Advanced timing options**. Not everyone likes being handicapped at 60 frames per second in a 3D game, so to sidestep this you only need to adjust the vertical refresh rate control to the desired value.

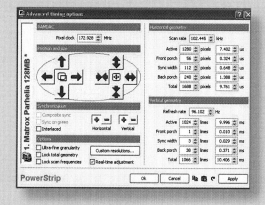

#7: PCI/AGP configuration

Graphics cards can sometimes be too aggressive in holding the bus, causing problems for other bus-master PCI devices, most notably PCI sound cards. *PowerStrip* offers a way to fix this here: **PowerStrip menu > Options > Adapter information**. Note the Read-only checkbox directly below the AGP transfer rates. When you uncheck this option, you will have access to two controls in particular that may assist in resolving compatibility problems. If the videocard's latency value is set to a very high value, like 248 clocks, reducing it to a more cooperative 80 clocks or even 64 clocks can significantly reduce any audio stuttering you may be experiencing. For those experiencing frequent crashes during 3D rendering, reducing the AGP transfer rate from 8x to 4x, or from 4x to 2x, can sometimes improve stability at only a small cost to performance.

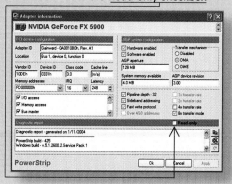

Windows XP
Demystified and Dissected!

Before we can crack into XP, we must first understand whence it came!

Windows
Timeline

➤ Microsoft shipped Windows 3.0 in 1990, but it wasn't until Windows 3.1 shipped that the industry began to accept the concept of a GUI on PC-compatible computers.

➤ Microsoft launched Windows 95 with incredible fanfare in 1995. The OS really was a leap ahead from Windows 3.1, but it still couldn't hold a candle to the Macintosh OS.

1983	1985	1987	1990	1993	1995	1996
MICROSOFT ANNOUNCES PLANS TO CREATE A GUI-BASED OS	WINDOWS 1.0	WINDOWS 2.0	WINDOWS 3.0	WINDOWS NT 3.1	WINDOWS 95	WINDOWS NT WORKSTATION

When XP was unleashed upon the masses in 2001, it proved itself to be the most stable, most flexible, and most attractive version of Bill's vaunted Windows OS to date. That's not to say XP is without its share of problems, annoyances, and challenges. It's just that while we all like to give Microsoft a hard time for what it does wrong, you have to give up some props for how well XP runs right out of the box.

Nowadays, thanks to XP, the Blue Screen of Death is all but a thing of the past, reserved mostly for truly traumatic events such as hardware failures, CPU mishaps, viruses, and random acts of God. So how does XP achieve this new-found level of stability? And how do we crack into it? Read on.

Blended OS

For years, MS has published two distinct versions of its OS: A more stable and secure—and harder to use—version for the corporate world called Windows NT, and a more user-friendly, "multimedia-ready" version, known as the Windows 9x series, for the average Joe. Windows XP takes these two previously disparate paths and merges them into a single OS, maintaining each platform's strengths. As a result, Windows XP—the XP stands for Experience, by the way—boasts the inherent stability and security strengths of NT's kernel (or code base; for more on this, see "Cracking the XP Kernel" on the following page) served up in Windows 9x's attractive, easy-to-use shell.

To avoid turning Windows XP into a jack of all trades but master of none,

Microsoft split the OS into several different versions: Windows XP Home, Professional, Media Center, and Tablet PC. Each edition shares a similar interface and runs the same software, but each specializes in delivering functionality for a specific audience. We'll be focusing on the two most popular editions here: Home and Professional. The primary difference between these two is that the Professional version is targeted at corporate users, and thus includes stronger security, backup, and networking features. Otherwise, it's identical to Home (unless otherwise noted). Most of the tips you'll find here will serve for both versions.

Window Panes

Regardless of which version you use, the new dynamic task-based user interface is the most immediately apparent and truly special aspect of XP, particularly to long-time Windows veterans—easily recognizable by their unbridled cynicism. Each opened window includes a new task pane that makes it easier for novices and old-timers alike to find files, features, and functions without hunting for them.

For example, open a folder using Windows Explorer and click a document file. The task pane will present you with options to e-mail, print, or publish the file on the World Wide Web. Click a digital photo file, and you'll be given the option to print the picture, create a slide show, or even order a print from an online service.

XP also makes it easier to find new files you create, too. Pen a new document with *Word* and the program will

automatically prompt you to save it in the My Documents folder. Similarly, pictures and downloaded files will route to the My Pictures and My Downloads directories, respectively.

Have XP Your Way

What's that you say? You don't want to save your files to the designated areas and you don't want to always manually locate your own directories? No problem, we'll show you how to customize your folder settings later. This brings us to what we really consider to be XP's greatest strength—its unparalleled level of customizability, at least when compared to previous versions of Windows.

Sure, WinXP is slick right out of the box. And once you get used to the basics of the new interface, it's easy to stick with the status quo, put up with all of XP's default settings, and bend to its will. But this is your PC and your OS, right? Bend it to *your* will—take control of Windows XP, today.

Throughout the following sections, which are jam-packed with tips and tricks—including many undocumented "hacks" and secrets about WinXP that Microsoft would rather you did not know, *Maximum PC* will show you exactly how to master the latest Windows OS in six straightforward steps. From tweaking how XP looks to hacking into the core of its Registry for customized operation, you'll find that there's much more to WinXP mastery than meets the eye. Your path to enlightenment begins here.

➔ *Windows 98 was an evolutionary step ahead for Microsoft, but most of the really important features, such as the Registry Checker, were hidden beneath the surface.*

➔ *Released in 2001, Windows XP represented a dramatic departure from previous versions of Windows. The dynamic task-based user interface made critical features much more accessible.*

1998	1999	2000	2001	2002	2003	2006?
WINDOWS 98	WINDOWS 98 SECOND EDITION	WINDOWS ME AND WINDOWS 2000	WINDOWS XP HOME AND PROFESSIONAL EDITIONS	WINDOWS XP MEDIA CENTER AND TABLET PC EDITIONS	WINDOWS XP "LONGHORN" PREVIEW	OFFICIAL RELEASE OF WINDOWS "LONGHORN"

Cracking the XP Kernel

Maximum PC dives under Windows XP's hood to show you what makes it tick!

For Windows 2000 users, Windows XP is an update with a new interface and some neat tools. Anyone moving up to XP from Windows 98 or ME is getting a brand-new operating system. You won't see the "Powered by NT" line on the box anymore, but an improved and updated version of the NT/Windows 2000 kernel lives at the heart of XP.

Think of the kernel as the engine of the operating system; it's the code that loads first, always stays in main memory, runs with special privileges on the processor, and provides the services that the rest of Windows and all of your applications use, such as managing memory and communications between your hardware and software.

The kernel is also responsible for doling out CPU resources to all of the applications you may be running simultaneously. The kernel uses "preemptive multitasking" to allot a share of processor time to each open app, and it also prevents any single program from monopolizing 100 percent of the CPU's resources.

In through the I/O Memory Door

All communications within Windows go through the kernel's Input/Output subsystem. Every device, driver, program, service, and Windows process has to have memory to run, and it gets that from the kernel's I/O process. Allocating and managing memory is vital to the way an operating system performs, and XP's kernel is much more robust than Windows 98 in this area. This new kernel features a "protected memory" procedure that gives each application or running process its own distinct area of memory to operate in. If said application or process crashes, it will not—in most cases—affect other software that may be running, including Windows itself. Windows can shut down the crashed program and reclaim its memory. In contrast, Win 98 had one memory space where applications had to fight for attention, and when one application crashed it tended to topple the whole house of cards.

Turn the Page: How XP Manages Memory

No matter how much physical memory you have—and we'd say 512MB is the minimum these days to get the most out of XP—there's never enough.

Because of this, Windows uses hard-disk space as "virtual memory." Windows uses physical memory—RAM—for code that needs to run the fastest, such as the virtual memory manager itself. The rest of your RAM is split up and matched to files being accessed on your hard disk. Each of these files is 4k in size and represents "one page" of memory, which Windows can "swap" to disk and back as you use one program or another. Windows tracks these files with a list of Page Table entries, and XP can track nearly 1.3GB worth of entries at a time, which is twice that of Windows 2000. This naturally translates into faster program response times for you.

XP is also better at working out which memory pages to load next so it spends less time loading information from disk; it no longer allocates more Page Table entries for storing files than the files actually need, and if an application has asked for more memory than it needs to run, XP can reclaim the unused portion for other programs.

The kernel's ability to manage memory is most crucial when your PC is running out of it, and XP raises the bar in this regard as well. In Windows 98/ME, a driver—and the Windows kernel—could demand memory even if there wasn't any available. If Windows couldn't allocate the memory, your system would hang, and you'd get the dreaded Blue Screen of Death. XP's kernel no longer allows these requests. As XP runs low on memory, it slows down passing information from memory to disk and back until there's more free memory. This also allows you to Alt-Tab between open apps to find one you can close without crashing the system.

These are just some of the primary upgrades the Windows kernel has received courtesy of XP. As you can see, WinXP's much more than just an update to Windows—it's a complete overhaul.

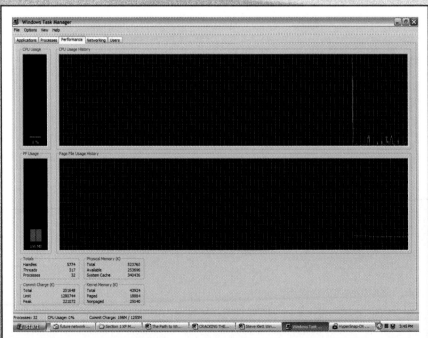

Win XP can manage 1.3GB of data at a time, which is twice that of Windows 2000. You can use the Task Manager to see everything XP's kernel is up to.

Windows XP Service Pack 2:
Improved Security, Wireless, and More!

We take an early look at Win XP's biggest upgrade yet and come away impressed with its enhanced security—and decreased annoyances

Microsoft is putting the finishing touches on a massive upgrade for Windows XP that addresses numerous security concerns, Wi-Fi connectivity, *Internet Explorer*, and even *Outlook Express*.

At press time, Microsoft developers were testing the second, and final, release candidate of SP2. What we've seen of this most significant upgrade managed to impress us. We'll be lining up on the day of SP2's release and here are nine reasons you should, too.

1

Messenger service is now off. Microsoft's insidious Messenger service, intended for network admins but most commonly known for its "UNIVERSITY DIPLOMA" pop-up spam, will be turned off by default.

2

A more powerful and configurable firewall. In SP2, Windows Firewall utilizes a more professional interface and now asks permit-or-deny questions about programs making unauthorized network connections. The firewall also runs during boot-up. Service Pack 1's firewall doesn't, which leaves a gap of vulnerability between the time Windows comes alive and the firewall service kicks in.

3

Improved Internet Explorer. For the first time in ages, Microsoft is substantially improving *IE*. The most significant additions are a built-in pop-up blocker and a "Manage Add-Ons" screen that lets you examine the third-party code modules that have integrated themselves with your browser. Troublesome modules (read: spyware) can be disabled, and *IE* now tracks crashes more carefully to help programmers debug problems. Furthermore, modules should have a harder time integrating themselves with *IE* without your knowledge or permission.

4

Simpler and more convenient Wi-Fi access. Win XP's wireless LAN client gets a new, streamlined look here. The original version became hard to manage as Windows discovered and kept track of more than a few access point configurations. Microsoft has also preconfigured hotspot profiles to make logging into various national services like Starbucks easier. An Automatic Connection feature allows you to easily hook into your preferred networks whenever you're in range. Finally, Bluetooth support now works better for simple connections like keyboards, mice, and PDA links, and shouldn't require external software to activate.

5

Local content zone lockouts. *Internet Explorer* will be more cautious about the permissions it gives to HTML files considered part of the "local content" zone. In the past, tricksters have loaded malicious code that never would have gotten through your web connection to your hard drive and prompted the browser to open the code from there. ActiveX and similar functions will be disabled by default for such local files, making it harder to develop and execute web Trojans.

6

Safer e-mail handling technologies. *Outlook Express* will include a plain text mode that will let you render incoming messages in plain text instead of HTML. This "rich edit control" mode—as opposed to Microsoft's MSHTML control method for HTML e-mail—should provide an additional barrier of effective protection against malicious code that is often transmitted via e-mail. In this mode, *Outlook Express* will not automatically execute infected HTML header scripts.

7

Buffer overruns get clamped down. Microsoft says SP2 clamps off a number of potential buffer overruns. These occur when hackers exploit an unchecked buffer in your program and overwrite the code with their own malicious code, which can take down a system faster than you can say "D'oh!" Time will tell.

8

Improved Windows Update. Microsoft's automatic update service receives a facelift in SP2, as well as the added ability to resume interrupted downloads. Because the rapid spread of viruses is largely a result of the high number of systems that aren't promptly patched, avoiding automatic update reminders will be discouraged.

9

Numerous internal changes. While SP2 also incorporates a slew of internal changes that mostly affect developers, one change we're closely watching is Execution Protection. This should help keep your programs running more smoothly in 64-bit or hybrid 32/64-bit environments. Given the very real potential for instability when 32- and 64-bit drivers get mixed, as well as the potential for certain 64-bit applications to crash when running on a system with huge memory capacities, Execution Protection may turn out to be one of the major perks for power users in SP2.

Customize Your Interface!

Who wants their desktop to look like everyone else's? Not us, and hopefully not you. Follow these tips to give your desktop a radical overhaul!

THINK

YOUR DESKTOP IS YOUR CANVAS

Warning: Proceed with Caution!

Some of the following tips involve changes to Windows XP's Registry settings and the use of third-party software not recommended or supported by Microsoft. Registry changes, and the installation of any new program, can result in system instability. Follow instructions carefully, and back up your system with a Restore point before proceeding **(See the section "Master the Dark Arts: Become a Power User").**

Howard Stern's fisticuffs with the FCC aside, freedom of expression and speech form the bedrock upon which this country was formed, and remains the tenant that the majority of us hold most dear. For some of us, it's the way we dress or style our hair. For others, it's body piercing and tattoos. Or it's as simple as the shoes we wear to a job interview, or the fuzzy dice hanging from the rear-view mirror of our cars. Regardless, most of us take advantage of these rights in some fashion, *every* day.

With this in mind, it's puzzling why so many people are content to let Microsoft dictate how their PC looks and feels. For shame! WinXP may be the slickest-looking form of Windows yet, but that doesn't mean it can't look better, or be made to conform to your personal style. One of XP's greatest and often-overlooked strengths is its flexibility in enabling us to exercise our expressive freedoms.

Thankfully, the first step in achieving true Power User status is also the easiest. There's a virtual cornucopia of simple ways to alter the appearance of your desktop. Your options range from basic tweaks using XP's built-in tools to total makeovers accomplished via third-party software. In some cases, you'll be able to hack XP's code to bend Windows to your will. From customizing the way your interface looks to adding a second monitor to expand your desktop real estate, we'll focus on showing you how to do things with your desktop that Microsoft would never tell you—and may even prefer you never heard about!

But before we jump into the thick of things, a quick note. We're assuming that you have some basic familiarity with changing XP's default desktop wallpapers, colors, and effects—this is a *Maximum PC* publication after all! For excellent walkthroughs on these basic elements, go to: www.microsoft.com/windowsxp/using/setup/customize/default.mspx and search under "customize your computer."

Tip One:
Give the Windows Desktop a Whole New Look!

You can use XP's Display Properties options to design your own themes from scratch, but wouldn't it be nice if there was a program out there that incorporated different theme/visual style templates and let you have all the fun while it did all the work? Well there are a few, of which *StyleXP* is perhaps the most useful, and easiest to use. Download a copy at www.tgtsoft.com and then hit up www.themexp.org for a bevy of visual styles to fit all tastes. You can select entire desktop themes, or just individual elements such as new mouse cursors. Once downloaded, unzip these elements to C:\Windows\Resources\Themes. Now you can select them from the Display Properties section of the Display Panel under appearances.

WindowsBlinds is another popular program for accomplishing the same effect, though it's limited to themes and visual styles, whereas *StyleXP* helps you tweak other areas of the desktop. However, due to a partnership between Microsoft and Stardock, the maker of *WindowsBlinds*, the app is integrated with XP's Display Properties control panel. You just have to download the program, and you instantly gain access to an array of new themes and visual styles.

StyleXP *is a handy utility for applying massive makeovers to Windows XP.*

WindowsBlinds *integrates with XP's built in display options to give you more pre-fab themes and styles to choose from.*

Tip Two:
Customize Your Account Icon

New themes are nice, but let's go a step further and change the default logon picture for your account by going to Start Menu, Control Panel, User Accounts. Click the account you wish to change, and select "Change my picture." You could choose one of the many generic premade options available at this screen, but that's dull, dull, dull! Instead select "browse for more pictures" and navigate to the image you'd like to use. XP will resize it for you. This image will appear on the Welcome screen for your account, as well as at the top of the Start Menu.

Ditch XP's pre-fab picture for your account in favor of some home-cooked options, like a pic of your dog.

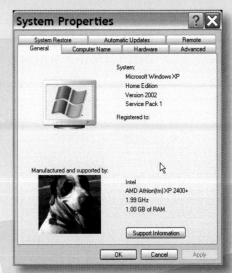

PC makers usually put their logo stamp in this space, but you can put your own logo here, too.

Tip Three:
Add an Image to Your System Control Panel

This tweak is a little more involved, and thus, a little more cool. Display any picture you'd like along with custom text in the System control panel by following these steps. First, take the image you want to use and resize it to 125 x 125 pixels (use your favorite photo editor), save it as "oemlogo.bmp," and copy it to C:\Windows\System32. Next open *Notepad* (Start Menu, All Programs, Accessories, Notepad) and type the following:

```
[General]
Manufacturer=
Model=
[Support Information]
Line1=
Line2=
Line3=
```

Fill in the lines after the equal signs with whatever text you wish, and save it as "oeminfo.ini" in the same C:\Windows\System32 folder. Now, right-click My Computer, select properties, and check out your work!

Tip Four:
Add Album Art to Music Folders

Windows XP will automatically add an album image to a folder housing music files as long as they're in Windows Media Audio format. If you're keen on using MP3 files for your digital music—most of the world is—you can still get the same effect. First, go to www. amazon.com and find the album you want to customize. Right-click its image, select "Save As," and save it in the folder containing the MP3 files for that album, then name it "folder.jpg." Now the folder will display the album image instead of the boring old folder icon. Pretty cool, huh? The same trick can be applied to your My Pictures folder, as well. Just make sure you're in the Thumbnail view or this trick won't work (in Explorer select View, Thumbnails).

Rename any image inside a folder to "folder.jpg" and it will appear instead of the folder icon!

Tip Five:
Get a Taste of Windows Longhorn Today, with SmartbarXP!

The next version of Windows, code named Longhorn and due in 2006, will have a new Quick Launch bar docked to the side of the screen that may be used to display time and weather, host tickers, and display memory, CPU, swap file, and network activity, as well as perform standard Quick Launch duties. But why wait? You can give the concept a whirl today thanks to a freeware app named *SmartbarXP*, which you can find online at www. smartbarxp.com.

Why wait until 2006 to try out one of Longhorn's new features, the "sidebar," when you can test it out now?

Tip Six:
Change your Bootscreen Image!

StyleXP is useful for much more than just applying new visual themes. It can also help you change the dull background image for the Windows logon screen. This hack has required blood, sweat, and tears to execute, but now *StyleXP* takes most of the work out of the equation. We still recommend you set a new restore point before proceeding, as the process does rename default Windows files and can result in instability if not done 100 percent correctly (see the "Master the Dark Arts: Become a Power User" section). Applying a new boot screen is as simple as downloading one to your desktop, pointing *StyleXP*'s browser to the file, and hitting "Apply." Presto—welcome to Win XP Homer Simpson Edition!

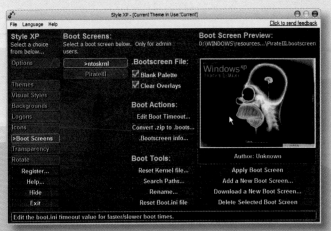

Altering your boot screen can be tricky, but utilities such as StyleXP make it safe and easy to accomplish.

Tip Seven:
Change Your Logon Screen Image

While we're at it, you should also learn how to set a custom image for your logon screen as well. This time, you'll have to do it manually, though you can also use *StyleXP* or a similar program if you wish. First, find the Logonui.exe file in C:\Windows\System32 and save a copy in another folder on your hard drive. Next, browse to www.themexp.com. Download a logon screen and extract its contents, which will include a new Logonui.exe file, into a temporary folder on your desktop. Reboot your PC in Safe mode by holding down F8 and restarting, and copy the new Logonui.exe file to C:\Windows\System32 replacing the existing, original Logonui.exe file, which you've backed up. Now restart your PC, and your new logon screen will appear.

XP's default logon screen is boring, unless you're in love with blue. Change it to suit your personality.

Get a 007 PC with DesktopX!

Turn your PC into the equivalent of James Bond with a nifty little program called *DesktopX* from Stardock, the company responsible for *WindowsBlinds*. With *DesktopX* you can outfit your desktop with all manner of objects, called "widgets," which perform a slew of useful or simply entertaining functions. These widgets range from balls you can toss around your screen to next-generation Windows Longhorn-style sidebars to weather stations, resource monitoring tools, and even fish that swim around your screen.

The free evaluation version (**www.stardock.com**) allows you to experiment with a generous array of toys. Upgrading to the full version will open up even more gadgets and desktop-customization options, such as allowing you to build your own widgets from scratch and design a completely new desktop.

DesktopX is not for the faint of heart. Using the various objects often requires patience and a trial-and-error approach; it all depends on the skills of the authors who scripted the objects you download. You will also likely encounter some DirectX compatibility issues—particularly with older programs or other GUI-tweaking apps. If you do, unloading the program from memory via the taskbar usually resolves most issues.

With DesktopX you can add all sorts of James Bond-style gadgets to XP's desktop, or give it a total redesign.

THINK
YOUR DESKTOP
IS YOUR CANVAS

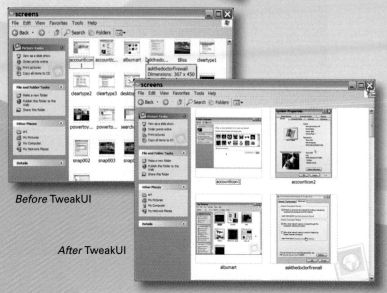

Before TweakUI

After TweakUI

Tip Eight:
Customize Thumbnail Size

The thumbnail view option in XP's swanky new version of Explorer lets you easily view suites of images. However, the default setting for the thumbs' image size may be tough on the eyes, particularly when your desktop is set to higher resolutions. You can alter the default size to your liking via the Registry, but that's needlessly difficult. Go to www. microsoft.com/windowsxp/downloads/powertoys/xppower-toys.mspx and download *TweakUI*, which we'll discuss in more detail later (for more on *Powertoys*, see "PowerToys for Power Users"). Open the Explorer tab and select Thumbnails. Change the pixel size of the thumbs from the default setting of 56 to a number between 32 and 256. Note: Enlarging the thumbs can slow down performance on slower machines. However, you can also tweak the image quality with the slider (located just above the pixel setting) to match the display capabilities of your machine.

Tip Nine:
Customize Default Window Title Size

We'll say it again: XP's default "Luna" interface looks great, but does come with trade-offs. For instance, if you have a smaller monitor, the default settings for Windows' title bars and the Open, Close, and Minimize control settings consume way too much screen real estate. To change them to a smaller, more friendly size for your desktop, go the Display control panel (right-click your desktop and choose Properties) and select Advanced. Now click on the bar of one of the sample windows and the Item and Font options should become active; if not, select Active Title Bar from the drop-down menu. Experiment with different pixel, font, and even color settings until you find what works for you. You may also notice that there are quite a few other toys to play with there, too...

If you don't like how much space the Windows title bar takes up, change it!

We love pinning apps to the Start menu. However, if your list gets too long, you can add separators to make your apps easier to find.

Tip Ten:
Add Separators to Your Start Menu!

If you've owned your PC for a while, chances are your Start menu is starting to look more than a bit cluttered with all the apps you've pinned. Put a little breathing space between all those apps with this handy hack.

Right-click your desktop and make a new shortcut. Select any .exe file as a target (it really doesn't matter which one you choose). Erase any text in the Name field and hold down the ALT key while entering "0160" on the number pad, which will give the shortcut an empty field for a name. Now click Okay. Right-click the new shortcut and remove the target. Next, click Change Icon and select a blank icon. Now simply drag this onto the Start button, and then drag it to the desired location.

2

Accelerate, Streamline, and Take Control of XP

Pretty desktops are fun and all, but speed is what turns us on. At *Maximum PC*, there's no such thing as a PC that moves too fast. With this in mind, here's how to give your system a performance boost, today.

So you've just completely pimped out your desktop, and now your PC is running slow as molasses? Hey, we told you not to go crazy. Whatever the case, if speed is what you're looking for, you've come to the right place. We'll show you how to trim your desktop's bells and whistles down to the bare necessities and accelerate your interface. We'll also fill you in on a host of other power-user tips that will make WinXP run more efficiently.

Additionally, if you can not only make a cup a coffee, but sit down, drink it, *and* read the sports pages while you're waiting for your machine to boot up in the morning, we'll outline exactly how to cut your PC's "wake-up" routine down to a mere 15 seconds. Now, getting you out of bed before 11:00 am...well, that's still *your* problem.

And, did you know that Windows XP comes standard with scores of background apps—all running by default—that may be sucking valuable game-crunching resources from your PC? Well, it does, and navigating though them unguided is like playing rugby in a minefield. See our extensive hard-core tips that not only expose what's going on beneath XP's surface, but also reveal how to regain control over these "services" and free your machine of those that you really don't need.

Tip One:
Speed Up Your Interface

We think WinXP's new interface is great, but we also run the latest hardware, so our machines easily fulfill the operating system's performance requirements. If the new Luna UI has got your older machine chugging along at 486 speeds, there are a few things you can do to pick up the pace.

First, go to the Display Properties Control Panel (right-click an empty spot on your Desktop and choose Properties). Now choose the Appearance tab and click the Effects button. Uncheck the following: "Use the following transition effect for menus and tooltips," "Use the following method to smooth edges of screen fonts," "Show shadows under menus," and "Show window contents while dragging." If this doesn't speed up your OS enough, you can turn off the next-gen interface altogether by selecting "Windows Classic Style" from the Windows and Buttons menu on the Appearance tab. In our Lab, this has given us 5 to 10 percent faster performance, as measured through our benchmark tests.

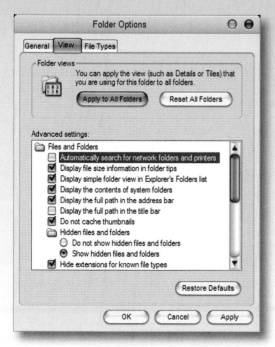

Tip Two:
See Your Icons Faster

Every time you open My Computer to browse folders, XP automatically searches for network files and printers, which can be causing a delay in how quickly your icons are displayed. Here's how to see them faster:

1. Open My Computer.
2. Click on the Tools menu and select Folder Options.
3. Select the View tab.
4. Uncheck the very first box that reads "Automatically search for network folders and printers."
5. Click "Apply" or "OK."

Tip Three:
Turn Off Indexing

Windows XP keeps a record of all files on the hard disk so that it can locate a particular file more quickly when you perform a search. The downside to this is that—since the computer has to index *all* of your files—it slows down normal file commands like open, close, etc. If you don't use the search feature much, turn indexing off: Control Panel>Administrative Tools>Services>Disable Indexing Services.

Tip Four:
Check for Signed Drivers

If it were up to the programming wizards at Microsoft, the entire world would run signed drivers. This is understandable—a significant number of crashes and system errors can be traced back to broken drivers. Signed drivers have passed through the Microsoft Hardware Qualification Labs and should be more reliable and robust than unsigned ones.

If your machine is crashing, and Windows is blaming it on a problem driver, go to the Run program under your Start menu, and run *sigverif. exe* to scan your system for unsigned drivers and other system files. Now visit your hardware manufacturers' web sites to find more up-to-date and signed versions of those drivers. Remember: Signed drivers are better, but unsigned drivers aren't necessarily bad, especially those that are updated frequently, like videocard drivers.

Tip Five:
Organize Your File View

If you have a big folder full of images from your digital camera or scores of unsorted MP3s, the "Show in Groups" folder option might be useful to you. It allows you to group your files in the Explorer window into similar categories instead of just listing them in the order you specify in the "Arrange by" menu. If you want to use "Show in Groups" to organize shots you took with your digital camera, choose "Arrange by Modified" to sort your snaps based on the day they were shot, then check "Show in groups" to group them by day. It's also convenient for music: Use "Arrange by Artist" with "Show in Groups" to group songs by the same artist together, or "Arrange by Album" to group songs from the same platter.

Tip Six:
Run Command Line Apps Fast, Fast, Fast

If you frequently run command-line applications, you should know about the Address bar's dirty little secret: Not only does the Taskbar's Address bar give you a quick way to launch your favorite web sites, but you also can run applications by typing the program's name into the Address bar.

Putting the Address bar onto the Taskbar is as easy as right-clicking the Taskbar, going to Toolbars, and selecting Address.

You can drag the bar to an empty, convenient place on your Taskbar, where it will live forever.

Don't know what to type to open your program? It's easy to find out. Right-click on the shortcut you use to open the program, go to Properties, and look in the Target box. All you need is the app's name, which usually ends with .exe, .com, or possibly .bat.

Tip Seven:
Optimize System Restore and the Recycle Bin

We really dig System Restore. If you install a driver that hoses your system, System Restore will frequently let you roll your system back to a time before that evil driver arrived. However, System Restore will eat 2 percent of your disk by default. That's not a big deal if you've got a puny 80GB hard drive, but if you just shelled out for a 250GB monster, 2 percent of that drive is 5GB.

To save your drive, open up System Properties again, go to the System Restore tab, and move the slider until you're a little happier with System Restore's disk space usage.

If you thought System Restore was a disk hog, the Recycle Bin consumes even more disk space—it occupies 10 percent of your drive by default! That's a full 25GB on our new 250GB drive. To turn down the Recycle Bin's disk usage, right-click the Recycle Bin, go to Properties, and move the slider from 10 percent to something a little more compatible with today's massive disks (we wonder when we're going to see a sub-1 percent option).

Tip Eight:
Don't Let Explorer Crashes Get You Down

If you're sick of a single Windows Explorer window crashing and then bringing down the rest of your OS with it, follow this tip: Open My Computer, go to Tools, then Folder Options. Click on the View tab, then scroll down to "Launch folder windows in a separate process" and enable this option. Just be aware that you'll have to reboot your machine for this tip to take effect.

Now, if Explorer does crash on you, taking your Taskbar and Start menu with it, it's easy to get them back. Just press Control + Alt + Delete. Then select File, New Task, and type `explorer.exe` to start a fresh version of your shell.

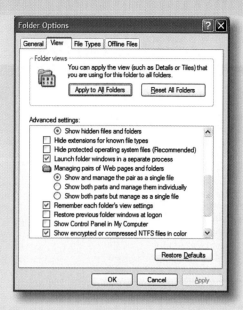

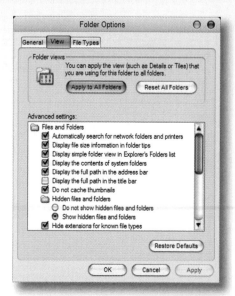

Tip Nine:
Delete MSN Explorer

If you're happy with *Internet Explorer* or another browser, and satisfied with your current e-mail and Internet service provider, you can save more than 13MB of hard drive space by deleting *MSN Explorer*. Windows Help says *MSN Explorer* is "software that makes it easy to get more from the web." That may be, but it's just a browser that integrates any Microsoft e-mail and messenger clients that require an MSN or Hotmail account. So if you're using another ISP, drop this duplicate browser like a hot potato. Open Control Panel, launch Add or Remove Programs, and on the left side of the dialog box, click Add/Remove Windows Components. Scroll through the list of Windows components and uncheck MSN Explorer. Read the warning and click Yes if you don't rely on MSN for your Internet connection. Click Next and follow the remaining on-screen prompts.

MSN Explorer is Microsoft's all-in-one Internet software solution. It includes a browser, email client, and messenger client. *MSN Explorer* requires an established MSN or Hotmail email account and an available Internet connection. The email client included with the software only supports Hotmail or MSN accounts. The software does not support external third-party email programs. As a result, you may not configure EarthLink email in the *MSN Explorer* settings.

Tip Ten:
Stop Windows from Saving the Thumbnail Cache

By default, Windows XP shows the thumbnail view of certain folders, whether you want it to or not. Even if you choose Details (or some other view) as your preference by going to Tools> Folder Options> View tab and click Apply to All Folders, Explorer may still revert back to the clumsy thumbnails view. It does this for any folder in which it finds the THUMBS.DB file; naturally, if you delete this file, it won't happen again.

The problem is that Windows seems to recreate the THUMBS.DB file automatically. Here's how to prevent this:

1. In Explorer, go to Tools> Folder Options or open the Folder Options icon in the Control Panel.
2. Choose the View tab, and turn off the "Do not cache thumbnails" option.

3. Click OK.

You also can change this setting in the Registry (see the "PowerToys for Power Users" section):

1. Open the Registry Editor (*Regedit.exe*).
2. Navigate to HKEY_CURRENT_USER\ Software\Microsoft\Windows\ CurrentVersion\Explorer\Advanced.
3. Double-click the DisableThumbnailCache value, or go to Edit -> New -> DWORD value to create a new value by that name.
4. Enter 1 (that's the number "1") for its value.
5. Click OK and close the Registry Editor when you're done; you'll have to log off and then log back on for this change to take effect.

SPEED LIMIT ∞

Lower Your Boot Speed to 15 Seconds

We'll start with the basic fast-boot tweaks. In the BIOS, disable "Floppy Drive Seek" and select the disk on which your OS is located as your First Boot Device. Empty your Start menu's Startup folder, and in the System Configuration Utility, clear the checkboxes of all but one or two of the most essential Startup items. Also, turn off any and all unnecessary Services (aim for a maximum of 25 Services set to Automatic and/or Manual—see the section "Windows Services Exposed and Expunged"). Finally, defrag your hard drive; then download and run *BootVis* (which is no longer available on Microsoft's site, but can be found via a half-second Google search.)

Now let's look at some of the other boot time-reducing modifications you can make.

- Our next order of business is to lose WinXP's "Luna" interface. It looks great, but it's slowing you down, pal. Click Start, right-click My Computer,

and select Properties. Navigate to the Advanced tab and click the Settings button under Performance. Select "Adjust for Best Performance" and click OK.

- Give your CPU and RAM a boost by taking down your wallpaper and removing all but one or two desktop icons. While you're at it, know this: Everyone but you finds your Windows sound scheme obnoxious. Spare their ears and improve your system's boot speed by clicking Start, navigating to Control Panel, and selecting Sounds and Audio Devices. Once there, click the Sounds tab, select "No sounds" from the Sounds scheme pull-down menu, and click OK.

- Now let's get rid of your fonts. The sad truth about fonts is that the more you have, the slower your boot time. This is especially true for machines with more than 500 fonts. If your font collection exceeds the 84 that XP comes stocked with, create a folder outside of the Windows directory and move the fonts there. You can move them back to the Fonts folder when they're needed.

- Disable the Windows Startup screen to shave off an extra second or two. Press Start, then Run, then type `msconfig`, and press Enter. Navigate to the Boot.ini tab and check /NOGUIBOOT. Click Apply, then OK.

- Generally speaking, the simpler

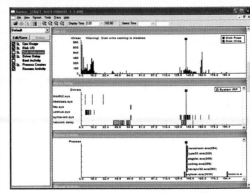

Improve Boot Speed

Bootvis analyzes your PC's boot process and checks for slow-starting drivers, apps, and even OS components. If all you want to do is make your PC boot faster, download *Bootvis* and run the program. Then go to Trace, then Optimize. If you want to see how much faster your PC is after *Bootvis* has done its job, go to Trace, Next Boot + Driver Delays.

Bootvis will restart your system and monitor the way each driver and TSR loads, then it will optimize their positions on your hard drive. *BootVis* is no longer officially supported by Microsoft, but it can be found by searching for it on Google.

Uncheck all unnecessary Startup items to make

your hardware setup, the quicker your machine will boot. If you have unused hardware devices listed in your Device Manager, disable them. Press Start, then Run, then type `devmgmt.msc`, and click OK. To disable a device, click on the device in question and select Disable. (Unused peripherals integrated into your mobo should be disabled in the BIOS.)

- One of the biggest culprits of a slow boot—and OS rot in general—is a mangled videocard driver install. Prior to your next videocard driver update, download and install Driver Cleaner (www.driverheaven.net/cleaner). This

XP Acceleration Resources

One of the most useful sites on the Net for learning all sorts of ways to customize XP for improved performance is www.tweakxp.com. Not only will you find scores of useful tips to try out, but also information about one of the more popular GUI-based XP tweaking-and-optimizing programs, *TweakXP*.

TweakXP bundles 48 different XP utilities into one handy program that lets you easily clean your registry, tweak your boot time, and back-up and restore your system—among many other useful functions.

Another popular program for tweaking XP's performance is Roemer Software's Optimum XP, which includes some 150 different XP hacks, tweaks, and tricks under one easy-to-use interface. (Visit www. roemersoftware.com for more info.)

Windows Services Exposed and Expunged

WinXP enables many resource-sucking background apps by default. Here's how to separate the wheat from the chaff and make XP run more efficiently in the process.

Compared with previous versions of Windows, XP is now packed with far more features than most people will ever use. Do you want to expand your Clipboard so it can share information with other users on a local network, for example? Or index the contents of files on your PC to speed up local searching?

Probably not, but that's just tough—Windows XP comes with these extras (and many others) built in. They're called Windows "services," and they're background programs that run under XP's hood, some of which are just begging for elimination.

This sounds like a bad situation, but the reality is Windows XP gives you all the tools you need to control these services. So if you would like a faster, leaner, more secure PC, learning the basics about services is a great way to start.

Gaining Control

To find out what's happening on your PC, launch the services console (Control Panel > Administrative Tools > Services, or just select Start > Run and enter `services.msc`). The console displays a list of all the services registered on your PC. Unusually for Windows, most services are accompanied by a lot of detail about what they do; make sure you click the "Extended" tab to view it all.

As you're scrolling down the list, pay particular attention to any services that have "Started" in the Status column. These are

currently running, and consuming at least some of your PC's resources. You could find 30 or more enabled—alarming, isn't it? Particularly because many are unnecessary for the kind of things you do with your PC.

Take a look at the "Startup Type" for each service, too. "Automatic" means the service starts on its own when required (or when Windows boots), while "Manual" services must be started manually (no surprise there). As you've probably guessed, services that are "Disabled" will not start under any circumstances.

The final column, "Log on as," illustrates a new security feature in Windows XP. Services that log on as "Local System" have full user privileges on your PC, which essentially means they can do whatever they like. However, services that log on as "Local Service" or "Network Service" have only the minimum privileges they need to carry out their tasks. So, even if a hacker manages to compromise one of these, the hacker will be limited in what he can do.

Don't start changing all your services to log on as "Local Service" or "Network Service." Many need the "Local System" account privileges, and changing their status could result in some strange behavior.

You've probably already spotted some services that look entirely unnecessary. Turning them off could save a little memory, reduce the time it takes your system to boot and close down, and even make your PC more secure. But make the wrong choice, and you could introduce a variety of odd and apparently unrelated problems. So which services are safe to remove, and what's the best way to do it? That's what we're here for.

Essential Services

Perhaps the best place to start is by detailing the services you really should keep running, regardless of how your system is configured. We think the following all qualify as essential services, so their settings should be left as "Automatic."

Antivirus Software You'll probably find that your antivirus program (perhaps your firewall, too) is running as a service. If you want to turn it off, though, it's best to do so via the "official" route (typically by right-clicking an icon in your system tray).

Cryptographic Services Even if you don't need the certificate services provided by this program, its other functions (like checking to see whether new drivers are digitally signed) are useful. We say leave it be.

Event Log This excellent feature records problems reported by other programs and services, which you can then view later (Control Panel > Administrative Tools > Event Viewer). Very useful, and we strongly recommend that you leave it running.

For the best overview of the services running on your PC, run the SysInternals Process Explorer (http://www.sysinternals.com/ntw2k/freeware/procexp.shtml).

Plug and Play You need this for your PC to recognize new devices as they are installed, or if you plug something into a USB or FireWire port, or even if your system has to redetect your hardware for some reason.

Remote Procedure Call Windows applications generally run in separate processes, which is a good thing (a crash in one application doesn't affect others, for example). Communication between processes can be handy, though, and that's the feature that RPC provides. Windows needs RPC to run, and disabling this feature is likely to cause very serious problems. So don't do it.

Task Scheduler You may never use this service to schedule night-time defrag operations, but it does have other handy applications, like the File Optimizations provided by the Windows XP Prefetcher (see the "Prefetch" section at **http://msdn.microsoft.com/msdnmag/issues/01/12/XPKernel/default.aspx**). Leave it set to "Automatic."

Windows Audio If you want to hear sound from your PC, allow the Windows Audio Service to stay running. And if you don't, just turn the volume down. This service should only be disabled if you don't have a soundcard or integrated sound on your motherboard.

Windows Management Instrumentation This service provides an interface that software can use to access and control various Windows functions (see "Programming Services"). Windows itself uses WMI, as do many other applications, so it's best to leave it set to "Automatic."

Workstation Allows access to remote files and other resources across a network, as well as provides support for some Internet services like "Background Intelligent Transfer." To be safe, whether you're networked or not, you really should leave this running.

Useful Services

One of the problems with the default Windows services settings is that they are configured in an unintelligent way. For example, services may be vital for a networked system and useless for anything else, but Windows will still launch them on a stand-alone PC. These are some of the services you may be able to do without, depending on your circumstances.

Application Layer Gateway Essential whether you're using Windows Internet Connection Sharing or the Internet Connection Firewall. Useless if you're not. (The same applies to "Internet Connection Firewall [ICF]/ Internet Connection Sharing [ICS]" and "Network Location Awareness.")

Automatic Updates If you prefer to not have Windows XP check for updates on its own, this service can safely be disabled. If you do disable it, however, don't forget to routinely check **www.windowsupdate.com** for updates.

Background Intelligent Transfer Used to download Windows updates in the background, so if you've disabled "Automatic Updates," this can be turned off as well.

COM+ Both the Event System and System Application Services help to administer Microsoft's Component Object Model system (see **www.microsoft.com/com/tech/COMPlus.asp** if you're interested). You may be running an application that needs it (even if you have a stand-alone PC), so leave it set to "Manual" if you know what's good for you.

DHCP Client Obtains an IP address from a DHCP server, either on a local network or (possibly) for your Internet connection. If you don't use DHCP, you can try disabling it, but restore it if you start having problems.

Help and Support Why is Windows Help a service? We have no idea. You can disable this if you like, but be aware that selecting Start, Help, or Support will restart it again.

HID Input Service Provides support for "hot buttons" on various input devices. Try turning this off, and restore it if you can't. For example, control Windows Media Player using the special buttons (Back, Next, Play, Stop, Volume) on your keyboard.

Logical Disk Manager If you want to manage your hard drives (right-click My Computer, select Manage, and then Disk Management), this needs to be running, along with the Logical Disk Manager Administrative service. As you might want to do this occasionally, we'd suggest leaving both services set at "Manual."

MS Software Shadow Copy Provider/Volume Shadow Copy Manages the copies of files (or complete volumes) provided by the Volume Shadow Copy service. Unless you use Microsoft Backup, or another imaging program that requires these services, they can both be turned off. Again, you can flip the switch back on if your backup program doesn't work correctly afterward.

System Restore It's nice to be able to "wind back" your system to undo the damage caused by installing a naughty driver, for example. Ideally, leave this service running. If you do decide to turn it off (Control Panel > System > System Restore), note that all your previous Restore Points will be lost as a result.

Telephony You definitely need this service if you use a conventional dial-up modem connection to the Internet. If you have a cable or ADSL connection, try setting this to "Manual" (it may still be required).

Webclient This allows you to browse to "Network Places" that are actually on the Internet, and lets Windows programs "create, access, and modify Internet-based files." As it reportedly can also slow down browsing on your local network, we recom-

Black Viper's voluminous web site, www.blackviper.com, is an excellent resource for more thoughts on how to configure your Windows Services.

mend disabling it, then monitoring what happens next.

Windows Image Acquisition If you don't have a scanner or webcam, then you can turn this off. And if you do, it may not require the WIA service, so turn it off anyway (or just set it to "Manual" and see what happens).

Windows Installer This tool handles any programs that install using .MSI files. You're likely to need it occasionally, though not often, so it seems a good candidate for the "Manual" setting (where the service will consume RAM only when it's required).

Wireless Zero Configuration Properties Handy if you've got any 802.11x wireless adapters installed (it helps set them up), but entirely useless if you haven't (and yet, bizarrely, it may still be running anyway.)

Nonessential Services

We've been fairly cautious so far, and with good reason—some services really are important for keeping your system running smoothly. This category is different, though, and the chance of your needing one of these services is very slim indeed.

Application Management This provides "Assign, Publish, and Remove software services," so turning it off might cause problems installing or removing some applications (particularly Microsoft's). However, as this service doesn't even exist on Windows XP Home edition, we're not sure how widespread these issues might be. Try turning it off and restoring the service to "Manual" if you have any problems.

Clipbook This feature lets you view the contents of the Clipboard, store them permanently, and share them with other users on your local network (use Start, Run, *clipbrd.exe* to see how this works). It can be disabled if you don't feel you'll use it.

Computer Browser Keeps track of the other systems currently connected to your network, so it can be safely turned off on a stand-alone system. Even if you're on a networked system, you only need a maximum of two PCs running this service, and perhaps none at all if all the networked PCs have Windows 2000 or XP-based systems.

Distributed Link Tracking Client This service lets you create a shortcut to a file on a remote PC, then updates it automatically if the file is moved later. If you're on a stand-alone PC, or if your networked systems don't use NTFS, or if you just don't need this feature, then turn it off.

Error Reporting Ever wonder what's responsible for those dialog boxes that pop up whenever an application crashes, asking if you want to send a report back to Microsoft? Well, this service is the culprit. It's high on the "nonessential" list. Whether you want to be a part of the Windows XP and application bug hunt is up to you.

Indexing A good idea in theory, this service creates a document index to speed up searches in Windows and *Office XP* (among other apps). However, in reality, it consumes more resources than it's worth, and you're better off disabling it. (Restore it later if searches start to seem too slow.)

IPSEC If you're a telecommuter and need to connect to a remote network via a VPN, then Internet Protocol Security (IPSEC) may be useful. Otherwise, it almost certainly is not. Turn it off and reclaim the resources.

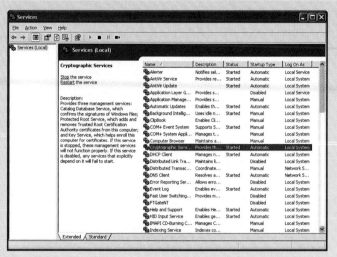

Unusually for Windows, most services provide a lengthy description of what they do. (Make sure you click the "Extended" tab to see it.)

Messenger No, not *Windows* or *MSN Messenger*. This is a service that sends messages between clients and servers across your network. It's obviously a superfluous feature for stand-alone systems, but home networks probably won't need it either. Turn the service off and see what happens.

Remote Registry Service Do you want remote users to be able to modify Registry settings on your PC? It's not as insecure as it sounds, but we'd still disable this feature, unless you have a good reason to do otherwise.

SSDP Discovery A component of "Universal Plug and Play." Whether you disable that or leave it running, you need to do the same with SSDP Discovery.

TCP/IP NetBIOS Helper Generally required only if your local network uses NetBIOS over TCP/IP. Turn it off, restoring the service if you have any subsequent network (or possibly Internet) problems.

Telnet Allows remote users to log on to your PC and run programs. Turn it off, unless you really need this service for some reason.

Uninterruptible Power Supply It's safe to disable this, unless of course you really do have a UPS.

Back Up Your Config!
If things go wrong, this is your "Plan B"

Does tweaking your services make you a little nervous? Are you concerned about how you can restore your current settings if something goes wrong? You should be. One answer is to back up the Services Settings held in the Registry; run REGEDIT, navigate to HKEY_LOCAL_MACHINE\SYSTEM\CurrentControlSet\Services, and use File > Export to save that data. Double-clicking the file it produces will restore your settings.

This is a good bit of insurance, but don't be complacent. Turn off a critical service like Remote Procedure Call and your PC may not even boot, making it impossible to use the backup file.

Universal Plug and Play Discovers devices attached to remote PCs on your network. May also be necessary if you use Internet Connection Sharing and allow others to modify the connection properties. Its security issues have now been resolved (**www.microsoft.com/technet/security/bulletin/MS01-059.mspx**), but unless you need this service, it's still wise to turn it off.

Windows Time Synchronizing your clock via an Internet time server is a good idea, especially if you have an "always on" Internet connection. But doing so via a Windows service that's running all the time is not the most efficient route.

WMI Performance Adapter Windows Management Instrumentation (WMI) is an essential service, but it can be slow. High performance (HiPerf) providers can speed things up massively, and the WMI Performance Adapter can be used to provide information on this. But unless you're a developer, this is of little utility, and can be disabled.

Proceed with Care

Compare our lists with the services running on your system, and you'll quickly pick out the ones that seem to be unnecessary. So what should you do next?

To avoid any potential problems, it's best to proceed with caution. Open the Services console (Start > Run > **services.msc**) and double-click one of the services you suspect is unnecessary. When

Services like "Help and Support" can be re-enabled unexpectedly, so keep an eye on your Service Settings to make sure they don't change.

the Properties dialog appears, select the "General" tab, change its "Startup Type" to "Manual," and click OK. (Change only one service at a time to avoid confusion.)

Once a service has been set to "Manual," it should only be launched if required by an application or another service. The good news is that this means you'll recover a little RAM for your other applications. The bad news? If the service really is required, there may be a noticeable delay at some point while it's launched.

To test this, reboot your PC and check the Services console again. If it's now showing as "Started," then this means another service or application requires it to function. Otherwise, try carrying out functions that relate to what the service is supposed to do (connect to the Internet, browse a networked PC, whatever it might be), then check the service status again. If your PC still works fine, and if the service is not shown as "Started," then it probably isn't required.

Don't let the potential risks put you off. Managing services isn't difficult, and is a great way to give your system a performance boost. ∎

Building Service Profiles
Quickly and easily turn whole groups of services on or off to suit your needs

You're about to play a resource-hogging game on your PC, and all the network-related services have been left running. So wouldn't it be better if you could turn them all off, play the game, then restore normal service when you're done?

To see one way of achieving this, open a DOS window, and enter **NET HELP SERVICES | MORE**. As you'll see, the NET command can be used to start (and stop) a variety of services.

Now open up Notepad and create a file called **STOPSERV.BAT** that contains the lines **NET STOP CLIPBOOK** and **NET STOP MESSENGER**. Then create a second file called **STARTSERV.BAT**, containing the lines **NET START CLIPBOOK** and **NET START MESSENGER**. Place the files on your desktop and you'll now be able to stop and start these with a double-click.

This works well, as long as you remember that some services rely on others. The Messenger Service depends on Workstation; when you're creating the restart batch file, this means that a NET START WORKSTATION

command must appear before NET START MESSENGER will work. Double-click on a service in the Services console, then select Dependencies for more information.

An alternative is to build one or more custom hardware profiles. To get started in Windows XP, select Control Panel > System > Hardware > Hardware Profiles, choose your current profile, click "Copy" and give it a name along the lines of "Minimum Services."

Next, choose Start > Run, and enter **services.msc** to start the console. Select a service that's running, but that you don't need. Double-click it, select the Log On tab, and ensure that it's disabled for the "Minimum Services" profile. Repeat this for every service you can do without.

Now, when you want to give a game or application everything you've got, just reboot your PC and choose your "Minimum Services" profile from the boot menu, And best of all, if something goes wrong, it's very easy to recover—just reboot again, and choose the regular hardware profile.

```
  MS-DOS Prompt

C:\WINDOWS>net help services
The syntax of this command is:

SERVICES
NET START can be used to start services, including

   NET START ALERTER
   NET START BROWSER
   NET START CLIENT SERVICE FOR NETWARE
   NET START CLIPBOOK
   NET START DHCP CLIENT
   NET START EVENTLOG
   NET START FILE REPLICATION
   NET START MESSENGER
   NET START NET LOGON
   NET START NT LM SECURITY SUPPORT PROVIDER
   NET START PLUG AND PLAY
   NET START REMOTE ACCESS CONNECTION MANAGER
   NET START ROUTING AND REMOTE ACCESS
   NET START RPCLOCATOR
   NET START RPCSS
   NET START SCHEDULE
   NET START SERVER
   NET START SPOOLER
   NET START TCP/IP NETBIOS HELPER SERVICE
   NET START UPS
   NET START WORKSTATION

When typed at the command prompt, service names of
be enclosed in quotation marks. For example, NET S
starts the net logon service.

C:\WINDOWS>_
```

The humble batch file is one of the best ways to speedily reconfigure your services.

3

Maintain a Healthy OS!

Windows XP can be a sickly OS, vulnerable to diseases like bloat, adware, viruses, and excessive clutter. Keep XP shiny and clean with these fail-safe, time-tested Maximum PC routines

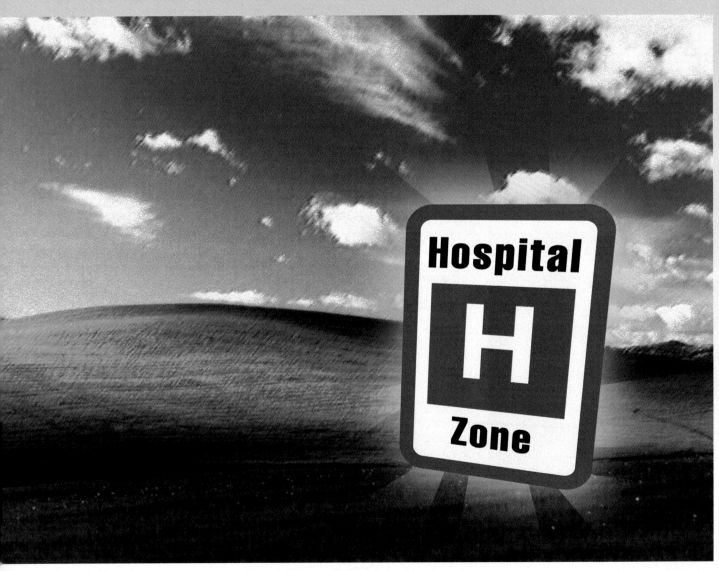

Hospital
H
Zone

Nothing beats a rollicking, speedy operating system that busts your programs open in seconds and blazes through games at dizzying frame rates. Windows XP is Microsoft's most stable and versatile operating system to date—but keeping it that way takes some time and effort on your part. Like an unkempt refrigerator, your OS can end up in a sorry state if you wait too long to clean it up!

For instance, as you add applications to your computer, they write entries in the Registry. As the Registry grows, Windows has more "stuff" to sort through when you want it do something. Net result: Windows gradually slows down over time.

Other factors contribute to Windows' gradual loss of performance. More files on the hard drive means more "junk" Windows has to muddle through to find what it's looking for. Without your due diligence, files can and will fragment, which means Windows may have to look in three different places on the hard disk platters to piece together a single file. This, of course, tosses efficiency out the window, and you suffer the associated performance penalties.

Like a newborn child, Windows XP has a weak immune system. Viruses, worms, spyware, adware, and other nasties can burrow their way into your computer's hard drive if you're not paying attention, resulting in all manner of anomalies. Disk problems can creep up any time, too. At best they're merely a nuisance. At worst, they're a destructive maelstrom that can corrupt files, resulting in total data loss, which is always only a stuck bit away—and usually occurs at the most inconvenient time.

Do we have your attention yet? Good. All's not lost. If you dutifully follow these preventative steps, your OS will thank you for it profusely, with years of trouble-free operation and top performance. As with your fridge or car regular maintenance of your OS is the key to keeping it clean. Institute these daily, weekly, and monthly tasks—as well as one Herculean yearly practice—into your PC regimen, *today*. Trust us, it's worth the effort!

Daily

Back-up Your files.

Transferring copies of your data to secure removable media, such as CDs or DVDs, is paramount. Your files are vulnerable to data corruption, hard drive seizures, malicious viruses, and all sorts of evil. Back up your files *every time you change them*. That means, if you brush up the resume in order to escape your soul-sucking job, back it up. If you finally get past all the damn snipers in the Stalingrad map of *Call of Duty,* back-up your game saves. If you get around to balancing your checkbook in *Quicken,* back up your files—heck, *Quicken* even includes its own, built-in backup system!

At the very least, use *Windows Backup,* which you have to install manually off of your XP CD (your CD drive:\valueadd\ msft\ntbackup). *Windows Backup* is easy to use; it contains backup and restore wizards to make the process painless, and it works with Windows' scheduling agent to automate backups to run whenever you'd like. Or pick up a more robust third-party app, such as *BackUpMyPC* (see the sidebar PC Backups made easy), which contains support for a wider range of removable media hardware, including CD/DVD-R drives.

Update Your Antivirus Program

You *are* using an antivirus program, right? If not, for shame. Go out and get yourself *Norton AntiVirus* or *McAfee VirusScan,* which are the two dominant antivirus programs available. Or, if you'd rather not shell out for these, head over to www. free-av.com and download *AntiVir.* It's free, it's effective, it's small, and it works. It lacks some of the bells and whistles that the commercial packages have, such as an e-mail scanner and heuristic detection, but its background agent catches viruses on the fly, making it nearly as effective as any antivirus program.

Most antivirus programs look for viruses, worms, trojans, and more. When a new virus hits the Net, antivirus developers scramble to update their wares to recognize and eliminate it. Take advantage of their vigilance and update your antivirus program daily. Some antivirus software lets you schedule automated updates. Do it.

Empty the Recycle Bin

Power users delete folders, files, shortcuts, and other stuff on a regular basis. Don't leave that junk to collect dust—and take up valuable disk space—by al-

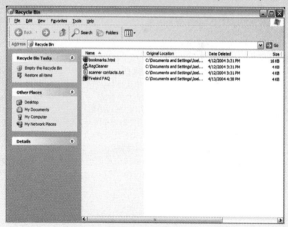

So obvious you can miss it: Hose out your Recycle Bin *on a daily basis to free up disk space.*

lowing it to languish in the Recycle Bin. Tank it. Check out Rich Levin's *T-Man* (short for Trash Man, www. rblevin.net/TMN_Index.htm). It's an itty-bitty program that can automatically flush the Recycle Bin when Windows shuts down. You can even elect to not have deleted items moved to the Recycle Bin, and instead have them deleted immediately. Click the Recycle Bin, right-click and select Properties, and check the box. Now just be careful when you hit that scary deletion-confirmation button!

The freeware AntiVir *virus scanner, like all antivirus programs, includes an Internet updater to keep it up to date on the latest viruses.*

Weekly

Defrag, Defrag...

Fragmented files can invoke a general PC malaise, which manifests itself as slowness, drive thrashing, poor posture, and halitosis. OK, maybe not those last two, but don't wait until your data is fragmented enough to notice a decline in performance; run Disk Defragmenter once a week. Fire it up through the Start menu/All Programs/Accessories/System Tools. It lets you analyze each partition of your hard drive, and it spits out a recommendation to either defrag the drive or leave it alone.

Update Windows

If you've disabled Windows' automatic update applet, it is imperative that you manually run Windows Update each week. Security "holes"—XP was perforated with 'em at launch—are exponentially more dangerous to your system than viruses are, and hackers find new ways to crack into Windows regularly. Microsoft continuously publishes patches for these security holes, so keep a look out for them. Launch Windows Update by clicking on its icon in Start/All Programs. *Internet Explorer* will launch and take you to the Windows Update web site, where you should elect to scan your copy of Windows XP for all available updates. After Update scans, it'll cough up a list of critical updates, optional updates, and driver updates. Be sure to install any critical updates; whether to install the others is your choice. Driver updates are almost always a good idea; read the descriptions of the other options carefully determine if you need them for your PC usage—the

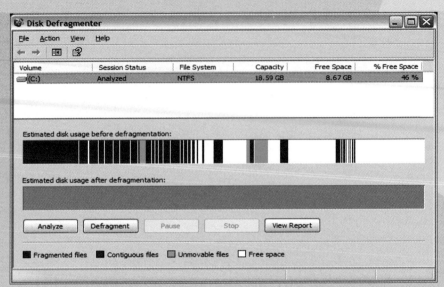

Disk Defragmenter *presents one of the easiest means to keep your PC running smoothly. Fragmented files hurt performance, so defrag your hard drive often.*

motto "don't fix it if it's not broke" exists for a reason.

Update Your Device Drivers

This can be a pain in the rear, but it's worth the bother. Manufacturers of motherboards, graphics cards, soundcards, modems, and other hardware tend to update their drivers on a regular basis. You should head to their web sites once a week and check for updates. Optimized drivers can boost the performance of your hardware—this is especially true of graphics cards. Drivers are the key to compatibility and performance and you should stay on top of them regularly. If the manufacturer of your hardware offers automatic e-mail updates informing you of new driver releases, sign up! Windows Update will

also inform you of new drivers, particularly for your graphics card.

Get Rid of Adware and Spyware

Adware and spyware not only snoop on how you use your system, but they also can impede performance. Run a free program called *Ad-Aware*, which can be found at www.lavasoftusa.com.

Run Disk Cleanup

Microsoft included a handy little applet called Disk Cleanup, which you launch through the Start menu in All Programs/Accessories/System Tools. It calculates how much disk space you can free up by compressing older files, clearing the browser cache, getting rid of temp files, and more.

PC Backups Made Easy

If Stomp's *BackUpMyPC* looks familiar, you've probably worked with Veritas *Backup Exec. BackUpMyPC* is based upon that ubiquitous application, and it allows you to hunt through a hard drive and networked storage devices to back up whatever you like.

BackUpMyPC has a simple, straightforward interface that lets you perform backups on the spot or schedule them to take place during off hours. It works with nearly any form of removable media, including recordable optical media, tape, Zip, Jaz, external hard drives, and more.

You can choose which files to back up or perform full system backups, which you can then catalog by date so if your PC's hard drive crashes, you're prepared to recover mission-critical data with a few swift strokes. For more information and a dowlnloadable trial version of *BackUpMyPC*, head to www.stompsoft.com/bump

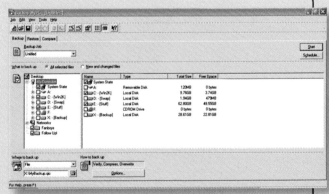

BackUpMyPC *features an awesome, smooth interface that lets the user back up and restore files in a jiffy.*

Disk Cleanup *analyzes your computer's hard drive and presents you with options to help you recover space, from compressing older files to wiping out your temp directory.*

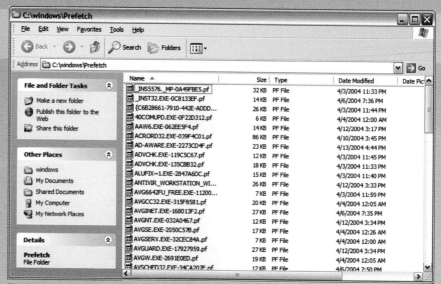

The Windows *prefetch gets clogged with data, and some of it pertains to programs that aren't even installed anymore. Clear the folder on a regular basis.*

Archive Old files!

Data that you create but end up not using languishes in folders, doing nothing but taking up hard drive space. Digital photos, *Word* documents, spreadsheets, movies, and other files you rarely open are your targets for this task: Archive them on removable media and delete them from your hard drive. Label the media clearly and consider making a spreadsheet listing of the files on each CD or DVD, or whatever you use, so that if you find yourself looking for something specific you can easily pinpoint its location.

Clear the Prefetch

Look in C:\Windows\Prefetch, and you'll find prefetch files for all the applications you run. Windows monitors how your programs operate and creates "prefetch" data, which operates much like a cache. The prefetch data consist

of items Windows thinks your programs will request; when they do, loading the data from prefetch is a bit quicker than finding it in other areas of the hard drive. Some of those applications might not be on the A-list of files you use all the time. It's safe to wipe out the contents of this folder completely; applications that need to store prefetch data will simply recreate it. Clearing the folder won't hurt performance, and it will free up disk space by getting ret rid of files that were dropped there by applications you rarely use.

Clean the Registry

It's a good idea to keep your desktop clear of icons, but in a powerful system you won't notice a difference in performance if your desktop is clean or cluttered. You might, however, notice a lag in the time it takes icons to appear on the screen, or in the animation of the Start menu. Clear the icon cache by locating the file IconCache. db. It usually resides in your profile directory (/Documents and Settings/<user name>/Local Settings/Application Data). Rename it, change its extension, and

reboot; Windows will automatically create a new, refreshed copy. Then, feel free to delete the renamed copy.

Clear Icon Cache

Programs that you install make entries in the Registry. Often, when you uninstall them, they maintain a ghost-like presence in the Registry, leaving orphaned entries and generally gumming up the works. Use a utility like *RegSupreme* from Macecraft Software (www.jv16.org, $12.95). It can find and eliminate unnecessary Registry entries. Just be sure to back up your Registry before you run it: launch RegEdit (click Start/Run, type in *regedit*, and hit enter), go to the Registry pulldown menu, select "Export Registry file," make sure the "All" radio button is selected, type in a name (such as the date; for example RegBackup_5-30-04), and hit Save.

Reinstall XP!

It may seem extreme, but once a year you should consider wiping your hard drive and installing a fresh, clean copy of Windows. You don't need to back up program files; you can reinstall your programs after you install Windows, so concentrate on your data files. You'll need to back up data files you can't live without. Make a thorough list—see our box-out for a good checklist

Back-up Everything

Back up these important files, and anything else you can think of, to CDs, DVDs, tape, or something else from which you'll be able to recover the data. You can use a backup program (discussed earlier) or

Shareware powerhouse RegSupreme *scours your system Registry looking for useless entries, which you can then delete.*

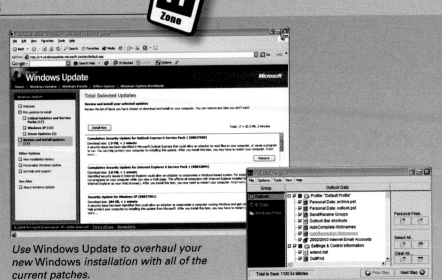

Use Windows Update *to overhaul your new* Windows *installation with all of the current patches.*

BackUpMyPC *is getting ready to create an exhaustive backup of our current Windows installation, parts of which we'll restore after reinstalling Windows.*

Microsoft's own backup tools are inadequate. You are well advised to use a third-party program like OutBack Plus.

simply copy the data to your removable media, or an extra hard drive. Remember that if you do use a backup program, you'll have to install it after you install Windows in order to regain access to your data. (Note: While you can export your e-mail and address book, *Outlook* doesn't include a method to export *all* of its settings, messages, contacts, and rules. For this, you must use a utility like *OutBack Plus,* available for $30 from AJ Systems at www.ajsystems.com.

Make sure you have any updated drivers you've downloaded for your hardware in a handy location—such as a folder on an alternate internal or external hard drive—before you begin. Have your installation software on hand for stuff like your modem, your network interface card, your motherboard, your soundcard, and your graphics card.

Delete Your Windows Partition

When you're absolutely sure you've backed-up everything, modify your CMOS setup program to tell the BIOS to boot off your CD drive first, and your hard drive second. Boot from the Windows XP CD. The Windows XP installation process will start. When the first setup screen appears, press Enter. Then the license agreement will pop up. Read it thoroughly (Yeah, right!) and hit F8 to sign your life away. The setup program will find your current installation of Windows and ask if you wish to repair it. Select no and move along to the partitioning screen.

The setup program will show your hard drive partitions. Unless you did some fancy partitioning when you last installed Windows, you'll probably see a single, large partition. Take a deep breath, and follow the prompts to delete the Windows partition. This is the part at which you destroy your current instal-

lation; there's no going back from here. Press D, then Enter, and then L.

The next screen will show unpartitioned space. Follow the prompts to create one huge partition, or, if you like several partitions. (On larger drives we like to set up one partition for our OS and another for programs, games, or digital pictures, for example.) The next screen will let you choose the file system; we recommend NTFS because it uses disk space more efficiently than FAT32. Let the setup program format the partition. Setup will then copy some files to the hard drive and reboot. When you see the "Press any key to boot the CD" prompt, don't do it! Let the system boot from the hard drive.

Follow the prompts, and Windows will launch a welcome screen, followed by a network setup screen. Windows may or may not have drivers for your modem or network interface card; in any case, you'll want to load newer drivers for them now. Next, Windows will prompt you to activate your installation. You have a 60-day grace period to activate Windows. If you don't activate now, Windows will only remind you later, so if your internet connection is up, get it over with.

Update Your Drivers

Next, you'll *finally* see the Windows desktop. The first thing to do is install your hardware's device drivers. When your drivers are all in, make your way to the Internet by running Network Setup Wizard (if you're using broadband) or by loading up your ISP's software and dialing out with your modem.

Check for newer drivers—or drivers you'd missed—for your equipment and install them now.

Next, head to Windows Update and install all of the critical updates, service packs, the latest DirectX version, and whatever else looks good to you. You'll probably have to run Windows Update more than once and reboot in between, as some updates must be installed separately from the others.

When Windows is up to date, install any applications you plan to use, such as *Microsoft Office,* games, and so on. Then, restore your backed up data. Windows Backup and *BackUpMyPC* let you specify a target directory when you restore data; plop your stuff wherever you like. If you copied stuff to removable media, copy it back onto your hard drive.

Piece of cake, right? Okay, maybe not, but if your spanking fresh XP installation isn't obviously faster than before, we'll eat our hats. ∎

Backup File Checklist

☑ Office documents: word processing files, spreadsheets, and presentations

☑ Email data – messages and address book

☑ Game saves

☑ Digital photos and other artwork

☑ Movies that you've created or edited

☑ MP3s, OGGs, and other music files

☑ Browser bookmarks/favorites

☑ Downloaded files you can't replace

☑ Passwords and security codes for web sites, *Quicken* files, and anything else that's encrypted

☑ Activation codes for applications that you downloaded and registered

Master the Dark Arts:
Be a Power User

You're not a true master of Windows XP until you have edited the Registry. Follow our tips to crack into the code, customize the OS to suit your style, and complete your transformation into a Power User.

W e've shown you how to revitalize your desktop, maximize your online connection, and accelerate, secure, and maintain your WinXP-powered PC. Now you're ready for the Big Show: Hacking the Windows Registry to further customize XP to meet your needs. This is where the true power users are separated from the wannabes.

If the mere thought of exposing XP's guts and editing its code makes you cringe—maybe you've heard horror stories of people who've tried and have hosed their OS' in the process—there's no need to worry. Really. You've got *Maximum PC* here to guide you through this last, vital step in earning your XP power-user stripes.

We've been dabbling in the "Dark Arts" for years, and have made all the mistakes already so that you won't have to. While operating on Windows' Registry admittedly has always been a risky and extremely complex procedure, it has never been as safe and straightforward as it is now with XP (provided you follow some basic guidelines, which we'll outline for you).

Essentially, you can think of the Registry as the Wizard of Oz that's behind the Windows graphical user interface you see every day. Others might tell you that you really don't want to see the wizard unless it's absolutely necessary. We're here to tell you different: Rolling up your sleeves and editing the Registry can be a very rewarding experience, particularly when a successful "hack" results in a more efficient way for you to interact with your PC. And it will definitely make you feel like you're in control of your OS, rather than the inverse.

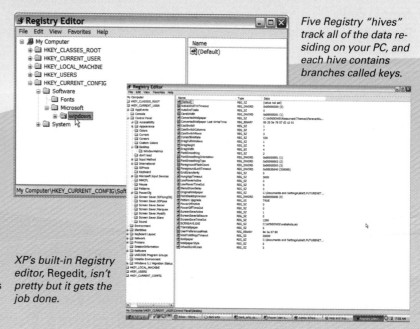

Five Registry "hives" track all of the data residing on your PC, and each hive contains branches called keys.

XP's built-in Registry editor, Regedit, *isn't pretty but it gets the job done.*

The Registry: An Introduction

It's possible you've been operating your PC for years without ever taking note of the Registry—oblivious to the OS potential you could unleash with some strategic modifications here and there. If so, a primer is in order.

The Registry is a Windows database that operates behind the scenes, storing information about everything happening within your computer. Whenever you make a change to your computer, be it installing new hardware or software, or changing your desktop background, this change is flagged in the Registry.

The Registry is hierarchical in structure, similar to the branch/tree structure used in hard drives. The main branches are called "hives," and the hives contain "keys." Within the keys are "subkeys" and values that reflect the actual data stored in the Registry. By tweaking these values you can alter the way XP looks, increase the speed at which it operates, and change many of its default settings to match your preferences.

For example, each time a new user logs on, a new hive is created for that user with a separate file for their user profile. Naturally, this hive is called the "User Profile Hive," and it contains specific Registry information about the user's application settings, desktop, network connections, etc. User Profile hives are located under the HKEY_USERS key.

The supporting file for the User Profile hive for a given user is located in HKEY_LOCAL_MACHINE\Software\Microsoft\ WindowsNT\CurrentVersion\ProfileList\SID\ProfileImagePath, and is named Ntuser.dat. The value of ProfileImagePath is a binary representation of the directory name of the user's profile, which includes the user's name. The Registry editor displays this binary value as a string. By altering the values in this string, as well as any other values contained in the rest of the Registry's keys and subkeys, we can change the way XP works or looks. There are a variety of third-party, GUI-based programs you can

use to do this, such as Macecraft Software's *jv16PowerTools* (www.jv16.org). However, for most of us, the Registry editor that comes with XP works just fine—though it's very low on bells and whistles. To access the editor, you simply click on Start Menu, Run, and type **Regedit**.

Cover Your Back With System Restore

Don't just go randomly pointing and clicking about. Changing some Registry settings could damage or disable critical XP components, and even prevent Windows from running at all. It's important that you proceed slowly and with caution, and that you don't make any changes unless you're absolutely sure of what you're doing. In fact, it's wise to perform a full system backup before diving into the Registry, particularly if you've no previous hacking experience.

At the very least, you should make prudent use of WinXP's System Restore procedure, which lets you set a "restore point" that you can use as a safety net. If your hacking efforts result in XP instability, or just in certain programs or functions not working as you'd like, you can just roll XP back to the last restore point and start over with a healthy OS—just like you stepped back in time.

Setting a restore point couldn't be easier, so there's no excuse not to take advantage of it. (You really should set a restore point before you make any type of significant change to your system, whether it's installing a new video card or even just installing a new game or version of *DirectX*.) And the best thing about the process is that rolling back to a particular restore point will not result in the loss of data you've created recently, such as email or *Word* documents, and the entire process is reversible. So if you select the wrong restore point and actually perform the rollback, you can easily fix your mistake. For a walkthrough of the process, see our sidebar "How to Set a Restore Point."

Start Slowly, with Basic Hacks

OK, now that we've covered the Registry basics, and set a restore point, it's time to take a deep breath, and wade into the hacking pool. We'll start off nice and slow—covering some simple Registry edits that alter XP's default organizational structure—and build up to more complicated hacks. By the time you finish plowing through our baker's dozen of hacks, you'll feel like a pro, and should be confident enough with the process to seek out your own tweaks to try out.

Hack One:
Remove Network Drive Options

After you've been using your PC for a bit, Explorer's menus tend to become pretty darn cluttered—and we bet that cleaning them up is right above organizing your sock drawer on your priority list. Here's a little hack that takes but a few seconds and will make things neater. We're going to remove two items from the Tools menu, the "Map" and "Disconnect" Network Drive options, which most of us don't give a hoot about anyways, as we're using a stand-alone PC. The first step, which will be the same first step for the rest of the tips and will be assumed after this point, is to fire up *Regedit* (Start, Run, type **Regedit**). Next, navigate to HKEY_CURRENT_USER\Software\ Microsoft\Windows\CurrentVersion\Policies\Explorer by simply using the drop-down menus under the HKEY_CURRENT_USER Hive. Create a new DWORD entry called "NoNetConnectDisconnect," and give it a value of 1. Do this by right-clicking anywhere in the right window pane, selecting New, and DWORD Value. Now, simply close *Regedit* and reboot. To re-enable these settings later, change the value to 0 or delete the entry.

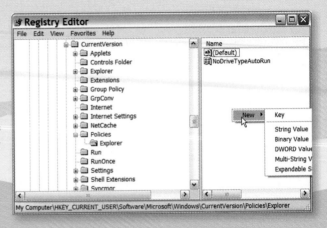

Hack Two:
Minimize Outlook to the System Tray

That wasn't tough at all, was it? Good. Here's another quickie that makes XP a bit more efficient if you rely heavily on *Microsoft Outlook*, which most of us do. You can have XP automatically minimize *Outlook* to the System Tray each time you start the program. Browse to HKEY_CURRENT_USER\Software\Microsoft\Office\10.0\Outlook\Preferences. Add a new DWORD value named MinToTray, and set it to 1. Next time you restart *Outlook*, it will automatically minimize to the System Tray.

How to Set a Restore Point
Keep yourself covered with XP's built-in safety net.

Roll your PC back in time, and even take it "back to the future" with XP's built-in System Restore utility. To access it, click Start, Help and Support, System Restore (listed under Additional Resources). Check the "Create a restore point" button, click Next, and then enter a name for your restore point. (Typically, it's a good idea to use the current date and time, or a description that reflects why you're setting the restore point, such as "Before My First Hack.") Now, click Create and you're done. If you get into trouble, just return to the System Restore home menu to select a restore point to activate, or to cancel a previous restoration.

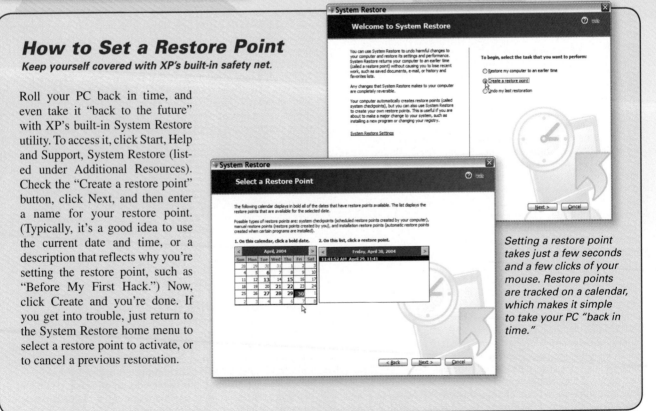

Setting a restore point takes just a few seconds and a few clicks of your mouse. Restore points are tracked on a calendar, which makes it simple to take your PC "back in time."

Hack Three:
Improve the Context Menu

So far, so good...and we bet you're starting to have a little fun, too. Nothing brings out your inner geek like editing the Registry. Next, we're going to add "Copy to folder" and "Move to folder" options to the right-click context menu, which should save you a lot of time, if—like us—you move a lot of files around on your PC. Go to HKEY_CLASSES_ROOT\AllFilesystemObjects\shellex\ContextMenuHandlers. Create a new key called "Copy To" and set its value to... deep breath: {C2FBB630-2971-11D1-A18C-00C04FD75D13}. Next, create another new key called "Move To" and set the value to... another deep breath: {C2FBB631-2971-11D1-A18C-00C04FD75D13}. Exit the Registry and the change is immediate. Now, when you right-click a file you'll be able to move or copy the file quickly using the new options.

Hack Four:
Kill Compression

The Disk Cleanup wizard is a handy way to find out what unused files you can get rid of to save disk space, but it also calculates the space you'll save by compressing your drive. We don't like to use compression, so we're going to disable it by browsing to HKEY_LOCAL_MACHINE\SOFTWARE\Microsoft\Windows\CurrentVersion\Explorer\VolumeCaches\CompressOldFiles. Clear the value from the Default key. The next time you start Disk Cleanup, it will skip the compression analysis.

Hack Five:
Secure Your Pagefile

The Windows swapfile (refers to Windows virtual memory) can contain anything that might be in RAM, including sensitive data like passwords. To set XP to automatically erase any info contained in the swapfile at shutdown, go to HKEY_LOCAL_MACHINE\SYSTEM\CurrentControlSet\ Control\Session Manager\Memory Management and add a DWORD value named "ClearPageFileAtShutdown." Set it to 1, reboot your PC, and your machine will automatically erase the contents of your pagefile when you shut down. Be aware that this will make your PC take longer to shut down, sometimes adding as much as 20-30 seconds to the process. If you find the trade-off's not worth the enhanced security, turn this option off by setting the value to 0 or by deleting the DWORD.

Kill the "My" Folders, Permanently

By default, you'll find a "My Pictures" folder in your My Documents folder, as well as My Music, My eBooks (blech!), etc. If you delete the folders as you normally would, they will "magically" appear the next time you start Windows. Annoying, to say the least, but you can do something about it with some hacking trickery. Open your My Documents folder and delete the My Pictures folder. Right-click an empty area, select New, and then Text Document. Name this document "My Pictures" (without a filename extension). Now, right-click your new My Pictures file, select Properties, turn on the Read-only and Hidden options, and you're done. WinXP may *try*, but it won't be able to create the "My Documents" folders next time you boot, because there cannot be two files with the same name in the same directory. Rinse and repeat to cleanse your My Documents folder or the rest of the "My" folders as you see fit.

You also can customize the folders listed in your Open dialog boxes: Whenever you open a file in Notepad or Paint, for example, there's a default list of folders on the left side of the window. Unfortunately, those folders are not that useful for most people. To customize them, point *Regedit* to HKEY_CURRENT_USER\Software\Microsoft\Windows\CurrentVersion\Policies\comdlg32.

Now we're going to get a bit trickier than simply modifying DWORDs and create a new key called "Placesbar." Inside that new key, create a String called "Place0" and point it to the folder you want to appear on the Open dialog, say, C:\Current Work. Create another String called "Place1" and point it to another location on your drive. You can use variables (%USERPROFILE% will point the folder to the profile of a currently logged-in user) or URI's, so you can even use network shares. This hack won't change the same dialogs in *Office*, but if you have *Office XP*, you can add new folders to the Placesbar by going to File, Open, and browsing to the folder you want to add. Once you have it selected, go to Tools and click "Add to My Places." If you have trouble with this route, you can use the PowerToy *TweakUI* to generate the same result—just look under the Common Dialogs options (for more on *TweakUI*, turn to the section "PowerToys for Power Users").

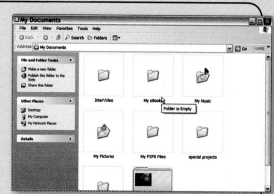

XP may say differently, but you don't have to keep the series of "My" folders under My Documents if you don't want them.

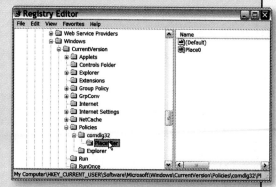

Make it easier to use folders the way you want to by customizing the Registry's Placesbar settings.

Hack Six:
Stop the WMP Recent Files List

If you want to keep what files you're playing in Windows Media Player a secret—and we can't imagine why—you can use the Registry to kill the "Recent Files" list. Navigate to the HKEY_CURRENT_USER\Software\Microsoft\MediaPlayer\Preferences Registry subkey. From the Edit menu, select New, Binary Value, and enter a name of "AddToMRU," then press Enter. Double-click the new value, set it to 00 to disable the list, or 01 to enable it, then click OK.

You can clear current entries from the most recently played files list by either deleting the HKEY_CURRENT_USER\Software\Microsoft\MediaPlayer\Player\ RecentFileList Registry subkey or deleting individual entries under this subkey. To clear streamed media entries, delete the HKEY_CURRENT_USER\Software\Microsoft\ MediaPlayer\Player\RecentURLList subkey.

Hack Seven:
Remove Unnecessary DLL's from Cache Memory

Sometimes XP keeps DLLs in cache memory even when the program that required them is no longer running, which can cut down on the memory available to other applications—particularly if your system is memory-deprived to begin with. This simple hack makes XP automatically remove these DLLs during shutdown. Navigate to HKEY_LOCAL_MACHINE\SOFTWARE\Microsoft\Windows\ CurrentVersion\Explorer and create a new DWORD value called "AlwaysUnloadDll." Give it a data value of 1. Exit the Registry and log off or reboot for the new setting to take effect. It should be noted that this setting may cause problems with some Windows programs—especially older 16-bit programs—and may generate error messages when you try to use this software. If so, delete the new key, or give it a value of 0.

Hack Eight:
Reject the Dumb Search Interface

Do you miss the simplicity of the old Windows 98/2000 search utility? Does it make you angry that Windows XP dumbed down your search options and gave you a bothersome Search mascot? Here's how to not only ditch the mascot, but also revert to the original, more powerful search interface.

Open *Regedit* by going to Start, Run, and typing **regedit** in the Open box. Then browse to HKEY_CURRENT_USER\Software\Microsoft\Windows\ CurrentVersion\Explorer\CabinetState\ and create a new String Value called "Use Search Asst." Then set the value to "no".

Hack Nine:
Turn off the Windows Picture and Fax Viewer

The *Windows Picture and Fax Viewer* is set as the default image viewer for all sorts of file types in Windows XP. Unfortunately, choosing a new program as the default in the File Types window won't change this, and there's no option in the Windows interface that can disable this component, which is extremely frustrating. Thankfully, we can fix Microsoft's blunder with a Registry hack: Navigate to HKEY_CLASSES_ROOT\SystemFileAssociations\image\ ShellEx\ ContextMenuHandlers. Delete the ShellImagePreview key. Close *Regedit* and the change takes place immediately.

Dual Backdrops for Dual Displays

To setup WinXP to use a different desktop image on each monitor in a dual-display setup, try this little hack: As always, be sure to use a high-res image to reduce dithering. Right-click your desktop, then select Properties. Under the Desktop section, select Customize Desktop, then select the web tab. To use an image file located on your hard drive, select New and browse to the file's location. Once you've selected the file you want, click OK and

it will appear on your desktop. Drag the image over to the second desktop and, from the image's pull-down menu in the upper left-hand corner, select Cover Desktop. Right-click and select "Arrange By" and "Lock web items on desktop." Now you can select a standard desktop for your primary display and use the web object to cover the standard desktop image on your second desktop with the image of your choice.

Hack Ten:
Set a Custom Resolution

If you hate being limited to XP's options for your desktop resolution, you can set your desktop to any display size you'd like. Just make sure you don't exceed the min/max recommendations for your videocard and monitor, as you can damage them if you do. Navigate to HKEY_CURRENT_CONFIG\System\CurrentControlSet\ Control\VIDEO\{Address of primary video card}\0000\. The DefaultSettings.XResolution DWORD represents the Y axis. Edit its value as a decimal to what you want it to be, such as "1152." Now, do the same to the DefaultSettings.YResolution DWORD, which is the X axis. Edit this value to match your Y setting, "863," in this case. Reboot your machine, and you're done.

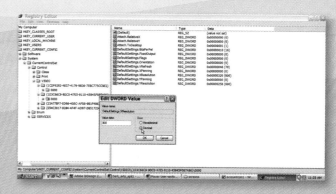

Hack Eleven:
Make Room for More Pinned Programs

As we've said, we love pinning our favorite programs to the Start menu—we just want more room to do it! This hack will kill Microsoft's pushy auto-generating list of Most Frequently Used Programs and give you extra real estate for your own. Go to HKEY_CURRENT_USER\Software\Microsoft\Windows\CurrentVersion\Policies\Explorer. Create a new DWORD called "NoStartMenuMFUprogramsList" with a value of "1." Reboot or log off and you'll have a nice big, blank hole to fill with new pinned programs.

Make Outlook Express News-only

To disable the e-mail capabilities within *Outlook Express* you can simply add /outnews to the end of the *Outlook Express* executable command. From the command prompt, type *msimn /outnews*. When you start the application in this mode, you'll notice the Inbox folder is missing and the Mail option under the Accounts menu is no longer available. You also can add the /outnews option to OE's shortcut to accomplish the same feat. Right-click the OE shortcut, select Properties, and change the info in the Target box to: "C:\Program Files\Outlook Express\ msimn.exe"/outnews.

Hack Twelve:
Disable CD Autoplay in XP Home and Pro

Sure, CD Autoplay can be convenient. However, having it on also means WinXP will automatically poll the CD drive at regular intervals, which can result in "hiccups" in video and music playback and even slower level-loading times. This feature is permanently disabled in XP Home with this Registry edit. Go to HKEY_CURRENT_USER\SOFTWARE\Microsoft\Windows\ CurrentVersion\Policies\Explorer and create a new DWORD called "NoDriveTypeAutoRun." Enter "b1" for the value data of the DWORD (making the value 0x000000b1 or decimal 177). What, you want to undo this change? Just set the value data back to "91" (decimal 145).

In Windows XP Pro it's a bit simpler: Click Start, Run, and type **GPEDIT.MSC**, which will launch the Group Policy editor. Then, go to Computer Configuration, Administrative Templates, System, and locate the entry for "Turn autoplay off." Modify it as you desire.

Hack Thirteen:
Kill Open Programs on Shutdown

How many times have you executed the shutdown sequence for your machine and left the office (or house) only to find it's still running when you get back? And then there's that "friendly" warning dialog box displayed telling you to close all open applications so that XP can shutdown? This happened to us all the time, but no longer, thanks to the following hack: Go to HKEY_CURRENT_USER\Control Panel\ Desktop. Modify the "AutoEndTasks" key to have a value of "1." If the key doesn't exist, simply create a new DWORD with the same name and a value of 1. To disable this hack, change the value back to "0," or delete the key entirely. ∎

How To Get Old Programs to Run on XP

Have your cake and eat it too by enabling your system to run multiple versions of Windows.

Windows XP has made big strides when it comes to backwards compatibility with programs developed for previous versions of Windows. Often, you can get a particularly stubborn legacy application to run via XP's Compatibility Mode (see sidebar).

However, there are still quite a few programs, particularly games designed for Win98 or Win95, that simply won't run on XP. In this case, you've got three choices:

1. Put the software on the shelf and start your own personal museum.
2. Run a second, older PC with Win95 or Win98 installed, using a KVM switch to share a single monitor, keyboard, and mouse. (See boxout.)
3. Set up a multiboot XP installation.

It can be tough getting older games, such as European Air War, *to run on WinXP. Multibooting can save the day.*

Multibooting XP with Win98

You can install two or more operating systems on your computer, and then choose the one that you want to use each time you boot your machine. This is known as "multibooting."

The first rule of thumb is to install the oldest operating system first, because if you don't, critical system files could be overwritten. And, before you can install a multiboot configuration, you must partition your hard drive. If you already have installed Windows 98, you can partition your drive—without wiping your data—using third party software such as *Partition Magic 8* (It's not exactly cheap, about $70, but it is quite useful. Browse to www.powerquest.com/partitionmagic).

If you're starting from a clean install, you can create multiple partitions that will each function as a separate, logical drive on a single hard drive by choosing Advanced Options during Setup and following the prompts—create one partition for Win 98 and a second for WinXP, which will typically be your C: and D: drives. Partition sizes of at least 10GB each are ideal. (Note: Make sure you have all the drivers you'll need to set up your hardware for each OS *beforehand*, preferably on a CD.) Install Win98 to the C: drive, which must use the FAT 16 or FAT 32 file system, and then WinXP to the D: drive, which should use the NTFS file system. When you want to use your old Windows 98 apps, reboot your PC and select Win 98 from the boot-menu, and you're off to the races.

It's a cumbersome process, but multibooting with WinXP is not that difficult—and the end result of finally getting to run a favorite old game again, such as *European Air War*, is worth it! For more excellent multibooting tips, go to **www.microsoft.com/windowsxp/using/setup/learnmore/multiboot.mspx.** ■

Easily Use Multiple PCs with a KVM Switch

Most of us have an old PC or two gathering dust in the basement. These make great secondary machines that you can use to run an older version of Windows, such as Win98 or WinSE. You can dramatically reduce required real estate with a device called a "KVM" (keyboard, video, mouse) switch, which will let you use the same keyboard, mouse, and monitor to control both—or even up to four—different systems. Prices typically range from $50 to $200.

KVM switches, such as logear's Mini-View III, make it easy to use multiple PCs simultaneously.

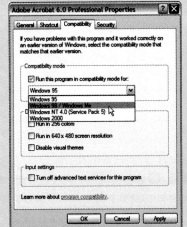

Before you resort to going the multiboot route, make sure to exhaust XP's built-in Compatibility Mode options, as these often can get a reluctant program kick-started.

Compatibility Mode Explained

If the legacy program in question won't even install, navigate to the setup file on the installation CD, usually called "setup.exe," and right-click on it. Select the Compatibility tab, check the Compatibility Mode box, and choose the OS the software was programmed for. Then try launching the set-up program as you normally would. If this doesn't work, try checking the rest of the options offered under the Compatibility tab, one at a time, re-launching set-up after each change.

So what do you do if the program installs just fine, but crashes to the desktop when you try to launch it? In this case, alter the Properties of the program's desktop shortcut the same as you did for the set-up executable. Right-click on the desktop shortcut, select the Compatibility tab, and check the appropriate boxes—you may have to try different combinations before it works. (You also can go online and try a Google search for tips from others who've had similar difficulties getting the same program to run under XP.)

PowerToys for Power Users

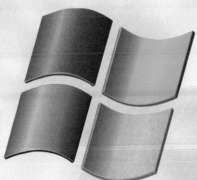

Don't have the time or desire to get your hands dirty messing with XP's innards? Microsoft's *PowerToys* will give you a high degree of customization options, without the mess.

No section on being a "power user" would be complete without mentioning Microsoft's own suite of nine software tools, known collectively as "PowerToys," which put a great deal of customization options in your hands. Released with each version of Windows, PowerToys for XP are available for download at **www.microsoft.com/ windowsxp/downloads/powertoys/ xppwertoys.mspx**. There's no charge for the download, just don't go asking MS for any PowerToys tech support—it doesn't provide it. Don't let that dissuade you from trying PowerToys out. XP's PowerToy lineup includes some of the handiest Windows utilities we've seen yet.

TweakUI
First and foremost is an excellent new version of *TweakUI*, which we've mentioned a few times already in this magazine. *TweakUI* is a small-but-powerful program that lets you change many Registry settings without having to get down and dirty with *Regedit*, which can be scary. Essentially, it lets you unlock

many of XP's hidden Registry features via a very simple point-and-click interface. And, you can use it to easily reconfigure many of XP's default UI and program settings. For example, you can use it to set which icons appear in the Start menu and on the desktop—it puts all the options in one place for you to pick and choose. You can use it to set how long the buttons in the Taskbar flash orange trying to catch your attention, or to tweak cursor shadows and menu fading. You can even use it to prevent programs from appearing on the Recently Used list in the Start menu. If you're only going to use one PowerToy, make it *TweakUI*.

Virtual Desktop Manager
Next up is the *Virtual Desktop Manager* Powertoy, which gives you the power to wield not two, not three, but four virtual

Give your desktop a 4X facelift with the Virtual Desktop Manager *PowerToy.*

desktops on a single monitor. So, if you don't have the desktop real estate for a true multimonitor display give it a whirl. This information is in a previous section titled "How to Set Up a Dual Display" (Part II). Each desktop features a copy of the Start menu, desktop, and taskbar—and each virtual desktop can be used to run different applications simultaneously. This is a great way for budding power users to strut their stuff and organize groups of open apps into their own desktops for fast switching amongst them all. For instance, you could have your *Office* apps open on one desktop, email apps on another, web pages on the third, and *Tetris* on the fourth.

Just right-click the Taskbar and select Toolbars>Desktop Manager to launch the Virtual Desktop Manager. A new toolbar, entitled MSVDM, will be added to the Taskbar, and you can use it to switch between the virtual desktops, which are numbered 1 through 4. Pretty cool, huh?

Use TweakUI *to par down XP's default file templates to reduce desktop clutter.*

TweakUI makes it easy to customize your Start Menu programs.*

Like to have lots of open apps on your desktop at once? The Alt-Tab Replacement toy makes it easier to find the one you want.

Alt-Tab Replacement
We used to think the default ALT+TAB application switching device built into XP was fine, until we saw this toy. *Alt-Tab Replacement* does exactly what the name implies—it replaces XP's default method with a one that gives you a thumbnail preview of all open applications in the task list. Just hit ALT+TAB as before, and continue to hit TAB while holding down the ALT key to select the app you want, then release ALT. Simple. However, if you've got an older PC that has its hands full just running XP you might want to give this toy a pass—generating and displaying the thumbnail images can bog down your system. For owners of newer PCs though, it's a definite plus.

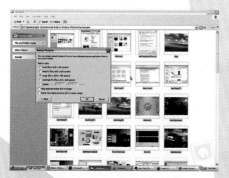

Finding it a pain to resize all those pics o' the kids for your web site? Image Resizer makes it painless.

Image Resizer
Digital cameras are great, but resizing your pics for use on the web, email attachments, or to display on your PDA can be an extremely tedious, time-consuming chore. It may not be the most sophisticated tool for the job, but the Image Resizer PowerToy is free and it's very adept at resizing groups of images efficiently. Resizer works similarly to the "Send Pictures via Email" options already

built-in to XP, but it ads the ability to process batches of images at the same time. Resized images are generated with filenames that are similar to the original image's and include a designation that denotes the new size, such as "medium" or "WinCE," which makes it easier to organize them in your folders.

CD and HTML Slide Show Generators
This is another tool that digital photo buffs are sure to find useful, particularly when it comes to sharing pics with Grandma and Grandpa out in Kansas who just got a new computer. Really two tools in one, the *CD Slide Show Generator* integrates into XP's CD recording wizard and adds the option to add a picture viewer to image-only CDs, which means Grandma and Grandpa can just pop the CD into their PC and view the slideshow, wheter it's running XP or not. Similarly, the *HTML Slide Show Generator* makes creating picture albums for display on the web a simple process.

Open Command Window Here
This toy is a shell enhancement, and an update to an old favorite. It adds an "Open Command Window Here" context menu item, which you access via right-clicking, to folders in My Computer or Explorer. If you never use the command line, you can ignore this toy. If you do, it's a must-have.

Power Calculator
While most of us might not care about it,

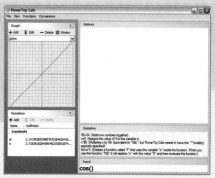

Make your PC extra-nerdy with the graphical calculator functions of the new, mighty Power Calculator.

the *Power Calculator* is a beefy alternative to XP's default tool that will please college students—particularly those equipped with laptops and take trigonometry. It lets you graph and evaluate functions, as well as perform many different types of conversions than the puny default XP calc can perform.

Taskbar Magnifier
Similar to the Magnifier tool that ships with Windows XP (Start>All Programs>Accessories>Accessibility) Taskbar Magnifier provides screen-magnification capabilities, but is relegated to the Taskbar, which can often be difficult to read at higher desktop resolutions.

Webcam Timershot
This tool can capture pictures from a web camera at specific intervals and automatically save them to custom locations such as an FTP or web site. It also can perform other useful duties, such as resize the images. ∎

Not the Only Power Game in Town
Microsoft's not the only player when it comes to making handy XP-tweaking tools. One of our favorite third-party utilities for Windows, *RegCleaner*, has been updated for Windows XP in the form of *JV16 PowerTools*. This software suite cleans up duplicate files, invalid shortcuts, and general Registry clutter – and it can be used to remove stubborn software,

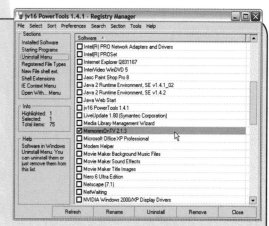

If there are features you wished TweakUI included, you'll likely find them in PowerTools.

which you might have deleted without "uninstalling," from the Add/Remove programs list. So give it a whirl and decide for yourself if it's worth the 30 clams. Find out more at **http://www.jv16.org/**.

Windows Longhorn Sneak Peak

We got our hands on an advanced preview version of Windows Longhorn and put the upcoming OS through the *Maximum PC* wringer. We came away duly impressed.

Let's get this out of the way right now: Don't expect to install Microsoft's next version of Windows, code-named "Longhorn," on your PC until 2006. But that's not too long to wait for what looks like the most ambitious operating system Microsoft has ever released, is it? We don't think so either.

What makes Windows Longhorn worth waiting for? Three key features: a new database-driven file system, a fancy-pants 3D user interface, and the usual host of feature-laden updates to the interface. We "acquired" a copy of an early alpha build of the OS and gave it a full run-through. Keep in mind that this is very early software, and any features mentioned here may or may not make the final cut. Crucial features like the new 3D user

Stacks are like context-sensitive folders for your data. Here, we did a search for all our Bob Dylan music, and then created stacks for each album. This is completely independent of the folder structure. The actual MP3s are spread all over our hard drive.

The Windows Address Book has been replaced with a Contacts Query. Once your contacts are set up, you can e-mail or IM a pal directly from here. Even cooler, you can associate images with people who are in them, so you can use queries to search for images of certain contacts.

Make WinXP 3D

Microsoft may not be showing screens of its new 3D interface for Longhorn yet, but that doesn't mean you can't get a taste of Windows' 3D future today. Several different organizations, including Microsoft, are currently working on prototype technologies with the goal of giving your desktop a complete 3D transformation.

Dusan Hamar's *SphereXP* is a work in progress that you can take for a spin yourself at www.hamar.sk/sphere/. Designed as a total replacement for XP's 2D desktop, *SphereXP* basically puts you in the center of a sphere, with all your apps and desktop objects revolving around you. You can pull objects to the foreground or push them back as you see fit. You're only allowed to change the sphere's background image, which ensures that every PC using *SphereXP* will operate exactly the same and that you'll only have to learn one environment.

Other 3D GUIs in progress include Microsoft's *TaskGallery* (http://research.microsoft.com/adapt/TaskGallery), and Vimana BV's *3DTop* (www.3dtop.com). Check 'em out!

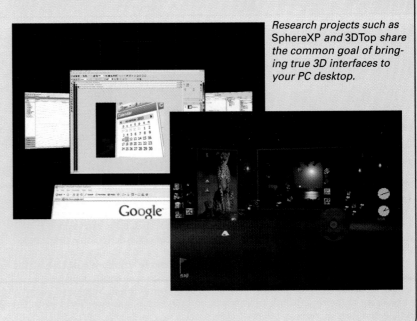

Research projects such as SphereXP and 3DTop share the common goal of bringing true 3D interfaces to your PC desktop.

The Longhorn desktop includes the Sidebar (top-right corner), a new place for always-running apps with dynamic updates to keep you informed. Expect to see your IM client, among others, here.

This handy window provides an easy way to sort, categorize, and even preview any digital photos or videos on your system.

interface are still absent in the build we tested, so treat this as the most tentative of previews. (The prospect of a 3D interface may scare you, which is understandable given how taxing the current default "Luna" scheme can be on typical machines. However, keep in mind that Bill Gates sees the "typical" machine having a 4GHz to 6GHz processor, more than 2GB of memory, and at least a terabyte of storage when Longhorn debuts.)

Despite the missing 3D interface, several new interface elements are present in Longhorn. We immediately noticed the new Sidebar, a super-sized version of the existing system tray that will give you instant access to important apps—like the clock, calendar, and instant messaging apps (To get a preview of this, check out www.smartbarxp.com). The sidebar takes up a lot of screen space, but can be set to auto-hide, just like the Taskbar. Or you can manually adjust the amount of space it uses.

After playing with it for a while, we're really stoked about the new WinFS file

system. Inside My Computer there's a new entry called the Default Store. When you drag any *Word* documents, *Excel* spreadsheets, images, music files, or videos onto the default store, Longhorn will extract the meta-data from the files and save it in a fast SQL-based database. All the info contained in your ID3 tags for music, EXIF data for images, and author and keyword information for *Word* docs will be instantly searchable.

Once your files are ensconced in the default store, you'll be able to easily use one of Longhorn's pre-built queries, which currently reside in the Start Menu. In the build we tested, we saw queries for Music, Documents, Photos and Videos, and Contacts. Each comes with several sorting options and is semi-configurable. In addition, you can save frequently used searches to the left side of the Query window. We expect that you'll be able to quickly write your own queries so you can sort any files stored on your computer anyway you want.

Several other new whiz-bang Longhorn features are worth mentioning. We're thrilled that Microsoft is finally

including an end-user interface to help you prevent unwanted Systray apps from loading every time you restart the machine. We also like the new features in *Internet Explorer*, which include an advanced download manager that supports resumed downloads and allows you to prioritize each active download, as well as a pop-up stopper. While tabbed browsing is nowhere to be seen, we still expect it to be present in the final version. ∎

New Windows OS = New DirectX = Good for Games

DirectX is the name for Microsoft's standard application programming interface (API) developers use to ensure that their software can "talk" to your hardware, with as little tweaking on your part possible. The plans for the new version of *DirectX*, to be made available with the release of Longhorn, are as ambitious perhaps as those for the OS itself.

For starters, the installation process is going to be streamlined, with games running entirely off of CD, or using a "silent setup" to copy to the hard drive unnoticed—just like the Xbox. A standard gamepad controller design—able to work with all types of games—is also in the works, as are built-in "patch update" notifications for all games installed on your hard drive, as well as the ability to set-up and launch online games with friends via *MSN Messenger*.

Other items on the *DirectX* team's plans include a built-in benchmark that will tell you what games your PC can run, which will also spawn a new "number-based" system for retail. You'd just need to run the benchmark on your PC at home, then look for games with the corresponding number on their box. Finally, the display driver process should be greatly simplified, allowing you to easily tweak settings without rebooting.

Expect Longhorn to give you one central portal for gaming on Windows. And we're not talking about the craptacular games that come with Windows either. We expect to see A-list games here.

How To...

MAKE CUSTOM Recovery Discs

Wipe away system build-up and create your own personalized recovery discs!

MAXIMUM PC
TIME TO COMPLETION
02:35
HOURS   MINUTES

BY JOHN TUMMINARO

WinXP utilities like *Disk Cleanup* and *System Restore* can be helpful in keeping your system in good health, but the truth is that there's no substitute for a top-to-bottom OS reinstall to make your PC feel like new. It's called a "clean start," and on the following pages, we'll show you how to perform one with the highest level of personal customization possible. We first did this project in June 2000 with Win98, and because the article was so well-received, we decided to update it for WinXP. Our time-tested (and improved) *Maximum PC* process involves backing up all your valuable files, wiping your system clean, reinstalling your OS along with all your personal settings and favorite apps, then creating a mirror image of this perfect system profile on CD-ROMs. It'll include all your OS preferences, all your networking settings, and all the software you use on a daily basis—ready to load at any time, and ready to rescue you from disaster.

After you're done, you'll be able to get that "fresh-out-of-the-shower" feeling anytime you want just by popping your recovery CDs and loading in your image. System feeling groggy? Virus attack? No problem. All you need is a clean start.

10 EASY STEPS

Lest you get antsy about the sheer scope of this project, check out how easy the process really is. Here's a brief outline of what you'll be doing:

1. Confirm that you can boot from CD. Most PCs shouldn't have a problem booting directly off of a CD, but some really old motherboards may have issues with this, so it's best to check.

2. Back up your data. All your files will be wiped clean during this project. Sorry, that's the nature of the beast.

3. Collect the essentials. Before you recklessly reformat your drive, you're going to make sure you have all the tools required for the project.

4. Format your drive. This is the point of no return. Anything not backed up is about to be offered as a sacrifice to the god of hard drives.

5. Install XP. This process is much easier than it was in previous Windows incarnations, but it's still the longest step here, so pay attention.

6. Windows Update. Microsoft's online resources will help you plug security holes and stomp out bugs.

7. Install drivers. Many people forget this step and end up wondering why their frame rates are in the toilet.

8. Tweak XP. Here's the part where you get to wring every last bit of performance from the OS.

9. Install apps. Your PC isn't going to be much use without some software to run.

10. Create restore discs. Finally, we're going to take a snapshot of your pristine, perfectly configured system.

WHAT YOU'LL NEED

▶ **CD-Rs or CD-RWs (at least three)**

▶ **Windows XP installation CD**

▶ **Norton Ghost 2003**

▶ **A CD burner**

STEP 1
Confirming That You Can Boot from CD

In order to restore your system without requiring a fragile floppy startup disk, your PC must be able to boot from a CD-ROM. Fortunately, almost all PCs that meet the minimum system requirements for WinXP are able to boot from the optical drive. Even so, you're still going to have to configure your BIOS so that your PC checks the CD-ROM for a bootable disc before turning to the hard drive. Here's how to do it.

Restart your computer. As soon as the screen that indicates your BIOS is loading comes up, you'll have a few seconds to press the correct key to enter the BIOS. The name of the key should appear on the screen (e.g., "Press F1 to enter the BIOS"), but if it doesn't, check your motherboard documentation. If you don't have a manual, try the Delete key. If that doesn't work, try pressing each of the function keys (F1, F2, etc.) and the Escape key until you hit the right one.

Once you enter your BIOS, check to see whether your BIOS is from Award or AMI by reading the title at the top. If you have an Award BIOS, enter the Advanced BIOS Features tab and scroll down to First Boot Device. It should be preset to Floppy. Because we aren't going to use the Floppy drive for boot purposes, press

```
          Phoenix - AwardBIOS CMOS Setup Utility
                   Advanced BIOS Features

   Virus Warning               [Disabled]          Item Help
   CPU L1 & L2 Cache           [Enabled]
   Quick Power On Self Test    [Enabled]        Menu Level    ▶
   RAID & SCSI Boot Order      [RAID,SCSI]
   First Boot Device           [CDROM]          Select Your Boot
   Second Boot Device          [HDD-0]          Device Priority
   Third Boot Device           [LS120]
   Boot Other Device           [Enabled]
   Swap Floppy Drive           [Disabled]
   Boot Up Floppy Seek         [Enabled]
   Boot Up NumLock Status      [On]
   Typematic Rate Setting      [Disabled]
 × Typematic Rate (Chars/Sec) 6
 × Typematic Delay (Msec)      250
   Security Option             [Setup]
   OS Select For DRAM > 64MB   [Non-OS2]
   Report No FDD For WIN 95    [No]
```

STEP 1 Once you're done with the "clean start" process, you can shave a couple seconds off your boot time by switching First Boot Device back to your hard drive.

Enter, select CDROM from the list, and press Enter again. Now press Escape until you're back at the BIOS entry screen. Select "Save & Exit Setup" from the menu, and press Enter.

If your BIOS is from AMI, select the Advanced BIOS Features tab, scroll to 1st Boot Device, and use the plus and minus keys until you've selected CDROM. Now press Escape, select "Save & Exit Setup," and press Enter.

Once you've done all this, you should be ready to boot off a CD.

✔ *OK, I've confirmed that my PC can boot from my CD-ROM, and I've made the CD-ROM my first boot device. I'm ready to move on.*

STEP 2
Back Up Data

Data backup can range from "quick and effortless" to "complete nightmare" depending on how organized your files are. If your personal documents are littered far and wide, let this be a lesson to you. Centralizing your data into one main folder—such as My Documents—can spare you the trouble of spelunking the depths of your system when you need to gather up coveted MP3s, JPGs, and AVIs.

Yes, you'll be tempted to use WinXP's Files and Settings Transfer Wizard. It purports to offer one-click backup of all the data you'll want installed on a new system. But trust us, it's not foolproof. The problem is that the wizard also transports all of the gunk—orphaned shortcuts, abandoned dial-up configurations, and so on—along with your data and settings. This of course defeats the purpose of performing a clean install!

So let's get down to business. On your desktop, create a folder that will eventually be copied to either removable media or a secondary hard drive. Into this folder, copy everything from My Documents along with any sundry files you might have created on your primary hard disk, be they text documents, videos, or MP3s—anything you want to save for posterity. Make sure you organize the files into sub-folders, and as long as you've got the opportunity

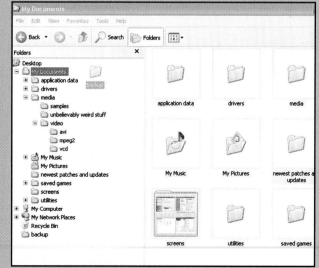

STEP 2 Don't miss any important files during a backup, because you can't come back for them after you reformat.

to tidy up things, make the most of it. Don't copy any personal documents that you're sure you'll never need. If you have a secondary drive that's unrelated to the primary drive (that is, it doesn't have any software installed on it and will not require reformatting), then you can leave files there for safekeeping.

You'll want to export your e-mail, as well. In *Outlook*, this can be done by opening up *Outlook* and right-clicking the Outlook Today icon in the list of mailboxes and selecting the "Properties for Outlook Today" option. Then click the Advanced button and copy the path from filename. The path will lead you directly to the file with all of your *Outlook* settings.

If you use a modem, you're going to need to copy down your ISP's phone number, as well as your username and password. This information can be found in Control Panel>Network Connections, but your password will be blotted out, so make sure you have it written down. Also, you'll need to record your username and password for any kind of broadband, such as PPPoE, that requires you to connect before using. If you use a static IP address, copy down all your IP settings, which can be found by going to Control Panels > Network Connections. Right-click Local Area Connections and select "Properties." In the new menu, highlight TCP/IP, click the Properties option, and you'll find your IP info.

Don't forget your saved games! If you can't figure out where they're stored by browsing game folders, you can try uninstalling the game. Before the uninstallation process begins, many games will offer to keep the saved-game files on your drive; these files can then be copied onto your new system when you reinstall the game. This isn't always going to work, though, so try first to find the right folder.

✔ **Alright, I've backed up all my data. I've double-checked that everything else on the drive is expendable. Yes, I'm sure. I'm ready to move on.**

STEP 3
Collect Your Project Tools

It never hurts to double-check your tool box, be-cause once you get moving, you won't want to be caught empty-handed. So make sure you have the following.

■ *Norton Ghost 2003*, the program we'll use to create the restore disc set. If you don't already own a copy, check your local software retailer or go to www.symantec.com for a boxed or downloadable version.

■ Your original Windows XP installation CD (either Home or Professional).

■ At least three CD-Rs or CD-RWs (it helps to have more on hand in case there are burning errors or you need more room).

■ An optical disc that contains all the drivers you need for your hardware. We suggest that you go onto the Internet and pull the latest drivers from vendor web sites. Usually the driver you've got on your CD is old and moldy, or even Windows XP–incompatible in some cases.

Try not to forget any components, because any driver that you don't update now will have to be updated every time you reinstall. So make sure you've got the most current driver releases for your videocard, motherboard chipset, soundcard, network card, USB 2.0 card, printer, and any specialized A/V cards you might have. We keep all our drivers on rewriteable optical discs. This way they all stay in one place and can be updated as necessary.

We'll warn you ahead of time that drivers are not always going to be digitally signed. Unsigned drivers aren't necessarily a bad thing as long as the company has a good reputation for making stable drivers.

You'll also need the original installation packages of all of the applications and utilities you'll want on your clean system mirror—*Office*, *Photoshop*, *ACDSee*, what have you.

Once you have all these parts collected, you can move on to the next step.

✔ **I've got Norton Ghost 2003, my Windows XP CD, plenty of CD-Rs, all the latest drivers for all my hardware, and I know which apps and utilities I want to install. Now what?**

STEP 4
Format Your Drive

This is it: the point of no return. Up until now, everything we've done has been simple preparation, but in this step you're going to actually erase files from your hard drive. If you've diligently backed up all your data, there's nothing to worry about.

Here's a final safety tip before we begin: If you used a removable drive to back up all your data and it's still connected to your PC, disconnect it now. When the XP install process begins and the formatting screen pops up, it will display the removable drive as the first partition. Many unhappy people have inadvertently formatted their removable drive—with all their backed-up data—instead of their hard drive. Whoops!

Drop the Windows XP CD into your optical drive and reboot. Since you've

already set it up to be the primary boot device, you should get a message that says "press Enter to set up Windows XP." Do this. Once you're in Windows Setup, wait until a "Welcome to Setup" screen appears. Follow the instructions and press "Enter to Set Up Windows XP."

When the EULA (end-user license agreement) appears, press F8 to continue. If Windows is already installed on your hard drive, then you'll need to press Escape to bypass the previous install, and install a fresh copy. Next you should see a list of the partitions you have on your PC. Before you do anything, you need to develop a plan for the final configuration of your partitions. Partitioning is basically dividing the disk space of a physical drive among several "virtual" drives called partitions. These virtual drives show up as separate drives (C, D, E) within Windows. While many people like to divide their drives into multiple pieces, we

recommend that you create a single partition for every physical drive you have.

Remember that there is no helpful redundancy in creating partitions, because if a physical drive fails, all of the partitions associated with the drive will die as well. It is also advantageous to create a single partition for your OS install because of the way Windows XP accesses its data. When a partition spans the entire disk, Windows XP automatically puts the large files onto the outside edge of the drive, where high seek times are mitigated by high throughput speeds. The smaller, more frequently accessed files use the inside edge of the disk platters, to take advantage of low access times. When you partition the drive into two pieces, you lose most of the advantages of this ordering scheme.

At the partition setup screen, find the partitions that are associated with your primary drive (Disk 0). Make sure this is the drive you want to format. If you have a physical hard drive that is 120GB, for example, and another 60GB physical drive that you backed up your old data on, look at the format screen and check the disk size—be absolutely certain that you are drawing a bead on the right drive. Once you're certain, delete them by pressing D, then Enter, then L.

Once this is done, you will have created a pool of all the free space on your hard drive and it will be ready for partitioning. Select the unpartitioned space, press Enter, and choose "Format the partition using the NTFS file system." For this task we want to avoid the Quick option since it simply rewrites the TOC to make the drive think it's empty instead of actually erasing anything. A full format goes through each hard drive sector and rewrites it, so if you have a bad sector on your drive, it will be exposed now rather than later.

Now let the drive format. This will take a long time.

✔ *I've formatted my drive and deftly avoided disaster. Windows XP is now ready to install itself. No sweat.*

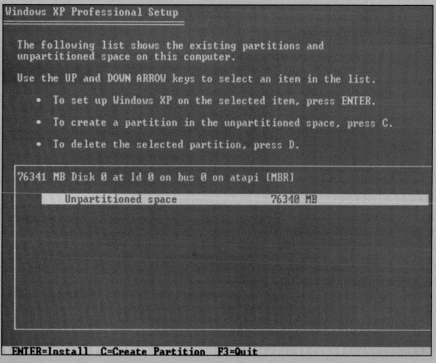

STEP 4 Now that you've pooled all your disk space, it's time to create a partition.

Install Windows XP

After the format of your hard drive, your PC will reboot, and the Windows XP install routine will swing into action. You'll be prompted along the way for basic information, and asked to enter your Product Key.

After Windows XP asks for your desired network setup option for broadband and modem connections, the rest of the installation will progress automatically. When it has finished and rebooted, you'll be prompted to change your display resolution. Follow the onscreen instructions and allow Windows to boot into the familiar desktop. You'll also receive a message asking if you want to register and activate Windows. (Note that activation is required, but registration is not.) If Windows was able to recognize your network card and you use a broadband connection, then you can probably activate now. Otherwise, you'll have to wait until after you have installed the network card or modem drivers (see the next step).

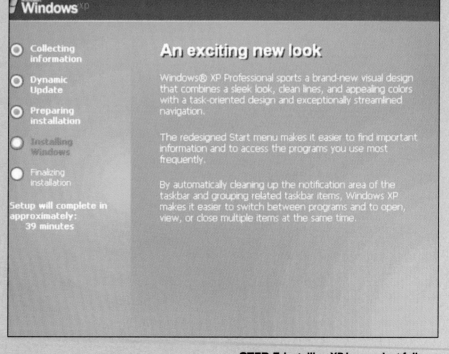

✔ *Okey-doke, a fresh copy of Windows is now completely installed. What do I do next?*

STEP 5 Installing XP is easy, just follow the directions onscreen.

STEP 6
Run Windows Update

Our first stop after installing Windows XP is Windows Update, Microsoft's one-stop online shop for security fixes, OS updates, and certified drivers.

If you're using a network card and you connect through a standard DHCP broadband connection, then you can skip to the next part about running Windows Update. But if you're using a modem, or if you need to install specialized network parameters (username and password) from your broadband ISP to connect to the Internet, then we'll need to visit the Control Panel before going to Windows Update.

Go to the Start Menu and click Control Panel. On the left-hand side there should be an option that says "Switch to Classic View." Click this and you'll see the familiar set of Control Panel icons. Double-click Network Connections, and on the sidebar choose "Create a New Connection," choose the "Connect to the Internet" option, then "Set Up My Connection Manually." From here you can choose to connect through dial-up or broadband with a username and password. Go through the desired menu selection and enter the information that you've copied down or that your ISP has supplied you with. After you're done, try to achieve a connection with your ISP. If you use a static IP, make sure you select that option in the Network Connection Wizard.

Once you're able to log on and access the Internet, go to the Start Menu on the Taskbar, select All Programs and click Windows Update. This will open an *Internet Explorer* browser that will automatically connect you to the Windows Update site.

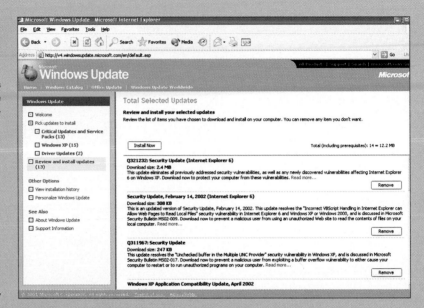

STEP 6 You'll need to go to Windows Update often—your OS is a work in progress.

Once the page comes up, click the "Scan for Updates" option and wait while your computer is gently probed.

Once your computer is checked, you'll have three different categories of updates available to you. The first section is Critical Updates, which will automatically be selected for download. You can click on that section to review what is going to be installed, but it's best to just leave it alone and let Windows Update patch whatever security holes the hacking gurus have come up with this week.

The second section contains noncritical software updates for Windows. We recommend installing everything you think you'll need, especially the Service Packs (SP2 includes SP1 updates and was nearly complete at press time) and all the rec-

ommended updates. Keep in mind that Windows will need to reboot several times for multiple updates and that some files are quite large. You might want to choose only a few at a time, especially for a dial up connection (note that Service Packs are available on CD for about $10).

The last section is Driver Updates, and it contains a sparse list of WHQL certified drivers for your hardware. These drivers will usually be a bit older than the latest ones you can find on your vendors' web sites. You may want to go with the latest update, even if it isn't sanctioned by Microsoft.

✔ *I've gone to Windows Update and brought my OS up to date. Are we done yet?*

STEP 7
Install Drivers

As we discussed earlier, having the latest drivers is extremely important to a well-functioning machine, but you'll want to be careful with some of the stuff you put on your freshly installed OS.

Vendor driver discs tend to contain tons of extras that most people neither need nor want. Creative Labs, for example, packs a dozen or so programs with its Sound Blaster Audigy driver CD, and it installs all of them by default. So when installing from vendor driver packs, make sure you always select the minimum

possible installation without all the extraneous software that's just going to muck up your pristine box. You can always add craplets later if you feel like you're missing out on something.

Most people use videocards based on either nVidia or ATI chipsets. Although your board maker may have a specialized driver pack, it's usually little more than a reference driver with a bunch of extra crap tacked on. To avoid this, just download the latest reference driver from either www.nvidia.com or www.ati.com. nVidia and

ATI make this especially easy by providing unified drivers that will work on any of its video chipsets since the TNT2 and Rage 128, respectively.

Your motherboard chipset will probably be based on either an Intel or VIA chipset, although it may also be one from SiS, ALi, nVidia, or AMD. Check the vendor's web page for the latest driver updates. Having the latest chipset driver is far more important than most people think.

These days, most everyone runs a soundcard from Creative Labs, although there are some other vendors still out there, as well as a ton of integrated audio chips. For integrated audio, check your motherboard vendor's web site and you should be able to find what you need. Audio card drivers are usually available as downloads from the vendor's home page.

Once you're done installing drivers, reboot your PC and go on to the next step.

 I installed all of the drivers necessary for my hardware, and I didn't forget to install updated chipset drivers for my motherboard. What's the next step?

STEP 7 Whenever possible, select the leanest driver installation option—you can always add programs later.

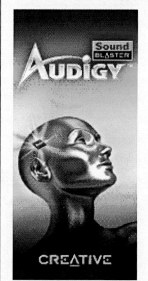

Setup Options

Please select the required setup type:

Full Installation:
When you want to create and experien multimedia contents.

Custom Installation:
For advanced users. You can choose individual components.

Drivers Only:
Only drivers are installed.

CRE∆TIVE

Tweak WinXP

This is the final step in your OS installation. Here's where you turn Microsoft's Windows XP into *your* XP by customizing its configuration and tweaking the settings for maximum performance.

If you didn't activate Windows during setup, do that first by clicking the key icon in your System Tray. Windows will generously offer to take you on a tour, install a Passport account, etc. Click all these reminders, then cancel them right away if you're not interested. This will prevent you from being bugged about them every time you reinstall.

Change the display resolution if you haven't already. In fact, while you're in Display Properties, take the time to set your power-management settings and Windows décor.

Set up directories for your personal data within My Documents, so you'll have a fairly easy method of backing it up later. Tweak My Documents to reflect the view you prefer (we prefer to see file details, not icons, so go to the View menu and select Details). If you want, you can go to Tools > Folder Options, select the View tab, and apply these settings to all your folders by clicking

General	Computer Name	Hardware	Advanced
System Restore	Automatic Updates		Remote

How do you want to be notified when updates are available for your computer?

Notification Settings

◉ Download the updates automatically and notify me when they are ready to be installed.

○ Notify me before downloading any updates and notify me again before installing them on my computer.

○ Turn off automatic updating. I want to update my computer manually.

Previous Updates

You can choose to have Windows notify you again about updates you previously declined.

Restore Declined Updates

STEP 8 Take the time to customize your settings. This includes folder views, update notification, and display properties, among other things.

"Apply to all folders."

Next, right-click the My Computer icon on the desktop and select Properties. When the Properties window opens, select the System Restore tab and adjust the slider to the amount of disk space you want to allocate to System Restore. Also make sure you examine the "Automatic Updates" and "Advanced" tabs in order to set preferences for Users, Windows Update, Performance, and Startup. Don't forget to go into *Internet Explorer* and specify your security settings (at Tools > Internet Options > Security). If you plan on using a software firewall, you can configure that now as well.

If you prefer a more comprehensive, one-stop approach, check out programs such as *TweakXP* that provide easy access to all the Windows XP tweaking options within one application.

Aye, Windows XP is tweaked to my tastes. No, I mean it. I've scrubbed through every dialog box and tab, including those within Internet Explorer, to reflect my preferences.

Let's carry on.

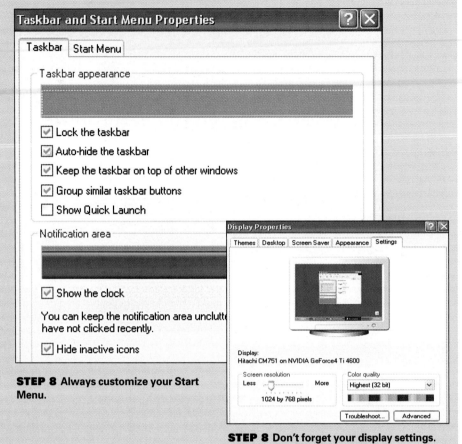

STEP 8 Always customize your Start Menu.

STEP 8 Don't forget your display settings.

STEP 9
Install Your Applications

The final step in building your custom OS image is to install all the key applications you want loaded whenever you do a clean-start reinstall. These apps should be installed judiciously, so wherever possible, select "custom" installations and limit the modules and install packages to just the ones you know you'll want to use.

Avoid installing programs that are frequently updated. For example, we're perfectly happy with *Office 2000* and don't have any plans to upgrade to *Office XP*, so we're going to add *Office 2000* to our base install. But with something like an instant-messaging client, which is updated almost obsessively, we prefer to install the latest version each time we go for a clean start.

Before you move on to the next step, make sure you try running all your programs at least once to ensure that the installs were successful.

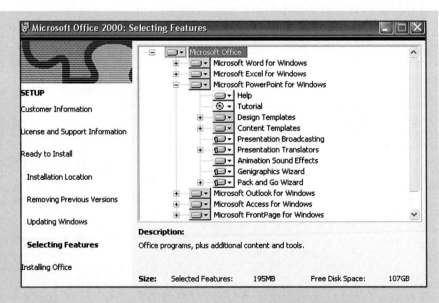

I've installed all the applications that I want on my pristine system image. And, yes, I've ensured the installations are as minimal as possible, selecting only the modules that I'll actually use.

STEP 9 Feel free to install *Office*, but leave the more commonly updated programs until later.

STEP 10
Create Restore Discs

You've gone through a long and tedious process to get here, but remember, you won't have to do it again for a long time. In this step, you're going to create the restore discs that will allow you to effortlessly refresh your system whenever you want.

Insert the *Norton Ghost 2003* CD into your drive, and run the setup program. It's really that simple!

The first thing you should do is create bootable rescue disks. Open *Ghost* and go to the Ghost Utilities section. Start the Boot Wizard and select all the default options. You'll probably need two floppy disks. These discs will help you re-image your hard drive even if you can't boot into Windows.

After you create the rescue discs, label them and open *Ghost*. Click on Backup. First you'll need to select the drive you want to image, and the destination for that image. We recommend you burn the image directly to a recordable CD or DVD. Press Next to continue.

Keep pressing Continue until you get to the Advanced Options page. Click Advanced Options, and then go to the compression tab. We recommend using the high-compression setting. High compression takes up less space but takes more time when creating the image. It makes no sense at all to use the no-compression option, unless you just like spending money on media.

You'll go through several more screens, before you're prompted to insert a blank CD into your burner. When that's done, click Next, pick your burner from the list, and click Finish. Make sure all your programs are closed, then press the Yes button to restart the machine and begin the imaging process. Your drive will now be compressed and the image will be saved to disc. Don't forget to label the discs consecutively when you're done. Well, golly, you've done it. You've made a complete image of a pristine system. Now, whenever you want a clean start, you can use one of the following methods to restore your system to its original state. *Remember that these processes will wipe out all your personal files, so make absolutely sure you repeat Step 2 and back up all your data.*

Restoring from Windows (easiest and best)
If you want to re-image your drive and can still boot into your old install, the process is an absolute snap. Just open up *Ghost* within Windows and cancel past the welcome screen. Insert disc one of your backup discs into the CD drive

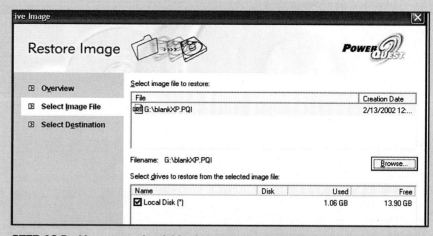

STEP 10 Backing up your hard drive is as easy as selecting it here, and telling *Ghost* where you want to save your image. *Ghost* will save the image to another hard drive, a network share, or even a CD-RW or DVD-RW.

and click the Restore button. Click "Select Image File" and point it to the .gho file on disc one. *Ghost* will ask you to insert disc two, then disc one again—just follow the directions. Once that's done, click Finish, and insert the discs as requested by *Ghost*.

Restoring from CD
If your PC just won't boot into Windows and you're loathe to use your set of floppies (if you even made them), then you can boot directly off the *Ghost* CD . The CD will drop you onto the command line. When you see the A:\> on your screen type: `c:\support\ghost.exe` then press the Enter key.

After the interface comes up, click the icon for Restore Image, then point it to disc one (which you should place in your drive now). Then just follow the instructions.

In case you were wondering, it's possible to make bootable CDs for your restore discs. But since you need the *Ghost* program to restore the image anyway, why not just boot from its CD?

Restoring from floppy disk
This is the same procedure as booting from CD, except that you will not need to enter DOS. Pop in the first of two floppies you made when you installed *Ghost* and reboot. *Ghost* will ask for the second floppy, and start up its GUI automatically.

Keeping Your Windows Clean

While even the most diligent housekeeper will find it impossible to keep a system absolutely free of data dust, there are still many ways to delay spring cleaning for up to six months or more, depending on your usage and degree of slovenliness. Your first defense is simple

common sense. Be judicious and selective about software installation packages, customizing their installs wherever possible. Avoid installing programs that have extensive spyware—and that means most file-sharing P2P applications (unless you can find one of the unauthorized, ad-free "lite" versions online).

Even if you don't use any of the traditionally suspect software, you should still use (and update frequently) Lavasoft's *Ad-aware* (www.lavasoft.nu) to get rid of commercial garbage dumped into your Registry and system folders.

You can also avoid strangling the pipes with cross-linked files and file fragments by shutting down Windows the right way. Use the Start Menu > Turn Off the Computer selection. Shutting down by simply flipping off the power switch can lead to data loss, file corruption, and the little droppings mentioned above. Trust us, take the extra five seconds and shut down the right way.

Virus checks and regular defragmentation of your hard disk are also essential to keeping your PC in top shape. System maintenance packages like *Norton Systemworks* contain numerous tools for Registry cleaning, disk defragmenting, virus checking, and removing old files and shortcuts. Likewise, McAfee's *QuickClean* (available for Windows 95b through XP) is a stand-alone utility that blows out the garbage from all of Windows' hiding places, deletes duplicate files and orphaned shortcuts, and safely "shreds" these files on their way out. And the next time you get a message saying that the uninstall is completed but "some elements could not be removed," *QuickClean* steps in and removes them for you. At this point, we think that's something everyone can appreciate. ■

Maximize Your
Broadband
Connection

Obtaining a fat online pipe is one of the best upgrades ever. Here's how to choose the right broadband service, and make sure it's performing at its optimum level.

W hether you go with satellite, cable, or DSL for your broadband connection, one thing will remain a constant: You're going to shell out hefty amounts of cash for the luxury. ISP providers make some bold speed claims in their marketing, but typically offer little in the way of guarantees. They're certainly not going to tell you when their product's not performing at its advertised rates, so it's up to you to do the detective work. In the following pages, we'll show you *exactly* how to make sure you're getting what you pay for.

Also, if you have more than one machine at home, even if that second machine is a notebook computer, there's absolutely NO reason you should be paying for more than one connection to the Internet. Naturally, your ISP will disagree, as most try to force you to pay an incremental up-charge to set up a connection to their broadband pipe for another one of your machines. Typically, this charge runs $10-$20 a month, which we're sure you could put to good use elsewhere, such as new games. With our help, you can easily set up a shared broadband connection with just a small investment of time and money. After all, why should you pay for what you can rightfully get for free?

Finally, while we all claim that we use our broadband connection for "work" reasons, let's be honest: Playing games is one of our top usages. Being able to go online and frag your buddies—or complete strangers—in *Quake III Arena* or *Unreal Tournament 2004* makes high-speed Internet access worth the extra cash. However, all broadband pipes and dial-up connections aren't created equally. And, even if they were, it's likely that many of your opponents have tweaked their settings to give themselves a slight performance edge, which can make

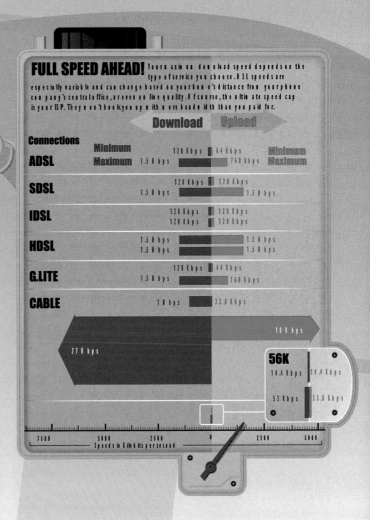

FULL SPEED AHEAD! Your maximum download speed depends on the type of service you choose. DSL speeds are especially variable and can change based on your home's distance from your phone company's central office, or even on line quality. Of course, the ultimate speed cap is your ISP. They won't hook you up with more bandwidth than you paid for.

There are a few semi-reliable online bandwidth tests, but the most reliable way to measure your connection's speed is to download files from a variety of servers and measure the average speed.

Give Dial-up a Boost!

Broadband access is becoming more ubiquitous these days. However, it's possible that some of you are still living so far out in the boonies—or maybe just a few feet beyond the reach of your local provider's DSL reach—that you're stuck with dial-up as your only means of online access. If so, we feel your pain. Still, we have a few tricks you can use to give your modem a kick in the pants. Check out the section "How to Give Dial-Up a Kick in the Pants."

BROADBAND TIP
How to Test Your Connection Speed

In addition to downloading multiple files from different servers and noting the download rates, there are also a few online connection tests that will give you a rough idea of your connection speed. However, because these online tests usually involve only one server they are not the best way to test your connection speed. Still, they provide a good frame of reference, and here are a few we have used that work well.

http://www.bandwidthplace.com
http://www.dslreports.com/stest
http://www.pcpitstop.com/internet/default.asp
http://www.dslreports.com/tools

all the difference between fragging, and being fragged. Make sure you're competing on a level playing field with our custom tweaks for eking the most performance out of some of today's most popular online games.

But before we get to all this juicy stuff though, it's important that you understand at least the basics behind the technology that powers your particular type of broadband pipe. Regardless of whether you use DSL, cable, or even satellite for your online connection, we'll break down the bits and bytes for you.

Digital Subscriber Line

One of the most common forms of high-speed Internet connection service is the Digital Subscriber Line, also known by its acronym, DSL. The technology uses your existing phone line to transmit data at high speeds, and requires only a DSL modem and an Ethernet card to operate. This technology is made possible by the fact that your little phone line is made up of a pair of copper wires that are capable of handling a lot more bandwidth than what is required by mere telephone con-

versations. DSL capitalizes on this excess bandwidth by using it to transmit data at a higher frequency than what is used for your telephone calls, so the two never get in each other's way. Think of your phone line like a bridge with an upper and lower deck; your calls roar along on the lower deck while data zips along on the upper deck.

DSL comes in a variety of flavors and configurations, but the most widespread form of DSL service for home users is known as ADSL, which stands for Asymmetric Digital Subscriber Line. As the name implies, this service boasts different speeds for uploading (sending data) than it does for downloading (receiving data). This is just fine for most people, since 90 percent of most people's time online is spent downloading web pages and files. A typical ADSL package consists of download speeds of up to 1.5 Mbps (150k/second), and upload speeds of around 128 Mbps (12k/second), though

DSL service requires you to attach filters to every phone or fax connected to the phone lines to make sure there's no interference. Luckily, most DSL packages include several filters for free.

most providers offer myriad speed packages that increase in price according to the amount of bandwidth provided. There is also VDSL, which is Very High Bit-rate DSL (very fast DSL, in other words), and

BROADBAND TIP

Open up the Pipe!

Windows XP is much better at handling high-speed Internet connections than the "made for dial-up" Windows 98, but there is still one little tweak that can increase your connection speed. The following tweak only works with Windows XP Professional edition:

- Click Start, Select "Run"
- Type "**GPedit.msc**"
- Expand the "local computer policy" branch
- Expand the "administrative templates" branch
- Expand the "network branch"
- Highlight the "QoS Packet Scheduler" in the left window
- In the right window, double-click the "limit reservable bandwidth" setting
- On the setting tab, check the "enabled" item
- Where it says "Bandwidth limit %," change it to read 0
- Close out of this window and reboot to make the new settings active.

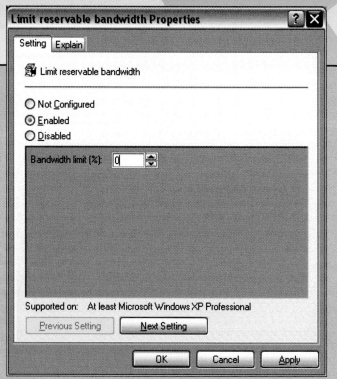

A little tweak in Windows XP Professional allows your operating system to utilize the full amount of bandwidth offered by your Internet connection.

SDSL, which is Symmetric Digital Subscriber Line (same speed up and down). These ultra-fast services are very expensive, and amount to overkill for most home users.

DSL technology is capable of sending data at a maximum rate of 8 Mbps, at a distance of about 6,000 feet, but how fast your individual service will be is determined by both the package you select as well as your proximity to the service provider's central office. DSL service is limited by a boundary of 18,000 feet, so if you are further away from the CO than this distance, you are out of luck and will not be eligible for service. Conversely, if you are extremely close to the CO, you might be able to obtain excellent speeds, whereas people at the very end of the line, around 15,000 feet away or so, might see lower speeds than expected.

The good news is that DSL service is a connection between your home computer and the central office, so there is no sharing involved whatsoever. This means you won't see your bandwidth drop during peak hours, and that, generally, you should be able to obtain the speeds promised by the provider most of the time. Of course, your download speeds are always determined by how fast other sites can send data to your computer, so you shouldn't expect 100 percent of your allotted bandwidth when downloading from websites across the world or from sites that are slow in general.

Cable Modem

Along with DSL, cable modem Internet service is the most popular form of high-speed Internet service among home consumers, due to its blazing speed and high level of availability. After

BROADBAND TIP

De-regulate Downloads

By default, the version of Internet Explorer that is included with Windows XP limits your number of simultaneous downloads to a paltry two downloads! This is pure bunk, but you can increase the number to whatever you like by hacking the registry. Our standard warnings apply here—before you fool around with your Registry, make sure you back it up.

- Click Start >Run and type "**Regedit**"
- Go to HKEY_CURRENT_USER \ Software \ Microsoft \ Windows \ CurrentVersion \ Internet Settings
- Select New > DWORD Value from the Edit menu
- Name the new value "MaxConnectionsPer1_0Server"
- Right-click the MaxConnectionsPer1_0Server value and choose Modify
- Under Base, click the radio button next to Decimal
- In the Value Data box, enter the number of simultaneous connections you want to set (10 is a good value), and click OK
- If you want to increase the number of connections to the server you can repeat steps 3 - 7 using the new value Max-ConnectionsPerServer
- Exit the Registry editor and log off, or reboot to make the new settings take effect

The Dish on the Dish

Aside from cable and DSL Internet, there is also the option of using a satellite dish to receive high-speed Internet service, though prices and plans, as well as availability, vary widely. The basic technology is pretty straightforward. The company beams its high-speed wireless service into the sky to a satellite orbiting the earth. Your satellite dish, mounted on the roof of your abode and facing south, points up into the sky and picks up the signal.

In general, satellite Internet connection speeds vary from a lowly 255 Kbps (five times faster than dial-up, but much slower than cable and DSL) to 500 Kbps. The downside to satellite Internet is that you have to buy or rent the dish, which is pricey. For example, basic satellite service from EarthLink includes a $350 equipment charge, $250 installation, and $70 a month for service. Second, bad weather often can interfere with the signal (despite what the companies say to the contrary). Also, satellite Internet is not the best solution for gaming, since it offers good throughput but high latency due to the distance the signal must travel (22,400 miles, and that's just one-way!), which means bad pings and no fun when playing games online.

In general, if you can't get cable or DSL, satellite Internet service is much more preferable than dial-up, but we only recommend it if you have no other choices.

all, the majority of American households already have cable TV service, so adding cable internet access (where available) is quite easy. And just like DSL, cable modem service has many benefits, but also a few drawbacks as well.

Cable modem service works by sending data at high speeds along the same coaxial cable that is used to deliver cable TV content to your home. This cable has several hundred megahertz of bandwidth, yet regular TV channels require only 6 MHz or so per channel, which is why you can have hundreds of channels delivered through one cable. Internet service, for all intents and purposes, is just another cable channel as far as the cable company is concerned.

Due to this excessive amount of available bandwidth, a cable modem Internet connection can reach a theoretical maximum of 30 to 40 Mbps, which is enormous compared to a standard DSL connection of 1.5 Mbps. However, there is a catch: Cable modem users are grouped in clusters and all share a finite amount of bandwidth. So, if nobody on your block is using the Net (say, at 4:00 in the morning), your Internet connection will be insanely fast, but at 8:00 pm on a weeknight you're likely to see it slow down to the speeds of DSL, or even slower depending on the amount of people using your cluster. The good news though, in comparison with DSL, is that a cable modem's bandwidth isn't limited by how far away you are from the provider's central office.

We've used both cable and DSL and can tell you that, from our experience, cable is a lot faster than DSL—sometimes as much as twice as fast. If you have the luxury of choosing between them, we recommend cable, although both are simply awesome compated to the soul-sucking wait times associated with dial-up modems. ■

Share Your Broadband Connection

DSL, cable, or satellite.
Here's how to pipe it through every PC in your home.

Most broadband Internet connections are fast enough to accommodate 10 stations, not just a single, lonely PC. So, if you have multiple PCs in your house, it's easy to share your broadband connection among them. And you're not limited to only PCs. Your broadband-fueled home network can connect to game consoles, MP3 players, and anything else that speaks TCP/IP.

In this article, we'll show you how to share your connection using NAT routing, a scheme that takes the single IP address assigned by your ISP and shares it with all your TCP/IP devices.

But before you get started, you need to decide what type of broadband router you want. You can either add a second network card to the PC that's already connected to the Net and use built-in Windows software to handle routing functions, or you can buy an inexpensive stand-alone router-in-a-box that does the same thing. The strategy you choose depends on your needs.

The router-in-a-box provides easy 24/7 Internet connectivity to every PC in your home, but may preclude you from hosting multiplayer game sessions for certain games. On the other hand, if you use your PC as the router, none of the other PCs on your LAN will have access to the Internet if your router PC isn't powered up. That's the bad news. The good news is that using an existing PC for routing functions is less expensive and easier to configure than the router-in-a-box method. Most routers-in-a-box cost between $100 and $150, and include an integrated hub with four or five Ethernet ports. For a couple bucks more, you can add a Wi-Fi connection to the device as well.

Some rules of thumb: If you have just two devices that will connect to the Internet, you should use an existing PC and the integrated Windows software. If you want to connect three or more devices, it will be more convenient to use a stand-alone router. There are also some more advanced options—such as using a dedicated Linux or Windows 2000 Server box to do your routing—but they're more difficult to configure and only add features (such as web and e-mail servers) that most home users will never need.

Step 1:
Make a Shopping List

Whether you choose to use a dedicated PC or a router, you'll need some additional parts, the first of which is a hub, a device with multiple Ethernet ports that lets you connect more than two devices to a network. You'll need a hub with one port for each device you intend to wire in. Wireless devices don't need their own ports, but your wireless access point does, unless it's integrated into your router. You can daisy chain multiple hubs together, but you should leave yourself some room for expansion.

In addition to the hub, you'll need an Ethernet network card (NIC) for each device you want to connect. Most PCs ship with Ethernet support built directly into the motherboard, but you should confirm that each candidate for your network is Ethernet-ready before you go to the store. An Ethernet port looks like a wide phone jack, and usually has a pair of lights beside it. You should be able to purchase a good PCI Ethernet card for

less than $30. And remember, if you're going to use your PC as the router, you'll

CAT-5 Ethernet cables

need two network cards for that machine.

Unless your network is going to be 100 percent wireless—which we don't recommend—you'll need a segment of CAT-5 Ethernet cable for each PC you intend to connect to the network. You'll also need one segment to connect the router to your broadband modem, and one segment to connect the router to the hub or wireless bridge (if it's not integrated in the router). Make sure you have some slack in the cables, especially if you plan to run them around at floor level. You don't want to trip over a cable and destroy your entire network.

If you want to network some PCs that are particularly far away from your router, it's easier to connect them wirelessly. Right

Linksys router

now, 802.11b and 802.11g wireless devices offer the best balance of speed, cost, and range. The newer 802.11g devices provide faster connections than 802.11b, but we've experienced some compatibility problems with all the 802.11g products we've tested to date. Regardless, if you want to make part of your network wireless, you'll need either a router that includes 802.11b or 802.11g support, or a stand-alone wireless bridge. Of course, you'll also need wireless network cards for each device you want to connect wirelessly.

D-Link DGE-500T Ethernet card

To sum up, here are your ingredients:
- Either a stand-alone router (like the Linksys WRT54G), or a PC with Windows ME, 2000, or XP and two network cards

- A broadband connection that uses Ethernet to connect to your current PC
- An Ethernet cable for each PC you intend to connect, plus one cable for the router and one for the hub
- A network card for each PC you intend to connect to the wired LAN
- (Optional) A Wi-Fi bridge and Wi-Fi network cards for each PC you want to connect wirelessly to the network
- If you're going to get a stand-alone router, feel free to skip Step 2B. Otherwise, read on.

Step 2a:
Configuring Your LAN Using an Existing PC and Internet Connection Sharing

Now that you've decided to use an existing PC as your router, it's time to get to work. Assuming the PC you want to use as the router is already hooked up to your broadband connection, all you need to do is install another network card in the PC, reconfigure some cables, and make a few minor software tweaks.

Power down your PC and open the case. Find an empty PCI slot and remove the slot cover. Install the new network card, screw it into place, and replace the case cover. If you have some sticky labels, it's a good idea to label the network connections, in case you ever have to disconnect everything. Label the card you just installed "Internal" and the original network card "External." Once you've restarted Windows and installed the drivers for your new card, you can move to

the next step, software setup.

Installing Internet Connection Sharing is very simple in Windows XP. Go to the Control Panel, then Network Connections, and right-click your *external* network connection. This will most likely be named Local Area Connection or Local Area Connection #1. Essentially, you want the network card that's connected to your cable or DSL modem. Go to Advanced, then check the box labeled "Allow other network users to connect through this computer's Internet connection."

That's all there is to it. Now you need to take one of the Ethernet cables you bought and run it from the Internal network card on the PC to the hub. If you can connect to the Internet—try browsing to **www.google.com** as a test—and see twinkling lights on the hub, you can safely proceed to Step 3.

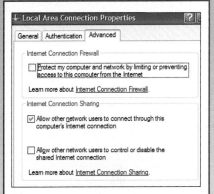

If you've got a couple of computers that need a network connection, and you don't mind running your main PC when they need access, Internet Connection Sharing is built into Windows, and is easy to use.

Step 2B:
Configuring Your LAN Using a Stand-alone Router

Before you begin configuring your router, you'll need your ISP's settings. When you first signed up for your broadband connection, you should have received an e-mail or letter with all the information about your settings. Most ISPs use dynamically configured IP addresses, but if you have a static address, or if you have to log in to your broadband connection using PPPoE, you'll need to have your IP info and login. If you can't find that info,

call your ISP's support line to request it.

Now you'll want to connect your PC to the router. Connect your cable or DSL modem to the port labeled "WAN" or "Internet" on the router. If you're using a stand-alone hub, you need to connect the router's LAN port to your hub and run another Ethernet cable from one of the ports on the hub to your PC's network card. If the hub's integrated into your router, you can just

run a line between your PC and a spare port on the router.

Now you should follow the instructions the manufacturer provides for configuring your router. In most cases, you'll need to point your web browser to a special, private IP address, and then enter the info your ISP provided. Once your router's set up, and you can connect to the Internet from your PC—try **www.google.com** to test—proceed to Step 3.

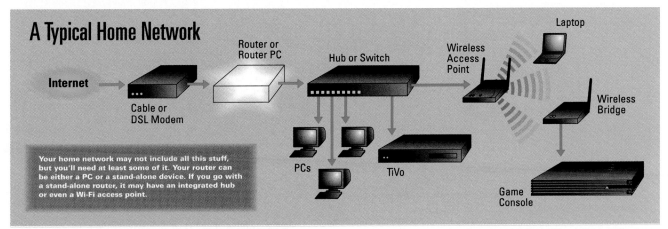

Step 3:
Running Cables

Now your local network has an Internet connection, but only one of your PCs is connected to it. What you need to do next is connect your other PCs and networked devices to the LAN. If they're in the same room, it's as easy as running a long Ethernet cable from the hub to the other PCs, but it's not always that simple.

There are a few tricks that can make longer cable runs easier. If your home has carpet, you can usually squeeze an Ethernet cable into the gap between the baseboard and the carpet. By doing this, you can get a cable from one side of a room to the other completely out of sight. Make sure you leave enough slack at both ends of the cable in case you need to move the PC or hub.

It's easy to run cables to a nearby room if you have a crawl space under your house, even if you don't want to drill holes in the floor. If you have central air or heat, and your home has floor registers, you can usually slide an Ethernet

Squeezing a cable into the gap between a heating duct and the floor is an easy and nondestructive way to get cables into your crawl space.

cable between the edge of the vent and the floor. Make sure you don't strip the cable when you're pulling it past the jagged metal vent.

If the above tips won't work in your home, you can run cabling around the perimeter of your room. Most hardware stores sell small clips that you can nail

into the baseboard to keep your Ethernet cables against the wall and out of the way. If you have to run a cable across a doorway, make sure you tape it to the floor so that no one will trip over it.

Remember: You can connect additional hubs to the first one. So, if you have a room a long way from your hub with two (or more) PCs, there's no reason to run two Ethernet cables to that room, just run one cable to that room, connect it to a hub, and then connect the devices to the new hub.

If you don't want to muck about in your crawl space, you can also use a wireless link to get the job done, but it will be expensive. If you already have a wireless access point, you'll just need to pick up a Wi-Fi bridge—they're frequently called Wireless Network adapters, and cost about $120. If you don't already have a wireless access point, you can get a pair of bridges and use them as a cableless cable.

Step 4:
Configuring Your Individual PCs

To configure your "peripheral" PCs to connect to the Internet, all you need to do is tell them to automatically get an IP address from your router. Go to the Control Panel, then click on Network Connections. Right-click the Local Area Network connection and select Properties. Double-click TCP/IP settings, and make sure both "Obtain an IP address automatically" and "Obtain

DNS server address automatically" are checked. Keep pressing OK until you're out of Network Properties. Some versions of Windows will prompt you to reboot after making this change. Test the Internet connection by going to a web site that's always up, such as **Google.com**.

Internet Protocol (TCP/IP) Properties ? X

General | Alternate Configuration

You can get IP settings assigned automatically if your network supports this capability. Otherwise, you need to ask your network administrator for the appropriate IP settings.

◉ Obtain an IP address automatically
○ Use the following IP address:

IP address:
Subnet mask:
Default gateway:

◉ Obtain DNS server address automatically
○ Use the following DNS server addresses:

Preferred DNS server:
Alternate DNS server:

Configuring your other Windows PCs to connect to the network is as easy as flipping a switch.

Step 5:
Share and Enjoy!

Once the router's up and running, you're not limited to connecting just PCs. Increasingly, home entertainment devices come with Ethernet ports, so you can connect them to the Internet as well. Xbox, PS2, and GameCube all offer Internet-based multiplayer gaming, and PVRs like ReplayTV and TiVo can download scheduling info over an Ethernet connection (which is nice because this doesn't tie up your phone line).

If sharing your network connection with every PC in your home isn't enough for you, it's easy to add an 802.11b or 802.11g access point to your LAN so you can have wireless access anywhere in the house. You can also add a basic file server to store your music, photos, and movies for easy access from anywhere in the house! ∎

How To...

PROTECT YOURSELF
With a Firewall

MAXIMUM PC
TIME TO COMPLETION
00:30
HOURS   MINUTES

Just because your computer is connected to the Internet doesn't mean you have to be a target for hackers. We show you how to properly configure your PC and use a firewall to make sure you stay safe

O ver the past few years, broadband usage has skyrocketed—and for good reason. Broadband can be more than 10 times faster than the speed of the average dial-up, and with a price of around $40/month, it's still fairly competitive in relation to the slower, more traditional method of logging on. But does using broadband open you up to new online dangers? Not if you're smart.

SIMPLY DISCONNECT
One common belief is that getting DSL can increase your chances of being hacked—i.e., that always-on technology means that your PC is vulnerable to attack 24 hours a day, which can be quite alarming. Fortunately, the reality is a little different.

The use of DSL doesn't mean that you have to be continuously connected to the Internet. While most ISPs let you stay logged on as long as you want— they generally don't employ timeouts that kick you off—it's ultimately your choice as to how often you're connected. You can log off at any time; in fact, it's a good idea to log off whenever you're not actively using your computer.

Furthermore, how you connect to the web is not the most important factor in your online security. Hackers can penetrate your system only if you're sharing files, perhaps across a home network, or are running server-type applications. Such activities put you at risk of being hacked, even if you're using a dial-up connection. And if you're running just one system, the chances of being hacked are pretty small, DSL or not.

SAFETY FIRST
While there's no need to be paranoid about broadband security, it's always wise to err on the side of caution and practice due diligence. Even if you have just one home PC, it's worth the time to carry out some basic checks to make sure your system is configured for optimum safety.

A good first step is to ensure that Windows XP is running only services that you really need and regularly use. To find out, select Start, Control Panel, Administrative

Tools, Services, and take a look at the list it presents. Services that may allow external access to your system include Telnet, the Remote Access Connection Manager, and support for FTP, WWW, or SMTP servers. To turn off any service that you don't need, right-click it, select Properties, and change Startup Type to "Disabled".

The default Windows XP network settings may also enable options that you don't need. Specifically, it's likely that NetBIOS is enabled, which could let remote users determine the network name and domain associated with your computer. To turn off NetBIOS, select Start, Control Panel, Network Connections, right-click your Internet connection, choose Networking, TCP/IP, Properties, Advanced, WINS, and clear the "Enable NetBIOS over TCP/IP" option.

The next step is to review your file shares at Start, Settings, Control Panel, Administrative Tools, Computer Management, Shared folders. The safest approach here is to avoid sharing whole drives or important system folders like C:\Windows. Right-click any file share you don't need to disable it or change its current permissions. If that doesn't work, the Microsoft support site has some great articles explaining File Sharing in Windows XP. Go to http://support.microsoft.com and search the knowledge base for 304040 for more on this topic.

The interface for *ZoneAlarm Pro* makes it easy to access all of the program's key options. Be sure to go through the included tutorial.

WINDOWS XP'S FIREWALL PROTECTION

Formerly known as Internet Connection Firewall (ICF), the new and improved Windows Firewall (the new name post SP2 installation) adds a more dynamic and aggressive approach to protecting you from potential threats. While stand-alone PCs aren't as likely to be hacked, there is some risk, especially with a broadband connection. Even if your machine is not the intended target, it can be used as a go-between for a larger-scale malicious endeavor. The point is that protection is better than no protection. Microsoft is keenly aware of these threats, which is why Service Pack 2 makes some significant changes with regard to security. At press time, SP2 wasn't quite ready so we'll take a look at what ICF does and point out a few of the key changes that Windows Firewall will (if all goes well) incorporate.

ICF works by maintaining a table of destinations you're trying to access online, such as the location of a particular web page or FTP server. Inbound traffic is allowed through only if ICF can see there's an unfulfilled outbound request; this means you can surf the web as before, but attempts by unknown systems to access your PC will simply be ignored.

If you decide to use ICF on a networked system, make sure you use it only on the Internet connection, or else it's likely to interfere with network traffic. The best idea is to choose one PC as your Internet gateway, connect that machine to the DSL line, and then share your broadband connection with the rest of the network.

ICF is a simple and powerful tool to protect your PC, but it does have one limitation—there's no check on outgoing connections.

This means that if a Trojan horse is installed on your computer, it could call home and communicate with its author and potentially give someone complete access to your PC. The best way to avoid this risk is by using a good antivirus program such as *Norton Antivirus*.

Generally, Windows Firewall is more aggresive than ICF. It is enabled by default and offers more in the way of inbound as well as outbound protection. Access at the port and application level is configurable and some ports will be blocked by default such as DCOM (Distributed Component Object Model), which has been used by worms. The interface allows you to select applications that will be given "exceptions" for access. Then, the ports will dynamically open and close as necessary. For instance, any app that attempts access initiates a dialog that allows you to configure what it can and cannot do. And, when you finish your online game of UT2004, Windows Firewall will automatically close the access port when the game is terminated. Pretty slick, right? Well, there's nothing terribly revolutionary about these implementations, but what Microsoft has done is provide more effective, built-in security that is relatively easy to work with.

THIRD-PARTY FIREWALLS

It's still too early for all of us to be using Windows Firewall, but whether you update XP or not, you'll still want to look into implementing a firewall. Several excellent software firewalls are available, and most are offered in a free version.

The best of the third-party firewalls is *ZoneAlarm*, from Zone Labs (**www.zonealarm. com**). This robust firewall provides a high degree of customization because it lets you track every program that asks for access to the Internet (you can set it so that com-monly used programs, such as *Internet Explorer*, are automatically granted access), and it also reports when someone is scanning your PC. (Hackers will perform scans of various IP addresses to look for vulnerabilities.)

Another advantage that *ZoneAlarm* has is that it can be set to automatically "lock" your PC's connection and deny all Internet access if your PC is idle for a period of time. This option is particularly helpful if your broadband connection is via cable modem, which often can't be easily disconnected or turned off.

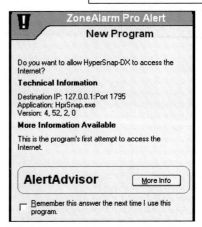

When a program tries to access the Internet, *ZoneAlarm* will tell you the name of the program and the IP address that it's trying to reach.

A stripped-down version of *ZoneAlarm* is available for free. If you want to try out the full-featured *ZoneAlarm Pro*, you can download a 30-day trial version.

CONFIGURE SECURITY SETTINGS

Adding a firewall to your system makes it more secure, but it doesn't address every possible vulnerability. In particular, you need to make sure that the security settings in your Internet applications are properly configured.

In *Internet Explorer*, for example, the Internet Zone security setting (Tools, Internet Options, Security) should ideally be set to either Medium or High. *Outlook Express* users can limit their exposure to viruses by selecting Tools, Options, Security, and choosing to work in the Restricted Sites Zone. Note that SP2 will include new features for IE and OE such as a lock down security zone and more secure default settings to help isolate vicious attachments.

No computer that's logged onto the Internet will ever be 100 percent secure, but by taking the steps outlined here, you've done everything you can to keep your PC safe and secure. ∎

Vulnerability Scanners

So you've tweaked your system and think it's hacker-proof. Just remember, there are always more ways to test your machine's vulnerabilities.

There are plenty of security tools that can help you find out if your system is at risk—they'll scan your PC and report back any potentially dangerous security holes.

One of the first sites that you should visit is the Gibson Research Corporation (www.grc.com). This site includes a lot of information about ensuring your PC's safety, and features tools that quickly and safely disable any security holes. There are also two web-based scanners on the site, *ShieldsUP!!* and *LeakTest*, which are very helpful

in determining how safe your PC really is.

Additional scanners are available, like those found at Sygate (scan.sygatetech.com) or BlackCode (www.blackcode.com/scan). *BlackCode* will also check your PC for over 1,500 Trojan viruses.

The most powerful tools available are the professional vulnerability scanners—applications that can check the setup of your PC for hundreds of different known security problems. *Shadow Security Scanner* (www.safety-lab.com/en) is one of the best: Just point it toward your PC's IP address and it looks for open ports, issues with open servers, password vulnerabilities, and more.

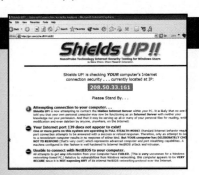

At $100, *Shadow Security Scanner* isn't cheap. But a 15-day free trial version is available so you can try it out at no cost, which definitely makes it worth the download.

5

Turn Your PC Into Fort Knox

Windows XP Professional edition, and to a lesser extent, Home edition, is equipped with powerful features to keep your data safe. We show you how to lock XP down.

L ate at night, while you are snug under your 600-thread-count sheets, someone—across the street, or perhaps in Hong Kong—may be wide awake and intent on breaking into your computer. Why? Who knows, and it really doesn't matter, does it? What does matter is that all of your data—your financial files, your email, the first chapter of that novel that's going to win you the Pulitzer Prize—are all sitting there, exposed and unguarded.

Countless would-be "hackers" are out there trying to expose the latest Windows XP security vulnerability, such as a heap-overflow bug that could allow them to author malicious code to execute on *your* machine. This code could take the form of a "Trojan horse" file, which could give a hacker full control of your PC's operating system via the Internet. Or maybe it's a rogue virus, spread through email, which could be deleting critical Windows system files on your machine as you snooze. Worse, someone could access your data, erase critical files, wipe out your hard drive, or use your computer as part of an attack on someone else's web site or service—just for "fun," and all while you're sound asleep.

Not on our watch! These issues may keep *us* up at night, as we strategize ways to thwart the next would-be hacker out there. However, you can continue to sleep soundly with the peace of mind provided in the following pages. We're going to make you aware of WinXP's security vulnerabilities, and provide you with all the vital information you need to safeguard your PC and lock it down as tight as Fort Knox.

Open Windows Invite Intruders

The Windows series of operating systems, up to and including WinXP, are huge, far-reaching programs. As such, they're incredibly complex, comprised of thousands of modules and millions of lines of code. This is a lot of code to keep track of, an almost insurmountable task for Windows programmers to dream of every possible avenue of attack a hacker might take—particularly before a new version of the OS is launched. Therefore, as is the case with any program of its magnitude, each new version of Windows is a fertile breeding ground for bugs, which may include errors of omission, unpolished code, or simple lack of forethought. XP is no exception. Because of

its vast installed base, Windows is also the most targeted operating system for virus writers, as it represents the largest billboard for them to broadcast their skills to the hacking "underworld."

As we've said, who really knows what motivates hackers? It might just be the novelty of pulling off annoying pranks, like defacing web sites, or the thrill of stealing the code of a major game before

Frankenstein XP

Windows XP inherited stability—and its core "engine" code—from Microsoft's more robust commercial operating systems: Windows NT Workstation and Windows 2000. Folder and file-encryption security was culled from Windows NT. XP's simplified folder view system can be traced back to Windows 95, and its window and cursor animations evolved from Windows 98. Last, but not least, XP's digital-media tools and the potentially life-saving System Restore utility were plucked from the much maligned, and short-lived, Windows ME.

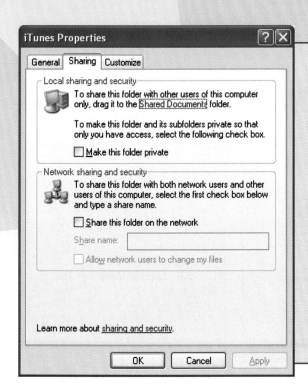

Make "Private" Folders Really Private!

Windows XP makes some pretty bold assumptions when you first install it. For instance, it automatically installs a bunch of *personal* folders for each user, but it doesn't bother to hide them from the other users. You can, and probably should, do this yourself. The tools are there!

However, you can only make folders contained in your personal profile private. These folders include your My Documents folder and anything within it, Desktop, Start Menu, Cookies, and Favorites—or any custom folder you create within your My Documents folder. Make them private by navigating to the file you want to privatize, such as My Pictures. (By default, you'll find most of them in a path like C:\Documents and Settings\<username>\My Documents\My Pictures.) Then, right-click the My Pictures folder, choose Properties, click the Sharing tab, and check the "Make this folder private" checkbox. From that point on, only people logged in to your user account will have access to those folders.

You can make your personal profile folders private, so that users logged in under other profiles can't access them.

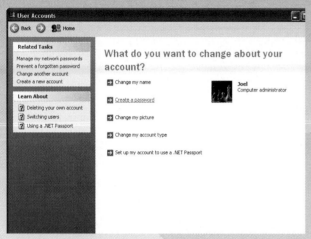

Password-protect user accounts in Windows XP through the Control Panel/User Accounts applet.

it's published, as was the case with Valve Software's *Half-Life 2*.

Last September, hackers exploited a security hole in *Microsoft Outlook* to gain access to Valve's internal network. They then swiped the source code to the hotly awaited *Half-Life 2*, which they compiled and leaked onto the Internet. Rumors still abound that this attack was a direct cause of the delay of *Half-Life 2's* release.

Typically, for each new "open window" hackers find to exploit, such as the *Outlook* back door noted above, Microsoft quickly responds with a patch to slam it shut. These fixes are made available via the Windows Update process. So we don't need to tell you this, right? But we will anyway, again: *Keep WindowsXP up to date!* Run Windows Update at least weekly. (See "Maintain a Healthy OS" in Part III).

Security Begins at Home

Of course, the latest security patch won't help you much if your PC's physical location makes it accessible to others when you're not around and you haven't set up safeguards. The easiest way, by far, for someone to steal information from or harm a PC is to sit down at the keyboard and go exploring, unimpeded. This may seem obvious, but keep your computer room secure. Lock the computer room door, if possible. Password-protect the computer's BIOS by entering the CMOS set-up program and configuring an administrator password. (The process depends upon the machine you're using, but look for a prompt to hit a key—typically "Delete," "F5," or "F2"—during the initial boot process, then navigate through the set-up program to find an

option to password-protect the PC). Just don't forget this password. Write it down, and keep it somewhere safe. Next, password-protect XP's screen-saver through the Display control panel. Use passwords for all of the user accounts on the PC. Configure these through Control Panel/User Accounts. Click on an account, each of which is accompanied by an icon in the bottom of the window. Then, on the next screen, click "Create a password," and follow the prompts.

Disable Simple File-Sharing

Simple file-sharing allows anyone to access your folders through the Guest account. Disabling it forces people on a network or that share your machine to authenticate, by supplying a password for an account controlled by a server, before they're able to access any shared directories and files on the network. If you're using Windows XP Professional, go to the Start button and launch My Computer. Click the Tools menu and select Folder Options. Click the View tab, look in the list labeled "Advances," and scroll down to the bottom. The last item is "Use simple file sharing." Clear

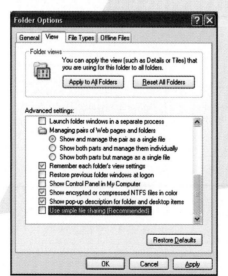

Uncheck the "Use simple file-sharing" box in XP Pro to prevent just any network user from accessing your shared folders.

Give your PC Terminator-class protection with a smart password scheme.

Passwords R' Us

It's not worth going through the trouble of password-protecting your BIOS, user accounts, personal folders, and encrypted files if you don't put some serious thought into the process. There are a lot of passwords here to remember, so a system is key—and no, using the name of each of your family pets or ex-wives isn't good enough. The passwords you select *must* be complex enough that no one will ever be able to guess them, but simple enough that you'll be able to remember them.

Here's a good strategy: Build a password system from things you remember by heart, such as a quote from your favorite movie. Take the phrase "Hasta la vista baby," from *Terminator 2*, for example. Drop everything but the first letter of each word, and add a number for extra security, and you've got "Hlv1b." Even better would be "Hlv1b#3"—even if a hacker knows you're a huge fan of the *Terminator* series, this would be near impossible to guess. The "1" and "#3" are also mnemonic clues. The "1" represents the first letter of Arnold's first name, and the "#3" stand for the number of *Terminator* movies. Pretty clever, eh?

Still, keeping track of multiple passwords is tough. Make sure to memorize the one you need to boot, and use it to also protect an *encrypted* file on your hard drive, or better still, on a floppy you keep in a secure location away from your PC, that lists the rest of your passwords for reference, should you forget 'em.

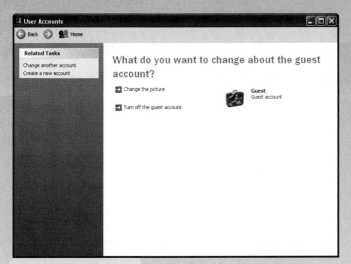

Windows XP allows you to switch off the Guest account to prevent indiscriminate local access to your PC.

Encrypt files and folders to prevent data theft. Even if your hard drive is physically stolen, thieves can't access your data without the proper keys!

the checkbox. (Note that this feature isn't available in Windows XP Home edition.)

Kill the Guest Account

The Guest account is a hacker's welcome mat, and it's enabled by default in both versions of XP. Its purpose is to simplify the sharing process in a simple network environment. Unless you're absolutely sure that your network is secure from any sort of intrusion—and, naturally, if your PC is not on a network—you should disable the Guest account immediately after installing XP. You can turn off the Guest account through Control Panel/User accounts. Note, however, that unless you're using XP Professional as part of a domain, turning off the Guest account with this method only removes it from the local-logon and fast user-switching

options; the Guest account remains active to network users.

Ban Remote Desktop

Remote Desktop is a feature specific to XP Professional that allows users to connect to a computer remotely and use it as if they were sitting in the chair in front of it—similar to applications like *PC Anywhere*. It's off by default, but verify that nobody turns it on by heading to Control Panel/System and clicking on the Remote tab. Be sure the checkbox next to the second heading is clear.

Enable Encrypted File System

Windows XP Professional contains a powerful encryption layer, called EFS (for Encrypted File System), that you

can apply to files and folders. Simply select a file or folder, right-click on it, and select Properties. In the General tab, click Advanced. Check the "Encrypt contents to secure data" checkbox. Note that Windows XP Home edition does not offer EFS, and Windows XP Professional can only encrypt files and folders stored on NTFS partitions. If you encrypt a folder with data already in it, Windows will ask if you wish to encrypt the entire contents of the folder. Windows encryption works by giving each file its own private key, while the machine has a public key. The keys have to match for the operating system to decrypt the file. On the local machine, encryption is transparent to the user. You can even store encrypted files, which would only be accessible to your computer, on remote servers. ■

Folder Guard *from WinAbility lets you hide or restrict access to files, folders and Windows XP resources.*

Protect Private Files with Folder Guard

If you want to beef up the security and privacy of various files, folders, and other resources, WinAbility's *Folder Guard* is a solid choice. This handy app puts you in control of exactly who can see what on *your* PC. (Check out the evaluation version at http://winability.com/folderguard.)

Folder Guard goes further than XP's own security tools with a suite of powerful options, such as the ability to hide folders completely from others when someone else uses your machine. It's as if the folders aren't even there! It's possible to lock files and folders with a master password, preventing others from accessing or changing them. If you don't want the

kids accidentally changing hardware or system settings, *Folder Guard* allows you to restrict access to the Control Panel, and to prevent others from formatting drives. You can even restrict access to removable drives and prevent other users of your machine from downloading stuff through *Internet Explorer.*

Folder Guard Standard v.6.0 for Windows9x and XP Home Edition runs $39.95; the *Professional* version, compatible with XP Pro, costs $59.95. *Folder Guard Lite* v.2.7 can hide and password-protect individual folders, which isn't a bad deal for $24.95.

All About Viruses

Being proactive and taking preventative measures can help keep yourself and your family free of nasty viruses, and the same's true for your PC. Here's how to keep XP inoculated.

A computer virus is a program designed to spread copies of itself onto multiple computers by infecting files or system areas of hard drives and floppy disks. Nasty viruses also can contain "payloads" in the form of malicious code that may alter, corrupt or delete files on a hard drive and make them inaccessible to you. Viruses typically try to operate invisibly, unbeknownst to you, until it's too late and the damage is done.

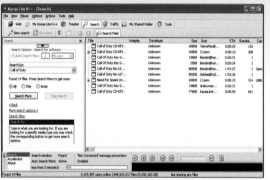

Kazaa Lite K++, *like any peer-to-peer file- sharing program, can't guarantee that the programs you download aren't laden with viruses. Use them at your own risk.*

And viruses aren't the only source of "colds" your PC can catch. You should watch out for two other infectious beasts: Worms (code that exists simply to replicate itself, not to damage files) and Trojan Horses (secret programs that allow access to a system through a remote connection). Worms are the least offensive of this terrible trio. Trojans, meanwhile, are in a different class. They're often spread the same way as viruses and worms (through email attachments or downloaded executables), but they require human intervention to be truly destructive.

The Never-Do List
In this day and age, there's really no reason anyone should fall prey to a virus, especially an executable virus. Viruses are programs, and programs can't execute themselves. They require some form of human activity to get them started, be it booting off of an infected floppy disk or running an email attachment from an

unknown source.

Protect your PC from yourself and *never* do the following:

• **Never Boot from a Floppy Diskette** without scanning it for viruses first. Viruses that reside in system areas of floppy disks can lie dormant for years in your desk, unused, only to wake up and infect your system when you boot off the diskette it calls home.

• **Don't Run Email-Attached Executables** without verifying their source and scanning them for viruses first. Viruses can't infect media files (AVIs, MPEGs, TIFs, JPGs, and so on), but they assault your PC as part of an executable file (file extensions such as EXE, COM, PIF, VBS, and more) or from templates that contain macros (*Word* document templates, for example). If you receive an executable as an email attachment, get in touch with the person from whom you received it. Make sure it's something he meant to send and that he knows what it is. Better yet, make a blanket rule against running executable files that arrive via email. Period.

• **Don't Download Pirated Software.** Downloading "safe" programs isn't usually a problem; rarely are product demos, freeware programs or authorized program updates infected. However, hackers love to plant viruses

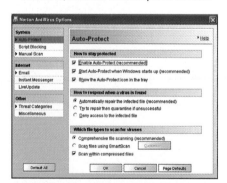

Norton AntiVirus *is one of the best antivirus programs available. Here's a look at its easy-to-use Options screen.*

and Trojans in pirated "warez," which is just one of the many reasons to stay away from them. By association, running file-sharing programs such as *Kazaa*, can be extremely risky as well. Use them at your own risk.

Use an Antivirus Program
It's absolutely vital, given the sheer number of viruses in existence, not to mention the new ones being bred daily, to get yourself a copy of Norton *AntiVirus*, McAfee *VirusScan*, or—at the very least—any one of a number of freeware antivirus programs (such as *AntiVir*, which can be found at www.free-av.com. See "Maintain a Healthy OS" for more on antivirus programs. ■

You're Infected!
If you receive a run32dll.exe error when you open Control Panel, your *run32dll. exe* file is corrupt or you've got a virus. To correct the error, begin by ensuring that you have an up-to-date virus-checker and perform a full scan of your system. Next, to restore *run32dll.exe*, insert your XP or installation CD-ROM, then go to a command prompt and type `"expand <CD-ROM:>\i386\rundll32. ex_ %Systemroot%\rundll32.exe"` to extract the file to your system. Restart your machine.

If your PC keeps rebooting with the message "This system is being shut down in 60 seconds by NT Authority/ System due to an interrupted Remote Procedure Call (RPC)" you've been wormed. This error is a symptom of the highly contagious *MSBlaster* (LoveSan) worm. Download and install the patch, which is available on Microsoft's Web site at http://support.microsoft.com and search for knowledge base article 833330. Next, remove running versions of the virus from your PC: Open Task Manager, select the Processes tab, then click End Process for all of the following processes: *MSBLAST.EXE, PENIS32. EXE,* and *TEEKIDS.EXE,* which are known variants of the Blaster worm.

How To...

STAMP OUT

Spyware

Lots of Internet companies want to track your every online move. We show you how to reclaim your privacy

MAXIMUM PC
TIME TO COMPLETION
00:12
HOURS MINUTES

Marketing firms and e-commerce sites are increasingly ramping up their efforts to gain market share on the Internet, and one of their most insidious techniques is the "consumer profile." Bet you didn't know that your online shopping habits are being tracked so that retailers can market their goods and services with greater precision. The thinking behind this practice stands to reason—after all, a consumer is much more apt to take notice of an ad that offers a special low price on an item of personal interest.

But the way the information for these profiles is collected has many Internet users concerned. That's because companies typically employ little files called spyware that are placed on your PC when you visit a specific web site.

Spyware can take many forms. The worst are basic cookies—files created by a web server that live on a user's PC for either the length of a web session or permanently on the user's hard drive. The goal of any spyware is to record your online activities, including the

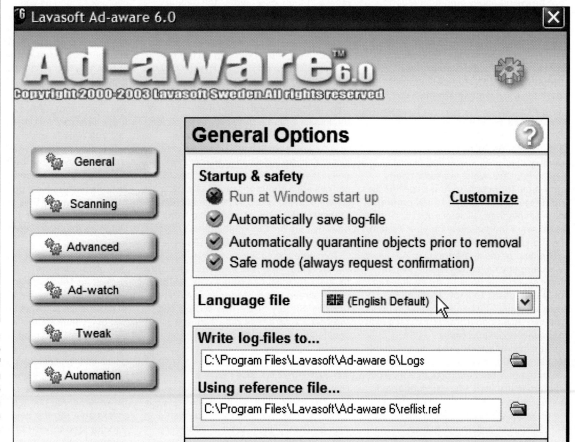

The options area lets you configure all aspects of *Ad-aware*, including whether or not the program will launch when Windows starts up.

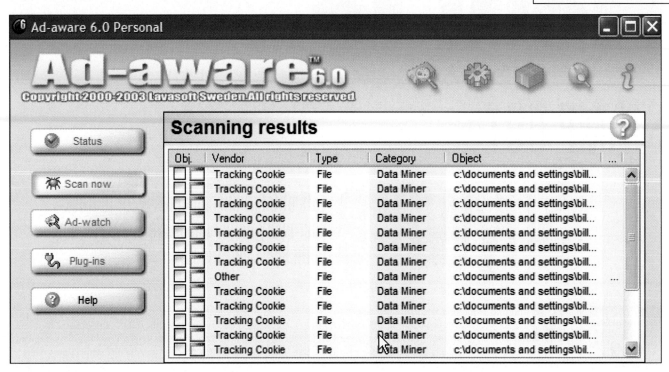

When a scan is completed, all suspected spyware on your PC will be listed. You can then go through the list and delete the files that you want gone.

sites you visit, collect information about your browsing habits, and then report that information back to the company that placed the spyware file on your PC.

As you'd guess, a lot of people don't want to give anyone that information, no matter how beneficial it might ultimately be. Unfortunately, getting rid of spyware isn't so simple.

ERADICATE SPYWARE

The problem is that most spyware is carefully hidden away in the nooks and crannies of your PC, including places like the Registry, which makes it nearly impossible for people to find a specific file and delete it. Thankfully, several programs are available that will scan your PC, find all the spyware lodged away on your system, and then offer you the option to delete it.

The best of these programs is *Ad-aware* by a company called Lavasoft. Lavasoft offers several versions of *Ad-aware*, and you'll be pleased to know that one of these is a fully functioning free version. (You can download it from Lavasoft's web site: www.lavasoftusa.com/.)

Installing *Ad-aware* is very easy—simply double-click the installation program and follow the onscreen instructions. Once the program is installed, you can configure it in several ways. If you wish, you can set the program so that it'll automatically scan and clean your system every time Windows starts.

To perform a manual scan, click Scan Now and then select either the default scanning method or the manual method. The default scan is completely automated, so all you need to do is start the scan and then sit back and let the app do the rest.

If you want to scan just a specific drive or folder, however, click Select Drives and then go in and click the box next to the drive you want to scan. You can expand and contract the folders within a certain drive by clicking the plus sign next to the drive's name.

If, for some reason, you don't want to install and use *Ad-aware*, *Internet Explorer* does let you go in and delete cookies. Since cookies are a common way to distribute spyware, this process can eliminate some of the files, although it won't delete the ones that are hidden in other areas of your computer or in your Registry.

To delete the cookies on your PC, simply launch *Internet Explorer*, then go to Tools, Internet Options. In the middle of the screen is a button that says Delete Cookies. Simply press that button and *Internet Explorer* will delete all the cookies that are being stored in that specific directory.

AD-SUPPORTED SOFTWARE

One final note about spyware is that some software companies will place files on your system so they can serve you ads within their products. This practice is especially common when the company gives away

"free" versions of its software, which you can use as long as you agree to view the ads that run within the software program.

A good example of this situation is the e-mail program *Eudora*. There is a sponsored version of this software that serves ads in a small window within the program while you check your e-mail. If you use this version of *Eudora*, *Ad-aware* will report that it found a spyware-related file in *Eudora's* directory.

If you choose to delete the file, *Eudora* will simply re-create it the next time you launch the program, but that might not be the case with all ad-sponsored software. For this reason, it's a good idea to refrain from deleting any files associated with free software installed on your computer. Doing so might prevent the programs from working.

(While our objective is to eradicate the bulk of spyware from our systems, we sometimes have to make exceptions. When you're getting software for free, it's only fair to provide the software company with some sort of revenue source—e.g., letting them serve you ads that may use spyware to cater to your needs. After all, it's very expensive to create and market new software.)

On the surface, spyware is a troubling issue, especially if you value your privacy. However, if you use a program like *Ad-aware* on a regular basis, you're taking a major step toward protecting your personal online habits.

Critical Security Tips

You're now well versed in protecting your computer, but we still have a few more tips for you to follow

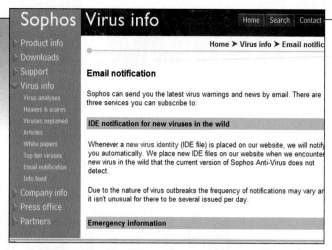

A new-viruses bulletin from **www.sophos.com/virusinfo/notifications.**

VIRUS PROTECTION

TYPES OF VIRUSES Any program that gets onto your PC and runs instructions without your knowledge is a "virus." You can get a virus by opening an infected document, running an infected file, or booting from an infected disk. "Worms" replicate themselves, often mailing themselves to every entry in your address book disguised as images, jokes, or even antivirus software. Trojans pretend to be another file altogether but don't replicate—someone has to trick you into downloading them.

REMOVE FLOPPIES Floppy disks left in your drive when you shut down or restart can spread "boot" viruses.

KEEP UP TO DATE Visit **www.norton.com** or **www.sophos .com/virusinfo/notifications/** for the latest virus-related news.

E-MAIL PROTECTION

BEWARE HTML MAIL Messages in HTML have the same problems as web pages (scripts, web bugs, etc.), so be careful where you click.

OUTLOOK SECURITY The Outlook Security Update stops you from opening "unsafe" file types, plus you'll get a warning if a script tries to read your address book or send e-mails without permission. Specify which file types can be opened with Attachment Options (**www.slovaktech.com/attachmentoptions.htm**).

DIGITAL SIGNATURE A digital signature proves the identity of the sender, and shows that the e-mail hasn't been tampered with. Get a free digital ID from Thawte (**www.thawte.com/certs/ personal/contents.html**) or a trial from VeriSign: In *Outlook*, choose Tools, Options, Security, Get a Digital ID.

BROWSER PROTECTION

CONTROL IE6 COOKIES *Internet Explorer 6* lets you choose whether to block or accept cookies, based on who they're from and the site's privacy policy: choose Tools, Internet Options, Privacy.

FINE-CONTROL COOKIES If you don't like the preset cookie schemes, or you want to find out which sites send cookies, click Advanced, Privacy, and create customized settings.

IT'S NOT OK Never click OK or Yes in a box without understanding what it's asking. If you're not sure, click No. If the site won't work, reload and try again.

CHECK LINKS To see where a link takes you before you click it, hover your mouse over it and look at the status bar above (if you can't see it, click on View, Status Bar), where the URL should be displayed.

PASSWORD STRATEGIES

DON'T PICK AN OBVIOUS PASSWORD Don't use your name, your dog's name, or your birthday. Hackers use programs that generate vast numbers of random passwords, so obvious ones are easier to guess. Use something obscure and almost literally unguessable.

PICK A GOOD PASSWORD Make up a word and add a number to it. Take two unrelated words and join them with punctuation or throw in some capitals. Or use the WinGuides Random Password Generator (found at **www.winguides.com/ security/password.php**).

PICK DIFFERENT PASSWORDS Don't use the same password for everything. If one site displays your password in error—or gets hacked by another user—other accounts will be vulnerable as well.

SPECIAL-OFFER PASSWORDS If a competition asks for your e-mail address and password, do not use a password that you use elsewhere. People use fake competitions to harvest these details.

SILENCE IE6 Don't let *Internet Explorer* remember your passwords. Go to Tools, Internet Options, Content, AutoComplete, and clear "User names and passwords on forms."

SIGN OUT OF PASSPORT If you share a PC or use an Internet café, tick the option for increased security when using .NET Passport (**www.passport.com**), so it deletes cookies and cached pages when you sign out.

IS IT SECURE? A headline saying "secure site" means nothing—especially if it's flashing. Look for https:// in the URL, or for a closed padlock in the status bar.

KEEP IT SECRET Never give out your password. Genuine technical-support people won't need to ask for it. And never change your password to one you're asked to use by someone else—it can lead to trouble. ■

How To...

ELIMINATE

SPAM

Tired of unsolicited e-mail flooding your inbox? We show you how to fight back

We're certainly no strangers to advertising. It's an integral part of mainstream media, a sad fact of modern life we've come to accept. But can't our e-mail boxes at least be sacred—reserved strictly for solicited business and personal communications, and not as another channel for product pitches? Apparently not, because unsolicited e-mail, aka spam, clutters our inboxes at an ever-increasing rate, promising lower mortgage rates, faster weight loss, herbal intoxicants, and what not. There is hope, however. With a little bit of footwork you can greatly diminish the spam that makes it into your life.

FILTERING

E-mail filters allow you to set parameters in your e-mail app that will help keep out unwanted correspondence. In *Outlook Express*, for example, go to Tools, Message Rules, Mail and select the first three boxes. This setup allows you to filter by sender, subject text, and message body text. Entering the words and addresses you want to filter one at a time can be a time-consuming process, but it'll save you from wading through piles of spam later on. (To get an idea of what kind of words to enter, simply look at a few spam e-mails you've received and enter text that is similar to the headers of those e-mails.) It's wise to have the offending messages sent to a designated folder instead of bounced or deleted, just in case a genuine e-mail message gets filtered by accident.

Keep in mind that even the best filters will be put under a mighty strain if you aren't careful with your e-mail address. Signing up for a newsletter, creating a personal web page, registering on a message board, signing up for Usenet, installing an instant messenger—

This is what can happen to your e-mail inbox if you don't keep spam in check.

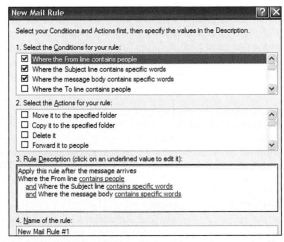

Basic filters will catch significant amounts of spam. We recommend filtering all mail that contains words such as mortgage, enlargement, and Viagra (unless of course you work for Pfizer).

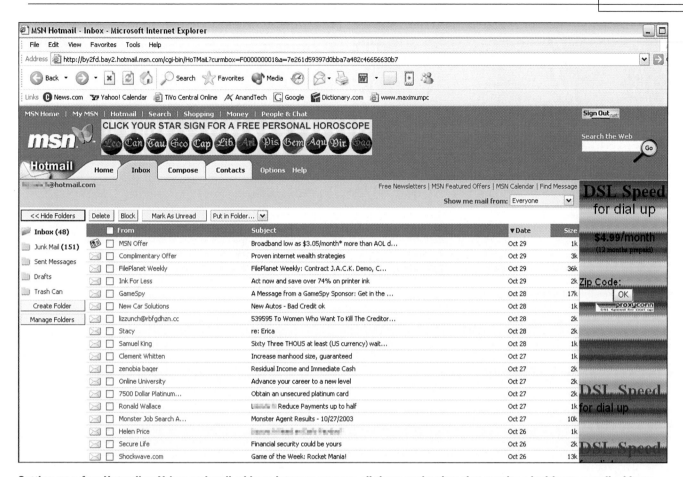

Setting up a free Hotmail or Yahoo webmail address lets you appease all those pesky sites that require a legitimate e-mail address, and prevents wiley spammers from getting your regular e-mail address.

all of these actions can open up your e-mail box to an army of unwelcome solicitors. For some of these services, you can submit a fake address. But oftentimes an e-mail will be sent to the address you provide, and your response is required to activate the service.

DIVERTING THE FLOW

A "dummy account" can help keep spam out of your regular e-mail account. Create an account that's only used for signing up for services and otherwise gaining access to parts of the Internet that require an e-mail address. If your Internet service provider doesn't offer additional e-mail accounts, Yahoo and Hotmail provide free e-mail accounts that are useful for this very purpose. You'll have just a few megabytes of space to work with anyway, so it's no big loss if this account is strictly a "spamcatcher."

You can also attach Hotmail to *Outlook Express* to make things more streamlined. In *Outlook Express*, go to Tools, Accounts, and click Add on the right, and then select Mail. This step will take you through the account-creation wizard. When you enter

a Hotmail or MSN address, the wizard will automatically adjust to give you options to receive web mail from those services.

You can also download a program called *YahooPOPs* that will let you receive Yahoo mail in *Outlook Express* (in addition to *Eudora* and several other e-mail clients). It's available at **http://yahoopops.sourceforge.net**.

Be warned: Some web-based services have begun to block Yahoo and Hotmail addresses from registration, due to abuse, in which case you have to use an extra e-mail address offered by your ISP, or use your primary account. Even if you get the paid, POP3 version of Yahoo mail, the web sites that block Yahoo block Yahoo, period.

OBSCURING YOUR PRESENCE

A lot of unsolicited e-mail gets to you via a "dictionary" method. Spammers will set up a system allowing them to issue an e-mail to every word in the dictionary, from aardvark@email.com to zebra@email.com.

Others create programs that harvest every e-mail on a web page, feeding it to their e-mail servers. That's why you

will see some people list their e-mail publicly as "suchandsuch AT suchandsuch DOT com," for example. This method fools the harvesting programs looking for "@" signs and ".com," ".net," and so forth. Another less automated method solicitors try is to send spam to corporate e-mail addresses by combining the first letter of a person's first name with their last name, so "Bob Jones" becomes bjones@mailbox.com.

Needless to say, it's a scatter-shot method, but it can quickly turn into a giant mess. For instance, if you reply to unsolicited e-mail—even once—you can almost guarantee yourself an avalanche of e-mail from that same source. That's because the people sending you the spam have determined that they're hitting a live target, and the ensuing onslaught can be unforgiving. For this reason, we recommend against replying to any form of spam, even if you're just trying to tell them to stop sending you e-mail.

(In fact, many unscrupulous spammers will tell you that if you send a removal message to a certain address, your name will be removed from their mailing lists.

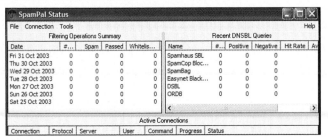

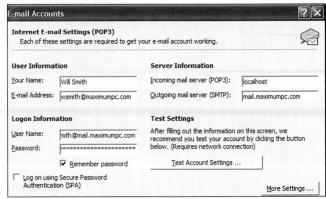

SpamPal scans the origin of all your incoming mail, and compares the server from which it came with known spam servers. Good mail is passed on to your e-mail client, spam messages are not.

Once you've installed *SpamPal*, you'll need to reconfigure the settings for all your e-mail accounts. Usually it's as simple as tacking @[yourmailserver'sname].com on the end of your username, and replacing your POP3 server's name with "localhost."

However, this instruction is often just another way to see if your address is actually valid and in use—the result is that the amount of spam you receive will increase, not decrease.)

What makes this situation especially frustrating is that many spammers will continue to e-mail you, even when you don't respond, as long as the e-mail message doesn't "bounce back", which would indicate that your e-mail address either doesn't exist or is indefinitely unavailable.

TAKING THE FIGHT TO THE SPAMMERS

Rudimentary filters and preventative measures can do only so much. Once spammers get your address, you need to take more active steps to stop the deluge of junk e-mail. There are several off-the-shelf packages that will help you filter spam from your legitimate e-mail, but our favorites are found exclusively on the web. *SpamPal* (**www.spampal.org**) works with any POP3 client, and will filter spam from your diet by comparing

every e-mail you receive to a list of known spammers. *Outlook* users will dig *Inboxer*. It uses advanced pattern-recognition software to determine which messages are spam and which are legitimate e-mail. Not sure which is right for you? We'll show you how to set up and configure both!

SPAMPAL

After you've downloaded and installed *SpamPal*, you'll need to do a bit of configuration. The installation wizard will walk you through the basic configuration steps. We recommend that you select the "medium" filtering option. The more aggressive filtering options use anti-spam blacklists that occasionally block large ISPs, like AOL and MSN, and can cause you to occasionally miss important e-mail. Once *SpamPal* is up and running, you can tweak this setting manually.

To get *SpamPal* up and running, you'll need to reconfigure your mail client's set-

tings. Instructions will vary based on the mail client you use (at **SpamPal.org** there are detailed directions for many different e-mail clients). You'll also want to follow *SpamPal's* instructions to set up a filter that will automatically copy messages labeled "spam" to an out-of-the way directory. Once *SpamPal* is online, the first thing you'll want to do is add important e-mail addresses to your whitelist. Messages from people on the whitelist are ignored by the spam filter, so you're assured of always getting this e-mail. You should add to the whitelist any addresses that you frequently receive e-mail from. You can use wildcards in the list too, to cover frequently used domains. For example, if you want to make sure you receive all e-mail from **Maximumpc.com**, you'd add *@maximumpc.com to the whitelist.

SpamPal's blacklist is the exact opposite of the whitelist. Any e-mail from

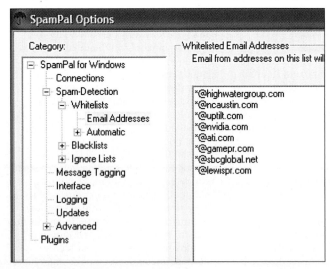

The SpamPal whitelist is made up of e-mail addresses you've deemed OK. E-mail from these addresses will be given automatic entry to your inbox.

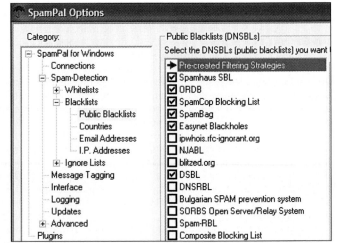

SpamPal uses a number of publicly available blacklists to determine which e-mails are and aren't spam. It looks confusing, but there are several preconfigured filtering settings that make *SpamPal* easy for anyone to set up.

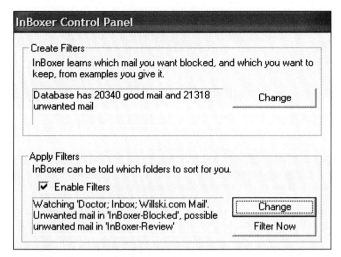

Inboxer works with Outlook, using Bayesian filtering techniques to catch spam. It builds a dynamic database of good and bad e-mails, and uses that to filter incoming mail.

You can configure the level of Inboxer's spam protection by adjusting these sliders. Moving the Review slider to a lower number will filter more spam, but may increase your chance of false positives.

an address on the blacklist will be summarily blocked, whether it triggers the other spam filters or not. You can also block entire domains, using the same wildcards as the whitelist. The blacklist is useful for filtering out spam you receive regularly but can't turn off, like those annoying coupon sheets and e-mail catalogs.

That's really all there is to running SpamPal. We recommend that new users occasionally check the folder holding all their sorted spam, to make sure no important e-mails are being sent to it. If you do get false positives, check the header, where you should see a line that looks like this: "X-SpamPal: SPAM SPEWS 4.18.48.119". That line tells you that the server at IP address 4.18.48.119 was listed in the SPEWS anti-spam list. If you notice a lot of false positives from one list or another, you can disable individual items in SpamPal's Options/ Blacklist menu.

INBOXER
Where SpamPal uses constantly updated online lists to determine which e-mails are spam and which aren't, Inboxer separates

the naughty from nice by analyzing the content of each message for spam-like patterns. Setting up Inboxer is easy, just install the app, open Outlook and get started. Remember, Inboxer works only with Outlook, so if you use another e-mail client, you're out of luck!

Inboxer adds a couple new buttons and a pair of folders to Outlook. For each message that's received, Inboxer assigns a probability that it is or isn't spam. By default, messages with a probability greater than 90 percent get put in the Blocked folder, while messages with a probability between 10 and 90 percent get put in a Review folder. The practical upshot is that the vast majority of spam gets dumped into the Blocked folder, a few messages end up in your Review folder, and the rest are valid e-mails.

What happens if a spam message gets through, or a valid message gets blocked? That's where the two new buttons come in. The Block button will let

you tag a message that Inboxer mistakenly designated as valid, and will move it to the Blocked folder. Inboxer will analyze that message, and add it to its extensive database. If you get a false positive, you will press the Keep button, and Inboxer will move the message back to your inbox, analyze it to see why the message was misidentified as spam, and keep like messages from getting wrongly tagged in the future.

If you'd like a free alternative to Inboxer, or you don't use Outlook, you should check into POPFile (popfile.sourceforge .net). It uses the same type of algorithms as Inboxer, but it's more difficult to get configured properly and running, especially if you get large volumes of spam. ∎

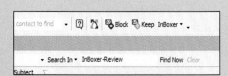

The Keep button shows up in your Blocked folder. It will let you mark a good e-mail that was accidentally filtered. Inboxer will also add that address to its database.

The Review folder will have both the Keep and the Block button. Expect to press Block frequently. Inboxer prefers to mislabel more spam as good, than good e-mail as spam.

The Block button shows up in all your normal e-mail folders. If Inboxer misses a spam e-mail, you can select it and press Block to banish it to your Spam folder.

Kill Pop-ups!

Use our expert tips to surf online unimpeded by unwanted ads.

Advertising is as much a part of the web as commercials are of network television. But since most of us mentally edit out the ads embedded in the pages we visit, advertisers have deployed another solution that's not so easy to ignore: The dreaded pop-up ad.

Pop-up ads are displayed in new browser windows that literally pop up on top of (or underneath) the page you really wanted to read. Chain pop-ups are even more annoying. Closing one new browser window opens one or more others, creating a seemingly inescapable nightmare of ads piled on ads. It's enough to make you want to shut your computer off, which is sometimes the only way you can escape the onslaught.

Take back the web by deploying a "pop-up blocker."

Stand-Alone Pop-Up Killers

There are a variety of solutions for jamming these intrusive pop-up pests. Several of Symantec's products have pop-up blocker modules, including *Norton Personal Firewall* and *Norton Internet Security*. McAfee's *Internet Security* program offers similar protection. Another solution is to switch to a web browser, such as *Mozilla*, that offers integrated pop-up ad blocking (see sidebar).

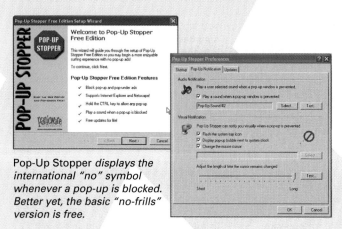

Pop-Up Stopper *displays the international "no" symbol whenever a pop-up is blocked. Better yet, the basic "no-frills" version is free.*

But if you don't need all the other tools you'll find in a commercial product, and you're not interested in switching browsers, you'll find a variety of free alternatives for killing pop-up ads, including Panicware's *Pop-Up Stopper: Free Edition*. (Note: This version only works with *Internet Explorer* and *Netscape* and can be found at www.panicware.com)

One of the best features of *Pop-Up Stopper* is that it remains completely invisible while you're visiting web sites that don't employ pop-up ads. If a web site does try to throw a pop-up window at you, *Pop-Up Stopper* shuts down the request and lets you know about it via a warning notification of your choosing, such as an audio alarm or a flashing icon in the Taskbar. One caveat: If you browse a lot of um... "advertising-heavy sites," pop-ups will fly so often that you'd be best advised to keep the notifications to a bare minimum; otherwise, the warnings will become as annoying as the pop-ups!

Not All Pop-ups Are Bad

Despite what you might have heard, you won't want to eliminate *every* pop-up browser window, because some of them will be elements of legitimate and useful web design. Online stores and financial institutions, for example, often use pop-ups to confirm transactions or provide critical information. If the site can't display its pop-up, you might not be able to complete your transaction.

Fortunately, pop-up blockers are becoming more and more sophisticated, and they usually can identify good pop-up windows from bad ones. One of the added attractions of a full-featured pop-up blocker, such as Panicware's *Pop-Up Stopper Professional,* is the ability to maintain lists of sites for which you *don't* want pop-ups blocked. (In the free version of *Pop-up Stopper*, you can allow specific pop-ups to execute by holding down the Ctrl, Alt, or Shift keys when you click on a web-page link.)

Pop-up ads are almost universally annoying, but with the right software, they can now be almost universally ignored. We've touched on a couple of ways you can build a wall between you and unwanted advertising, but there are many others. Give one of these solutions a shot and see if it doesn't improve your web-browsing experience. ■

The Browser Alternative

If you don't like the idea of installing yet another utility program on your computer, you should consider switching to a web browser that has a pop-up blocker built right in. The non-profit Mozilla Organization's *Mozilla* project is one solid choice, and the software is free.

Once you've installed *Mozilla*, click on the Edit menu and choose Preferences. In the left-hand pane, click on the plus sign next to the heading Privacy & Security. Next, click on the Popup Windows menu item. In the right-hand side of the window, put a checkmark next to the item that reads "Block unrequested popup windows."

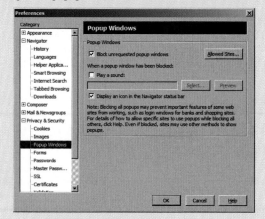

A solid alternative to Internet Explorer, Mozilla *offers built-in pop-up protection.*

How To...

PROTECT YOUR
Wireless LAN

Keep the neighborhood snoops, sniffers, and data thieves off your 802.11 network

MAXIMUM PC
TIME TO COMPLETION
00:40
HOURS   MINUTES

BY WILL SMITH

Every month, you pay five sawbucks for a broadband Internet connection, and your favorite way to savor the lightning-fast downloads is via a wireless Internet connection. But danger lurks in this high-speed, free-range utopia. Just consider how many seedy online guides explain how to get "free broadband" by leaching off someone else's precious Wi-Fi bandwidth!

Stolen bandwidth isn't the only problem. Once thieves can leech your net connection, they can also get access to files on your PC, track the sites you browse, and even read your private e-mails and instant messages. Yikes! *It sucks to be you.*

But that's where we come in. We're here to save you from bandwidth pirates and other pimply ne'er-do-wells. Whether you use 802.11b or 802.11g, the precautions for wireless safety are about the same. We'll show you how to lock down your data and minimize the chances that a wireless snooper will leech from your LAN.

Wireless networking entails that every data packet to and from your PC be broadcast over the airwaves, so there's always a chance that someone will be able to sniff your data. If you want to make your LAN 100 percent secure, you'll have to disconnect it from wireless technology entirely. Still, the tips in this article will protect you from all but the most determined miscreants.

What You'll Need

▶ **802.11b or 802.11g access point**

▶ **802.11b or 802.11g cards to access the LAN**

▶ **100Mbit Ethernet hub**

▶ **NetStumbler (www.netstumbler.com)**

▶ **Laptop computer**

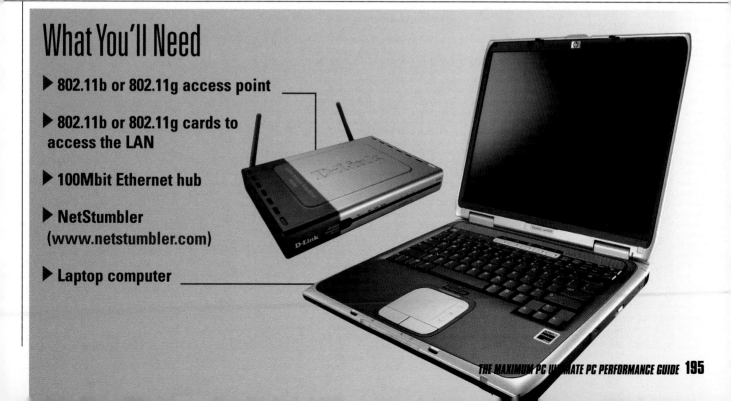

Give Your Network a New Name

Your network's name can actually be a weak spot. In order to gain access to your network, an intruder has to know its name—commonly called an SSID. Most access points from a single manufacturer ship with the same SSID (preset at the factory), and the easy setup programs that come with the hardware don't always encourage users to change the SSID.

What can you do to fix this? Change your network's SSID! Open up the configuration program that was provided with your access point, and change the SSID to something completely unique and obscure. We recommend that you *not* use anything obvious, such as your hardware manufacturer's name, or words like "default," "wireless," "802.11," "network," "home," or anything else that may be easily guessed after just a few tries.

While you're changing the SSID, make sure to change the password for your AP's administration account. No matter how secure you make your AP, it's wide open if a cracker can just log in using the username and password printed in the instruction manual.

Changing your SSID is the first step you need to take, but it's certainly not the end of your lockdown routine.

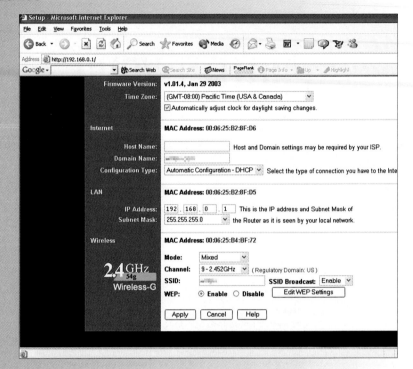

Get WEP Working

Enabling WEP—wired equivalent privacy—is the second-most important thing you can do to stymie would-be wireless freeloaders. WEP isn't 100 percent secure, but cracking the encryption technology isn't a simple exercise. In fact, it presents more trouble than most common bandwidth thieves are willing to wrestle with.

First things first: If your access point and your Wi-Fi card support 128-bit encryption, use 128-bit encryption. A 128-bit key can indeed be cracked, but even under perfect circumstances, a cracker will have to sniff packets from your wireless network for six or more hours in order to get enough data to generate a WEP key. And we repeat: That's in an *ideal* situation. It can actually take days or longer to sniff enough packets to crack a 128-bit key.

Of course, a 128-bit key won't help you if it's just 1111 1111 1111 1111 1111 1111 11. Interfaces for entering keys will differ from access point to access point. Some APs require that you enter the key in hexadecimal, while

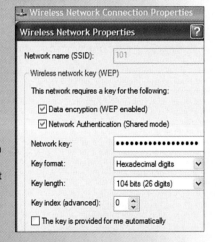

others prefer plain ASCII text. Luckily, the Windows wireless control panel lets you enter your key in either format, so make sure you enter the key in the same format in both places!

When you create your key, remember that hex keys can include the digits 0 through 9 and A through F. ASCII keys can be any letter of the alphabet or any number. For maximum security, avoid repetition or any kind of pattern.

You Gotta Keep'em Separated

Now that your access point is reasonably secure, it's time to separate your networks. By separating them, you'll deny access to your wired LAN even if a cracker manages to break into your wireless network. The process involves getting a hub in addition to your router/gateway as well as a second IP address from your ISP.

First, you'll need to rewire your wired network. Connect your new hub to your DSL or cable modem, then connect your wired LAN to one port on the hub and the access point to another port. Next, configure your access point with the new IP address. Now you have two separate networks—one wired and one wireless—running off of the same broadband modem.

Of course, your wired network shouldn't be altogether vulnerable with the router/gateway as the connectivity device. At any rate, it's still a good idea to have a good software firewall such as *ZoneAlarm* running on all of the computers in the LAN.

Disable SSID Broadcasting

The SSID is your network's name. By default, most access points are set to broadcast their SSIDs to a compatible Wi-Fi device in the vicinity. So not only can crackers discover vulnerable wireless LANs by driving around with Wi-Fi enabled laptops, they can also get network names at the same time!

Most access points, however, include an option to disable SSID broadcasting. It's generally a good setting to disable, but we have had some problems maintaining connectivity when using the Windows built-in wireless configuration

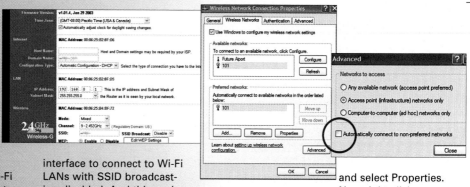

interface to connect to Wi-Fi LANs with SSID broadcasting disabled. And this problem is exacerbated if other people in your neighborhood have wireless LANs set up.

If you're noticing interference after disabling SSID broadcasting, there's a setting you can change to minimize the problem. Right-click My Network Places

and select Properties.

Now right-click your specific wireless connection, and select Properties. Go to the Wireless Settings tab, and select the Advanced option. Uncheck the "Automatically connect to non-preferred networks" option.

Super Security

Most access points are able to deny wireless access to unknown computers. You see, each network card has a unique number assigned when it's manufactured. This "MAC address" is a 12-digit code, and no other piece of network hardware will share the same code. By telling your wireless LAN to grant access only to network cards that have known MAC addresses, you can prevent unknown users from gaining entry.

Each AP will handle MAC address filtering differently, so you'll need to consult your instruction manual. The Linksys interface is pictured above. Just remember, any time you want to add a new authorized user to your wireless LAN, you'll have to get the MAC address, go into your access point's

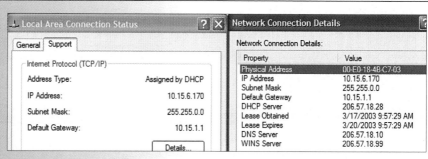

configuration screen, and manually enter it.

To get the MAC address from a Windows XP system, right-click My Network Places and select Properties. Next right-click your wireless network connection and select Status. Go to the Support tab, and press Details. The MAC address is labeled Physical Address in the window that pops up.

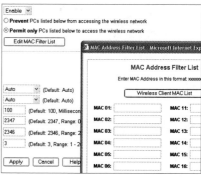

Check Your Back

If you've followed all our instructions, your wireless LAN should be reasonably secure. If the National Security Agency wants into your wireless LAN, there's not much you can do to stop it, but our tips should keep little Billy next door from

using your DSL line to download gigabytes of Trent Reznor MP3s.

Regardless, you should still install *NetStumbler* (www.netstumbler.com) on one of your wireless PCs, and see if your LAN shows up. *NetStumbler* is the

most common 802.11 network sniffer. Most likely, it's what your enemies will be using to discover and compromise your LAN. If you configured everything correctly, your access point shouldn't even show up in this utility's window. If you don't see it, the freeloaders probably won't either, and will just move on to easier prey. ∎

Give Dial-up a Kick in the Pants

Just because you use a dial-up connection doesn't mean that you're left out of the speed-tweaking party. Use these tips to shift gears and get your modem moving.

Someday, broadband Internet connections will become as ubiquitous as the old fashioned dial-up connections of yesteryear. Until then, most online surfers will continue to get their Internet fix through a modem and a phone line, which means World Wide Web translates to "World Wide Wait" for many of you.

Still, all hope's not lost: Here are a few tricks you can use to give your dial-up connection a speed boost today.

Tweak those settings

One of the easiest things you can do to improve your connection is download and install the latest drivers and firmware for your modem; these usually can be found on the manufacturer's website, and may offer improved performance and features. You also can find optimized initialization strings for your modem that may give you a performance boost; check with your modem's manufacturer for more information.

Now that you've gotten your modem software up to date, it's time to tweak your network settings. There are sev-

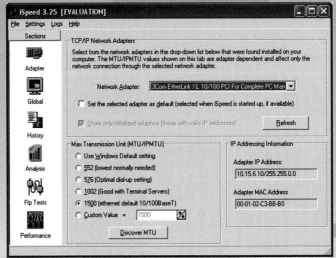

Programs such as HMS Software's iSpeed *can automatically tweak your settings to maximize your dial-up connection*

eral well-documented hacks that can help make your connection more efficient. They mostly deal with modifying various settings to your TCP/IP stack and Registry, and can be found online at numerous websites. Techspot.com's Windows XP Modem Tweak Guide is particularly informative and can be found at **www.techspot.com/tweaks/winxp_modem/index.shtml**.

There are also several programs that will automatically change these settings for you if you don't feel comfortable fiddling with your PC, such as HMS Software's *iSpeed*. You can download a trial version at **www.hms.com/ispeed. asp**.

Bonding...modem bonding

You may be able to *really* kick your dial-up into high gear with modem bonding, which is a technique that melds two separate dial-up connections into one, delivering a maximum connection speed that is equal to the con-

nection speed of the two modems combined. This means that two 56k modems can be bonded together to produce a connection capable of delivering 112k of throughput.

First, you'll need to purchase and install two separate modems. Note that the modems don't need to be the same speed or from the same manufacturer. You can also mix an internal modem with an external one if you like. The only other things you will need are two separate phone lines to connect the modems to, and an ISP that allows for bonded connections, which can be very tough to find. Your best bet is to call the tech support lines for all the ISPs offering dial-up service in your area.

While a bonded connection can be significantly faster than standard dial-up, it can cost as much—or more—than broadband when you factor in the second phone line and second dial-up connection charge for your ISP. However, if no other broadband technologies are available in your

Download Managers

A useful tool that every dial-up user should keep on their hard drive is a download manager. These handy programs are useful for their ability to resume interrupted downloads, an important feature when downloading large files over a slow connection.

Download managers such as Headlight Software's GetRight *can be invaluable to the dial-up user for their ability to resume interrupted downloads*

Internet Accelerators

Many major ISPs now offer free "accelerator" technology that they claim will allow you to surf the Net at speeds up to five times faster than standard dial-up. The latest version of the AOL software is called *AOL Top Speed*, EarthLink offers the aptly named *EarthLink Accelerator* and NetZero offers *NetZero Hi-Speed Internet*. In each case, the technology uses compression to reduce the time it takes to load a web page's graphics and text, essentially trading image quality for speed. It also uses caching to store elements of frequently visited sites in order to reduce load times.

While accelerator technology won't actually make your physical connection any faster, it can make it *appear* faster, which could translate into a more enjoyable online experience.

How To...

MAXIMUM PC

TIME TO COMPLETION

01:30

HOURS   MINUTES

HTMLify YOUR DESKTOP

Embed images, bookmarks, and even entire web sites into your Windows background

BY WILL SMITH

Here's one of our favorite desktop customization tricks—adding HTML elements to the background. Check out the screenshot below. The elements are fixed in place (they can't be moved by an errant mouse swing), but they're also fully active, and ready to roll as soon as you boot up. The folders on the left side of the screen can be opened and closed. The browser window featuring Slashdot is fully operational, but it's embedded in the wallpaper. The bookmarks on the right launch web sites in a separate browser window. The cartoon and

picture of Gina don't do any fancy tricks, but they are cropped and positioned in a way that can't be done with Windows' normal wallpaper controls.

For this project we'll be manipulating HTML tables; go to **www.w3schools.com/html/** for a good primer. You can also use a fancy web editor like *FrontPage,* but you'll probably need to fire up *Notepad* as well to manually tweak the code. Your Windows OS must be able to accept HTML for its desktop. That means WinME, 2000, XP, or Win98 with Active Desktop enabled.

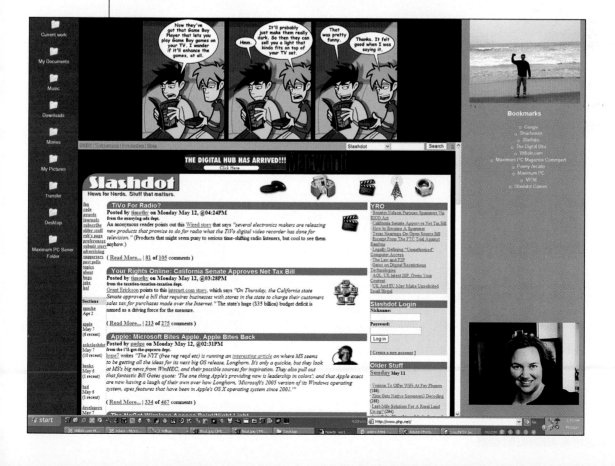

1 Getting Started

First, you need to decide what elements you want on your desktop. We chose a favorite digital photograph, a cartoon, commonly used bookmarks, links to favorite folders, and an embedded browser window. (If you use a lower-reso-lution display, you might not be able to cram in as much content.) Second, create a directory named "Desktop" on your C: drive to hold all the image files you plan to use. Finally, check out our sample HTML file. It's available at **Maximumpc.com**.

It contains all the code (but not all the images) used in our project.

2 Setting Up HTML Tables

Our HTML desktop is divided into four basic areas, each of which is a cell of an HTML table. Whether you create your table with a WYSIWYG editor like *FrontPage* or pound it out in *Notepad*, you'll want to size it perfectly so that it occupies all the available space on your desktop. You can either manually specify your desktop's height and width in the `<table>` tag that you use to create the table, or you can set the width and height to 100 percent. We recommend setting it to 100 percent. This will prevent your tables from getting borked when you change resolutions.

When you open our sample HTML file, you'll see that we used variable widths for all three columns. If you're using a low resolution, you might want to set a fixed width for whichever column you plan on filling with web content (remember that your web page cell should be at least 800x600 pixels). We also recommend setting a long vertical cell for your folder shortcuts. It's difficult to get the folders lined up properly in a horizontal layout. Open your HTML file in *Internet Explorer* to see how it looks after each step.

This is what the straight tables look like with no content at all.

3 Choosing Images

Now it's time to pick images for your desktop. They can be JPEGs, GIFs, and PNG files, and stored on either your local PC or an Internet server (which means one of your embedded images can be a constantly updated web cam feed). Just remember that if you use an image stored online, it will show up as a broken link when you aren't con-nected to the net.

Linking to images on your hard drive is something most web editors just don't do well, so you'll probably need to open *Notepad* to create those links. In your image tags, you'll use `file:` `///c:/path/to/image/here` in the SRC field of the link. Make sure you use three slashes, and use forward slashes in the path instead of backslashes. It's also a good idea to specify the pixel width and height of your image inside the `<IMG>` tag.

If the above paragraph doesn't make any sense, take a look at our sample HTML file to see how we placed our images in different cells of the desktop table.

This image of Gina is static, but if you want to, you can have a web cam feed your desk-top with constantly updated images. Just keep it clean, if you know what we're say-ing, and we think you do.

Making Folders and Bookmarks

Now it's time to make shortcuts to frequently used folders. First, create an image to use for the folder icon. You can make something nontraditional (like a GIF image of a filing cabinet or bucket), or you can grab the traditional image we used (folder.gif) from our web site.

We created links to various directories on our hard drive by using the `<a>` (anchor) tag. Instead of using an online URL in the HREF= section of the anchor tag, we used another call: `file:///`. Make sure you type the entire path to the folder you want to link to using forward slashes instead of backslashes, and substituting `%20` for any spaces in the folder names. For

example, to link to your Program Files directory, you'd type: `<a href=file:///c:/Program%20Files/>`. You can find the locations of elusive directories by right-clicking them, going to Properties, and grabbing the path from the Target tab.

Our right-column bookmarks are straightforward HTML links in an unordered list. If you want to add your own bookmarks, you can replace the URLs in the HREF= section of each `<a>` tag with the URL of the web site you want to bookmark, then change the name between the `<a>` and `</a>` to reflect your new bookmark.

```
Untitled - Notepad
File  Edit  Format  View  Help
<a href="file:///c:/Desktop/Current%20work/" class="nwhite">
   <img border="0" src="file:///c:/Desktop/folder.gif" align="center" width="43" height="39">
      <font face="Arial" size="2">
         <span style="vertical-align: middle"><br>
            Current work
         </span>
      </font>
</a><br>
```

We made our icon look-alikes by using a small GIF file and this snippit of HTML code.

Testing It Out

Now that you have most of the basic elements in place, give your work a test run. Right-click your desktop and select Properties. Go to the Desktop tab, and press the Browse button. Browse to your HTML file, and press Open. Now press Apply and watch your desktop transform.

Your initial design will likely require tweaking. Images will be out of place, columns might be too wide or narrow,

and you may have some broken links. Also, it's difficult to tell when the desktop has been refreshed with changes from your HTML file, but there are two surefire ways to force reloads: Log off Windows and log back on, or change the resolution of the display.

Embedding a Web Page

To embed a web page in the large empty center area, once again open Display Properties, and go to the Desktop tab. This time, select Customize Desktop and click the Web tab. Click the New button, then type in the URL of the web site you want to embed.

When you exit the dialog, the web window will pop up on your desktop. You should be able to resize it and position it by clicking the edges of the page and dropping and dragging. If you can't do this, you can right-click an empty area of the desktop, and go to Arrange Icons By, and uncheck Lock Web Items. Move and resize the web page until you are satisfied with its placement, then recheck Lock Web Items.

You're Done!

That's all there is to it. You've set up a basic desktop template using HTML. This is only a start, though. Using what we've done here as a basic template, you should be able to add scripts that grab content dynamically from the Internet—news headlines, random images, stuff like that. For hardcore HTML hackers, the sky's the limit. ■

How To...

MAKE A
LINUX ROUTER

Why throw away that old PC, when you could turn it into a high-speed Internet router?

MAXIMUMPC
DIFFICULTY RATING
EASY
HARD
XXX

Shopping List:

■ **Internet connection (dial-up, DSL, or cable)**

■ **BBI Agent Router: free at** www.bbiagent.com

■ **386 or newer PC with 8MB or more of RAM**

■ **1.44MB floppy drive and diskette**

■ **Two supported Ethernet or NE2000 compatible network cards (see** www.bbiagent.net/en/hardware.htm **for a list of compatible adapters)**

■ **Network hub or switch with enough ports to connect all your PCs to your router**

■ **Assorted Ethernet cables**

BY CHRISTIAN "WOLFMANN" LESEMANN

D o you want to put more than one PC on your high-speed Internet connection? It's easy to do if you have a router. Sure, you could just use the Internet connection software that's built into Windows, but then you'd have to leave your main PC running all the time. You could also go to CompUSA and plunk down $150 for a stand-alone boxed router, but that would mean buying new, expensive equipment. And this would be a crying shame, considering that most PC geeks already have most of the hardware they need sitting in a closet, just collecting dust. In the following nine steps, we show you how to turn your ancient, long-forgotten PC into a state-of-the-art Linux-based router.

As with any how-to, make sure you read and understand all the instructions before you begin. You don't want to get halfway through the project, then realize you're in over your head. This advice is even more relevant when you're dealing with a powerful but finicky operating system such as Linux.

For this how-to, we'll use a floppy-size distro of Linux known as *BBI Agent*. It doesn't require any major computer hardware, just a 386-class machine with 8MB of memory. We selected *BBI Agent* because it supports everything you'll need to get your network running, it also includes a *Netfilter* (www.netfilter.org) firewall, and is stupidly-simple to set up. And unlike most of the router/gateways sold on the open market, the router we're configuring will even work with external dial-up connections.

Now, we know what you're thinking: "Sounds too good to be true—there must be a downside." Fear not, skeptics. *BBI Agent* has all the features of a residential gateway/router yet is highly configurable and extremely stable. It even has advanced features that consumer-based gateways/routers don't have and can support up to 60,000 clients

Step 1: Prepare Your Network

This article assumes you're comfortable with Windows-based home networking and have an existing network. We'll assume that you currently have two computers networked and are using a hub to connect them. If you're using a broadband connection, you'll first need to install two NICs in your router box. Remember to verify that those NICs are compatible with *BBI Agent*. You should also make sure your PC has enough PCI or ISA slots to install two NICs. One NIC will be the WAN (wide area network) NIC and will connect to the Internet. The other will be your LAN (local area network) NIC and will connect to your network. Connect the WAN NIC to your cable/DSL modem, and the LAN NIC to the hub/switch. All of your network PCs should also be connected to the hub/switch. For initial setup you should have a monitor and keyboard on the router to configure the PC. Keep a serial port enabled for an external modem if you require dial-up access. Once you have everything connected, turn on the networked PCs and make sure that the lights on all the networked NICs are lit.

> **Online User Guide: www.bbiagent.com/en/docs/explorer/000.htm**

Step 2: Configure Your Router's Network Cards

Your router can only include the NICs supported by *BBI Agent*, which is based on the 2.4 Linux kernel. (Any NIC with Windows drivers will work in your desktop machines.) Most NICs bought at BestBuy or CompUSA in the last few years should be supported. See the shopping list for a link to a definitive selection and do your homework first! Your motherboard will also have to be able to support two network cards, which may be an issue with older mobos. Plug-and-play is not supported, so you'll need to change your NIC and BIOS to manually assign their own resources by disabling the PnP OS Option, usually found under "Integrated Peripherals." Install the cards you wish to use into the router computer: Be careful, some older ISA slots are tight. Use firm pressure, but not enough to bend the mobo. You'll temporarily need a monitor and keyboard (or preconfigure the cards in another computer—but that's not recommended) to boot the computer off a DOS disk; use the cards' provided configuration utilities to assign I/O Address and IRQ. The standard DOS-based NIC configuration utility has limited options and is self-explanatory. You can remove the monitor and keyboard once the router is up and running, but some computers don't boot without a keyboard, or lock up once the keyboard is removed.

Step 3: Create the Boot Image for Your Router

Now we'll begin configuring and downloading your router's operating system. From any computer with a Java-compatible Internet browser, open **www.bbiagent.com** and click the Download tab. The web site has exhaustive instructions and support on how to set up the floppy boot image, but we'll walk you through the basics and explain what everything means. Scroll down the page, and click Applet (in red text). On the first applet page click Next, then select the type of CPU and amount of RAM used by your router.

On this screen, you'll also set the IP address and subnet mask of your router. We recommend using 192.168.0.1 as the IP, and 255.255.255.0 as your subnet mask. A subnet mask of 255.255.255.0 will allow about 253 users. A subnet mask of 255.0.0.0 will allow a possible 60,000 machines to connect to the router, but we doubt your machine would support that kind of traffic. The IP address range starting with 192.168 is a private IP, and is for use on private networks only.

After you've chosen your IP address and configured your CPU and RAM info, you're ready to proceed to the next step.

> **The common private IP address ranges are 192.168.x.x and 10.15.x.x. Those addresses are reserved for use on private LANs and can't be accessed by machines on the Internet.**

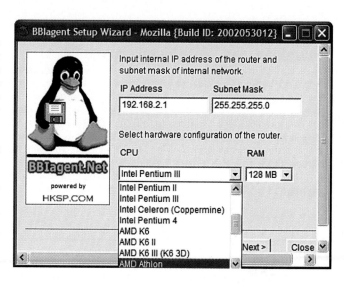

Step 4: Configure Your Router's Connections

Now we need to configure your LAN-side NIC. This is the card that will be plugged into your hub. First, select the card's manufacturer and model. Then set the IRQ and I/O address that either the BIOS assigned or that you configured using the DOS utility in Step 2. Once you've done that, move on to the next screen.

Here you'll want to select your connection protocol. This controls how your PC connects to the Internet via your ISP's network. The most common setup is a standard dynamic IP address assigned via DHCP. If your DSL or cable connection requires you to run a small application that accepts your username and password before you can connect to the Internet, you'll need to choose the PPPoE option. Finally, if your ISP assigned you a static IP address, choose the last option (Ethernet with Static Address).

If you're going to connect to a dial-up connection through the router, you should select the PPP option. If you still aren't sure which protocol to select, ask your ISP. After you click Next, you'll be presented with another config screen that will either configure your WAN-side NIC or your external modem. Follow the instructions on the screen to configure your connection to the Internet.

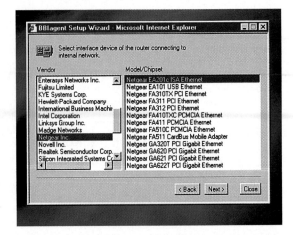

Sometimes when your net connection isn't working, the problem is the result of a bad DNS server rather than a flawed pipeline to the Internet. In 1997 a small problem with DNS information snowballed into one of the largest Internet outages ever! Most .com and .net addresses were totally unreachable!

Did you select PPPoA instead of PPPoE? You can change the connection protocol in the Administration WAN Connection setup menu once the router is functioning! Groovy!!

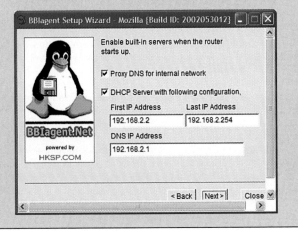

Step 5: Configure DNS/DHCP Server & Connection Protocol

The next step allows you to configure some advanced options: DNS proxy/cache and DHCP server. The DNS proxy/cache is really optional, but we recommend it for most people, especially dial-up users. The DHCP server, however, is a must-have and a no-brainer.

The first option on this page is the DNS proxy. A DNS proxy contains a cache that simply stores DNS entries, which are the IP addresses of domain names, such as **www.maximumpc.com**. We recommend enabling the DNS cache for better performance.

The DHCP server assigns IP addresses to each of the machines on your private network. So unless you want to do that on each machine manually, you'll need to enable the DHCP server.

After you've selected your protocol, click Next to continue.

Step 6: Verify Settings, Download, and Write Floppy Image

We're almost done with the initial config. On this screen, you can verify your settings and download the Linux floppy image. After you click the download button, save the image in a convenient place on your c:\ drive. To write the image to floppy, you'll need BBIwrite.exe for Windows95/98/ME or Rawrite.EXE for DOS. (Head to www.bbiagent.com and download them there.) We couldn't get either of the image writing apps to work in Windows XP or 2000, so you'll need to bust out the trusty DOS boot disk again.

All done? Throw the floppy in the router box, power it up, and you're good to go.

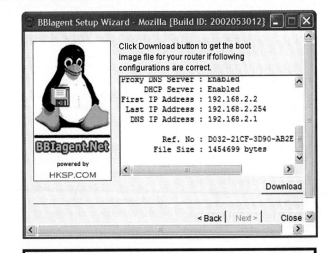

How does *BBIAgent* fit everything you need for running a router onto a 1.44MB floppy disk? By running a totally stripped down Linux kernel, devoid of support for 3D acceleration, 2D acceleration, a fancy graphical UI, sound, and anything other than a pair of network cards and *Network Address Translation* software.

In case you didn't know, Linux is an Open Source operating system. Therefore, anyone who wants to can download the source code of the OS and modify it to suit his needs. Of course, you do have to make the source code for any of your modifications publicly available too!

Step 7: Configure the Router

To further configure the router, you'll need to access it via a web browser from another computer. This means you can ditch the monitor and keyboard on the router.

To administer the router, you'll need to download BBIAgent Explorer (BBIAgent.jar) from the BBIAgent site. Once you have the JAR file, enter the router's address in your browser. This will typically be 192.168.0.1. When you get a dialog box requesting the "BBIAgent Explorer" file, browse to it. The default password is "BBIagent."

Once you're in the config app, change your router's password immediately. Go to Configuration, click Password, and change it.

Then click WAN Connection, and it will tell you if the router is configured properly by showing you the IP Address, DNS Server, Default Gateway, etc. The most important part will be configuring any passwords or settings you will need to connect to and communicate with your ISP. Once that information is entered you can select Connect in the Setup menu. From the Administration page you can also establish and set the parameters for any virtual services, such as DNS and DHCP, and you can configure the firewall and security rules. After that, your connection should be good to go! Remember to hit "Save to Diskette" after you make any changes!

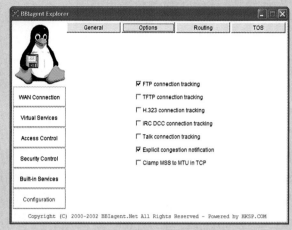

Step 8: Set Up Windows Clients

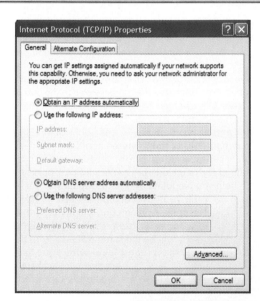

If you enabled the LAN-side DHCP server on the router and your machines are not already set up to accept a DHCP connection, then do so now. To set up DHCP-client in Windows, go to the network properties of the network adapter's TCP/IP setting and select "Obtain IP Address Automatically." If the DHCP server on the router is working properly, you shouldn't have to enter any parameters. You may have to reboot clients for the changes to take effect.

If each of your machines was set up with its own IP address, DNS, and default gateway, then you can safely wipe out all these values after you write them down. The great thing about this router is that it uses *NAT* and includes a packet-inspecting firewall. You shouldn't need any other protection on your network; however, installing personal firewalls on each client is still advisable, as most outbound connections are not blocked, only inbound connections.

> **Your IP address** is not only a unique identifier for your current connection to the net, it also describes where on the net your PC lives. There are about 16 million computers that can share the first number in your IP address, but just 65,000 that can share the first two numbers. Only 256 computers can share the first three numbers.

Step 9: In the Event This All Explodes in Your Face...

HKSP (makers of *BBIAgent*) includes on its web site a small Java-based walkthrough of the installation and administration of the router. Its customer support is prompt and knowledgeable. Don't be afraid to use it! We've included solutions to some of the most common problems we've encountered:

Burning the floppy image fails or won't start! Windows95/98/ME, MS-DOS, and Linux are the only supported OSes. Grab a DOS boot disk from a friend and use it.

My network cards aren't initializing and/or I get a kernel panic! Recheck your vendor/model selections. Did you set your NICs properly? Set resources that are not used on your computer. Disable any serial ports; leave one if you need dial-up. Change the order of the cards in their slots.

I can't connect to the Internet! Check the WAN Connection settings on the router. If there are IP, DNS, and Gateway entries from the ISP, the router has configured itself. If not, press Connect. If it won't connect, verify that the cable is plugged into the WAN NIC, and that the NIC is initialized properly with the correct driver. Reboot the router and contact your ISP to see if there are any outages. Try switching your network cables. You may have mistakenly associated the wrong NIC with the wrong connection. ∎

How To...

SET UP YOUR
5.1 Speaker Rig

BY ROB PRATT

Everything you need to know about getting the best audio from your PC theater setup

If you already have a 4.1 surround-sound speaker system for your PC, you might assume that setting up a 5.1 system is a slam-dunk—but you'd be wrong. Sure, the Dolby Digital 5.1 spec adds only a middle channel to the traditional 4.1 mix, but 5.1 systems actually demand a degree of fine-tuning that belies their ostensible simplicity. Regardless, positioning your 5.1 speakers for optimal effect is well worth the trouble: The improvement in sound imaging that occurs when you jump to 5.1 is dramatic, especially for DVD movie playback. Your 3D soundscape suddenly comes alive with perfectly positioned music and sound effects.

The Dolby Digital 5.1 spec was developed for movie theaters and was never intended to be shoehorned into living rooms or the rooms that typically host PCs. The 5.1 audio format anticipates listeners sitting in much larger spaces, much farther away from their speakers. Small, tight spaces lessen the reverberation that's integral to 3D sound imaging and shrink one's "sweet spot" (that is, one's ideal listening position).

But fear not. Even if you live in a small hutch or hovel, you still may be able to make your PC theater system sound like the local multiplex. We asked pro audio engineers for advice on how to place 5.1 rigs in four different perplexing PC theater environments. Learn what you can from our case studies and apply your new knowledge at home.

TEST YOUR 5.1 SPEAKER PLACEMENT

There is no set formula for determining the precise placement of 5.1 PC speakers, so you'll need to place the speakers, gauge results, then tweak, gauge, tweak, and so forth. First off, make sure your speakers are wired correctly and that they're set at equal volume. The front left signal from your PC's soundcard should come out the front left speaker, the rear right signal should come out the rear right speaker, and all speakers (except the subwoofer) should sound like they're playing at the same volume.

Your speakers' "phase" (that is, their polarity) is crucial

to creating a good audio field. If your speakers connect with RCA jacks, and you never have to insert a bare wire into a spring-lock or clamp-down connector, then you probably don't have to worry about phase problems. But if you do have to connect bare wires at some point, you should verify that you've connected the correct wires to the correct connectors. Out-of-phase speakers produce audio that seems to be playing on top of your head instead of between your ears, and bass oftentimes seems nonexistent. The *Video Essentials* DVD (a home-stereo configuration disc available at many video rental stores) and most THX-certified DVDs include pre-generated pink noise that will help you pinpoint out-of-phase speakers.

After you've tackled phase, take a look at your speaker placement. Ideally, all three front speakers (left front, middle, right front) will be the same distance from the floor and level with your listeners' heads. Rear speakers should be slightly higher than the front speakers and needn't to be pointed directly at the listening area.

Since bass frequencies are nondirectional, your subwoofer can go almost anywhere, but is usually best placed on the floor near the front speakers or in a convenient corner. To find the best subwoofer placement in our tests, we put the sub in the sweet spot (that is, the exact place where we intend to be sitting), disconnected all the speakers but the sub, then played a music track with a lot of bass. We crawled around the room until we found the place where the subwoofer sounded best, then positioned the sub in this location. You'd be surprised by how well this trick works.

Final adjustments are based on subjective observations. For the clearest 3D definition from the front speakers, angle them toward the sweet spot. For a smaller sweet spot, angle the front speakers in toward each other even more. For a larger sweet spot (which will accommodate more listeners), use wider, more obtuse angles. Rear speakers can be placed facing the sweet spot or angled toward the top-rear corners of the room to maximize effectiveness.

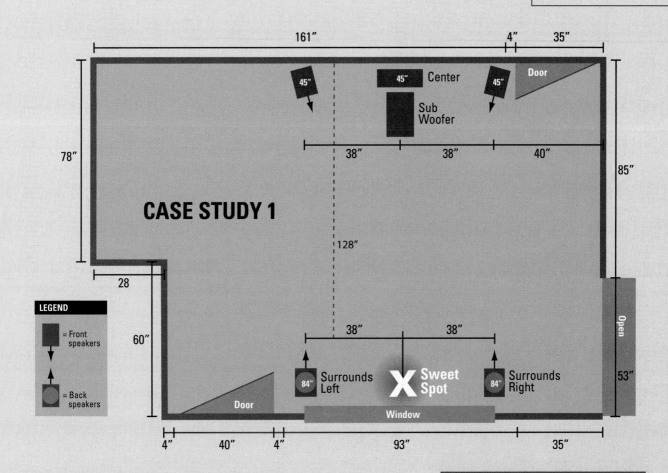

Figure: Floorplan diagram of Case Study 1 with measurements and speaker placements.

Labels in diagram:
- 161"
- 4"
- 35"
- 45" (Front speaker, top left)
- 45" Center
- Door
- Sub Woofer
- 45" (top right)
- 78"
- 85"
- CASE STUDY 1
- 38" 38" 40"
- 128"
- 28
- 60"
- LEGEND
  - = Front speakers
  - = Back speakers
- Open
- 53"
- 38" 38"
- 84" Surrounds Left
- X Sweet Spot
- 84" Surrounds Right
- Door
- Window
- 4" 40" 4" 93" 35"

CASE STUDY 1

A Living Room from "L"

Over the next three pages we'll show you how to deal with quandaries ranging from bass traps to rooms with excessive echo. Of course, these are just guidelines. Unless you have rooms that are identical to these, you'll need to set up your speakers, then tweak their orientation.

The worst listening environments are perfectly square rooms and rectangular rooms where the long dimension is twice as long as the short dimension. Both spaces are highly prone to generating "room modes" or "standing waves," which emphasize certain frequencies, diminish others, and generally shoot to hell the smooth frequency response of a good set of speakers. The slightly L-shaped space of our first case study—a living room in a modern apartment—has characteristics of both these troublesome models. Even worse, our intended sweet spot abuts the rear wall, which meant we had limited options for positioning the rear speakers.

Front speaker and sub placement was relatively straightforward. The front speakers were placed far apart and angled slightly inward to provide a wide sound field at the sweet spot and still give some positional cues. We placed the subwoofer directly in front of the PC.

Placement of the rear surround speakers proved more challenging. Aiming the rear speakers directly inward at the listening position sounded too harsh, but turning them outward caused uneven reflected sound. When turned outward, away from the sweet spot, the rear left sounded great, because it reflected off a nearby wall. The rear right, however, aimed directly into another room, and long reverberations from the open space made for lopsided surround effects, especially when paired with the crisp-sounding, quick reflection from the left. The best-sounding solution was to mount the speakers high on the rear wall (roughly three feet above the sweet spot) and directly in line with the front left and front right speakers. Tilted toward the ground at a 45-degree angle, the rear speakers then delivered an enveloping surround-sound effect.

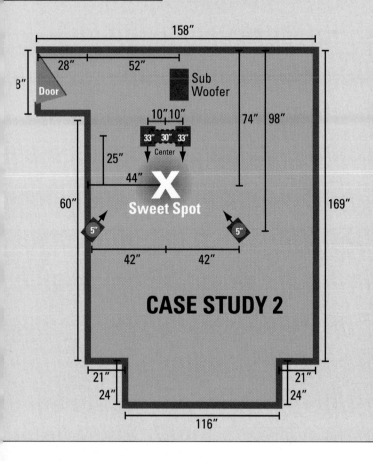

CASE STUDY 2

The DVD Desktop

We were pleasantly surprised by how easy it was to fine-tune this small listening space—a computer den with the floor space of a two-car garage. Our biggest problem wasn't even related to acoustics; it had more to do with cramming so many speakers into such a small area. The whole system—speakers and all—had to fit into an area about three feet wide.

Because the desktop space was so narrow, we had little opportunity to do anything more than position the front speakers on either side of the PC monitor and place the center speaker on the tabletop between the front edge of the monitor and the back edge of the keyboard. We turned up the center speaker volume by 2dB to account for its occlusion by the keyboard.

By using our subwoofer test, we found two spots underneath the desk that were good for the sub. To keep the subwoofer close to our PC and minimize wire-runs, we sacrificed leg room and put the subwoofer directly beneath the PC monitor.

Typically, the optimal placement of rear speakers is directly aside the listening position, aimed inward, and a little higher than head-level to soften the directionality of the surround speakers. By placing the rear left and rear right on the floor, we got close to this optimal placement, though our speakers ended up below head level. The result, however, was the most convincing surround sound of all our case studies.

CASE STUDY 3

Corner Pocket

Take the tight configuration of a desktop space, then cram it in the corner of a large room. Can you still have a great PC theater? In our third case study—a game testing room at our publishing company—a corner workstation configuration forced us to make an extra effort to get our rear speakers positioned and balanced. A low ceiling and asymmetric room shape only compounded our difficulties, as did the occupant of an adjoining workstation, who didn't like the idea of a rear speaker planted on his desk.

Limited corner desktop space forced us to make a trade-off between the spread of the front speakers and desktop workspace. If we set up the front left and right for a wider spread, then positioning the center-channel speaker to be in line with them would use up all of our available desktop space. So we compromised by going with an arrangement that gave us roughly four feet of separation between the front left and front right speakers, and about two square feet of desktop space in front of the center speaker.

Positioning the rear speakers was more of a challenge, because of the presence of another workstation. Eventually, we created tiny shelves for our speakers, placed them slightly higher than head-level, and aimed the speakers directly inward. The vast spread between the two rear surround speakers worked well to create a cocoon of sound—even though both speakers were angled directly at our listening position. For subwoofer placement, we determined that a spot three feet to the left of the corner offered the tightest sound (direct corner placement was too loud and boomy). To fine-tune the subwoofer, we boosted its volume by 6dB to compensate for the fact that our workstation's desktop occluded earshot to the subwoofer from the listening position.

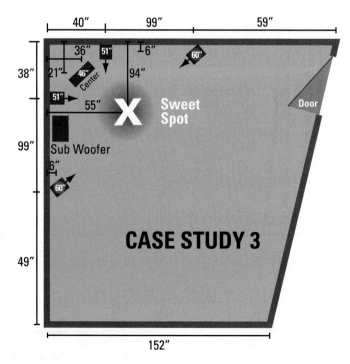

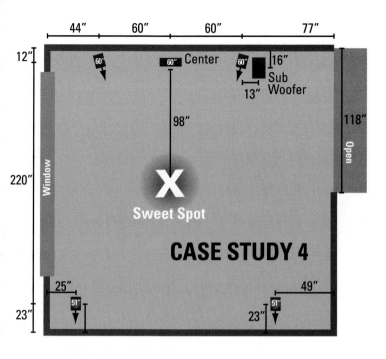

44" 60" 60" 77"

12"

60" 60" Center 60" 16"
Sub
Woofer
13"

98"

118"

Window 220" Open

X
Sweet Spot

CASE STUDY 4

25" 49"

23" 51" 51" 23"

CASE STUDY 4

Space, the Final Frontier

A gorgeous picture window that takes up one full wall. Brand-new hardwood floors. A ceiling two floors high. All of these factors made us think we'd have a tough time getting our second living-room case study to do more than echo-echo-echo when we cranked up our PC theater rig. However, in the end, the wide-open space and reflective surfaces allowed us to set up our 5.1 speakers almost exactly to the recommended configuration, with great results.

With plenty of room to spread out, we placed the front left and front right speakers a whopping five feet from the center channel on either side. This gave us a wide sweet spot. We positioned our subwoofer in the front of the room, near the right speaker. The space to the right of the subwoofer—a small alcove with a low ceiling—turned out to be quite a nifty bass trap. It reinforced low frequencies and added a massive presence to the gunfire, explosions, and thumping techno soundtrack of *The Matrix*.

Aiming the rear speakers directly at the sweet spot created sound cues that were a bit too direct. We remedied this situation by turning the surrounds backward and adding a 3dB boost in volume. The final effect wasn't as clear and precise as the close-in desktop theater configuration of Case Study 1, but it did provide the most convincing sensation of depth.

READING BETWEEN THE LINES

PROTECT YOUR STEREO!

The center speaker of Dolby Digital 5.1 speaker rigs can sometimes enhance the imaging of stereo audio in MP3 files and music CDs. But because most stereo music already contains elements that are mixed to sound like they're in the center when played on two speakers (vocals, guitar solos, and kick drums, for example), a center speaker can often overpower the front left and right speakers. For this reason, we sometimes disable the center channel when playing stereo recordings.

HAVE BASS, WILL TRAVEL

The ".1" in Dolby Digital 5.1 refers to the fact that the data bandwidth for the low-frequency effects (LFE) channel is only one-tenth the bandwidth of any one of the other five channels (the LFE channel adds subwoofer oomph to explosions and other environmental effects during DVD movie playback). In Dolby Digital 5.1 speaker systems built for PCs, however, the subwoofer often works much harder. Because "multimedia speaker" satellites are usually small units that don't have good bass response, their crossover is typically set up so that the subwoofer takes care of all

the low frequencies. During regular music playback, the sub handles only the normal allotment of low frequencies, but during DVD movie playback, the sub handles regular low frequencies *and* whatever is assigned to the LFE channel—and the result can be alarmingly loud. So, when switching between movies and music, adjust the subwoofer volume.

THE TERROR OF TRIPWIRES

The audio delight of surround sound cannot exist without the hassle of long speaker-wire runs. But you need not risk life and limb for good sound. In a carpeted room, stuff the wires between the baseboard and the carpet fiber. In a hard-floored room, tack the wires to the baseboard. You can also run flat speaker wire (available at home-improvement stores) underneath carpet or on "over-the-top" runs through walls and attic crawl spaces.

STAYING IN PHASE

Avoiding a phase cancellation problem is as easy as pie if you pay attention to your wire's color coding when you hook up everything. Even speaker wires that aren't color-coded

usually have indicators for which wire goes where: Some use a stripe on one of the two conductors, and others print text (usually stating the gauge and type of wire) on one of the conductors.

GROUND, GROUND, GET A GROUND, I GET A GROUND

PC-based entertainment centers are prone to ground loop hum. One of the most common causes of ground loop hum is the gigantic electrical circuit that's created when you connect your PC to a set of speakers and a TV. All three connect to an AC power wall outlet, and the ground loop comes from a trickle of electricity that flows in one device (for instance, into your PC), then into another device (such as out of the audio connectors and into your speakers) before returning to the wall outlet. Completely stamping out ground loop hum often requires a lot of specialized electrical wiring, but you can get rid of most of it simply by making sure you plug all your PC theater components into the same wall outlet or power strip. ■

How To...

OPTIMIZE YOUR PC FOR
Multiplayer MAYHEM

MAXIMUM PC
TIME TO COMPLETION
00:45
HOURS   MINUTES

A few computer tweaks here and there can make you a force to be reckoned with in online games

BY JOEL DURHAM JR.

The battle is joined! You find yourself in war-torn France with a small squad of combat-hardened soldiers, seeking out Nazis while wading through the smoking ruins of a rustic village. A dingy gray haze of smoke obscures the landscape and even seems to dull the distant thumping of mortar shells that pummel the landscape, leaving craters in their wake.

There's movement up ahead. Without warning, a shot rings out and you hear a cry to your left: One of your comrades in arms hits the ground with a thud. There's no time to mourn: You race for cover as bullets zing past your head. You duck into what used to be a bakery and peer cautiously through the shattered window.

There, ahead, is the assailant. He doesn't see you. You raise your rifle and aim just behind his ear.

And suddenly, he vanishes. A tenth of a second later, he's behind you, unloading lead into your sorry car-

cass, and you die a wholly unheroic death. What is this, some sort of secret Nazi experiment in teleporting?

No, it's latency—the time between initiating an instruction, such as firing on the enemy, and its actual execution. It just ruined your game of *Medal of Honor: Allied Assault.* You check your stats and find that your ping has hit 550 milliseconds. The game stutters like an old movie in a bad projector.

What can you do about this travesty? Enemies are popping in and out of sight, bullets seem to be fired from phantoms, and there's a general lack of cohesiveness in the world around you. You have to put a stop to this, but how?

Well, since you asked… We'll show you some tried and true methods for making your PC better equipped to handle the pressures of online gaming.

Hints for Every Occasion

FIND A LOW PING SERVER

It *seems* obvious. The one factor that will affect your multiplayer gaming performance more than anything else is your ping. Ping measures how long it takes a packet of data to make it to a server and back. It's further complicated by the packet's trip through your system's architecture. For instance, using a software-controlled modem (*Winmodem*) will result in higher pings compared with high-quality, hardware-

controlled modems because software-controlled modems have to wait for processor time. The higher your ping is in relation to a given server, the more latency you'll experience.

When you're browsing for a server, sort the list by ping (you can usually do this by clicking the Ping header at the top of the list). Find a server with a low ping, but don't trust it right away. Refresh it, if the game allows you to refresh a single server, or refresh the list, two or three

Surfing through a *Quake III Arena* server list for a low ping server.

times. If the server's ping is consistently low, try logging on to it.

At the very beginning of the game,

watch players for signs of latency. Check the player list and see if anybody there has pings of more than 400 milliseconds. If the server is overrun by high pingers, you're likely to see them freeze and jump around and be hard to target, then when you kill them they'll complain and call you an LPB (low-ping bastard). You, of course, respond by calling the victim an HPW (high-ping whiner).

When you find a server with a low ping populated by other players with sub-200ms pings, you've found a winner.

GET RID OF THE ROUTER
More and more homes have multiple computers and small, often wireless LANs. In many cases, they share a broadband Internet connection with a router such as the Linksys Wireless-B Broadband Router. This is a huge convenience: A single Internet connection can serve any number of computers in a household. However, for gaming, it's best to bypass the router and connect directly to the cable or DSL modem.

You see, the router adds another translation layer between your lean, mean gaming machine and the Internet, where all the servers reside. In our tests, the addition of a router increased pings by 10 to 20 milliseconds, a significant margin if you're a competitive player.

If you don't want to deprive the rest of your housemates of high-speed Internet access, see if your Internet provider offers a second IP address for your

broadband connection. You'll also need a high-speed hub or switch. Hook the cable modem, your computer, and the router all to the hub, and you're set.

MAX OUT YOUR MODEM
In Windows 9x and ME, there are two Registry settings you can tweak to squeeze better performance from your modem. They are the MTU (maximum transmission unit) and the MSS (maximum segment size). The former defines the largest packet size that can be transferred in a single frame. MMS indicates how much data can be crammed into each packet. MMS is usually smaller than MTU to allow for packet routing information and other semantics.

First, you have to determine the details of your Dial-Up Adapter. Open your Registry editor by selecting Start\Run, typing regedit, and hitting Enter. In the left pane, navigate to HKEY_LOCAL_MACHINE\Enum\Root\Net.

Open each subkey, numbered 0000, 0001, and so on, and look for the entry DeviceDesc with the value Dial-Up Adapter. Expand the Bindings subkey and you will find a string name like MSTCP\XXXX (with each X being a

number). Jot down the four digits after MSTCP\. Navigate to HKEY_LOCAL_MACHINE\Enum\Network\MSTCP and expand the subkey with that same four digit number.

Find the entry Driver with the value NetTrans\XXXX. Jot down the four-digit number following NetTrans\. Navigate to HKEY_LOCAL_MACHINE\System\

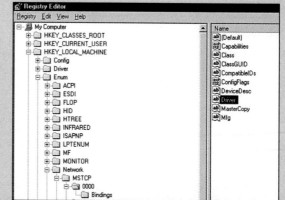
Tweak the Registry to get the most out of your modem.

CurrentControlSet\Services\Class\NetTrans. Expand the key with the name equal to the four-digit number you just jotted down.

Now, create two new string values named MaxMTU and MaxMSS. Set the former to 576 and the latter to 536. Exit the Registry and restart the machine.

There's an excellent article on this process at www.winguides.com/registry/dis-

Tips for Quake III Arena Engine Games

The granddaddy of multiplayer gaming, *Quake* rocked the world when it was originally introduced in 1996. With each new *Quake* title, and the incremental patches that have accompanied them, Internet play has become smoother and more streamlined. That does not mean, however, that there aren't still tweaks to make any Quake III engine game even better.

LAG-O-METER
The Lag-O-Meter is a splendid tool for gauging your net performance and detecting latency and dropped packets. Fire it up by bringing down the console (press the ~ key), typing \cg_lagometer, and hitting Enter. Be sure to include the preceding backslash or you'll end up broadcasting the word "cg_lagometer" to everyone else on the server.

The Lag-O-Meter, located in the bot-

tom right corner of the screen, consists of two important components. The top line indicates how synchronized your machine is to game world updates. Blue dots indicate that your computer is drawing frames at or better than the rate that the server is sending updates. When yellow dots appear, it indicates that your graphics card is getting ahead of the server's world updates. This can cause signs of latency, like when enemies are there one second and gone the next. You can combat this through your snaps setting, discussed later.

The second line indicates how packets are being received from the server. Ideally, it should remain green, meaning that packets are arriving intact and on time. Yellow blips indicate late packets, and red blips mean packets are being dropped. You can optimize this some-

The Lag-O-Meter in the bottom right corner gives you a clear indication of how well your current connection is working out.

what by tweaking your rate setting, discussed next.

THE RATE COMMAND
The "rate" console command sets the maximum data rate the server will send to the client in bytes per second. Normally the server won't use the entire pipe, but this command sets the cap.

Since we're using a broadband connection to play *Medal of Honor* online, we increase our "rate" setting.

If your client uses a dial-up connection, the rate should be relatively low—in the 3000 to 4000 range. Lowering the rate at the first sign of latency can smooth out the lag symptoms. It's a good practice to experiment with different rate settings while keeping an eye on the Lag-O-Meter; as the meter shows greater lag and more late or dropped packets, you should lower the rate. Adjust the rate by opening the console and typing \rate X, with X being the new value, and then hitting Enter.

Faster, broadband connections benefit from a higher rate. Try setting it to something in the 25,000 range. Then prepare to level your enemies by popping railgun charges through their craniums.

There is not one perfect value for the rate variable that will work on every server. You'll have to experiment each time you log on, and if you stay on the same server for a long time, you may have to fiddle with it at regular intervals.

THE SNAPS COMMAND

In earlier *Quake* games, the rate at which a client received updates depended on its frame rate, giving people with faster machines or more powerful graphics cards an advantage. *Quake III Arena* introduced a new architecture, updating the world in accordance with the "snaps" variable. The snaps setting tells how many world updates are received from the server per second.

Utilize the snaps command by opening the console and typing \snaps and hitting Enter. This will show you your current snaps setting. Enter \snaps followed by a number (for example: \snaps 30) to change the value.

Normally, the snaps default setting of 20 is fine. If you wish to experi-

Use the "snaps" command in *Return to Castle Wolfenstein* to tweak world update frequency.

ment, the rule of thumb is the faster your Internet connection, the higher your snaps setting should be. Consider keeping it around 20 with a 56K dial-up connection, and 30 to 40 if you PC is fitted with a broadband connection.

Also, use the Lag-O-Meter to help you find your ideal snaps setting. Depending on Internet traffic and lag, you might adjust snaps several times in one play session. When the Lag-O-Meter starts to show red lines (dropped packets) on its bottom graph, you might try lowering the snaps settings. Thus, if the snaps setting is 35 and the Lag-O-Meter starts filling up with red bars, lower the snaps

Tips for Half-Life Engine Games

The *Half-Life* engine was originally based on the *Quake* and *Quake II* engines, but it's so heavily modified that it's taken on a life of its own. Besides the actual *Half-Life* game, the Valve classic is the subject of what may be the most popular game mods ever: *Team Fortress Classic, Day of Defeat,* and *Counter-Strike.* None of these or other mods stray too far from the core code of the *Half-Life* engine, so net play tweaks that work on one will likely work on all three.

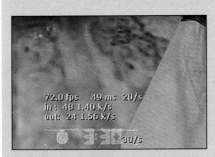

The Netgraph, shown here in *Counter-Strike*, gives an indication of how laggy or lag-free your online experience is.

As is the case with *Quake III Arena,* you enter commands at the console. If you're using Valve's Steam service, the console is accessed by simply pressing the ~ key in-game. If you're not using Steam, you have to add the -console switch to your *Half-Life* icon's property sheet. Right-click your *Half-Life* icon on the desktop or in the Start menu, select Properties, and at the end of the Target text (outside the quotes), type -console. Then launch *Half-Life* normally; you can now access the console in-game with the ~ key.

THE NETGRAPH

One of the most useful tools to monitor your network performance and determine the effectiveness of any optimization tweaks, is the Netgraph. Start the netgraph by opening the console and typing NET_GRAPH X, where X is 1 for the standard netgraph, 2 for an enhanced netgraph, or 3 for a small, abbreviated version of the netgraph.

You can tweak the size and placement of the netgraph. In the console, type NET_GRAPHWIDTH X to adjust its width (default is 192) and NET_GRAPHHEIGHT

X to tweak its height (default is 64). Type NET_GRAPHPOS X to place the graph where you wish it to appear on your screen: substitute X with 1 for the bottom right, 2 for the bottom center, or 3 for the bottom left.

The graph shows several details: the frame rate in frames per second, the current latency in milliseconds, in and out packet sizes in bytes, in and out data rates in kilobytes per second, and more. The graph portion itself shows latency through the height of the green line, and red vertical lines show dropped packets. The very bottom graphs how quickly the client is rendering frames. Dropped packets and infrequent server updates will cause the client to extrapolate data, represented by yellow, orange, and red appearing in the graph. When the graph starts to get colorful, the game will become choppy.

THE CL_RATE COMMAND

This is similar to the *Quake III* engine "rate" variable described earlier. It has to do with data transmission from the

You can use the "rate" command in *Day of Defeat* to iron out some lag.

We used "cl_updaterate" in *Team Fortress Classic* to raise the rate for our fast cable modem.

should lower the rate.

If your client has a broadband connection to the Internet and the server you're playing on has a low ping, try increasing the cl_rate to 10,000 or more, and start the hunt. That gives you a chance to tear up enemies' hides with a machine gun before they have a chance to draw a bead on you.

THE CL_CMDRATE AND CL_UPDATERATE COMMANDS

The console commands "cl_cmdrate" and "cl_updaterate" can be used in conjunction with the netgraph to streamline Internet gaming.

The first command, cl_cmdrate, determines the maximum number of packets that get sent to the game's server each second. By default, the cl_cmdrate is set at 30, which is fine for 56K modems with connections higher than 50Kbps. If your connection speed is slower and you start to experience lag, try lowering the value by opening the console and entering cl_cmdrate X. Set X at 30 and work your way down to 20. Alternately, users of broadband connections can expect smoother play by

game server in bytes per second. You adjust the rate by opening the console and typing cl_rate X, where X being is the new value.

Slow connections should get lower rates. With a modem connection, you'll probably want the cl_rate to hover around the 3000 to 4000 range. Use the netgraph to watch for signs of latency, and lower the cl_rate by increments of 100 or 200 at a time to smooth out the connection. Experiment with different rate settings, using the netgraph to help you out; as it shows greater lag, late packets, and dropped packets, you

increasing the rate to 35 or 40.

The cl_updaterate is the opposite of the cl_cmdrate. It indicates the maximum number of packets that get sent from the server to the client per second. Its default setting is 20. That should be considered the minimum setting; users of dial-up connections won't likely benefit from lowering the rate. If you have a broadband connection, consider raising it to 30 or 40 by opening the console and entering cl_updaterate X, with X being the new setting.

Experiment with these variables to find the most silky-smooth settings possible.■

How To...

KICK ASS AND TAKE NAMES IN
FIRST-PERSON SHOOTERS

BY WILL SMITH

There is no honor in online first-person shooters. Cheating is rampant, naughty language is the rule, and he who frags best wins the game. So if you're nothing but fragbait, pay attention to the lessons on this page. We can't turn you into the greatest deathmatcher of all time, but we can keep you from living in that permanent vacation home at the bottom of the frag board.

Know Your Enemy's Location
Pay attention to everything around you. Listen closely for footsteps and the sounds of enemies equipping their weapons. Headphones are especially helpful for pinpointing sounds in a 3D space. Also, take care to conceal your position. Walk softly and don't pick up weapons or ammo that you don't need. Those sounds can give you away.

Never Take a Knife to a Gunfight
We call this the Sean Connery Rule. If you come face to face with an enemy and you're low on health, armor, and ammo, you should retreat. Run away, man! Run like the wind! Re-equip yourself, *then* attack. On the flipside, never hesitate to finish off a weakened enemy. Sure, it's not a fair fight, but what do you care? A frag's a frag.

Master the Circle Strafe
By using your mouse for aiming and your movement keys to step left and right, you can circle an enemy while always keeping your weapon on-target. Practice on bots, then take your mad strafing skills to more intelligent prey.

Check Your Corners
When you're entering a new room, make sure no one is lurking in the corners before you completely expose yourself. Remember, these are 3D games, so look up and down too.

Control Yourself
That craptastic mouse that came with your PC just won't cut it for a firefight, so get yourself a real weapon like the Microsoft Intellimouse Explorer or the Logitech MX700. Just make sure to try before you buy. Once you have your mouse, experiment with the cursor speed and acceleration settings to determine what works best for your play style. Snipers might want the high precision of a low mouse speed, while run-and-gun fraggers usually prefer a higher speed. You might also try disabling mouse acceleration for more predictable aim.

Get Down with the Lingo
The language of the online FPS community, or l33tspeak, is frightening and difficult to master. If you say the wrong thing, you'll be marked as a n00b (newbie player) and targeted for easy frags. Here are some phrases that should help you fit in: "y0 bish, I totally pwned j00!" (Hey,

man, I really kicked your butt just then.); "j00 are mah bish" (I can frag you wherever and whenever I like.); "y u h8 me?" (Why do you kill me over and over?)

Caution: If you can't master this phraseology with utmost fluency, we recommend against using l33tspeak at all. It's better to be silent and thought a fool than to open your mouth and prove it.

Basic Rules for Team Games
DO NOT SHOOT YOUR TEAMMATES. If you're playing on a teamplay server, the object is to beat the other team. You will not beat the other team if you spend your time shooting your teammates in the back. Even if your squad is trudging across Iwo Jima in *Battlefield 1942* and you haven't seen an enemy for 10 minutes, it's not acceptable to unload into your pal.

Set Up an Ambush
Whether you're playing in a team game or in an online fragfest, setting up an ambush is a time-honored tradition in FPSes. Go to a key area of the map—it can be a weapon spawn, an ammo dump, or just a choke point between two objectives—and find a nice dark corner to wait in. When an enemy approaches, wait until you've lined up a sure shot, then frag 'em. The losers call it camping, but we call it winning. Advanced tip: It's a good idea to set up on an enemy spawn spot. Even the best deathmatcher is disoriented and weak after respawning!

How-To Win at Unreal Tournament
Some guns rock, some will get you rocked. Use the flak cannon, the shock rifle, and the lightning gun to kill your enemies quickly. When your adrenaline meter hits full, you can perform combos to give you special powers. To speed up, tap move-forward four times quickly. To regen your health, tap move-backward four times quickly. Try right, right, left, left and forward, forward, back, back for more fun.

How To...

MASTER DIGITAL
PHOTOGRAPHY

BY BRAD DOSLAND

MAXIMUMPC
DIFFICULTY RATING
EASY
HARD
XXX

Think you know how to take digital pics? Think again. This guide will reveal everything you don't know about picking the right camera and getting the most from your hardware, software, and digital files.

There was a time when photography was an arcane art. Just getting an image to actually appear required vast experience and dangerous chemicals. But those days are over. Today, the latest digital cameras allow anyone to capture sophisticated images with the press of a finger. Instant image preview on your camera's built-in LCD screen ensures that you never miss the moment. Special effects such as sepia toning and montaging are a click of the mouse away. Fixing classic problems—such as eliminating the red-eye effect created by on-camera flash—is equally simple; all you need is an image-editing program. This should be the golden era of photography, right?

Wrong.

Despite all the powerful tools at our disposal, digital photography is still just photography, and photography will always be a subtle art form. Anyone can take a good picture with a bit of luck, but it requires specialized knowledge to end up with a great picture. The software bundled with your new digital camera may allow you to add effects to your pics, but to realize your ultimate vision, you'll need to master the tools at your disposal. You must call the shots. And that's where we come in. On the following pages, we're going to expose you to all the information and techniques you'll need to transform your mundane snapshots into memorable images.

These two models from Olympus illustrate the trade-offs between camera body size and lens size. While the actual aperture mechanisms are roughly identical (as illustrated by the yellow circles) the C-4040 on the left has nearly double the glass of the compact D-40 on the right (as illustrated by the red circles). Unfortunately, the superior C-4040 is too big to fit in most pockets.

Find the Right Megapixel Range

In case it ever comes up on a test: "Megapixels are to a digital camera as megahertz are to a PC." True enough, but just like the computer buyer who spends top dollar on a screaming system and then uses it just to check e-mail, digital camera shoppers often waste their money on more megapixels than they need.

In a nutshell, cameras with 1 megapixel of resolution or less (for example, webcams or the camera built into Sony's Clie Handhelds) are best suited for very rudimentary shots. We're talking about reference images for insurance claims, or mug shots for a company web site. Most people will be disappointed by 1-megapixel image quality, even when compared with disposable film cameras.

Cameras rated in the 3-megapixel range are becoming affordable, with street prices around $140 (depending on features) for name brands such as Kodak or Olympus. These cameras will suit the typical digital photographer wishing to make standard size prints. 5×7 (and up to 8×10) prints made from a 3-megapixel camera are high quality and will satisfy all but the most critical of photo experts. (Of course, a good photo printer is necessary to get the most from any image's resolution.) Also note that while 4- and 5-megapixel cameras are coming down in price, there is often a trade-off for quality with the lens and zoom capabilities (among other features). It will pay to do a little research at sites like www.digicamhelp.com to ensure value. And, unless you're planning on shooting for a print

publication (which requires additional resolution to reproduce the dot pattern used in the print process) or need very large prints, leave the 6-megapixel and higher cameras (along with the high prices) to the pros.

Buy the Best Lens

Since all photography is really just about capturing the light, it should come as no surprise that the lens used to focus that light is one of the most critical components of any digital camera. Sadly, many big-name companies skimp when it comes to their lenses, and image quality suffers as a result.

The first shortcut some camera makers take is to forgo a glass lens for an inferior plastic version. The imperfections inherent to plastic make it a lousy choice for a camera lens. To avoid distortion and uneven focus, stick with a glass lens. Also, when it comes to lenses, the more the merrier. While a camera can operate with a single piece of glass over the aperture—acting like a sort of contact lens—cameras with multi-element lens assemblies generally produce vastly superior images. More lenses in the assembly straighten and correct the light image before it reaches the recording surface of the camera.

Finally, size matters. Bigger glass allows more light to enter, making the camera more sensitive and better able to record images in lower light conditions, and that's a good thing. Extremely compact digital cameras typically use small lenses as a matter of necessity, so buyer beware.

Pick the Right Removable Media

Size also matters when it comes to removable media. Currently the shelves are glutted with an unnecessary variety of removable memory formats, from CompactFlash to the thinner Memory Stick to the even slimmer SmartMedia to the even smaller MMC and SD cards. Which format your camera uses makes a huge difference.

The youngest of formats, the xD-Picture Card, was introduced by Olympus and FujiFilm a few years ago. The card is tiny, but keep in mind that the physical size of the memory card isn't the most important factor when selecting a digital camera. Understand that a 3-megapixel camera can store nearly 1,000 images on a single 1GB card, while only about 100 images would fit on a 128MB piece of media. Bump this up to a 6-megapixel unit and you're talking 320 images for the 1GB card and a measly 40 images on the 128MB media. At press time, the xD format topped out at 512 MB, which is a reasonable capacity for most applications. However, if you are taking your camera on the road with little or no opportunity to offload images, you would probably like to have fewer of these previous slivers of media to risk losing. Therefore, choosing a camera that accepts 1GB CompactFlash cards might make sense given the current comparable price for xD media that's half the capacity.

Finally, you will notice that the companies that make removable media will tell you that the speed of the media makes a big difference. True and false. On a high-end camera, you can tell a difference between standard CompactFlash and the 40x High Speed version. But that margin is negligible on most consumer cameras since the record mechanism bottlenecks the potential of the media. Still, camera models are specific with regard to supported media type as well as speed (or version) of that media so you'll want to be sure what you are getting.

These pictures illustrate the difference in resolution between a sub-megapixel image and a 4-megapixel image. Details are completely lost in the sub-megapixel photo (bottom), while details in the 4-megapixel photo (top) stand up to magnification many times over.

	MMC	SM	MS	SD	CF (4x)
64MB	$50	$40	$40	$50	$40
128MB	$80	$60	$60	$70	$50
256MB	n/a	n/a	$100	$90	$60
512MB	n/a	n/a	n/a	$160	$120
1GB	n/a	n/a	n/a	n/a	n/a

	MSPro	xD	CF HS	CF Pro	SD HS
128MB	n/a	$80	$60	n/a	n/a
256MB	$120	$130	$70	n/a	$100
512MB	$300	$230	$130	$150	$180
1GB	$600	n/a	$260	$300	$430
2GB	n/a	n/a	n/a	$610	n/a
24GB	n/a	n/a	n/a	$1400	n/a

This chart illustrates the choices available in removable media, based on prices listed at LexarMedia.com as we went to press. We chose to feature Lexar for pricing comparisons, because it's one of the few vendors that sell all the different formats under its own brand. Notice the size and cost benefits of the CompactFlash format.

Pick the Right Battery

Batteries may seem like a low-tech consideration, but no other component will have a bigger impact on your shooting. Unfortunately, no other choice you make when buying a camera will be less clear-cut.

Digital cameras are notorious juice hogs. It's not uncommon for a camera to drain a brand-new set of standard batteries in less than 20 shots. Ouch. The problem is that digital cameras need batteries to be "topped off." When the current falls below a certain threshold, the camera thinks its batteries are dead, though they may still be able to provide hours of life in a less demanding device, like a portable MP3 player. For this reason, standard batteries aren't the best possible choices for digi-cams. They really have only one saving grace: They're available for purchase almost everywhere you go.

Deciding between the convenience of rechargeable Nickel-Metal Hydrides (left), the efficiency of proprietary Lithium-Ion cells (center), and the mixed-skills of specialized Lithium-Ion batteries (right) is a difficult call. But most casual enthusiasts go for off-the-shelf batteries in a pinch.

On the flipside, proprietary Lithium-Ion batteries last longer than standards and can be quickly recharged, saving massive money compared to disposables. But if you're shooting on the road and you run out of juice without an outlet or your proprietary charger around, you're screwed. One option is to buy and charge a backup battery, but backups can be very expensive ($50 to $100) and can drain as well.

The best compromise for some people might be a camera that uses rechargeable Nickel-Metal Hydride batteries. These cells sport a relatively long life (typically a charge is good for hundreds of shots) and are economical. Only you can make the call.

Choose Bells and Whistles Wisely

The ads for digital cameras are littered with esoteric specs. Some of them are important, some aren't. Here's a quick overview of what to look for and what to ignore.

Serial connection? USB? FireWire? Who cares? Get with the program and invest in an inexpensive external media reader. Some are available to read all media formats.

■ Zoom lenses will allow you to get closer to the action, and most good cameras include at least a 2x or 3x optical zoom. But beware of the digital zoom; it only degrades picture quality and should be shunned.

■ The ability to record short video clips is becoming more and more common, but don't be misled. Digital cameras are not yet a substitute for an actual camcorder. Your video clips will be short and chew up vast real estate on your removable media, and the quality tends to be dismal. Many cameras don't even capture audio with the clip.

■ Direct-print features that allow you to make prints directly from the camera can be handy, but only if you invest in a special DP-capable printer.

■ When it comes time to download images from your camera to your computer, make sure you have at least a USB option. Serial connections are just too slow and buggy. If a FireWire or USB 2.0 connection is available, go for it.

■ Many cameras come with a bevy of auto-exposure modes and/or exposure bracketing. Most of these are useless, so you'll want to make sure your camera has the ability to manually override the exposure to compensate for backlighting.

■ The last thing to consider is the camera size itself. Small cameras make certain sacrifices (smaller lenses, small LCD preview screens, awkward grip), but compensate by being easier to pocket. An old photo truism says it all: "The best camera is the one you have with you."

Find the Right Image Editor

You can't beat the price of bundled editing software, but you may not want to suffer through the buggy, underpowered crap that ships with some cameras. While many cameras include excellent name-brand software from companies such as Adobe, others toss in low-rent programs that can actually damage your precious images. Don't be afraid to bail on the bundled shovelware for one of these alternatives.

■ Adobe's venerable *Photoshop* does everything you can imagine, and better than any other contender. Many people swear that *Photoshop* is the most perfect piece of software ever, in terms of power and grace. But that perfection comes at a steep price. Tipping the scales at more than $600, *Photoshop* is not for everyone.

■ With a price tag of less than $100, *Photoshop's* little brother—Adobe *Elements 2.0*—is for everyone. We reviewed this app and found that it sacrificed just a few high-end pro features of its big brother, but for a $500 savings. *Elements* will help you crop, color-correct, stylize,

There are many choices when it comes to image-editing software, but dollar for dollar, it's hard to beat Adobe *Elements 2.0*. Calling it "Photoshop Junior" does this robust app a great disservice.

catalog, and infinitely tweak your digital pics ad nauseam. It rocks, which is why we gave it a Perfect 10 verdict.

■ Another viable sub-$100 alternative is JASC's *Paint Shop Pro*, in its eighth iteration. This program spares no power when it comes to image editing, but comes up a tad short when compared with the more intuitive interface of Adobe's offerings.

■ Ulead's *PhotoImpact XL* costs less than $100 and is another excellent alternative, but the company's *Photo Express* software is woefully underpowered for all but the most rudimentary fixes. This is also true of other bargain-bin software, such as Micrografx (ne Corel) *Picture Publisher*, ArcSoft *PhotoImpression*, MGI *PhotoSuite*, and Microsoft *Picture It*.

Finally, If you post your pictures online, you may want to consider Macromedia's *Fireworks MX 2004*. While the $300 price tag is intimidating, webmasters swear by this indispensable tool.

To Print or Not to Print, What Are Your Image-Sharing Options?

Many digital photographers have a hard time breaking out of the "FotoMat Paradigm," the inclination to make 3x5-inch prints of every picture snapped. It doesn't have to be this way, folks. You have a PC—so use it!

If you want to avoid dusty shoeboxes and faded prints, but still want to share your images with friends and family, fire up a free online account such as the one provided by Yahoo! These services allow your peeps to see your pix from anywhere in the world, and they can even order prints.

For starters, viewing images on a big PC screen is a much better choice than squinting at small prints. The color onscreen is brighter, the detail is richer, and the image is bigger. And if you're not content with seeing your images on a computer monitor, most modern digital cameras include a cable to toss pictures on a big-screen TV, which is perfect for sharing vacation slide shows with unwitting visitors.

Another great option is using online photo-sharing web sites, such as Kodak's Ofoto.com. These free services allow you to upload your images to a web page, where they can be viewed by anyone with net access. They also offer additional services (usually for a fee), such as to print orders by mail. (This puts the ball back in the court of relatives who are always pestering you for reprints of the baby.) Yahoo! offers an excellent version of this service at Photos.yahoo.com. Shutterfly.com is another veteran service with a good reputation. There are many other photo-sharing options, but going with one of the reputable names helps ensure that the time you invest uploading images won't be wasted when the site goes under in a month or two. Also, always remember to keep backup copies of all your images. Even the established sites could go out of business, and you don't want to lose your images if that should happen. Finally, shop around. These sites frequently offer free prints and other perks for new sign-ups.

If you do decide to print your pictures from your desktop, test the printer before you buy if possible. Specs alone do not tell the whole story. Some printers are simply better for photos. Many modern inkjet printers make excellent photos, especially when used with dedicated photo paper. Splurge for the good paper and your prints will also last longer, and not fade away.

Indispensable Utilities

It doesn't take long to begin filling a folder on your hard drive with digital images, but without the right tools, you might as well be stuffing them into a dusty shoebox. A cataloguing utility will help you find just the pictures from that trip to Vegas, or only the images of college friends, or any particular images you're looking for. And when you've found what you're looking for, many of these utilities will compile the images into a custom web page or screensaver, or burn them to a CD. There are tons to choose from, and you may want to try

Man does not live by image editing software alone, so be sure to check out utilities such as Xecute Software's *Smart Pix Manager*. This awesome tool allows you to catalogue your images in a robust database that makes it easy to find just what you're looking for.

a few to see what fits your taste, but start with database-driven choices such as Fookes Software's *Album Express*, *Smart Pix Manager v5.52*, or Harry Doldersum's *PictureBook v1.4*.

While the new *Photoshop CS* and *Elements 2.0* do include a long-overdue thumbnail browser, a dedicated image browser is a must for any digital photographer. ACD Systems' *ACDSee* is the best. Among the staggering amount of features in the latest 4.0 version are: the ability to create ZIP archives within the program; support for video files and video frame capture; and slideshows with text, sound, and transitions. Plus, there's even a mobile version of the program for the Palm platform. *ACDSee* is the complete package, and it's amazingly fast. When you want to see a JPEG, don't wait for *Photoshop* to crawl to a start. PhotoDex's *CompuPic* is similar to *ACDSee* and is $10 cheaper, but lacks some of *ACDSee's* grace.

Lastly, you may want to buy an expensive piece of software you hope you'll never use. German developer Convar makes *PC Inspector Smart Recovery*, which recovers files that have been accidentally deleted from a camera's removable media (assuming you haven't already overwritten the media with new pictures). It's pricey at $140, but if it helps you save that picture of the Loch Ness monster...

Getting the Shot

You've got the gear and you've got the software, now the hardest part: Getting the shot. Now, we can't teach you in a scant few paragraphs all the mojo that artists spend years developing, but we can turn you on to a few simple techniques guaranteed to make your pictures better.

Photography is all about filling the frame with good stuff, then putting it together in an interesting way. What makes something interesting enough to take its picture? Ultimately this is a matter of taste, but there are some easy guidelines. First, is it unusual? People are more interested in seeing the rare than the common. And if you're shooting the commonplace, shoot from an uncommon angle: eye-level with a dog or looking down on a street scene.

Next, there's contrast. This means putting the very big next to the very small, the very strong next to the very fragile, the dark next to the light, and so on. A prime example of this principle is pattern-breaking. Imagine a photo where everyone in the stands of a tennis match is looking to the left—except one person who is looking to the right. That's contrast. Same thing works for color. Imagine a bright red flower in a field of green.

But where to put your subject? There are endless options, but a great rule is to avoid the middle. Too often people use the target in the center of the viewfinder as a bullseye when it should be just the opposite. Follow the "Rule of Thirds" and place the horizon, the person, or whatever your subject happens to be about one-third of the way in from the top, bottom, left, or right of the frame. When taking a close-up portrait of a face, place the eyes at the top third.

Shedding Light on the Subject

Learning photographic lighting techniques could easily demand a lifetime of practice, but here are a few simple tips that will dramatically improve your pictures.

First and foremost: Don't flash. The tiny built-in flash on your camera is the worst enemy of good photography. Because it's mounted so close to the lens, you get the red-eye effect that makes people look like they're possessed. Sure, you can use the special no-red-eye mode that sends out a disco strobe of flashes before the picture is actually taken, but this results in your subject looking stunned. A classic no-win situation.

Then there's the flash light itself: cold, shallow, and flat. Most on-camera flashes are limited to a range of 10 feet or so. This means you either put your subject against a wall and get an obnoxious halo shadow, or you stand them

By positioning this troupe of Tunisian dancers in the open shade, with indirect light reflecting on them from the white building and steps, you can create very flattering light that typically requires a studio setup to achieve. Depending on your camera's white balancing, you may need to correct the color slightly for the blue tones of the shadows.

away from any walls and your subject appears to be floating in a black void. Again, no win.

Shooting in low light is a problem, but shooting in direct sunlight is too. Direct mid-day sun creates harsh shadow lines on your subject, which can be effective with dramatic architectural studies but not very flattering on people. And the old trick of putting the sun behind your shoulder usually just results in pictures of people squinting. Ironically, if you absolutely have to take a picture in direct sunlight, be sure to use the flash (in fill-flash mode, if your camera supports it) to fill in the harsh shadows.

Oftentimes, the best place to shoot outdoors is known as "open shade." This is an unobstructed area in the shade where sunlight can reflect off surrounding buildings, walls, sidewalks, etc. This creates even, pleasing light. The best light, however, can always be found at dawn and dusk. This perfect light is what the professionals use, and the only thing that can get a supermodel out of bed before noon. But the peak moments are brief, so be prepared.

Tricking the Camera into Taking the Shot You Want

With today's automated cameras, many of the trickier aspects of photography have been taken out of your hands. While this does make getting a shot easier, it

These images illustrate the advantages of placing your subject (and horizon line/background object) away from the center of the frame. Using the "Rule of Thirds" results in much more visually engaging photographs.

can make getting the shot you want much harder.

A great example is a room with daylight flooding in from the windows. If you let the camera's auto-exposure handle matters, you'll end up with a dark room with glowing windows. Some higher-end digital cameras have manual override features that allow you to compensate for hot spots, but here's a simple technique that's faster and works on nearly all cameras: Before you take the picture, point the camera at a part of the room where there are no windows in the frame. Press the shutter halfway to get an exposure lock and hold it there, then pan back to the shot you want to take, and press the shutter com-

AUTO-EXPOSED LIGHTING

TRICKED LIGHTING

The camera's automated exposure is great for most situations, unless you have backlighting. In the first pic, the camera's light meter read the bright light of the window and exposed for the window, not the subject. A quick solution is to tilt the camera down, so the window's not in the frame, then get an exposure lock by pressing the shutter halfway. Now tilt back up to your original frame and take the shot.

pletely. Simple but effective. Just make sure the object you use for exposure-locking is roughly the same distance from the lens to avoid any focus issues.

Another common conundrum is the "person in front of the landmark." Here's the deal. For smaller objects, such as animals in a zoo, have the person get as close as possible to the background, then use the telephoto feature to zoom in as tight as possible. Back up to get everything in the frame. The telephoto effect will compress the person in the foreground with the background object. The opposite applies to larger background objects, such as Mount Rushmore. In these cases, you want to zoom the lens to the widest setting and have the person come close to the camera so they fill up either the right or left-hand third of the frame. Trust us, this works.

Beyond the "Auto" Settings

The great thing about the state of digital photography is that the editing programs themselves have evolved. The tedious tasks you most often need to perform have been automated, often to a single click of the mouse. And believe it or not, these Auto settings can be remarkably effective in a majority of cases—so if you're a digital photographer, don't reflexively snub your software's "Auto" options.

That said, when you do need to get "hands on" with your pictures, consider the following.

Many burgeoning photographers like the Variations tool in *Photoshop* and *Elements* (other programs have similar tools, but we'll limit ourselves to Adobe terminology for this section). This tool allows you to actually preview a bunch of editing options, such as color shifts, and allows you to set the intensity for these changes. This helps you learn how to visualize the possibilities for image correction, but it can also be tricky picking the right direction when all the choices appear side by side. One technique is to decide which correction you think you want, then look away at a normal photo (such as a poster or one in a magazine), then look directly back at your selection. This helps clear your eye—just like a sorbet might clear a gourmet's palate.

Once you're beyond the Variations tool, consider going straight to the Levels tool. At first, this interface may appear very foreign, but it's really just a linear, visual display of all the data intrinsic to an image. The data is graphed on an X-Y axis, and by adjusting different appropriate levels, you can manipulate color shifts, brightness, and contrast. It will take a bit of time to become familiar with the white-point, black-point, and mid-point sliders underneath the graph, but once you get the hang of it, control becomes intuitive. *Photoshop* also has a Curves tool, which is handy for quick contrast and brightness adjustments, but this amenity is sacrificed in *Elements*.

In terms of actually applying manual image adjustments, two pointers are in order. First, always work on a copy. Sometimes genius work just looks hokey the next day. Second, when applying an effect, use our "too-far-and-back" technique: Crank the settings until the image preview definitely looks wrong, then go back to the midpoint between "all wrong" and where you started. This is an easy way to teach yourself the moderation that's required to become a great image editor.

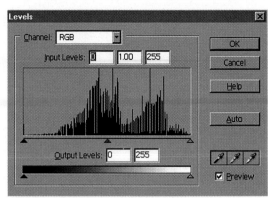

After you become comfortable with the automated tools provided by your image editing software, you'll want to try your hand at more ambitious manual corrections, such as Adobe's Levels tool. With a slide of the arrows below the image graph, you can control brightness, contrast, and color corrections with amazing accuracy.

Tools You Should Never Use

Not every tool available in the basic image editing interface serves a useful purpose, so let's just leave you with this: Stay away from gimmicky filters! You know the ones we're talking about: brush filters, distortion filters, stained glass filters, solarize filters, and (god forbid) lens flare filters. The list goes on and on. We know some of them can look kind of cool, and there's bound to be some instances where they're actually applicable. But in an effort to beat down visual clichés, you should make a promise to yourself to use each special effect filter just once in your lifetime. In magazine publishing the filters

If you want to completely disfigure *Maximum PC* contributing editor T. Liam McDonald, apply some wacky *Photoshop* filters to his photo. Just don't call it art.

are used every now and then, but rarely for actual photography. Instead, you're more likely to see the filters applied to logo treatments or background texture—visual devices that are often supposed to look surreal. ■

How To...

BURN YOUR
Videotapes TO DVD

Save your precious video memories before they're lost forever

MAXIMUM PC
TIME TO COMPLETION
03:00
HOURS   MINUTES

BY RICK POPKO

BIO:
Rick Popko is a former *Maximum PC* editor. He's currently the Managing Editor of Web Services at Pinnacle Systems, and in his free time, he's a filmmaker. His first feature, *Monsturd*, created with partner Dan West, was purchased by Blockbuster Video. Their second feature, tentatively titled *RetarDEAD* is currently in production. Rick can be reached at **Rick@4321films.com**

Did you know that analog videotape has a shelf life of approximately seven years? After that, the stock itself begins to deteriorate. If your tapes are that age or older, chances are you're going to begin seeing noticeable degradation in picture and audio quality. At first you may experience slight tracking problems, then grain and snow will be introduced to the picture, and ultimately the colors will bleed and fade altogether. Audio that sounded perfect when you first made the videotape will start to sound like it was recorded through an empty coffee can. If that isn't reason enough to transfer all of your old videos to DVD, we've got a few more.

9 MORE REASONS WHY IT'S A GOOD IDEA TO BACK UP YOUR MOVIES ONTO DVD:

▶ Blank bulk DVDs cost less than videotapes.
▶ DVDs are lighter, meaning they cost less to mail.

If you don't take the time to convert your old videotapes to DVD now, this is what could become of your home movies down the road.

▶ DVDs take up less shelf space.
▶ You can make perfect copies of your DVDs without any loss to picture quality.
▶ DVD media lasts longer than videotape (some brands allegedly last up to 50 years).
▶ You can build interactivity into your DVDs, allowing viewers to jump to any spot on the disc in moments.
▶ Unlike videotape, a DVD won't wear out easily if you play it a lot.
▶ Unlike videotape, a DVD won't get stuck in the player.
▶ Unlike videotape, a DVD isn't easy to record over.

Another benefit to transferring your videos to DVD is that once the video is on your computer, you can use a software video editor to turn your ho-hum home videos into exciting movies! A good software video editor lets you cut out all the boring parts, add titles, music, narration, special effects, and then author a DVD that will play in most consumer set top DVD players.

In this feature, we're going to explain how to back up your older analog videotapes (this includes VHS, S-VHS, 8mm, and Hi8) onto DVD using Pinnacle Systems' *Studio 8* and MovieBox USB. We're going to briefly explain the concept of digital video editing (how it works and why you want to do it), and then we'll delve into the process of creating a fully interactive DVD. All you need for this how-to is a reliable PC, a CD-R/RW or DVD-R/RW drive, a copy of Pinnacle Systems' *Studio 8*, and the proper analog-to-digital video converter. With that, let's get started.

Is Your PC is Up to the Task?

Digital video requires hefty system resources. You can get away with a 1GHz machine with 256MB RAM, but if you're going to do real-time MPEG-2 encoding (MPEG-2 is the video format used on DVDs) from a DV source, you'll want at least a 2GHz machine with 512MB RAM.

External real-time MPEG-2 encoders, such as Pinnacle's MovieBox USB, do all of the video processing in the box, so you can get away with lesser system specs. Also, digital video takes up a lot of hard disk space. If you're encoding real-time MPEG-2, then your bit rate will be pretty small (between 2 and 10mbits per second), but if you're encoding DV video (with a bit rate of 3.6MB per second), then you'll most likely want to invest in a second hard drive for video capture and playback. Hard drives are pretty inexpensive these days. For example, you can get a 120GB Western Digital for around $100—that's less than a dollar a GB!

Choose the Right Converter

**Pinnacle Systems'
USB MovieBox**

To back up your analog videos onto DVD, you're going to need an analog-to-digital video converter. Note: Some miniDV camcorders can convert analog video onto miniDV tape. If your camcorder can do this, then you can skip to Step 3.

Of the multitude of analog converters out there, 99 percent of them will fit in one of the following three category types:

TYPE 1: External device that converts analog video to a DV-compliant video stream that is fed into your computer's FireWire port.

TYPE 2: External device that converts analog video to an MPEG-1 or MPEG-2 video stream that is fed into your computer's USB-1 or USB-2 port.

TYPE 3: Internal PCI card that has analog (RCA and S-video) connectors and converts video to an M-JPEG AVI, a DV-compliant AVI, or MPEG-1 or MPEG-2 stream.

For this story, we looked at three products from Pinnacle Systems (MovieBox DV, MovieBox USB, and Studio Deluxe). Each product fits into one of the aforementioned category types and all three include the full version of Pinnacle's *Studio 8* editing software. Note: Before you decide on a solution, make sure your PC has the requisite port.

Ready, Set, Capture

At this point you should have the analog converter of your choosing and a copy of Pinnacle's *Studio 8*. Your analog camcorder (or VCR) should be attached to the converter and, if you're using an external converter, that converter should be attached to your PC's USB or FireWire port.

If you're not ready to make a commitment to a particular converter solution, you can still play along at home with the trial version of *Studio 8* software. You can use any MPEG-1 video you happen to have on your hard drive.

CONFIGURE YOUR SETUP OPTIONS
Upon launching the *Studio* app, enter Setup Options to set your video capture device and capture format (i.e., are you going to capture DV video or MPEG video?). Note: Setup options will differ slightly depending on the type of converter you're using. You can also set durations for transition effects and titles, and set your voice-over input source and recording quality.

From the Capture Source tab shown above, select which type of scene

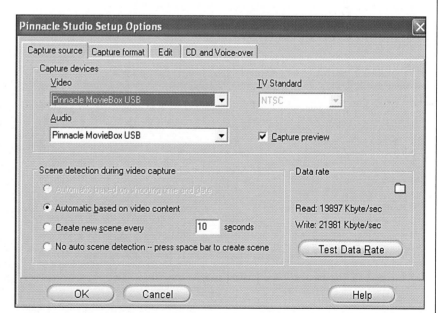

detection you'd like to use. If you choose "Automatic based on video content," the software analyzes your footage as it's being recorded to your hard drive. When you stop capture,

the software separates each scene and gives you a helpful visual icon of each shot. These icons can make it very easy when it comes time to edit your favorite clips together. You can also

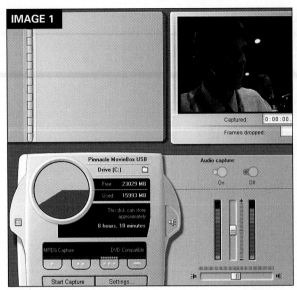

IMAGE 1

IMAGE 2

choose, "No auto scene detection," so your file is not broken up into individual scenes.

CAPTURING YOUR VIDEO

Begin playing your source video. Video should appear in the "video preview" window [image 1]. If you do not see the video, then something is not configured properly. Recheck your Capture Source settings and make sure you have the right input on the converter selected. When you get to a spot in the video that you'd like to capture, click the "Start Capture" button.

After you've captured all the video clips you want to use in your DVD project, click the Edit tab at the top of the screen [image 2]. This takes you to the video editing area of the application.

Your shots appear in the order you captured them in the Album folder. *Studio* lets you edit in three different modes, "storyboard," "timeline" and "text view." Try each one to see which you prefer (we're using "timeline" in image 2.) To change the editing mode, click on the View menu at the top of the screen, and select a different mode.

4 Edit Your Video

Editing video is the most exciting part of the whole DVD creation process. This is where you begin to craft your story. This is your opportunity to edit out all the bad takes and bloopers. And while you're at it, this is the perfect time to punch up the content. The editing interface is where you add fade-ins/outs, music and narration, special effects, and titles (as seen in the screenshot). You can view the results of your changes in the preview monitor (shown in previous step). When you've finished editing, you can do several things with your video. You can export your movie to any number of file formats including DV AVI, MPEG-1, MPEG-2, RealVideo, and Windows Media. Depending on the video converter you purchased, you may also be able to export your movie back to tape.

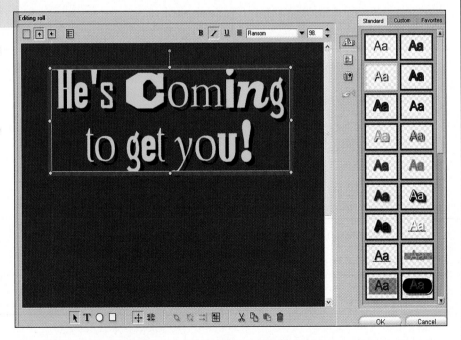

5 Build Your DVD

To begin building your DVD, click the "Show Menus" tab (the bottom left tab of the Album window). This opens all of the pre-built DVD menus available to you. Select a style that appeals to you and drag it to the beginning of your timeline. A pop-up window asks if you'd like *Studio* to create chapters at the start of each scene and if you would like to automatically return to the menu after each scene is finished playing. These choices are entirely up to you. If you're making a compendium of short films, then you'll probably want to go back to the main menu after you get to the end of each short. Do not select this if you just want to make chapter jumps for longer videos.

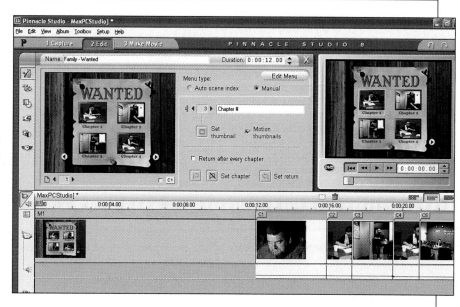

MODIFYING CHAPTER THUMBNAILS

After you've selected how you want your chapter marks inserted, you're ready to customize your chapter thumbnails. The thumbnail customization window should open automatically, but if it doesn't (or you've closed it accidentally), double-click the menu you've dropped onto your timeline. *Studio* uses the first frame in each of your clips as a thumbnail, however, that might not be the best reference for a user. Maybe you faded in from black, or maybe you're beginning your shot on the back

of someone's head. To fix a thumbnail reference, click the chapter thumbnail you want to change in the preview window on the right. The video (within that chapter) will play. When you see a good reference image, click the "set thumbnail" button. Continue this process with all of your chapters until you're happy with your selection of thumbnails. If you're not happy with a chapter point on your timeline, place your cursor over it, select it, right-click and delete it. You can add chapters by clicking on a scene in the timeline, right-clicking and select-

ing "Set chapter."

To create a motion chapter thumbnail, select "Motion thumbnails." You will need to render the menu in order to see the motion thumbnails in action. If you don't see a progress bar at the top of your timeline (indicating that the menu is being rendered), then you need to enable background rendering. To do this, click the Setup menu at the top of the screen, select Edit, then select "Render as a background task."

Once you're happy with your menu, you're ready to burn a disc.

6 Burn Your DVD

To burn a disc, click the Make Movie tab at the top of the screen. Select the Disc tab at the lower left of the Make Movie window. To preview/test the interactivity of your movie before you burn it to disc, click the "DVD" logo in the lower left-hand side of the preview monitor [image 1]. If everything looks good, then click the Settings button in the upper right-hand corner of the Make Movie window, select your output format (either VideoCD, S-VCD, or DVD). In Settings select the drive and media you're going to write to, and click OK [image 2].

Back in the Make Movie window click the green "Create disc..." button. At this point your video clips will be rendered, which may take a few moments depend-

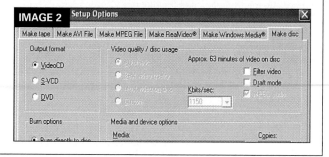

ing on the length of your video and the number of effects you added in the editing process, and then burned to disc.

Be aware that not all set-top DVD players work with recordable DVDs.

Advanced DVD Creation

Now that you know the basics of creating and burning an interactive DVD, we're going to tell you how to spice up your movies even more. For example, you may want to have an intro movie play before the viewer gets to the DVD menu (like those FBI warnings you get on all studio released DVDs). You might also want to create a menu from scratch, add a motion background, and import your own music to loop as long as the menu is displayed onscreen. Read on.

CREATE A PRELUDE TO THE MENU

If you'd like a video or still image to appear before a viewer gets to your menu, you'll need to import the content you want to use into your Album. For

video, click the "folder" icon on the left side of the album and import the desired video. For a still image, click the "camera" icon to import the image you want to use.

From the album, click and drag the video or image to your timeline and insert it before the menu. If it's a still image, you can stretch it to last as long as you'd like by clicking the right-hand side of the image and dragging it to the left or right. Note: Before importing your image, be mindful of its size (resolution). If you're making a DVD, you'll want the image to be 720x480. If you're creating a VCD or S-VCD, you'll want the image to be 320x240.

CUSTOM MENUS

If you don't like the pre-built menu templates that are included with *Studio*, create your own. To do this, click the Edit Menu button in the Menu Interface.

To get to the Menu Interface screen, double-click the menu that's in your timeline.

From the menu editor, you can rename your chapters using the text tool, import your own background (still or motion), change the buttons and frames, and import new still images into your chapter thumbnails. To create a motion background, click the "background" icon (the little picture of the cactus and sun), click the "folder" icon, and open the video clip that you'd like to loop in the background.

CREATE SUBMENUS

If you want to get really creative, you can create submenus within your DVD. For example, from the main menu you may want to give people the option of watching your movie, or viewing all of the bloopers that you cut from the flick.

To create a submenu, click the Show Menus tab (the bottom tab on the left-side of the album window. Grab the second menu you want to use (or create your own—see instructions above), and drag

and drop it on your timeline to the right of your first menu. Next, double-click the first menu on your timeline (this brings up the menu editor), then click and drag the second menu from your timeline to the menu-editor preview window and drop it in the chapter button of your choosing.

ADD MUSIC

To add your own music to a menu, click the "speaker" icon on the left side of the album window, then click the "folder" icon towards the top of the window and import the music clip that you'd like to play while people are soaking up your

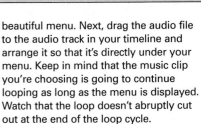

beautiful menu. Next, drag the audio file to the audio track in your timeline and arrange it so that it's directly under your menu. Keep in mind that the music clip you're choosing is going to continue looping as long as the menu is displayed. Watch that the loop doesn't abruptly cut out at the end of the loop cycle.

As a time-savings feature, *Studio 8* includes a utility called SmartSound that automatically generates music to fit any required clip length. To use this feature, click the "speaker" icon in the left corner of your timeline, and then click the "notes" icon. From the SmartSound window you can choose from a number of different styles of music, preview the selection, and send then send to your timeline. To apply music to your menu, select the menu in your timeline, select the Style, Song, and Version, and click the "Add to Movie" button. The song will be auto-

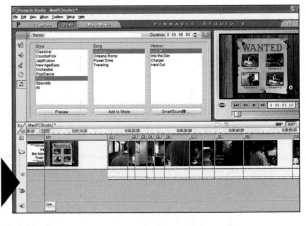

matically added to the timeline.

There you have it: The tools you need to make your own DVD titles look as good (if not better) than most discs coming out of Hollywood today. ■

MAKE
Your OWN DVD

Don't sweat it, it's easier than you think

Now that recordable DVD drives cost under $200, there's no longer any reason to fumble around with pathetic videotapes. In this how-to, we'll show you how to create a DVD-Video out of your own analog or digital footage that can be played on most set-top DVD players and PC DVD-ROM drives.

Luckily, the software that comes with most DVD burners handles most of the hard work, such as compressing your video and creating the proper file structure for the disc. This leaves you more time to do what you've always wanted to do—direct!

The Essentials

In order to create your own DVD, you'll need a DVD burner, the appropriate type of recordable media and content creation software. (Check your drive's manual for specific media recommendations.) If you're going to be sharing your DVD with others, keep in mind that the write-once formats (DVD-R and DVD+R) and far more compatible with set-top players than the rewriteable formats (DVD-RW and DVD+RW).

If you have a FireWire-equipped DV camera, you can plug it into your PC and import the footage directly into your video-editing or DVD-authoring application. But if you want to archive footage from analog sources—such as videotapes or an analog camcorder—you'll need a video-capture card that converts the analog signal to a PC-friendly digital signal. For our project, we used Dazzle's Digital Video Creator II video capture kit, which supports real-time compression of video to the DVD-compliant MPEG-2 standard and is ideal for DVD-Video.

For DVD mastering, we used MyDVD 5.0 (www.sonic.com), a capable and easy-to-use application bundled with many consumer DVD burners.

1 Cinematography

We used the Dazzle capture kit to digitize footage of our favorite pooches, Lucy and Greta, from a Sony Hi-8 Handycam. The DVCII provides preset recording templates for sending video to specific formats. In our case, we selected DVD/MPEG-2, which is the highest-quality setting for creating DVD-Video-compliant video.

2 The Director's Chair

It's time to fire up MyDVD 5.0. At the introductory screen, select "Create or Modify a DVD-Video Project." Again, if you have a FireWire-equipped DV camera, you can record directly to DVD from within MyDVD by selecting "Transfer Video Direct-to-DVD," but you won't be able to customize the menus or edit footage, other than at the beginning or end of clips. In our case, we knew we'd need to edit more extensively—for example, Lucy's embarrassing bathroom break in the middle of one take—using Dazzle's video-editing capabilities.

3 Preproduction

After selecting "Create or Modify a DVD-Video Project," you'll be presented with the DVD-authoring equivalent of a blank canvas. Don't worry about customizing the template just yet—you can modify your work later with different fonts, backgrounds, and button styles after you've imported your video.

4 Making Sub Menus

Of course, there were a number of gripping sequences that didn't make it into our final cut, so we're going to let viewers in on some of the behind-the-scenes action by dropping in a menu button to access these other clips. To do this, we clicked "Add Sub-Menu" on the toolbar to the left, and MyDVD created a menu button that we renamed "outtakes." We just double-clicked the new menu button to access the new, blank menu, and then followed the same procedure as above to add more video to this submenu. To return to the first screen, just click on the "Home" icon in the DVD display window.

5 Set Dressing

Now you can tailor the video by editing the menu style. Click on the "Edit Style" button on the toolbar at the top of the window. Here's where you'll find the options to switch your menu to a different theme, and to customize these themes with your own fonts, background image, background music (MP3s encoded with a constant bitrate are OK), and even the option to animate your menu buttons with looping video from your own footage! The only things you cannot do are move the button positions off the "grid" alignment and change the appearance of the sub-menu button..

6 Dress Rehearsal

Now we want to see how our disc will work in a DVD-ROM drive or set-top player. MyDVD lets you audition discs before they're burned to media by clicking "Preview." A remote control pops up and you can click anywhere on the screen, just as you could with a software DVD player. Or, to emulate the set-top experience, use the remote-control-style buttons at the bottom of the window. This way, you can confirm that menus behave the way you want them to, and that your titles are correct. If not, the project is still fully editable at this stage, so feel free to delete buttons, add menus, and tweak the style to the rewriteable media.

7 The Final Cut

When you're happy with the results you've auditioned within MyDVD, exit the preview by clicking the "Stop" button at the bottom of the window. Then click the "Burn" button and save your project to your hard drive (this allows you to edit or update the project later, or simply to reuse your edited style). Click "OK" in the "Make Disc Setup" dialog, and MyDVD will begin the process of building your menus, transcoding the video into the proper format and burning the project to disc.

Epilogue

Although MyDVD is extremely easy to use from start to finish, it's somewhat light on features (particularly video editing) and customization (you can't move the positions of menu buttons, for example). So once you get the hang of the process of capturing and encoding your footage, consider trading up to a more full-featured product, like Adobe's excellent DVD-authoring app, Encore DVD ($550, www.adobe.com). High-end authoring packages will allow you to create menu interfaces that are indistinguishable from professional products. How professional the movies themselves are, well, that's up to you.

How To...

MAKE A FEATURE FILM ON YOUR PC

All you need is talent, a good PC, basic DV equipment, and a bunch of willing friends

BY RICK POPKO

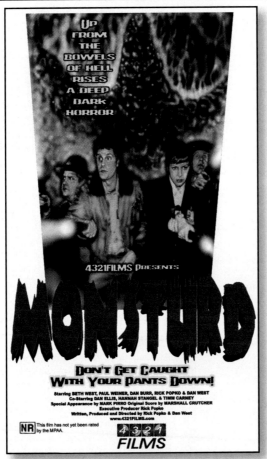

UP
FROM
THE
BOWELS
OF HELL
RISES
A DEEP
DARK
HORROR

4321FILMS PRESENTS

MONSTURD

DON'T GET CAUGHT
WITH YOUR PANTS DOWN!

Starring BETH WEST, PAUL WEINER, DAN BURR, RICK POPKO & DAN WEST
Co-Starring DAN ELLIS, HANNAH STANGEL & TIMM CARNEY
Special Appearance by MARK PIRRO Original Score by MARSHALL CRUTCHER
Executive Producer Rick Popko
Written, Produced and Directed by Rick Popko & Dan West
www.4321FILMS.com

NR This film has not yet been rated by the MPAA.

4321 FILMS

Rick's film even has a pro-caliber VHS label.

Digital video has evolved to the point where anyone with a decent DV camcorder, a fast computer, a good script, and a handful of friends (who'll act for free) can make a feature film for practically nothing. That's right: A full-length feature film. Don't believe me? Well, my friends and I just did it. It's called *Monsturd* (yes, it's about what you think it's about!).

Monsturd was shot with Canon's GL-1 DV cam (it can be found for about $2,000), and edited on a 500MHz Micron rig with 250MB RAM (which cost $1,500 two and a half years ago). We used a Pinnacle Systems DV500Plus editing package ($650), which includes the full version of Adobe *Premiere*. Our hard drive was a 7200rpm, 100GB Western Digital ($200). Our production budget (aside from the aforementioned gear) included tape stock, costumes, props, beer, some food, and a one-day cop car rental—all for just about $3,000.

Locations: $0. Actors: $0. Permits: $0. Insurance: $0.

So you see, with the tools at your disposal today, you *can* make a movie. Now we're going to walk you through the process...

Step One: The Script

Before you recruit all your friends and rush headlong into a feature-length project, you'll need a script. There are two ways to get your hands on one. You can (A) write one yourself, or (B) option one from someone else. If you choose A and have never written a screenplay before, there are several books that can get you started. Word on the street is that Syd Field is the man most people turn to for advice on the subject of screenwriting. See www.sydfield.com for more info on his books. When you're ready to type it out, spend the extra dough on a screenplay formatting app. It'll make your life a lot easier. We used *Final Draft* (www.finaldraft.com) and were very happy with its features and functionality. Keep in mind that one page of formatted script equals approximately one minute of film time, so a 90-page script would equal an hour and a half.

If you're going to option a script from someone else, you'll need a limited license agreement (meaning you purchase the rights to someone's script for a predetermined period of time), but there are inexpensive workarounds. For instance, you could try to solicit up-and-coming screenwriters, or you could look for an undiscovered talent on Francis Coppola's Zoetrope Screenwriter web site (www.zoetrope.com).

Step Two: Cast and Crew

■ ACTORS

Now that you've got a script, it's time to assemble your cast and buy your gear. Luckily for us, we have a wide circle of friends who are hams and don't mind acting for free. If you're not so fortunate,

No, the two hams above aren't "real" actors. They're former *Maximum PC* editor Brad Dosland (top) and current senior editor Gordon Mah Ung (bottom)! Secret bonus info: Dosland turns into poo.

post a flyer at your local community college's drama department, take out a small classified ad in your local paper, talk to the barista at your neighborhood Starbucks, or join some Internet independent filmmaker forums, such as www.indieclub.com. You'll be surprised how many people will jump at the chance to be in a movie (even if it doesn't pay).

■ EQUIPMENT

When buying a DV cam, make sure it has at least three CCDs (charge-coupled devices). Each CCD is responsible for recording each color (red, green, and blue) separately. Cheaper camcorders have just one CCD. A three CCD camera takes a richer picture, and captures sharper details. Plus, if you plan on selling your movie to a distributor, you're going to want the highest-quality picture you can get. Bottom line: If you're making a feature film, you can't settle for a cheapie.

We chose Canon's GL-1 because it can shoot in what is called "Frame" mode (i.e., progressive mode), meaning the camera can record 30 frames per second (non-interlaced). Most camcorders shoot 30 frames per second *interlaced*, meaning that each frame is made up of two fields. Interlaced video gives you a clearer, smoother picture;

With three CCDs the GL-1 is a decent choice. Just make sure to shoot in "frame" mode.

however, it looks like video, and we wanted to avoid that. "Frame" mode makes your video more film-like. (Note: Since the filming of *Monsturd*, Canon Canon developed and released a second-generation camcorder called the GL-2).

Along with a good camcorder, you'll want to purchase a good microphone—never use a camcorder's built-in mic (oftentimes a camera's onboard mic will pick up camera motor hum as the tape's recording). We bought a $300 Audio-Technica AT835b shotgun from B & H Photo (www.bhphotovideo.com). A shotgun mic is directional, meaning you have to point it directly at an actor to pick up his or her voice, thus audio from behind the mic will not be audible. If your camcorder doesn't have an XLR mic input jack, you'll need an XLR-to-1/8-inch adapter plug.

Some other wise investments are a solid tripod, some lights (we bought three el cheapo halogens for $20 a piece from Home Depot, and they worked great for the duration of our shoot), and some gels (for interesting lighting effects). There's just one more thing every filmmaker should have in his or her arsenal: a smoke machine. We used the smoke machine for at least 15 different shots in *Monsturd*. You can usually pick up a decent one from your local head shop for $110 (get a couple bottles of liquid smoke, too).

You'll also need a ton of miniDV tapes. MiniDV tapes are typically 60 minutes each in SP mode; about 90 in LP mode. LP mode is not advised, however. Because you're running the tape over the head more slowly, if you hit an anomaly on the tape stock, you're going to get severe audio and video dropouts. DV tapes cost about $5 each if you buy in bulk from an online retailer or Costco, and about $8 from your local drug store. Stay with the same brand throughout the shoot. It's been said that mixing tape stocks can clog your camcorder's heads.

Step Three: The Shoot

■ SCHEDULING

OK, so you've got your script, your cast, and your gear. You're ready to start shooting. A caveat about using volunteer actors: You'll have to work around their schedules, not the other way around. And don't count on anyone memorizing his or her lines. Remember, they're doing you a favor. Fortunately, because DV tape stock is so cheap, you can feed an actor a line while you're filming and have it parroted back the way you'd like it. If he doesn't get it right the first time, try again. You can keep the tape rolling until the line is voiced to your satisfaction. That's what we did for most of our shoot. The downside to this approach is having to watch hours and hours of actors saying the same stupid line over and over and over again!

■ SECURING LOCATIONS

Whenever possible, think big, meaning get a cool exterior shot before you cut to the inside of a room. Try to not film all your scenes indoors (your viewers will start feeling claustrophobic).

Here's a secret that not a lot of filmmakers know: There are many people

HELPFUL HINTS

■ Be prepared for the time commitment. Unless you and your actors can work on the film full-time, it's going to take awhile. *Monsturd* was two years in the making (including editing).

■ When it comes to editing, the best way to learn what's possible is to watch lots of movies, then practice, practice, practice.

■ Avoid making scenes more than a minute and a half in length.

■ Keep your shots and your scenes interesting. If you have a slow scene, figure out some way to make it compelling: a strange character, a non sequitur, something that makes the viewer think, "huh?"

out there who are willing to help you for free in exchange for a screen credit. We were able to get footage of a helicopter taking off from an airstrip because we promised the owner of the helicopter a plug for his company in the end credits. In fact, we got a lot of good locations using that technique.

■ INSURANCE

If you've got a real film company and a real budget, then get insurance, because if someone gets hurt on your shoot, you can (and will) be personally liable. My partner and I were broke when we started our movie, so we didn't have much to lose. Still, it helps to play it safe. Don't ever put your actors in a life-threatening

situation. If you need someone to drive a car off a cliff, hire a stuntman for the day, or drive off the cliff yourself.

■ PERMITS

Professional Hollywood productions have to secure permits to film in public places. Permits cost money—anywhere from a few hundred dollars a day to several thousand, depending on the level of your production (i.e., will you be closing off streets, diverting traffic, blowing up things?).

Did we get permits to film *Monsturd*? Heck no! Basically, the worst thing that can happen if you get caught filming on the city street with a cast and crew is that the police will ask for your permit. If you can't provide one, they'll ask you to break down your equipment and move along. Word of advice: If you're going to eschew permits, don't do anything that's going to call a lot of attention to yourself. Also, don't linger for too long. Get in, get your shot, break it down, and get out of there fast! If you're filming the outside of a business, get permission from the business to use it as an exterior. It's OK to show a business in passing, as long as you don't focus on it for more than a moment.

■ RELEASE FORMS

Before yelling "action," make all your actors sign release forms. This will protect you should your film make a million dollars and one of your actors comes forward and says, "Hey, I never wanted to be in your movie!" He or she can then sue you. A release form says it's OK to use an actor's name and likeness in the movie. Generic release forms are readily available on the Internet; just try searching Google. (You may have to modify them to fit your production.)

■ PRE-STRIPING TAPES

Tape striping is a technical term for laying down time code on your digital video tape. Time code works similarly to the counter on a cassette deck, but uses realtime increments instead of simply ticking off sequential numbers. So, for example, if you're looking for a shot that's 30 minutes into one of your DV tapes, you'd simply put the tape into your camcorder and forward it to the 30 minute mark.

True, even without pre-striping, a camcorder will lay down time code any time you hit Record; however, if you were to stop recording, eject the tape, then put it back in your camcorder, the camera will think it's a new tape, and the time code that's generated will restart at zero.

When your time code gets broken like that it's hard to find the shots you're looking for. To stripe your tape, put a blank miniDV tape in your camcorder, put the camcorder's lens cap on, and record for the duration of the tape. When you're done, rewind the tape and you're ready to go. You now have time code on your tape and it won't get broken (even if you eject the tape from the camcorder).

Step Four: Editing

■ THE CAPTURE CARD

The only equipment you need for editing is: a good PC, an OHCI-compliant FireWire card, at least 512MB RAM, an extra hard drive (for storing and playing back your captured video), and a software editor. There's a lot of speculation on the Internet as to why some FireWire cards are $1,000 and some are just $30. The difference comes down to hardware acceleration and software bundle. A cheap FireWire card simply acts as a transport mechanism, dragging data from your camcorder to your computer's hard drive. But a $500 to $1,000 capture board will have extra chips that allow you to view realtime transitions and effects on your TV screen while you edit. Less expensive editing packages force you to render all effects and transitions before viewing, which can be a cumbersome process, especially with a feature-length project. As a general rule, the more a FireWire card costs, the more realtime effects you can expect.

We edited *Monsturd* on a 500MHz PC using Pinnacle Systems' DV500Plus capture card and Adobe *Premiere* editing software. The DV500 is one of the few realtime hardware cards out there that can use more than one software editor. In fact, you can buy the DV500 with Pinnacle's *Edition DV* software as well.

If you're on a budget, you can buy a more consumer-oriented package such as Pinnacle's Studio DV version 8 package, which, for $130 comes with an OHCI-compliant FireWire card and the *Studio 8* editing software. Whatever software you choose, read the box carefully. Some consumer software says realtime "previews" on the outside of the box. What that means is that you can drop a cross dissolve between two video tracks and see the effect in realtime on your computer monitor, not on your TV. Big difference. You can't always gauge how things are going to look between the two. This is especially true when you're doing color adjustments.

A couple things to keep in mind before buying a FireWire card: You'll get a better

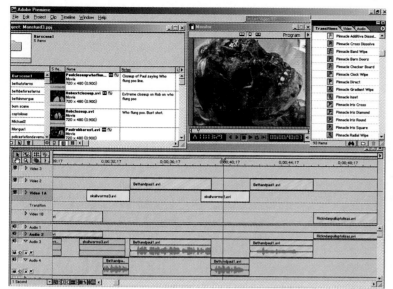

Adobe *Premiere* provides all the tools you'll need to meld your video and audio into a single, cohesive unit. Of course, you'll still need editing talent!

deal if you buy the FireWire card and the editing software together as a bundle. And most video editing software companies offer a free demo/30-day trial version you can download or order as a CD. Read reviews and see what others are saying about the software out there.

■ LOGGING CLIPS

Before you dump all your raw footage into your hard drive, you're going to want to go through all your tapes and log them. This is where time code comes into play. Put a DV tape in your camcorder and play the whole thing back from the beginning of the tape. You should have a text doc open to jot down every shot and its time code. If you find a particular shot that you know you'll use, note that as well. After you've logged all your shots you should know where everything is on all of your tapes. You're now ready to capture.

■ CAPTURING CLIPS

Capturing is the process of recording material from your camcorder to your computer's hard drive. Capture only what you need. DV takes up a ton of hard drive space (3.6MB per second, to be exact). So don't just dump the entire contents of your miniDV tape to your hard drive, or you're going to fill it up fast (and it's a pain in the neck to go back and delete what you don't need).

■ MUSIC

We investigated how much it would cost to use a song by Sisters of Mercy on a previous film we were making. BMG said it would be $2,500 for the song rights for the first 1,000 or so tapes, then

Yes, this would be the Monsturd.

5 cents for every copy thereafter. That didn't include fees to the band (should they have wanted any) or permission from the band to use the song. Whatever you do, don't steal the music. You'll get a cease-and-desist order and you'll be charged for using the copyrighted song in question. There is a "fair use" clause that lets you use some recorded music legitimately, but there are rules. The song can't play for more than 10 seconds, and it can't be the focal point of the scene (it can be used only as background). You really shouldn't have to pay for music up front anyway. There are thousands of talented musicians and bands who are eager to help out in exchange for a credit, or a cut of the back end. For *Monsturd*, we went with Emmy Award winning composer Marshall Crutcher, who not only scored the film, but also did our audio mix. Marshall was kind enough to work for nothing in exchange for 10 percent of the film's profits. He would normally charge $90,000 for the amount of work he did for us.

■ BACKUP

Buy an extra 100GB hard drive to back

up your project files and video clips. One in 100 hard drives crashes unexpectedly, and Murphy's Law says it's going to be yours. Don't take any chances. We didn't back up our movie until three months after we started editing. Looking back, that was very stupid. If our hard drive had crashed, we would've lost three months of editing and had to start all over again.

Step Five: The Master Copy

Once you've completed all your editing chores (a time-consuming artistic process best left for another story), you should have your entire movie on one timeline. You're now ready to lay master copies to miniDV or DVCAM tape.

If you've shot a feature that's 90 minutes or less, the only way you're going to squeeze it onto a 60-minute tape is to record in EP mode (just remember, if you hit a glitch in the tape, you may lose bits of audio and video). MiniDV can work for your own master tape, but no distributor will accept it. We ended up renting a DVCAM deck from our local photo-supply store for $95 a day, plus tapes. (DVCAM tapes are roughly $30 a piece. They're more robust than miniDV tape stock and come in lengths longer than an hour.) You'll want to make at least three master DVCAM tapes. (You never know when your house might burn down.) It's a good idea to give one of your extra copies to your parents or a trusted friend. Now you're ready to find a distributor! ■

Rick Popko is a former Maximum PC *editor. Since 1985, he's written 10 feature-length screenplays, one of which was co-written with Dan West, and optioned by Francis Coppola. Popko and West are currently working on a feature tentatively titled* The Blockheads in: Mask of the Weenie Wagger. *Rick can be reached at rick@4321films.com.*

How To...

MAKE MP3s

LIKE A MASTER AUDIO TECHNICIAN

Only newbies create MP3s with a single mouse click. Here's everything you need to know about ripping and encoding digital music like a true PC power-user

BY LOGAN DECKER

If you're the type who brings a portable MP3 player to the gym just to counter the excruciating boredom of a cardio workout, then the MP3 creation software that came with your player is fine. After all, how good can any music sound over the din of a Stairmaster? Just as long as you're encoding at 128kbps and using an optical drive that's capable of digital audio extraction (in other words, virtually any brand-name drive made in the last several years), you'll find nothing to complain about.

But if you want your MP3s to sound as good on your badass stereo system as they do on your solid-state player, you'll need to do more than just reach beyond the 128kbps bitrate minimum. You'll need power-user tools to get the most accurate digital audio extraction, and a high-end encoder that gives you total control over your MP3 compression. The good news is that the software you need is available for free online. First up, audio extraction from mass-produced music CDs. After that, we'll get into the fine details of precision MP3 encoding.

What you'll need:

CD media

Optical drive with C2 error capability

SOFTWARE: Exact Audio Copy, LAME, RazorLAME

Step 1: Extracting Every Last Drop

Your best defense against extraction errors is an optical drive with good hardware error-correction—specifically a drive that can report C2 error information to your PC. When data is obscured (oftentimes due to a scratch or smudge on your audio CD's surface), an optical drive must compensate by replacing the error with a "best guess" of what belongs there. C1 was the first error-correction scheme; it fills in missing data based on the data that's directly before and after the error. C2 error correction performs an analysis similar to C1 error correction, but across many interleaved frames instead of within just one frame. This makes C2 capable of more accurate data correction.

Our favorite burner is Plextor's 52/32/52A, closely followed by Lite-On's SOHR-5238S (also 52/32/52), both of which feature buffer underrun protection. When ripping from an audio CD that we mangled with scissors, Plextor's drive finished the task just seconds faster than the Lite-On, although both managed to correct all the audible errors. Plextor also optimized its circuits for cleaner power and went with a black CD tray to absorb laser light. It's difficult to discern whether these features actually improve CD ripping, but Plextor says they reduce error rates overall.

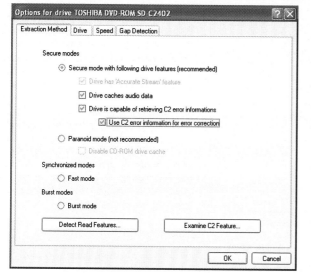

Step 2: Exact Audio Copy

Even if you're using an old 16x burner that doesn't extract every digital bit correctly, you can still get high-quality results using a program called *Exact Audio Copy* (www.exactaudiocopy.de). During the install, you'll be prompted to insert an audio CD to test the features of your drive. After the testing is finished, you'll be offered the option of selecting Beginner or Advanced mode. The Advanced options are really advanced, and you're likely to be paralyzed by the astounding number of tech terms and strange settings. There will be plenty of time for experimentation later, so select Beginner mode for now.

It's time to drop in the CD containing the audio you want to extract. Go to EAC > Drive Options. Make sure the Secure mode is checked (it's under the Extraction Method tab). This allows *EAC* to receive information from your drive's advanced error-correction hardware (assuming it's capable of reporting it). Make sure all the boxes you see in the screenshot (to the left) are checked if they're available. Leave the other options alone.

Step 3: And… Action!

Now we're ready to rip. Highlight the tracks you want to extract in the main window, then go to Action > Copy selected tracks, and in the dialog box specify what folder you want the tracks placed in. Don't touch the filename area, even though it says "Filename will be ignored." This advisory is a little misleading: If you don't enter a filename, it will use the track names you see in the main window.

The first thing you'll notice about *EAC* is that it's slow. In fact, extracting a heavily damaged CD can take hours, especially if your hardware has poor error correction. But we're going for quality, not speed. The process is sluggish because *EAC* reads each block a minimum of 16 times, and of those reads, eight must match exactly. It will read and reread your disc, essentially scrubbing the CD for accurate data, until it gets uniform results. If it cannot read the block correctly, then the software will do its best to correct the error, and will report to you which track had a "suspicious position." You can then listen to the track yourself to determine if the error resulted in an audible defect (which often won't be the case).

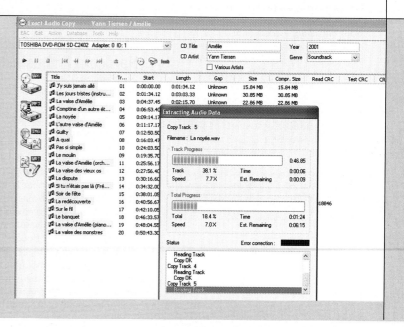

This is what you will face if you want to use the DOS-based *LAME* executable on its own. Command line switches…it's not pretty.

Just drag your files—even folders—onto the window, and *RazorLAME* queues them up for you.

Step 4: Put the Squeeze On

Now that you've mastered extraction, you'll want to compress your resulting WAV files in a way that squeezes file sizes down to manageable proportions, with as little negative effect on sound quality as possible. All snooty audiophiles agree that the very best compressor/encoder is *LAME*, a free piece of software that stands for "LAME Ain't an MP3 Encoder." Of course, it really *is* an MP3 encoder, but when it was first released, it couldn't produce MP3 streams. Long story. Anyway, *LAME* on its own is an extremely complicated command line-based executable. If you don't mind entering a lot of text in a DOS box with handfuls of simultaneous switches, go for it. We, however, prefer to pair it up with the friendly GUI front-end called *RazorLAME*.

If the one-click encoder that came with your portable MP3 player is akin to *Microsoft Paint*, then the *LAME/RazorLAME* combination is the equivalent of Adobe *Photoshop*. You can jump in right away and do high-quality encoding without much difficulty, but rest assured, a description of all available sound-tweaking options could fill an entire book.

> Download the latest versions of the LAME encoder executable from www.hot.ee/smpman/mp3/ and the RazorLAME front end from www.dors.de/razorlame/docs.php.

RazorLAME setup is a piece of cake. Just extract the contents of the ZIP file you downloaded into its own folder, and drop the LAME executable into the same folder.

Step 5: Decompression

First, decompress the RazorLAME file into its own folder. There's no install routine, so put it wherever you want. Now open the *LAME* encoder zip file and extract LAME.exe to the same folder (all the other files are administrative documents). Launch the *RazorLAME* executable. At this point, you could easily drag your audio files right into the window and hit Encode. This is what's so great about *RazorLAME*—it takes a command line program and let's you start working right away without touching your keyboard. But we want to customize our settings for MP3 files that will be rendered in absolute high-fidelity on the best stereo equipment….

The "Lame Options" at the bottom of the screen shows you which command line switches have been activated by your preferences.

Step 6: High-End Settings for Hardcore Enthusiasts

Go to Edit > LAME Options. Here you'll see the familiar bitrate setting. We're going to pull the slider to the right for 256kbps recording. We honestly can't tell the difference between 256kbps and the maximum rate of 320kbps, but if we were encoding classical music with lots of delicate strings, we'd probably default to 320kbps. "Joint Stereo" is the stereo mode by default. Unless you're encoding at 128kbps or below, change this to "Stereo." Joint stereo discards redundant information between the left and right channels. You won't notice the difference at low bitrates, but at higher ones you might begin to notice a swooshing flange effect. (You've probably already noticed this in many crappy MP3 files you've downloaded—well, joint stereo is the culprit.)

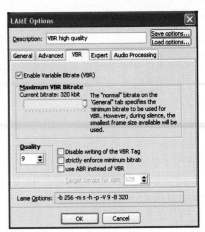

VBR can give you better results than CBR, often at lower file sizes, but may not be compatible with older MP3 players.

Step 7: VBR—Maybe

Now go to the Advanced tab, and under Optimization select "Quality." Do not check "Delete source file after processing" (if your PC hangs during the encoding process, or if you don't like the results, your original files will be toast). If you want, you can select the VBR tab to encode at variable bitrates. In this mode, pauses and silences are encoded at very low bitrates, and complex passages are encoded at the maximum bitrate. Please note that some MP3 hardware players still choke on VBR-encoded MP3s, so we're going to emphasize compatibility for now. Save your options by giving them a descriptive title and clicking "Save options" so you can duplicate the results later without having to memorize all the settings.

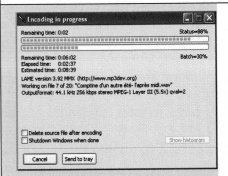

Step 8: Making Music

Now, all you have to do is drag your files (or folders) into the *RazorLAME* window, press Encode, and the program immediately begins grinding out your MP3s. On a slow P-III system, the process could take a long time. But a quick A/B test between your old and new files on a quality stereo system should prove that it's time well spent.

As an added bonus, if *RazorLAME's* status bar indicates that the process is going to take hours, you can select "Shutdown Windows when done" (see screenshot)—even during the encoding process. ∎

TURN YOUR
PC INTO A Rock N' Roll RECORDING STUDIO

Are you ready to rock? If the answer is "yes," we're going to show you how to connect your "axe" to your PC. Once hooked up, you'll be able to "lay down tracks" to your heart's content, providing you have enough hard drive space and the chops to make it worth saving. Let's rock!

PC RECORDING BASICS

First off, note that you cannot simply connect your guitar to the back of your soundcard. The signal needs to be boosted by an amplifier or pre-amplifier to what is called "line level." The definition of line level is that it's the standard voltage level accepted by an amplifier, mixer or recording device. The signal will not become distorted if it is within this line level tolerance.

Most preamps and some amplifiers offer a line level output, meaning you can run a cable from the amp or preamp into your soundcard, but do not confuse "line level output" with "speaker output." A lot of less expensive amps offer speaker output so that you can send your guitar tone to a set of speakers, but if you plug this into the delicate "line level" input of your soundcard you could fry the soundcard or worse, the motherboard that it is attached to as well. On amplifiers that have the appropriate output, it is simply labeled "line out."

What you'll need:

> A guitar
> A preamp (effects pedal, etc)*
> Soundcard with line level input or Microphone input
> A 1/4" to 1/8" minijack cable *
> Recording software

* This is dependent on your setup.

METHOD 2: USING A PREAMP OR EFFECTS BOX

One way to kill two birds with one stone is to send the signal into a preamp/effects box with a line level output. This accomplishes the task of letting you tweak your tone while sending the signal in the proper format to the soundcard. These boxes sit in between your guitar and soundcard, processing the signal and sending it along its way for the soundcard to pick up. When shopping for one of these units, the key consideration is what kind of effects you are looking for as well as price.

Most soundcards offer an analog in port for plugging in a microphone.

Let's Jam!

METHOD 1: RECORDING FROM A MICROPHONE

If you currently play through an amplifier, there are two ways to get the sound to your PC. One way is to connect a microphone to your soundcard's Mic in port and then place the microphone in front of your amplifier. The benefit of this approach is it is relatively affordable since microphones are rather inexpensive. This is also a good route if you've spent years tweaking your amp's tone to the point where it's perfect and don't want to bother with reconfiguring your tone via a new preamp or effects box. The downside is the mic could pick up ambient noise in your recording area, which will have to be edited out via software, adding complexity and additional expense to your project.

Recording your amp's output with a mic is an easy way to record with your PC.

METHOD 3: THE BEST OF BOTH WORLDS

As stated in the previous section, the most efficient way to customize your tone and send it to the soundcard at the appropriate signal strength is to use a preamp. In our opinion, the best model on the market is the Guitarport from Line6 (www.guitarport.com).

This little red devil works through your computer's USB port and an online software interface to deliver an avalanche of awesome preset tones, effects, amps and features. Here's how it works: You plug your guitar into the front of the unit, then plug the Guitarport into a USB port and connect it to your speakers or plug in headphones. Next you run the included cable from the unit's line out into your soundcard's line input and you're literally ready to rock.

The Guitarport from Line6 is an all-in-one "solution" for playing a guitar through your PC.

The Guitarport's connections include a USB port for power, headphone jack, line out and stereo RCA jacks as well.

Once you fire up the software it connects to the Guitarport online interface (a Net connection is required to use it) and it's like standing on a stage with 50 different amps at your disposal.

The software "models" 15 different amplifiers and 18 effects pedals for an enormous variety of tones, all available at the click on your mouse. It even includes a chromatic tuner!

Once you're up and running, you can play along with audio files saved to your hard drive or play along with lessons available via the online software. The software even lets you slow songs

down to half-speed without changing the pitch, making really tough sections easier to figure out. You can even type in "Van Halen" and the software will change the current tone to match Eddie's! It's really an incredible combination of hardware and software that takes all the guesswork and frustration out of this entire process. We can't recommend this product highly enough!

PUTTING IT ON WAX

The final step in this process is recording your tracks, which must be done via software. There is an enormous number of software packages on the market to fulfill your recording needs, ranging from the most basic to so advanced they'll make your head spin. If you want the most basic package available, remember that all versions of Windows include a Sound Recorder (Start Menu, Programs, Accessories, Entertainment, Sound Recorder). This rudimentary recorder works fine in a pinch but is so lacking in features we don't recommend it. Our personal favorite due to its ease of use is *Audio Record Wizard* from NowSmart Software. It's nowhere near as advanced as many software packages on the market, but that's why we like it. It has an intuitive interface and can even save your tracks as MP3 which can save you disk space.

Audio Record Wizard is a splendidly simple audio recording package.

If you're looking for a more advanced software suite, check out the following programs and URLs.

Guitar Tracks — http://www.cakewalk.com
SoundForge — http://mediasoftware.sonypictures.com/
n-Track Studio — http://www.fasoft.com/
Adobe Audition — http://www.adobe.com
A great all-around resource — http://www.guitarists.net

SPEAKERS

Now hear this!

Q How do "flat-panel" satellites work, and what are their pluses and minuses?

Some of the more interesting products on the PC audio landscape are flat-panel speakers, which are less than an inch thick and can even be hung on a wall like a portrait. Unlike traditional speakers, which use heavy magnets attached to cone-shaped drivers to create sound, flat-panel speakers employ what's called "planar magnetic technology." This design is like a magnetic sandwich, in which a conductive plastic diaphragm is the meat and two rows of magnets are the bread. Current is sent to the magnets from the amplifier, causing the diaphragm to vibrate, creating sound.

The benefits of flat-panel speakers are mainly aesthetic, in that they take up less space than traditional speakers and look very high-tech. They aren't all looks though, and actually offer surprisingly good sound quality. The only real downside to this technology is that flat-panel speakers tend to cost a bit more than regular speakers while not offering any significant performance or sound-quality advantage. If space is a concern, or if you like the sleek exteriors, flat-panel speakers are technologically sound. However, with so many superb "regular" speaker systems on the market, we have a hard time justifying the additional cost of them simply for their perceived "wow" factor.

Back in the good old days, we were able test speakers in the *Maximum PC* lab during working hours. Not anymore. Today's PC audio systems are almost powerful enough to be measured not on a musical scale, but on the Richter scale. We're talking mega-wattage, earth-shaking bass, glass-shattering highs and surround sound so immersive you'll never go to a movie theater again. Of course, everyone has different needs (and space constraints), so luckily there are many different configurations of speakers available, from basic to bombastic.

First, almost all speaker systems include subwoofers these days—some with enormous 8-inch drivers—and most offer surround sound capability as well, including the 7.1 speaker systems from Creative Labs (that's eight speakers total!). Still, the most common speaker configuration these days is the 2.1 system, which translates to two satellites and a subwoofer. The satellites are the small speakers that go on your desk and reproduce the high and midrange tones, while the subwoofer tackles all the low tones and is usually placed under the desk somewhere. The phrase "2.1" refers to the two satellites, represented by the number "2," and one subwoofer, represented by the ".1." Using the same nomenclature, a 4.1 speaker system has—you guessed it—four satellites and a subwoofer. A 4.1 system is great for gaming because it includes a front and a rear channel, so you can hear enemies approaching behind you and watch the action in front of you at the same time. However, 4.1 leaves big audio gaps directly in front and behind you, which led speaker manufacturers to introduce 5.1 systems. These are now the de facto configuration for today's high-end PCs, mainly due to the fact that DVD movies are encoded in 5.1 surround sound, so a 5.1 speaker system is required to reproduce the movie theater experience. But that still isn't enough for the hardcore crowd, and thus 6.1 and 7.1 speaker systems have been launched as well.

Surround sound systems like Creative Labs' Gigaworks S750 bring new levels of immersion to the desktop.

All the specs and tech lingo explained

Crossover
A circuit that filters away audio signals that fall outside a certain range. This is used for preventing a speaker from receiving sound signals it cannot accurately reproduce. A crossover usually consists of one or more pairs of inductors and capacitors.

Dolby Digital
A Dolby Laboratories format for representing sound in six discrete channels—five positional channels and a subwoofer channel. This is a popular digital surround sound format, and is used in most DVD movies.

DTS Sound
Digital Theater System. A multi-channel surround sound format that competes with Dolby Digital and also delivers sound in discrete channels—five positional channels and a subwoofer channel. DTS movies are encoded at a higher bit rate than that used by Dolby Digital, so more information about the sound is used during recording (in other words, more bits of data are used).

Frequency Response
The frequency range within which the speaker will actually produce sound.

Mini-jack
The small audio connector frequently used by headphones and computer speakers. Sony invented the Mini-jack when it discovered that the large audio connectors used in the old days were unsuitable for portable audio applications.

Peak Power Rating (Burst)
The peak power a speaker can handle for a very brief period. This is usually higher than the RMS power rating.

Power Per Channel
The power rating of each individual speaker output.

RCA Plug
The traditional plug used in audio and video cables. RCA connectors are normally coded red for right-side audio, white for left-side audio, and yellow for video. RCA stands for Radio Corporation of America.

RMS Power Rating
Root Mean Square power rating. This is a speaker's maximum continuous power output, or how much power it can sustain indefinitely. This is a more accurate—and realistic—assessment of a speaker's power than Burst power (see item above).

Satellites
Speakers (usually small ones) that reproduce high and midrange tones, and that are designed for convenient placement.

S/PDIF
Sony/Phillips Digital Interface. A format for transferring digital audio data without first converting it to an analog signal.

Generally, there are two kinds of S/PDIF connectors: one that accepts a coaxial RCA-type cable and one that uses an optic fiber TOSlink cable.

Subwoofer
A speaker designed to deliver very low-frequency sound. Because the human ear cannot distinguish the direction of very low-frequency sound, a subwoofer's placement does not affect the stereoscopic staging of music.

Surround Sound
The delivery of sound in more than two channels, with multiple speakers positioned in locations that "surround" the listener. The basic surround sound setup uses four speakers; two in front and two behind the listener.

THX Certification
A certification granted to theaters, home cinema and multimedia products indicating that they have met a level of quality deemed sufficient to faithfully re-create a movie theater experience. THX is essentially a quality label created by Lucasfilm, and was named after George Lucas's first feature film, *THX-1138*.

TOSlink/optical
A digital interface that uses a beam of light carried through a cable to transmit digital data to a speaker system. It uses a fiber optic cable, hence the name. It's sometimes referred to as TOSlink because it was developed by Toshiba.

2.1, 4.1, 5.1, and 6.1
Abbreviations used to denote the number of sound channels in a speaker system. The number before the decimal point indicates the number of regular audio channels and the number after the decimal point denotes the subwoofer (low-frequency) channel. For example, 5.1 means five regular channels and one subwoofer channel.

Since this Logitech Z-2200 system has two satellites and one subwoofer, it's designated as a 2.1 system. If it had two more satellites, it'd be a 4.1 system.

SPEAKERS

You've got questions, we've got answers

Question: What do I need to play movies in Dolby Digital surround sound?

A: In order to listen to true "discrete" Dolby Digital multi-channel audio on your PC, which is sound that is sent to separate channels from the sound source, all you need is a piece of hardware to decode the sound into its separate channels and a 5.1 speaker system. It's really that simple. A Dolby Digital audio stream is a digital signal that includes six audio channels, but these signals have to be sorted by a decoder and sent to their respective channels in order to get that movie-theater sound separation where you hear bullets whizzing from the front channel to the rear channel. This decoder can either be built into the soundcard or the speakers, or it can be a separate add-on unit.

> In order to get discrete multi-channel audio, you'll need a Dolby Digital decoder like this sexy unit from Creative Labs.

Question: How much power do I need?

A: A realistic assessment is that speaker systems that crank out 100 watts are sufficiently loud for home use, or 200 watts for a surround sound system. However, ultra-high-wattage speakers that are capable of 500 watts or more sound better at moderate volumes since there is absolutely no stress to the speaker's components at lower levels, whereas lesser speakers can become considerably stressed at lower volumes. The real reason for speakers to have high wattage ratings isn't to actually use those high levels of output, but to ensure distortion-free playback at lower volumes. As a yardstick, the 2.1 Logitech Z-2200 speakers are capable of pumping 200 continuous watts and are pure sonic fury. We almost went deaf testing them.

There is a wattage war going on right now, and Creative is winning with its 700-watt Gigaworks S750.

Question: Does it matter where I place the subwoofer?

A: A subwoofer produces tones that are so deep the human ear is unable to pinpoint their location, which is why the conventional wisdom is to put the sub anywhere you like. Your ears can't tell the difference if it's three feet behind you or five feet to your right. However, there will always be a "sweet spot" in your listening area where the subwoofer sounds best, so we recommend playing a bass-heavy DVD (*Saving Private Ryan's* opening sequence is a good choice) or some thumping music and then moving the subwoofer around the room while returning to your listening area to see how it sounds. Once you've pinpointed the "sweet spot," invite your friends over to show your home theater off a bit! For tips on speaker placement, you also can read the article on the next page of this very issue.

A speaker system's subwoofer really lets you feel its power. For maximum impact, care should be taken in choosing its placement.

Question: I have a 5.1 speaker system, but am seeing advertisements for 6.1 and even 7.1 speaker systems now. Is it worth it to upgrade?

A: Although the addition of one little speaker behind you or two on the sides may not seem like it would make a big difference, it does. The traditional 5.1 surround sound speaker system sounds fantastic but leaves huge gaps in the sound field behind you and on the sides as well. The only catch to upgrading to 6.1 or 7.1 is that Creative Labs is the only manufacturer selling such speaker systems, but it offers both a budget 7.1 speaker system called the Inspire T7700 as well as high-end 6.1 and 7.1 systems as well (named Megaworks and Gigaworks). You can also buy Creative Labs' S700 5.1 system, which is upgradeable to 7.1 for an extra $100. Also note that you'll need a soundcard that supports 7.1 sound, but there are several models on the market currently that offer this feature.

6.1 and 7.1 speaker systems are all the rage these days, and are a fantastic upgrade from a 2.1 or 4.1 speaker system.

How To...

BUILD YOUR OWN
Arcade Machine

Jump every barrel, munch every dot, and slaughter every alien in sight—just like the old days

MAXIMUM PC
TIME TO COMPLETION
CANCEL YOUR VACATION PLANS

BY ERIC BRATCHER

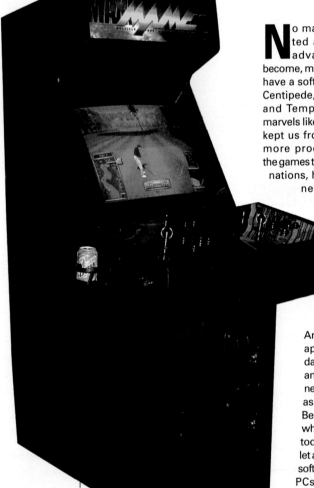

No matter how sophisticated and technologically advanced video games become, most gamers will always have a soft spot for the classics: Centipede, Pac-Man, Asteroids, and Tempest. Before modern marvels like *SimCity* and *Half-Life* kept us from doing something more productive, these were the games that captured our imaginations, honed our reflexes to near-feline efficiency, wowed us with their technological brilliance, and siphoned off our meager allowances, 25 cents at a time.

True, those were simpler times. Arcade games tended to appeal to the more fundamental, baser instincts, and as such, are nowhere near as deep and elaborate as most games of today. Besides, the graphics stink when compared with even today's cell-phone games, let alone the bleeding-edge softworks our ever-evolving PCs are now capable of

handling. Despite all this, the fact remains: Many of those games flat-out rocked.

In fact, they still do. Thanks

> *Gamers will always have a soft spot for the classics: Centipede, Pac-Man, Asteroids, and Tempest.*

to *Maximum PC*, the wonders of modern technology, and the faithful efforts of a few talented die-hard gamers, it's easier than ever to convert an old PC into an arcade machine that can play nearly every arcade game ever made, right in your living room! Be forewarned, building your own arcade cabinet is technically challenging. You'll need to do custom wiring, mounting, and even a little work with power tools, wood, and Plexiglas. With that in mind, let's get to work building your nostalgic monument to video game history. Put your quarter on the glass—you've got next game.

Do Your Homework

A journey of 1,000 miles begins with a single step. Good thing too, because it'll be quite awhile before you're allowed to walk any further than the nearest Internet-enabled PC. You should ask a ton of questions before you dive into the building process, and chances are you don't even know what the questions are yet.

Park your browser at the web site Build Your Own Arcade Controls (**www. arcadecontrols.com**). BYOAC is the ultimate site for everything related to home arcade machines, and we couldn't have written this story without it. Read the step-by-step newbie guide, examine at least a few of the 700+ example cabinets

on the site's database (we studied at least 400), and then start lurking about the forums. The guys there are the true experts, and have forgotten more about arcade cabinets than we'll ever know. Take lots of notes, browse the old postings, and even consult the sages directly, if you like. Just don't post inane, newbie questions like, "Where can i get tha ROMz for every game evar?" BYOAC doesn't tolerate illegal ROM requests—Google will serve you well for those purposes.

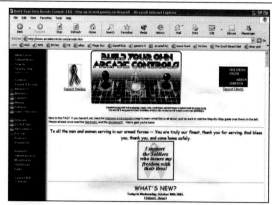

Incidentally, we'll admit that the line between legal and illegal can be murky at times, but everything we talk about in this article is 100 percent allowed by law.

The Cabinet: Buying Used vs. Building New

There's an old saying: "If you want to confuse a computer genius, give him a hammer." Okay, so we made that up, but it's important to consider when answering the next question: Do you want to buy a used arcade machine and repurpose it, or would you rather play carpenter and build the entire shell yourself?

Our recommendation is to buy. It's more authentic, much of the hard work has already been done, and it's often cheaper. Most importantly, your rescued cabinet will probably come with quite a few spare parts that you would either pay top dollar for or completely overlook

if you had to buy them piecemeal. For example, our cabinet, a Mortal Kombat machine with some serious miles on it, cost a whopping $50. It came with a coin door, monitor mounting brackets, cabinet handles, panel latches, a marquee glass and trim, and countless other odds and ends that would have totaled at least $150 new.

If you still want to build your own cab, there are several sets of plans freely available for download at BYOAC, in the "Cabinets" section. Arcade Flashback by LuSiD is easily the most popular.

Make a Budget and a Plan

Before you go any further, check your wallet and decide exactly how much money you can spend on your cabinet. It's fairly easy to build a cabinet cheaply, but it's even easier to spend a fortune on it. Making a budget now and sticking to it will save you from making tough cutbacks later on.

Done? Then it's time to come up with the overall design for your cabinet. What games are you going to want to play? Who will be using it besides you? What controls do you want? How should it look? It's important to plan these things now to avoid saying "D'oh" later. For example,

you may be dead-set on having a four-player control panel, so all your friends can play at once. Great idea! Unless you've already rushed out and bought an old Asteroids cabinet—its control panel simply doesn't have room for four sets of controls. You don't necessarily need to etch everything in stone, but having a well thought-out plan now can both help you decide the best way to spend your budget and save you from buying something you can't use. By the way, never rush when building an arcade cabinet—in the long run, it takes less time to do some-

thing right than it takes to do it over (if that's even an option).

4 Scrub Your Cabinet

OK, so you finally bought your used cabinet from a local arcade operator, a nearby auction, or eBay, where you paid through the nose to get it shipped to your house. Next: gut it. Whether it's a vivisection or an autopsy, you need to clean it out and start with a blank slate. Remove every part and clean it—if your machine is anything like ours, which lived outside for a time, it'll be filthy. Take careful inventory as you do this, saving small parts in plastic bags and labeling, possibly even photographing, everything. If you've done your BYOAC homework, this is also a good time to start noticing what parts are missing or need replacing.

5 Choose and Mount the Monitor

There are two choices here. You could buy a real arcade monitor, but a PC monitor will also work. Real arcade monitors are obviously authentic, but have disadvantages: They tend to max out at 640x480 resolution, they often have unique hookup or power considerations, and if you try to handle one without following the proper degaussing procedure, you could be in for a serious electrical shock. On the other hand, a PC monitor is safer, easier to hook up, and higher-res. However, its picture is so sharp that some arcade games will actually look odd on it. For now, we'll go with a standard 19-inch Viewsonic, which will rest on a shelf we mounted using the original monitor brackets and some furniture leg levelers.

6 Give It a Makeover

Now that we've hung the monitor shelf, we know where bolts will jut out of the cabinet. Take them all out, use wood putty to fill in any unused holes, and let's refinish the outside. Once again, you have several options. You can pick up some real arcade machine side-art decals from eBay or another online vendor. Some people just use vinyl laminate or contact paper. We decided to save some cash by simply painting the cabinet. After all, we can always apply decals later. Conventional wisdom holds that you should use a foam roller and sand the surface smooth between coats, but we liked what happened when we specifically didn't sand. It produced a nice, bumpy texture that actually hid many of the numerous dings and dents our cabinet had acquired during its rough life.

7 Install the PC and Speakers

Every Frankenstein monster needs a brain, right? A good rule of thumb is to remember that it doesn't usually take much to emulate an arcade game, but more horsepower is always welcome. We're going to go with a 1.3GHz P4 with 256MB RAM, a 30GB hard drive, and a GeForce2 videocard. We mounted our PC on the floor of the cabinet, but left it in its case. Some builders doff the case altogether and screw the mobo right into the cabinet's sidewall, but we prefer to use the case. For speakers, we found an old Logitech 2.1 system, set the subwoofer on the cabinet floor, and anchored the two satellites in the appropriate place using the decidedly low-tech approach of Velcro, poster board, and duct tape. Metal pipe tape works well, too.

8 Add the Trim

If you have a coin door, you can remount it now. The same goes for cabinet handles, marquee trim, and especially t-molding. For those who don't know, t-molding is the plastic trim that wraps around every edge of an arcade machine. It's called t-molding because it actually has a T shape, with the top of the letter being the visible part and the stem being the ridge that slips into a slot on the wood and holds the trim in place. There are several widths and colors available at **www.t-molding.com**, and it's easily cut with a razor blade or kitchen shears. If you need to cut the slot yourself, we recommend you use a router, Dremel, or Roto-Zip with a 1/16-inch or 3/32-inch straight cut bit.

9 The Marquee and the Window

Every arcade machine needs a marquee at the top. You can purchase one from eBay, but you can also make your own. We simply cranked up *Photoshop* and merged both the *MaximumPC* logo and the MAME emulator logo. Then, it was just a matter of printing a couple copies on nice paper and mounting it with mounting clips behind the monitor glass (all of which came free with the cabinet). The light from behind is a plain-old, $10 under-cabinet fluorescent light from Home Depot. This is also a great time to make a monitor bezel out of black poster board and get a piece of glass, Plexiglas, or Lexan for the monitor glass.

10 Design Your Control Panel

That old Mortal Kombat button layout worked fine for MK, but it's lousy for many other games, so we'll make a new one. Think about what games you want to play, and list the necessary controls. Pac-Man? Just a four-way stick and a start button will do. Street Fighter II? You'll need two eight-way sticks and six buttons each, plus the start button. Plot out a good size and button placement—we prefer to leave about 3/16-inch between each button. For the moment, we'll stick with a fairly basic layout: two eight-way joysticks, each with one start button and seven action buttons.

11 Choose Your Joysticks and Buttons

There are two kinds of buttons: leaf switch buttons and microswitch buttons. Both do fundamentally the same thing, but there are some subtle differences. Microswitch buttons are modern, durable, and fuss-free, mount at any depth, and make a clicking sound when pressed. Leaf switches are an older design, make very little noise, but are more finicky about mounting depth, and need occasional adjusting. For novices, we recommend microswitch buttons, which run about $1.80 each. There are also several kinds of joysticks. Here's the breakdown: The best eight-way sticks are Happ Perfect 360 opticals, but they run about $40 each. You can get by with Happ Super joysticks for about $14.20 each. Strangely, the Super sticks are of far higher quality than the Happ "Ultimate" joystick.

12 Place a Parts Order

Now it's time to order the joysticks, buttons, microswitches, and any other parts you'd like for your control panel. There are two major online vendors from which to choose: Happ Controls (**www.happcontrols. com**) has the largest selection, but also some high prices. Wico (**www.wicothe-source.com**) has nearly as much, including translucent leaf switch buttons, but its joysticks can't compare and service can be inconsistent. We like Bob Roberts (**www. therealbobroberts.com**), a one-man operation that stocks the most common of both Happ's and Wico's items. He's beloved by the BYOAC crowd for his slightly lower prices, down-to-earth demeanor, and exemplary customer service. Whichever vendor you choose, make sure you add a pushbutton wrench to your order—it's the best $2.35 you'll spend.

13 Order a Keyboard Encoder

One critical item we haven't yet mentioned is the keyboard encoder, which translates the signals from your control panel into the keystrokes that the computer can understand. There are a few competing models: the Hagstrom KE-72, and GroovyGameGear's KeyWiz, but we chose the I-Pac from Ultimarc ($39-69 at **www.ultimarc.com**. It's extremely easy to use, it's fully programmable, and it has a very cool "shift-key" feature, which removes the need to add buttons for Esc, Enter, and other PC functions on your panel. When you order the I-Pac, add in the super-handy $19 Wiring Kit. It combines wire clippers/strippers, tons of wire, cable ties, and .250 female quick connects.

14 Practice Building the Control Panel

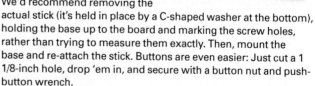

Draw out your control panel on a sheet of cardboard and cut the necessary holes with an Xacto knife. Usually joysticks work best with a 1 1/8-inch hole in the center and one screw in each corner of their 3.5 x 3.08-inch footprint. We'd recommend removing the actual stick (it's held in place by a C-shaped washer at the bottom), holding the base up to the board and marking the screw holes, rather than trying to measure them exactly. Then, mount the base and re-attach the stick. Buttons are even easier: Just cut a 1 1/8-inch hole, drop 'em in, and secure with a button nut and pushbutton wrench.

Now, pretend to play a few games, making sure that all the buttons and joysticks are positioned properly. Are the buttons spaced sufficiently apart from one another and the joysticks? Are the controls far enough from the panel's edge? Now is the time to refine your design. You may even want to skip ahead to Step 17 and actually play-test it.

15
OK, Now Actually Build the Control Panel

Satisfied with your layout? Then grab yourself a sheet of 3/4-inch wood, either plywood or MDF. MDF is medium density fiberboard; it's much easier to work with than ply. Redraw your panel onto the wood, then cut your new top panel. For button holes, just use a spiral saw or a drill with a 1 1/8-inch spade bit or hole saw. Before you paint or cover the top panel with contact paper, reinstall your hardware again, to make sure everything fits. Once you've made your final adjustments, remove the hardware and paint your panel, then reinstall all the hardware again. Then, attach the top panel to your panel box—this is usually done by screwing it to a large hinge mounted on the panel's front edge. Once the hinge is on, you can lock it down with a panel latch on each interior sidewall, accessible from the coin door or the cabinet's rear.

16
Wire and Mount the Control Panel

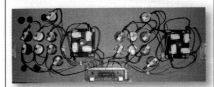

This step isn't nearly as scary as you might guess, thanks to the I-Pac. Here's the logic: Every microswitch, on both buttons and joysticks, has three exposed terminals, marked NO, NC, and Com. The NO is your positive (figuratively speaking), and the Com your ground. Thus, to wire Player 1, Button 1, you simply take a strand of 20-24 gauge wire, strip off about 1/8-inch from each tip. Then attach a .250 or .187 female quick connect to one end and stick it onto the NO terminal, screwing the other end into the terminal marked 1 SW1 on the I-Pac. Do this for every switch on both buttons and joysticks. When you've got all the positives run, let's start on the ground wires. Make a daisy chain, using quick connects to link the Com terminal of each switch to the Com terminal of the switch next to it, with each end of the chain terminating in one of the two GND slots of the I-Pac. That's it! Why daisy chain? That way, it will take two bad connections to short out your panel and you'll know right where they are because only the switches between the shorts will fail.

17
Connect the Panel and Fire It Up!

Now, all that's left is to anchor the panel box to the cabinet itself, using either heavy-duty Velcro or carriage bolts driven through the rear and floor of the panel box. If you have a used cabinet, the guide holes should already be drilled. Assuming your PC is operational, just plug your keyboard into the I-Pac, and then use the included cable to plug your I-Pac into the PC's PS2 keyboard socket. Hit the gas on the PC, choose your preferred game, and you should be ready to play!

The bare-bones hardware for your MAME cab is now done, so you can skip ahead to the last pages of this feature to see just a sampling of the software available to you. However, this isn't a mean machine—it's a bargain basement jalopy. If you want a real cabinet to be reckoned with, keep reading and consider mixing in at least a few of our optional upgrades!

The Alternative

Building your own arcade cabinet is all fine and dandy, but what if you're one of those players who would rather play than plan? No worries. There are several companies that sell pre-made arcade cabinets, or even just arcade control panels that you can hook up to your PC. See www.hanaho.com, www.custom-arcade.com, www.dreamauthentics.com, or simply type MAME into eBay. Buy pre-made if you must, but we have to recommend against it. There are too many big drawbacks: It's hard to find the exact configuration you want, it's more satisfying to do it yourself, your cabinet is unoriginal, and most important, it's much more expensive. Sure, it's easier, but if you wanted easy, you'd just buy a PS2 and the latest arcade collection.

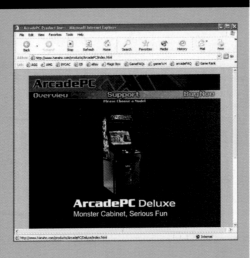

18 Build a New Control Panel Box

We've got plans—big plans. We need a much larger control panel, so we've built a new control panel box, measuring 34x17-inches, out of 3/4-inch MDF. We got a little fancy, using "wood squares" to hold the sides together, giving the top a slope, and routing out little areas on top so the joystick bolts would lay flush with the surface. But the carpentry here is still blessedly basic: Make a box with a hinged lid and holes in the back to reach through to latch the lid down. We cut our t-molding grooves using the methods from Step 15. We've also added a very simple keyboard drawer, made by cutting a hole in the front of the box, attaching a sheet of 1/4-inch plywood to the resulting piece of wood, and then sticking it back in place with Velcro mounted along the bottom edge. The plywood is a couple inches wider in the rear than in the front to keep it from falling out, and "L" shaped brackets mounted to the floor on the inside of the box keep the drawer from flopping downward when it's pulled out. Oh, and there's a shelf inside the box—more on that later.

18 Upgrade Those Joysticks

Believe it or not, you really need a dedicated four-way stick for oldies like Pac-Man and Dig Dug—they control poorly with an eight-way stick. Either track down a Wico four-way leaf switch stick (a challenge, but worth it. See Step 23 for leaf switch wiring) or spring for Happ's Ms. Pac-Man replacement stick ($21.45) and bolt it in.

We also want to upgrade those eight-way sticks to Happ Perfect 360 Opticals ($40.50 ea.) They mount like any other stick, with one added step: They need a 5V power source. To get it, find a Molex power extension cable from your local PC shop, the same ones you use to power hard disks and optical drives inside your PC. With the computer unplugged, insert the male end of the Molex cable into your PC's power supply. On the other end, cut off the female connector, which would normally connect to, say, your hard drive. Then, using 16- or 18-gauge wire and electrical tape or connectors, extend the exposed red wire and one of the black wires, connecting them to the red and black wires on both sticks. It's that easy. We also swapped in cool, custom ball-top handles purchased from eBay.

20 Add a Trackball

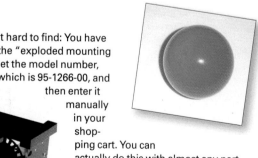

Any true classic gamer will tell you that playing Centipede with a joystick is blasphemy. To avoid gamer's hell, we added the finest trackball currently on the market: a 3-inch High Lip from Happ ($93). It's the exact ball used in brand-new Golden Tee arcade machines. We also spruced it up a little. First, we grabbed one of Happ's trackball mounting plates, which keep the bolt heads from showing through the panel's surface ($24). Then, we bought a shorter lid for the trackball housing ($3.55). This enables a little more of the trackball to stick up through the panel, just like Happ's "High-Ball" model. (This part is a bit hard to find: You have to look at the "exploded mounting view" to get the model number, which is 95-1266-00, and then enter it manually in your shopping cart. You can actually do this with almost any part on Happ's site, which is nice.) Finally, we dropped in a blue translucent ball ($21.30), simply because it looks awesome. You'll need to cut a strangely shaped hole in the top panel to mount your trackball, and we'll get to wiring it in Step 22.

21 Add a Spinner

Any true classic gamer will tell you that playing Tempest, arguably the best video game of all time, with anything other than a spinner is not only sacrilegious, but practically pointless. There are two good choices here: The SlikStik Tornado ($90 from **www.slikstik.com**), is an engineering marvel that spins for literally minutes at a time, and the Oscar Controls Vortex (approx $73 from **www.oscarcontrols.com**, depending on which knob you choose), is a near-exact replica of the original Tempest spinner. In our opinion, the Vortex actually edges out

the more expensive Tornado for three reasons: First, the Tornado spins so freely that you can sometimes move it by accident when letting go of it—not good during a heated Tempest match. Second, we love the Vortex's Tempest heritage. Third, and most important, Oscar Controls owner Kelsey is yet another vendor who, like Bob Roberts and Ultimarc's Andy Warne, has earned an absolutely stellar reputation for fairness and customer care. Whichever spinner you choose, mounting them is as easy as drilling three holes and twisting first a screwdriver, then a very tiny Allen wrench.

22 Wire the Trackball and Spinner to an Opti-Pac

Once the trackball and spinner are mounted, we need an encoder. There are a few out there, but we chose the Opti-Pac from Ultimarc. Just as the I-Pac convinces your PC that the joysticks and buttons are actually a keyboard, the Opti-Pac swears to it that trackballs and spinners are your mouse. It connects simply to your PC via a USB or PS2 port. We used a PS2 cable, because some DOS programs don't read USB. Just how you connect trackballs and spinners to the Opti-Pac differs slightly from one device to the next, but if you follow the directions provided by your vendors and Ultimarc,

you shouldn't have any problems. In our case, we simply cut the connector off the trackball harness, stripped the tips of the newly exposed wires, and screwed them into the corresponding slots of the Opti-Pac. We did have to swap a couple wires around to make sure up was up and down was down, but it was a simple procedure, as was wiring the spinner afterward. We even

wired the left and right mouse buttons to buttons on the control box's sides, which proved very handy both in Windows XP and when playing pinball games like Adventure Pinball Forgotten Island.

23 Upgrade Your Buttons to Translucent Leaf Switches

Leaf switch buttons are more authentic than microswitch buttons, and they're also available in see-through colors, which was the main selling point for us. Unfortunately, leaf buttons also require button holders to hold the button and leaf switch in place. The leaf switches also come in two lengths, the shorter of which is designed for metal control panels, so you may have to use a router to cut out some of your control panel in order to make it thin enough to use leaf buttons. Because we didn't want to rout out too much of our control panel, we cheated a bit and discarded the button holders—they're too tall, and if we used

them, we'd have to carve out so much of the panel it wouldn't be strong. Instead, we fashioned crude collars from spare Lexan to use as button holders, and then screwed the leaf switches right into the wood, aligning them by hand. It isn't pretty, but it beats routing the panel so thinly that it could crack. Once mounted, wiring leaf switches is even easier than wiring microswitches. There are only two poles, and they're interchangeable. Just choose one for the NO and one for the Com, and wire them

up with .187 female quick connects. Were the leaf switches worth all the trouble? Absolutely—wait 'til Step 29.

24 Upgrade the Monitor

Back in Step 5, we described two choices for your monitor. We chose the PC monitor, because it's smaller and safer than authentic monitors, but the arcade screen is also a compelling choice, despite a max resolution of 640x480 and funky hookup requirements (a 15Hz refresh rate, for instance). There is a third option,

though: the Wells-Gardner D9200, a gorgeous, huge 27-inch (or 31-inch, if your cabinet can fit it), multi-resolution arcade monitor that plugs into a regular wall outlet and attaches to your PC via a normal, VGA-style cable. At about $580 after shipping from **www.wellsgardner.com**, it's not cheap, but it's worth every penny. Mounting it turned out to be easy—we simply set the D9200 on the existing monitor shelf, which we hung in the cabinet using the original monitor brackets, and then unceremoniously nailed a 2x4 brace across the top. One giant precaution: **NEVER, EVER TOUCH THE BIG, RED WIRE COMING OUT OF THE MONITOR'S REAR!** This is where the monitor stores enough electricity to light up Manhattan. If you do need to handle your monitor, always unplug and discharge it using a degaussing coil or the D9200's built-in degausser.

25 Upgrade the Videocard

If you have a D9200, you'd be very wise to consider switching your videocard to an ArcadeVGA from **www.ultimarc.com**. Based on the ATI Radeon 7000 chipset, this card is specially designed to work in tandem with the D9200. Regardless of the card you use, make sure you force the resolution down to 640x480 before you connect the D9200. Windows XP's default resolution 800x600 can damage the D9200 (until the Arcade VGA is installed), so you need to go to Properties/Settings/Advanced/ Adapter/list all modes and set your resolution to 640x480 before switching to the D9200. After this, open your case and install the Arcade VGA, plug the D9200 into its middle

socket, and fire up the PC in Safe Mode (press F8 repeatedly as the PC boots). Install the Arcade VGA's drivers, then install the D9200 utility and *Quickres*, both downloadable from the Ultimarc web site. Reboot your PC, reset the resolution to 640x480 just to be safe, and you're good to go.

27 Add a Second Power Button on the Roof

Your PC's motherboard connects to the case's power button via a single, two-stranded wire. Find it, and splice in

another strand on each wire, so that both have two forks; one that goes from the mobo to the case's power switch as it should, and another fork that juts out. Now run another pair of wires from the new ends you spliced to a normal arcade momentary switch mounted on the top of the arcade cabinet. One of the strands is the NO, and the other the Com, or ground. Which one's which? Look at the wires leading from the case to the mobo's sockets for power LED, hard drive LED, and so on. There should be one color, usually black, that recurs in each wire—that's your ground.

26 One-Button Power Up

By now, you're probably really tired of powering up each piece of your cabinet individually by hand, right? Never fear, we can make your startup much easier and far cooler. Some folks will tell you to hack a relay into your surge protector, but we just sprang for a Smart Strip from Bits Limited ($30 at **www.bitsltd.net**). This power strip designates one outlet as the "control", and turns on all the other outlets when it senses the "control" power up. Thus, we plug our PC into the control outlet and when it turns on, so to will the monitor, lights, and speakers. When it's time to quit playing, the Smart Strip powers everything off the second Windows shuts down.

28 Give the Cabinet a New Makeover

We decided to redo the cabinet's surface to make it look a little less hooptie. **Partsexpress.com** sells high-quality, vinyl, speaker laminate at $12 per 2x10-foot roll that goes on smoothly and looks badass. We chose a cherry wood grain pattern for the sides, but wanted to do something a little different for the control panel. We covered a piece of poster board with the plain, black laminate. We then carved it into shape and inserted it between the surface of our control panel and

an overlay made of Lexan we bought at Home Depot ($40) and cut ourselves using a spiral saw. Finally, we dropped $40 on a real monitor bezel from Happ to replace our poster board frame, and made the marquee look better by hiring Kinko's to print our design on a special medium called "backlight film."

29 Light It Up!

Now's the time when the translucent buttons and trackball become worth the trouble. We've replaced our PC's original, wimpy power supply with a new 550-watt behemoth. Why? Because it's the cabinet's time to shine—literally. Remember that shelf we put in the new control panel box? Let's set some lights on it. First, four white, cold-cathode tubes (Approx $8 each) to light those beautiful, translucent leaf switch buttons. Next, a single blue Lazer LED cannon ($2 from www.svc.com) to brighten up the trackball. It may seem like this is overkill; after all, wouldn't a normal fluorescent fixture be cheaper and just as good? Actually, no. One must be careful with under-panel lighting, because the heat from incandescent, and even fluorescent bulbs, can cause the trackball to expand. This, in turn, makes the ball less accurate when in use.

There's more. We also got two red Lazer LED cannons and used duct tape (again: low tech, but effective) to mount them in place behind the coin switches. Best of all, each of these lights is powered by standard Molex cable plugged into spare outlets on the PC power supply. We didn't even have to splice or cut a single cable.

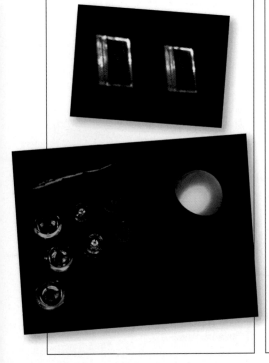

30 Add Atari "Volcano" Start Buttons

Remember these? They adorned such masterpieces as Missile Command, Asteroids, and the greatest game of all time, Tempest. Lucky for us, they can occasionally be found on eBay, but don't pay more than $25 each. There are two types of these buttons, five-prong and six-prong. If the button has five prongs, three will be marked NO, NC, and C, so wire them just like you would a microswitch button. If you get the six-pronged variation, the four terminals will be marked NC, NC, NO, and NO. In this case, connect your wires to the two NO terminals. In both models, the two unmarked prongs power the button's light. If you want them to blink in accordance with coin insertion, they can be powered via the I-Pac. We wanted constant illumination, so we just wired them straight into our power supply. Run a red 5V and black ground wire from a Molex connector just as you did in Step 19 for the Perfect 360, but wire a 330A resistor in place between the red wire and the prong. It's not too tough—we literally clamped a quick connect to each end of the resistor and covered the whole thing with heat-shrink tubing. There are no markings that say which prong is which, so just attach red to one and black to the other, then switch them if it fails to light.

31 Make the Coin Slots Work

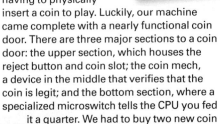

Nothing says "arcade machine" like actually having to physically insert a coin to play. Luckily, our machine came complete with a nearly functional coin door. There are three major sections to a coin door: the upper section, which houses the reject button and coin slot; the coin mech, a device in the middle that verifies that the coin is legit; and the bottom section, where a specialized microswitch tells the CPU you fed it a quarter. We had to buy two new coin  mechs ($12 each), which slid right into place. After that, it was a simple matter of connecting the NO and Com terminals of the microswitches—check the markings, by the way—to the waiting sockets on the I-Pac. Ka-Ching!

32 The Final Touch: Drink Holders

We don't know which cabinet builder was the first to think of this final, greatest upgrade, but we worship him just the same. Once your cabinet is finally up and running, you'll probably be logging some marathon gameplay sessions, which can make a gamer very thirsty. Thus, each side of our cab's control panel is decked out with one of these deluxe cup holders. They usually go for about $13 each on eBay. Made in Germany by Fischer Automotive Systems, this is the very same drink holder you'll find in a Mercedes E class. They're collapsible, they resize themselves to match beverage containers of any size or alcohol content, and they even act as their own drip trays. Overkill? Maybe, but who cares? Drink holders are pimp.

33 Troubleshoot, and Dream of Future Upgrades

Actually, the drink holders weren't the final touch—there's no such thing. No matter how well you did, there's always troubleshooting to be done. For instance, our joysticks tended to work loose until we rechecked the mounting hardware and found that some of the nuts and bolts were mismatched. If you're like us, your cabinet will be in a constant state of upgrade. We're already thinking of better

speakers, and USB ports for a steering wheel, flight stick, or dance pad. You can even upgrade your control panel to a rotating or swappable design. If that's not enough, you can always set up specialized controllers for games like Q*Bert and 720, or install a laser-etched window in the cabinet with neon inside. Your project never has to end. Luckily, neither does the fun. Play on!

Game Time! What to Play (Legally) on Your Arcade Cabinet...

EXISTING ARCADE GAME COMPILATIONS

It sounds too obvious to even write down, but the easiest thing to play on your arcade machine is definitely actual arcade games. Microsoft's Return of the Arcade yields *Pac-Man*, *Dig Dug*, *Pole Position*, and *Galaxian*; however, the best package going is the Atari Arcade Classics collection published by Infogrames, now renamed Atari. It features arcade-perfect and cabinet-ready versions of *Missile Command*, *Asteroids*, *Centipede*, *Tempest*,

Millipede, *Asteroids Deluxe*, *Gravitar*, *Pong*, *Warlords*, *Super Breakout*, *Crystal Castles*, and *Battlezone*. Both trackball and spinner are easily configured to work flawlessly, and there's plenty of supplemental material: pictures of promotional patches and print ads, interviews with original Atari founder Nolan Bushnell, and so on.

LEGALLY PURCHASED ROMS

Shortly before this article went to press, the BYOAC crowd discovered **www.starroms.com**, a site that enables gamers to legally purchase arcade games (called ROMs, after the chips on which the games were physically stored in real arcade machines). These ROMs work with emulators like MAME and cost about $2 each. Through a

partnership with Atari, StarROMs currently offers nearly 60 games from which to choose, including everything in the Atari Arcade Classics collection (except, oddly, Pong) as well as: *Toobin'*, *Paperboy*, *Tetris*, *APB*, *720 Degrees*, *Gauntlet*, *Cyberball*, *Escape from the Planet of the Robot Monsters*, *Marble Madness*, and many more. Hopefully they'll

enter into agreements with other arcade machine manufacturers and offer more ROMs soon.

TWO WORDS: GOLDEN TEE

If there's a game more fun than Golden Tee for good friends to play over a pint at the local pub, we've not seen it. We're not alone, either—it's so popular, you can actually go to manufacturer Incredible Technologies' web site and look up the

location of the nearest Golden Tee machine. The PC version, clumsily titled *Peter Jacobsen's Golden Tee*, was released several years back, so it's no beauty queen. However, it's undeniably Golden Tee, and controls perfectly as long as you have your trackball acting as your mouse, and have both right and left mouse buttons wired somewhere on your panel. Ours are on the sides, beside the pinball buttons.

OTHER COMMERCIAL GAMES

For that matter, there are dozens of existing PC games that run flawlessly on an arcade cabinet with only minor tweaking. As long as the controls are re-mappable and the resolution can be set at 640x480 (or higher if you're using a regular PC

monitor instead of an arcade screen), you've got a good chance of getting it going. We had great luck with sports titles like *Madden NFL* and *Tiger Woods 2004*, and action games like *Beyond Good & Evil* also tend to fare well, as long as your PC is fast enough. Granted, arcade controls are rarely suited to first-person shooters, but Encore's *Pinball Madness 4* (and our side-mounted pinball buttons) helped ease the pain.

DRAGON'S LAIR

We're not talking about the botched, 3D iteration of Dragon's Lair that broke our hearts last year. No, we mean the charming, hand-animated original, which

was a laser disc-based, technological marvel when first released way back in 1983. It takes some tweaking and MPEG ripping, but with an emulator named DAPHNE, it's possible to get Dragon's Lair up and running beautifully on a PC-based arcade cabinet. We haven't room to detail the whole process here, so just hunt down the 20th Anniversary DVD-ROM version of the game (*not* the regular DVD) and visit **www.daphne-emu.com**, specifically the documentation page, to start reading up about how to make it happen.

SHAREWARE, FREEWARE, AND REMAKES

There are about a million programmers out there just cranking out arcade-style games perfectly suited for an arcade cabinet. We haven't room to list all the URL's, but links to most of these can be found in the Software forum of the BYOAC

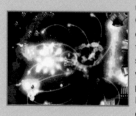

message boards. Check the thread called "Links to pretty cool software ...," which is always pinned in place. Here are a few of our favorites: the retro-psychedelic Asteroids clone *Spheres of Chaos*, available at **www.chaotica.u-net.com**; Pompom's Robotron-like *Mutant Storm* (**www.pompom.org.uk**) and the deeper, anime-styled shooter *Starscape* (pictured) from **www.moonpod.com**. There are also entire sites, like **www.game-remakes.com/**, that are devoted to creating legal-to-own clones of yesteryear's hits. Cool. ■

How To...

CREATE A 3D MODEL

Let's use the free version of 3ds max to create a futuristic police cruiser

BY FRED RUFF AND PAUL PERREAULT

MAXIMUMPC
DIFFICULTY RATING
EASY
HARD
XXX

NOTE:

Before starting this how-to, consult your software's help file for basic info.

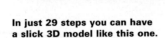

In just 29 steps you can have a slick 3D model like this one.

I f you play PC games, chances are you've heard about "mods." A game mod is nothing other than a partial or complete modification of a shipping game. It can include new textures, new models, new maps, new gameplay elements, and even a new theme. A game "modder" may edit or add new content, change the behavior of in-game objects, or both. Mods play a huge role in several PC game genres, and many titles are designed with modding in mind. Game mods are fun to create, and give people much more bang for their gaming buck.

Game developers and publishers have taken note of the modding trend, and now many new titles ship with some form of game editor bundled in. More often than not, these editors give gamers the power to create unique, playable environments (for example, users can rearrange game content, and script unique interactions between characters). *Dungeon Siege* and *Neverwinter Nights* are two examples of very modifiable games.

A few years ago, Discreet released *gmax*, a consumer-level design- and content-editing app based on *3ds max* (a pro-level application used by many game developers). The only differences between gmax and *3ds max* are price (*gmax* is free), and the fact that *gmax* lacks a renderer, which will prevent you from creating movies. There are several "*gmax* ready" games available that will let you use gmax to add new content. Gmax is now supported by Turbo Squid and you can download your own copy at **www.turbosquid.com/gmax** (note it's about 19MB and you must register).

Creating a game-ready model with *gmax* is a perfect way to get your feet wet if you want to give the world of game modding a try. Just be aware that this how-to will make no sense whatsoever unless you have *gmax* up and running. The instructions might seem difficult at first, but if you follow along, you'll soon be a *gmax* master.

Step 1: Units

First fire up *gmax*. Before we do anything, we'll need to pick a scale to work in. We don't want to create a police cruiser that's as big as a house, or as small as a toy. We want our cruiser to comfortably accommodate two 6-foot individuals.

The default scale for gmax is a generic integer system, but let's switch it to feet and inches so we can get an idea of our scale. Go to Customize>Units Setup, and change the units to feet with decimal inches (see image). Activate the perspective view port by clicking in it. Now go to the command panel, Create>Geometry>Standard Primitives>Box and draw out a parametric box primitive that's 2-feet wide by 2-feet long by 6-feet in height. (Tip: Click on the Keyboard Entry rollout and enter values for length, width, and height.)

Think of the box as a reference object representing a 6-foot-tall man. When you're roughing out your cruiser model, you can put this box next to it to imagine your model in context. Feel free to delete, freeze, or hide the box once you're happy with the scale of your model.

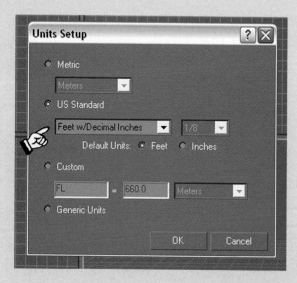

Step 2: Drawing out the Cruiser's Hull

We like using Patch Surfaces: Using patches allows you to create a smooth surface and provides features to interactively up-res and down-res the mesh. In any active view port, you can change to Front view by pressing F. Once you've done this, press the W key—this toggles full-screen mode.

Create a Circle shape with a radius of 2.5 to 3 feet. Collapse the primitive to an Editable Spline by right clicking the circle (this brings up the Quad Menu) and selecting Convert To...Editable Spline. Now delete one half of the circle: Click the Modify panel and click the Segment sub-object mode. Select and delete two segments, which will result in the creation of an arc. From there, use the Create Line command to draw out the other lines using the vertical origin line as an imaginary mirror plane.

Now use the Mirror command within Editable Spline to make a second copy of the spline: Select the Spline sub-object mode, select the spline, find the Mirror button, and make sure to click the Copy checkbox. Click the Mirror button, then drag the mirrored copy into place. Choose "Yes" when *gmax* asks to weld the endpoints.

Step 3: Laying Out the Surface Splines

Now we'll take the hull shape and make several copies of it, scaling each to create something like the shapes in the screenshot (the shapes look like straight lines because we're viewing them in Top view). Click the Hierarchy tab, and click the Affect Pivot Only button. Now click the Center To Object button, then click the Affect Pivot Only button to complete the operation.

Be sure to save your work frequently!

Click the shape to make it active. Now hold down the Shift key, and click and hold the Y-axis manipulator. Drag upward (along the Y-axis) a few units, then release the mouse button. This action will pop up the Clone Options dialog window. Enter 7 in the Number of Copies field, click the Copy radio button, then hit OK. This procedure will create 8 shapes. Scale each line shape using the Scale tool on the main toolbar. The result should look like our screenshot.

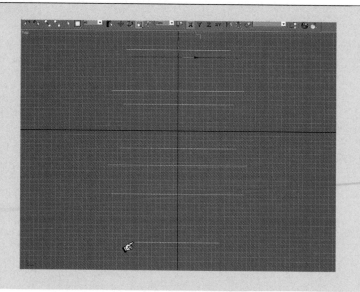

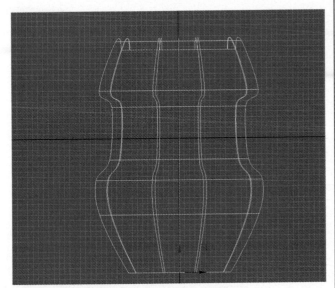

Step 4: Making the Cross Sections

Before we attempt to make the cross sections to complete the spline surface, we'll need to attach all the splines together in the proper order. When we attach the splines we should start from the bottom of the screen (with the original shape) and work our way up. Just don't attach the last two splines; we will attach the last two splines out of order. This will cause the surface to wrap back in on itself creating a nice rear engine area. The order should be: 1, 2, 3, 4, 5, 6, 8, 7.

Do this now: Click the spline at the bottom, go to the Modify panel and click the Attach button. Now click each spline object to attach it to the "root" spline (remember the order for the last two splines). With the resulting shape selected, go to the Modify panel, and apply the Cross Section modifier. If the option for Smooth is not chosen, click it.

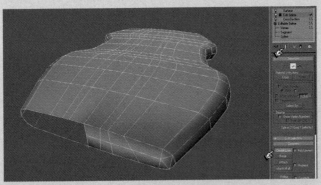

Step 6: Capping the Surface

Select the surface and click the Edit Spline modifier in the Modify Panel. Now turn on Show End Result (the small "pipe" icon below the Stack View area). Enabling this feature will allow you to see the full effects of the modifier stack. Go into Vertex mode within Edit Spline. Look for the PolyConnect checkbox and uncheck it. Look for the 3D Snap icon at the bottom of the *gmax* interface (this looks like a magnet with a 3 next to it). Turn it on, then right click the button to bring up the snap options dialog box. Select Vertex and deselect Grid Points.

Close the dialog box and click Create Line in the Modify panel. When you mouse over the splines, you should see a blue cross at each of the vertex locations. On the front and back of the vehicle, connect the six top and bottom vertices. For example, click the top middle vertex then the bottom middle vertex. Right click anywhere in the scene (this ends the Create Line mode). If the surface flips "inside out," adjust the Flip Normals option in the Surface modifier.

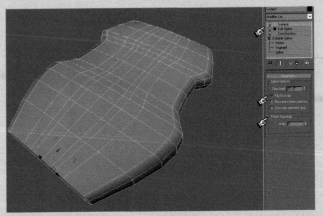

Step 5: Making the Surface

Before applying the Surface modifier, apply an Edit Spline modifier so we can cap the sides, but not the ends, of the surface. Now apply the Surface modifier so we can see the result with uncapped ends. Press F3 to toggle between Wire Frame and Smooth + Highlights in the view port. Since we want a nice balance of polygons and performance, we'll turn the Patch Topology Steps to 1. At this point, the surface might look "inside out." You can turn on Flip Normals to fix the problem, but later, it might flip back the other way, so if it does, come back here and turn it on and off as needed.

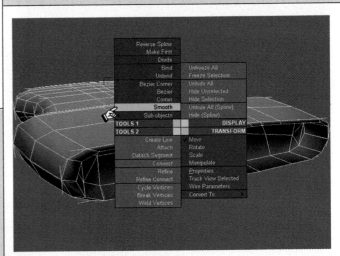

Step 7: Tweaking the Surface

Once your caps are created, you might notice that the polygon edges are not straight. To fix this, enter Vertex sub-object mode, select all vertices within the Edit Spline modifier, then right click over one of the vertices to bring up the Quad Menu. Choose the Smooth option in the upper left hand Quad. This will smooth the spline handles creating a smoother surface.

If you want to adjust the overall surface, now is a good time to do so. To move or scale a cross section, enter Spline sub-object mode in the base Editable Spline object and select the spline shape you want to transform. Your surface should update showing you immediate results. (Remember: The S key toggles 3D Snaps on and off). Now collapse the object to an Editable Mesh: Select the Surface modifier at the top of the Modifier Stack and right click—select Collapse All. This Patch modeling technique is an extremely powerful approach for most modeling jobs. If you want to be really crazy, you could add another Edit Mesh modifier on top of the Surface modifier to retain the modifier stack. This would allow you to retain full control over every aspect of your procedural model.

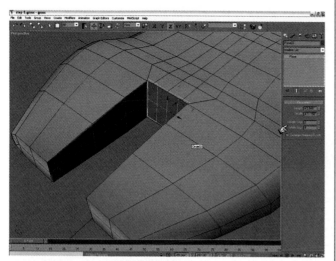

Step 8: Making the Front

Now, we'll delete faces on the surface of the ship, then weld multiple Plane objects back into place. In the Top view port, select a group of polygons (Face sub-object mode) on the front section and delete them. This will create the two "prongs" of the ship.

Now create three Plane objects (Create>Geometry>Plane) for the cutaway interior. The front facing panel will need to be 2 Length Segments x 4 Width Segments (you can adjust these parameters in the Plane Length and Width parameters), and the side planes will need to be 3x2 segments. This will give us a matching number of vertices on the model.

After the three Plane objects are roughly in place, select the Editable Mesh object, then use the Attach command to attach the Plane objects. Use Move and Scale tools to adjust the Plane objects while keeping them nice and flat. Once all the vertices are lined up, select all vertices and set your Weld Threshold to 1.0. Then press Weld Selected. If your vertices don't weld properly, increase the Weld Threshold or manually tweak the positions of the vertices that don't look right.

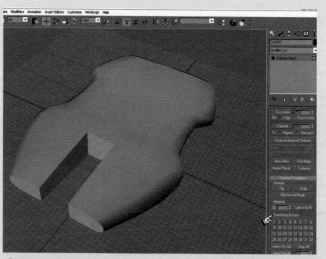

Step 9: Smoothing

Once we've welded all the vertices in place, the surface smoothing may look strange—like it's trying to smooth an edge without enough polygons. Let's fix that. Turn on the selection option called Ignore Visible Faces. This will select all polygons that are within a preset (45-degree) angle. Now pick one face on one of the Planes that you welded into place. It should select the whole flat area.

Go to the bottom of the Command Panel, and you should see a list of buttons with a matrix of numbers. These are your Smoothing Groups. When two polygons have the same group, they will look smooth. Change each of the planes to have different smoothing group numbers. Once you've figured that out, do that same for the front vents and the rear engine. (Don't forget to turn off the Ignore Visible Edges option when you're done).

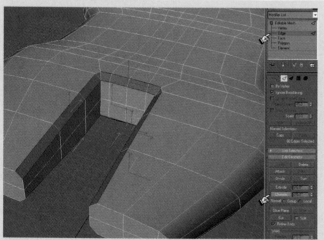

Step 10: Chamfering

The Chamfer tool is not only great for smoothing sharp edges, it can also act like a refinement tool, creating a polygon where an edge once was. First, make a nice chamfered edge around the front rim of the prongs: Select all the edges on the top and bottom of the front rim, and use the Chamfer tool to create a chamfer edge. Next, we want to extrude out some detail in the front wall we added. We want to extrude out a poly right in the middle, so let's chamfer the middle edge, leaving a new center strip for us to extrude. Select the edges on the back wall including two edges along each side and chamfer those to make a new strip of polygons for extruding.

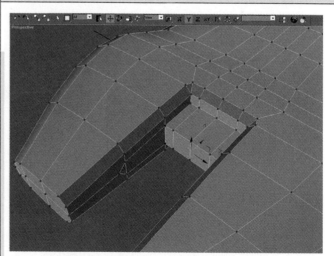

Step 11: Extruding

To create the details in the front, we'll use the Extrude tool, but we'll have to delete faces ahead of time to ensure that we don't end up with two faces next to each other that are never seen. The first faces to delete are on each side of the front wall we created. We'll be extruding the middle row of polygons, so go ahead and delete the two polygons on the side walls of the prongs. Next, select the back row of four faces and Extrude them out so they cover the holes you created on the side. The Extrude tool can be accessed via the Quad Menu (right-click the selected face). Finally, select all the close vertices and Weld them together. (Remember you can increase the Weld Threshold if necessary).

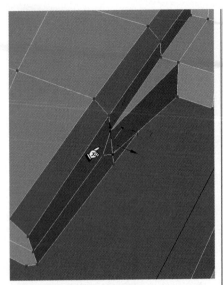

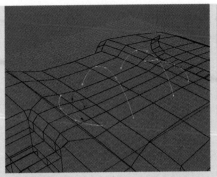

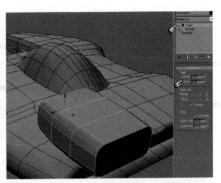

Step 12: Making the Front Interior Vents

Next we're going to extrude out the front interior vents. These will overlap the two faces on each side of the extrusion you just made, so let's delete those polygons. Now select two polygons adjacent to the deleted faces and Extrude out the two vents. Again, Extrude them out so they overlap the hole you created by previously deleting those faces. Once this is done, Weld the vertices to close the hole you made. Now, go into Vertex mode and click the Target button in the Weld group. Last, take the other end of the vent and target weld the vertices back to the original surface.

Step 13: Creating the Canopy

Create the canopy with patches using the same techniques we used to create the body of the cruiser. Start by using the Arc object (located in the Create>Geometry>Shapes panel) for our initial spline shape. Draw out an Arc for your canopy in the front view. Scale and rotate the objects till they look like the screen shot. After you position your shape objects, collapse them to Editable Splines. Use the Attach command to join the splines together, in order, and apply a Cross Section modifier and a Surface modifier. Set the steps to 1 this time. You may need to Flip the normals if the resulting surface appears "inside out."

Your modifier stack should look something like this: Surface, Edit Spline, Cross Section, Editable Spline.

Step 14: Creating the Boosters

Activate the Front view and draw out a Rectangle shape (Create>Geometry>Shapes) for the booster engines. Go to the Modify panel and turn up the Corner Radius until the shape looks the way you want it. Now change the Interpolation Steps to 1. (The default is 6 and creates more polygons than we really need). Now apply an Extrude modifier to give it some depth. Increase the segments as well (4 will do). Now apply a Taper modifier to the booster and increase the Curve Amount spinner. Take a look at the modifier stack for reference. If you are unclear about what some of the controls do, feel free to tweak them until you get the desired output.

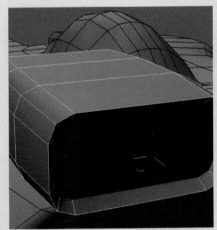

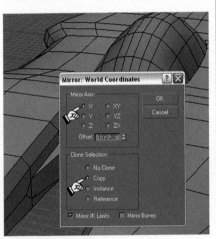

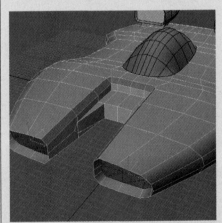

Step 15: Adding Booster Vents

Select the booster if it's not already selected, and collapse it to an Editable Mesh. Select the two ends of the booster, and use the Bevel tool to bevel them inward. If the results aren't smooth, then use Ignore Visible Edges to select the inner ring and smooth it out.

Step 16: Finishing the Boosters

To finish off the boosters, select a face on the bottom and extrude it out to attach it to the ship. We moved it forward for a more interesting sleek look. After the booster looks correct, use the Mirror tool on the main toolbar to mirror it along the X-axis. Choose the Instance option and use the spinner to offset the copy to where you want it. You might need to make adjustments with the Move tool afterwards.

Step 17: Making the Front Intakes

The front vents are easy to make; we will use the Bevel tool again. Enable Polygon sub-object mode. Select the polygons on each side of the front of the ship and Bevel them inward. (The Bevel tool can be found in the Quad Menu or in the Edit Geometry rollout). After beveling the faces, use the Ignore Visible Edges selection tool to select all the newly created ring faces, and make them share the same smoothing group.

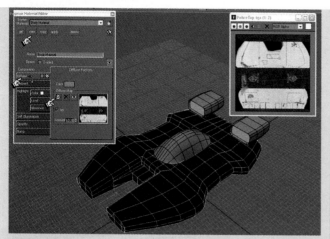

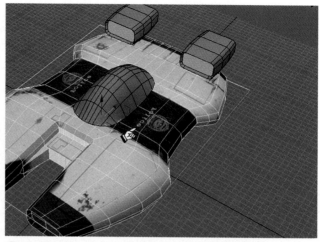

Step 18: Assigning a Material

Now that the body section is finished, let's make a new material for it so we can texture map it. We created our textures in Photoshop, but you can use any image editor. Realistic textures can make a good model look great—and low quality textures can make even the best model look bad. Once you've created your textures, save them in TGA format. Now press "m" on the keyboard. This opens the Material Editor. Click New to make a new material, and give it a name (properly naming objects and materials will save you time and grief later).

Now select the body and click Apply. This will apply your texture map to the model. In the Diffuse tab, click the Pick Map File button (look for the icon with the checkerboard in the folder). Open the *gmax* Material Navigator (the Navigator and the Material Editor work hand in hand). You can use the Navigator as your Material Library: Every texture you make will be visible in the Navigator. To edit a material double click a material in the Navigator. This will "activate" it in the *gmax* Material Editor.

Step 19: Applying Texture Coordinates

Once you've applied a material to your ship, it might look very strange since we never applied mapping coordinates. Mapping coordinates are the instructions that position the textures on sections of geometry. Texture mapping is as much art as it is science, and only loads of practice will hone your skills.

Select the ship body and apply a UVW Map modifier from the modifier drop-down list. Once the modifier has been applied you will need to determine the best projection type. Change the Alignment radio button to Y instead of Z. Now that it's projecting in the right direction, we want to make it fit over the body. You can press the Fit button to fit it to the mesh, or use Move, Scale, and Rotation tools to position the modifier correctly.

Step 20: Mapping a Selection

As we hinted at before, texture mapping is a complex task. In the previous step we applied a texture to a whole model. In this step we will apply a texture to a selection of faces. The texture we created contains the word "Police." Now check the screen shot from step 19. If you've made that text read left to right in the last step, take a look at the other side of your model. The other side will read backwards! This problem is easy to fix. First, collapse the body to an Editable Mesh.

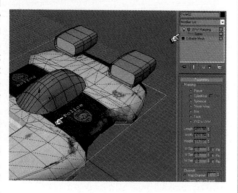

Note that the UVW Map modifier that you applied previously gets "baked into" the editable mesh when you collapse the stack. Now, select all the polygons on the side of the ship where the text reads backwards. Apply another UVW Map modifier, and this time it will map the selection rather than the whole object. Enable the Gizmo sub-object mode and rotate the UVW Map Gizmo 180 degrees in the Y-axis so that both sides have the text projecting the proper way. Repeat these steps for the bottom of the ship.

Step 21: Mapping the Front Intakes

Start again by collapsing the body to an Editable Mesh. Now, before mapping the front intakes and rear exhaust ports, let's create another new material and apply it to the faces of the intakes. Select the front intakes, and the rear exhaust port. (Use the Ignore Visible Edges tool for the flat surfaces with multiple polygons.)

Open the *gmax* Material Editor and click New. Don't forget to give it a name. Click the Pick Map File button and browse for your intake texture. Now click Apply while in Polygon sub-object mode, and the new material will be applied to the selected set of faces. 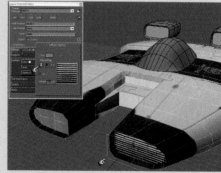 You'll need to select each group of faces and apply UVW Map modifiers to each of them at a time. Use the Alignment and Fit tools to get the UVW Map Gizmo in the right place. Try experimenting with the Normal Align tool and the Region Fit tool.

When you apply a texture to a sub-object selection, *gmax* automatically creates a "Multi/Sub-Object Material." You can read more about materials in the *gmax* User Reference.

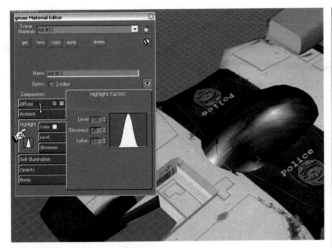

Step 22: A Shiny Canopy

Select the canopy object. If you haven't already applied a UVW Map modifier to this object, do so now. Once again, in the *gmax* Material Editor click the New button to make a new material for the canopy. Give it a name. Choose the bitmap that you want to use for the diffuse component using the Pick Map File button. Apply the material to the canopy object.

After you apply the material to the canopy, select the Highlight component in the *gmax* Material Editor. Set the highlight Level to 100 and the Glossiness to 45. This will give the canopy a more shiny appearance. Keep in mind that this highlight effect shades the vertices of the mesh, so the more polygons, the smoother it will look. (But since this is a low-res game style model, low polys are good!)

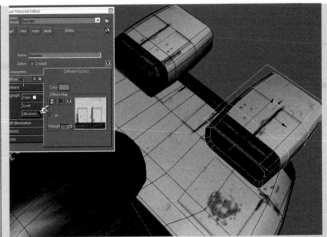

Step 23: Mapping the Boosters

The boosters should be texture mapped using the same techniques described in the steps above: Load texture, select faces, apply UVW Map modifier. Since the second booster was created as an instance of the other, anything done to one will automatically be applied to the other. Keep in mind that collapsing the stack on either object will destroy this relationship.

Make a new material in the *gmax* Material Editor for the boosters. Pick the appropriate texture map. Select both boosters and click Apply. Since the boosters are instanced, select one of them and add a UVW Map modifier. We changed the alignment to the Y-axis, used the Fit tool, and even checked the Flip option for V Tile.

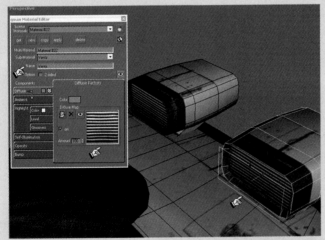

Step 24: Booster Intake Vents

We already made a vent material and applied it to the body of the ship, so let's find it and use it again here. Open up the Material Editor and select the body of the ship. Click the Get button to get the material from the ship. This is a Multi/Sub-Object Material, so pick the intake vent material from the drop-down list within the Material Editor. (This illustrates why it is important to name your materials accurately.) Select one of the boosters, collapse it to an Editable Mesh, and select the faces where the vent texture should go and click Apply in the *gmax* Material Editor. While those faces are selected, add a UVW Map modifier and repeat this for the second booster.

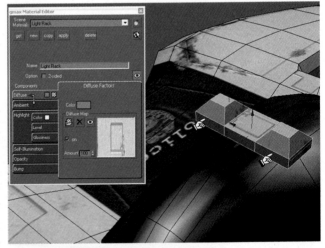

Step 25: Creating the Light Rack

Since the most recognizable feature of a police car is its rack of colored lights, we'll build a futuristic set for this 21st century police cruiser. Activate the Top view (press the T key in any active view port), and make a Box primitive to use as the base of the light rack. Make it rectangular and give it three Width Segments. Collapse this to an Editable Mesh and select two of the top faces on either side of the center face. You can use the Polygon sub-object mode for this operation. Use the Bevel tool to bevel out the two lights. Create a new material in the Material Editor, and choose the appropriate texture map. Exit subobject mode and add a UVW Map modifier to the light rack.

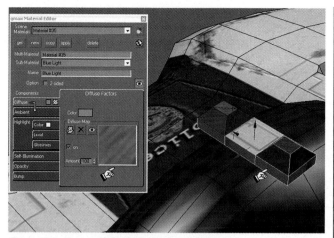

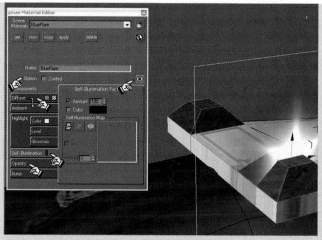

Step 26: Face Mapping the Lights

Now we'll employ another texture mapping technique: face mapping. Select the light rack and collapse it to an Editable Mesh. Select the five faces on one of the bevels that you created in the last step. Create a new material in the Material Editor and choose the red light texture for the diffuse component. Notice how the texture we created has a glass-like effect to it.

While the beveled faces are selected, click Apply. This will apply a single texture to the entire selection—which isn't the effect we want. Now apply a UVW Map modifier to this selection. The UVW Map modifier has a mapping option called Face; select this option now. This type of mapping will apply your texture to each of the selected faces and align the texture map one-for-one on each of the faces. Repeat this for the blue light as well.

Step 27: Creating the Light Flares

We can use transparency with textures to create interesting effects. In this step let's create light flares for the red and blue rack lights. Activate the Right view, and create a Plane object with one length segment and one width segment. To constrain the Plane object to a square while in create mode, hold down the Ctrl key as you drag out the shape.

Move the plane object to the center of one of the lights. Create a new material and pick the blue flare texture for the Diffuse component. Next, click the Opacity component. Pick the FlareOpacity.tga texture for the opacity component. This texture will act as an alpha mask for the Opacity channel. Make sure the plane object is selected and click Apply. The object should automatically become transparent. If it doesn't, click the top "eye" icon. Since this is a flare that gives off light, it should "self-illuminate." Click the Self-Illumination channel and set the Amount to 100. We also want the flare to be seen from both sides, so check the 2-Sided checkbox in the material editor.

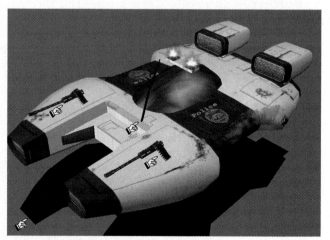

Step 28: Finishing the Flares

Now that we have one flare all ready to go, let's copy it and rotate it so that we see a flare from all angles. Select the flare object, and while holding down the Shift key, rotate it 90 degrees on the Z-axis, so it faces the front. By holding down the Shift key, you can quickly copy, instance, or reference an object while transforming it. We used this same technique earlier—so this should be familiar territory. Do this again with the new flare, this time rotating along the X-axis. You should now have three flares that look something like the screenshot. Create another material using the red flare texture, and copy the three planes over to the other side.

Step 29: Use What You've Learned

Now that you've learned a few modeling and texture mapping techniques, add your own accessories to the model. We added machine guns, an antenna, and even a polyshape for the shadow on the ground. All of the textures required for building this model have been made available on the bundled CD for you to play with and tweak. A good beginning project would be to texture map the bottom of the model (we didn't cover this step in the tutorial). We've also included the final model for reference. A more advanced project would be to prepare this model for export for one of the *gmax* ready games. Imagine flying this cruiser around in *Command & Conquer: Renegade!* ■

What is currently Intel's finest?

If you're looking for a new CPU, there are only two choices for ultimate performance on the PC: Intel and AMD. Intel is still king of the hill in the microprocessor business in terms of volume, but some would argue that it no longer has a lock on the performance crown. Intel's flagship CPU today is the Pentium 4 Extreme Edition (P4EE), which has transistors that are 0.13-microns thick. This chip packs quite a punch thanks to its 2.5MB of onboard L2 and L3 cache, which is used for storing frequently used data and instructions. If 2.5MB of cache sounds good, then temper that with the painful street price of about $1,000 per chip. It's painful even when you keep in mind the fact that Intel sells virtually the same chip (in the form of the Xeon) to guys in business suits for use in corporate servers for about four times that price. The P4EE is now offered at speeds up to 3.4GHz.

The emergence of the P4EE took many by surprise, since it was introduced shortly after Intel launched an improved version of the standard Pentium 4 (non-extreme, in other words). Code-named Prescott, the revamped P4 packs new instructions for better performance in gaming and multimedia, as well as improved Hyper-Threading (Intel's fancy way of saying "virtual dual processors.") There's also 1MB of cache, vs. 512KB of cache in the older Pentium 4, and it's more efficient at processing long instructions. Unfortunately, software must be specifically coded to take advantage of the features in the "new" Prescott Pentium 4, so we don't expect it to shine until it's up near the 5GHz range.

What is currently AMD's finest?

In the AMD camp, the company continues to turn heads with the catchy phrase "64-bit computing," referring to its new 64-bit CPUs. You can expect all of AMD's top-of-the-line and mid-range CPUs to contain 64-bit capabilities. What's the big deal with 64-bit computing? Well, there are two advantages to 64-bit computing: The first is it supports craploads of RAM. If you want 8GB, you can have it with the Athlon 64 series. The second is 64-bit data types. By processing data 64 bits at a time, you can essentially double the amount of processing power of a 32-bit processor. The only problem is that software, including Windows XP, has to be coded to take advantage of the 64-bit CPUs, and we don't expect to see a lot of movement on this front until 64-bit CPUs are a bit more common.

Fortunately, the Athlon 64 is still freakishly fast in 32-bit code. Most of this is due to its large 1MB L2 cache and integrated memory controller. The memory controller in most traditional PCs (such as the Athlon XP and Pentium 4) is handled by a separate chip called the north bridge. The North bridge chips and memory controllers run at far lower speeds than the CPU core. By attaching the northbridge chip directly to the CPU core, AMD is able to run its memory controller at the core speed, meaning that, with the 2.4GHz Athlon 64 FX-53, you have a 2.4GHz memory controller. That gives the chip splendid memory latency and incredible bandwidth.

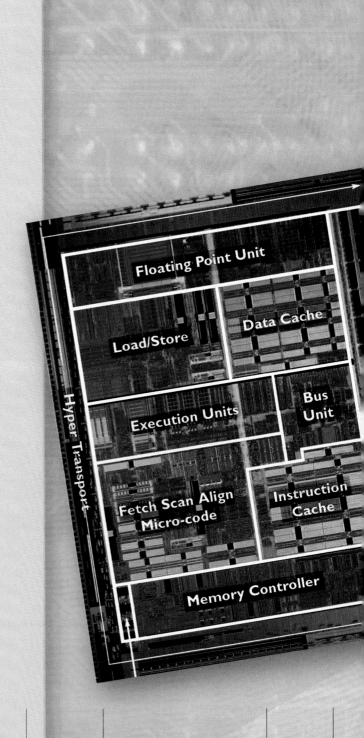

CPUs & COOLING

The need for speed still

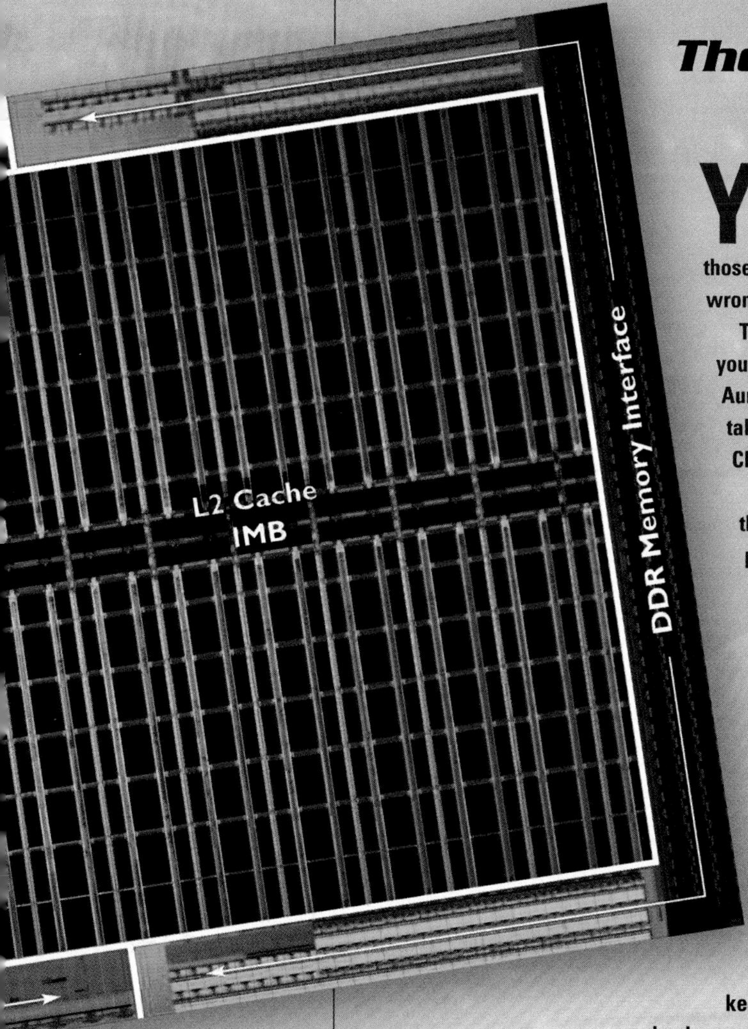

L2 Cache
1MB

DDR Memory Interface

A CPU up close looks a lot like the floorplan for your average one bedroom apartment.

You may have heard that nobody will ever need more power than a 60MHz processor. Yeah right. Those same PC-power naysayers said the same thing at 500MHz, 1GHz, and 3GHz. As always, those negative nabobs were flat-out wrong then, and they're flat-out wrong now.

The primary spec of a CPU is pretty basic: Clock speed. If it takes you overnight to render a home movie for a DVD you're authoring for Aunt Fannie, or if batch conversions of pictures from your new digital camera take longer than brewing a pot of coffee, then a faster CPU will be just about the most valuable upgrade you can make.

Trying to decode the megahertz madness isn't an easy job, though. Even though clock speed still matters, today it's entirely possible that in some applications and games, a 1,000MHz slower CPU can be faster. To wit, despite its 1GHz clock speed disadvantage when compared head-to-head with Intel's finest, AMD's Athlon 64 FX series is generally recognized as the better CPU for gaming. That doesn't make the Pentium 4 a wimp, though, because in just about any MP3 encoding apps, the P4 still rules the roost.

To discover the fastest processor for your needs, just think about what you do with your PC. Does your boat float on scientific applications that are floating-point intensive? Then look to AMD. Do you edit video with the latest version of Adobe *Premiere*, or are you a *Photoshop* fiend? Then the Pentium 4 is your elixir of choice.

Before you drop some ducats on a new processor, also keep in mind that sweeping changes are about to overtake the PC landscape. What changes? Follow along as we walk you through what's going to happen in the next 12 months in the land of the CPU.

All the specs and tech lingo explained

BGA
Ball Grid Array. This is a method of packaging a chip in which the chip is attached to the printed circuit board by means of solder balls instead of pins or leads. This method of attachment offers better electrical contact than using leads or pins.

Branch Prediction
A method of improving CPU performance by predicting the results of likely computations and speculatively executing subsequent code. With branch prediction, the CPU tries to guess which direction the program is heading next and executes code based on that guess. If the CPU guesses right, it saves time by not having to wait for the computational result before proceeding. If it guesses wrong, it pays a price in wasted work and clock cycles.

Clock Speed
The frequency at which a CPU executes instructions. Clock speed is usually expressed in megahertz (MHz) or gigahertz (GHz).

Floating Point Instruction
Instructions that involve data with decimal points. For example, 3.266 is a floating point number. The "point" is the decimal, which "floats" by changing places as the numbers being computed change.

Front-Side Bus Speed
The speed of the connection between the CPU and the main memory (RAM) on the motherboard. Front-side bus is frequently abbreviated into its acronym, "FSB," and is usually expressed in MHz.

Gates
Transistors in a CPU are also known as gates because they are essentially switches that open and close to control the flow of signals to the processor.

Hyper-Threading
An Intel technology that permits the CPU to execute two program threads in parallel, as if it were two separate CPUs. A Hyper-Threaded CPU shows up as two separate processors in the operating system.

L2 Cache
Like all CPU caches, Level 2 cache (aka L2) functions as memory that stores frequently used data and instructions. When the CPU can't find the data or instructions it requires in L1 cache, it turns to the slightly slower-- but considerably larger--L2 cache for answers.

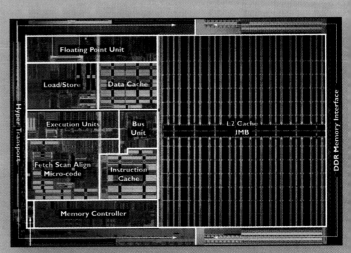

L2 cache is where a CPU stores information for fast retrieval. Building it into the CPU reduces latency (the time the CPU has to wait for instructions) and improves performance.

Integer Instruction
Instructions that involve calculating whole numbers. For example, the numbers 0, 1 and 2 are integers.

L1 Cache
A tiny amount of extremely fast memory used for storing instructions and/or data. L1 cache is built into the CPU itself, and information on it is immediately available to the CPU with practically no delay.

L3 Cache
After the CPU looks for information in the L1 and L2 caches, it turns to the L3 cache. In comparison to the L1 and L2 caches, it takes more time to get to information on the L3 cache. Nonetheless, the L3 cache is dramatically faster than main memory. Not many CPUs include an L3 cache, but Intel's Itanium processors and some of its Xeon CPUs stand out as notable exceptions.

Micron
A metric unit equaling one millionth of a meter. One micron is about 100 times thinner than a human hair. Modern processors like the Pentium 4 and Athlon 64 feature wire traces that are 0.13 microns thick!

Multiplier
A function built into a CPU that, when combined with a system's front-side bus speed (FSB), determines the CPU's speed. For example, a 100MHz front-side bus coupled with a multiplier of 8x produces a CPU that runs at 800MHz.

Pipelines
In modern CPUs, instructions are broken down into several parts to allow for more efficient processing, and these parts are executed in a CPU's pipelines. The number of pipelines a CPU has determines how many steps an instruction can be broken down into. For example, a Pentium 4 has a 20-stage pipeline.

Register
A special, high-speed storage area within a CPU. Data must be placed in a register before it can be processed. CPUs are sometimes categorized by the size of their registers; a 32-bit CPU has registers that are 32 bits wide.

SSE2
Streaming Single-instruction-multiple-data Extension 2. These are special instructions built into a processor that

correspond with "hooks" built into software to allow for more efficient processing of multimedia tasks. Software has to be coded to take advantage of these features, and SSE2 is one example of this.

Transistors Count
The number of microscopic transistors that make up the CPU chip. Modern CPUs typically contain tens of millions of transistors. For example, a Pentium 4 is made up of 55 million transistors, while an Athlon 64 packs 106 million.

Cooling Terms:

Active Cooling
An arrangement in which a fan is used to ensure a steady flow of air over the heatsink.

HSF
Heatsink and Fan. Most processors require a heatsink and fan to keep temperatures low and maintain reliable operation.

Passive cooling
An arrangement in which nothing is used to ensure a steady flow of air over the heatsink. This typically means that just a heatsink is used, rather than a heatsink/fan combination.

Phase Change
A process in which a coolant is evaporated and condensed (usually with the help of a compressor). Cooling systems that utilize phase change can reduce temperatures below the ambient room temperature. A refrigerator is a phase-change device.

Heat Spreader
A piece of metal—usually aluminum or copper—placed on top of a CPU die to improve transmission of heat away from it. Both the Pentium 4 and Athlon 64 feature heat spreaders.

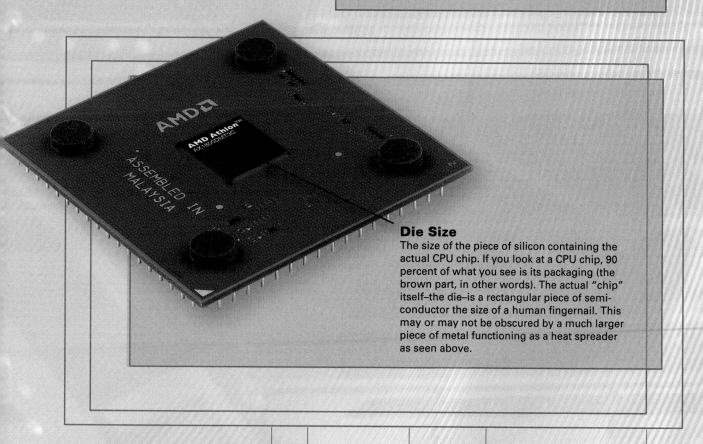

Die Size
The size of the piece of silicon containing the actual CPU chip. If you look at a CPU chip, 90 percent of what you see is its packaging (the brown part, in other words). The actual "chip" itself—the die—is a rectangular piece of semiconductor the size of a human fingernail. This may or may not be obscured by a much larger piece of metal functioning as a heat spreader as seen above.

CPUs & COOLING Cheat Sheet

You've got questions, we've got an-

Question: Which company, Intel or AMD, is selling the fastest CPU, and which company is selling the best-valued CPU?

A: Sadly, this depends on how you define "fast." Today, having software that's properly coded for a CPU's architecture is almost as important as the CPU's clock speed. In general, the 3.4GHz Pentium 4 Extreme Edition is faster in most audio, video,

Intel's Pentium 4 Extreme Edition may be the fastest CPU in captivity, but the Athlon 64 FX 53 is just a bit slower and costs less than half the price.

and general applications than the 2.4GHz Athlon 64 FX-53. However, the Athlon 64 FX-53 is faster in gaming thanks to its on-die memory controller. Overall, the P4EE gets the nod for being speed king, while the Athlon 64 FX-53 gets it for pricing, since it's about $200 (at press time) cheaper than the P4EE and runs faster in some apps and games than the P4 solution. AMD CPUs, in general, have always been less expensive than Intel's, and are a favorite of the "build it yourself" crowd, while the "money is no object" crowd usually favors Intel silicon.

Question: What is thermal paste and how do I properly apply it?

A: Thermal paste is the Cheez Whiz-like substance that you are supposed to spread between a heatsink and CPU to promote better heat transfer between them. The paste fills in the tiny gaps between the heatsink and CPU, and greatly increases the conductivity between the two. Failure to put paste on the CPU could lead to system major instability. The amount of paste to apply depends on what brand of paste you're using and whether you are putting it on a CPU with a heat spreader or on the core itself. If you're putting the paste on a heat spreader, you'll generally need just a bb-sized dollop of paste in the center of the heat spreader. On CPUs without heat spreaders, like the Athlon XP, you're not supposed to apply it directly to the core. Instead, put it on the heatsink, spread it out with a plastic bag, and then apply it to the CPU. Also, be careful not to apply too much paste, which is messy and will ooze out all over your CPU like a smashed PBJ sammich. Second, remember some thermal paste is conductive, and getting a bunch of it on your CPU or motherboard could lead to short circuits. Third, too much paste defeats the purpose. We recommend Artic Silver (http://www.arcticsilver.com/) because it works great and is affordable.

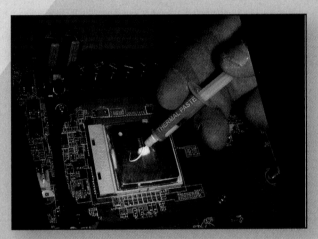

Applying thermal paste to the CPU greatly increases thermal conductivity and is a must for today's hot, hot, hot CPUs.

Overclocking voids your warranty, but excessive overclocking could void the CPU itself.

Question: How easy is it to damage a CPU during either overclocking or improper installation?

A: Most overclocking (running your CPU above its rated speed) hijinks usually don't permanently damage the CPU in the short term. However, excessive overclocking, especially with inadequate cooling, can greatly shorten the life of the processor. A stock CPU from Intel or AMD will usually give you many years of service before dying. However, an overclocked CPU could fail after several months, or after two or three years of overclocking. It's really a crap shoot. We've seen cases in which the CPUs simply stopped running at the overclocked speed after two years of service, but still ran fine at the stock speeds. Minor overclocking feats usually won't hurt much, though, and in cases where you're overclocking a lower-bin part (say, a 2.4GHz Pentium 4C) to higher speeds, you can probably get away with it for some time without any ill side effects.

The Athlon 64 FX-53 will come into its own when applications actually support its 64-bit architecture.

Question: What are the real-world benefits of 64-bit computing, and will I be able to reap those benefits today, a few months from now, or a few years from now?

A: Does 64-bit computing really matter yet? Yes and no. Taking advantage of the 64-bitness in the Athlon 64 series requires an operating system that supports 64-bit transfers. As of this writing, Windows XP 64-Bit Edition was only shipping with Itanium-based systems with the promise of a wider release (at least to OEMs) later this year. When available, the first major benefit will be large memory support, which means if your system supports 8GB of RAM, you can run it. Obviously, more beneficence comes from the 64-bit application support.

Question: What upcoming technologies will allow us to keep pace with Moore's Law, and guarantee that circuit paths will continue to shrink?

A: Moore's Law, which says transistors on a chip would double every 24 months, will likely continue for many more years. One area that's expected to go through a change within the next few years is the technology used to draw the circuits. Today, trying to draw the circuits used to make 90-nm CPUs is like trying to write calligraphy with a paint roller. By 2007, we should have the first chips (including CPU, GPU, and RAM) using Extreme Ultraviolet lithography or EUV. EUV is expected to be useable on chips down to at least 30 nanometers.

This year, we should see the first PC CPU to use strained silicon. Intel literally stretches the silicon in its chips to reorient the atoms in a manner that allows for the faster flow of electricity. As a practical matter, many believe Moore's Law will see an end by the year 2020, when we're pushing 16-nm chips.

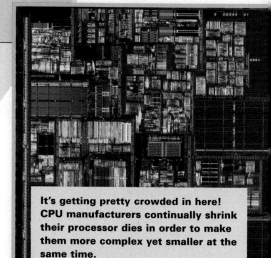

It's getting pretty crowded in here! CPU manufacturers continually shrink their processor dies in order to make them more complex yet smaller at the same time.

Processor Spec Finder
Your source for specs on Intel® processors

Intel® Pentium® II Xeon™ processors at 450.00 MHz

🛈 This processor is no longer shipping

Results

sSpec Number	SL36W		
Processor Frequency	450.00 MHz	CPUID String	0653
Package Type	S.E.C.C.	Core Voltage	2.0V
Bus Speed	100 MHz	Thermal Guideline	34.5W
Core Stepping	B1	Thermal Spec	75°C
L2 Cache Size	512K	Manufacturing Technology	0.25 micron
L2 Cache Speed	450 MHz	Bus/Core Ratio	4.5
Spec Update			
Notes			

More information can be found in the Pentium® II Xeon™ processor Spec Update.

The processor's L2 cache has a 64GB address range.

The L2 cache's ECC cannot be disabled on this processor.

Intel's online database will tell you everything you ever wanted to know, and then some, about your CPU.

Question: How can I determine the exact voltages and temperature thresholds of my CPU?

A: This takes a little bit of work. First, open up your PC, remove your heatsink, clean off the thermal paste, and look for the S Spec on the heat spreader (or, even esier, look at the box your CPU came in). On a 3.2GHz Pentium 4 Extreme Edition, for example, the S-spec is SL7AA. Assuming you have another computer that works nearby, point your browser to http://processorfinder.intel.com/. Once there, you can punch in your S-spec and Intel will tell you the core stepping, thermal spec (64 degrees Celsius), and voltage (maximum of 1.550 volts). On the Prescott Pentium 4, Intel has taken CPU temperatures to a new level. Each processor will be able to tell the computer what its maximum temperature threshold is.

On Athlon XP CPUs, you also need to remove the heatsink to find the processor's "ordering part number" or OPN. On an Athlon XP 3200+, for example, it's AXDA3200DKV4E. The AX means the chip is an Athlon XP. The DA means it's a 0.13-micron part, the D indicates it uses an organic PGA package, the K tells you its operating voltage of 1.65 volts, the V is maximum die temperature (85 degrees Celsius), the 4 is the amount of cache (512KB), and the E tells you it is a 400MHz bus processor. If you want to check out your Athlon XP, visit: http://www.amd.com/gb-uk/assets/content_type/DownloadableAssets/Processor_Recognition_Rev05_ENG.pdf.

ADDING AN AFTERMARKET
Fan TO YOUR Pentium 4

1. Choosing a Fan

Any retail CPU package will include a stock heatsink that has been approved for use by the CPU's manufacturer, but the upgrader in you may desire more cooling, less noise, or both. A high-speed fan will provide better cooling for your P4, but may sound like an airplane taxiing down the runway. Meanwhile, a fan with multiple speed settings will allow you to strike a balance between cooling and noise. Most fans have a noise-level specification printed on the box—anything around 32 decibels or lower should be tolerable.

Fan speed aside, there are two characteristics you should look for in a CPU cooler: First, you'll want either an all-copper heatsink or an aluminum heatsink with a copper base; all-aluminum heatsinks don't transfer enough heat to meet the demands of today's fastest processors, but copper does a terrific job. Second, the larger the diameter of your CPU fan, the more air it will move at a given rotational speed.

2. Installing the Fan

The heatsink/fan isn't the only part of the CPU cooling equation—the thermal compound you apply between the processor and the heatsink is just as important. At Maximum PC, we prefer Arctic Silver 5 (www.arcticsilver.com). Carefully clean off any residual thermal compound from both your CPU and heatsink using rubbing alcohol before applying a new layer or Arctic Silver.

To install a new P4 heatsink/fan, you'll need to follow the instructions in the box, since installation procedures may vary. (Most Pentium 4 coolers will somehow lock on to the plastic frame surrounding the CPU socket.) Once your new cooler is mounted, don't forget to plug the fan into the power header on your motherboard! We recommend monitoring your CPU temperatures for a little while after installing a new heatsink/fan, especially if you're overclocking. You can do this in the BIOS (usually on the Health screen), or from within Windows using a free utility like Motherboard Monitor (included on the CD). In general, a Pentium 4 processor should not exceed 115 degrees Fahrenheit under a heavy workload.

Pentium 4 heatsink/fan contraptions reside within a plastic frame with four posts. Each post clips into a bracket surrounding the CPU socket on the motherboard.

3. The Awesome Blossom

Our top pick for a Pentium 4 cooler is the Zalman CNPS7000A-Cu (www.zalman.co.kr). This flower-like heatsink/fan offers two speed settings ("silent" and "normal"), both of which are pretty quiet. And at the "normal" setting, the CNPS7000A-Cu delivers enough cooling power for moderate overclocking.

This Zalman fan/heatsink moves a lot of air, and is one of the best CPU cooling solutions on the market.

4. Megahertz for Nuthin'

Overclocking is the dark art of running a chip above its rated speed. Sometimes it works, sometimes it doesn't—and it could potentially damage your hardware, so don't try overclocking unless you're comfortable with the risks. However, careful overclocking can often yield extra performance for little or no extra money.

Your CPU's speed is determined by multiplying the speed of your front-side bus (FSB) with the processor's multiplier ratio. For example, an 100MHz FSB times a multiplier of sixteen equals a 1.6GHz processor (100 x 16 = 1600). Make sense? You can usually overclock a CPU by changing either the FSB speed or the multiplier ratio (or both). Unfortunately, all Pentium 4 processors ship with their multipliers locked, leaving the FSB as the only overclocking option. Most motherboards allow you to change the FSB speed from within the BIOS (this option is usually located on the Frequency/Voltage Control menu). We recommend increasing the FSB speed a few megahertz at a time (for instance, going from 200MHz to 203Mhz) and monitoring CPU temperature and system stability after each bump up. A word of warning: Unless your mobo supports independent FSB, memory, AGP, and PCI clock speeds, overclocking the FSB will overclock the latter three as well, potentially causing reliability problems.

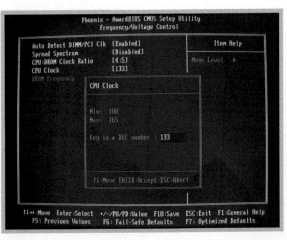

These days, overclocking is usually done by adjusting the FSB speeds in our system's BIOS.

ADDING AN AFTERMARKET
Fan TO YOUR Athlon CPU

1. Choosing a Fan

Picking a heatsink/fan for your CPU inevitably involves a tradeoff between noise and cooling performance. You can either have massive cooling with a lot of noise or less cooling and quieter operation. If noise pollution is a concern, look for a fan that generates 32 decibels of noise or less (most manufacturers provide a decibel rating on a fan's retail box). There are two features you should look for in any Athlon cooler: First of all, a big fan will offer better cooling than a small one without spinning as fast. However, some Athlon motherboards have capacitors positioned very close to the CPU socket, preventing the installation of large coolers. Second, choose a heatsink that features a copper base or an all-copper design, as these are better at wicking away heat than all-aluminum heatsinks.

Our recommendations? The Zalman CNPS7000A-Cu (www.zalman.co.kr) is an excellent heatsink/fan that's compatible with both the Athlon and the Athlon 64 and can be set to either "silent" or "normal" modes. Meanwhile, the Thermaltake A4002D (www.thermaltake.com) is an inexpensive cooler that utilizes new Tip-Magnetic driving fan technology that funnels air directly to the heat source for better performance with less noise.

2. Installing the Fan

The thermal compound between your cooler and the surface of your CPU is just as important as the cooler itself. Here at *Maximum PC*, we've used Arctic Silver (www.arcticsilver.com) for years, and it remains our favorite thermal compound. Before applying new thermal compound, don't forget to clean off any leftover compound from both your CPU and heatsink using rubbing alcohol.

Installing an Athlon heatsink/fan for the first time can be tricky. Apply a small amount of thermal compound to the heatsink and then place the heatsink directly on top of the die. Clip one side of the heatsink to the CPU socket, then grab a flat-head screwdriver and push the other clip down and slightly outward, hooking it onto the CPU socket. Be very careful not to push too hard, or you might inadvertently crush your processor's delicate core! Finally, don't forget to plug the fan into your motherboard's fan power connector.

Once your new cooler is installed, keep tabs on your CPU temperatures. You can do this through the Health screen of the BIOS on most mobos, or through Windows using a program such as Motherboard Monitor (mbm. livewiredev.com). In general, an Athlon shouldn't exceed 130 degrees Fahrenheit during heavy usage.

The stock Athlon heatsink/fan will work just fine, but if you are overclocking you're going to need more juice.

Be careful placing the heatsink on your Athlon XP CPU. Since they lack heatspreaders, their delicate cores are exposed and can be damaged easily.

3. Let's Overclock!

Overclocking—the practice of running a computer chip above its rated speed—is a dark art that could damage your system and will void your warranty. Sounds like fun, no? When it works, overclocking can squeeze extra performance out of an aging system for little or no money, and one thing's for sure: It's easier on an Athlon than on a Pentium 4.

Your CPU's clock speed is determined by multiplying the speed of the system's FSB. Overclocking can thus be accomplished by changing the FSB speed, the multiplier ratio, or both. Like P4s, Athlons are multiplier-locked at the factory—but unlike P4s, most Athlons can be unlocked. The unlocking process is beyond the scope of this article, but the best place to start is an unlocking kit from HighSpeed PC (www.highspeedpc.com).

Most mobos allow FSB speed tweaks in the Frequency/Voltage Control menu of the BIOS. We recommend upping the FSB a few megahertz at a time and monitoring CPU temperatures and testing for stability after each increase. Also, unless your mobo allows separate FSB, memory, AGP, and PCI clocks (few do), overclocking the FSB will overclock the other three too, potentially limiting your success.

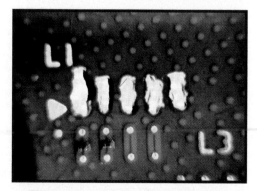

These connected circuits of this Athlon XP CPU tells us it's "unlocked" and ready for overclocking!

HOT OR NOT?
Is the heatsink/fan that came with my CPU sufficient or should I buy a better heatsink/fan?

The heatsink that came with your CPU is certified by the manufacturer of the CPU to offer sufficient cooling for running the CPU at its standard clock speed. If you plan on overclocking, however, it is wise to purchase an aftermarket cooling solution to handle the increased temperatures that overclocking produces.

MO' MEMORY
I was wondering how much of a performance boost the AMD XP CPUs get from running on a 166MHz FSB (333MHz) in conjunction with 333MHz DDR RAM? I've seen some websites that claim there's no significant performance gain. Is this because of the 64-bit CPU-to-memory data path that the Athlon XP uses?

The Athlon XP does experience a fair boost when its FSB is increased from 266MHz to 333MHz DDR. While clock speeds continue to climb at a crazy pace, memory bandwidth has not. The Athlon is handcuffed a bit by its narrower bus (the P4 has a 256-bit CPU-to-memory data path), but still benefits from the added bandwidth. In general, we recommend running your system's FSB and memory at the fastest speeds they'll tolerate.

CLOCK CONUNDRUM
I recently noticed that my AMD 1.1GHz processor has changed speed. It has operated at 1.1GHz for over a year and a half, but now it's operating at 850MHz. I haven't fooled with anything in the case, and no one else has used my system. How did this happen?

Your system's CMOS likely was reset. We've seen systems occasionally "forget" their configurations, and it usually indicates a bad connection on the CMOS battery, static build-up, or a dying CMOS battery. (The CMOS battery is that coin-cell on your motherboard.) What you need to do is go into your BIOS and

Although you might think a bundled heatsink/fan with a CPU would be bunk, they actually work quite well.

verify that the system bus is running at 133MHz. When the CMOS lost its contents, it probably defaulted to a 100MHz bus. The math backs this up: 8.5x100=850MHz; 8.5x133=1100MHz. The other possibility is that your system builder used a remarked Athlon. That is, he or she took an 850MHz Athlon, shorted the L1 bridges, and reset it to 1.1GHz. Over time, the material that's used to unlock the bridges can wear away, and the CPU can default to its stock 850MHz speed. The Doctor believes that your problem is more likely the first scenario than the second.

TOO HOT TO HANDLE
What is an acceptable temperature for my CPU to run at, and what is the best way to monitor its temperature?

In general, a Pentium 4 CPU should never go above 115 degrees Fahrenheit, and an Athlon should stay below 130 degrees. If either CPU is hovering above these levels, it would be wise to invest in a bigger, more efficient cooling mechanism for the CPU. The best way to check your CPU's temperature is to either look in your BIOS (there's usually a screen that displays the CPU temp and fan rotation speed, among other things.), or to use a program called

Motherboard Monitor

Motherboard Monitor, which is on the disc that accompanies this magazine.

DOUBLE TROUBLE
I was told that if you have dual CPUs, you can dedicate certain processes to each CPU. I was wondering if this would work for Intel's Hyper-Threading (HT) technology. Can I set background processes to run on the virtual second CPU, and everything else to run on the primary CPU? Would this boost performance?

Yes. Having a dual-processor or HT-enabled machine indeed makes it possible to dedicate workloads for processes and applications via Windows XP's Task Manager to the two "virtual" CPUs. However, keep in mind that Hyper-Threading is not the same as two physical CPUs. The single CPU still has the resources of a single CPU, it's just a little more efficient at doling them out when in HT mode. If, for example, you run two applications that both require the same functions of the CPU, the performance will be no better, and may even be worse, if the applications are not optimized for Hyper-Threading. On the other hand, if you run multiple applications that use different functions of the CPU, you can see quite an efficiency boost. HT isn't the magic bullet of computing, but it does work very well at some things.■

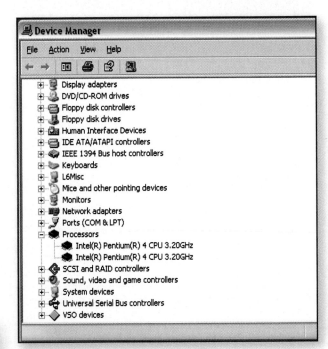

An Intel Hyper Threading-enabled CPU appears as two physical processors to the OS, but isn't as efficient as actually having two procs.

MAXIMUM... BOOKS?

300 PAGES EACH!

ALL COLOR! NO ADS!

Yes. It's true. *MAXIMUM PC* introduces the next generation in computer books!

Maximum PC Guide to Building a Dream PC

It's the biggest, meanest, *most complete* PC building guide we've ever created! Not only do we show first-time PC builders *everything* they need to know about assembling a computer from scratch, we also divulge the truth behind competing hardware technologies, and show you how to make the smartest parts choices. Includes configuration plans for six different Dream Machine archetypes. *By Will Smith, technical editor*

● **$29.99; AVAILABLE IN SEPT 04; ISBN 0-7897-3193-2**

Maximum PC 2005 Buyers Guide

Get an insider's peek at 2004's most exciting Lab experiments, plus forward looks at the gear you *must* know about in 2005. Includes the hidden story behind *Maximum PC* benchmarking, and a full compendium of our most positive—and brutal—2004 product reviews. Special Ask the Doctor and Watchdog wrap-ups make this a veritable *Maximum PC* almanac! A must-have reference book for faithful readers of the magazine. *By George Jones, editor-in-chief*

● **$29.99; AVAILABLE IN SEPT 04; ISBN 0-7897-3194-0**

Maximum PC Guide to PC Hardware Hacking

The most complete, most descriptive, most *helpful* book on case-modding ever published! Loaded with stunning illustrations and 100 percent *actionable* instructions, we show you how to construct a mind-blowing mod of your own. Painting, lighting, drilling, cutting, cooling... *every* topic is covered! Case-modder extraordinaire Paul Capello shares the tricks and insights that have made him a legend among hardware hacking experts. *By Paul Capello & Jon Phillips*

● **$29.99; AVAILABLE IN DEC 04; ISBN 0-7897-3192-4**

ALSO
Maximum PC Ultimate PC Performance Guide

All of *Maximum PC's* "newsstand only" special issues bound into a single book! Five issue's worth of content—a must-have treasure for *Maximum PC* fanatics.

● **$29.99; AVAILABLE IN SEPT 04; ISBN 0-7897-3317-X**

Q

What are the basic functions handled by my north bridge and south bridge chips?

The north bridge chip resides near the top of the mother-board, near the CPU socket, and serves as a four-way inter-section connecting the CPU, memory, video card (AGP) bus, and its partner, the south bridge chip. This means the north bridge chip allows the CPU to retrive information from memory, lets the videocard send commands from the AGP bus to the CPU and also lets all those plugged-in peripherals like your modem or network card down in the lower half of the motherboard communicate with the CPU and memory via the south bridge chip.

Most of a motherboard's "value-added" features—such as the IDE controller, USB controller, and onboard sound and Ethernet—are handled by the south bridge chip. It's worth noting that some core-logic chipsets, such as nVidia's nForce3, integrate all their functionality into a single chip, thus doing away with the north bridge/south bridge construct. Also, AMD's new Athlon 64 CPUs have integrated the memory controller diretly into the CPU, alleviating those duties from the north bridge chip.

Q

What are the pros and cons of onboard sound, video, RAID, and Ethernet support?

Back in the day (2001), motherboards included nothing but the basics—a PS2 port, serial, paral-lel and maybe, if you were lucky, a USB port. Nowadays though, motherboards include every pos-sible add-in feature you could ask for: Networking, sound, video, RAID (a technology for letting several hard drives work together as a single drive), FireWire, multiple USB ports, and more. In some case, such as with onboard RAID and Ethernet, you get the same level of functionality and performance you'd get from an add-in card. Having these features built into your motherboard is usually a good thing, since it frees up the PCI slots and could save you some money as well.

Integrated sound is a mixed bag though, with most chipsets offering poor-quality built-in sound that decreases overall performance by consuming valuable CPU cycles for audio processing. The notable exceptions are nVidia's nForce chipsets, which sound fantastic and even offer real-time Dolby Digital encoding and decoding capability!

Finally, onboard video may save you some money, but you'll pay a massive price in performance. For one, add-in cards have their own onboard memory to use in games, but integrated graphics chips usually just steal some of your system memory. Sure, they say it's "shared" but you don't want to share your precious memory with anyone or any-thing, trust us. More importantly, integrated video just plain sucks for today's demanding 3D games. If you must have integrated graphics, we can half-heartedly recommend ATI's Radeon 9100 IGP since it's the only chipset that boasts pro-grammable shaders demanded by next-generation games like *Half-Life 2* and *Doom 3*.

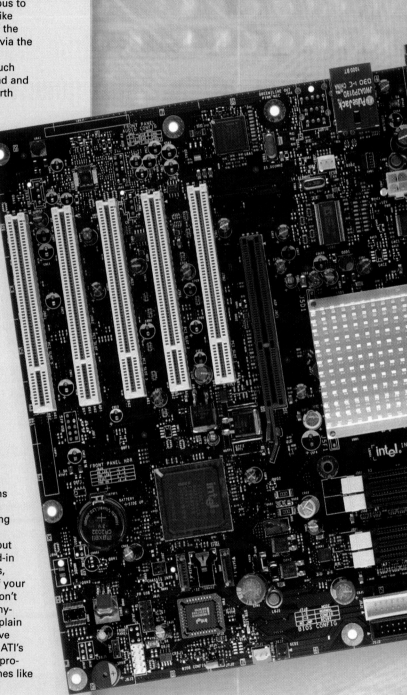

MOT

HERBOARDS

The motherboard is the Grand Central Station of your PC. All aboard!

Intel sells its motherboard chipsets to other vendors, but also makes Intel-branded boards as well, such as this 875P model.

The biggest mistake a budding PC enthusiast can make is to underestimate the importance of a well-designed, properly-configured motherboard. A PC's motherboard is the technological equivalent of Grand Central Station—virtually everything in the computer connects to it, and in order for your PC to "do" anything the commands always have to be routed through the motherboard. A motherboard determines all future upgrading options, limits how much performance you'll ever extract from your rig, and is the number one factor in your system's overall level of stability.

Now, upon close examination of a motherboard you will note two distinct pieces of silicon. One is near the top of the motherboard and the other is near the bottom. These two chips are what is called the "core-logic chipset," and they are the ones who are really running the show. One of these chips controls things on the top-half of the motherboard, while the other handles the talking on the bottom-half. Together they comprise all the features, doodads and doohickeys that are "onboard," meaning stuff you won't have to buy because it's already on the motherboard such as a LAN port, modem, audio and so forth.

Oh, but it doesn't end there! If you're in the market for a new motherboard, you must also worry about what new technologies are looming on the horizon, threatening to make your shiny new purchase obsolete before you can even get home from the store. And right now is both the worst time and the best time in years to invest in a new mobo! It's the worst time because in the next few months we'll see the emergence of an entirely new memory technology (DDR2), peripheral bus (PCI Express), and motherboard formfactor (BTX), as well as new CPUs from both AMD and Intel that may not be compatible with all current mobos. These new technologies will make everything on the market currently "yesterday's news" overnight. The good news, however, is that once this newfangled hardware arrives today's top-of-the-line hardware will suddenly become extremely affordable. Can you say, "fire sale?" We knew you could.

If you're considering building your first PC or are simply looking to understand more about the specie Personalus Computerus, the motherboard is an excellent place to begin. Since every single component plugs into the motherboard or plugs into something attached to the motherboard, understandings its connections and how it works with other components will give you a good overview of how a PC works.

MOTHERBOARD Tech Terms

AGP Slot

Accelerated Graphics Port. AGP is a graphics card interface developed by Intel which provides the graphics controller direct access to the PC's main memory. The AGP interface has been improved over the years and is now denoted as 2x, 4x and 8x AGP. 8x AGP indicates that the interface provides a theoretical bandwidth eight times higher than that of the original AGP standard.

ATA

Advanced Technology Attachment. This is the parallel interface used to attach hard drives, CD ROMs, DVD drives, etc to the majority of PCs on the market. This term is used interchangeably with IDE.

BIOS

Basic Input-Output System. The BIOS is the first program the computer executes when it is turned on and is typically contained in a ROM chip on the motherboard. It allows the computer to perform rudimentary self-diagnostics and allows access to the hard drive so that the Operating System can load.

DDR memory

Double Data Rate Memory. Memory which transfers data on both the rising and falling edge of the clock and therefore is capable of transfering twice the amount of data for any given clock speed. DDR memory is the most common type of memory used in PCs today.

DIMM

Dual Inline Memory Module. The most commonly used memory modules today are DIMMs. These have electrical contacts arranged in two long lines on both sides of the module's bottom edge. Most conventional SDRAM DIMMs have 164 pins, whereas DDR DIMMs have 184 pins.

Dual Channel

Dual Channel memory interface. An arrangement where the memory controller has two separate pathways by which it can access main memory, giving potentially twice the bandwidth. For the dual channel interface to function, memory modules must be installed in pairs that are identical in both capacity and speed.

Fan Headers

The connectors on the motherboard onto which the CPU, power supply and system cooling fans can be attached. Some fan headers are capable of controlling the speed of the fan connected to it based on temperature readings taken by sensors on the motherboard.

Form Factor

The specification for the physical size and layout of the motherboard. Form factors permit the standardization of motherboards so that they will fit in a wide variety of enclosures. The most commonly encountered form factors today are ATX, Micro-ATX and Flex-ATX.

Frequency clock

The quartz timing device that provides precise electric pulses that drive and synchronize everything in the computer.

Front Side Bus

The connection between the CPU and the main memory (RAM) on the motherboard.

IDE Port

Integrated Drive Electronics port. For all practical purposes, IDE is ATA. While IDE refers to the interface architecture and ATA is the actual specification, the difference is lost to most users. IDE port and ATA port refer to the same 40-pin connector on the motherboard. ATA drives are also commonly called IDE drives.

I/O Controller

Input/Output Controller. In the context of motherboards, the I/O Controller is, for most intents and purposes, another term for the Southbridge chip. There are some technical differences in the implementation of Southbridge chips and I/O Controller Hub chips, but they serve the same functions.

Memory Controller

The part of the Northbridge chip, or the CPU, which controls the exchange of data between the CPU and the main memory.

Northbridge

The component of the core logic chipset that primarily functions a memory controller, allowing the CPU to interface with main memory and the video card (AGP) slot (if the PC has one). In some systems, such as those based on the Athlon 64 processors, the memory controller is built into the CPU.

PC2700-3200

A labeling on DDR memory that denotes its bandwidth. PC2700 memory has a theoretical throughput of 2700MB/sec

PCI Slot

Peripheral Component Interconnect Slot. A multi-purpose interface that allows the computer to accept all manners of expansion cards. The original PCI slot is 32-bits and operates at 33MHz. Today, there are 33 and 66MHz PCI slots, and slots which operate with 32 and 64-bits interfaces, but generally the slots are backwards compatible with older cards.

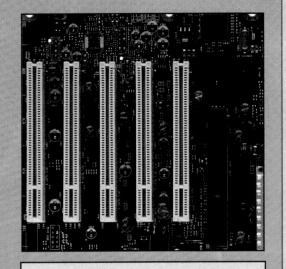

The standard interface for add-in cards is the PCI slot, which is white in color and runs at 33MHz.

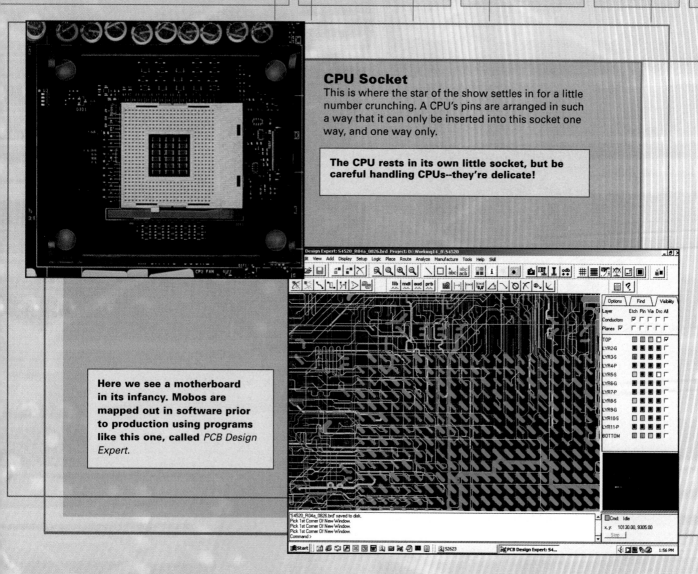

CPU Socket
This is where the star of the show settles in for a little number crunching. A CPU's pins are arranged in such a way that it can only be inserted into this socket one way, and one way only.

The CPU rests in its own little socket, but be careful handling CPUs--they're delicate!

Here we see a motherboard in its infancy. Mobos are mapped out in software prior to production using programs like this one, called *PCB Design Expert*.

---

whereas PC3200 memory serves up 3200MB/sec. PC2700 memory is also known as DDR333 memory because it runs at 333MHz, while PC3200 and DDR400—which runs at 400MHz—are one and the same.

PCB
Printed Circuit Board. A board on which circuits are etched and chips are attached. A PCB is typically green in color but motherboards and video cards have appeared with a wide array of colored PCBs as of late.

PCI Express
This is the successor to the PCI slot, and will become the new standard for connecting peripheral cards to the PC in the next few years. Unlike the parallel PCI bus, PCI Express is a serial bus. PCI

Express slots and cards are not interchangeable with conventional PCI cards.

Power-On Self Test (POST)
The diagnostic tests that a computer performs on itself prior to booting its operating system. The Integrity of RAM and I/O interfaces are usually tested as part of the Power-On Self-Test regimen.

SDRAM
Synchronous Dynamic Random Access Memory. Memory that synchronizes itself with the CPU's memory bus. Although DDR memory is technically a type of SDRAM, the term SDRAM typically refers to PC66/100/133 memory used in older computers.

Serial ATA
Serial Advanced Technology Attachment. This is a serial interface used for connecting storage devices to the computer, and it will replace the ATA interface, which is parallel. It uses a seven-pin connector that is much smaller than the 40-pin ATA interface cable. The first generation of Serial ATA interface is capable of a 150MB/s transfer speed as opposed to 100MB/s for ATA/100.

Southbridge
The component of the core logic chipset that provides the interface between the north bridge and the slower interfaces in the PC such as the PCI slots, USB, IDE and other I/O interfaces. In other words, everything other than main memory and AGP falls under the charge of the southbridge chip.

Rear connectors

PCI slots

CPU

Front airflow

The all-new BTX formfactor (above) should eventually replace the aging ATX spec, promising improved airflow, among other benefits.

Q uestion: What is the ATX spec and what are the details on its likely successor, the BTX spec?

A: The ATX (Advanced Technology eXtended) spec was developed nearly a decade ago as the successor to the Baby AT standard. It is the most popular motherboard formfactor in use today, but it's starting to show its age. ATX's main shortcoming is that its designers did not anticipate the massive amount of heat generated by today's PCs. To address this problem, Intel developed the BTX (Balanced Technology eXtended) spec to replace ATX.

The biggest differences between a BTX and an ATX motherboard is its layout. For instance, whereas the CPU socket on an ATX board is positioned towards the rear of the case, BTX places the CPU socket at the front of the case, right next to an intake fan. This allows the CPU to get cool air before any other component in the system. The CPU will also be enshrouded by a "thermal module" which directs air from the intake to other parts of the system.

While BTX motherboards began appearing this year at trade shows, the adoption rate by manufacturers has not been as rapid as Intel had hoped. After all, a new formfactor requires a new case and power supply in addition to the motherboard. There is speculation that some ATX power supplies will work with BTX boards, but the jury was still out at press time. When BTX becomes available to consumers, they will appear in the standard size (similar to current ATX mid-towers) as well as the increasingly smaller microBTX and picoBTX.

Q uestion: What are the key differences among all the popular mobo formfactors?

A: Most of the motherboard formfactors in widespread use today are variants of the ATX spec. Plain-Jane ATX is by far the most common, and is characterized by the placement of the CPU and memory sockets above the expansion slots and a connector plate that includes all the basic I/O ports. The MicroATX formfactor retains the same basic design as its big brother, but is about 25 percent smaller. MicroATX mobos are primarily intended for smaller computers and typically feature integrated audio and video. Meanwhile, FlexATX is very similar to MicroATX but is even smaller, and is often found in one-piece computers or mini-systems.

Q uestion: What features will the next generation of motherboards have?

A: Several new technologies have emerged this year and more are just around the bend. PCI express blows away the 133MB/sec transfer rates of the PCI bus with a bandwidth cap of up to 4GB/sec in each direction. Also keep an eye out for the PCI Express graphics solutions, which replace AGP and may be available as you read this (ATI has already announced their Radeon X lineup of PCI Express cards). Meanwhile, in the memory department, the next generation of RAM has surfaced in the form of DDR2. You'll find all three of these technologies in Intel's 915 chipsets (Grantsdale) and various incarnations from others like VIA and nVidia. Aside from that, look for next-generation motherboards in the BTX formfactor.

Q uestion: What are the benefits of moving the memory controller off of the motherboard and onto the CPU, as in the case of the Athlon 64? Will Intel follow AMD's suit soon?

A: The most obvious benefit is much faster memory access. The old method of using a motherboard-based memory controller caused data flowing between the controller and CPU to travel a relatively long distance, and be subjected to considerable signal noise from other components along the way. This limited the speed at which the FSB could reliably operate, and also increased latency, or the amount of time the CPU spends waiting for memory to respond to its requests. An on-die memory controller handily solves both of these problems. Whereas the Pentium 4's FSB canters along at 800MHz, the Athlon 64's runs at full CPU speed—that is, 2.2GHz for a 2.2GHz processor. Furthermore,

AMD estimates that its integrated memory controller gives the Athlon 64 a latency of just 50 nanoseconds, or about half that of a Pentium 4 running on an 800MHz bus.

Given the very tangible benefits of an integrated memory controller, it would seem obvious that Intel would follow AMD's lead in the near future, right? Wrong. Chip design is all about making tradeoffs—adding more circuitry (such as a memory controller) to a CPU can make it faster, but it simultaneously decreases production yields and drives up the cost of the processor. For the time being, it would seem Intel has chosen to focus on other methods of improving CPU performance. Intel could plausibly add an on-die memory controller in the future, but it would be more of an economic decision than anything else.

WHO'S IN THE DRIVER'S SEAT?

I've seen you stress the importance of chipset drivers many times in Ask the Doctor. So I decided to update the drivers on my old Dell Dimension 4100. Using an Intel chipset identification utility, I discovered that I had an 815 Intel chipset and found at least five driver updates for it on the Intel web site.

However, Intel tells me that my system is an OEM version of an Intel Desktop Board BIOS and advises me not use its drivers, but to instead call my PC manufacturer for advice. That's right, you guessed it! Dell does not offer chipset update drivers. Is it safe to precede with the Intel drivers?

The Doctor thinks you're confusing two different things: chipset drivers and your motherboard's BIOS. We don't recommend you try to install a BIOS—the software that resides in a chip on your mother-board and tells your OS how to access all the nifty features of your PC—for any board other than the one that's specified. That's a sure-fire way to kill your PC. It sounds to us like you're interested in updating your Dell mobo with an Intel BIOS, which would be bad.

On the other hand, chipset drivers work on any boards that use the chipset in question. Most of the chipset vendors make one driver that will work with all their modern chipsets for convenience.

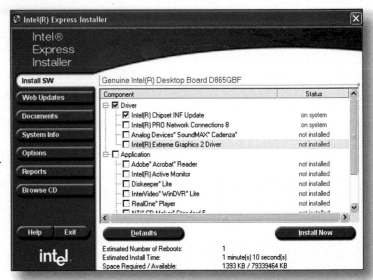

Intel lets you update chipset drivers manually or automatically over the Internet.

WINDOWS ACTS WACKY

I'm having trouble getting my new PC working. It's an Athlon XP 1800+, with 256MB of RAM, and a pair of 40GB Maxtor drives in a RAID 0 array. I can't get the machine to work properly. When I try to install Windows to the RAID array, Windows locks up, even though I am using the correct drivers for my RAID controller.

If I install Windows to one of the drives without RAID, Windows works OK for a while, but eventually I get crashes when I'm playing Battlefield: 1942. The system won't reboot, and I get an error in NTFS.sys or kern32.sys. Please help!

The Doctor had a similar problem with one of his machines recently. Assuming you're not overclocking, which can really bork 3D and PCI devices, we'd bet your problem is bad memory. A bad stick of RAM or a faulty slot on the mobo is the most common cause for this sort of problem.

To test it, open your case and remove one stick of RAM, then fire up the PC, and see how things run. If that fixes your problem, the RAM you removed is likely faulty. If it's still wonky, swap the stick you removed with the stick that's still in the system, and try again. You should also try moving the memory to the other slots in your mobo.

If your RAM tests OK, your motherboard could be faulty. The only way to confirm that is to swap your mobo with another mobo, and see what happens.

CAN'T TAKE THE HEAT

Q: I just installed a new processor, and as soon as I start playing 3D games my PC just shuts off. What is happening?

Sounds like you didn't install the CPU's heatsink properly, as random shutdowns are almost always due to overheating. Some motherboards have built-in temperature sensors that will shut the PC off once temperatures breach preset thresholds in an attempt to save your CPU from meltdown. Our advice is to remove the heatsink/fan from your CPU, make sure it is being mounted correctly, and remount it. Also, if you aren't using any type of thermal compound to increase the efficiency of your CPU's heatsink we highly recommend applying a dab onto the top of the CPU prior to mounting the heatsink.

THE CASE FOR ATX

I am looking to buy a new case, but how do I know for sure that my motherboard will fit properly?

If your system shuts off randomly, it's probably due to excessive heat. If your CPU's heatsink/fan aren't doing their job, you may need an aftermarket unit like Thermaltake's Volcano.

All cases and motherboards are designed to a certain specification, which is called it's "formfactor." There are several formfactors, but as long as the one for your case matches the one for your motherboard you will be fine. The most common formfactor for desktop machines is called ATX and it's what you would call the typical "tower" PC, that stands a few feet tall and is quite large. The majority of both cases and motherboards conform to the ATX specification, and are all interchangeable. That is, any ATX motherboard will fit into an ATX case. In fact, an ATX case will fit several variants of the ATX specification, but it makes little sense to buy a big ATX case if you want a smaller Micro-ATX motherboard. The bottom line for matching cases to motherboards is to make sure the specifications match—it's that simple.

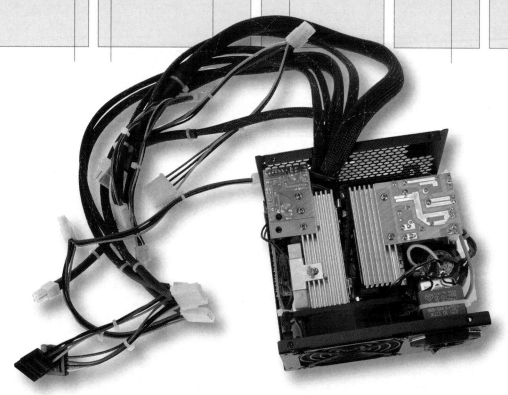

The power supply is one of the most important, yet most often-overlooked, components in a PC.

MEMORY BOOSTER?

I have an Athlon XP board running PC2700 (333MHz). should I upgrade to PC3200? Is it worth it?

The first question here is actually, "will my motherboard support a 400MHz bus?" Not all Athlon XP motherboards support this faster bus speed, so be sure to consult the website of your motherboard manufacturer to see what bus speeds are supported. If a 400MHz bus is supported, by all means upgrade away! nForce 2 motherboard owners should pay special attention to this situation as some nForce 2 motherboards shipped with support for a 333MHz front side bus, but are able to go up to 400MHz with an updated BIOS from nVidia. Once again, be sure to check nVidia's website to see if your board revision will support the faster bus speed. Also note that if you are currently running PC2700 you will have to upgrade your memory as well since PC2700 only runs at 333MHz. You'll need PC PC3200, which is also known as DDR400, to run at 400MHz.

MORE POWER SCOTTY!

How important is the power supply when upgrading?

Extremely important. In fact, if you're considering a major upgrade (CPU and motherboard), the power supply is the best place to start. Today's CPUs require a lot of juice, and when you consider that you might have to plug your videocard into the power supply as well, along with all your other add-in cards, you begin to understand how a steady supply of ample power will go a long way towards creating a stable system. As a baseline we always recommend a 350 watt power supply for most "power user" type systems. In general, that should be more than enough power to run a very fast system with as many peripherals plugged into it as your heart desires. You should also purchase a high quality power supply from a known company, rather than some cheapo unit that might save you a few bucks. We highly recommend power supplies from Antec (www.antec.com) as well as PC Power and Cooling (www.pcpowerandcooling.com) ∎

Currently, the ATX formfactor is the de rigueur standard for today's performance-oriented desktop machines, as demonstrated by this gorgeous system from Falcon Northwest.

Q If I buy a top-of-the-line videocard today, how long will it be a viable solution for good gaming?

In general, a high-end videocard should be extremely capable for at least a year, and maybe longer depending on what kind of frame rates you demand and the kind of features you'd like to be able to use. There are actually games out today that run just fine on 3-year-old cards, but that's only because the 3D engine used in the game came out at roughly the same time as the card. Play a next-gen game on this same card, though, and it will be like watching a slide show, if the game runs at all.

While the videocard industry generally relies on a six-month refresh cycle for all of its cards, the game development industry moves at a much slower pace. You see, all games use a certain 3D engine, which is a massive pile of code that determines the visual quality of the game you see on the screen. These engines take years to develop and are as for-ward-looking as possible, meaning they are designed to run on whatever hardware will be in consumers hands several years down the road. Because of the 3D engine's life cycle, these engines are brutal on hardware when first released, but over time the hardware catches up and eventually surpasses the 3D engine's capabilities. A classic example is id software's *Quake III* engine. When it was first released several years ago, nothing but the most high-end card available could play that game at 30 frames per second. Today, the latest hardware runs that engine at over 200 frames per second! All that is about to change, though, as id software is preparing to release its all-new engine for its upcoming game, titled *Doom 3* and that will surely drop any videocard on the market to its knees. Then, in three more years, we'll laugh at the *Doom 3's* engine's simplicity.

Q Is there anything I can do to extend my videocard's lifespan?

There is indeed a way to extend a videocard's life cycle, and it's called "overclocking." This practice allows you to run a videocard's processor and memory at faster speeds than the stock settings, but, like CPU overclocking, it voids your warranty and can be detrimental to your videocard's life expectancy. Also, overclocking won't help you when a massive jump in frame rates is required to play a next-gen game. At best, you'll see a 5 percent to 10 percent increase in performance, but if a next-gen game is released and you have older hardware, it might just be unacceptably slow.

EOCARDS

The one component that's almost worth its weight in gold!

I f there's one overarching need for a PC that is powerful enough to be classified as a weapon of mass destruction, it's gaming. Having a super-fast CPU, lightning-quick memory, and enough fans to cause a brown out doesn't do much for Microsoft *Word* or *Instant Messenger*, but for today's games, you simply cannot bring a knife to a gunfight.

The most important weapon in your gaming arsenal is, of course, the videocard. Although there used to be two separate types of videocards—2D cards for desktop work and 3D cards for games—today's videocards do everything in one sexy silicon package. And over the years, as games have become increasingly complex and more lifelike, videocard development has accelerated rapidly in an attempt to bring *Finding Nemo* graphics to the desktop. While that day is still far off in the future, modern videocards are technological wonders that are just as complex (and just as expensive, unfortunately) as high-end CPUs.

The consumer videocard market is currently owned by two companies—ATI and nVidia. While nVidia held the speed crown all by itself for the past few years, ATI has come on like gangbusters during the past year. Until recently, these two rivals' top products—ATI's Radeon 9800XT and nVidia's GeForce FX5950 Ultra—were neck-and-neck in terms of performance and price. However, we'd advise those in the market for a new videocard to enter a holding pattern until a few things are cleared up in the upcoming year.

Both nVidia and ATI have released all-new product groups this year. ATI's new core (dubbed R420) is at the heart of the new X800 boards while nVidia's new tech (NV40) powers the GeForce 6800 line. Both companies typically release a product family and then launch incremental speed increases for the 18 months following the initial release. NV40 and R420 are all-new technology though, and, as such, should represent a huge leap forward in graphics processing technology.

These new cards could not have arrived at a more prescient time, either, because of the two major game engines—used in many of the games on the market today—are being completely overhauled in 2004 (we hope), with the release of *Half-Life 2* and *Doom 3*. Both of these games include every next-gen feature available and will be serious ballbusters for low-to-midrange videocards. These games are so eagerly anticipated, in fact, that their release will spawn a wave of upgrading across the PC landscape.

nVidia's GeForce FX 5950 videocard is a 3D processing behemoth with 256MB of onboard memory and a cooling solution big enough for a small four-cylinder engine.

All the specs and tech lingo explained

AGP

Accelerated Graphics Port. A graphics card interface developed by Intel that provides the graphics controller direct access to the PC's main memory. The AGP interface has been improved over the years and is now denoted as 2x, 4x, and 8x AGP. 8x AGP indicates that the interface provides a theoretical bandwidth of 2.1GB/sec, eight times higher than that of the original AGP standard.

AGP Fast Write

AGP Fast Write is a scheme that allows data to be sent directly from the CPU to the videocard without first placing it in main memory. This affords a small performance boost but works only if it is supported by both the videocard and the motherboard.

Anisotropic Filtering

A function performed by the videocard that reduces the tiresome shimmering effect that is common when high-resolution textures are moved from the foreground to the background.

API

Application Programming Interface. A set of protocols, subroutines, and data structures that makes it easier for a programmer to produce a sophisticated program by presenting what is akin to ready-made building blocks. Microsoft's DirectX is an API, as is OpenGL.

Bilinear/Trilinear Filtering

Two axes and three axes filtering, respectively. A bilinear filtering process only takes into account nearby pixels on a single mip-map level, whereas trilinear filtering considers proximate pixels on more than one mip-map level.

Core Clock Speed

The speed at which the GPU, or "videocard core," operates.

DDR

Double Data Rate. DDR refers to the memory technology that transfers data on both the rising and falling edge of the clock, thereby permitting twice the

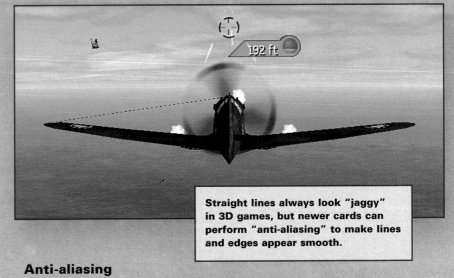

Straight lines always look "jaggy" in 3D games, but newer cards can perform "anti-aliasing" to make lines and edges appear smooth.

Anti-aliasing

A technical term that translates loosely to the blurring or smoothing of graphics. Anti-aliasing reduces the appearance of "jaggies" in straight lines in a game scene. Anti-aliasing can reduce the jagged appearance of graphics, but it also results in a reduction in sharpness.

amount of data to be transferred for any given clock speed. DDR memory is a common type of memory used in graphics cards today.

Direct3D

A graphics API developed by Microsoft for processing and displaying 3D graphics. Direct 3D is supported by practically all modern videocards.

DirectX

DirectX is a cross-platform code base written by Microsoft that allows game programmers to access hardware features on a computer without exact knowledge as to what kind of hardware is installed. This allows developers to work on next-generation effects years before they're officially supported by videocards that are available to the public.

Drivers

The software that is required for the videocard to work properly with the operating system. Performance and compatibility problems with a videocard frequently can be addressed by installing the newest drivers.

DVI

Digital Visual Interface. An interface that connects a monitor with a videocard. Most LCD displays support the DVI interface, and produce better image quality when it is used. Despite the word "Digital" in its name, a DVI connector actually outputs both digital video signals and the legacy analog video signals. An adapter can be used to hook a traditional VGA connector to the DVI interface.

Floating Point Color

Floating Point Color allows color information to be defined more accurately, with the use of decimal points. This is one of the new features introduced with DirectX.

Hardware T&L

Hardware Transform & Lighting. The hardware acceleration of T&L functions provided by a videocard. This process, during which a scene is constructed in wire frame mode and lit, used to be performed by a system's CPU but is now accomplished by a videocard's GPU. The offloading of this work from the CPU frees it to perform other tasks, ultimately improving performance.

Memory Speed

The speed at which the dedicated graphics memory on the videocard operates.

Memory Bandwidth

The rate at which the memory on the videocard can be accessed by the GPU. Memory bandwidth is usually expressed in gigabytes per second (GB/sec), with the best videocards boasting figures over 20GB/sec.

Open GL

A graphics API first developed by Silicon Graphics Inc. for processing and displaying 3D graphics.

Programmable Shaders

Programmable shader units are the areas of GPUs that can run generalized programs rather than fixed 3D functions. There are two basic types of programmable shader units: pixel and vertex.

RAMDAC

Random Access Memory Digital-to-Analog Converter. Circuitry that converts data from the video memory into analog signals that can be displayed by the monitor. A fast RAMDAC is necessary to produce flicker-free images at high resolutions.

Vertex Shader

A programmable shader unit that specializes in geometry calculations. Vertex shaders handle terrain morphing, some lighting calculations, and some shadow calculations.

Vertical Sync

Vertical Synchronization or *V-Sync*, is the signal that tells the monitor when to draw the next vertical line. The rate at which V-Sync occurs is also known as the "refresh rate." Enabling V-Sync in a game prevents the game from running faster than the monitor's refresh rate, which can cause textures to "tear" or look distorted.

GPU

Graphics Processing Unit. A specialized chip on the graphics card that accelerates mathematically intensive graphic tasks such as applying effects and textures to 3D objects. Just like a CPU does all the computing for basic desktop tasks, the GPU does all the heavy lifting in 3D gaming.

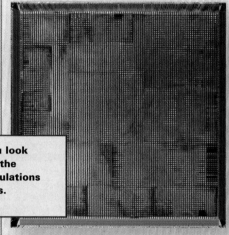

This is what a GPU looks like if you look really, really close. It's the heart of the videocard and performs all the calculations needed to draw a game's 3D images.

Pixel shaders are the foundation of every next-generation game in the pipeline, and allow for incredible special effects such as the orange tint cast on the walls by these flaming skulls.

Pixel Shader

A programmable shader unit that manipulates individual pixels. Pixel shaders can create bump maps (a layer of "skin" that goes on top of a texture, allowing for dimples or bumps to appear on a model), reflective surfaces, dynamic shadows, and all sorts of "Wow!" effects.

VIDEOCARDS Cheat Sheet

You've got questions, we've got answers

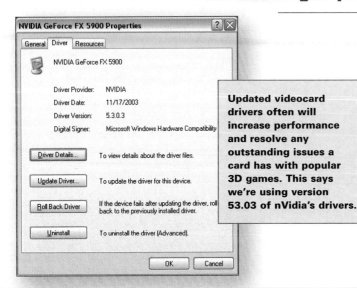

NVIDIA GeForce FX 5900 Properties

General | Driver | Resources

NVIDIA GeForce FX 5900

Driver Provider: NVIDIA
Driver Date: 11/17/2003
Driver Version: 5.3.0.3
Digital Signer: Microsoft Windows Hardware Compatibility

Driver Details... | To view details about the driver files.

Update Driver... | To update the driver for this device.

Roll Back Driver | If the device fails after updating the driver, roll back to the previously installed driver.

Uninstall | To uninstall the driver (Advanced).

OK | Cancel

Updated videocard drivers often will increase performance and resolve any outstanding issues a card has with popular 3D games. This says we're using version 53.03 of nVidia's drivers.

Question: Which drivers should I use? The ones from the card maker or from the chipset manufacturer?

A: It's generally best to use the latest drivers from the maker of your videocard's chipset, since these drivers are constantly being updated to add new features and to improve performance. Plus, the videocard you purchased could have been sitting on the store shelf for a few months, so the drivers on the included CD may be quite old. nVidia and ATI have both kept a breakneck pace of driver development as of late, with new revisions coming out almost monthly, so check the maker of your videocard chipset's web site often for new drivers.

Question: I have a 2-year-old computer. Should I upgrade to a top-of-the-line videocard or upgrade my CPU/motherboard instead?

A: It makes no sense to upgrade to the fastest videocard in the world when you have a last-gen CPU that's incapable of keeping the GPU supplied with fresh instructions. Your best bet is to spread your upgrading money around by staying one or two rungs below the top-of-the-line and getting a new CPU *and* videocard. For instance, if you have a Pentium 4 1.6GHz and a GeForce 2 videocard, rather than spending all your money on a new videocard or a 2.8GHz CPU, buy a 2.4GHz CPU and a midlevel videocard like the GeForce FX 5700 or Radeon 9600XT. That way your CPU and videocard will both receive an upgrade and will be quite evenly matched. Also, if you are only running 256MB of memory, you should definitely consider a RAM upgrade prior to upgrading other key components, as adding more memory to your system is one of the best "bang for the buck" upgrades you can perform.

The CPU works to supply the videocard with instructions during gaming, so teaming a next-gen card with a last-gen CPU is an exercise in futility— the CPU simply won't be able to keep up.

Question: What is the lowest refresh rate I should be running?

A: For CRTs, any refresh rate less than 75Hz is too low, and we prefer 85Hz. Higher refresh rates are better for your eyes, and won't give you the blinding headache that comes as a result of screen flicker. DVI flat panels are a slightly different story because they don't have a refresh rate, per se. Your DVI panel likely will default to 60Hz, and that's just dandy.

Plug and Play Monitor and NVIDIA Quadro FX 500 P...

Color Management | Quadro FX 500
General | Adapter | Monitor | Troubleshoot

Monitor type

Plug and Play Monitor

Properties

Monitor settings

Screen refresh rate:

85 Hertz

☑ Hide modes that this monitor cannot display

Clearing this check box allows you to select display modes that this monitor cannot display correctly. This may lead to an unusable display and/or damaged hardware.

OK | Cancel | Apply

As a rule of thumb, you should always set the refresh rate higher than 60Hz. Anything less can cause flickering and lead to headaches.

Question: What is the key difference between different versions of DirectX?

A: Microsoft's DirectX is a programming language game developers use to create 3D scenes and special effects in games. As such, videocard manufacturers create hardware support in their products for these effects. As new specifications for DirectX come out, they are built into videocards. Therefore, a DirectX 8 videocard only supports the effects included in that revision of DirectX, and will not be able to render the effects included in DirectX 9, for example. The latest version of DirectX is 9.0b, but it's expected that version 10 will ship with the next version of Windows.

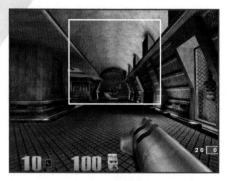

This nVidia board is a DirectX 8 card, and will play DirectX 9 games just fine, except it won't be able to render some of the whiz-bang visual effects.

Question: What's the difference between bilinear, trilinear, and anisio filtering?

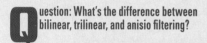

A: Each filtering strategy is designed to make the bit-map textures stretched over polygons look more realistic. Simply put, if 3D objects and environments weren't filtered, they'd look pixelated and jaggy, and no one would be very impressed by 3D games. But filtering strategies also have a particularly important relationship to mip-maps.

Mip-maps are sets of different textures of varying quality. For example, when you stand stationary in a 3D scene, the textures stretched over objects in the background are low-res, low-quality mipmaps, and the textures stretched over objects in the foreground are high-res, high-quality mipmaps. As you walk forward in the scene and begin to get closer to the previously far-away objects in the background, those objects' low-res mipmaps automatically swap out for higher-res versions. This rendering strategy is helpful to frame rates because low-res, low-quality textures demand less memory bandwidth than higher-quality textures. But here's the rub: The demarcation lines between mipmap levels of varying quality can be visually distracting if they're not adequately filtered.

To give you a better idea of how the different filtering modes affect mipmaps in 3D games, we fired up *Quake III*, and set it to show different mipmaps in "false colors" (the command is "r_colormiplevels 1" if you want to try for yourself). In the pictures you see below, each mip level appears as a different color. The first level represents the highest texture quality and

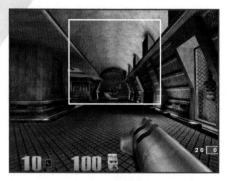

has normal color. In the images below, the second mip level (of slightly lesser quality) is red, and then the levels are green, then blue, and then back to red again, accordingly. We'll show you the effect different filtering types have on the transitions between different mipmap levels so you can judge what to enable for yourself.

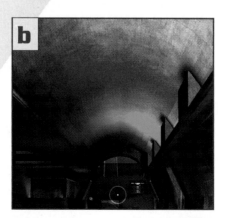

Image A shows only bilinear filtering. Notice that seams between textures are smoothly blended, but there's no blending between different mipmap levels. In image B, trilinear filtering is enabled. Note that the transitions between mipmap levels are smoothly blended, which will eliminate the visible seams between mipmaps. Image C shows you the same scene with anisotropic and trilinear filtering are enabled. With aniso on, the mipmaps are perspective-corrected, which creates the stair-stepping effect you see as you look from the sides to the top of the arch.

WORST-CASE SCENARIO

What is the worst possible outcome of a failed attempt at videocard overclocking? How likely is a "failure" when attempting this?

The worst outcome is that your board will simply stop working, which could be a big deal or a little deal depending on its value. However, catastrophe can largely be avoided simply by overclocking in very small increments. For example, try increasing your board's memory or clock speed in 5MHz increments. After each bump up, play a 3D game for a while and watch for signs of excessive heat, such as graphical artifacts and other anomalies. Once you start seeing weirdness in your games or your PC's behavior, back the clock speed down a notch and you should be just fine. Just remember—overclocking your videocard could shorten the card's overall lifespan.

ARE ONBOARD GRAPHICS REALLY THAT BAD?

Are integrated graphics any good? Will they be able to run *Doom 3*?

Integrated graphics—that is, graphics that are built directly into a motherboard—are designed to provide minimal 3D performance in exchange for reduced cost. Integrated chips are not designed for gaming, but rather for simple 2D desktop work. As such, anyone serious about gaming should never consider using integrated graphics.

VEXED BY AGP 8X RADEON

I'm in the market for a new videocard and the card I'm looking at is AGP 8x Radeon, but my motherboard only supports AGP 4x. Will this hold my videocard back quite a bit?

Do you need an AGP 8x mobo to get the max performance from the Radeon? Yes. Do you need an AGP 8x mobo to get the max performance from today's games? Not really. You see, current games aren't able to saturate the AGP 4x bus, which can pump about 1.06GB/sec of info from the videocard to main memory. Our testing backs this up.

We tested the Radeon 9800 Pro in a board that allowed us to disable

We're finally seeing games that really stress a 256MB buffer like that on the Radeon 9800 Pro.

AGP 8x. And, as far as our benchmarks go, there was no significant difference between 8x mode and 4x mode. We do expect to see games this year that will stress the 4x AGP bus.

NEW DIRECTX WITH AN OLD CARD

Is it ok to install DirectX 9 on my system if I only have a DirectX 8 videocard?

Yes, it is ok, and it's also a good rule of thumb to make sure you always have the latest version of DirectX as well. All games require a certain version to run, so if you haven't updated your DirectX installation in a while and want to play a brand-new game, you could have problems. Usually, games that require an upgrade to a new version of DirectX will include it in the installation, but not always, so be sure to check.

IS 256 JUST FOR KICKS?

Do I really need a videocard with 256MB of onboard memory for today's games?

You don't need a 256MB card, since there are a few games on the market that can actually fill such a massive frame buffer. With *Half-Life 2* and *Doom 3* on the horizon, you're going to need that extra memory eventually, so if you're upgrading now, it's a good idea to get a 256MB card to ensure its usefulness into 2005 and beyond.

TOWERS OF POWER

What are those brown cylindrical towers all over my videocard?

Those are capacitors, and their job is to make sure the GPU always receives a steady stream of power from the power supply without any major spikes or dips. You should be

You should always keep both your videocard drivers and your version of DirectX up to date, as newer versions typically offer increased performance and stability.

extremely careful when handling your videocard, since the capacitors are only attached at their base and can snap off quite easily.

NEED MORE FUNKY FLOW
I need to know how to upgrade the fan on my videocard. I need more cooling for my videocard, and this seems like the only way, since the fan is glued on and the connector cables are soldered to the card.

You usually cannot remove the heatsink/fan that is included with your videocard, since it is usually glued to the chip with some alien substance that does not want to come off. However, we've heard of people who have had success putting the card in the freezer, and then, once frozen, popping the heatsink right off. We haven't personally tried it, though, and applying any kind of force to your GPU could cause permanent damage.

If your fan's wires are soldered to the board, you need to first remove the solder using either a wick or a solder sucker, then reattach the new fan to the same leads. (Just pulling them could cause permanent damage to your board.) If this level of hardware-hacking sounds scary, you can always install a PCI fan in the slot directly

Today's high-end videocards all include heatsinks on top of the GPU that are difficult, if not dangerous, to remove. Dangerous to the card, that is.

below your videocard for more cooling. You also should make sure there is a case fan directly above the AGP slot blowing warm air out of the case. You can mount a fan on the case door as well, so that when it's closed, the fan is blowing directly onto the PCI slots. Some cases even include these fans, but most require drilling a hole to mount them.

CRASH COURSE
I'm experiencing random crashes in games. What's my basic troubleshooting strategy?

First, if you're overclocking anything in your system, stop. Even slight overclocking can cause instability. If that doesn't fix your problem, then go to your motherboard or system vendor's web site, and get their latest motherboard chipset drivers (do not confuse chipset drivers with a BIOS update). Install the chipset drivers, making sure you reboot as prompted. Now install the latest videocard drivers appropriate to your videocard—most likely from ATI.com or nVidia.com. Updating these two drivers in this order will fix 90 percent of all crashes in games.

If you still have problems, you should open your PC and make sure that you've got good airflow around the videocard, and that its onboard fan is working properly. You should also ensure that your finicky game doesn't have known issues with your 3D accelerator by checking the game's support page (the URL is usually listed in the game manual). Finally, don't rule out other components, such as your network card or soundcard. Again, check the game's support site for known issues.

Games like *Far Cry* bring most older videocards to their knees. If you can't afford to upgrade, you'll have to turn down the eye candy.

TIME TO UPGRADE
I get errors when I try to play some new games, but my computer meets all the games' system requirements. What's wrong?

The system requirements listed on the side of game boxes aren't always accurate. Frequently, a game will state that it requires a 32MB 3D accelerator, but what that really means is that you need a 3D accelerator with hardware T&L. For the record, all the GeForce and Radeon lines include hardware T&L. As we move forward, games are beginning to require programmable shaders support too, so eventually you're just going to have to upgrade just to play newer games—it's unavoidable!

A SWEET TOOTH FOR EYE CANDY
I'm running my favorite game with all its effects turned to the max—and it's dog slow. What's your opinion on which visual settings should be set to the max whenever possible, and which settings I should sacrifice, and

in which order they should be sacrificed?

The easiest way to increase frame rates is to lower your resolution. For example, at 1600x1200, the minimum number of pixels that your 3D card will draw per frame is 1.92 million. And, if you enable antialiasing, texture filtering, and other features, your card will draw considerably more than that. In contrast, at 640x480 the minimum number of pixels the card draws is about 307,200. Even at 1024x768, the card draws only about 800,000 pixels. The upshot is that lowering your resolution might even allow you to run all the fancy visual effects at full blast.

If running at low resolutions is anathema to you, try disabling antialiasing and anisotropic filtering. Both of those features are performance hogs. Decreasing texture quality and turning down the number of mip-map levels can further increase performance, but they will also severely impact your image quality.

Q What makes a hard drive "fast"?

Many factors define a hard drive's raw speed potential, but the most important is the rotational speed of its platters. All drives store their data on internal platters, and the data is retrieved when the platters spin under read/write heads. The faster these little platters spin, the faster the data can be accessed. Today's standard desktop drives rotate at 7200rpm, and these drives are very fast. There is also a handful of 10,000rpm drives, which are insanely fast due to their rotational-speed advantage. On the server side of things, where performance is king and money is no object, 15,000rpm drives reign supreme. These drives are the absolute pinnacle of performance, but not practical for desktop tasks due to their high cost and relatively small capacity.

The size of a drive's onboard memory plays a distinct role in its overall performance as well, with the rule of thumb being "the bigger the better." Onboard memory buffers range in size from 2MB to 8MB, and drives with these large buffers deliver up to 30 percent faster performance, on average, than drives with smaller buffers. Typically, data is delivered from the buffer as fast as the interface allows, so the more data a drive can wedge into its buffer, the faster it can perform typical desktop tasks.

Q What is Serial ATA?

Take a look at a machine equipped with Serial ATA, and the most striking feature will be the skinny data cables. While skinny cables have a positive impact on a case's internal airflow, this isn't the main reason why the PC industry is dropping parallel ATA (and its flat, wide cables) for SATA. The main reason is that the current parallel interface is facing a performance wall.

Parallel ATA cables send data along multiple wires within the same wide ribbon. Each piece of data must travel along the length of the familiar ribbon cable, and arrive at the same time in order to maintain data integrity. In order to get more speed from this scheme, the only option is to push the data to higher frequencies or make the data path wider. That's where the problems lie. Making the data path wider is impractical, as there are already 80 conductors in the ribbon. And increasing speed adds to the likelihood of data corruption.

Because serial interfaces don't have to deal with coordinating multiple lanes of data, we're able to push them to much higher speeds. SATA is currently rated for 150MB/s, slightly higher than the 133MB/s offered by the fastest parallel ATA spec (which still hasn't been widely adopted). SATA will eventually double to 300MB/s by the end of 2004, and then again to 600MB/s by 2007.

Although current hard drive transfer rates fall far short of the maximum throughput of even parallel ATA specs, companies are laying the foundation for the future. You don't, after all, wait for the traffic jam before you try to build the roads (unless you run the state of California).

Serial ATA drives have separate cables for data (above) and for power (below).

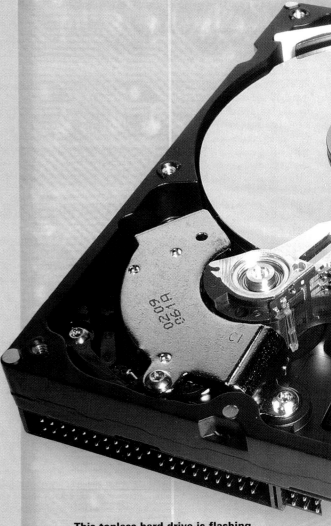

This topless hard drive is flashing its platters like it's Mardi Gras. The silver arm over the platters is the read/write head.

HARD DRIVES

Every PC needs a hard drive, but the options are mind-boggling. Follow along as we unboggle them for you.

The hard drive is truly the unsung hero of PC components. You know the type; the kind of component that labors away in the background while all the flashy components like the CPU and videocard get all the credit. Yet the hard drive is the one single component that is used in almost every single task you'll ever perform on your PC.

Whether you are trying to access folders on your hard drive, surfing the web or copying content from one location to another, your hard drive is constantly in use. Even when you are just sitting in front of your computer, staring at the screen, the hard drive's platters are spinning furiously as the drive's read/writer heads eagerly await your next command. The millisecond you click on a folder, these heads leap into action to deliver the data you've requested, and as soon as they complete your request, they return back to their "ready and waiting" status. You could say the hard drive is the Labrador retriever of the PC, waiting patiently with its tongue hanging out and tail wagging as you decide what trick you'd like it to perform next. As soon as you toss the bone and say "fetch!" it's off and running. And the good news is, drives promise to become even faster over the next 12 months thanks to the emergence of an all-new hard drive interface named Serial ATA.

This new interface doesn't offer any *major* benefits over the old interface, which was called "parallel ATA," other than that it offers more bandwidth for future drives to take advantage of, and is easier to add to a system due to its smaller cables and lack of jumpers. Parallel ATA drives have to be correctly configured via jumper pins as Master or Slave prior to use, but the newer drives have no such limitation—just plug them in and they work. Nonetheless, eventually all hard drives will use the Serial ATA interface, so if you are in the market for a hard drive today, you'd be wise to consider a SATA drive in order to make your system as future-proof as possible. Plus, drive manufacturers are only releasing their top-of-the-line drives in SATA form these days, so if you buy one, you can be sure it's the cream of the crop (for now).

All the specs and tech lingo explained

Areal Density

Areal Density, also called "Bit Density," is the amount of data that can be stored on a given surface area on a hard drive's platter. Increasing Areal Density is the most common method used by manufacturers to increase hard drive performance.

Burst Speed

Today's hard drives include onboard memory that is called a "buffer." When a piece of data is stored in this buffer and then requested by the operating system, it's delivered directly from the buffer, which is much faster than having the disk's mechanical apparatus retrieve the data. This process of delivering data from memory is called "bursting," and how fast a drive can deliver data from its buffer is its "burst speed," which typically is slightly slower than the maximum speed allowed by the interface.

Capacity

The storage capacity of a hard drive. Today, this is typically between 10 and 300 gigabytes (GB).

Data Transfer Rate

The average speed at which data can be transferred to and from a hard drive across a drive's entire capacity. A drive's data transfer rate is the single best specification to use in determining how "fast" a particular drive is.

Drive Head

These are tiny mechanical arms that float over a drive's platters and perform read/write operations. The tiny heads float just a few microns over the surface of the platter.

IDE

Integrated Drive Electronics. A hard drive that has its electronics integrated onto the drive itself, rather than requiring a separate plug-in card in order to function. For all practical purposes, IDE is ATA. While IDE refers to the interface architecture, ATA is the actual specification. This difference is lost to most users, however. An IDE port and ATA port refer to the same 40-pin connector on the motherboard.

ATA

Advanced Technology Attachment. This is the parallel interface used to attach hard drives, CD ROMs, and DVD drives to the majority of PCs on the market. The term "ATA" is used interchangeably with the term "IDE." Officially, there are the ATA-1 through ATA-6 specifications, which usually are written as 'ATA', and then the interface's maximum throughput. For example, the final spec of parallel ATA is ATA/133, which allows for data transfers of up to 133MB per second.

The de facto hard drive interface for the past several years has been this 40-pin cable dubbed ATA or IDE.

IDE Channel

This has been the primary channel for hard drives for many years now. An IDE channel (also called ATA) is a parallel interface with 40 pins that supports two drives per channel. A typical IDE controller found on a motherboard has two IDE channels and can support four devices.

Logic Board

The circuit board on the hard drive where the controller chip(s) and other electronic components are attached.

Master/Slave

A single IDE channel supports two devices, and each must be configured to be the Master or the Slave. Neither designation has any superiority over the other, but these designations are required in order for each device to be recognized on the channel.

Master Boot Record

This is the first sector(s) that a hard drive

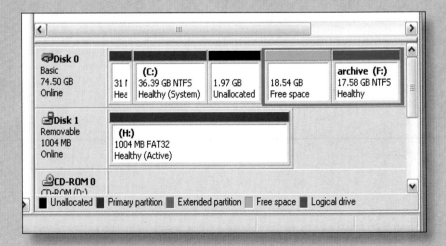

This 75GB hard drive (Disk 0) has been sliced and diced into two partitions (C: and F:). Most people prefer to have two partitions on a drive: one for regular use and one for backup.

reads. It contains information on how the hard drive is formatted, how it is partitioned, and where an operating system can be located and loaded. Because it contains the partition table and its associated information, the Master Boot Record is sometimes called the "Partition Sector."

Onboard Memory
The memory included on a hard drive. This memory is used to store incoming data, and allows the drive to accept small amounts of data at a faster rate than it can actually write onto the disk. Since data can be transferred much faster from this memory than from the actually physical disk, hard drives with a large amount of onboard memory (8MB, for example) offer better performance than drives with less memory (typically, 2MB).

Partitions
A hard drive's capacity can be divided into multiple portions that are called "partitions." Each partition will appear as a separate disk to the operating system and user, but can be located on the same hard drive.

Platters
Metallic discs inside the hard drive where information is stored. The rigid nature of these discs gave rise to the name "hard drive" or "hard disk."

Read/Write Assembly
A hard drive typically has two read/write heads for each platter it contains. These are mounted near the tip of the access arms. The "whole enchilada" of the access arm and read/write head is called the "read/write assembly."

Random Access Speed
How fast a drive is able to locate a random piece of data, expressed in milliseconds. It includes the time it takes for the drive to locate the requested piece of data, move its read/write head to

the proper location and then access the correct piece of data.

Rotational Speed
The speed at which the platters in a hard drive rotate. Rotational speeds of contemporary hard drives generally fall between 4,700 and 15,000 revolutions per minute (rpm). Higher rotational speeds typically yield higher performance at the expense of generating more heat and noise.

SCSI
Small Computers System Interface. A parallel interface that exists alongside the less expensive ATA interface. Up to seven or 14 devices can be connected on each SCSI channel. The interface also can be used to connect other high-bandwidth devices, such as scanners to the PC. Due to its high cost and ability to support a large number of drives, SCSI is primarily used in high-end server and RAID solutions.

The seven-pin Serial ATA connector plugs directly into the ports on the motherboard and drive, and doesn't require any jumpers to be set!

Serial ATA
Serial Advanced Technology Attachment. A new interface used for connecting drives to the computer. With seven pins instead of 40, Serial ATA cables are much slimmer than ATA cables. The first generation of Serial ATA interface is capable of a 150MB/s transfer speed, as opposed to 100MB/s for ATA/100.

Sector
The smallest unit on a drive that can be accessed. When a hard drive is formatted, it is divided into numerous concentric rings called "tracks," with each track being divided into numerous arcs called "sectors."

S.M.A.R.T.
Self-Monitoring Analysis and Reporting Technology. A feature built into hard drives that monitors and reports a drive's overall health, and also can let a user know if a drive is about to fail.

RAID
Redundant Array of Inexpensive Disks. An arrangement whereby more than one hard drive is combined to form a single storage volume. Depending on the configuration, better performance, better security, or both can be attained.

The only way to practically double a hard drive's speed is to add a second drive and divide up the work between them. It's a process called "R.A.I.D.," and here we see a four-drive array (the fifth drive is the primary volume).

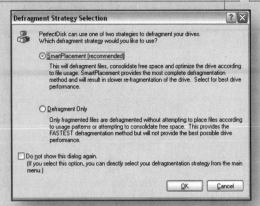

One of the first rules of responsible hard drive ownership is to defrag often.

Question: What's the best hard-drive defragmenting utility?

A: When your hard drive saves data, it can't always put all the pieces of data in sequential blocks right next to one another. Sometimes it has to put a piece here, another piece there, and other pieces scattered way over yonder. As this happens over and over again, a drive becomes "fragmented," which slows your system down because the drive has to search high and low to fetch the data you've requested. To combat this, there are "defragmentation" programs that rearrange all the bits on your hard drive so that related units are next to one another, which speeds up transfer times. If you are using Windows 2000/XP, the Microsoft-supplied defragger is better than nothing, but if you want better performance and faster results, go with *PerfectDisk* (www.raxco.com). *PerfectDisk* can complete a full defrag with as little as 5 percent free space on the disk, will defrag all Windows system files, and supports scheduling and network drive defragging. Another popular defragmentation utility is *Diskeeper* (www.executive.com), which is from the company that created the defrag utility that ships with Windows.

Question: My drive's filling up, but I can't tell what's hogging the space. What's the best way to keep track of hard drive data?

A: Windows isn't nearly as helpful as it should be when it comes to red-flagging your overstuffed folders. Sure, you can search for big files, but you'll never know what folders might be glutted with small files that add up to big trouble. Grab *SpaceMonger* from www.werkema.com to get a handle on the situation. *SpaceMonger* gives you a graphical, proportional look at your drive's contents, and lets you "drill down" into those big folders to see what's taking up so much darn space.

How did that get in here? *SpaceMonger* offers a to-scale representation of your drive's files and folders for easy cleaning.

Question: How often do hard drives fail?

A: Not often, but even once is one time too many. In practice, if you take care of your drives, they should easily outlast the other components in your PC.

Manufacturers used to measure reliability in MTBF, which stands for "Mean Time Between Failures," which is like a product's half-life. These numbers could run into the hundreds of thousands of hours for quality drives (and there are only 8,760 hours in a year!), but since these numbers resulted from a ton of guesswork, they've been supplanted by Annualized Failure/Return Rate (AFR or ARR) and Component Design Life (CDL). Typically, the AFR or ARR on any given drive model is 1 percent or below, meaning that 99 of 100 drives shipped to the field run happily. CDL from most manufacturers is five years. After that, they're not so sure all those moving pars can be trusted, and you're best off transferring your data to a new home.

To make sure you don't get caught in a "hard drive down" scenario, make sure S.M.A.R.T. is enabled in your BIOS (if offered). It will keep an eye on your drive's self-reported diagnostics. Every six months, scan your disk for trouble (go to My Computer, right-click the drive, and select "Tools" then "Error-checking"). If your drive continually indicates a lot of bad sectors, consider it a swan song.

Question: How much damage can a hard drive take? What precautions should one take when handling a hard drive?

A: If you drop a drive from any distance, there's a good chance there will be some damage. If you're very lucky, the drive will bounce in your favor. If you've gotten away with dropping a drive several feet, we salute you, but the fact is that a drop of just a few inches can be enough to damage a drive. One very certain fact is that drives can take relatively more abuse when they're turned off than when they're running, since the drive's head is usually parked in a safe location off the disk when the drive is turned off.

If you're working on a drive that is removed from the PC, try to work on and over a padded surface. When the drive is inside your PC, be sure to securely mount the drives using all four screw holes in order to dissipate vibrations evenly across the mechanism.

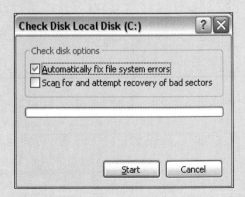

Excessive vibration can throw a drive's read/write head off the scent when it's searching for data, leading to reduced access times. Always mount a drive securely, with *at least* two screws per side.

Be sure to check your hard drive for errors every few months, and be sure to always backup your important files!

NEW DRIVE DILEMMA

I just installed a new hard drive. What is the easiest way to move all my data onto this new drive and then use my old drive for MP3 storage?

Most retail hard drive packages include utilities for transferring your old data to the new drive. However, we always recommend a fresh install of Windows with a manual update instead. The reason for this is that if your old installation of Windows was clogged with crap, the last thing you want is all that junk on your brand-new drive. So start fresh—you won't regret it.

PUSHING THE SIZE LIMIT

I just bought a 200GB hard drive and Windows XP is only recognizing 137GB. What's wrong?

The specification for your hard drive's ATA interface allows only 28 bits for addressing data on a disk, which means the maximum it can "see" is 137GB. Now that hard drives are twice as large, the specification has been updated to 48 bits to reflect this jump in capacity. In order to take advantage of this new size limit, you'll need *Service Pack 1 (or SP2)* from Microsoft for your operating system and possibly an updated BIOS as well. With those installed, you will be able to access all of your hard drive's capacity. Also, one way to sidestep this issue is to use an add-in PCI controller for your hard drives

Hard drives typically include data migration utilities, but we recommend a fresh install of Windows on a new drive for peak performance.

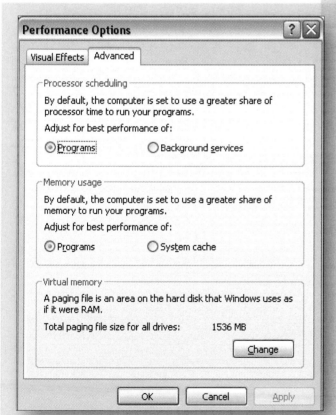

You can tell Windows how much hard drive space to use as a swap file, but given how cheap RAM is these days, why not just add more memory if you need it?

rather than connecting them to the motherboard.

IS ATA/133 WORTH IT?

I have an ATA100 hard drive. Should I upgrade to ATA/133 or Serial ATA 150?

Not unless you are looking to buy a bigger drive anyway. If that is the case, then go ahead and get the newer interface, but don't do it thinking you'll see any recognizable speed increase. In fact, most ATA/133 drives are exactly the same internally as ATA/100 drives. Remember: The number after the "ATA" is the maximum transfer rate for *the interface,* not the drive.

MASTER YOUR DRIVE CHAIN

Does it matter if my hard drive is the Master or Slave on its channel? Should I put it on the same chain as my CD-ROM?

If possible, it's best to install any IDE device on its own channel in order to give each device full control of that channel's resources. The reason it's bad to put a CD-ROM on the same channel

as a hard drive is that the channel can only send and receive data from one device at a time, so if you are using your CD-ROM and the hard drive needs something, it'll have to swap back and forth between then, slowing down both drives. Try to make your primary hard drive the Master on the primary IDE channel, and your CD-ROM the Master on the secondary channel.

SWAPPING OUT YOUR SWAP FILE

What is my hard drive's swap file? Do I need it?

Your hard drive's swap file is a portion of the hard drive that is used when your system's memory is completely full. While you work at your PC, programs that are in use store their data in your system's memory so that you can access it very rapidly. But if you have a lot of applications open and not enough memory, programs will begin to store their data on your hard drive, which is quite slow compared to your PC's lightning-fast memory. If you do a lot of multitasking and have scant memory, you'll need a swap file. If you have a gigabyte of RAM, you probably don't need a swap file.

OPTICAL DRIVES

Here's a burning sensation you'll love!

Q Does it make any difference what color or brand of media I use?

Which one should you use? That's easy. Check the documentation that came with your optical drive, or the manufacturer's website for media recommendations. These recommendations didn't come about as a result of back-alley deals or bribes of exotic whiskey. You'll find some media brands recommended over others because these discs have been specifically tested with the manufacturers' drives. The proper laser strength for each type of media has been evaluated and programmed into the drive's firmware.

In general, we do not recommend buying cheap spindles of off-brand media, no matter how inexpensive they are. El Cheapo vendors aren't worried about brand loyalty, so they skimp on quality control and you pay the price in discs that are error-prone or that won't retain their data for very long.

When the compact disc was introduced by Philips and Sony in 1979, vinyl records had the misfortune to be standing directly in its path. These black, circular monstrosities—with their fragile surfaces and analog data—couldn't compete with the CD's deadly combination of digital clarity and rugged portability. A few years later, engineers figured out how to adapt audio CD technology for use with computer data by adding strong error detection and correction schemes, which led to the downfall of the floppy disk. This storage medium then evolved to DVD, which has taken over as the standard to distribute audio, data, and video to consumers. Today, it continues to evolve at an astounding pace.

Both CD and DVD drives fall under the banner of "optical storage." These drives contain a laser, and when a disc is inserted the laser "looks" at the surface of a disc, where information is encoded in a single spiral track that begins in the center of the disk and moves outward toward the edges. The laser is looking for variations in the surface of the disc, from which it derives digital data (ones and zeroes, in other words). The spiral track in a commercial CD-ROM contains a series of bumps and flat surfaces called "pits" and "lands" embedded in a clear layer just below the disc's outer surface. These "pits" and "lands" represent ones and zeroes and are the building blocks of data. Recordable CDs, or "burned" CDs, work in a similar way. Commercial, write-once and recordable DVDs use these same principles to store information.

In the upcoming year the basic optical technology won't be coming in for any major overhauls, but we certainly expect to see big increases in both DVD recording speeds (they are currently pegged at a relatively pokey 8x) and disc capacities. We're not sure how quickly manufacturers will be able to ramp up recording speeds, but in terms of capacity increases, just look to Sony, which released the first dual-layer recordable drive this year. These drives will be able to encode data on a semitransparent disc layer, and then refocus to encode more data on the layer immediately beneath—nearly doubling the capacity of current recordable DVDs!

Plextor's PX-708A is unique among DVD burners in that it can burn relatively inexpensive 4x media at 8x speeds! You gotta love that.

OPTICAL DRIVES Tech Terms

Audio Extraction

The process of copying audio data from a CD (also known as "ripping"). Audio CDs include far less formatting and error correction data than data CDs, so audio extraction must be supported by the drive and accomplished via a specific software program.

Blue Laser

A new technology that uses a blue laser beam to boost DVD capacity to 27GB. Due to the much shorter wavelength of the blue laser compared to the red laser, a lot more information can be burned onto a blank DVD using a blue laser than with the thicker red laser.

Buffer

Memory that is built into an optical drive to ensure continuous flow of data to the drive's laser during recording. Data is taken from its source, fed into the drive's buffer, and then spooned to the drive's laser for uninterrupted writing.

Buffer Underrun

When a disc is being "burned," the drive's laser is being fed by the disc's buffer. If the source feeding the buffer is interrupted and the buffer empties, the recording process stops. This is known as a buffer underrun. Today's CD-R and DVD-R drives have technology that prevents this from happening by halting the recording process until the buffer is full again, but drives without this feature must abort the recording process, rendering the disc unusable.

Combo Drive

An optical drive that offers both DVD-R/RW and CD-R/RW burning functionality.

DVD+R/RW

DVD+Recordable/Re-Writable called "plus RW." It's one of two competing recordable DVD formats (the other is "dash RW") whose disks can be played in standard DVD players. DVD+R/RW is supported by a group of companies that includes Philips, Sony, Hewlett-Packard, Dell, Ricoh, and Yamaha.

DVD-R/RW

A DVD rewritable format called "Dash RW," which is supported by the DVD Forum and companies, like Panasonic, Toshiba, Apple Computer, Hitachi, NEC, Pioneer, Samsung, and Sharp.

Dual-Format DVD Burner

DVD burners that can read both DVD+R/RW and DVD-R/RW discs, as opposed to single-format drives that only can read +R or –R disks.

Dual-Sided

Some factory-pressed DVDs contain data on both sides of the disc. These are essentially two DVDs placed back to back, and need to be flipped manually for data on the opposing side to be accessed.

Firmware

The software built into a drive that regulates its operation. Firmware is usually stored in EPROM or flash memory on the drive. It can be updated in most drives, but updates normally are not performed on a regular basis.

Packet Writing

Packet Writing is an alternative process for writing data to a CD. It varies from the standard method of writing information in a single, continuous track around the CD. Packet writing allows data to be written in small, individual chunks. Discs must be formatted before packet writing can be used on them.

Random Access Time

How long it takes for a drive to locate and access a random piece of data on a disc, usually measured in milliseconds.

Red Laser

The conventional red laser beam used in today's DVD players and recorders. The size of the red laser beam restricts a rewritable DVD's capacity to around 4.7 GB per layer.

Dual-Layer

Some factory-pressed DVDs contain data on two layers for a total capacity of around 9.4 GB. While all DVD players, including DVD-ROMs, can fully access dual-layer discs, only the Sony DRU-700A can record using them...thus far.

This dual-layer DVD has been separated to show its separate layers, but retail discs look like a standard DVD recordable disc.

You've got questions, we've got answers

Kiss Technology's DP-500 Networked DVD Player represents an end-run around the DVD format wars because it reads all of them!

Question: What's the best DVD-burning format for making DVD-Video discs that will play in my set-top DVD deck?

A: Our tests have shown that the format with the highest compatibility among set-top players is DVD-R, followed by DVD+R, DVD-RW, and then DVD+RW. But the compatibility difference between DVD-R and DVD+R is very slight, and newer models of set-top players are tweaked to recognize all or most of these formats. So the most reliable approach is to spend a little extra cash for a dual-format burner and experiment with different types of media.

Alternatively, you can buy a newer-model DVD player that will not only read all the recordable formats, but that also will offer niceties like progressive scan playback.

Question: Are non-combo, non-dual-format drives even relevant anymore? Why would anyone ever buy a dedicated DVD-ROM drive, CD-ROM drive, or CD-RW burner in this day and age?

A: Today's optical storage market is divided among drives that record to CD-R, DVD-R, or both. Drives that do both are known as "combo" drives, while drives dedicated to recording in one format are called, "dedicated" drives. A general rule of thumb is that dedicated drives tend to offer higher speeds than combo drives, but the speed differential is often negligible. But there are still good reasons to look at dedicated or single-format drives. For example, Plextor's ultra-foxy PlexWriter Premium CD-RW drive doesn't burn DVDs, but it offers a staggering amount of one-of-a-kind features, like the ability to tweak laser strength for higher compatibility with your audio equipment, and to "overburn" discs so that ordinary CDs can contain as much as 1GB of data.

Another reason to covet a dedicated drive is price. For example, if you know your set-top DVD player can read DVD-R discs, don't waste your money on a dual-format burner when you can buy a less expensive single-format burner.

Single-purpose drives, like Plextor's incredibly fast and featurific PlexWriter Premium, can still be sexy.

Next-generation DVD burners will use blue lasers to create an ultra-high capacity storage medium, but they won't arrive until the end of 2004.

Question: What's the difference between red-laser and blue-laser optical drives?

Well, there's the color, for one thing. Ahem. Red lasers are used in today's garden-variety CD and DVD burners. CD burners use an infrared laser that has a wavelength of 780nm (nanometers) to burn discs. DVD burners user a red laser with a wavelength of 650nm, which is why you can write so much more information on a DVD. Think of it like writing with a sharp pencil instead of a dull crayon; you'd be able to fit many more words on a piece of paper.

Next-generation optical drives are being designed with blue lasers that have a wavelength of only 405nm, so they are able to fit even more information on a single disc. Blu-ray is a long way away, though. Due to this ambivalence, we'd advise to just stick with straight-up DVD-R for the time being.

SOUNDCARDS

Whether you love music, games or movies, nothing brings your PC to life like a killer soundcard. Listen up as we dissect the latest technology!

It's fairly common these days to purchase a motherboard with onboard audio, which means that a chip on the mobo does audio processing so you don't have to buy a separate soundcard to get audio from your system. Like most free lunches though, there is a catch: Onboard audio usually doesn't offer a high level of sound quality, and is lacking in features, compared to an add-in soundcard. In many cases, the onboard audio doesn't even contain a digital signal processor (DSP), which means it must offload the actual audio processing to your CPU, which can cost valuable frames per second in 3D games, lowering the framerate by as much as 5 percent.

In most cases, the biggest limitation of onboard audio is the number of speakers it supports. Most motherboard audio chips contain three minijacks: one for stereo-out, one for microphone-in, and one for line-in, meaning you're going to be stuck with only two speakers. Meanwhile, every soundcard on the market supports at least four speakers, with some supporting up to eight!

One exception to the "onboard sound is crap" rule is the nForce. This onboard solution is fully digital and supports 5.1 Dolby Digital surround sound. Its audio quality is excellent as well, so if you buy an nForce 2 or nForce 3 motherboard, you won't need an extra soundcard to handle audio duties.

It's true that a lot of people simply use whatever soundcard came with their PCs, figuring that as long as the sound comes out of the speakers, it's good enough. We're here to tell you it's not. There's absolutely no reason to settle for "good enough" when you could be enjoying multi-channel surround sound and audio fidelity so pure your ears will feel dirty listening to it, and all for a relatively modest price.

At the core of today's high-quality soundcards is an audio processing unit that does the majority of the sound processing. Soundcards also can contain surround sound decoders, which separate digital sound streams from DVD movies into discrete channels or analog sounds into separate channels for games. This is called "3D sound," or "positional audio," and a soundcard's ability in this arena is dictated by the hardware or software support for audio code specifically programmed into games. These different types of surround sound for games include Creative Labs' EAX, and Microsoft's DirectSound3D. Some soundcards even have specific optimization for MP3 playback.

The sound card usually will contain a CD pass-through interface that allows the CD or DVD drive to be connected to the soundcard (usually with a thin, gray cable), so that you can play music CDs through the system's speakers. Sound cards usually support at least four speakers: front, left, and right satellites; and surround left and right channels. Some sound devices also provide dedicated support for center/subwoofer channels. Furthermore, most audio hardware includes digital outputs, coaxial, optical, or both.

The biggest trend in sound hardware in upcoming months is support for more speakers. More speakers means a more convincing sound field, and already, Creative Labs is pushing a 7.1 speaker solution with the SoundBlaster Audigy 2 ZS, while Hercules is offering two 7.1 soundcards. This trend will take a while to saturate the market, however, as 7.1 speaker systems are only just beginning to trickle out.

Creative Labs' Audigy 2 ZS is the pinnacle of current technology, offering pristine sound quality and features up the wazoo.

24-Bit Audio

Sound that is represented by 24-bits of data every time it is sampled. Traditional CD-quality audio is 16-bit. Using 24 bits improves resolution and fidelity.

API

Application Programming Interface. A set of protocols, subroutines, and data structures that makes it easier for a programmer to produce a sophisticated program by presenting what is akin to ready-made building blocks.

DirectSound 3D

A Microsoft API for representing, manipulating, and delivering sound in three dimensions. DirectSound 3D often is used in software that offers positional sound effects.

Dolby Digital 5.1

A Dolby Laboratories format for representing sound in six discrete channels—five positional channels and a subwoofer channel. This is a popular digital surround sound format, and is used in most DVD movies.

DSP

Digital Signal Processor. The chip that digitally process audio data.

DTS

Digital Theater System. A competing format to Dolby Digital that also delivers sound in discrete channels—five positional channels and a subwoofer channel, albeit at a higher bitrate. DTS is used in

some DVD movies and is developed by Digital Theater System, Inc.

DVD Audio

A budding format that uses DVDs to deliver audio with exceptional fidelity. Unlike CDs, which are limited to 16-bit samples at 44.1 KHz, DVD Audio can deliver sound that is sampled at up to 24 bits and 192 KHz.

Game Controller

A joystick, gamepad, or other device used predominantly for gaming purposes. Many soundcards feature a connector for hooking up such devices, which is logically called the "Game Port."

Hardware Channels

The number of separate audio streams that the audio hardware can handle simultaneously. Additional channels often can be simulated in software, but at a significant cost in processor attention.

Host-Based Processing

This is the term that's used to refer to audio processing that's done by a system's CPU rather than a processor found on the soundcard. Since it is expensive to design a soundcard with its own onboard processor, some less expensive models simply skip this step and offload all the process-

ing work to your CPU, which can degrade overall system performance due to heavy CPU utilization levels.

S/PDIF

Sony / Philips Digital Interface. A format for transferring digital audio data without first converting it to an analog signal. Generally, there are two kinds of S/PDIF connectors: one that uses the traditional RCA cable and one that uses a fiber optic cable.

Sampling Frequency

The number of times the sound data is sampled per unit time. Traditional CD audio is sampled 44,100 times a second, and hence has a sampling frequency of 44.1 KHz.

Signal-to-Noise Ratio

The ratio of audio signal strength to that of unwanted background noise. A higher signal-to-noise ratio usually indicates a superior audio product.

Surround Sound

The delivery of sound to more than two channels, and with multiple speakers positioned in locations that "surround" the audience. The basic surround sound setup uses four speakers—two in front and two behind the audience.

CMSS

Creative Multi-Speaker Surround. A standard developed by Creative Technologies for delivering surround sound by sending a two-channel signal to mutliple channels.

> Creative Lab soundcards ship with a nifty technology called CMSS that lets you send a stereo signal to multi-channel speaker systems.

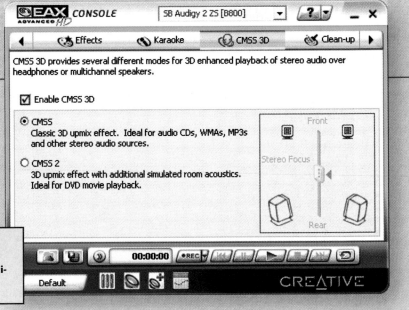

SOUND CARDS | Cheat Sheet

You've got questions, we've got answers

The M-Audio Revolution soundcard is a typical "dual use" card in that it offers digital output as well as multi-channel analog output.

Question: What is the difference between a surround sound card for home theater and a card for gaming and music? Is there any?

A: The primary difference between gaming and home theater is the connections required for each type of sound output. For example, in order to get positional audio from a DVD movie, a soundcard needs a Digital Out connector to send the DVD's audio signal to the speakers. At some point, this digital stream of audio has to be "decoded" into its separate channels, and this decoding can take place either in the soundcard or in the speakers. 3D games are a different story, though, as they typically produce sound that is analog and thus is sent to the soundcard in multiple channels (as opposed to the single-channel digital stream from a DVD movie). To produce these sounds accurately, a soundcard must have different jacks for the front speakers, the center channel, and the rear channel. So today's soundcards need analog output jacks for games and digital output for movies. Luckily, most decent soundcards on the market today offer both types of outputs, making most "gaming" soundcards suitable for home theater as well.

Question: What's the difference between 24-bit/192KHz audio and 16-bit/44.1KHz audio?

A: 16-bit/44.1KHz audio is the specification for CD-quality audio, whereas 24-bit/192KHz sound is recorded at a higher bit rate, meaning it includes more information (or bits of data) about the sound than 16-bit/44.1KHz audio. With a higher bit rate, sound is produced with increased resolution and is able to convey more subtle nuances than with a lower bitrate. Unfortunately, it will be a while before 24-bit/192KHz media becomes commonplace, simply because 16-bit/44KHz is excellent sound quality by most people's standards. Another roadblock to the adoption of 24-bit/192KHz audio is that if you play a CD that was engineered at 16 bits, it won't sound better with a soundcard that's capable of 24-bit resolution. Most 24-bit soundcards do let you record at that resolution, though, which is a nice feature if you do a lot of music recording.

High-res 24-bit audio is available in high-end soundcards and is used mainly in the still-developing DVD-audio specification as well. It provides extremely high levels of musical fidelity.

Buyer beware! This Mad Dog Entertainer 7.1 soundcard looks like a typical high-end card, but it doesn't even have an onboard DSP!

Question: In specific terms, how badly might my 3D gaming frame rates suffer if I use a "host-based" card that relies on my CPU for audio processing chores?

A: Most onboard sound chips (and even some add-in soundcards) offload audio number crunching to the system's CPU, which is generally bad. This is because, during a 3D game, the CPU has its hands full feeding instructions to the videocard, so the last thing it needs is more work. We know how it feels! However, by most benchmarks, the difference in frame rates for a system using a host-based card and an add-in card is usually less than 10 frames per second. If you have a monster gaming rig that has frames to spare, you can afford to send some more work to the CPU. However, if you're running a "budget" system, an add-in card with its own audio processor is the way to go for maximum gaming performance.

CRTs & LCDs

Do you prefer perfectly flat or totally fat?

If you think Hell is a 640x480 VGA monitor, just remember that the very first PC displays couldn't show full-color images whatsoever—we just had green text on a black background, and we loved it! The display currently gracing your desk is a work of art compared to the very first monitors, for it gives you a clear picture of your digital world—every mouse move, every keystroke, every pop-up window, every confirmed frag.

Because they're built to last, modern full-color monitors have a delightfully long life in an age of disposable CPUs. And because their job is simply to show you the information outputted by your videocard, your monitor is blissfully uninterested in being upgraded to keep pace with your motherboard, memory, hard drive, and so on. Also, because Cathode Ray Tubes (CRTs) in particular typically weigh close to a metric ton, they are expensive to ship and a pain to get home in your Toyota Prius. So there's a lot of built-in incentive to buy a display you'll be happy with for a long, long time.

However, like a "life partner" who's been packing on the pounds lately, it's sometimes hard to notice that a monitor has outlived its best years until you spy something better. Indeed, while all CRT and LCD technologies work on the same basic engineering principles, the technologies have indeed improved over the years, and displays engineered in the 1990s just don't look as good as their modern counterparts. The rest of the world might be passing you by with higher resolutions and better color accuracy, and the urge to upgrade becomes irresistible.

There are plenty of good reasons to upgrade your display, but don't deep-six your current display for the flavor of the month without understanding more about the two types of monitors.

The arrival of super sexy LCDs has sounded the death knell for the beloved CRT.

What is a CRT?

The term stands for Cathode Ray Tube. CRT monitors are just fancy implementations of the same technology used in common TV sets: An electron beam originating from the base of a vacuum-sealed tube scans across the tube's screen, which is covered with a layer of phosphor material. A metal grating or wire mesh limits how much of the electron beam can hit individual phosphor clusters, thus leading to an acceptably sharp image. When the phosphor material becomes excited, it glows either red, green or blue. Mix up several differently colored phosphor clusters (pixels by any other name), and suddenly you have millions of colors. Although it is possible to make flat or nearly flat cathode ray tubes, most older models exhibit some curvature, at least around the corners. Most flat CRTs are based on aperture grille technology, but some use shadow-mask technology (both are explained on the next page).

What is a LCD?

Liquid-Crystal Displays are modern alternatives to CRTs. LCD manufacturing starts with a flat pane of glass, which is then layered with a grid of small transistors; the transistors are arranged in groups of three, and each triad describes a screen pixel. When excited by electricity, these transistors can be made to open and shut. Put a backlight behind the transistor grid and, behold, you have an image. Well, that's the shamefully simplistic version of how LCDs work, but it should be enough to give you the basic concept.

All the specs and tech lingo explained

Aperture Grille

A type of CRT that uses a grille of extremely fine wires to focus the electron beam precisely on the right phosphor clusters. Sony introduced this technology with its Trinitron line of displays. An Aperture Grille-based screen typically displays more vivid and brighter colors than a Shadow Mask display.

This aperture "grille" is thrashed, but we can still see the vertical phosphor stripes that determine how much light hits the display.

Brightness

This spec is simply a measurement of how brightly a monitor can display its images. It is often expressed in candelas per square inch: cd/in^2.

CRT

Cathode Ray Tube. A traditional monitor and TV screen technology that produces a picture by using an electron beam to excite phosphors behind a glass screen.

Dot Pitch

The distance between each individually colored phosphor dot on a Shadow Mask CRT screen. A smaller dot pitch allows for a sharper image. Dot pitch is usually measured in millimeters. For example, a pitch of 0.28mm isn't as sharp as a pitch of 0.25mm.

Grille Pitch

The distance between individually colored phosphor stripes on an Aperture Grille screen. A smaller pitch allows for a sharper image. Like dot pitch, grille pitch is also measured in millimeters, and smaller pitch numbers are better.

LCD

Liquid Crystal Display. The main advantage of LCD screens is that they can be made very slim, and are always perfectly flat. Unfortunately, unlike CRTs, LCDs have only one native resolution, and can look distorted when running non-native resolutions.

Pixel Pitch

The size of each colored pixel on an LCD or plasma display.

Pixel Response

The time required for an LCD pixel to change color. A slow response time can lead to blurriness during video playback and 3D gaming. CRTs do not suffer this particular brand of blurriness.

Refresh Rate

The number of times a CRT's electron beam sweeps across the screen during a full second. Refresh rate is measured in kilohertz (Hz), with the lowest acceptable value being 75Hz. (Any rate lower can cause eyestrain.)

Shadow Mask

A metal sieve placed behind a CRT display to ensure that the display's electron beam hits precisely the right phosphor dots. A Shadow Mask CRT is typically bulbous in shape.

Viewing Area

The portion of a display that can actually show image content; typically expressed in inches, and measured from one corner of a screen to the diagonally opposite corner.

Display Resolution

The number of pixels a monitor can display. Resolution is usually expressed in the form of a horizontal value followed by vertical value. For example, a resolution of 1280x1024 means that the monitor can display 1280 pixels horizontally and 1024 pixels vertically—1,310,720 total pixels.

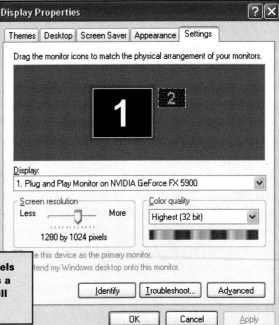

Your display's resolution is the number of pixels that appear on the screen. More pixels equals a sharper image, whereas a lower resolution will appear blurry and dithered.

You've got questions, we've got answers

The 19-inch CRT is starting to look like a product of a bygone era, what with affordable 21-inch CRTs now the norm.

Q: What type of display is the best for gaming?

A: The knee-jerk recommendation has long been "a primo 19-inch CRT." Why? Because CRTs are better suited for gaming than LCDs (they offer better color accuracy as well as support for multiple resolutions without visual-quality degradation), and because 19-inchers have always been great values,

price-wise. However, in today's modern age of affordable 21-inch CRTs, we say the bigger the better—unless, of course, you need to transport your display to LAN parties. If that's the case, then an LCD with a proven, fast pixel response time might make sense. Just be aware that if you try to run the LCD at a non-native resolution, your screen content might look a bit jaggy and blurry.

Q: What is an optimal refresh rate?

A: On an LCD, this is a no-brainer—use whatever refresh rate the manufacturer tells you to use for the native resolution of the panel (this is the resolution the display *has* to run at in order for everything to look normal, i.e., not stretched out, squished, or jaggy). This is almost always 60Hz, even if the monitor may be able to handle higher. Don't worry—LCD pixels don't fade and strobe the way CRT pixels do, so 60Hz won't cause eyestrain.

CRTs are a little trickier. While some

would answer "as high as a resolution as the CRT will allow," we recommend taking a more cautious approach. First, make sure you've loaded the Windows drivers for your particular display before you mess with the refresh rate settings. With the driver loaded, Windows won't let you choose a rate higher than the monitor can display without damage to its circuitry. Our advice is to stay away from 60Hz, but 75Hz or higher will be just dandy.

A monitor's refresh rate is the number of times the on-screen image is updated every second. The key is to set it high enough that you don't notice the flickering.

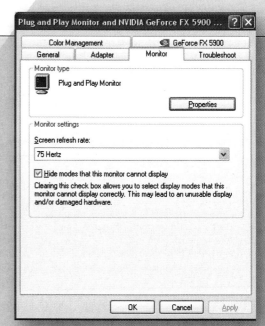

A high-end aperture grill CRT offers the perfectly flat screen of an LCD with the resolution range needed for gaming.

Q: What is the benefit of an Aperture Grille CRT over a Shadow Mask CRT?

A: Shadow mask CRTs can have bulbous screens, which is a by-product of their basic design—the screens of older models must be curved a bit for proper electron beam deflection. Also, the core masking technology that makes shadow mask CRTs different from aperture grille CRTs allows for relatively fewer electrons to hit the phosphor layer. This, in turn, leads to relatively dimmer screens and less brilliant colors than what one might find in an aperture grille display.

Aperture grille CRTs are generally

considered finer pieces of technology, and, indeed, most CRTs intended for high-end image editing and design work are aperture grille displays. The best aperture grille monitors offer perfectly flat, non-bulbous screens, and this reduces glare from ambient light. And, as noted earlier, the aperture grille allows for more electrons to hit the phosphor layer, and this allows for brighter screen content and more brilliant colors. Aperture grille isn't perfect technology, however. The grille itself is held in place by two very thin wires, which can be manifested as two extremely thin lines crossing the screen horizontally. These wires can be distracting if you're the obsessive-compulsive type.

Putting your PC to work

CHOOSE A
CRT Monitor

The right CRT for you

There are many factors to consider when buying a CRT monitor. High-end CRTs cost an arm and a leg. Budget CRTs will give you headaches. Here's how to find a happy medium.

Screen Size and Resolution

The first decision point is picking a screen size. Sizes are generally specified by the diagonal size of the CRT tube. The most common are 17", 19", and 21", with a 4:3 Aspect Ratio, which specifies the width vs. the height of the screen. Note that the viewable part of the screen inside the monitor bezel is generally about one inch less than the tube size. Pay attention to the "viewable" size, since it's the part you actually see. If you can afford it, bigger is generally better, but too large a screen may cause eyestrain, so try several out for size before you buy. In general, we steer clear of 17" monitors (too small) and 24" monitors (too big), so 19" or 21" is the sweet spot. One of the great advantages of CRTs is that they perform well over a wide range of resolutions, but for optimum image quality, you should aim for the following:

17"	1024 x 768	to	1152 x 864
19"	1152 x 864	to	1280 x 1024
21"	1280 x 1024	to	1600 x 1200

Connectors

All CRT monitors come with a VGA-style DB-15 connector. Some high-end monitors also include five BNC connectors for individual RGBHV connections. These are recommended if you're running cable lengths over 15 feet.

Shadow Mask or Aperture Grille or Slot Pitch

There are two common types of CRT tubes: Shadow Mask and Aperture Grille. Shadow Mask tubes have a screen made up of round red, green, and blue phosphor dots. Aperture Grille tubes have alternating vertical stripes of red, green, and blue phosphors. Which type is better? They're both suitable for most applications, but there are differences. Shadow Mask tubes can show finer detail, but they also tend to produce stronger Moiré interference patterns on-screen (which look like rainbow colored swirls). Aperture Grille tubes generally produce images that are brighter and higher in contrast, with colors that are somewhat more vibrant and saturated, but they tend to be more expensive. They also include two very fine horizontal damper wires that are generally invisible to most users but that drive others crazy.

Dot Pitch or Slot Pitch describes the spacing between the RGB phosphors in millimeters. In general, the smaller the better, but this spec is much-abused and misunderstood, so always take this spec with a grain of salt. Note that you can't compare the pitch values between Shadow Mask and Aperture Grille tubes since they are completely different. In fact, you shouldn't compare the pitch values between different manufacturers or tube designs.

Flat or Curved Screen and Anti-Reflection Coating

The natural shape of all CRT monitors is curved, but they are now manufactured in flat versions at somewhat higher cost. Flat screens are better because they minimize visual distortions and glare. However, the flatter the tube, the more likely there will be some geometric distortion and reduction in sharpness, particularly in the corners. When viewing a "perfectly flat" CRT at the computer store, pay close attention to the corners of the display to determine if the distortion levels are acceptable to you.

You'll also want to make sure a CRT has an anti-reflection coating, because without it, you'll see a mirror image of everything in front of the CRT, including yourself and everything behind you. Not only is this distracting, but it significantly reduces the contrast and readability of the screen. Anti-reflection coatings range from the cheap and relatively ineffective frosting (which also reduces image sharpness) to dielectric layers like those on high-quality lenses. If you work in a relatively darkened room, anti-reflection will be much less important than if you work in a brightly lit environment.

CHOOSE A
LCD Monitor

The right LCD for you

Just like with a CRT, the first decision point is picking a screen size. Sizes are generally specified by the diagonal size of the screen. The most common are 15", 17", 18", 19", and 20", with a 4:3 or 5:4 Aspect Ratio, which specifies the width vs. height of the screen.

The most important point to be aware of is that each LCD is manufactured with a fixed pixel resolution format, called its "Native Resolution." You need to use the LCD in its native resolution; otherwise there will be a substantial and generally unacceptable degradation in image quality. That's because the LCD must internally convert other resolutions into its native format in a process is called "rescaling," which always degrades the image, especially when there is text and graphics.

The native resolution varies with screen size.

Typical values are:

15"	1024 x 768
17"- 19"	1280 x 1024
21"	1600 x 1200

Response Time and Motion Artifacts

LCDs also have a relatively slow response time compared with CRTs, and they suffer from varying degrees of motion-smear, motion-flicker, and other motion artifacts. Most panels include a response-time specification in milliseconds. In general, the smaller the better, but this spec is "spun" by manufacturers sometimes, so be cautious. Some manufacturers quote separate (and smaller) rise and fall times. Also, the times refer to transitions from peak white to black, whereas the more common gray-gray transitions are much slower. The faster panels generally show greater motion-flicker, which is often more of a visual problem than motion-smear. To check on the degree of motion-flicker, go to www.displaymate.com/dwshots.html. Slowly and smoothly move the scrollbar up and down. Look for flicker in any of the test patterns and in the navigation bar text in the on the left side of the screen.

In order to minimize additional motion artifacts, make sure that you set your refresh rate to the native refresh rate of the panel, which generally is 60Hz. This should be in the monitor's spec sheet. Setting it to a different value (particularly a higher value like 75Hz) will reduce image quality in analog mode and may introduce strobing effects and some image break-up when there is motion.

Analog or Digital

Most LCDs are connected to the computer via the same analog VGA DB-15 connector as CRTs. That makes them an easy replacement for CRT monitors. However, LCDs operate at a fixed pixel-resolution format, so the monitor must analyze the analog signal and try to extract and measure each individual pixel in the image. That's easier said than done, and if it's not done exactly right, the LCD image actually will appear a bit fuzzy and include some digital noise as well. Some LCD monitors also include a digital or DVI interface that transmits the signal to the monitor digitally, which largely solves this dilemma. Monitors with DVI inputs are more expensive, though, and you'll need a graphics board that has a DVI output and connector.

Image Quality Issues

LCDs can have outstanding image and picture quality. When properly adjusted, they can produce a perfectly sharp image, something that is beyond the capability of a CRT. But there are some areas where LCD performance may be weak: They have trouble producing pitch-black and usually produce some level of dark-gray instead, and they may have trouble reproducing intensities near peak white (called "white saturation") . The gray-scale may be uneven, with irregularities and bumps, particularly at low intensities, and the Gamma may be way off, resulting in color-calibration errors, that can affect digital photographs. The *DisplayMate* test patterns (on the disc included with this magazine) will let you check and evaluate all of these issues..

PERFORMANCE ISSUES AND DISPLAYMATE

There are considerable differences in performance between different monitors. Even if you know what to look for, it's hard to make a decision without the right tools and test patterns. *DisplayMate* is the computer industry standard for testing and evaluating monitors. *Maximum PC* uses the advanced *DisplayMate Multimedia* Edition for testing and reviewing all of the magazine's monitors. There are also end-user versions, designed to help users set up and tune up their monitors for optimal image and picture quality. They are also very good for monitor testing and evaluation. In addition, DisplayMate and *Maximum PC* are making available a free limited-function demo version of *DisplayMate*, with six sample test patterns to help you get started. Use them to perform some basic tests on any monitor you're thinking about buying. It's available on the magazine's website, www.maximumpc.com.

Your PC is sick, we've got the cure

CABLE QUERY

If I upgrade from a CRT to an LCD, do I need to upgrade my videocard as well? Will there be any issues connecting my current videocard to my new display?

It depends on your hardware, but probably not. The standard connection for a CRT is an analog DB-15 cable, and most LCDs include this type of connector. However, some LCDs are capable of sending a digital signal, so they use a DVI (Digital Visual Interface) connector. In order to use this type of connector, it must be supported on your graphics card. Luckily, most modern videocards sport both types of connectors.

OUCH...MY HEAD!

I have a CRT monitor, and sometimes, after using the computer for a while, I get headaches. Is this normal?

Headaches are a common side effect of an improperly set up workstation, but there are a few things you can do to mitigate the effects. The first thing you should do is to make sure your monitor's refresh rate is set to a proper level. If it's set too low, the screen will appear to be flickering and will give you a headache in no time. Once the monitor is set to a higher refresh rate, the screen will flicker so fast that it will largely be imperceptible, which will alleviate the problem. To change your refresh settings, right-click the desktop and select Properties, then click on the Settings tab. Next, click on the Advanced tab in the lower right-hand corner and then click on Monitor. Your refresh rate will be displayed in this screen, so simply change it to the highest setting possible.

It's also wise to

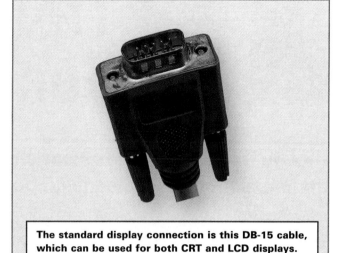

The standard display connection is this DB-15 cable, which can be used for both CRT and LCD displays.

make sure there is adequate light in your work area. Some people like to work in the dark because it makes the images on the screen seem more vivid. But it's common knowledge that this will hurt your eyes over time, and will definitely contribute to headaches as well.

Finally, be sure to take breaks. As a general rule, you should take a break every half-hour. Close your eyes, roll your neck around, and don't look at a computer screen for a few minutes if possible.

IS DUAL DISPLAY OK?

What do I need in order to run dual displays?

Well, besides two displays, you need either a videocard with dual outputs or two physical videocards. Luckily, most mid-range to high-end videocards released in the last few years have included both an analog DB-15 connector as well as a DVI connector for an LCD. If you have one of these videocards and want to run two LCDs, you'll have to acquire a DVI to DB-15 adapter, which are available at Radio Shack.

If your videocard only has one output, you'll have to run the second display from a second physical videocard. Dual-displays are

supported in Windows XP, so as soon as you plug in the second display XP will recognize it and allow you to set its resolution from the Display Settings menu (right-click on the desktop and select Properties, then Settings).

If you're concerned about gaming issues with dual-displays, remember that when you fire up a game it will automatically run on the gaming card and be displayed on one monitor, so the secondary display will just be for desktop work.

Almost every videocard made in the past few years is suitable for dual-displays thanks to its dual-outputs. The round port between the DVI and DB-15 ports is a TV-Out jack.

This VGA to DVI adapter lets you plug a standard DB-15 monitor cable into a videocard's DVI-out jack.

XP Troubleshooting Secrets

How to fix your OS woes using XP's built-in troubleshooting and diagnostic tools

BY SCOTT MUELLER

WARNING!
HAZARDS
AHEAD

Your car has, oh, about 50,000 individual parts. That's 50,000 opportunities for something to go wrong, and 50,000 guesses at what your problem might be.

Windows XP, on the other hand, has more than 45 million lines of code. If you think of these lines as "parts" within the OS, and consider that these "parts" are often altered by apps you install or corrupted by disk failures, brownouts, or bad juju, then you can see why your system goes awry so often.

Fortunately, getting WinXP back up to speed is a lot less expensive and painful than doing the same with your comparatively simple automobile. That's because Microsoft includes error-reporting features, diagnostic programs, and utilities that can help you root out the cause of a system snafu—all before resorting to the dreaded reinstall.

We're going to show you how to decode the error messages left behind by Windows XP after it crashes, and explain how to use the tools built into the OS to become your own mechanic. You'll be diagnosing problems, recovering from system mishaps, and maintaining a working machine in no time.

What Is Windows XP Trying to Tell Me?

The most serious PC problems are caused by corrupt files and buggy software, as well as defective or incorrectly configured hardware. These problems often result in a STOP or Blue Screen of Death. The resulting "screen dump" is a frustrating and cryptic string of letters and numbers. But often these messages can be decoded to provide some useful information. For example, say you're working on a system that STOPs (blue-screens) with the following message:

```
STOP: 0x0000002E
(0x00699F11, 0x04EBD77F,
0x00000000, 0x80ADD9C8)
DATA_BUS_ERROR
```

The best thing to do when you get a STOP or blue-screen error like this one is to look up the error code (the first string of letters and numbers after STOP:) in the Microsoft Knowledge Base at http://support.microsoft.com. There you'll find articles that will help you decode the specific error you're receiving, and helpful information about troubleshooting the problem.

The Knowledge Base tells us that the 0x0000002E code indicates a parity error detected in memory. An error like this is normally caused by problems with memory, but can also be caused by other

hardware such as a videocard, a failing hard disk, a boot sector virus, or even a defective device driver. The message in our example includes four parameters (in the parentheses) that provide valuable information. The parameters for this error are decoded as follows:

- *Virtual address of the fault (0x00699F11)*
- *Physical address of the fault (0x04EBD77F)*
- *Processor Status Register contents (0x00000000)*
- *Faulting Instruction Register contents (0x80ADD9C8)*

Of these, the second one (the physical address) is the most useful, as it indicates the exact location in memory where the fault occurred. In this case, the address is 0x04EBD77F, which is a hexadecimal number that translates to 82,564,991 in decimal, which if you divide by 1,048,576 (number of bytes in a megabyte) places the error at 78.74 as a megabyte address, which is the same as saying the error is in the 79th megabyte (addresses start with 0). If you have two 128MB DIMMs in the system, then this places the error in the first bank of the two installed.

Now if this error reoccurs, and the address is the same every time, then the problem is most likely the memory mod-

ule, which should be replaced. If the error reoccurs but the address is always different, then I would suspect other hardware or software in the system instead of just the memory modules.

While not all STOP errors utilize the parameters in the same manner, the first place to start is always the Microsoft Knowledge Base. Hey, they're the ones that came up with these codes in the first place!

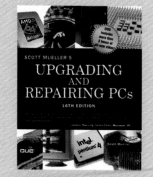

ABOUT THE AUTHOR
Scott Mueller is the author of Upgrading and Repairing PCs, *now in its 16th edition. This 1,600 page, "Geek Tested and Approved" manual is a favorite reference among the* Maximum PC *editors.*

WARNING! HAZARDS AHEAD

Better Living Through Device Management

The Device Manager is the software component of the plug-and-play standard, and it should be the first place you look if you're having problems installing a new piece of hardware, or to resolve conflicts between devices. You can use Device Manager to see a graphical view of the hardware that's installed in your computer, get detailed listings of resource usage, update hardware device drivers, change settings, and troubleshoot problems. To open Device Manager, select Start > Control Panel > Performance and Maintenance > System. On the Hardware tab, select Device Manager.

The primary uses for Device Manager include:

• *Check to see if the installed hardware is recognized and working properly.*
• *Change hardware resource configuration and device settings.*
• *Identify installed drivers.*
• *Install updated drivers.*
• *Enable, disable, or uninstall hardware devices.*
• *Roll back to a previous driver version.*
• *Print a summary of the devices that are installed on your computer.*

Normally, the automatic plug-and-play features in Device Manager will properly configure all the installed hardware in such a way that there are no conflicts. This is especially true in systems running WinXP. It's rare that you'll need to manually edit or modify the resource allocation of devices. In general, the settings should be left on automatic. By setting resources manually, you risk causing problems, and your system may even lock up. If that happens, try starting in Safe mode: Reboot the PC, and hold down the F8 key while the system restarts to access the Safe mode option, then open the Device Manager and reset everything back to automatic. Once you restart, the plug-and-play routines will take over and should resolve any critical conflicts.

Another useful feature of the Device Manager is that it lets you see resource usage at a glance. For example, to check for any IRQ resource conflicts, go to the View menu, select Resources by type, and then click Interrupt Request.

An IRQ is a signal that a device uses to gain the attention of the processor. Most all devices that communicate data to and from the system will require an IRQ, since they will need to request the attention of the processor as data comes in. Without this type of design, buffers on the device may overflow before the processor decides to check to see if the device needs attention. Older ISA bus devices can't normally share IRQs, while PCI devices can share them. Problems can occur if you have a lot of older ISA bus devices in a system, since there are only 16 total IRQs, and many of them are reserved for specific uses. In my system, there's only one free IRQ (IRQ 10), meaning I can add only one more ISA bus device before I'll have allocation problems. On the other hand, I can add more PCI-based devices because they can all share IRQ 9. Note that the PCI bus is designed to remap shared IRQs (called IRQ steering), so having multiple devices on a single IRQ doesn't present a problem.

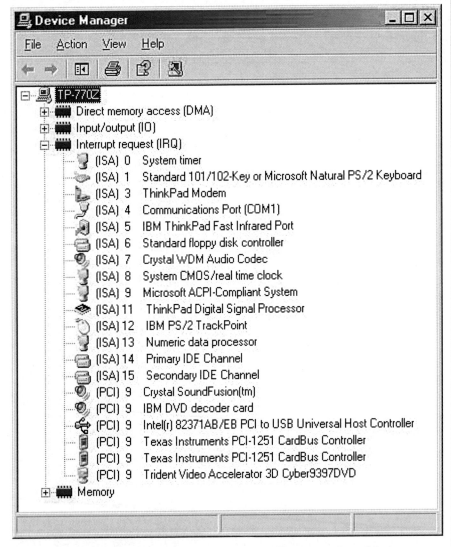

If you look at the Device Manager for our system, you'll see a number of devices sharing IRQ 9, for example, since all of those devices are PCI based.

Getting the 411 from System Information

WinXP includes a powerful System Information utility that can display system configuration information for both local and remotely connected computers. To run System Information, select Start > Programs > Accessories > System Tools > System Information. The main display in the System Information program includes the following categories:

- *Hardware Resources (similar to Device Manager)*
- *Components (hardware)*
- *Software Environment (installed drivers, programs, services)*
- *Internet Settings*

System Information will not only display the information on the screen, but it can also save or print a complete report about your system. This can be very useful if somebody is helping you troubleshoot the system remotely. By sending along the file or printout, the troubleshooter will have a lot of important information about your system that may be useful in diagnosing a problem. System Information can also be used as a launching point, from the Tools menu, for several other valuable utilities that are described in the following sections.

Network Diagnostics
Network Diagnostics is designed to collect and display information about your hardware, operating system, Internet browser and e-mail program configurations, modems, and network cards. It should be your first stop in diagnosing

"connectivity" problems, and will often point you directly to the culprit.

System Restore
System Restore is a very useful tool that's designed to store and track changes made to your system. WinXP will normally create what's called a "restore point" automatically whenever you install new hardware, drivers, or software. You can also use the tool to manually create restore points anytime you like. This is similar to how many game programs allow you to save your current position, so if you "die" in the game, you can reset to the previously saved position rather than having to start over. In working with PCs, this can be a valuable timesaver. Once restore points are created, you can use the System Restore program to restore your computer to an earlier state.

File Signature Verification
The system files and drivers provided with Windows XP have a special digital signature by Microsoft, which indicates that they are original, unaltered files that have been approved by Microsoft for use with Windows. Problems can arise when installing new software or drivers on your computer, as in some cases your original files can be overwritten by unsigned or incompatible versions.

To check for problems with critical files, Windows XP provides the File Signature Verification utility, which is designed to identify and display the following information

for any unsigned files on your system:

- *Filename*
- *Location*
- *Modification date*
- *Type*
- *Version number*

By clicking on the Advanced options, you can also root out third-party drivers that haven't been digitally signed, which means these drivers haven't necessarily been approved by Microsoft for use with WinXP. If you find drivers like these, check the manufacturer's web site for updated drivers, especially ones that have received WHQL (Windows Hardware Quality Labs) certification.

DirectX Diagnostic
Graphics and sound applications commonly use the DirectX API (application program interface) to run under Windows. Because of the variety and complexity of

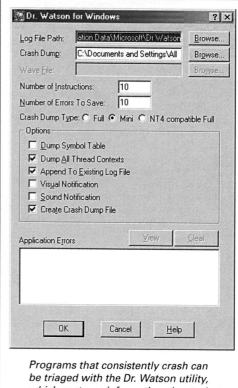

Programs that consistently crash can be triaged with the Dr. Watson utility, which captures information about what went wrong for examination later.

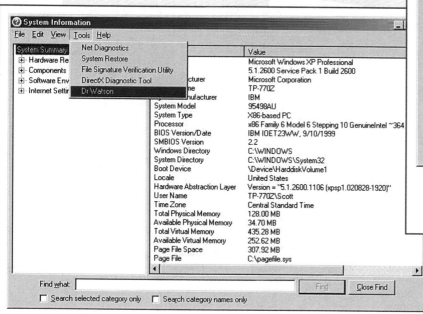

The System Information utility isn't just a great resource for information about your PC. It's also a launching point for a host of great diagnostic tools.

graphics hardware and software, there can sometimes be problems with various videocards, drivers, and programs that work with DirectX. The DirectX Diagnostic tool can give you information about the DirectX components and drivers on your system. This tool enables you to test sound and graphics output and enables you to adjust or disable certain hardware acceleration features for compatibility and testing purposes.

Dr. Watson

Dr. Watson for Windows is a software error-debugging tool designed to log information when errors occur. A text file (Drwtsn32.log) is created whenever an error is detected, and can be printed or sent to Microsoft or other software companies to help verify and resolve bugs in software.

Dr. Watson is automatically installed in your system folder when you install Windows. If a program error occurs, Dr. Watson will automatically log the error. You can also start Dr. Watson manually to change the configuration and settings for the program.

Perform Open Heart Surgery with DiskProbe

Microsoft includes a very powerful set of support tools located in the \Support\Tools folder on the XP Professional CD (these are unfortunately not included in the XP Home version). For descriptions of all the tools, Microsoft provides online documentation via release notes and a help file. Also, there's more information on these tools in the Windows XP Resource kit, which you can view online at www.microsoft.com/windows/reskits/default.asp.

One of the more powerful and interesting programs included in the Windows Support Tools package is *DiskProbe*, a sector editor utility. *DiskProbe* allows you to read and write individual physical or logical sectors on a drive, and has special features for decoding and editing the Master Boot Record (MBR), partition tables, and volume or partition boot sectors. Because these structures are literally outside of the file system on a drive, they are not accessible through most other applications. With this tool, a knowledgeable user can restore these important data structures if they are damaged, for example by a boot sector virus.

In addition to editing, you can also use *DiskProbe* for preventive maintenance, by making backups of these critical sectors as files, which can be stored on another disk (such as a floppy, for example). Once saved, they can be later restored in the event that these sectors are corrupted on your hard drive.

To run *DiskProbe*, first make sure you have installed the Windows Support Tools from the Windows XP Professional CD. Then select Start > Windows Support Tools > Command Prompt. At the prompt, enter **Dskprobe**. The program will then launch in a window. Optionally you can run the program by opening Windows Explorer and navigating to the \Program Files\Support Tools folder, then clicking Dskprobe. The documentation for the program is available via the Help command on the menu bar.

Note that editing critical sectors such as the MBR is like performing open-heart surgery on your system. *DiskProbe* and other sector editors like *Norton DiskEdit* function at a level below the Windows file system, which means that the standard safety protocols are not in effect. *DiskProbe* gives you access to every byte on the physical disk without regard to normal security or access privileges, which makes it possible to damage or overwrite critical areas of the disk. If you change so much as a single byte incorrectly, you could render your system non-bootable and possibly render the drive unrecognizable even if the system is booted from a floppy or CD!

Fortunately, *DiskProbe* defaults to read-only mode, which means you can run the program to view sectors without worrying about accidentally making changes. Before you do make any changes with a low-level tool

such as *DiskProbe*, make sure you have a backup of any important data.

I have specialized in data recovery for many years, and in that line of work I regularly use sector editors like *DiskProbe* to restore critical boot sectors on hard drives that had otherwise been inaccessible to Windows.

In a recent example, a client of mine appeared to have lost hundreds of hours of video footage due to a hard drive crash. To solve the problem, I did a manual inspection of the MBR and partition boot sectors. The drive had been formatted with the FAT32 file system, and I very quickly discovered that somehow the first sector of the three-sector long FAT32 partition boot sector, which was at Logical Block Address (LBA) 63, had been overwritten with zeros. I knew from experience that FAT32 keeps a backup copy of the primary partition boot sectors at LBAs 66 through 68. So I used *DiskProbe* to copy sector 66 and paste it to sector 63, thereby solving the problem.

A job like this would cost hundreds to possibly thousands of dollars if sent to a professional data recovery service. Now you see why most people who know data recovery don't like to teach it.

Except me, that is.

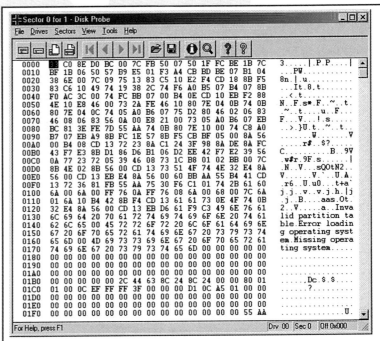

If you have a steady hand and some experience with hex editing, DiskProbe can rescue you from major hard disk calamities.

MAXIMUM... BOOKS?

300 PAGES EACH!

ALL COLOR! NO ADS!

Yes. It's true. *MAXIMUMPC* introduces the next generation in computer books!

Maximum PC Guide to Building a Dream PC

It's the biggest, meanest, *most complete* PC building guide we've ever created! Not only do we show first-time PC builders *everything* they need to know about assembling a computer from scratch, we also divulge the truth behind competing hardware technologies, and show you how to make the smartest parts choices. Includes configuration plans for six different Dream Machine archetypes. *By Will Smith, technical editor*

● **$29.99; AVAILABLE IN SEPT 04; ISBN 0-7897-3193-2**

Maximum PC 2005 Buyers Guide

Get an insider's peek at 2004's most exciting Lab experiments, plus forward looks at the gear you *must* know about in 2005. Includes the hidden story behind *Maximum PC* benchmarking, and a full compendium of our most positive—and brutal—2004 product reviews. Special Ask the Doctor and Watchdog wrap-ups make this a veritable *Maximum PC* almanac! A must-have reference book for faithful readers of the magazine. *By George Jones, editor-in-chief*

● **$29.99; AVAILABLE IN SEPT 04; ISBN 0-7897-3194-0**

Maximum PC Guide to PC Hardware Hacking

The most complete, most descriptive, most *helpful* book on case-modding ever published! Loaded with stunning illustrations and 100 percent *actionable* instructions, we show you how to construct a mind-blowing mod of your own. Painting, lighting, drilling, cutting, cooling... *every* topic is covered! Case-modder extraordinaire Paul Capello shares the tricks and insights that have made him a legend among hardware hacking experts. *By Paul Capello & Jon Phillips*

● **$29.99; AVAILABLE IN DEC 04; ISBN 0-7897-3192-4**

ALSO
Maximum PC Ultimate PC Performance Guide

All of *Maximum PC's* "newsstand only" special issues bound into a single book! Five issue's worth of content—a must-have treasure for *Maximum PC* fanatics.

● **$29.99; AVAILABLE IN SEPT 04; ISBN 0-7897-3317-X**

WARNING!
HAZARDS
AHEAD

The XP Doctor Is In!

Your PC is sick, we've got the cure

Installing Windows XP from Upgrade CD

Can I do a full install of Windows XP on a clean hard drive with an upgrade XP version? I want to start from scratch with a new drive and not install Windows 98 first.

You never need to install an older version of Windows in order to upgrade it with a newer version. If you use an upgrade version of Windows XP on a blank system, Windows will prompt you to insert a valid Windows 98, ME, or 2000 disk near the beginning of the install process.

Double Disks?

Can I install Windows XP to two of my home computers, or do I have to purchase two installation disks?

Unfortunately for consumers, Microsoft's licensing rules for Windows XP allow the OS to be installed on only one machine at a time. However, if you already have a copy of XP and want to upgrade another machine, you can save a few bucks by buying an extra license without the CD and manuals. You can order additional licenses for XP Home or Professional at http://shop.microsoft.com/. A Home upgrade costs $84 and a Professional Upgrade costs $184.

Windows XP Activate!

I am always tweaking my computer with hardware upgrades. Now it's reached a point that whenever I make a change to something in my computer that is hardware related, I have to re-activate my copy of Windows XP. This was fine the first few times when I could do it online, but now I have to call to get the activation code. I know they do this to prevent piracy and to prevent you from loading the software on more than one computer, but I am always making some type of change to my computer and it's getting rather annoying. Is there anyway around this?

Unfortunately, there's no legitimate way around Windows XP's product activation, however we have to wonder how frequently you're upgrading your hardware to encounter constant reactivation requests.

On our test systems, the only way we can force a reactivation request is to upgrade a lot of hardware. We've seen activation requests when we've upgraded more than two of the following components: the motherboard, CPU, network card, or hard drive. Even *Maximum PC* editors stick with a system for at least six months.

Saving Patches and Hot Fixes for Later

I have a question about patches and hot fixes. I thought I could download all the patches to a directory and apply them when I wanted, but they always install themselves and I have no idea how to save them so at some future date I can wipe my hard drive and reinstall Windows and then reinstall all the fixes without having to download them again. Is this possible, and if so how?

The site you want is download.microsoft.com. Click the Windows (security and updates) option on the left side of the page. Make sure you download all the updates listed—you'll need to click "Next 45" at the bottom of the page to see them all. The Doctor recommends you download all the security updates for your version of Windows to one folder. After you've done that, you can save them to CD, DVD, or whatever format you'd like for future use.

FireWire Failure

Why does Windows XP sometimes fail to recognize my FireWire (IEEE 1394) hard disk after a restart?

This is a known problem in XP in which the disk fails to start on approximately every fifth attempt. No fix is currently available. The only solution is to unplug the disk, wait 15 seconds, and then reconnect the device. If this solution doesn't work, try powering off the computer, wait five seconds, then restart the machine.

Messenger Messages are Driving Me Mad

I have a home LAN using Windows XP Home Edition. My family and I will be playing online games or watching a movie in the living room when, all of a sudden, we get a pop-up message on our desktop. Can I fix this problem without resorting to third-party software?

The Windows Messenger service—not to be confused with Windows Messenger, the IM client—is the latest front in the war against spam. Luckily, these messages can be stopped by activating XP's built-in firewall.

All you need to do is open up the Properties for your Internet connection, go to Start> Control Panel> Network Connections, and then right-click the icon for your Internet connection. (If you use a cable modem or DSL, it will probably be a Local Area Connection, but if you use an analog modem it will be named after your ISP.)

Windows (Security & Updates)

Most Popular Downloads

1. Mydoom (A, B) and Doomjuice (A, B) Worm Removal Tool (KB836528)
2. Security Update for Windows XP (KB823980)
3. Internet Explorer 6 Service Pack 1
4. Blaster Worm Removal Tool for Windows XP and Windows 2000 (KB833330)
5. Cumulative Security Update for Internet Explorer 6 Service Pack 1 (KB832894)

⊟ Next 45

6. Security Update for Windows XP: KB828028
7. Security Update for Windows 2000: KB828028
8. Security Update for Windows XP 64-Bit Edition (KB823980)
9. Security Update for Windows 2000 (KB823980)
10. Security Update for Windows XP (KB824146)
11. Cumulative Security Update for Internet Explorer 6 (KB832894)
12. Security Update for Microsoft Windows 98 and Windows 98 Second Edition (KB823559)
13. Windows XP Home Edition Utility: Setup Disks for Floppy Boot Install
14. Software Update Services 1.0 with Service Pack 1
15. Windows XP Professional with Service Pack 1 Utility: Setup Disks for Floppy Boot Install
16. Windows 2000 Service Pack 4 Network Install for IT Professionals
17. Security Update for Windows NT Workstation 4.0: KB828028
18. Cumulative Security Update for Internet Explorer 6 Service Pack 1 (KB824145)
19. Security Update for Microsoft Windows XP: KB828035
20. Internet Explorer 5.5 Service Pack 2 for Windows Me
21. Security Update for Windows NT Server 4.0: KB828028

If you find yourself frequently installing Windows on new machines, you can save yourself a lot of downloading hassle by keeping copies of all the Windows patches on a CD.

Click Properties, and then click the Advanced tab. Check the box labeled "Protect my computer and network by limiting or preventing access to this computer from the Internet." Note that installing Service Pack 2 will enable Windows Firewall and disable Windows Messenger service by default.

Legacy App Woes

I have used a database program for years, but it won't work with Windows XP. It originally was a DOS program, and there is an updated version that works with Windows 98. I have tried to use the emulator in XP, but the app just won't run. How can I get a Windows 98-compatible program to work with Windows XP?

Like Kenny Rogers sings, you gotta know when to hold 'em, and know when to fold 'em…. The Doctor knows it's difficult to bid adieu to an application that's served you well for years, but Richard, it's time.

The sad fact is, some applications work with the Windows XP compatibility tools, and some don't. We recommend you find a way to export your data from your old database app into a more commonly recognized format. Almost every application lets you import from comma- or tab-separated text files, so you should dump your old database into a .CSV (comma separated value) file from a Windows 98 machine, and then import it into your new database app.

Activating XP's built-in firewall options should eliminate evil Messenger-spawned spam.

Perennial Performance Problems

I've had WinXP since the first month it was out, and I've noticed a sporadic problem. My PC slows down to the point of crawling at times. When I check the Task Manager, I notice that the "system" process is running at 100 percent. A reboot stops the slowdown, but it inevitably comes back.

What puzzles me the most is that I've had this problem consistently over the last two years spanning three motherboards, four processors, and 20 fresh reinstalls of WinXP. All of my hardware (including floppies) has been changed out during the course of my upgrades, so it can't be a hardware problem. I'm a stickler for trying to keep current, so all the hardware is flashed to the newest versions and all my drivers are the latest builds.

Please help!

We've seen this before and it's usually the fault of either a badly written driver or an especially unpleasant virus. Another suspect is spyware running distributed computing—similar to Seti@Home—in the background and disguising that CPU usage as a System process. We've also heard reports of a bug in Windows XP Service Pack 1 having the same effect.

Because you've updated all your hardware, it's likely either a virus or spyware that is causing your problem. Get a virus scanner, such as *McAfee VirusScan* or *Norton Antivirus*, update your definitions, and do a full system scan. If that doesn't turn up anything, start with a clean install of Windows XP, then add one piece of software at a time to your system. First test the system with no other software installed. Then install Service Pack 1 (or SP2) and test again. Finally, install the other software you use, one item at a time, and test them individually. If you're still experiencing problems, disconnect your PC from the network and see if that fixes the problem.

When conducting your tests, the Performance applet comes in handy. It's located in Start > Control Panel > Administrative Tools > Performance. Open up the Performance Logs section, then click Counter Logs. In the right pane, right-click and select New Log Settings. Give your log a name, and then click the Add Counters button. Change the Performance object to Process and select the % Processor Time counter from the counter list, and then choose the System process from the list of different processes. The Performance tool will record the CPU usage for the particular process you're troubleshooting while you run your tests. To see if it spiked while you were testing, open the Performance applet again and press Ctrl+L to open a log file. If you click the Add button and select the log you've created, it will show you a graph of the CPU usage for the process you selected.

Make sure you disable any counter logs you create when you're done with them, as some can seriously degrade your PC's performance.

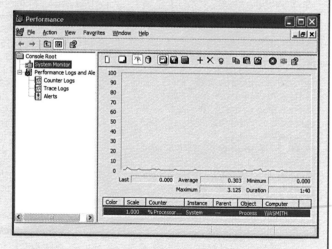

The Performance tool is your best bet for isolating misbehaving applications. You can easily isolate the CPU usage for a single process and track it over time.

Index

3D acceleration, Media Center PCs, 81
3D audio formats, soundcards, 7
3D games, videocards, 35–36
3D interfaces, Longhorn, 162
3D models, creating, 252–260
  boosters, 256, 258
  canopies, 256
  chamfering, 255
  cross sections, 254
  extruding, 255
  intakes, 256
  light rack, 258
  lighting, 259
  mapping selections, 257
  materials, 257
  patches, 253
  smoothing, 255
  splines, 253
  texture, 257
  unit setup, 253
  vents, 256
4-megapixel images, compared to sub-megapixel images, 216
24-bit audio, 296–297
64-bit computing, 265

A

Abit motherboards, 27
AC Power Loss, 95
accelerators, 198
access points, securing, 196
Account icon, customizing Windows XP desktop, 131
ACDSee, 218
acid, painting cases, 87
active cooling, 263
actors (creating movies), 231
AD EXT/SPDIF_IO, 39
Ad-Aware, 148, 171, 187–188
ADC, soundcards, 7
add-on soundcards, 295
Adobe Audition web site, 238
Adobe Elements 2.0, 217–220
Adobe Illustrator, 85
Adobe Premier, 230
ADSL (Asymmetric Digital Subscriber Line), 174
Advanced Technology Attachment (ATA), hard drives, 288
AGP, 280, 284
  configuration, 125
  Fast Write, 280
  Pro, 77
  settings, 94
  slots, 25, 272

airflow, testing case fans, 64–66
ALi ALADDiN-P4 chipset, 23
ALi MAGik 1 chipset, 21
Alt-Tab Replacement, 161
AMD
  760 chipset, 21
  Athlon XP, 17
  compared to Intel, 18
  CPUs, 17, 260, 264
    memory, 268
  Duron, 17–18
  Opteron, 18
  overclocking CPUs, 117
amenities
  cases, 12–13
  motherboards, Athlon, 29–30
  power supplies, 58
  selecting motherboards, 26–27
analog speaker rigs, Media Center PCs, 83
analog videotapes. *See* videotapes
Anisotropic filtering, 280
Antex, hard drive cooler, 62
Athlon 64, 18
Athlon XP, 17
  chipsets, 19
  Rev A, chipsets, 19
  Rev B, chipsets, 19–201
antivirus software, 90, 142, 186, 189
  Windows XP, updating, 147
aperture grille CRTs, 47, 300
APIs, 280, 296
appearance, cases, 13
application integration, 109
Application Layer Gateway, 143
Application Management, 144
application position recall, 109
arcade machines. *See also* games
  building, 242–251
    budget, 243
    buttons, 245
    cabinets, 243–244, 247, 249
    coin slots, 250
    Control Panel, 245–247
    drink holders, 250
    joysticks, 245, 247
    keyboards, 245
    lighting, 250
    marquees, 244
    monitors, 244
    parts, 245
    speakers, 244
    spinners, 248
    start buttons, 250
    trackballs, 247
    translucent leaf switches, 248

  trim, 244
  troubleshooting, 251
  games, 251
archives, Windows XP, 149
areal density, hard drives, 8, 288
Arrange by Artist option, 139
Arrange by Modified option, 139
Arstechnica.com, 91
art, adding to Music folders, 132
artwork, painting cases, 85–86
assembling
  entertainment centers, 80–83
  Media Center PCs, 82–83
  PCs, 68–78
  PCs, BIOS setup, 74
  PCs, cable installation, 71
  PCs, connecting drives, 73
  PCs, connecting power supply, 72
  PCs, CPU installation, 70
  PCs, IDE drives, 71
  PCs, inserting motherboards into cases, 72
  PCs, installing drives, 72–73
  PCs, installing soundcards, 73
  PCs, installing videocards, 73
  PCs, installing Windows XP, 75
  PCs, memory installation, 71
  PCs, mounting motherboards, 70
  PCs, removing motherborad tray, 70
  PCs, safety tips, 77
  PCs, troubleshooting tips, 77
  PCs, wire installation, 71
Asymmetric Digital Subscriber Line. *See* ADSL
ATA (Advanced Technology Attachment)
  BIOS, disabling, 98
  hard drives, 288
  motherboards, 272
  ports, 25
Athlon
  64 3700+, 15
  overclocking CPUs, 30, 120–121
  selecting motherboards, 28–30
  XP, 16, 119, 267
ATI Radeon IGP
  320 chipset, 21
  330 chipset, 23
  340 chipset, 23
Audigy 2, 40–41
Audigy 2.ZS, 295
audio
  24-bit, 296–297
  channels, soundcards, 7
  CODEC, motherboards, 24
  digital extraction, CD burners, 50–51

Dolby Digital 5.1 speakers, setup, 206–209
DVD, 296
extraction, 293
MP3s, 234–236
onboard, 40, 295
RazorLAME, 236
studio recordings, creating, 237–241
Audio Copy, 235–236
Audio Record Wizard, 238
auto painting, 86
auto-sensing, NICs, 4
Automatic Updates, 143
aux-in (soundcards), 39
auxiliary power connectors, 33
Azalia, 41

B

Background Intelligent Transfer, 143
BackUpMyPC, 148
backups
BackUpMyPC, 148
burning videotapes to DVDs, 222–227
data, creating custom recovery discs, 165–166
movies, 233
Windows XP, 147, 149–150
Bargon Athlon XP, 17
batteries, digital cameras, 217
Bay Cool, 62
BBI Agent, 202–203
benchmarks, overclocking CPUs, 120
Bevel tool, 256
BGA (Ball Grid Array), CPUs, 262
bilinear, videocards, 280, 283
BIOS, 24
AC Power Loss, 95
AGP settings, 94
cache, 96
CAS latency, 93
correcting CPU speed, 92–93
correcting memory, 92–93
disabling ATA BIOS, 98
disabling memory checks, 98
disabling Serial ATA, 98
enabling PCI IDE BusMaster, 98
faulty fans, 95
hard drive failures, 95
legacy hardware resources, 96
memory timing, 93
minimizing component interference, 96
motherboards, 272
overclocking CPUs, 116–117
PCI bus performance, 94
peripherals, 94
protecting PCs from viruses, 95
setup, 74
standby state, 96
streamlining boot sequence, 98
switching hard disks to user-defined, 97
system temperatures, 95
unused resources, 95
Black Viper web site, 143

Blue Laser, 293
blue-screen error (Windows XP), 305
boosters, 3D models, 256, 258
boot images, creating for routers, 203
booting
CDs, confirming boots, 165
PCs from diskettes, 186
PCs, streamlining boot sequence, 98
PCs, troubleshooting, 76
Windows XP, changing bootscreen image, 133
Windows XP, Compatibility Mode, 159
Windows XP, multibooting, 159
Windows XP, optimizing speed, 141
Bootvis, 141
branch prediction, CPUs, 262
bridges, WLANs, 6
brightness
CRTs, 105–106
LCDs, 49
monitors, 299
broadband connections, 172–179
cable modem, 175
dial-up, increasing speed, 173, 198
DSL, 174–175
satellite connections, 175
sharing, 176–179
testing speed, 173
broadcasting (SSID), disabling, 197
browsers, 90
Mozilla project, 194
protecting, 189
budgets, building arcade machines, 243
buffers, 293
hard drives, 8
optical drives, 5
underrun protection, CD burners, 50
burning
DVDs, 292–294
videotapes to DVD, 222–227
burst speed, hard drives, 288
Buss-Cool, 63

C

C1/C2 errors (audio extraction), 235–236
cabinets (arcade machines), building, 243–244, 247–249
cable modem connections, 175
cables
installing, 71
monitors, 302
safety tips, 77
shared Internet connections, 178
cache memory, removing DLLs from, 156
cache, BIOS, 96
cameras
automatic camera features, 219
batteries, 217
Canon GL-1 DV cam, 230
Image Editor, 217
lenses, 216
megapixels, 216
Olympus, 215

removable media, 216
selecting, 216–220
Canon GL-1 DV cam, 230
canopies, 3D models, 256
capacitors, 32
power supplies, 58
videocards, 33
capacity
hard drives, 8, 288
memory, 4
capture cards, shooting movies, 232
capturing video, burning videotapes to DVD, 223–224
Card Cooler Sunon fans, 63
CAS (custom address strobe), 93
latency, 93
memory, 4
case studies
airflow tests of case coolers, 65–66
Athlon XP Barton 3000+, 119
Athlon XP Palomino 2000+, 119
Dolby Digital 5.1 speaker setup, 207–209
overclocking CPUs, 118–119
P4 Northwood, 118
cases, 10–13. See also mini-systems
amenities, 12–13
appearance, 13
cooling, 78
cooling features, 10
fans, positioning, 64–66
front-mounted I/O ports, 11
Lian Li's PC 6070A, 13
Media Center PCs, 82
modding, 13
painting, 84–89
power supplies, 13
price, 13
quality, 10
selecting, 12–13
structural design, 12
upgradeability, 11, 13
Xoxide UV-reactive, 12
cathode ray tubes. See CRTs
CC-DAs, 5
CCDs (charge-coupled devices), 231
CD Autoplay, disabling, 157
CD burners
Lite-On, 51
selecting, 50–51
speed, 51
Yamaha CRW-F1, 50
CD Slide Show Generator, 161
CD-Extra, 5
CD-I, 5
CD-in (soundcards), 39
CD-ROMs, 5
CD-ROMXA, 5
CD-Text, 5
CDs
booting, 165
restoring from, 171
Celeron, CPUs, 17
central processing units. See CPUs
chamfering, 3D models, 255
channel outputs (soundcards), 40

chipsets, 19–23
    Athlon, 20–21
    Media Center PCs, 81
    north bridge compared to south
      bridge, 269
    Pentium 4, 21–23
    selecting for Athlon motherboards,
      28–29
    selecting for motherboards, 26
    soundcards, 7
    videocards, 3
choosing. *See* selecting
cl_cmdrate command, 213
cl_rate command, 212
cl_updaterate command, 212
cleaning Registry, 149
clear coat, 88–89
clearing prefetch files, 149
clients, Windows, setup for Linux
    router, 205
Clipbook, 144
clocking
    CPUs, 261–262
    system buses, 74
clocks
    generators, 25
    speed, 280
    videocards, 34–35
CNPS6500B-CU (Zalman), 61
CNPS7000A-CU, 266
coin slots, arcade machines, 250
COM+, 143
combo drives, 293
Comer Pocket, Dolby Digital 5.1 speaker
    setup, 208
Command Panel, 255
command-line applications (Windows
    XP), running quickly, 139
communications streaming architecture
    (CSA), 27
CompacFlash cards, 216
Compatibility Mode (Windows XP), 159
components, minimizing interference,
    96
compression
    disabling, 155
    Disk Cleanup Wizard, 91
    utilities, 90
Computer Browser, 144
configuring
    DHCP, 204
    DNS proxy, 204
    LANs for Internet connection shar-
      ing, 177
    Linux router, 205
    network interface cards (NICs) for
      router creation, 203
    PCs for shared Internet connections,
      178
    router connections, 204
    Windows XP, custom recovery discs,
      169–170

connections
    broadband, 172–179
    dial-up, modem bonding, 198
    routers, configuring, 204
connectors
    input, speakers, 6
    motherboards, 25
    power supplies, 57
    soundcards, 7
Context menu, adding options, 155
contrast, CRTs, 105–106
Control Panel, arcade machines,
    245–247
convergence, CRTs, 107
converters, burning videotapes to
    DVDs, 223
cookies, disabling, 187–189
cooling
    cases, 10, 78
    CPUs, 263, 268
    hard drives, 62
    mini-systems, 14
    overclocking CPUs, 113
    selecting, 60–63
    slots, 63
Cornerstone P1750, 47–49
costs. *See* prices
CPU Critical Temperature, 95
CPUs
    AMD, 17, 260, 264, 268
    Athlon 64, 18
    Athlon XP, 16–18, 267
    BGA (Ball Grid Array), 262
    branch prediction, 262
    Celeron, 17
    clocking, 261–262
    coolers, selecting best, 60–63
    cooling, 263, 268
    Duron, 17–18
    floating point instruction, 262
    FSB (front-side bus speed), 262
    gates, 262
    hyper-threading, 262
    installing, 70, 264
    Intel, 17, 260, 264
    Media Center PCs, 81
    microns, 262
    multipliers, 262
    Opteron, 18
    overclocking, 111–123, 264–267
    Pentium 4, 17
    Pentium 4 Willamette, 16
    pipelines, 262
    register, 262
    selecting, 16–23
    sockets, 25
    speed, 16–17, 92–93, 261–267
    gSSE2, 262
    temperature, 265
    thermal paste, 264
    transistors, 263
    troubleshooting, 77, 264–265
    voltage, 265
    Xeon, 17

crashes, Windows Explorer, 140
Creative Labs, 295
    Audigy 2, 40–41
    Audigy 2.ZS, 295
    Sound Blaster, 40
    speakers, 239–241
crossover, 240
crossover points, speakers, 6
CRT type (monitors), 2
CRTs (cathode ray tubes), 47, 298–303.
    See also monitors
    aperture grille, 300
    brightness, 105–106, 299
    compared to LCDs, 47
    contrast, 105–106
    convergence, 107
    degaussing screens, 105
    DisplayMate, 107
    DisplayMate software, 105
    dot pitch, 299
    geometry, 106–107
    grille pitch, 299
    moiré control, 107
    optimal refresh rate, 300
    pixel pitch, 299
    pixel response, 299
    position, 106
    refresh rate, 299
    refresh rates, 104
    resolution, 105
    selecting, 301
    shadow mask, 47, 299–300
    size, 106
    specifications, 48
    troubleshooting, 302
    viewing area, 299
cryptographic services, 142
crystal (videocards), 33
CSA (communications streaming archi-
    tecture), 27
Curve Amount spinner, 256
custom address strobe (CAS), 4
custom menus, creating DVDs, 226
custom recovery discs, creating,
    164–171
    application installation, 170
    configuring Windows XP, 169–170
    confirming CD boot, 165
    data backups, 161–166
    formatting drive, 166
    install drivers, 168–169
    installing Windows XP, 167
    restoring discs, 171
    running Windows Update, 168
    tools, 166
custom resolutions, setting, 157
customizing
    desktops, with HTML, 199–201
    folders, 91
    Windows XP, 90
    Windows XP desktop, 130–134

D

DAC, 7, 39
DAE speed, optical drives, 5
data backups, creating custom recovery discs, 165–166
data buffer size, optical drives, 5
data transfer rates
    hard drives, 288
    optical drives, 5
data transmission rates, WLANs, 6
Dazzle Digital Video Creator II, 228–229
DDR (double data-rate), 3, 272
decompression, RazorLAME, 236
Defrag, 90
defragging utilities, 90
degaussing CRT screens, 105
deleting
    MSN Explorer, 140
    My folders, 155
    partitions, 150
    recent files list, Windows XP, 156
Dell XPS B733r, airflow test, 66
design, mini-systems, 14
desktops
    customizing, with HTML, 199–201
    Dolby Digital 5.1 speaker setup, 208
    embedding web pages, 201
    hard drives, 46
    modes, monitors, 109
    Virtual Desktop Manager, 160
DesktopX, 133
device drivers, updating, 148
device management, 306
Device Manager, 90, 306
DHCP
    client, 143
    configuring, 204
dial-up connections
    increasing speed, 173
    modem bonding, 198
die size, 263
digital 5.1 speaker rigs, Media Center PCs, 83
digital audio extraction, CD burners, 50–51
digital cameras. See cameras
digital photography, 215–221
    creating feature films, 230–233
    lighting, 219
    printing, 218
    selecting cameras, 216–220
digital signal process. See DSP
Digital Signal Processor (DSP), 296
Digital Subscriber Line. See DSL
Digital Theater System (DTS), 240, 296
digital-out connector (soundcards), 38
digital photography, automatic camera features, 219
DIMM (Dual Inline Memory Module) motherboards, 272
diodes, videocards, 33
Direct3D, videocards, 280

DirectSound 3D, 40, 296
DirectX, 280–286, 284
DirectX Diagnostic, 307–308
disabling
    CD Autoplay, 157
    compression, 155
    fans, 101
    file sharing, 184
    guest account, 185
    spyware, 187–188
    SSID, 197
disc-at-once mode, optical drives, 5
Disk Cleanup, 91, 148, 155
Disk Defragmenter, 148
disk media, 43
diskettes, booting from, 186
DiskProbe, 308
Display Properties Control Panel, 138
Display Properties options, customizing Windows XP desktop, 131
DisplayMate, 105, 107
Distributed Link Tracking Client, 144
DLLs, removing from cache memory, 156
DMA, 90
DNS proxy, configuring, 204
Dolby Digital 5.1 speakers, 240, 296
    playing music, 241
    setup, 206–209
dot pitch (monitors), 2, 48, 299
double data-rate. See DDR
double-sided DVD-RAM, compared to dual-layer, 54
download managers, 198
Dr. Watson, 308
Dragon's Lair, 251
drink holders, arcade machines, 250
drivers
    installing, custom recovery discs, 168–169
    selecting videocards, 36
    updating, Windows XP, 150
    videocards, 36, 280
drives
    DMA, 90
    formatting, custom recovery discs, 166
    heads, hard drives, 288
    installing, Media Center PCs, 82
    optical, 292–294
    troubleshooting, 77
DRU-500A (Sony), 53–54
DSL (Digital Subscriber Line), 174–175
DSP (Digital Signal Processor), 7, 296
    chipsets, soundcards, 7
    soundcards, 39
DTS (Digital Theater System), 240, 296
dual channel memory interface, motherboards, 272
dual displays, 108–110, 302
    hardware, 108
    hotkeys, 110
    nView compared to HydraVision, 108

profiles, 110
    special effects, 110
dual-format DVD burners, 293
dual-layer DVD-RAM, compared to double-sided, 54
dual-sided DVDs, 293
Duron, 17–18
DVD+R/RW, 293
DVD burners, 52–54
    interface PCB (printed circuit board), 52
    Plextor PX-708A, 292
    selecting, 53–54
DVD desktop, Dolby Digital 5.1 speaker setup, 208
DVD+R/W, 53–54
DVD-R/RW, 293
DVD-R/W, 53
DVD-RAM, 53-54
DVDs, 293
    audio, 296
    burning, 292–294
    burning videotapes to, 222–227
    creating, 226, 228–229
    troubleshooting, 294

E

ECC (error corrections code), 4
Editable Mesh, 256
editing
    movies, 232
    videotapes, burning videotapes to DVD, 224
effects boxes, recording from, 237
EFS (encryption file system), 185
electro magnetic interference (EMI), power supplies, 55
email
    executables, 186
    spam filters, 190–191
embedding web pages on desktops, 201
EMI (electro magnetic interference), power supplies, 55
emptying Recycle Bin (Windows XP), 147
enabling WEP, 196
encoders, LAME, 236
encryption, 183–184
encryption file system (EFS), 185
engineering, mini-systems, 14
entertainment centers, creating, 80–83
    installing drives, 82
    installing videocards, 82
    output options, 83
    required parts, 80–81
    software, 83
equipment
    arcade machines, 245
    creating movies, 231
Error Reporting, 144

errors
    C1/C2 (audio extraction), 235–236
    error corrections code (ECC), 4
Ethernet, 269
Ethernet 10BASE-T, 4
Event Log, 142
executables, 186
expansion, mini-systems, 15
external interfaces, WLANs, 6
external media readers, 217
extraction, audio, 235–236, 293
Extrude tool, 255
extruding 3D models, 255

F

Falcon Northwest, painting cases, 84–89
fans
    buses, Nexus, 13
    Card Cooler Sunon, 63
    cases, positioning, 64–66
    cooling tips, 78
    disabling, 101
    faulty, 95
    headers, 24
    headers, motherboards, 272
    installing, 266–267
    Pentium 4, 266
    power supplies, 55
    quieting PCs, 101
    selecting, 60–63, 266
    troubleshooting, 268
faulty fans, 95
Fax Viewer, turning off, 156
feature films
    creating, 230–233
    editing, 232
features. *See* **amenities**
files
    organizing (Windows XP), 139
    sharing, disabling, 184
filters
    quieting PCs, 101
    spam, 190–191
finding. *See* **selecting**
firewalls, 90, 180–181
FireWire, 24
    Windows XP, 310
firmware, 293
first-person shooter games, 214
Flash, optical drives, 5
flat-panel speakers, 239
flex circuits, 43
Flexisign Pro, 85
Floating Point Color, videocards, 280
floating point instruction, CPUs, 262
floppy disks, restoring from, 171
Floppy Drive Seek option, 98
floppy image (Linux), 204
floppy ports, motherboards, 25
Folder Guard, 185

folders
    creating shortcuts to, 201
    customizing, 91
    My folders, deleting, 155
    organizing (Windows XP), 139
form factor, 272
formats
    3D audio, soundcards, 7
    optical drives, 5
formatting drives, custom recovery discs, 166
Formfactor, memory, 4
forums (Maximum PC), mini-systems, 14
freeware, arcade games, 251
frequency clock, motherboards, 272
frequency range, WLANs, 6
frequency response, 6, 240
front side bus, motherboards, 272
front-mounted I/O ports
    cases, 11
    mini-systems, 15
front-panel connectors, 24
front-side bus speed (FSB), CPUs, 262
FrontPage, 199
FSB (front-side bus speed), CPUs, 262

G

games. *See also* **arcade machines**
    arcade machines, 251
    controllers. *See* joysticks
    creating 3D models, 252–260
    first-person shooters, 214
    Half-Life 2, hacker attack, 184
    Half-Life 2, tips for multiplayer performance, 212–213
    Half-Life 2, videocards, 35
    keyboards, 59
    monitors, 300
    mouse, 59
    multiplayer games, optimizing PCs for, 210–213
    New DirectX, 163
    Quake III Arena Engine, tips for multiplayer performance, 211–212
    sound cards, 297
gates, CPUs, 262
GeForce 6800 videocard, 15
GeForce FX 5800, 34
GeForce FX 5950, 279
geometry controls, power strips, 125
geometry, CRTs, 106–107
GhostCD, 171
Gigaworks, 239
Gizmodo.com, 91
GlobalWin I-Storm II, 62
gmax, creating 3D models, 252–260
    boosters, 256, 258
    canopies, 256
    chamfering, 255
    extruding, 255
    intakes, 256

    light rack, 258
    lighting, 259
    mapping selections, 257
    materials, 257
    patches, 253
    smoothing, 255
    splines, 253
    surfaces, 254
    texture, 257
    unit setup, 253
    vents, 256
Golden Tee, 251
gondolas, 73
Google.com, 91
GPUs, (graphics processing units), 33–36, 281
graphics
    adding to HTML tables, 200
    cards, PCI/AGP configuration, 125
    painting cases, 85–86
    videocards, 284
graphics processing units. *See* **GPUs**
grille pitch (monitors), 48, 299
GroovyGameGear KeyWiz, 245
ground loops, Dolby Digital 5.1 speaker setup, 209
Guess account, disabling, 185
Guitar Tracks web site, 238
Guitarists web site, 238
Guitarport, 238
guitars, connecting to soundcards, 237–238

H

hackers
    firewalls, 180–181
    security, 183
hacking Registry, 91, 153–154
Hagstrom KE-72, 245
Half-Life 2
    hacker attack, 184
    tips for multiplayer performance, 212–213
    videocards, 35
Hamar, Dusan, 162
hard disks, user-defined, 97
hard drives, 42–46, 287–291
    areal density, 288
    ATA (Advanced Technology Attachment), 288
    burst speed, 288
    capacity, 288
    coolers, 62
    cooling tips, 78
    data transfer rates, 288
    disk media, 43
    drive heads, 288
    failures, 95
    flex circuits, 43
    Hitachi, 44
    IDE (Integrated Drive Electronics), 42, 288

installing, 72, 73
logic board, 42, 288
master boot record, 288–289
master/slave jumpers, 43, 288
memory, 289
parallel ATA, 45
partitions, 289
platters, 289
power connectors, 43
random access speed, 289
read/write head assembly, 43
S.M.A.R.T. (Self-Monitoring Analysis
and Reporting Technology), 289
SCSI, 289
sectors, 289
selecting, 44–46
desktop *versus* server drives, 46
speed, 44–45
Serial ATA, 45, 58, 286, 289
specifications, 8
speed, 286, 289
spindle motors, 43
troubleshooting, 77, 290–291
troubleshooting performance, 286
voice coil, 42
hardware
audio channels, soundcards, 7
channels, 296
dual displays, 108
mini-systems, 14–15
specifications, 2–9
voices, soundcards, 7
Hardware Transform and Lighting,
videocards, 280
HDTVs, Media Center PCs, 83
headers, fans, motherboards, 272
heat spreaders, 263
heatsinks
cooling tips, 78
overclocking CPUs, 113
power supplies, 55
safety tips, 77
selecting, 60–63
troubleshooting, 76
Help and Support, 143
HID Input Service, 143
history, Windows XP, 126–127
Hitachi hard drive, 44
Hornet Pro mini-system, 15
host-based processing, 296
hotfixes (Windows XP), 310
hotkeys
HydraVision, 109
monitors, 110
HSF (Heatsink and Fan), 263
HTML
customizing desktops, 199–201
Slide Show Generator, 161
HydraVision
assigning hotkeys, 109
compared to nView, 108
hyper-threading
CPUs, 262
mini-systems, 14
Hyperdictionary.com, 91

I

I-Pac, 245
I/O controller, motherboards, 24, 272
I/O ports, front-mounted, mini-systems,
15
IC7-G, 27
icons (Windows XP), viewing quickly,
138
IDE (Integrated Drive Electronics)
Cables, 42, 73
drives, master/slave jumpers, 71
hard drives, 288
ports, 25, 272
Image Editors (digital cameras), 217
Image Resizer, 161
images, adding to HTML tables, 200
Inboxer, 192–193
indexing (Windows XP), turning off, 138
Indexing service, 144
input capacitors, power supplies, 55
input connectors
soundcards, 7
speakers, 6
input options, Media Center PCs, 81
installing
applications, custom recovery discs,
170
cables, motherboards, 71
CPUs, 70, 264
drivers, custom recovery discs,
168–169
drives, Media Center PCs, 82
fans, 266–267
hard drives, 72, 73
memory, 71
PCs, arcade machines, 244
soundcards, 73
videocards, 73, 82
Windows XP, 75
Windows XP, creating custom recovery discs, 167
Windows XP, from Upgrade CD, 310
Windows XP, reinstalling, 149
Windows XP, troubleshooting, 76
insurance, shooting movies, 232
intakes, 3D models, 256
Intel
845 chipset, 21
845E chipset, 21
845GE chipset, 21
845GV chipset, 21
845PE chipset, 21
850 chipset, 22
850E chipset, 22
Azalia, 41
compared to AMD, 18
CPUs, 17, 260, 264
CSA (communications streaming
architecture), 27
IC7-G, 27
interfaces
Longhorn 3D interfaces, 162
NICs, 4

optical drives, 5
PCB (printed circuit board), 52
Windows XP, increasing speed, 138
WLANs, 6
interlacing, 231
Internet
accelerators, 198
broadband connections, 172–179,
198
intruders, preventing, 183–184
IPSEC, 144

J

JASC PaintShop Pro, 218
Jedi Academy OpenGL tests, Hornet
Pro 64, 15
Jonestown massacre, 88
joysticks, 296
arcade machines, 245–247
headers, 39

K

kernel, Windows XP, 128
keyboards, 90
arcade machines, 245
selecting, 59
KeyWiz, 245
KVM switches, multiple PCs, 159

L

LAME, 236
LAN Party Pro875, 26
LANs, configuring for Internet connection sharing, 177
laser optics (DVD burners), 52
latency, CAS, 93
Lavasoft Ad-aware, 171, 187–188
LCDs (liquid circuit displays), 48–49,
298–303
brightness, 299
compared to CRTs, 47
dot pitch, 299
grille pitch, 299
optimal refresh rate, 300
pitch, 299
pixel response, 299
refresh rate, 299
selecting, 301
shadow mask, 299
troubleshooting, 302
viewing area, 299
LEDs (light-emitting diodes), NICs, 4
legacy hardware, resources, 96
legacy problems (Windows XP), troubleshooting, 311
lenses (digital cameras), 216
Levin, Rich, 147
LFE (low-frequency effects), Dolby
Digital 5.1 speaker setup, 209
Lian Li's PC 6070A case, 13
light rack, 3D models, 258
light-emitting diodes (LEDs), 4

lighting
3D models, 258
arcade machines, 250
creating movies, 231
digital photography, 219
line-conditioning circuitry, power supplies, 55
line-in (soundcards), 38
Linux, routers, creating, 202–205
Lite-On CD burner, 51
living room case study, Dolby Digital 5.1 speaker setup, 207
loading tray motor (DVD burners), 52
locations, shooting movies, 232
logging clips, creating movies, 233
logic boards, 42, 288
Logical Disk Manager, 143
logon screen (Windows XP), changing images, 133
Longhorn, 132, 162–163
low-frequency effects (LFE), Dolby Digital 5.1 speaker setup, 209

M

M-Audio Revolution soundcard, 297
MAC addresses, securing WLANs, 197
mapping 3D models, 257
marquees, arcade machines, 244
mass storage, Media Center PCs, 81
master boot record, hard drives, 288–289
master copies, movies, 233
master/slave jumpers, 43, 71
materials, 3D models, 257
Max data transfer rate, optical drives, 5
Max distance between terminals, WLANs, 6
Max resolution, videocards, 3
Maximum output, speakers, 6
Maximum PC Commport.com, 91
Maximum PC forums, mini-systems, 14
maximum refresh rate (monitors), 2
McAfee VirusScan, 147
Media Center PCs, creating, 80–83
installing drives, 82
installing videocards, 82
output options, 83
required parts, 80–81
software, 83
media, optical drives. See optical drives
megahertz, CPUs, 16–17
megapixels (digital cameras), 216
memory
AMD XP CPUs, 268
CAS (custom address strobe), 4
controller, motherboards, 272
correcting, 92–93
DDR, motherboards, 272
disabling memory checks, 98
hard drives, 289
installing, 71
management, Windows XP, 128

Media Center PCs, 81
mini-systems, 15
specifications, 4
timing, 93
videocards, 3, 35, 281
Memory type, videocards, 3
Messenger, 144
Mic-in (soundcards), 38
microns, CPUs, 262
microphones, recording from, 237
Microsoft Hardware Qualification Labs, 139
mini-jack speakers, 240
mini-systems. See also cases
cooling, 14
design, 14
engineering, 14
expansion, 15
front-mounted I/O ports, 15
hardware, 14–15
Hornet Pro, 15
Maximum PC forums, 14
memory, 15
selecting, 14–15
technology, 14–15
miniDV tapes (creating movies), 231
minimizing Outlook, 91, 154
Mirror tool, 256
modding, cases, 13
modem bonding, 198
modems, multiplayer games, 211
moire control, CRTs, 107
monitors. See also CRTs; LCDs
aperture grille, 47
application integration, 109
application position recall, 109
arcade machines, 244, 249
assigning hotkeys, 109
cable, 302
Cornerstone P1750, 47–49
desktop modes, 109
dual displays, 108–110, 302
games, 300
hotkeys, 110
LCDs, 48–49
position, 108–109
profiles, 110
selecting, 47–49
shadow mask CRTs, 47
special effects, 110
specifications, 2, 48–49
troubleshooting, 302
virtual desktops, 109
Monsturd (film), 230–233
Moore's Law, 265
motherboards, 24–31, 271–277
Abit, 27
AGP slots, 25, 272
amenities, Athlon, 29–30
ATA, 25, 272
audio CODEC, 24
BIOS, 24, 272
clock generator, 25

CPU sockets, 25
DDR memory, 272
DIMM, 272
dual channel memory interface, 272
fan headers, 24
Firewire, 24
floppy ports, 25
form factor, 272
frequency clock, 272
front side bus, 272
front-panel connectors, 24
I/O controller, 24, 272
IC7-G, 27
IDE ports, 25, 272
inserting into cases, 72
installing cables, 71
installing memory, 71
LAN Party Pro875, 26
memory controller, 272
mounting, 70
MSI K8N NEO Platinum Edition, 31
nForce2, 29
nForce3 250Gb, 31
NICs, 25
north bridge, 272
overclocking, 27
PC2700-3200, 272
PCB, 273
PCI Express, 273
PCI slots, 24, 272
POST, 273
power connectors, 25
RAID, 24
RAM, 25
removing tray, 70
SDRAM, 273
selecting, 26–30
Serial ATA, 24, 27, 273
Shuttle, 14
southbridge, 273
trays, cases, 11
troubleshooting, 274–277
mounting motherboards, 70
mouse, selecting, 59
movies
burning to DVDs, 222–227
creating, 230–233
editing, 232
MP3s, 234–236
MS Software Shadow Copy Provider, 143
MSI K8N NEO Platinum Edition, 31
MSN Explorer, deleting, 140
MultiDrive II (Panasonic), 53
multiplayers, optimizing PCs for, 210–213
multiple PCs, KVM switches, 159
multipliers, CPUs, 262
music
creating DVDs, 226
creating movies, 233
Dolby Digital speakers, 241
MP3s, 234–236
RazorLAME, 236
studio recordings, creating, 237–241

Music folders, adding art to, 132
MusicMatch tests, Hornet Pro 64, 15
My folders, deleting, 155
MyDVD 5.0, 228–229

N

n-Track Studio web site, 238
National Security Agency, 197
NET_GRAPH X, 212
Netfilter, 202
NetStumbler, 197
Network Diagnostics, 307
Network Drive options (Registry), hacking, 154
Network Interface Cards. See NICs
networks, SSIDs, 196
New DirectX, 163
Nexus fan bus, 13
nForce2, 29
nForce3 250Gb, 31
NICs (Network Interface Cards), 4, 25
    configuring for router creation, 203
noise, quieting PCs, 100–103
    fans, 101
    noise-dampening materials, 102
    replacing power supplies, 102
north bridge
    chips, compared to south bridge, 269
    motherboards, 272
Norton AntiVirus, 147
Norton Ghost 2003, 166
Norton Internet Security, 194
Norton Personal Firewall, 194
Notepad, 199
NTFS, 90
nVidia
    GeForce FX 5950, 279
    nForce 420-D chipset, 21
    nForce2 chipset, 21
nView, compared to HydraVision, 108

O

Olympus, cameras, 215
onboard audio, 40–41, 295
onboard graphics, videocards, 284
onboard RAM, 33
onboard sound, 269
onboard video, 269
Open Command Window Here menu, 161
Open GL, 281
Opteron, 18
optical drives, 292–294
    connecting, 73
    specifications, 5
    troubleshooting, 294
optics control PCB (printed circuit board), 52
optimal refresh rate (monitors), 300
optimizing
    PCs for multiplayer games, 210–213
    Recycle Bin, Windows XP, 139

System Restore, Windows XP, 139
Windows XP boot speed, 141
Optimum XP, 141
Outlook, minimizing, 91, 154
Outlook Express, disabling email, 157
output capacitors, power supplies, 55
output connectors, soundcards, 7
output options, creating Media Center PCs, 83
output, speakers, 6
overclocking, 124
    Athlon motherboards, 30
    CPUs, 111–123, 264–267
    CPUs, AMD, 117
    CPUs, Athlon, 120–121
    CPUs, benchmarks, 120
    CPUs, BIOS, 116–117
    CPUs, case studies, 118–119
    CPUs, coolers, 113
    CPUs, heatsinks, 113
    CPUs, preparations, 115
    CPUs, requirements, 114–115
    CPUs, steps, 115–116
    CPUs, videocard velocity, 117
    motherboards, 27

P

P4 Northwood case study, 118
packet writing, 5, 293
pagefiles, securing, 91
painting cases, 84–89
    acid, 87
    artwork, 85–86
    auto painting, 86
    clear coat, 88–89
    disassembly, 87
    graphics, 85–86
    Jim Saling, 89
    paint options, 86
    toxins, 87
    vinyl, 85–86, 88
    weeding, 86
Panasonic, MultiDrive II, 53
panels, Display Properties Control, 138
parallel ATA, 45
parity (memory), 4
partitions
    deleting, 150
    hard drives, 289
passive cooling, 263
password protection, 91, 184, 189
patches
    3D models, 253
    Windows XP, 310
PC Inspector Smart Recovery, 218
PC Power and Cooling Buss-Cool, 63
PC2700-3200, motherboards, 272
PCB, motherboards, 273
PCI
    bus, performance, 94
    slots, 24, 272
PCI Express, motherboards, 273
PCI IDE BusMaster, enabling, 98

PCI/AGP configuration, graphics cards, 125
PCs
    BIOS setup, 74
    booting, from diskettes, 186
    building, 68–78
    cable installation, 71
    memory installation, 71
    mounting motherboards, 70
    removing motherboard tray, 70
    configuring for shared Internet connections, 178
    connecting drives, 73
    connecting power supply, 72
    CPU installation, 70
    IDE drives, 71
    inserting motherboards into cases, 72
    installing, 244
    installing drives, 72
    installing hard drives, 73
    installing soundcards, 73
    installing videocards, 73
    installing Windows XP, 75
    Media Center, creating, 80–83
    installing drives, 72
    installing hard drives, 73
    installing soundcards, 73
    installing videocards, 73
    installing Windows XP, 75
    safety tips, 77
    troubleshooting, 76–77
    wire installation, 71
peak power rating, 240
Penny-arcade.com, 91
Pentium 4, 17
    chipsets, 20–23
    fans, 266
    Willamette, 16
Pentium 4B, chipsets, 20
performance problems (Windows XP), troubleshooting, 311
performance, PCI bus, 94
peripherals, 94
permits, shooting movies, 232
phase cancellations, Dolby Digital 5.1 speaker setup, 209
phase change, 263
Photo-CDs, 5
photography. See digital photography; photos
PhotoImpact XL, 218
photos, adding to HTML tables, 200
Photoshop, 217–220
ping servers, 210
pinning programs, Start menu, 157
pipelines, CPUs, 262
pirated software, 186
pixels
    LCDs, 49
    pitch, monitors, 299
    response, monitors, 299
    shaders, videocards, 281
platters, hard drives, 289

Plextor PX-708A DVD burner, 292
Plug and Play, 143
pop-up ads, killing, 194
Pop-Up Stopper, 194
Popko, Rick, 233
ports
   I/O, cases, 11
   SB1394 (soundcards), 38–39
position
   case fans, 64–66
   CRTs, 106
   monitors, 108–109
POST (power on self test), 76, 273
power buttons, arcade machines, 249
Power Calculator, 161
power connectors, 25, 43
power factor correction circuits, power
   supplies, 55
power on self test (POST), 76
power per channel (speakers), 240
power supplies, 55–58
   capacitors, 58
   cases, 13
   connecting, 72
   connectors, 57
   EMI (electro magnetic interference),
     55
   fans, 55
   heatsinks, 55
   input capacitors, 55
   line-conditioning circuitry, 55
   output capacitors, 55
   power factor correction circuits, 55
   replacing, 102
   safety tips, 77
   selecting, 57–58
   speakers, 6, 241
   troubleshooting, 76
   voltage, 58
powering on PCs, troubleshooting, 76
powerstrips, 124–125
PowerToys, 160–161
pre-striping tapes, shooting movies, 232
preamps, 237–238
prefetch files, clearing, 149
prices, cases, 13
printing, digital photography, 218
private folders, securing, 183
problems. See troubleshooting
processors, 19–23. See CPUs
profiles
   monitors, 110
   videocards, 125
   Windows Services, 145
PSUs (power supply units), selecting,
   57–58

Q

Quake III Arena Engine games, tips for
   multiplayer performance, 211–212
Quick Launch, 90
quieting PCs, 100–103
   fans, 101
   noise-dampening materials, 102
   replacing power supplies, 102

R

RAID, 24, 269
RAM, motherboards, 25
RAMDAC (random access memory digital-to-analog converter), 281
   videocards, 3
random access memory digital-to-analog converter. See RAMDAC
random access speed, hard drives, 289
random access time, 293
RAS, 93
Razor's Edge vinyl shop, 85
RazorLAME, 236
RCS plugs, 240
read/write head assembly, 43
recording modes, optical drives, 5
recordings, creating studio recordings,
   237–241
recovery discs
   creating custom discs, 164–171
   creating custom, data backups,
     165–166
Recycle Bin (Windows XP)
   emptying, 147
   optimizing, 139
Red Laser, 293–294
Reeves, Kelt (president of Falcon
   Northwest), 84–89
refresh rates (monitors), 2, 104, 299
RegCleaner, 161
Regedit, 160
register, CPUs, 262
Registry, 91
   cleaning, 149
   hacking, 153–154
   setting changes, customizing
     Windows XP desktop, 130
release forms, shooting movies, 232
Remote Desktop, 185
Remote Procedure Call (RPC), 143
Remote Registry Service, 144
removable media, 216
removing
   DLLs from cache memory, 156
   motherboard tray, 70
replacing power supplies, 102
requirements, burning videotapes to
   DVD, 223
resolution
   CRTs, 48, 105
   LCDs, 49
   setting custom resolutions, Windows
     XP, 157
   videocards, 3, 125
resources, unused, 95
restore points (Windows XP), 154
Roberts, Bobs, 245
Roemer Optimum XP, 141
ROMs, arcade machines, 251
routers
   boot images, 203
   configuring, 205
     connections, 204
     LANs as stand-alone routers, 177

Linux, creating, 202–205
multiplayer games, 211
WLANs, 6

S

S.M.A.R.T. (Self-Monitoring Analysis
   and Reporting Technology), hard
   drives, 289
S/PDIF, 240, 296
safety tips, 77
Saling, Jim, painting cases, 89
sampling frequency, 296
satellite connections, 175
satellites, 240
SB1394 port (soundcards), 38–39
scanners, vulnerability, 181
screensavers, password protection, 91
scripts (creating movies), 231
SCSI, hard drives, 289
SDR, (single data-rate), 3
SDRAM (synchronous dynamic RAM), 4,
   93
   motherboards, 273
SDSL (Symmetric Digital Subscriber
   Line), 175
search interface (Windows XP), reject-
   ing, 156
sec Dolby Digital 5.1 speaker setup, 209
sectors, hard drives, 289
security
   access points, 196
   antivirus software, 189
   configuring settings, 181
   disabling file sharing, 184
   disabling Guess account, 185
   eliminating spam, 190–193
   encryption, 183–184
   executables, 186
   firewalls, 180–181
   Folder Guard, 185
   intruders, preventing, 183–184
   killing pop-up ads, 194
   pagefiles, 91
   password protection, 184, 189
   private folders, 183
   protecting computers from viruses,
     186
   swapfile (Windows XP), 155
   tips, 189
   Trojan horse files, 183
   vulnerability scanners, 181
   WLANs, 195–197
seek time
   hard drives, 8
   optical drives, 5
selecting
   cases, 12–13
   CD burners, 50–51
   coolers, 60–63
   CPUs, 16–23
   CRTs, 301
   DVD burners, 53–54
   fans, Pentium 4, 266

hard drives, 44–46
    desktop *versus* server drives, 46
    speed, 44–45
keyboards, 59
LCDs, 301
mini-systems, 14–15
monitors, 47–49
motherboards, 26–31
    amenities, 26–27
    Athlon, 28–30
    chipsets, 26
mouse, 59
power supplies, 57–58
soundcards, 40–41
videocards, 34–36
    clock speeds, 34–35
    drivers, 36
    GPU, 35–36
    memory, 35
    shaders, 36
Serial ATA (SATA), 24, 27, 98, 286, 289
    disabling, 98
    hard drives, 45
    motherboards, 273
    power supplies, 58
    RAID, 24, 27
server hard drives, 46
servers, ping, 210
Service Pack 2 (Windows XP), 129
session-at-once mode, optical drives, 5
settings, BIOS, 92–98
    AC Power Loss, 95
    AGP settings, 94
    cache, 96
    CAS latency, 93
    correcting CPU speed, 92–93
    correcting memory, 92–93
    disabling ATA BIOS, 98
    disabling memory checks, 98
    disabling Serial ATA, 98
    enabling PCI IDE BusMaster, 98
    faulty fans, 95
    hard drive failures, 95
    legacy hardware resources, 96
    memory timing, 93
    minimizing component interference, 96
    PCI bus performance, 94
    peripherals, 94
    protecting PCs from viruses, 95
    standby state, 96
    streamlining boot sequence, 98
    switching hard disks to user-defined, 97
    system temperatures, 95
    unused resources, 95
setups, BIOS, 74
Shacknews.com, 91
Shaders, 36, 281
shadow mask, monitors, 47, 299–300
Shadow Security Scanner, 181
shareware, arcade games, 251
sharing
    broadband connections, 176–179
    files, disabling, 184
shooting movies, 232

shortcuts, creating, 201
Show in Groups folder option, 139
shutting down Windows XP, killing open programs, 157
Shuttle, 14
signal-to-noise ratio, 296
signature verification (Windows XP), 307
signed drivers, Windows XP, 139
signs, Flexisign Pro, 85
silicon chips, 19–23
single data-rate. *See* SDR
SiS
    645 chipset, 22
    645DX chipset, 23
    648 chipset, 23
    650 chipset, 23
    733 chipset, 21
    735 chipset, 21
    745 chipset, 21
    R658 chipset, 23
size
    buffers, hard drives, 8
    CRTs, 106
    default windows (Windows XP), customizing, 134
    monitors, 2
    thumbnails (Windows XP), customizing, 134
Slashdot.org, 91
SlickStik Tornado, 248
slots, coolers, 63
Small Computers System Interface. *See* SCSI
SmartbarXP, 132
smoke machines, 231
smoothing 3D models, 255
Snaps setting (Quark III Arena Engine games), 212
software, 90
    antivirus, 90, 186
    browsers, 90
    compression utilities, 90
    creating Media Center PCs, 83
    defragging utilities, 90
    DisplayMate, 107
    DisplayMate software, 105
    firewalls, 90
    pirated, 186
Sony, DRU-500A, 53–54
sound
    MP3s, 234–236
    onboard, 269
    quieting PCs, 100–103
        fans, 101
        noise-dampening materials, 102
        replacing power supplies, 102
    RazorLAME, 236
    studio recordings, creating, 237–241
soundcards, 38–41
    24-bit audio, 296
    AD EXT/SPDIF_IO, 39
    API, 296
    Audigy 2, 40–41
    aux-in, 39
    CD-in, 39

channel outputs, 40
compared, 295–297
connecting guitars to, 237–238
DAC, 39
digital-out connector, 38
DirectSound 3D, 296
DSP, 39, 296
DTS, 296
gaming, 297
hardware channels, 296
host-based processing, 296
installing, 73
Intel Azalia, 41
joystick headers, 39
line-in, 38
M-Audio Revolution, 297
Mic-in, 38
onboard audio, 40–41
S/PDIF, 296
sampling frequency, 296
SB1394 port, 38
selecting, 40–41
specifications, 7
surround sound, 296
TAD, 38
SoundForge web site, 238
southbridge, motherboards, 273
spam, 190–193
    email filters, 190–191
    Inboxer, 192–193
    SpamPal, 192–193
SpamPal, 192–193
speakers, 239–241
    arcade machines, 244
    Dolby Digital, 240
    Dolby Digital 5.1, 206–209, 296
    flat-panel, 239
    frequency response, 240
    mini-jack, 240
    power, 241
    rigs, Media Center PCs, 83
    S/PDIF, 240
    satellites, 240
    specifications, 6
    subwoofers, 240
    surround sound, 240
    THX certification, 240
    TOSlink/optical, 240
    troubleshooting, 241
    troubleshooting sound, 76
special effects, monitors, 110
specifications
    hard drives, 8
    LCDs, 48–49
    memory, 4
    monitors, 2, 48–49
    NICs, 4
    optical drives, 5
    soundcards, 7
    speakers, 6
    videocards, 3
    WLANs, 6
speed
    broadband connections, 173
    CD burners, 51
    clocks, videocards, 34–35

CPUs, 16–17, 261–267
  hard drives, 8, 44–45, 286, 289
  memory, 4
  optical drives, 5
  Windows XP boot process, optimizing, 141
  Windows XP interface, 138
SphereXP, 162
spindle motors (DVD burners), 43, 52
spindle speed, hard drives, 8
spinners (arcade machines), 248
splines, 3D models, 153
spyware, 148, 187–188
SSDP Discovery, 144
SSE2 (Streaming Single-instruction-multiple-data Extension 2), CPUs, 262
SSIDs, 196–197
standards
  NICs, 4
  WLANs, 6
standby state, 96
start buttons, arcade machines, 250
Start menu (Windows XP)
  adding separators to, 134
  pinning programs, 157
static, safety tips, 77
Status tab, 74
stop errors (Windows XP), 305
Streaming Single-instruction-multiple-data Extension 2 (SSE2), 262
structural design, cases, 12
Studio 8 software, 223
studio recordings, creating, 237–241
StyleXP, 131–133
sub-megapixel images, compared to 4-megapixel images, 216
submenus, creating DVDs, 226
subwoofers, 207, 239–240
SuperMicro SC-750A, airflow test, 65
surfaces, 3D models, 254
surround sound, 240, 296
sustained transfer rate, hard drives, 8
swapfile (Windows XP), security, 155
sweet spot, Dolby Digital 5.1 speaker setup, 207
switches, KVM, multiple PCs, 159
switching regulators, 32
Symmetric Digital Subscriber Line (SDSL), 175
system buses, clocking, 74
System Control Panel (Windows XP), adding images to, 132
System Health tab, 74
System Restore, 139, 143, 153, 307

T

tables (HTML), 200
TAD (soundcards), 38
Task Scheduler, 143
Taskbar Magnifier, 161
TaskGallery, 162
TCP/IP NetBIOS Helper, 144
technology, mini-systems, 14–15
Telephony, 143
televisions, Media Center PCs, 83

Telnet, 144
temperature
  CPUs, 265
  system, 95
terminals, WLANs, 6
tests
  broadband connection speed, 173
  case fans, 64–66
  Jedi Academy OpenGL, Hornet Pro 64, 15
  Lite-On CD burner, 51
  MSI K8N NEO Platinum Edition, 31
  MusicMatch, Hornet Pro 64, 15
texture, 3D models, 257
Theinquirer.net, 91
themes, Windows XP, 131
thermal paste, 264
third-party firewalls, 181
thumbnails
  modifying, burning videotapes to DVD, 225
  stopping from saves, Windows XP, 140
  Windows XP, customizing, 134
thumbscrews, cases, 12
THX certification, 240
timing, memory, 93
tools, creating custom recovery discs, 166
TOSlink/optical, 240
toxins, painting cases, 87
track-at-once mode, optical drives, 5
trackballs (arcade machines), 247
transfer rates
  hard drives, 8
  optical drives, 5
transistors (CPUs), 263
translucent leaf switches (arcade machines), 248
transmission rates, WLANs, 6
trays, motherboards
  cases, 11
  removing, 70
tRCD (RAS to CAS delay), 93
trilinear, videocards, 280, 283
trim, arcade machines, 244
tripwires, Dolby Digital 5.1 speaker setup, 209
Trojan horse files, 183
troubleshooting
  arcade machines, 251
  cooling, 78
  CPUs, 264–265
  CRTs, 302
  DVDs, 294
  fans, 268
  hard drive performance, 286
  hard drives, 290–291
  LCDs, 302
  monitors, 302
  motherboards, 274–277
  optical drives, 294
  PCs, 76–77
  speakers, 241
  videocards, 278, 282–286

Windows XP, 304–311
  blue-screen error, 305
  device management, 306
  DirectX Diagnostic, 307–308
  DiskProbe, 308
  Dr. Watson, 308
  FireWire failures, 310
  hotfixes, 310
  installing from Upgrade CD, 310
  legacy problems, 311
  Network Diagnostics, 307
  patches, 310
  performance problems, 311
  signature verification, 307
  stop errors, 305
  System Restore, 307
  Windows Messenger, 310
tubes (monitors), 2
turning off
  Fax Viewer, 156
  Windows Picture, 156
TV tuners, 32
TweakUI, 160
TweakXP, 141

U

Ultimarc I-Pac, 245
underrun buffer, 293
underrun protection, CD burners, 50
Uninterruptible Power Supply (UPS), 144
unit setup, creating 3D models, 253
Universal Plug and Play, 145
unused resources, 95
updates
  device drivers, 148
  drivers, Windows XP, 150
  Windows XP antivirus software, 147
upgrades, cases, 11, 13
UPS (Uninterruptible Power Supply), 144
user-defined hard disks, 97
UVW Map Gizmo, 257

V

Vantech Exhaust PCSC-100, 63
VBR tab (encoding), 236
velocity, videocards, 117
ventilation, cases, 12
vents, 3D models, 256
vertex shaders, 281
vertical synchronization, videocards, 281
VIA KLE133 chipset, 20
VIA KT133 chipset, 20–21
VIA KT133A chipset, 20
VIA KT266 chipset, 20
VIA KT266A chipset, 20
VIA KT400 chipset, 21
VIA P4X266 chipset, 22
VIA P4X266A chipset, 22
VIA P4X400 chipset, 22
VIA ProSavage
  KM133 chipset, 20
  KM133A chipset, 20

KM266 chipset, 21
P4M266 chipset, 22
video
  CDs, 5
  games. *See* games
  onboard video, 269
videocards, 32–36, 279–286
  3D games, 35–36
  AGP, 280, 284
  AGP Fast Write, 280
  Anisotropic filtering, 280
  API, 280
  arcade machines, 249
  auxiliary power connectors, 33
  bilinear, 280, 283
  capacitors, 32, 33
  clock speed, 280
  crystal, 33
  DDR, 280
  diodes, 33
  Direct3D, 280
  DirectX, 280
  drivers, 280
  Floating Point Color, 280
  GeForce 6800, 15
  GeForce FX 5800, 34
  GPU, 33
  GPU (graphical processing unit), 281
  Hardware Transform and Lighting, 280
  installing, 73, 82
  memory, 281
  onboard graphics, 284
  onboard RAM, 33
  Open GL, 281
  overclocking, 124
  pixel shaders, 281
  powerstrips, 124
  profiles, 125
  RAMDAC, 281
  resolution, 125
  selecting, 34–36
    clock speeds, 34–35
    drivers, 36
    GPU, 35–36
    memory, 35
    shaders, 36
  shaders, 281
  specifications, 3
  switching regulator, 32
  trilinear, 280, 283
  troubleshooting, 278, 282–286
  TV tuners, 32
  velocity, 117
  vertex shaders, 281
  vertical synchronization, 281
  workstation, 36
videotapes
  burning to DVD, 222–227
  editing, 224
viewable image size (monitors), 2
viewing
  desktop changes, 201
  Windows XP icons, 138
viewing area
  LCDs, 49
  monitors, 299

vinyl, painting cases, 85–88
Virtual Desktop Manager, 160
virtual desktops, 109
viruses
  protecting computers from, 186, 189
  protecting PCs from, 95
voice coil, 42
voltage
  CPUs, 265
  memory, 4
  power supplies, 58
Volume Shadow Copy, 143
vulnerability scanners, 181

W

water-cooling systems, 60–61
web editors, FrontPage, 199
web pages, embedding on desktops, 201
web sites, 91
  Black Viper, 143
  Windowsupdate.com, 90
Webcam Timershot, 161
Webclient, 143
weeding, 86
weld thresholds, 255
Wells-Gardner, 249
WEP, enabling, 196
Wikipedia.com, 91
Willamette, 16
Windows, restoring from, 171
Windows Audio, 143
Windows Explorer, crashes, Windows XP, 140
Windows Image Acquisition, 144
Windows Installer, 144
Windows Management Instrumentation, 143
Windows Media Audio format, 132
Windows Messenger, troubleshooting, 310
Windows Picture, turning off, 156
Windows Services, 142–145
  antivirus software, 142
  Application Layer Gateway, 143
  Application Management, 144
  Automatic Updates, 143
  Background Intelligent Transfer, 143
  Clipbook, 144
  COM+, 143
  Computer Browser, 144
  cryptographic services, 142
  DHCP client, 143
  Distributed Link Tracking Client, 144
  Error Reporting, 144
  Event Log, 142
  Help and Support, 143
  HID Input Service, 143
  Indexing service, 144
  IPSEC, 144
  Logical Disk Manager, 143
  Messenger, 144
  MS Software Shadow Copy Provider, 143
  Plug and Play, 143

  profiles, 145
  Remote Procedure Call, 143
  Remote Registry Service, 144
  SSDP Discovery, 144
  System Restore, 143
  Task Scheduler, 143
  TCP/IP NetBIOS Helper, 144
  Telephony, 143
  Telnet, 144
  Uninterruptible Power Supply (UPS), 144
  Universal Plug and Play, 145
  Volume Shadow Copy, 143
  Webclient, 143
  Windows Audio, 143
  Windows Image Acquisition, 144
  Windows Installer, 144
  Windows Management Instrumentation, 143
  Windows Time, 145
  Wireless Zero Configuration Properties, 144
  Workstation Windows Service, 143
Windows Time, 145
Windows Update, 148, 168
Windows XP
  antivirus software, updating, 147
  archives, 149
  backups, 149–150
  booting, 141, 159
  cleaning icon cache, 149
  cleaning Registry, 149
  configuring, custom recovery discs, 169–170
  creating custom recovery discs, 164–171
  customizing, 90
  customizing desktop, 131–134
  deleting, MSN Explorer, 140
  deleting, partitions, 150
  deleting, recent files list, 156
  Disk Cleanup, 148
  Disk Defragmenter, 148
  emptying Recycle Bin, 147
  encryption security, 183–184
  Fax Viewer, turning off, 156
  file backups, 147
  firewalls, 181
  history, 126–127
  icons, viewing quickly, 138
  installation, troubleshooting, 76
  installing, 75
  installing, creating custom recovery discs, 167
  installing from Upgrade CD, 310
  interface, increasing speed, 138
  kernel, 128
  Longhorn, 162–163
  Media Center Edition, 80
  memory management, 128
  optimizing Recycle Bin, 139
  optimizing System Restore, 139
  organizing files, 139
  panes, 127
  PowerToys, 160–161
  reinstalling, 149

Registry setting changes, 130
restore points, 154
running command-line applications
  quickly, 139
Service Pack 2, 129
setting custom resolutions, 157
shutting down, killing open programs, 157
signed drivers, 139
SmartbarXP, 132
stopping thumbnails from saving,
  140
swapfile, security, 155
System Restore, 153
troubleshooting, 304–311
turning off indexing, 138
updating drivers, 150
Windows Explorer crashes, 140
Windows Picture, turning off, 156
Windows Services, 142–145
Windows Update, 148
WindowsBlinds, 131
Windowsupdate.com, 90–91
wireless LANs. *See* WLANs
Wireless Zero Configuration Properties,
  144
wizards, Audio Record, 238
WLANs (wireless LANs)
  security, 195–197
  specifications, 6
WMP (Windows Media Player), deleting
  recent list, 156
workstation videocards, 36
Workstation Windows Service, 143

X

xD-Picture Card, 216
Xeon, CPUs, 17
Xoxide UV-reactive case, 12
XPC SB51G mini-system, 14

Y–Z

Yamaha CRW-F1, 50

Zalman CNPS7000A-CU, 266
Zalman, CNPS6500B-CU, 61
ZoneAlarm, 181, 196
ZoneAlarm Pro, 181